Rhetoric in an Antifoundational World

Rhetoric in an Antifoundational World

language, culture, and pedagogy

•

Edited by Michael Bernard-Donals
and Richard R. Glejzer

yale university press   new haven and london

Copyright © 1998 by Yale University.
All rights reserved.
This book may not be reproduced, in whole or in
part, including illustrations, in any form (beyond
that copying permitted by Sections 107 and 108 of
the U.S. Copyright Law and except by reviewers
for the public press), without written permission
from the publishers.

Designed by Sonia L. Scanlon
Set in Adobe Garamond
Type by Keystone Typesetting, Inc.
Orwigsburg, Pennsylvania
Printed in the United States of America by
Thomson-Shore, Inc., Dexter, Michigan.

Library of Congress
Cataloging-in-Publication Data
Rhetoric in an antifoundational world : language,
culture, and pedagogy / edited by Michael
Bernard-Donals and Richard R. Glejzer.
p.   cm.
Includes bibliographical references and index.
ISBN 0-300-07022-5 (alk. paper)
1. English language—Rhetoric—Study and
teaching—Theory, etc.   2. Language and
culture—English-speaking countries.   3. English
language—20th century—Rhetoric.   4. Language
and languages—Philosophy.   5. Knowledge,
Theory of.   I. Bernard-Donals, Michael F.
II. Glejzer, Richard R.
PE1404.R494   1998
808'.042'07—dc21   97-19675
CIP

A catalogue record for this book is available from
the British Library.

The paper in this book meets the guidelines for
permanence and durability of the Committee on
Production Guidelines for Book Longevity of the
Council on Library Resources.

10 9 8 7 6 5 4 3 2 1

Contents

Acknowledgments · ix

Introduction · 1
Michael Bernard-Donals and Richard R. Glejzer

Part I
Antifoundationalism and Rhetoric

1
Rhetoric · 33
Stanley Fish

2
The Contingency of Language · 65
Richard Rorty

3
A Short History of Rhetoric · 86
Terry Eagleton

Part II
Theoretical Elaborations

4
Language Obscures Social Change · 101
Melanie Eckford-Prossor and Michael Clifford

5
Toward a "Materialist" Rhetoric:
Contingency, Constraint, and the Eighteenth-Century Crowd · 128
Michael Hill

6
The Decentered Subject of Feminism:
Postfeminism and *Thelma and Louise* · 147
Linda Frost

7
Habermas's Rational-Critical Sphere and
the Problem of Criteria · 170
Patricia Roberts

8
Foundational Thuggery and a Rhetoric of Subsumption · 195
Frank Farmer

Part III
Extensions and Complications

9
Hymes, Rorty, and the Social-Rhetorical Construction of Meaning · 227
Robert E. Smith III

10
"Too Little Care":
Language, Politics, and Embodiment in the Life-World · 254
Kurt Spellmeyer

11
History and the Real · 292
Charles Shepherdson

12
The Subject of Invention:
Antifoundationalism and Medieval Hermeneutics · 318
Richard R. Glejzer

13
The Royal Road: Marxism and the Philosophy of Science · 341
Michael Sprinker

Part IV
Teaching and Writing (in) an Antifoundational World

14
Beyond Antifoundationalism to Rhetorical Authority:
Problems Defining "Cultural Literacy" · 371
Patricia Bizzell

15
Composition Studies and Cultural Studies:
Collapsing Boundaries · 389
James A. Berlin

16

What We Need to Know about Writing *and* Reading,
or Peter Elbow and Antifoundationalism · 411
Ellen Gardiner

17

Teaching as a Test of Knowledge:
Passion, Desire, and the Semblance of Truth in Teaching · 423
David Metzger

18

Composition in an Antifoundational World:
A Critique and a Proposal · 436
Michael Bernard-Donals

Contributors · 455

Index · 457

Acknowledgments

This book was assembled over many years and at several institutions, so we have many people to thank. We are especially grateful to our colleagues at Albertson College of Idaho and the University of Missouri, who provided encouragement to see this project through. We also need to thank our departments, which provided time and funding for the completion of the project. The Research Council at the University of Missouri, Columbia, was instrumental in providing funding for the book in its final stages. Thanks to Linda Frost and Ellen Gardiner, who not only contributed to this book but also helped us to complete it through their enthusiasm and wise counsel. We are happy to acknowledge those at Yale University Press who made the transition from manuscript to print more manageable: to Jonathan Brent, who bore with us; to Cynthia Wells for her patience; to JoAnn DiCera, who calmed frayed nerves. Special thanks go to Ruth Veleta and Margaret Otzel, whose work on the manuscript made the final editing a pleasure rather than a chore. Finally, we are most grateful to our families, without whose help and wisdom this book could not have been completed.

We wish also to acknowledge those presses and institutions that have generously granted us permission to reprint essays. Thanks to Stanley Fish and Duke University Press, Durham, North Carolina, for permission to reprint "Rhetoric," from *Doing What Comes Naturally: Change, Rhetoric, and the Practice of Theory in Literary and Legal Studies* (471–502), copyright © 1989. "A Short History of Rhetoric," from *Walter Benjamin* by Terry Eagleton, is reproduced by kind permission of the publisher, Verso. Thanks to the *New Left Review* for permission to reprint Michael Sprinker's "The Royal Road," and to the National Council of Teachers of English for permission to reprint Patricia Bizzell's "Beyond Antifoundationalism to Rhetorical Authority" and Robert Smith's "Hymes, Rorty, and the Social-Rhetorical Construction of Meaning," both of which appeared in *College English*. James Berlin's "Composition Studies and Cultural Studies," from *Into the Field: Sites of Composition Studies,* was reprinted by permission of the Modern Language Association. Richard Rorty's "The Contingency of Language," which appeared in *Contingency, Irony, and Solidarity,* was reprinted with the permission of Cambridge University Press. Kurt Spellmeyer's essay, " 'Too Little Care': Language, Politics, and Embodiment in the Life-World," appeared in a much different form but under the same title in *College English*. Charles Shepherdson's "History and the Real" appeared in different form in *PostModern Culture.*

Introduction

Michael Bernard-Donals
and Richard R. Glejzer

In an essay on antifoundationalism and the teaching of writing, Stanley
Fish defined the term *antifoundationalism* as the assertion "that matters [of
fact, truth, correctness, validity, and clarity] are intelligible and debatable
only within the precincts of the contexts and situations or paradigms or
communities that give them their local and changeable shape" (Fish 344).
The foundations that had previously been assumed to be objective or
neutral or value-free—for Fish, in this essay, the idea that language communicates real situations; for others, that we can have unmediated knowledge of historical events, or that we can move unproblematically between
written language and human intention—had, in the literary critical academy at least, become radically contested. The antifoundational paradigm
saw language not as a transparent medium but as a construction that itself
was the result of a combination of material and discursive forces. The
result for the literary critical academy was that—if it did not know it by the
time Fish first published his essay in 1987—interpretation was not a matter of correctness but of understanding the forces that give it shape and
that other cultural products (including both literary and historical texts,
and other nontextual productions like film, performance art, and community practices and rituals) were open to the same kind of investigation.

Of course, in 1987 Fish was announcing something that most of us in
the literary critical community had known for about twenty years. Barthes
and later Derrida had suggested to us that the epistemological certainty
with which we read texts, the result of which taught us to examine language for its communicative value, was rather naive, not only because these
certainties had for so long gone unexamined, but because they were themselves the result of historical contingencies and choices made in the context
of local communities of thought. Derrida, in a very limited example,
suggests in "Signature Event Context" that our understanding of language
as communicative is at least in part a misreading of the need for an absent
interlocutor, which becomes apparent when examining texts by Condillac,

Rousseau, and J. L. Austin (Derrida 311–27). If our knowledge of writing is shaped by a misunderstanding of the term *absence,* then it is possible to overturn the epistemological assumption that writing functions differently from speech and is parasitic on it; this assumption then overturns much of what we assume about the transparency of the written, about inscription, and about linguistic knowledge. Foucault and Lacan had also, in different ways, understood that the real is not reflected by language but is deferred and misrecognized in language. In an essay entitled "Science and Truth," for example, in which Lacan notes the distinction between psychoanalysis and science, he asserts that "there is no such thing as a meta-language (an assertion made so as to situate all of logical positivism), no language being able to say the truth about the truth, since the truth is grounded in the fact that it speaks, and that it has no other means with which to do so" (16). The "truth" that science desires to arrive at is achieved by means of a language that can only manage to understand itself as a language; the relation between "truth" and the real is a relation between the naming of an object or state of affairs and that object's or state's distance from the truth. That is to say, Lacan understands language as functioning not as a reflection of the real but as something that substitutes for it, which implies, as Fish did twenty-two years later, that we can understand notions of "fact" or "truth" only in relation to contexts or paradigms within which they are created, which themselves are constructed.

Derrida, Lacan, and Foucault announced something like antifoundationalism in Europe a full fifteen to twenty years before it was readily accepted in the United States, and even here, as Fish wryly notes, "it would be *too much* to say that the foundationalist argument lies in ruins," because without foundations, traditionalists or foundationalists fear that by abandoning "truth" or "fact" we also abandon "rational inquiry and successful communication" (345).[1] Still, the antifoundational paradigm was announced on the American stage once and for all by Richard Rorty and his *Philosophy and the Mirror of Nature,* which was published in 1979. In it, Rorty questions whether epistemological questions that have been asked by philosophy for the last several hundred years do not misunderstand the relation between "world" and "truth." It is impossible, suggests Rorty, to be able to say anything about a world "out there," separate from the sentences we use to describe it, and so it is equally impossible to say anything about truth, since truth is always relative to a scheme which is itself an artificial construct. What is needed is to replace epistemology—in an antifoundational "world without mirrors"—with hermeneutics, "an expression of hope that the cultural space left by the demise of epistemology will not be filled—that our culture should become one in which the demand for constraint and confrontation is no longer felt" (Rorty, *Philosophy* 315). Hermeneutics operates discursively; in it interlocutors "play back and forth between guesses about how to characterize particular statements or other events, and guesses about the point of the whole equation, until gradually we feel at ease with what was hitherto strange" (319), namely, a set of statements that are unrecognizable within the constraints of the initial conversation. People change their minds—and descriptions of the world can be said to progress—not when they are convinced that one set of statements more closely approximates a state of affairs unmediated by language, but when the equation can be restated in terms recognizable enough by both interlocutors. This changes not just the state of affairs, but also the interlocutors, whose definitions of themselves also changed during the conversation.

This antifoundational view of the world was attractive to Fish and others in the literary critical academy because it gives up the difficult (if not impossible) task of finding objective criteria with which to adjudicate truth claims without giving up on a notion of progress and emancipation. Truth, in other words, becomes a set of practices in a world of descriptions rather than an object of discovery, and at a stroke the threat of chaos resulting from a world without foundations is dispelled in favor of a more humane world in which order is available though contingent, and in which understanding is reached through debate and something that looks like communication. Because of the central role of debate and "keeping the conversation going" in Rorty's American antifoundational model, an investigation into the components of conversation becomes imperative. If knowledge is formed by language (not the other way around), and if language is constructed socially out of contexts, situations, and communities, then what is needed for antifoundationalism is a methodology that understands language as constructed, contingent, and constitutive of social orders.

It is for this reason that a majority of those who have become known in the United States as antifoundationalists have come to see a role for rhetoric in their formulations of knowledge as discursive. Rhetoric could be described roughly as the use of language to produce material effects in particular social conjunctures—a description that can be found in Plato's *Gorgias* and *Phaedrus,* as well as in Aristotle's treatises on rhetoric and ethics—and that has changed little in rhetoric's various incarnations since around 300 B.C.E. (including its denigration at the hands of the early church fathers and Peter Ramus, its reincarnation and resurrection as belles lettres, and its full-fledged renaissance as rhetoric and composition studies in the latter half of the nineteenth and into the twentieth centuries). What is important to note in this understanding of rhetoric is that it takes as axiomatic language's capability to exert power in observable (and reproducible) ways, that as a form of praxis it can produce real social change, and that rhetorical analysis can yield information about language's power and its relation to the material world from which, in part, it derives that power. A rhetorically situated methodology, then, would not only seem capable of understanding the negotiations of normal and abnormal discourse and their effect on subjects' "worlds" as well as those subjects themselves, but also—because of antifoundationalism's assumptions about the constitutive power of discourse on all forms of production, discursive and nondiscursive—seem capable of theorizing the relations between cultural forms and the polises that create them, and between those polises and their material and discursive constraints.

What is uncertain in this argument is the *degree* to which rhetoric and rhetorical analysis are a valuable methodology for understanding the human social order and its relation to its various constructions of "the world." If it is true that because all human knowledge of the world is created, not discovered, and is thus contingent, then all we have at our disposal are various "discourses" from which to make sense of "the world," and what Stanley Fish says is true: we must decide which analysis of the world is more acceptable by dint of its rhetorical *force*. While it seems clear that rhetorical analysis is probably the *only* methodology capable of understanding a human relation to a discursively constituted world, it is not clear that it is only discursive force that allows or forces us to change our minds (and our selves). It is possible, for example, to read Plato's *Gorgias* less as a refutation of rhetoric and more as a consideration of the world in which rhetoric and dialectic must function. In *Gorgias,* Socrates makes the point that in a rhetorical argument about whether doing harm or suffering harm is the more rational choice, one is compelled to choose either one or the other alternative, though "I would rather avoid both" (469). This is not a choice provided by dialectic or rhetoric, though it would seem to be one available to Socrates, as would his choice of recanting his teachings in the face of imminent execution. Most people have been perplexed by this point in Plato's dialogue, but we believe it can be resolved by suggesting that Socrates is here acknowledging that states of affairs are compelling not simply by dint of their rhetorical force, but also by some extra-rhetorical or material force (such as the fear of suffering harm, or the impending threat of death—in Rorty's terms, the dangers that come from "the scarcity of food and from the secret police" [*Philosophy* 389]). If we take rhetoric as the preeminent methodology in an antifoundational paradigm for investigating the constitutive effect of language on knowledge, then we are also forced to deal with rhetoric's excess—material, extra-discursive force—and we need then to reexamine seriously the extent to which the changing descriptions of "a world" affect that world's effect on the interlocutors doing the describing.

The essays collected in this book begin by inquiring about the sources of rhetorical power by calling into question whether it is true, as Richard Rorty suggests, that language "goes all the way down." As Terry Eagleton has tried to assert,[2] and as Roy Bhaskar, among others,[3] has tried to prove, language derives its power from the polis, an organized social whole that is at once constrained by the very language it is trying to understand and by various material forces over which it is not in complete control. In this view of rhetoric, one needs to explain not only the force of language but also the *extra*-discursive constraints within which it operates. This collection will suggest the possible results of the claim that analysis of material constraint would seem to fall outside the purview of rhetoric and to the various "hard" or "objective" sciences, which take as their domain the world of unmediated material reality. Because one of the primary tenets of antifoundationalism is that there is no unmediated access, scientific or otherwise, to material "reality," then it is quite possible that while knowledge of the world has two "domains" (the realm of the certain, of science, and the realm of the contingent, of rhetoric), as suggested by Rorty, scientific knowledge is impossible without a study of how it is formed socially (that is, rhetorically), as suggested by Kuhn.[4] In short, this book tries to answer the question, What happens to literary studies and theory, and to the study and teaching of writing, if we go along with the antifoundational understanding of the world as discursively organized, and what are some alternative strategies for human understanding once we grasp some of antifoundationalism's problems and aporias?

Before we talk about the structure of the book and examine its arguments, it is important to contextualize the essays not only theoretically but also temporally. While antifoundationalism can be seen as evolving directly out of the confrontation of literary study with French phenomenology's treatment of the real and the Anglo-American pragmatist reaction to epistemology, we also need to take seriously the claim that as critical practice antifoundationalism functions as a conversation with contemporary contexts and communities, while it also shifts the ground of those contexts and communities. Doing so requires a brief accounting for some of the strands that, woven together, constitute the current conjuncture of rhetorical and literary theory in the United States. Two of the more important strands that should be considered are the different "spins" rhetoric has acquired in the last ten years' discussions of the subject, and the reaction against theory that has taken place in the American academy since the middle 1980s. These strands might each be divided further. Though calls for a resurrection of rhetoric in literary studies have been most clear since the early 1980s, the term *rhetoric* has been valorized negatively as the last best tool available for language study in a world beset by theory (and antifoundational theory at that), or as a tool to be used only when more reasonable criteria for observation and investigation of cultural products cannot be found. Other scholars, however, suggest that rhetoric does have the capability for understanding the material dimension of cultural facts, and as such should be seen as a valuable means not only for investigating culture, but for transforming it. The reaction against theory might also be subdivided as follows: though many in the literary academy have clapped their hands with glee at the demise of poststructural and postmodern paradigms of literary investigation, they have failed to notice that these methodologies have found a home in theoretical orientations like New Historicism and cultural studies. Moreover, though theory seems to have died a quiet death as a subject for study on university curricula on most campuses, it remains alive and well in our approaches to pedagogy, which have taken for granted the idea that epistemology does not sufficiently explain the relation between "art" and "life," and which see language as that which structures the realities of both our students and the authors they read in our classes.

First, the positive valorization of rhetoric. In what has become a standard introduction for undergraduate and graduate students to the last seventy years of theoretical work in literary studies, Terry Eagleton, in *Literary Theory: An Introduction*, concludes his overview of the field with a recommendation that we replace literary theory altogether with "a different kind of discourse—whether one calls it of 'culture,' 'signifying practices,' or whatever is not of first importance—which would include the objects ('literature') with which these other theories deal, but which would transform them by setting them in a wider context" (205). This discourse is rhetoric, which "from ancient society to the eighteenth century, examined the way discourses are constructed in order to achieve certain effects." He notes rhetoric's affinity to formalism and structuralism, suggesting that it understands the devices of literary and nonliterary languages and works to discern their effects in various wider social and historical structures; and he notes its affinity to poststructural and psychoanalytic theories in its "preoccupation with discourse as a form of power and desire" and that discourse can be "a humanly transformative affair" (206). In one move, Eagleton here has broadened the classical understanding of rhetoric, at least in its Aristotelian incarnation, by suggesting not only that we read the first and third books of *Rhetoric,* with their examinations of human stereotypes and catalogue of figures, but also that we read the eighth and ninth chapters of the first book closely and attend the epistemic function of rhetoric (as Bizzell and Herzberg remind us that William Grimaldi has done), so as to see language as constitutive of the structures of the polis, and to see language, in Burke's turn of phrase, as related to—and consonant with—action, or praxis.[5] Eagleton took this reading even further in his earlier book on Walter Benjamin in an essay entitled "A Short History of Rhetoric" (see chapter 3 herein) by going beyond Aristotle to Plato, who links rhetoric to dialectic (in Eagleton's perhaps overbroad terms, he links "agitation" to "propaganda") to inform a broader theory of phronesis, or social knowledge. In the earlier essay, Eagleton, by linking language to social action, sees rhetoric as bordering on the revolutionary, in that any act of language is transformative not only of subjects but of those subjects' lived relations with one another and thereby their "world." By valorizing rhetoric as a form of social action and by understanding rhetoric as explicitly tied to what Fish calls "contexts or situations or paradigms or communities," Eagleton sees for rhetoric a seminal role in an antifoundational world, because unlike "theoretical" knowledge (the classical concept of *sophia*) or even scientific knowledge, assumed to be relatively objective (the classical *episteme*), rhetoric is a theory of "the polis as a whole." Rhetoric is the culmination of practical knowledge, in its function to provide individual polises or communities with knowledge useful to their aims, and in its function to understand broader human activity in a world that functions with some regularity and that, for better or worse, devises a "law" (either a law of nature, or a code of civil law, or a spoken or unspoken and insidious set of conventions or ideologies) which may or may not approximate those regularities. It understands itself not epistemologically as a way to adjudicate truth claims according to the yardstick of "the real," but in ways akin to Rorty's hermeneutics as a way to see both truth claims and the criteria against which they are measured as subject to inquiry and negotiation.

But where Eagleton (and Tompkins) see rhetoric's role as positive and revolutionary, in both its classical and its contemporary functions, others see rhetoric as at best a stopgap measure in a world where there are no criteria with which to establish truth claims, and where the truth—inasmuch as we can recognize it from within our "own" interpretive communities or vantage points—is irrelevant to discussions of "the world." Ironically, it is Stanley Fish whose view of rhetoric and its function in an antifoundational world (or, as he puts it, a world in which we have irreversibly gone down the "anti-formalist road") is perhaps the most impoverished of those who have staked out anti-foundationalism to begin with. Throughout the essays that make up his book *Doing What Comes Naturally,* Fish seems to argue—in what appears to be complete accordance with Rorty's thesis in *Philosophy and the Mirror of Nature* and *Contingency, Irony, and Solidarity*—that languages and their connection to what we understand as "the world" "are made rather than found, and that truth is a property of linguistic entities, of sentences" (Rorty, *Contingency* 7). For this reason, rhetorical analysis and the practice of rhetoric are all there is.

Fish builds his apparent defense of rhetoric on Aristotle's own, which appears in the first book of the *Rhetoric.* The strength of rhetoric, for Aristotle, is that it enables speakers to understand that there *are* in fact different situations in which one can use different rhetorical strategies. Rhetoric is thus elevated from the mere choosing of which trope to use when, to the analysis of the situations that dictate those tropes. That is to say, rhetoric is removed from the realm of the haphazard—as the toolbox from which one could choose discursive strategies in a chaotic world—and is reinstated in the realm of the life-world. Fish goes on to suggest that, like antifoundational philosophies, rhetoric can be taken to task *for reason of* this defense, since it is through Aristotle's defense that we once and for all understand rhetoric to be at several removes from any discussion of what is known to be true once and for all. Rhetoric is the anti-foundational methodology par excellence because it understands the world as radically contingent, and simultaneously it is that radical contingency that dooms rhetoric to be forever part of the phrase "mere rhetoric," because in spite of the persuasiveness of the antifoundational paradigm theorists most often fall back into the familiar epistemological assumptions about foundations and objective knowledge. Rhetoric, by saying out loud that the world is constituted by language spoken in more or less local contexts, is both the hero and the demon of the contemporary critical academy.

Rhetoric's mixed fortunes in such a view are the result of a peculiar reading of some seminal rhetorical texts, most notably the *Gorgias* and *Phaedrus* by Plato, and to some extent the *Rhetoric* of Aristotle. Michael Sprinker, in an essay on literary theory's falling stock in the antifoundational academy, suggests that in part, rhetoric's negative valorization is due—in Fish's book—to an "incapacity to distinguish between sophistry and deliberative rhetoric, between more or less venal, *ad hoc* rationalization and reasoning toward a conclusion not known in advance" ("The War against Theory" 112; see also his "Knowing, Believing, Doing"). This may overstate the case somewhat, but it is curious to note that Fish takes Plato's Socrates seriously when, in the *Gorgias*, he argues that "rhetoric [need not] know the facts at all, for it has hit upon a means of persuasion that enables it to appear in the eyes of the ignorant to know more than those who really know" (quoted in Fish 472). The point is that even on its best days rhetoric has to contend with the accusation that, given its antifoundational starting point—what the antisophistic Plato and the anti-antirhetorician Fish have in common—it deals with reality only insofar as reality is that which is useful in particular situations. But what Fish (and those who, like Chaim Perelman and Stephen Mailloux, understand all situations as discursive and therefore rhetorical) fails to note is rhetoric's connection with other forms of knowledge, none of which is "objective" in the sense that it is unmediated, but which nevertheless occupy some middle ground between the absolute certainty afforded by a metaphysics and the absolute skepticism that some see as the upshot of antifoundationalism and its rhetorical world.[6] In the same way that Eagleton and others take pains to emphasize the connection between rhetorical knowledge and its potential revolutionary capacity in larger social formations, Fish deemphasizes this connection, thereby weakening rhetoric at the very moment when it would most likely seem to be a candidate for apotheosis in a radically antifoundational literary academy.

The two other contemporary moments in the antifoundational academy that need to be mentioned are the rehabilitation of pedagogy and the simultaneous wake being held for theory in the academy. I say "wake" because while some are disappointed at the untimely demise of theory as a subject for speculation and others are dancing on theory's coffin in jubilation, theory "wakes" much as does Finnegan in another capacity in Joyce's book of the same title. These two contemporary moments made themselves apparent to us during the

year we were assembling the material for this collection. The first was announced when Bernard-Donals taught, in the fall of 1993, a course entitled
"Introduction to Literary Studies." Part of the description of the course, listed
in his department's section of the undergraduate bulletin, read as follows:
"Introduces students to two or more literary theories and two or more literary
genres." Bernard-Donals, in his syllabus for the course, aimed to highlight
theoretical questions as the class read the texts on the reading list. Several recent
books on the teaching of theory and the theoretization of pedagogy have
recently claimed that we should do more than just teach theory as a subject, and
instead should imbricate "theory" with "pedagogy" or "the classroom" (terms
that, interpreted loosely, have to do with what goes on in our teaching).[7] But it
wasn't always clear just what the essays in those books had to do with the
realities of teaching or the value of theory, as Bernard-Donals found as his
course progressed.

The second articulation of this moment was announced in a fairly recent
article in the *Chronicle of Higher Education,* "Scholars Mark the Beginning of
the Age of 'Post-Theory,'" which suggests that Theory with a capital *T* is no
longer the rage in the (literary) academy. Instead, it has become just another
part of the literary enterprise—along with periods, genres, literary history, and
the like—that has gained a certain amount of legitimacy in literary scholarship.
Questions of Theory (about the stability of texts, the legitimacy of meaning,
the politics of the institution) have taken a back seat to questions of theory (the
construction of meaning in particular historical eras, texts, and cultures).

Both these articulations can be seen as characteristic of the place of theory
in the academy in an antifoundational world. The first event—teaching a
course that "familiarizes students with at least two literary theories"—suggests
that theory can be considered an object of study separate from the texts that can
also be taught during a course. One could have taught, say, three novels and
three volumes of poetry, alongside semiotics and poststructuralism, in an introduction to literary studies course. And, one could make a case to teach *Lolita,*
for example, poststructurally, in order to show the intertextuality of the various
tropes of the novel; to suggest the instability of the various narrative structures
used by Nabokov and, in turn, Humbert; and to show the "absent center" that
is Lolita herself. That segment of the course has gotten "theory" into the
"classroom."

The second event suggests a more complicated relationship between theory and pedagogy, and between the antifoundational moment and the method-

ologies with which we believe we can teach it. The *Chronicle* article suggests that the field of literary studies has so self-consciously adapted the highly theoretical, continental version of antifoundationalist (read here, poststructuralist) claims that textual structures are built arbitrarily and mean contingently that everything we do—including everything we do in the classroom—is theoretical. We do not just teach poststructuralism as our favorite flavor of theory and deploy it in analyzing texts to which it seems particularly well-suited (like *Lolita*). Rather, we acknowledge the situatedness and arbitrariness of the literary enterprise itself, so that we see the artificiality of the classroom setting and the practices that define it, and acknowledge, with our students, the forces that built the setting as well as the assumptions guiding literary analysis. That is what the imbrication of rhetoric with antifoundationalism (à la Fish, Rorty, and Eagleton) is about: to see theory not as a "technology of interpretation" but as a commitment "to various forms of writing [and] . . . to complex discursive practices" (Nelson xiii). Morton and Zavarzadeh, in *Theory/Pedagogy/Politics,* go even further to suggest that "all discursive practices are pedagogical, in the sense that they propose a theory of reality—a world in which those discourses are 'true' " (vii). Theory is not just another subject to bring, kicking and screaming, into our classrooms. Rather, it should be seen as a way to reorient the classroom itself and to understand it as embedded in other discursive practices (institutional, political, economic) that propose their own, often contradictory, versions of what is real.

Has theory really become so much a part of what we do as scholars and teachers that it structures not only what we teach but how we teach? If one takes the reorientation of theory and pedagogy implied by these two situations to suggest a wholesale retooling of the literary academy, then the answer is surely no. We answer this way because we know what goes on in many classrooms, and we know that whether we take Theory as a subject or as a paradigm, it is just not out there yet. We also see, however, a tension in even the desire to bring theory (which has presumably been interiorized in the contemporary antifoundational moment) and pedagogy (as a strategy of textual analysis and for social reorientation) together at all, a tension between treating the full pedagogical and political implications of "theoretizing" the classroom as praxis and treating theory as a tool for literary analysis. For someone like Cary Nelson or Bruce Henricksen and Thais Morgan, theory is generally treated as a way to understand literature differently, and, as a by-product of this new understanding, to see students and the classroom differently. For those like Kecht or Morton and

Zavarzadeh, theory is understood as a means by which pedagogy might be reformulated along interdisciplinary lines, and they understand this reformulation in explicitly political terms. But if the latter view can be said to be more "political" in that it attempts to change more than just the theoretical tools, it also provides far less understanding of the implications this reformulation has for individual students, classrooms, and English departments. In short, the connection between theory and pedagogy implied by the reactivation of rhetoric in an antifoundational world suggests that we have finally arrived at the place announced by the article in the *Chronicle of Higher Education;* but that connection also hints at the host of problems involved in questioning the assumptions by which the literary academy works and in problematizing the criteria of adjudication with which rational decisions about a life in the polis can be made.

This book falls into four sections. The first, "Antifoundationalism and Rhetoric," serves as an introduction to three of the most important works in Anglo-American theory that explicitly treat the connection between rhetoric and antifoundational theory. It is perhaps Rorty's essay, "The Contingency of Language," that most clearly articulates the connection between pragmatic philosophy, an antifoundational worldview, and the role of language. Here Rorty suggests that "language goes all the way down," providing the slogan for antifoundational thought that advises that it does not make sense for us to attempt to theorize a world "out there" independent of language, and instead urges theorists to understand how language is constitutive of that world. It is this slogan, also, that is the most controversial in the eyes of several contributors to this book, since it appears to collapse ontology into an epistemology, obviating the need, in the words of Eckford-Prossor and Clifford, to discover just what it goes all the way down *into.* Stanley Fish's essay examines the fortunes of rhetoric, whose stock in the current conjuncture at least is quite high. "Rhetorical man," notes Fish at the end of that essay, is one who "thinks of truth horizontally—as the culminating reinterpretation of our predecessors' reinterpretation of their predecessors' reinterpretation," who thinks of truth, goodness, and beauty "as artifacts whose fundamental design we often have to alter" (Rorty, *Consequences of Pragmatism* 92; quoted in Fish 54). Because truth is contingent on the temporal contexts of its discursive locations, it is rhetoric—the examination of those locations—that allows us to understand humans not as radically free, but rather as highly constrained, and that provides the tool with which we can understand, if only partially, those constraints. Terry Eagleton, whose essay "A Short History of Rhetoric" is quoted with approval by Fish, takes something of a different view. Less certain than Fish or Rorty that language goes all the way down, Eagleton suggests that the role of rhetoric should act *both* as an indicator of the local inscriptions of political ethics and their change over time, and as a means of understanding the material effects (discursive and extra-discursive) of language on social orders. Whereas Fish and Rorty understand rhetoric as subsuming the extra-rhetorical realm, Eagleton—perhaps more in keeping with Plato than with Aristotle—is more willing to understand the material and the discursive as relatively autonomous and as mutually affective. Rhetoric, for Eagleton, becomes a way to examine changes that exceed discursive change, and a way to organize knowledges that may be better excavated by scientific (or other, extra-rhetorical) means.

The book's second section, "Theoretical Elaborations," undertakes an examination of antifoundationalism as a literary and cultural theoretical stance. Most of the essays in this section take for granted an antifoundational worldview as proposed by Rorty and/or Fish, and attempt to understand its theoretical consistency by investigating the extent to which language can be seen as the means by which to understand the world (or, alternately, "the world"). Most of the essays, while granting the persuasiveness and the inevitability of the antifoundational paradigm, nevertheless work to resolve certain contradictions or correct erroneous assumptions about the way language works to "order" our understanding. In "Language Obscures Social Change," for example, Melanie Eckford-Prossor and Michael Clifford invert the notion that language can be seen as something like an indicator for change. Foundations or no foundations, studies of the philosophy of language have traditionally argued a connection between social change and changes in language (whether it be in terms of sentences, semantic structures, or meaning). Antifoundationalism makes the connection much more tenuous: though changes in language are tantamount to changes in our understanding of the world—and in Rorty's understanding, changes in one are equal to changes in the other—it is harder to understand the extent of the relation, because any that might be established is at once subject to the same inquiries as was the original object of inquiry. Changes do occur, however, and it is left to antiformal theorists to decide how to gauge them.

But Eckford-Prossor and Clifford turn this conundrum around. Archaeologies of knowledge may in fact reveal how social change has occurred—and these archaeologies most often take place at the level of language—but these archaeologies are needed in the first place because in its actual use by subjects, language does not indicate or promote change at all. This essay suggests that the "impenetrability and density" that Rorty attributes to language is consistent with the idea that it is less "a deep repository of possible meanings" than it is "'transparent' in its immediacy and in its meaning" for the atemporal now. Users of language may assume that by using language, they are shaping their world; but this activity looks less like the building of fabulous castles of sand on a beach than like the building of an edifice with an erector set, following the directions in the box all the while. Although it is true that archaeologies yield the unused or unarticulated possibilities of a text, Eckford-Prossor and Clifford's point is that it may be more worthwhile to understand the reasons why archaeologies are necessary or, even more interesting, to understand why, at certain crisis points, conventionally used language has so much pressure put on it that it becomes clear the extent to which language acts as a stumbling block to understanding. For example, during the 1992 Republican National Convention, terms like *family* and *normal sexuality* became so overloaded as to make clear their connection and disconnection to an extra-discursive real. More to the point, the possibility of such clarity suggests—as much in accord with Rorty as it is with one of Rorty's paragons of hermeneutic philosophy, Martin Heidegger—that it may be necessary, even in a postfoundational world, to retain a category that is extra-discursive and yet unknowable, unarticulable, or at the very least inaccessible by way of rhetoric.

Michael Hill's "Toward a 'Materialist' Rhetoric: Contingency, Constraint, and the Eighteenth-Century Crowd" and Linda Frost's "The Decentered Subject of Feminism: Postfeminism and *Thelma and Louise*" both begin with the premise that language works simultaneously to indicate change on the one hand and to problematize our understanding of it on the other. For Hill, the eighteenth-century novel serves as a locus within which one can understand "the various and uneven conditions under which it becomes possible (and necessary) to write about female emergencies," and the crowd (as opposed to the consciousness of the individual) serves as a trope used by novelists that describes at once the public for whom they write and the limit of identity (and the articulation of that identity) of the reading and writing subject. That is, the "crisis" in which women find themselves—as depicted in eighteenth-century novels like *The Monk*—is the product of a particular moment in history, which is itself comprised of various competing ideological (political-rhetorical) claims and which is therefore contingent; and yet the crowd, though "novelized" by the eighteenth-century literary ideology, is a historical *effect* that can be explained only by "mov[ing] in various ways *between* traditional epistemological and ontological distinctions" (emphasis added) in order to have at least partial access to the extra-rhetorical "cause" of history. Frost's account of the postfeminist reading of *Thelma and Louise* also takes as its point of departure the antifoundational and decidedly postmodern idea that discourse is both destabilizing in its contingency and indicative of social phenomena that in part constitute it. Feminism is a contested site in a postmodern world in which it "becomes not only a threat to patriarchal authority, but a site of its own cultural authority, itself a decentered subject with multiple and . . . discordant voices speaking in it." *Thelma and Louise,* as a film that "was positioned as self-evidently—and therefore problematically—'feminist' " in its popular reception, becomes for Frost both a text that simultaneously conceals and reveals the discursive "worlds" that give it shape, and the impetus for the production of various postfeminist texts that, in their reaction to the gender- and literary-ideological constructions of women of the film, provide what Rorty would call the incommensurable, or abnormal, discourses that work against the decentering discourses of feminism. Perhaps most interesting about Frost's essay is that, in its juxtaposition of the "feminist" *Thelma and Louise* and its postfeminist receptions—both contingent discourses—it is possible to move from the realm of the discursive (or, if you prefer, the realm of rhetoric) to the realm of the extra-discursive which, as in Hill's description of the novelization of the crowd, is visible mainly in its effect.

Frost's article also articulates the juncture between various feminisms on the one hand and the antifoundational world on the other. "The Decentered Subject of Feminism" takes for granted that feminism is positioned both as a discourse that has acknowledged boundaries and as a practice that transgresses those boundaries. In part, its discussion of *Thelma and Louise* highlights Fish's thesis that the lack of foundations (or, in Frost's case, a center) is not equivalent to the absence of constraints or an object of knowledge in an antifoundational world. Rhetoric, Fish claims, comes with its own rules and regulations, even if they are only those that come within the context of the contemporary moment. Frost's essay is illustrative of the risks that accompany the benefits of a constantly contested field of inquiry.

It is the problem of criteria—those rules and regulations—that concerns Patricia Roberts in "Habermas's Rational-Critical Sphere and the Problem of Criteria." In this essay, Roberts argues that the American Puritans' form of argumentation can be seen as an example of Habermas's understanding of the indisputable nature of logic, and that by examining the consequences of the Puritans' arguments in times of crisis, one gets a sense of how authoritarian (or of how such logic can *become* authoritarian) is Habermas's understanding of a public sphere. This rereading of Habermas ironically places him as something of an absolutist-foundational thinker, a reading that runs counter to his depiction as an antifoundationalist in line with Gadamer because of (1) their acknowledgment of the bias of the historical observer, (2) their understanding of social movement as occurring through a multidirectional dynamic of communication and argument (that is, slow as opposed to revolutionary movement), and (3) their view of culture as polyglot. But in Roberts's reading, Habermas misconstrues logic as axiomatically transcendent of culture, as is illustrated by the suggestion that the Puritans—in a move symptomatic of Habermas's logical argument—link pure rationality to Scripture, without investigating whether its authority is culturally derived. The argument put forward by Habermas tries to do away with the elitism of Gadamer's hermeneutic (based as it is on the notion of the superiority of classical art) by pointing to a democratic ideal of argument and conversation (thereby suggesting an antifoundational alternative to it); but by oddly pointing to criteria of self-evident reasonableness, Habermas goes Gadamer one better on the foundationalism scale and tends toward what can only be called a logical fundamentalism. This reassessment of Habermas illustrates just how difficult it is to take an antifoundational (or social constructivist) position that is theoretically consistent.

This same problem is at issue in Frank Farmer's "Foundational Thuggery." In rehearsing the debate on hermeneutics between Habermas and Gadamer, Farmer calls attention to the rhetorical formulations of each thinker. Though both argue the need to understand the relation between the world as it effects our interpretations of it and the complexities of those interpretations themselves—a thoroughly antifoundational enterprise—the arguments themselves become foundational. As Farmer points out, both in the Habermas-Gadamer debate and in the subsequent choosing up of sides in the debate by people like Fish and Rorty, the primary mode of argument in theoretical and practical debates about what counts as a truth-claim is "subsumption," in which the claims made by your opponent are shown to be thinkable only in terms of some other, prior, claim: the one you have been making. Like Roberts, Farmer notes that it is no wonder anyone (Habermas and Gadamer included) has trouble making his or her claim stick if we rule out foundational claims to truth. The inevitable result seems to be a rhetorical thuggery, but the question then becomes—implicit in Farmer's conclusion—whether there is not some ethical way in which to deploy rhetorical analysis in such a way that it "subsumes" less than it contributes to what Oakeshott called the "conversation of humankind."

The third section, "Extensions and Complications," begins with the assumption that though we live in an antifoundational world, we may need to reconfigure rhetoric in ways that allow it to work as it did for Plato and Aristotle, namely, as an overlapping of conceptual, scientific, and contingent (or situation-specific) knowledge and its deployment as practice. What this practice is takes different forms in the five essays of this section. In the first two, Robert Smith and Kurt Spellmeyer put forward the idea that the methodology that would appear to be most successful given the antifoundational paradigm in the human sciences is ethnography. Smith, who takes as a given nearly every aspect of Rorty's turn to hermeneutics, imbricates Dell Hymes's work in anthropology and Richard Rorty's in language theory. From Hymes, we learn that ethnography's starting point is the "analysis of the communicative habits of a community in their totality," in which the communicative event "is central (in terms of language proper, [this] means that the linguistic code is displaced by the speech act as focus of attention)" (quoted in Smith). From Rorty, we learn that in the current conjuncture, we cannot use the "ocular metaphor"—in which philosophy gives us language with which we can gain direct access to the world, in which philosophy is the "mirror" of nature—and so we must embark on the project of describing our own worlds, without insisting that our world is *the* world. The result, for Smith, is that since we are all "descriptors—as opposed to merely the described or even *seekers* after descriptions (and those descriptions no more than reflections mirrored from some elsewhere)—then, in a very real sense, we are all, already, anthropologists." Smith then reinvokes the move that Kuhn made over twenty-five years ago, suggesting that instead of adjudicating descriptions on the basis of what we believe to be a neutral "scientific" language of meta-descriptions, we should understand them as speech events. Thus to understand fully that one is not necessarily superior or inferior to the other, but simply that they derive from distinct, local custom and worldviews, we need to think of the work we do as understanding speech acts as community-generated and as attempts to forge responsible links among various communities.

The story that links all the various aspects of Smith's essay together is that of the Shuar father, retelling the story of the hummingbird's gift of fire to his son. The Shuar, native peoples of the Amazon Basin, are in jeopardy of being lost to the encroachment of Western science and technology in the search for land and raw materials. For Smith, there is an urgency in his—and Rorty's—rhetorical project: the antifoundational paradigm renders terms like *superior* and *inferior* when used to describe culture as arbitrary and contingent, and so lest we relegate the Shuar to the status of marginal and therefore expendable, we must understand their community as integrally connected to ours by way of the ethnographic (and, at its heart, the rhetorical) project. That is, we need to reconsider rhetoric as a methodology that gives us a way to understand the practical and political consequences of our language, as a way to map social change to change in descriptions, and as a guard against scientist or foundational metaphors that risk returning us to the binary of either/or, which raise progress over understanding and which regularize the process of marginalization.

Something of the same urgency, and the same fear, runs throughout Spellmeyer's essay, " 'Too Little Care': Language, Politics, and Embodiment in the Life-World." It is laced with descriptions of the encounter between Western "ocularists," who see science, philosophy, and their accompanying reason as tools with which to demystify the practices of "uncivilized" peoples and who insist on the dissemination of neutral observation language as the currency of the culture of the center. He also discusses non-Western cultures whose language is descriptive of a world in which the subject and the subject's world are not radically distinct, and in which politics is "a deep politics of experience, 'deep' because it unfolds at the boundary between life-worlds in dialogue or contestation." For Spellmeyer, who also takes for granted the contested paradigm of antifoundationalism, it is surprising that we have neglected this deep politics, since theorists like Rorty, Kuhn, Polanyi, and others have been telling us about it for years, and since our understandings of the body and of class—to mention only two examples—have been thoroughly questioned and have provided a hint of the contested and contestatory world in which we have lived for the last thirty years. Rather than use the dissemination of language and reason as rhetorically agonistic—as argument—Spellmeyer urges us to consider working and teaching with another kind of "reason," one that values an experiential pluralism: "not the liberal pluralism that perpetuates estrangement by ignoring or suppressing difference, but one that values difference as a common resource for the enlargement of life-worlds through an endless, uncoercive exchange." Here we have a restatement of Rorty's rhetorical hermeneutics, in which understanding is negotiated in a spirit of community rather than argued with an eye toward who wins and who loses. And yet at some level Spellmeyer understands that this is, like Habermas's ideal speech situation, belied by the actualities of the contemporary world. It may be our hermeneutic world calls for a rhetoric of deep reason rather than teleological reason, but the fact is that it is easier said than done, because "education and colonization have become too closely allied for any immediate and painless change in our thinking about the uses of knowledge" (34). Spellmeyer then reconsiders the move toward a rhetoric of the life-world in the essay's second half, in which he grants that perhaps clarion calls to rhetoric are not enough, and that rhetorics of embodiment have to begin not across polises but within them, perhaps one person at a time, in "this place where I live and [with] the people to whom I am bound by concern, love, mutual dependence, and the power of memory." Like Smith's, Spellmeyer's project, which also looks something like an ethnography, is local and painstakingly gradual.

The next two essays—Charles Shepherdson's, entitled "History and the Real," and Richard Glejzer's, entitled "The Subject of Invention: Antifoundationalism and Medieval Hermeneutics"—take a rather different view of the nonfoundational world. Rather than exhibiting, in Fish's words, "theory hope," the desire to fill in the gap left by the demise of foundational or neutral observation languages with which we can understand "the world," Shepherdson and Glejzer note that such a move misses the point and the possibilities afforded by Rorty's doing away with epistemology. Whereas Smith and Spellmeyer—and to some extent Frost, Bizzell, Bernard-Donals, Berlin, and others—see Rorty's hermeneutics as a challenge because of its untidiness and because of its failure to give credit to the material and extra-discursive elements of the life-world that may be only marginally accessible through a study of language, both Shepherdson and Glejzer suggest that Rorty provides a challenge because he (perhaps unwittingly) *opens up a space* in which we can observe the extra-discursive effect of language, but in which we must observe it also as a *cause* of our anxiety about its failure and of our misrecognition of language as that which is forced to do the job of science and philosophy in the now marginalized paradigms. Shepherdson connects readings of Foucault, Lacan, and Derrida to suggest that Rorty is moving in the same direction as Foucault—not simply to construct "a more accurate history (the truth about the past—that of the historian) or to erect a great theoretical edifice (a universal truth—that of the philosopher), but to dismantle the narratives that still organize our present experience (a truth that bears on the position of enunciation)." In the case of Victorian sexuality as inscribed by Foucault or by Freud (via Lacan), throwing away standard versions of the law of sexuality and custom does not emancipate human subjects so that they may "enjoy" more freely, more spontaneously, the pleasures of sex; rather, transgression—the drive in humans to enjoy—is in fact a function of the law (which we think of in terms of repression) itself, producing not liberation, but rather the limit of enjoyment (we can enjoy only that which we have been prohibited) as well as a "perverse productivity," the production of that which exceeds the law and its transgression by working against the law.

It is this "excess," this irrational drive—a drive that is not outside culture but rather a direct result and component of culture—that can be read as content but which can also be understood as both symptom and cause of a structure of that which works at the limits of language, at the limits of rhetoric. Whether we call this the unconscious, or the ideological, or the trans-historical, it is the element that, for Spellmeyer and Smith at least, is accounted for by ethnographic methodologies, but which, for Shepherdson, is not accessible at all except as it is understood as symptom, unless we work "at undoing the structure that produced these two related sides" of pleasure and moral constraint, of science and life-worlds, of philosophy and hermeneutics. Glejzer's essay considers how this "undoing" works at the level of a text, collectively known as the Middle Ages. By taking history as the "subject" of the "new Middle Ages," he claims, scholars in Medieval Studies have lately claimed to provide new possibilities to the study of the period, replacing its traditional content with a new set of possibilities by contesting that very content. This allows medievalists to forego the period's own terminologies and contingencies, "foreclosing an investigatory practice of examining how the contextual is itself constituted, a methodology that would allow for an ontological dimension of/in knowledge and meaning." Glejzer contends that this move, however, places the Middle Ages in the realm of the knowable rather than the possible, in that it forecloses the possibilities of meaning in terms of what can be inscribed. And yet medieval theologians and writers themselves seemingly always arrived at the point of impasse, the point at which describing the world in terms of its foundations always fell into the abyss of the impossibility of inscribing those foundations. Medieval scholars, in other words, constantly found themselves at the point of the unwritable, and yet write they did. Glejzer goes on to connect this medieval impasse with the misrecognition of the Middle Ages as a contextualizable entity, and in so doing argues that it is at the contemporary point of misrecognition that we can move from the idea that the Middle Ages is an absence that demands to be filled with a content to the idea that it is this *demand* that is symptomatic of the structure of knowledge. That is, in interrogating not just the subject of invention—content—but the invention of the subject—the structure of knowledge—we have limited access not only to medieval knowledges, but also to contemporary knowledge, neither of which is inscribable, and yet both of which are inscribed. Whereas Spellmeyer and Smith have suggested there are methodologies that allow us to take responsible action and build a communitarian knowledge at the level of discourse, in a way compatible with Rorty and Fish and yet going beyond them in their inclusion of the materiality of the world that escapes inscription, Shepherdson and Glejzer tell a different story: it is discourse that deflects the construction of a communitarian knowledge, and yet in this deflection we have access to the extra-discursive drive that operates in consciousness and produces the discontinuities that lie between socially and individually constituted subjects.

The section concludes with Michael Sprinker's essay, "The Royal Road: Marxism and the Philosophy of Science," in which Rorty's antifoundational paradigm is acknowledged, and yet in which Rorty's hermeneutics is seen as highly problematic and functionally unproductive. In a sense, Sprinker moves beyond Eagleton: it is not clear that even rhetoric will work to produce change in an antifoundational world, because although rhetoric has a link to the material world, it does not provide conceptual or scientific knowledge of the kind that allows change to take place at a social level beyond that of interpretation. While rhetoric may be useful, it needs to be supplemented by a philosophy of science that understands itself as ideologically inscribed and yet functions in spite of this fact. Invoking Roy Bhaskar's critical realism and taking direct aim at Rorty, Sprinker notes that hermeneutics guts the project of the human sciences, in that it waters down human agency so far that it eliminates the possibility of any real, measurable change through a hermeneutic reading. It is *because* language goes all the way down that a rhetorical or hermeneutic redescription can change only individual instances of material life rather than the structures—which exist trans-linguistically—that are in part responsible for it. Putting it in terms of Shepherdson's and Glejzer's essays, while Rorty would allow for a reassessment of the content of the subject's relation to other subjects, he theorizes no way to reassess those relations in anything other than linguistic terms: change takes place at the level of language, but it is hard to see how language may be the effect of other structures that exist somewhere else. Against Stanley Aronowitz's claim that it is not possible to assert that the objective world possesses "an independent power which can be discovered through scientific investigation, specifically through experiment" (quoted in Sprinker), a claim consistent with Kuhn and Rorty (and to some extent, Fish), Sprinker asks if it is possible to believe "that there were no subatomic particles in the universe before their existence was experimentally registered at the end of the nineteenth century, or that such particles cease to exist after they have passed through a cloud chamber and their 'tracks' are recorded." Hermeneutics on Rorty's account—and the rhetorical redescription that attends it to produce change—does not allow for a human agency that can exert any pressure on the structures within which those agents exist, because he separates rhetorical and hermeneutic power from science's explanatory capacity by subsuming that capacity beneath hermeneutics. Sprinker claims that, if we are to do valuable work in the antifoundational paradigm, rhetoric—the study of language and its effects—may not be enough, and that to clear the ground so that the emancipatory work for change may be accomplished, we may need to understand rhetoric as at least having to work alongside other forms of knowledge that reflexively allow agents to understand the nature of those material and linguistic forces that exert pressure on them, or as having at its disposal, because of its connection to events in the polis and to the conceptual knowledge afforded by the human sciences, a method of accounting for and accurately describing the structures of knowledge not accessible through discourse.

The section entitled "Teaching and Writing (in) an Antifoundational World" concludes the book and presents several practical arenas in which the antifoundational paradigm has affected the dissemination of language and knowledge, and examines how the paradigm's theoretical constitution may limit or enhance teaching in traditional and critical incarnations. What becomes clear in this section is that the antifoundational paradigm has perhaps more firmly taken hold in pedagogical circles than it has in theoretical ones—or, at least, it has become a topic for debate from within that it is an object to be resisted from without—and that, by dint of its connection to rhetoric, the study of writing and the practice of teaching have become antifoundational through and through. It also becomes apparent here that the theoretization of pedagogy, as opposed to the teaching of theory, acknowledges the divergent readings of rhetoric that are only touched on in many of the theoretical discussions (see Fish especially), suggesting that rhetoric is a much richer tool (or methodology, or epistemology) than is often assumed.

In "Beyond Antifoundationalism to Rhetorical Authority," Patricia Bizzell uses a discussion of E. D. Hirsch's *Cultural Literacy,* which became a lightning rod for discussions of diversity and the canon immediately after its publication in the mid-1980s, to wonder whether those responsible for the dissemination of knowledge and the teaching of writing understand fully the implications of the antifoundational model. She suggests that Hirsch's book is much more important for what it tells us about a kind of cultural angst: discussions of what constitutes a canon of American culture are symptomatic of a greater fear that is characteristic of antifoundationalism—namely, that without a clear view of what serves as foundational "text," it will be impossible for us to teach "what students need to know" because we cannot say which texts are better or worse *compared to some standard.* If it is not clear that Melville and Twain are superior to Snoop Doggy Dogg and the Stone Temple Pilots, then why should we include the latter pair on course syllabi and not the former; further, if there is not a standard for adjudicating the superiority of standard or academic discourse to nonstandard or everyday discourse, then there is no reason for spending so much time in the writing classroom with our students.

Bizzell, though, sees such worries as groundless and counterproductive, both in their argument and in their counterarguments. They are groundless because, as Fish has said before, there are always constraints to discourse and to discussions of what is standard or in the canon. It is just that these constraints are not handed down from on high but generated from the arguments students and teachers alike have in the classroom and in the journals. The fear that antifoundationalism leads to a loss of criteria for adjudication is baseless, since those criteria are negotiated along with the texts we are trying to place within or outside the canon. But what is perhaps more important, for Bizzell, is that worrying about the consequences of antifoundationalism is counterproductive. In calling Hirsch's supporters essentialists in their attempt to concretize an "American canon," many scholars invoking a cultural studies perspective—in which the object for investigation is not the text so much as the dynamic of text, culture, ideology, and history—seem to fall backward into what Reed Dasenbrock calls in another context a "new essentialism," which valorizes difference over sameness but nevertheless fails to understand the instantiations of power that require such an alternative in the first place. For our purposes, Bizzell's essay suggests not a moral discussion of canonicity and "literacy," but a distinctly *rhetorical and political* one that is "not [seen as] an alternative to moral preoccupations: it is these preoccupations taken seriously in their full implications." Bizzell takes this quotation directly from Eagleton's invocation of rhetoric in his book on literary theory, and in doing so she provides a way of seeing antifoundationalism and rhetoric as intimately conjoined: if language is productive of the social, and if rhetoric is the articulation of political expediency that takes account of commonly held opinions as well as material (discernable and palpable) states of affairs, then the definition of "a rhetorical situation . . . leaves room for change because none of the parties in the conversation is wholly determined either by material circumstances, such as biological gender, *or* by discursive constructions, such as the current cultural interpretations placed on gender" (emphasis added). Bizzell here challenges Rorty's understanding of language as going all the way down, and challenges teachers to get their students to understand that even though language is their only access to the world, the world also "pushes back" on language so as to have effects that go beyond the articulable or "interpretation."

It is from this re-vision of the antifoundational that David Metzger's "Teaching as a Test of Knowledge: Passion, Desire, and the Semblance of Truth in Teaching" begins. The difference between our assumptions that language has effects on the world and that language constitutes the world is akin to the difference Metzger sets up as the one between the semblance of the truth and the "true." What happens when one begins from the antifoundational assumption that the world is (at least in part) constituted by language—which is itself a vexed medium if we also begin (how else could we?) from the structuralist-poststructuralist assumption of language-function through difference—is that teachers may misunderstand students' semblances of the truth for the true; or we may insist that students provide us with "knowledge" when instead they refuse—because they see the teacher's mistake—and instead "dissemble." This is the end of teaching:

Imagine the following conversation:

Teacher: You realize that you don't really prove any of your statements about O. J. Simpson in your paper.
Student: Yes, of course.

A teacher might go on to ask why the student chose not to support his or her assertions about O. J. Simpson. The student could then demonstrate that every problem the instructor had with the paper was the result of a . . . choice . . . not to communicate or not to learn.

The impasse occurs when the instructor fails to theorize resistance or—in Žižek's terms—cynicism in his or her students, and misunderstands the student's semblance of truth for what he or she thinks is the student's "truth." The impasse could be said to be that between "knowing *x*" and "knowing how to do *x.*" Teachers who begin with the antifoundational insistence that language (at least in part) constitutes "the truth," need, Metzger insists, to get beyond assuming that these two are the same, and must instead surprise the student by acknowledging that they understand the difference and are capable of working against the easy equation. In other words, if a student cynically refuses to "do" *x,* and the teacher insists that this refusal stems from a misunderstanding of the task, then teaching ends. In this scenario, the teacher assumes that the truth of the matter ends with the refusal, and that the refusal is equivalent with the real. But if the student who refuses is confronted by a teacher who understands that the refusal is not commensurate with knowledge "of" *x,* then that moment of surprise may provide the student with knowledge of the difference and the willingness to move from one to the other. In a sense, what Metzger is getting at in his essay is that by suggesting that dissemination is the object of pedagogy in the current antifoundational conjuncture, we overemphasize the discursive properties of rhetoric without properly understanding that there are limits to the discursive that our student may at some level recognize and use, but which we also must work into our teaching.

Both Ellen Gardiner and James Berlin make the same point as Metzger, but from a different perspective. In "Composition Studies and Cultural Studies: Collapsing Boundaries," Berlin again invokes Eagleton's call for a reclamation of rhetoric and suggests that "cultural studies might then be described as the examination of the ways discursive formations are related to power or, alternately, the study of language's uses in the service of power." Cultural studies' underpinnings are possible only on a poststructural or antifoundational construal of philosophy: not only cultural understandings and products but also "subjectivities are produced, not given, and are therefore the objects of inquiry, not the premises or starting points" (Richard Johnson, quoted in Berlin). It is necessary, then, to understand the writing of pedagogy as involving not just the production of texts, but also the production of subjects, always bearing in mind that the study of both requires careful attention to "economic, social and political considerations that are always historically specific," and that in studying the reception of texts, the aim is to work toward an openly democratic society "that promises a space for open and free critique and yet denies it at every turn." Rhetoric is the ideal methodological tool for this two-pronged study, since it was, after all, "invented to resolve disputes peacefully, as an alternative to armed conflict, and it remains the best option in a perilous time." Whereas Metzger sees rhetoric—or at least the dissemination of knowledge as a rhetorical act—as a troubled practice unless one recognizes the aporia between the truth of the world (and its material, extra-discursive dimension) and what appears to be true, Berlin suggests that the two are so intimately related as to allow a change in one's interpellation by discursive means to affect change in one's social and material circumstances. Yet it is not altogether clear whether, first, rhetoric was not in its own way violent, and second, if it was not, whether it was at all successful in providing a useful "alternative to armed conflict." Even Rorty, toward the end of the most hopeful section of *Philosophy and the Mirror of Nature,* suggests that there is a difference between one's discussions about "the world" and those material dangers represented by "the scarcity of food [and] the secret police" (389), which might be interpreted as leaving open room for extra-discursive phenomena that may nevertheless only be inscribed rhetorically. Moreover, though rhetoric might be seen as liberatory in an antifoundational world in which the argument over principles of adjudication might allow us to understand the constraints within which we operate, Plato in the *Gorgias* (Eagleton's model) has Socrates wondering whether the reasonable articulation of an ethical praxis could prevent human suffering and a violent world.

Given such a world, and wondering, like Metzger, how to confront students who are much more savvy about their place in a world of semblances, Ellen Gardiner asks whether Peter Elbow's expressivist rhetoric and liberatory motives work against the grain of a constructivist or epistemic pedagogy. The heart of the matter, in "What We Need to Know about Writing *and* Reading, or Peter Elbow and Antifoundationalism," is whether Elbow's critics are right when they label him a foundationalist, or, if they are not right, whether his iconoclasm and anti-institutional rhetoric do not hide a naïveté to the intransigence of ideology and its material traces. Elbow's pedagogy works to empower students by investing them with a certain authority: students have had experiences in a world of work and play, and they have access to a language that they know has an effect and can influence peers, parents, friends, and teachers. At the same time, he places limits of what some have called "politeness" on the kinds of responses that peers might provide to writing produced in the classroom but which is meant to replicate the "real world" situation. Gardiner concludes that such a dual purpose presents a paradox in "Elbow's rhetoric of reading [such] that to recuperate authentic motives for reading and writing, to make the exchange between the writer and reader more authentic, he actually prevents the relationship between writer and reader from being authentically social by excluding the possibility of the kind of negotiation that happens in ordinary conversation." Like the problem that many have pointed to in Fish's understanding of the antifoundational world and in Rorty's hermeneutics of "normal and abnormal discourse," Elbow's pedagogy enjoins students to understand that they already know how to communicate in the world "out there," and yet removes a way to know that world through any discourse but an institutionally provided and institutionally guided one that renders rhetoric neither connected nor wholly disconnected from the constraints students experience both inside and outside the institution.

"Composition in an Antifoundational World: A Critique and a Proposal" marks a transition between assuming that current antifoundational models of the world suffice and providing other ways of negotiating a world that constitutes and is constituted by the discursive. In this essay, Michael Bernard-Donals outlines the two prevalent versions of the antifoundational paradigm in composition studies: a "weak" version, like Elbow's and Bruffee's social constructionist (or, in Elbow's case, a mix of expressivist and social) views of the self; and a "strong" version, like Bizzell's, which suggests that while language may go all the way down, so do extra-rhetorical facts, though they are explainable only in unscientific and ideological ways. Teaching writing, in the stronger version of the paradigm, involves situating students differently and in unorthodox relations to one another such that they are able to "rearticulate" their subjectivities and "view the world" through different eyes. Bernard-Donals suggests that this is not enough, since it does not provide a way for students—or, for that matter, their teachers—to understand the ways in which those extra-discursive facts may exert an equally extra-discursive power. He also advances a theory of "transcendental realism," derived from a realist philosophy of science proposed by Roy Bhaskar and elaborated here by Sprinker, as a way to examine the material constraints within which discourses are made through a process of observation and testing, modeled after the experimental sciences. While this model attempts to match the rigorous method of science, it nonetheless understands the process to take place *alongside* (though not necessarily within) the realm of the discursive and the ideological. In other words, Bernard-Donals puts forward the idea that there really does need to be something which language goes all the way down *into,* and that this "something" can be plumbed rhetorically only if we understand rhetoric as having both a material and a discursive dimension. Though rhetoric may have, in this view, a significant role in an antifoundational world, it must also be paired with a method that understands language as tethered to the material-real, and that we must understand the effects of the real on us even if we are not able to understand those effects in an unmediated, neutral-observation language.

Notes

1. Though truth and fact are dying a slow death by antifoundationalism, foundationalist philosophers fear, belief lives on. Fish's point is that the acceptance of antifoundationalism nevertheless has no consequences for rational inquiry and successful communication except for a change in the claims made about such inquiry and success. The valid procedures for inquiry and the criteria for successful communication can change from community to community, era to era, but some such procedures and criteria are always in place at any particular historical moment. It remains to be seen whether these procedures remain in the province of the human sciences, or whether we must rely on more rigorously scientific methods in order to salvage them for critical inquiry (see the chapters by Bernard-Donals, Sprinker, and Metzger).

2. See Eagleton's "A Short History of Rhetoric," herein; it also appeared in *Walter Benjamin: or, Towards a Revolutionary Criticism.*

3. See, for example, Roy Bhaskar's "Rorty, Realism, and the Idea of Freedom," in *Reclaiming Reality;* Donna Haraway's *Simians, Cyborgs and Women;* Sandra Harding, "Rethinking Standpoint Epistemology"; Michael Sprinker, *Imaginary Relations;* Michael Bernard-Donals, "The Rodney King Verdict, the New York *Times,* and the 'Normalization' of the Los Angeles Riots."

4. It will be part of the task of this book to inquire as to whether, as regards the accessibility to the material-real, (1) all disciplines of inquiry use rhetoric, so rhetorical analysis is significantly relevant to analyzing all disciplines and their claims to accessing the material-real, or (2) rhetorical analysis is useful for analyzing contextualized language use but there is more at work in the practices of inquiry beside language, making rhetoric's contact with the material-real severely restricted.

5. See also Jane Tompkins's early essay, "The Reader in History," in which she makes similar claims for the relevance of rhetoric in a "post-theoretical" world. She claims, however, a somewhat more limited role for rhetoric as the protoreception theory, suggesting that the similarity between contemporary understandings of language and a classical is "the common perception of language as a form of power," though it is mainly the power of interpretation rather than the power of compulsion (226). Where Eagleton speaks favorably of Tisias, Corax, and Plato, each of whom in one way or another connected rhetoric to both philosophy and praxis, Tompkins begins her discussion with Longinus's understanding of interpretation and hints that Plato's expulsion of the poets in *The Republic* was the result of his primarily aesthetic rather than rhetorical understanding of language.

6. See Chaim Perelman, *The Realm of Rhetoric,* especially his chapters entitled

"Quasi-logical Arguments" and "Arguments Based on the Structure of Reality," both of which have a hard time distinguishing between rhetorical figure and the "reality" on which it is based; and see Stephen Mailloux, *Rhetorical Power.*

7. See, for example, Cary Nelson's *Theory in the Classroom;* Bruce Henricksen and Thais Morgan's *Reorientations: Critical Theories and Pedagogies;* Donald Morton and Mas'ud Zavarzadeh's *Theory/Pedagogy/Politics;* and Maria-Regina Kecht's *Pedagogy Is Politics.* See also Bernard-Donals's essay "Teaching Theory."

Works Cited

Bernard-Donals, Michael. "The Rodney King Verdict, the New York *Times,* and the 'Normalization' of the Los Angeles Riots; or, What Antifoundationalism Can't Do." *Cultural Critique* 27 (spring 1994): 61–87.

——. "Teaching Theory." *Minnesota Review* NS 41–42 (fall 1993–spring 1994): 298–309.

Bhaskar, Roy. *Reclaiming Reality: A Critical Introduction to Contemporary Philosophy.* New York: Verso, 1989.

Derrida, Jacques. "Signature Event Context." Trans. Alan Bass. *Margins of Philosophy.* Chicago: University of Chicago Press, 1982: 307–30.

Eagleton, Terry. *Literary Theory: An Introduction.* Minneapolis: University of Minnesota Press, 1983.

——. "A Small History of Rhetoric." *Walter Benjamin: or, Towards a Revolutionary Criticism.* New York: Verso, 1981: 101–13.

Fish, Stanley. *Doing What Comes Naturally: Change, Rhetoric, and the Practice of Theory in Literary and Legal Studies.* Durham, N.C.: Duke University Press, 1989.

Haraway, Donna. *Simians, Cyborgs and Women.* New York: Routledge, 1991.

Harding, Sandra. "Rethinking Standpoint Epistemology: What Is 'Strong Objectivity'?" *Centennial Review* 36.3 (fall 1992): 437–70.

Henricksen, Bruce, and Thais Morgan, eds. *Reorientations: Critical Theories and Pedagogies.* Urbana: University of Illinois Press, 1990.

Kecht, Maria-Regina, ed. *Pedagogy Is Politics: Literary Theory and Critical Teaching.* Urbana: University of Illinois Press, 1992.

Kuhn, Thomas. *The Structure of Scientific Revolutions.* Chicago: University of Chicago Press, 1969.

Lacan, Jacques. "Science and Truth." Trans. Bruce Fink. *Newsletter of the Freudian Field* 3.1–2 (spring/fall 1989): 4–29.

Mailloux, Stephen. *Rhetorical Power.* Ithaca: Cornell University Press, 1989.

Morton, Donald, and Mas'ud Zavarzadeh, eds. *Theory/Pedagogy/Politics: Texts for Change.* Urbana: University of Illinois Press, 1991.

Nelson, Cary, ed. *Theory in the Classroom.* Urbana: University of Illinois Press, 1986.

Perelman, Chaim. *The Realm of Rhetoric.* Notre Dame, Ind.: University of Notre Dame Press, 1982.

Plato. *Gorgias.* Trans. Walter Hamilton. London: Penguin, 1960.

Rorty, Richard. *Consequences of Pragmatism.* Minneapolis: University of Minnesota Press, 1982.

——. *Contingency, Irony, and Solidarity.* Cambridge: Cambridge University Press, 1989.

——. *Philosophy and the Mirror of Nature.* Princeton: Princeton University Press, 1979.

Sprinker, Michael. *Imaginary Relations.* New York: Verso, 1986.

——. "Knowing, Believing, Doing: How Can We Study Literature, and Why Should We Anyway?" *ADE Bulletin* 98 (spring 1991): 46–55.

——. "The War against Theory." *Minnesota Review* NS 39–40 (fall 1993–spring 1994): 103–21.

Tompkins, Jane. "The Reader in History: The Changing Shape of Literary Response." *Reader Response Criticism: From Formalism to Post-Structuralism.* Ed. Jane Tompkins. Baltimore: Johns Hopkins University Press, 1980: 200–232.

Winkler, Karen. "Scholars Mark the Beginning of the Age of 'Post-Theory.'" *Chronicle of Higher Education* (13 October 1993): A 8–9, 16–17.

I
Antifoundationalism and Rhetoric

1
Rhetoric

Stanley Fish

> . . . up rose
> *Belial,* in act more graceful and humane;
> A fairer person lost not Heav'n; he seem'd
> For dignity compos'd and high exploit:
> But all was false and hollow; though his Tongue
> Dropt Manna, and could make the worse appear
> The better reason, to perplex and dash
> Maturest counsels: for his thoughts were low; . . .
> . . . yet he pleas'd the ear,
> And with persuasive accent thus began.
> —*Paradise Lost,* II, 108–15, 117–18

For Milton's seventeenth-century readers this passage, introducing one of the more prominent of the fallen angels, would have been immediately recognizable as a brief but trenchant essay on the art and character of the rhetorician. Indeed in these few lines Milton has managed to gather and restate with great rhetorical force (a paradox of which more later) all of the traditional arguments against rhetoric. Even Belial's gesture of rising is to the (negative) point: he catches the eye even before he begins to speak, just as Satan will in Book IX when he too raises himself and moves so that "each part, / Motion, each act won audience ere the tongue" (673–74). That is, he draws attention to his appearance, to his surface, and the suggestion of superficiality (a word to be understood in its literal meaning) extends to the word *act,* that which can be seen. That act is said to be "graceful," the first in a succession of double meanings (one of the stigmatized attributes of rhetorical speech) we find in the passage. Belial is precisely *not* full of grace; that is simply his outward aspect, and the same is true for "humane" and "fairer." The verse's judgment on all of his apparent virtues is delivered in the last two words of line 110—"he seem'd"—and the shadow of "seeming" falls across the next line, which in isolation might "seem" to be high praise. But under the pressure of what precedes it, the assertion of praise undoes itself with every janus-faced word (the verse now begins to imitate the object of its criticism by displaying a pervasive disjunction between its outer and inner meanings; indicting seeming, it itself repeatedly seems): "compos'd" now carries its pejorative meaning of affected or made-up; "high" at once refers to the favored style of bombastic orators and awaits its ironic and demeaning contrast with the lowness of his thoughts; "dignity" is an etymological joke, for Belial is anything but worthy; in fact, he is just what the next line says he is, "false and hollow," an accusation that repeats one of the perennial antirhetorical topoi—that rhetoric, the art of fine speaking, is all show, grounded in nothing but its own empty pretensions, unsupported by any relation to truth. "There is no need," declares Socrates in Plato's *Gorgias,* "for rhetoric to know the facts at all, for it has hit upon a means of persuasion that enables it to appear in the eyes of the ignorant to know more than those who really know" (459), and in the *Phaedrus* the title figure admits that the "man who plans to be an orator" need not "learn what is really just and true, but only what seems so to the crowd" (260).

This reference to the vulgar popular ear indicates that rhetoric's deficiencies are not only epistemological (sundered from truth and fact) and moral (sundered from true knowledge and sincerity) but social: it panders to the worst in people and moves them to base actions, exactly as Belial is said to do in the next, famous, run-on statement, "and could make the worse appear / The better reason." This is an explicit reference to a nest of classical sources: the most familiar is Aristotle, *Rhetoric,* II, 1402, 23, condemning the skill of being able to make arguments on either side of a question: "This . . . illustrates what is meant by making the worse argument appear the better. Hence people were right in objecting to the training Protagoras undertook to give them" (Roberts 14). Socrates makes the same point in the *Phaedrus:* "an orator who knows nothing about good or evil undertakes to persuade a city in the same state of ignorance . . . by recommending evil as though it were good" (260). Behind Belial (or descending from him; the direction of genealogy in *Paradise Lost* is always problematic), is the line of sophists—Protagoras, Hippias, Gorgias— shadowy figures known to us mostly through the writings of Plato where they appear always as relativist foils for the idealistic Socrates. The judgment made on them by a philosophic tradition dominated by Plato is the judgment here made on Belial; their thoughts were low, centered on the suspect skills they taught for hire; the danger they represented is the danger Belial represents: despite the lowness of their thoughts, perhaps *because* of the lowness of their thoughts, they pleased the ear, at least the ear of the promiscuous crowd (there is always just beneath the surface of the antirhetorical stance a powerful and corrosive elitism), and the explanation of their unfortunate success is the power Belial now begins to exercise, the power of "persuasive accent." Encoded in this phrase is a continuing debate about the essence of rhetoric, a debate whose two poles are represented by Gorgias's praise in the *Encomium of Helen* of rhetoric as an irresistible force and the stoic Cato's characterization of the rhetorician as a good man skilled at speaking (*vir bonus, dicendi peritus*). The difference is that for Gorgias the skill is detached from any necessary moral center and represents a self-sustaining power ("persuasion allied to words can mould men's minds"), while for Cato the skill is a by-product of a focus on goodness and truth (thus the other of his famous aphorisms, "seize the thing, the words will follow"—*rem tene, verba sequentur*—which later flowers in the Renaissance distinction between *res et verba*). In one position eloquence is the hard-won creation of a special and technical facility, a facility one acquires by mastering a set of complicated—and morally neutral—rules; in the other eloquence is what naturally issues when a man is in close touch with the Truth and allows it to inspire him. Born, it would seem, in a posture of defensiveness, rhetoric has often gravitated toward this latter view in an effort to defuse the charge that it is amoral. Quintilian's formulation (itself gathered from the writings of Cicero) is one that will later be echoed in countless treatises: "No man can speak well who is not good himself," *bene dicere non possit nisi bonus* (*Institutio Oratoria*, II, xv, 34). As a defense, however, this declaration has the disadvantage of implying the superfluousness of rhetoric, an implication fully realized in Augustine's *On Christian Doctrine,* where eloquence is so much subordinated to wisdom that it disappears as a distinct and separable property. Belial, in contrast, is wholly defined by that property, by his ability to produce "persuasive accents." "Accent" here is a powerfully resonant word, one of whose relevant meanings is "mode of utterance peculiar to an individual, locality or nation" (OED). He who speaks "in accent" speaks from a particular *angled* perspective into which he tries to draw his auditors; he also speaks in the rhythms of song (etymologically, accent means "song added to speech"), which as Milton will soon observe "*charms* the sense" (II, 556). "Persuasive accent" then is almost a redundancy: the two words mean the same thing, and what they tell the reader is that he or she is about to be exposed to a force whose exercise is unconstrained by any sense of responsibility either to the Truth or to the Good. So dangerous does Milton consider this force that he feels it necessary to provide a corrective gloss as soon as Belial stops speaking: "Thus *Belial* with words cloth'd in reason's garb / Counsell'd ignoble ease and peaceful sloth" (II, 226–27). Just in case you hadn't noticed.

I have lingered so long over this passage because we can extrapolate from it almost all of the binary oppositions in relation to which rhetoric has received its (largely negative) definition: inner/outer, deep/surface, essential/peripheral, unmediated/mediated, clear/colored, necessary/contingent, straightforward/angled, abiding/fleeting, reason/passion, things/words, realities/illusions, fact/opinion, neutral/partisan. Underlying this list, which is by no means exhaustive, are three basic oppositions: first between a truth that exists independently of all perspectives and points of view and the many truths that emerge and seem perspicuous when a particular perspective or point of view has been established and is in force; second, an opposition between true knowledge, which is knowledge as it exists apart from any and all systems of belief, and the knowledge that, because it flows from some or other system of belief, is incomplete and partial (in the sense of biased); and third, an opposition between a self or consciousness that is turned outward in an effort to apprehend and attach itself to truth and true knowledge, and a self or consciousness that is turned inward in the direction of its own prejudices, which far from being transcended, continue to inform its every word and action.

Each of these oppositions is attached in turn to an opposition between two kinds of language: on the one hand, language that faithfully reflects or reports on matters of fact uncolored by any personal or partisan agenda or desire, and on the other hand, language that is infected by partisan agendas and desires, and therefore colors and distorts the facts that it purports to reflect. It is use of the second kind of language that makes one a rhetorician, while adherence to the first kind makes one a seeker after truth and an objective observer of the way things are. It is this distinction that, as Thomas Kuhn notes, underwrites the claims of science to be a privileged form of discourse because it has recourse to a "neutral observation language" (Kuhn 125), a language uninflected by any mediating presuppositions or preconceptions, and it is the same distinction that informs Aristotle's observation that "nobody uses fine language when teaching geometry" (*Rhetoric*, III, 1404). The language of geometry—of formal rules with no substantive content—is contrasted by Aristotle to all those languages that are intended only to "charm the hearer," the languages of manipulation, deception, and self-consciously deployed strategy.

It is this understanding of linguistic possibilities and dangers that generates a succession of efforts to construct a language from which all perspectival bias (a redundant phrase) has been eliminated, efforts that have sometimes taken as a model the notations of mathematics, at other times the operations of logic, and more recently the purely formal calculations of a digital computer. Whether it issues in the elaborate linguistic machines of seventeenth-century "projectors," or in the building (à la Chomsky) of a "competence" model of language abstracted from any particular performance, or in the project of Esperanto or some other artificial language claiming universality (see Lange), or in the fashioning of a Habermasian "ideal speech situation" in which all assertions express "a 'rational will' in relation to a common interest ascertained without deception" (*Legitimation Crisis* 108), the impulse behind the effort is always the same: to establish a form of communication that escapes partiality and aids us in first determining and then affirming what is absolutely and objectively true, a form of communication that in its structure and operations is the very antithesis of rhetoric, of passionate partisan discourse.

That desideratum and the fears behind it have received countless articulations, but never have they been articulated with more precision than in these sentences from Bishop Sprat's *History of the Royal Society of London* (1667):

> When I consider the means of *happy living,* and the causes of their *corruption,* I can hardly forbear . . . concluding that *eloquence* ought to be banish'd out of all *civil societies,* as a thing fatal to Peace and good Manners. . . . They [the ornaments of speaking] are in open defiance against *Reason;* professing not to hold much correspondence with that; but with its slaves, *the Passions:* they give the mind a motion too changeable, and bewitching, to consist with *right practice.* Who can behold, without indignation, how many mists and uncertainties, these specious *Tropes* and *Figures* have brought on our Knowledge? How many rewards, which are due to more profitable, and difficult arts, have been snatch'd away by the easie vanity of *fine speaking?* (quoted in Howell, 111–13)

The terms of banishment are exactly those invoked by Plato against the poets in Book X of his *Republic:* Homer, Socrates says, may be "the most poetic of poets and the first of tragedians, but we must know the truth [and] we can admit no poetry into our city save only hymns to the gods and the praises of good men; for if you grant admission to the honeyed Muse . . . pleasure and pain will be lords of your city instead of law and that which shall . . . have approved itself to the general reason as the best" (607a). The "honeyed Muse" is precisely what Belial becomes when his tongue drops Manna (113), a quintessentially idolatrous act in which he substitutes his own word for the word sent down to us by God and therefore deprives us of the direction that God's word might have given us. Although the transition from classical to Christian thought is marked by many changes, one thing that does not change is the status of rhetoric in relation to a foundational vision of truth and meaning. Whether the center of that vision is a personalized deity or an abstract geometric reason, rhetoric is the force that pulls us away from that center and into its own world of ever-shifting shapes and shimmering surfaces.

Of course, the allure of surfaces and shapes, of "specious *Tropes* and *Figures,*" would not be felt if there were not something already in us that inclined to it. Rhetoric may be a danger that assaults us from without, but its possible success is a function of an *inner* weakness. The entire art, as Aristotle explains regretfully, is predicated on "the defects of our hearers" (*Rhetoric,* III, 1404a), on the assumption that members of the audience will be naturally susceptible to the rhetorician's appeal. The antirhetorical stance can be coherent only if it posits an *in*coherence at the heart (literally) of the self that is both rhetoric's victim and its source. That self is always presented as divided, as the site of contesting forces; in Christian terms the forces are named the carnal and the spiritual; in secular psychologies the names are passion and reason or the willful and the rational; but whatever the names, the result is a relationship of homology between the inner and outer landscapes, both of which contain a core element of truth and knowledge that is continually threatened by a penumbra of irrationality.[1] If tropes and figures "give the mind a motion too changeable," it is because the principle of change, in the form of the passions, already lives in the mind, and it follows then that banishing eloquence and the poets from your republic will only do half the job. As Milton puts it in the *Areopagitica,* "they are not skillful considerers of human things who imagine to remove sin by removing the matter of sin" (297); policing the outer landscape will be of little effect if the inner landscape remains host to the enemy, to sin, to error, to show.

It is the view of the antirhetoricians that this double task of inner and outer regulation can be accomplished by linguistic reform, by the institution of conditions of communication that at once protect discourse from the irrelevancies and contingencies that would compromise its universality and insulate the discoursing mind from those contingencies and irrelevancies it itself harbors.

Bishop Wilkins proposes to fashion a language that will admit neither *Super-fluities*—plural signifiers of a single signified, more than one word for a particular thing—nor *Equivocals*—signifiers doing multiple duty, single words that refer to several things—nor *Metaphor*—a form of speech that interposes itself between the observer and the referent and therefore contributes "to the disguising of it with false appearances" (Howell 17–18). The idea is that such a language, purged of ambiguity, redundancy, and indirection, will be an appropriate instrument for the registering of an independent reality, and that if people will only submit themselves to that language and remain within the structure of its stipulated definitions and exclusions, they will be incapable of formulating and expressing wayward, subjective thoughts and will cease to be a danger either to themselves or to those who hearken to them. In this way, says Wilkins, they will be returned to that original state in which the language spoken was the language God gave Adam, a language in which every word perfectly expressed its referent (on the model of Adam's simultaneously understanding the nature of the animals and conferring upon them their names), a language that in course of time and "emergencies" has unfortunately "admitted various and *casual alterations*" (19).

In the twentieth century, Wilkins's program is echoed point for point (absent the theological scaffolding) by Rudolf Carnap, who would admit into the lexicon only words that can be tied firmly to "protocol" or "observation" sentences, sentences that satisfy certain truth conditions and are therefore verifiable by reference to the facts of the world. The stipulation of this criterion, Carnap asserts, "takes away one's freedom to decide what one wishes to 'mean' by [a] word" (63). The freedom of individual speakers and hearers would be further taken away if the words of a verifiable lexicon were embedded in a grammar that "corresponded exactly to logical syntax," for if that were the case "pseudo-statements could not arise" (68). That is, no one could be misled either by the words of another or by that part of one's consciousness inclined to wander from the path of truth; the tendency of language to perform in excess of its proper duty—to report or reflect matters of fact—would be curbed in advance and the mind's susceptibility to the power of a language unconstrained by its empirical moorings would be neutralized. In short, the danger posed by rhetoric, both to the field of discourse and to the discoursing consciousness, would have been eliminated. Of course there are important differences to be noted between the idealism of Plato, the antienthusiasm of a Restoration bishop, and the logical positivism of a member of the Vienna Circle, but together (and in the company of countless others) they stand on the same side of a quarrel that Plato was already calling "old" in the fifth century before Christ. That quarrel, the quarrel between philosophy and rhetoric, survives every sea change in the history of Western thought, continually presenting us with the (skewered) choice between the plain unvarnished truth straightforwardly presented and the powerful but insidious appeal of "fine language," language that has transgressed the limits of representation and substituted its own forms for the forms of reality.[2]

To this point my presentation has been as skewered as this choice, because it has suggested that rhetoric has received only negative characterizations. In fact, there have always been friends of rhetoric, from the sophists to the anti-foundationalists of the present day, and in response to the realist critique they have devised (and repeated) a number of standard defenses. Two of these defenses are offered by Aristotle in the *Rhetoric*. First, he defines rhetoric as a faculty or art whose practice will help us to observe "in any given case the available means of persuasion" (1355b) and points out that as a faculty is it not in and of itself inclined away from truth. Bad men may abuse it, but that after all "is a charge which may be made in common against all good things." "What makes a man a 'sophist,'" he declares, "is not his faculty, but his moral purpose." To the anticipated objection that rhetoric's potential for misuse is a reason for eschewing it, Aristotle replies that it is sometimes a necessary adjunct to the cause of truth, first because if we leave the art to be cultivated by deceivers, they will lead truth-seekers astray, and second because, regrettable though it may be, "before some audiences not even the possession of the exactest knowledge will make it easy for what we say to produce conviction," and on those occasions "we must use, as our modes of persuasion and argument, notions possessed by everybody" (1355a). That is, because of the defects of our hearers the truth itself must often be rhetorically dressed so that it will gain acceptance.[3]

Aristotle's second defense is more aggressively positive and responds directly to one of the most damaging characterizations of rhetoric: "We must be able to employ persuasion, just as strict reasoning can be employed, on opposite sides of a question, not in order that we may in practice employ it in both ways (for we must not make people believe what is wrong), but in order that we may see clearly what the facts are" (1355a). In short, properly used, rhetoric is a heuristic, helping us not to distort the facts, but to discover them, and moreover, adds Aristotle, the setting forth of contrary views of a matter will have the beneficial effect of showing us which of those views most accords with the truth because "the underlying facts do not lend themselves equally well to the contrary views." By this argument, as Peter Dixon has pointed out, Aristotle "removes rhetoric from the realm of the haphazard and the fanciful" (14) and rejoins it to that very realm of which it was said to be the great subverter.

But if this is the strength of Aristotle's defense, it is also its weakness, for in making it he reinforces the very assumptions in relation to which rhetoric will always be suspect, assumptions of an independent reality whose outlines can be perceived by a sufficiently clear-eyed observer who can then represent them in a transparent verbal medium. The stronger defense, because it hits at the heart of the opposing tradition, is one that embraces the accusations of that tradition and makes of them a claim. The chief accusation, as we have seen, is that rhetoricians hold "the probable (or likely-seeming, plausible) in more honour than the true" (*Phaedrus* 267a). The sophist response is to assert that the realm of the probable—of what is likely to be so, given particular conditions within some local perspective—is the only relevant realm of consideration for human beings. The argument is contained in two statements attributed famously to Protagoras. The first declares the unavailability (not the unreality) of the gods: "About gods I cannot say either that they are or that they are not." And the second follows necessarily from the absence of godly guidance: "Man is the measure of all things, of the things that are that they are, and of the things that are not that they are not." What this means, as W. K. C. Guthrie has pointed out, is "that the Sophists recognized only accidental as opposed to essential being . . . the conditional and relative as opposed to the self-existent" (193). This is not to say that the categories of the true and good are abandoned, but that in different contexts they will be filled differently and that there exists no master context (for that could be occupied only by the unavailable gods) from the vantage point of which the differences could be assessed and judged.

The result is to move rhetoric from the disreputable periphery to the necessary center: for if the highest truth for any person is what he or she believes it to be, the skill that produces belief and therefore establishes what, in a particular time and particular place, is true, is the skill essential to the building and maintaining of a civilized society. In the absence of a revealed truth, rhetoric is that skill, and in teaching it the sophists were teaching "the one thing that mattered, how to take care of one's own affairs and the business of the state" (Guthrie 186). Rhetoricians are like physicians; it is their job "to diagnose the particular institution and prescribe the best course of action for a man or a state under given conditions" (Guthrie 187); and when Socrates asks Protagoras whether he is "promising to make men good citizens," the reply is firm: "That . . . is exactly what I profess to do" (*Protagoras* 319a). Of course in this context words like *good* and *best* do not have the meanings a Plato or Socrates would want them to have—good and best in any and all circumstances; rather they refer to what would appear to be the better of the courses that seem available in what are generally understood to be the circumstantial constraints of a particular situation; but since, according to the sophist view, particular situations are the only kind there are, circumstantial determinations of what is good are as good as you're going to get.

That is, as I have already said, the strongest of the defenses rhetoric has received because it challenges the basic premise of the antirhetorical stance, the premise that any discourse must be measured against a stable and independent reality. To the accusation that rhetoric deals only with the realms of the probable and contingent and forsakes truth, the sophists and their successors respond that truth itself is a contingent affair and assumes a different shape in the light of differing local urgencies and the convictions associated with them. "Truth was individual and temporary, not universal and lasting, for the truth for any man was . . . what he could be persuaded of" (Guthrie 51). Not only does this make rhetoric—the art of analyzing and presenting local exigencies—a form of discourse no one can afford to ignore, it renders the opposing discourse— formal philosophy—irrelevant and beside the point. This is precisely Isocrates' thesis in his *Antidosis*. Abstract studies like geometry and astronomy, he says, do not have any "useful application either to private or public affairs . . . after they are learned . . . they do not attend us through life nor do they lend aid in what we do, but are wholly divorced from our necessities" (261–62). Indeed he goes so far as to deny to such disciplines the label "philosophy," for "I hold that man to be wise who is able by his powers of conjecture to arrive generally at the best course, and I hold that man to be a philosopher who occupies himself with the studies from which he will most quickly gain that kind of insight" (271). Men who want to do some good in the world, he concludes, "must banish utterly from their interests all vain speculations and all activities which have no bearing on our lives."

What Isocrates does (at least rhetorically) is shift the balance of power between philosophy and rhetoric by putting philosophy on the defensive. This same strategy is pursued after him by Cicero and Quintilian, the most influential of the Roman rhetoricians. In the opening pages of his *De Inventione* Cicero elaborates the myth that will subsequently be invoked in every defense of humanism and belles lettres. There was a time, he says, when "men wandered at large in the field like animals," and there was "as yet no ordered system of religious worship nor of social duties" (I, 2). It was then that a "great and wise" man "assembled and gathered" his uncivilized brothers and "introduced them to every useful and honorable occupation, though they cried out against it at first because of its novelty." Nevertheless, he gained their attention through "reason and eloquence" (*propter rationem atque orationem*) and by these means he "transformed them from wild savages into a kind and gentle folk." Nor would it have been possible, Cicero adds, to have "turned men . . . from their habits" if wisdom had been "mute and voiceless"; only "a speech at the same time powerful and entrancing could have induced one who had great physical strength to submit to justice without violence." From that time on, "many cities have been founded . . . the flames of a multitude of wars have been extinguished, and . . . the strongest alliances and most sacred friendships have been formed not only by the use of reason, but also more easily by the use of eloquence" (I, 1). Whereas in the foundationalist story an original purity (of vision, purpose, procedure) is corrupted when rhetoric's siren song proves too sweet, in Cicero's story (later to be echoed by countless others)[4] all the human virtues, and indeed humanity itself, are wrested by the arts of eloquence from a primitive and violent state of nature. Significantly (and this is a point to which we shall return), both stories are stories of power, rhetoric's power; it is just that in one story that power must be resisted lest civilization fall, while in the other that power brings order and a genuine political process where before there was only the rule of "physical strength."

The contrast between the two stories can hardly be exaggerated because what is at stake is not simply a matter of emphasis or priority (as it seems to be in Aristotle's effort to demonstrate an *alliance* between rhetoric and truth) but a difference in worldviews. The quarrel between rhetorical and foundational thought is itself foundational; its content is a disagreement about the basic constituents of human activity and about the nature of human nature itself. In Richard Lanham's helpful terms, it is a disagreement as to whether we are members of the species *homo seriosus* or *homo rhetoricus*. On the one hand, *homo seriosus,* or serious man,

> possesses a central self, an irreducible identity. These selves
> combine into a single, homogeneously real society which

constitutes a referent reality for the men living in it. This
referent society is in turn contained in a physical nature
itself referential, standing "out there" independent of man.
Man has invented language to communicate with his fellow
man. He communicates facts and concepts about both nature and society. He can also communicate a third category
of response, emotions. When he is communicating facts or
concepts, success is measured by something we call *clarity*.
When he is communicating feelings, success is measured by
something we call *sincerity, faithfulness to the self* who is
doing the feeling. (1)

On the other hand, *homo rhetoricus,* or rhetorical man,

is an actor; his reality public, dramatic. His sense of identity
depends on the reassurance of daily histrionic reenactment.
He is thus centered in time and concrete local event. The
lowest common denominator of his life is a social situation. . . . He assumes a natural agility in changing orientations. . . . From birth, almost, he has dwelt not in a single
value-structure but in several. He is thus committed to no
single construction of the world; much rather, to prevailing
in the game at hand. . . . He accepts the present paradigm
and explores its resources. Rhetorical man is trained not to
discover reality but to manipulate it. Reality is what is accepted as reality, what is useful. (4)

As rhetorical man manipulates reality, establishing through his words the imperatives and urgencies to which he and his fellows must respond, he manipulates or fabricates himself, simultaneously conceiving of and occupying the
roles that become first possible and then mandatory given the social structure
his rhetoric has put in place. By exploring the available means of persuasion in a
particular situation, he tries them on, and as they begin to suit him, he becomes
them.[5] "I hold," says Isocrates, "that people can become better and worthier if
they conceive an ambition to speak well," for in the setting forth of his position
the orator "will select from all the actions of men . . . those examples which are
the most illustrious and the most edifying; and habituating himself to contemplate and appraise such examples, he will feel their influence not only in the

preparation of a given discourse but in all the actions of his life" (*Antidosis* 275, 277). What serious man fears—the invasion of the fortress of essence by the contingent, the protean, and the unpredictable—is what rhetorical man celebrates and incarnates. In the philosopher's vision of the world rhetoric (and representation in general) is merely the (disposable) form by which a prior and substantial content is conveyed; but in the world of *homo rhetoricus* rhetoric is *both* form and content, the manner of presentation and what is presented; the "improvising power of the rhetor" is at once all creating and the guarantee of the impermanence of its creations: "To make a thing beautiful or unbeautiful, just or unjust, good or bad is both a human power and a sign of the insubstantiality of these attributes" (Streuver 15, 12). Having been made they can be made again.

Which of these views of human nature is the correct one? The question can be answered only from within one or the other, and the evidence of one party will be regarded by the other either as illusory or as grist for its own mill. When presented with the ever-changing panorama of history, serious man will see variation on a few basic themes; and when confronted with the persistence of essentialist questions and answers, rhetorical man will reply as Lanham does by asserting that serious man is himself a supremely fictional achievement; seriousness is just another style, not the state of having escaped style: "In a fallen cosmetic world, [plain Jane] is asking *not* to be considered, wants to be overlooked—or perhaps to claim attention by contrast. She is as rhetorical as her made up sister, proclaims as loudly an attitude. Thus the whole range of ornament from zero to 100 is equally rhetorical, equally deep or equally superficial" (30). That is to say, for rhetorical man the distinctions (between form and content, periphery and core, ephemeral and abiding) invoked by serious man are nothing more than the scaffolding of the theater of seriousness, are themselves instances of what they oppose. And on the other side, if serious man were to hear *that* argument, he would regard it as one more example of rhetorical manipulation and sleight of hand, an outrageous assertion that flies in the face of common sense, the equivalent in debate of "so's your old man." And so it would go, with no prospect of ever reaching accord, an endless round of accusation and counteraccusation in which truth, honesty, and linguistic responsibility are claimed by everyone: "From serious premises, all rhetorical language is suspect; from a rhetorical point of view, transparent language seems dishonest, false to the world" (Lanham 28).

And so it *has* gone; the history of Western thought could be written as the history of this quarrel. Indeed, such histories have been written and with predictably different emphases. In one version written many times, the mists of religion, magic, and verbal incantation (all equivalently suspect forms of fantasy) are dispelled by the Enlightenment rediscovery of reason and science; enthusiasm and metaphor alike are curbed by the refinement of method, and the effects of difference (point of view) are bracketed and held in check by a procedural rigor. In another version (told by a line stretching from Vico to Foucault) a carnivalesque world of exuberance and possibility is drastically impoverished by the ascendancy of a soulless reason, a brutally narrow perspective that claims to be objective and proceeds in a repressive manner to enforce its claim. It is not my intention here to endorse either history or to offer a third or to argue as some have for a nonhistory of discontinuous *episteme* innocent of either a progressive or a lapsarian curve; rather I only wish to point out that the debate continues to this day and that its terms are exactly those one finds in the dialogues of Plato and the orations of the sophists.

As I write, the fortunes of rhetorical man are on the upswing, as in discipline after discipline there is evidence of what has been called the interpretive turn, the realization (at least for those it seizes) that the givens of any field of activity—including the facts it commands, the procedures it trusts in, and the values it expresses and extends—are socially and politically constructed, are fashioned by humans rather than delivered by God or Nature. The most recent (and unlikely) field to experience this revolution, or at least to hear of its possibility, is economics. The key text is Donald McCloskey's *The Rhetoric of Economics,* a title that is itself polemical since, as McCloskey points out, mainstream economists do not like to think of themselves as employing a rhetoric; rather they regard themselves as scientists whose methodology insulates them from the appeal of special interests or points of view. They think, in other words, that the procedures of their discipline will produce "knowledge free from doubt, free from metaphysics, morals and personal conviction" (16). To this McCloskey responds by declaring (in good sophistic terms) that no such knowledge is available, and that while economic method promises to deliver it, "what it is able to deliver [and] renames as scientific methodology [are] the scientist's and especially the economic scientist's metaphysics, morals, and personal convictions" (16). Impersonal method then is both an illusion and a danger (as a kind of rhetoric it masks its rhetorical nature), and as an antidote to it McCloskey offers rhetoric, which, he says, deals not with abstract truth, but with the truth that emerges in the context of distinctly human conversations (28–29). Within those conversations, there are always "particular arguments good or bad. After making them there is no point in asking a last, summarizing question: 'Well, is it True?' It's whatever it is—persuasive, interesting, useful, and so forth. . . . There is no reason to search for a general quality called Truth, which answers only the unanswerable question, 'What is it in the mind of God?' " (47). The answerable questions are always asked within the assumptions of particular situations, and both question and answer "will always depend on one's audience and the human purposes involved" (150). The real truth, concludes McCloskey, is that assertions are made for purposes of persuading some audience and that given the unavailability of a God's-eye view, "this is not a shameful fact," but the bottom-line fact in a rhetorical world.

At the first conference called to consider McCloskey's arguments, the familiar antirhetorical objections were heard again in the land, and the land might have been fifth-century Athens as well as Wellesley, Massachusetts, in 1986. One participant spoke of the path to extreme relativism which proceeds from Kuhn's conception of the incommensurability of paradigms to the idea that there are no objective and unambiguous procedures for applying rules since meanings of particular actions and terms are context-dependent. Other voices proclaimed that nothing in McCloskey's position was new (an observation certainly true), that everyone already knew it, and that at any rate it did not touch the core of the economists' practice. Still others invoked a set of related (and familiar) distinctions between empirical and interpretive activities, between demonstration and persuasion, between verifiable procedures and anarchic irrationalism. Of course, each of these objections had already been formulated (or reformulated) in those disciplines that had heard rhetoric's siren song long before it reached the belated ears of economists. The name that everyone always refers to (in praise or blame) is Thomas Kuhn. His *Structure of Scientific Revolutions* is arguably the most frequently cited work in the humanities and social sciences in the past twenty-five years, and it is rhetorical through and through. Kuhn begins by rehearsing and challenging the orthodox model of scientific inquiry in which independent facts are first collected by objective methods and then built up into a picture of nature, a picture that it itself either confirms or rejects in the context of controlled experiments. In this model, science is a "cumulative process" (3) in which each new discovery adds "one more item to the population of the scientist's world" (7). The shape of that world—of the scientist's professional activities—is determined by the shapes (of fact and structure) already existing in the larger world of nature, shapes that constrain and guide the scientist's work.

Kuhn challenges this story by introducing the notion of a paradigm, a set of tacit assumptions and beliefs within which research goes on, assumptions which rather than deriving from the observation of facts are determinative of the facts that could possibly be observed. It follows then that when observations made within different paradigms conflict, there is no principled (that is, non-rhetorical) way to adjudicate the dispute. One cannot put the competing accounts to the test of fact, because the specification of fact is precisely what is at issue between them; a fact cited by one party would be seen as a mistake by the other. What this means is that science does not proceed by offering its descriptions to the independent judgment of nature; rather it proceeds when the proponents of one paradigm are able to present their case in a way that the adherents of other paradigms find compelling. In short, the "motor" by which science moves is not verification or falsification, but persuasion. Indeed, says Kuhn, in the end the force of scientific argument "is *only* that of persuasion" (94). In the case of disagreement, "each party must try, by persuasion, to convert the other" (198), and when one party succeeds there is no higher court to which the outcome might be referred: "There is no standard higher than the assent of the relevant community" (94). "What better criterion," asks Kuhn, "could there be?" (170).

The answer given by those who were horrified by Kuhn's rhetoricization of scientific procedure was predictable: a better criterion would be one that was not captive to a particular paradigm but provided a neutral space in which competing paradigms could be disinterestedly assessed. By denying such a criterion, Kuhn leaves us in a world of epistemological and moral anarchy. The words are Israel Scheffler's: "Independent and public controls are no more, communication has failed, the common universe of things is a delusion, reality itself is made . . . rather than discovered. . . . In place of a community of rational men following objective procedures in the pursuit of truth, we have a set of isolated monads, within each of which belief forms without systematic constraints" (19). Kuhn and those he has persuaded have, of course, responded to these accusations, but needless to say, the debate continues in terms readers of this essay could easily imagine. The debate has been particularly acrimonious because the area of contest—science and its procedures—is so heavily invested in as the one place where the apostles of rhetorical interpretivism would presumably fear to tread.

At one point in his argument, Kuhn remarks that in the tradition he is critiquing scientific research is "reputed to proceed" from "raw data" or "brute experience"; but, he points out, if that were truly the mode of proceeding, it would require a "neutral observation language" (125), a language that registers facts without any mediation by paradigm-specific assumptions. The problem is that "philosophical investigation has not yet provided even a hint of what a language able to do that would be like" (127). Even a specially devised language "embodies a host of expectations about nature," expectations that limit in advance what can be described. Just as one cannot (in Kuhn's view) have recourse to neutral facts in order to settle a dispute, so one cannot have recourse to a neutral language in which to report those facts or even to report on the configuration of the dispute. The difference that divides people "is prior to the application of the languages in which it is nevertheless reflected" (201). Whatever report a particular language (natural or artificial) offers us will be the report on the world as it is seen from within some particular situation; there is no other aperspectival way to see and no language other than a situation-dependent language—an interested, rhetorical language—in which to report.

This same point was being made with all the force of philosophical authority by J. L. Austin in a book published, significantly, in the same year (1962) that saw the publication of *The Structure of Scientific Revolutions*. Austin begins *How to Do Things with Words* by observing that traditionally the center of the philosophy of language has been just the kind of utterance Kuhn declares unavailable, the context-independent statement that offers objective reports on an equally independent world in sentences of the form "He is running" and "Lord Raglan won the battle of Alma" (47, 142). Such utterances, which Austin calls "constative," are answerable to a requirement of truth and verisimilitude ("the truth of the constative . . . 'he is running' depends on his being running"); the words must match the world, and if they do not they can be criticized as false and inaccurate. There are, however, innumerable utterances that are not assessable in this way. If, for example, I say to you, "I promise to pay you five dollars" or "Leave the room," it would be odd were you to respond by saying, "True" or "False"; rather you would say to the first, "Good" or "That's not enough" or "I won't hold my breath," and to the second, "Yes, sir" or "But I'm expecting a phone call" or "Who do you think you are?" These and many other imaginable responses would not be judgments on the truth or accuracy of my utterance but on its appropriateness given our respective positions in some social structure of understanding (domestic, military, economic, and so on). It is only if the circumstances are of a certain kind—if five dollars is a reasonable rather than an insulting amount, if the room I order you to leave is mine not yours—that the utterances will "take" and achieve the meaning of being a promise or a command. Thus the very identity, and therefore the meaning, of this type of utterance—Austin names it "performative"—depends on the context in which it is produced and received. There is no regular (in the sense of reliable and predictable) relationship between the form of the linguistic marks (the words and their order) and their significance. Nothing guarantees that "I promise to pay you five dollars" will be either intended or heard as a promise; in different circumstances it could be received as a threat or a joke (as when I utter it from debtor's prison) and in many circumstances it will be intended as one act and understood as another (as when your opinion of my trustworthiness is much lower than my own). When the criterion of verisimilitude has been replaced by the criterion of appropriateness, meaning becomes radically contextual, potentially as variable as the situated (and shifting understandings) of countless speakers and hearers.

It is precisely this property of performatives—their force is contingent and cannot be formally constrained—that is responsible for their being consigned by philosophers of language to the category of the "derived" or "parasitic," where, safely tucked away, they are prevented from contaminating the core category of the constative. But it is this act of segregation and quarantining that Austin undoes in the second half of his book when he extends the analysis of performatives to constatives and finds that they too mean differently in the light of differing contextual circumstances. Consider the exemplary constative, "Lord Raglan won the battle of Alma." Is it true, accurate, a faithful report? It depends, says Austin, on the context in which it is uttered and received (142–43). In a high school textbook, it might be accepted as true because of the in-place assumptions as to what, exactly, a battle is, what constitutes winning, what the function of a general is, and so forth, while in a work of "serious" historical research all of these assumptions may have been replaced by others with the result that the very notions "battle" and "won" would have a different shape. The properties that supposedly distinguish constatives from performatives—fidelity to preexisting facts, accountability to a criterion of truth—turn out to be as dependent on particular conditions of production and reception as performatives. "True" and "false," Austin concludes, are not names for the possible relationships between free-standing (constative) utterances and an equally free-standing state of affairs; rather they are situation-specific judgments on the relationship between contextually produced utterances and states of affairs that are themselves no less contextually produced. At the end of Austin's book constatives are "discovered" to be a subset of performatives, and with this discovery the formal core of language disappears entirely and is replaced by a world of utterances vulnerable to the sea change of every circumstance, the world, in short, of rhetorical (situated) man.

This is a conclusion Austin himself resists when he attempts to isolate (and thereby contain) the rhetorical by invoking another distinction between serious and nonserious utterance. Serious utterances are utterances for which the speaker takes responsibility; he means what he says, and therefore you can infer his meaning by his considering his words in context. A nonserious utterance is an utterance produced in circumstances that "abrogate" (21) the speaker's responsibility and therefore one cannot with any confidence—that is, without the hazard of ungrounded conjecture—determine what he means: "A performative utterance will, for example, be . . . hollow or void if said by an actor on the stage, or if introduced in a poem, or spoken in a soliloquy. . . . Language in such circumstances is in special ways . . . used not seriously, but in ways *parasitic* upon its normal use. . . . All this we are *excluding* from consideration. Our performative utterances . . . are to be understood as issued in ordinary circumstances" (22). The distinction then is between utterances that are, as Austin puts it later, "tethered to their origin" (61), anchored by a palpable intention, and utterances whose origin is hidden by the screen of a theatrical or literary stage setting. This distinction and the passage in which it appears were taken up by Jacques Derrida in a famous and admiring critique of Austin. Derrida finds Austin working against his own best insights and forgetting what he has just acknowledged, that "infelicity [communication going astray, in an unintended direction] is an ill to which *all* [speech] acts are heir" (Derrida, "Signature" 180). Despite this acknowledgment, Austin continues to think of infelicity—of those cases in which the tethering origin of utterances is obscure and must be constructed by interpretive conjecture—as special, whereas, in Derrida's view, infelicity is itself the originary state in that any determination of meaning must always proceed within an interpretive construction of a speaker's intention. The origin that supposedly tethers the interpretation of an utterance will always be the product of that interpretation; the special circumstances in which meaning must be inferred through a screen rather than directly are the circumstances of every linguistic transaction. In short, there are no ordinary circumstances, merely those myriad and varied circumstances in which actors embedded in

stage settings hazard interpretations of utterances produced by actors embedded in other stage situations. All the world, as Shakespeare says, is a stage, and
on that stage "the quality of risk admitted by Austin" is not something one can
avoid by sticking close to ordinary language in ordinary circumstances, but is
rather "the internal and positive condition" of any act of communication (Derrida, *Positions* 190).

In the same publication in which the English translation of Derrida's essay
appeared, John Searle, a student of Austin's, replied in terms that make clear the
affiliation of this particular debate to the ancient debate whose configurations
we have been tracing. Searle's strategy is basically to repeat Austin's points and
declare that Derrida has missed them: "Austin's idea is simply this: if we want to
know what it is to make a promise we had better not *start* our investigations
with promises made by actors on stage . . . because in some fairly obvious way
such utterances are not standard cases of promises" (204). But in Derrida's
argument, the category of the "obvious" is precisely what is being challenged or
"deconstructed." Although it is true that we consider promises uttered in everyday contexts more direct—less etiolated—than promises made on a stage, this
(Derrida would say) is only because the stage settings within which everyday
life proceeds are so powerfully—that is, rhetorically—in place that they are in
effect invisible, and therefore the meanings they make possible are experienced
as if they were direct and unmediated by any screens. The "obvious" cannot be
opposed to the "staged," as Searle assumes, because it is simply the achievement
of a staging that has been particularly successful. One does not escape the
rhetorical by fleeing to the protected area of basic communication and common sense, because common sense in whatever form it happens to take is
always a rhetorical—partial, partisan, interested—construction. This does not
mean, Derrida hastens to add, that all rhetorical constructions are equal, just
that they are equally rhetorical, equally the effects and extensions of some
limited and challengeable point of view. The "citationality"—the condition of
being in quotation marks, of being *in*direct—of an utterance in a play is not the
same as the citationality of a philosophical reference or a deposition before a
court; it is just that no one of these performatives is more serious—more direct,
less mediated, less rhetorical—than any other. Whatever opposition there is
takes place within a "general" citationality which "constitutes a violation of the
allegedly rigorous purity of every event of discourse or every *speech act*" ("Signature" 192).

Searle points out (205) that to achieve a "general theory of speech acts," one must perform acts of exclusion or idealization like Austin's; but it is the possibility of a general theory—of an account that is itself more than an extension of some *particular* context or perspective—that Derrida denies. His is the familiar world of rhetorical man, teeming with roles, situations, strategies, and interventions, but containing no master role, no situation of situations, no strategy for outflanking all strategies, no intervention in the arena of dispute that does not expand the arena of dispute, no neutral point of rationality from the vantage point of which the "merely rhetorical" can be identified and held in check. That is why deconstructive or poststructuralist thought is supremely rhetorical: it systematically asserts and demonstrates the mediated, constructed, partial, socially constituted nature of all realities, be they phenomenal, linguistic, or psychological. To deconstruct a text, says Derrida, is to "work through the structured genealogy of its concepts in the most scrupulous and immanent fashion, but at the same time to determine from a certain external perspective that it cannot name or describe what this history may have concealed or excluded, constituting itself as history through this repression in which it has a stake" (*Positions* 6). The "external perspective" is the perspective from which the analyst knows in advance (by virtue of his or her commitment to the rhetorical or antifoundational worldview) that the coherences presented by a text (and an institution or an economy can in this sense be a text) rest on a contradiction it cannot acknowledge, rest on the suppression of the challengeable rhetoricity of its own standpoint, a standpoint that offers itself as if it came from nowhere in particular and simply delivered things as they really (nonperspectivally) are. A deconstructive reading will bring those contradictions to the surface and expose those suppressions and thus "trouble" a unity that is achieved only by covering over all the excluded emphases and interests that might threaten it. These exclusions are part of the text in that the success of its totalizing effort depends on them. Once they are made manifest, the hitherto manifest meaning of the text is undermined—indeed is shown to have always and already been undermined—as "the rhetorical operations that produce the supposed ground of argument, the key concept or premise" are deprived of the claim to be *un*rhetorical, serious, disinterested (Culler 86).

Nor is this act performed in the service of something beyond rhetoric. Derridean deconstruction does not uncover the operations of rhetoric in order to reach the Truth; rather it continually uncovers the truth of rhetorical operations, the truth that all operations, including the operation of deconstruction itself, are rhetorical. If, as Paul de Man asserts, "a deconstruction always has for its target to reveal the existence of hidden articulations and fragmentations within assumedly monadic totalities," care must be taken that a new monadic totality is not left as the legacy of the deconstructive act. Since the course of a deconstruction is to uncover a "fragmented stage that can be called natural with regard to the system that is being undone," there is always the danger that the "natural" pattern will "substitute *its* relational system for the one it helped to dissolve" (249). The only way to escape this danger is to perform the deconstructive act again and again, submitting each new emerging constellation to the same suspicious scrutiny that brought it to light, and resisting the temptation to put in place of the truths it rhetoricizes the truth that everything is rhetorical. One cannot rest even in the insight that there is no place to rest. "Rhetoric," says de Man, "suspends logic and opens up vertiginous possibilities of referential aberration" (10). But the rhetorical vision is foreclosed on and made into a new absolute, if those "vertiginous possibilities" are celebrated as the basis of a new wisdom. The rhetorical beat must by definition go on, endlessly repeating the sequence by which "the lure of solid ground" is succeeded by "the ensuing demystification" (Ray 195). When de Man approvingly quotes Nietzsche's identification of truth with "a moving army of metaphors, metonymies and anthropomorphisms," a rhetorical construction whose origin has been (and must be) forgotten, he does not exempt Nietzsche's text from its own corrosive effects. If Nietzsche declares (well in advance of Kuhn and Austin, but well after Gorgias and Protagoras) that "there is no such thing as an unrhetorical, 'natural' language" for "tropes are not something that can be added or subtracted from language at will," the insight must be extended to this very declaration: "A text like *On Truth and Lies,* although it presents itself legitimately as a demystification of literary rhetoric, remains entirely literary, and deceptive itself" (de Man 113). The "rhetorical mode," the mode of deconstruction, is a mode of "endless reflection," since it is "unable ever to escape from the rhetorical deceit it announces" (115).

That, however, is just what is wrong with deconstructive practice from the viewpoint of the intellectual left, many of whose members subscribe to Nietzsche's account of truth and reality as rhetorical, but find that much of poststructuralist discourse uses that account as a way of escaping into new versions of idealism and formalism. Frank Lentricchia, for example, sees in some of de Man's texts an intention to place "discourse in a realm where it can have no responsibility to historical life" and fears that we are being invited into "the realm of the thoroughly predictable linguistic transcendental," the "rarified region of the undecidable," where every text "speaks synchronically and endlessly the same tale . . . of its own duplicitous self-consciousness" (310, 317). Terry Eagleton's judgment is even harsher. Noting that in the wake of Nietzschean thought, rhetoric, "mocked and berated for centuries by an abrasive rationalism," takes its "terrible belated revenge" by finding itself in every rationalist project, Eagleton complains that many rhetoricians seem content to stop there, satisfied with the "Fool's function of unmasking all power as self rationalization, all knowledge as a mere fumbling with metaphor" (*Walter Benjamin* 108). Operating as a "vigorous demystifier of all ideology," rhetoric functions only as a form of thought and ends up by providing "the final ideological rationale for political inertia." In retreat "from market place to study, politics to philology, social practice to semiotics" deconstructive rhetoric turns the emancipatory promise of Nietzschean thought into "a gross failure of ideological nerve," allowing the liberal academic the elitist pleasure of repeatedly exposing "vulgar commercial and political hectorings" (108–9). In both his study of Benjamin and his influential *Literary Theory: An Introduction,* Eagleton urges a return to the Ciceronian-Isocratic tradition in which the rhetorical arts are inseparable from the practice of a politics, "techniques of persuasion indissociable from the substantive issues and audiences involved," techniques whose employment is "closely determined by the pragmatic situation at hand" (*Walter Benjamin* 104). In short, he calls for a rhetoric that will do real work and cites as an example the slogan "Black is beautiful," which he says is "paradigmatically rhetorical since it employs a figure of equivalence to produce particular discursive and extra-discursive effects without direct regard for truth" (112). That is, someone who says "Black is beautiful" is not so much interested in the accuracy of the assertion (it is not constatively intended) as he or she is in the responses it may provoke—surprise, outrage, urgency, solidarity—responses that may set in motion "practices that are deemed, in the light of a particular set of falsifiable hypotheses, to be desirable" (113).

For Eagleton, the desirable practices are marxist-socialist and the rhetoric that will help establish them has three tasks: "First, to participate in the production of works and events which . . . so fictionalize the 'real' as to intend those effects conducive to the victory of socialism. Second, as 'critic' to expose the rhetorical structures by which non-socialist works produce politically undesirable effects. . . . Third, to interpret such words where possible 'against the grain,' so as to appropriate from them whatever may be valuable for socialism"

(113). It is the second of these tasks that presents conceptual and cognitive problems. If all cultural work is, as Eagleton says in the sentence just before this passage, rhetorical, then how does one's own rhetoric escape the inauthenticity it discovers in the rhetoric of others? Eagleton's answer is contained in his assumption of the superiority of the socialist program; any rhetorical work in the service of that program will be justified in advance, while conversely any rhetorical work done in opposition to socialist urgencies will flow from "false consciousness" and will deserve to be exposed. This confidence in his objectives makes Eagleton impatient with those for whom the rhetoricity of all discourse is something to be savored for itself, something to be lovingly and obsessively demonstrated again and again. It is not, he says, "a matter of starting from certain theoretical or methodological problems; it is a matter of starting from what we want to *do,* and then seeing which methods and theories will best help us to achieve these ends" (*Literary Theory* 211). Theories, in short, are themselves rhetorics whose usefulness is a function of contingent circumstances. It is ends—specific goals in local contexts—that rule the invocation of theories, not theories that determine goals and the means by which they can be reached.

There are those on the left, however, for whom the direction is the other way around, from the theoretical realization of rhetoric's pervasiveness to a vision and a program for implementing it. In their view the discovery (or rediscovery) that all discourse and therefore all knowledge is rhetorical leads or should lead to the adoption of a *method* by which the dangers of rhetoric can be at least mitigated and perhaps extirpated. This method has two stages: the first is a stage of debunking, and it issues from the general suspicion in which all orthodoxies and arrangements of power are held once it is realized that their basis is not reason or nature but the success of some rhetorical-political agenda. Armed with this realization one proceeds to expose the contingent and there-fore challengeable basis of whatever presents itself as natural and inevitable. So far this is precisely the procedure of deconstruction; but whereas deconstructive practice (at least of the Yale variety) seems to produce nothing but the occasion for its endless repetition, some cultural revolutionaries discern in it a more positive residue, the loosening or weakening of the structures of domination and oppression that now hold us captive. The reasoning is that by repeatedly uncovering the historical and ideological basis of established structures (both political and cognitive), one becomes sensitized to the effects of ideology and begins to clear a space in which those effects can be combatted; and as that sensitivity grows more acute, the area of combat will become larger until it encompasses the underlying structure of assumptions that confers a spurious legitimacy on the powers that currently be. The claim, in short, is that the radically rhetorical insight of Nietzschean/Derridean thought can do radical political work; becoming aware that everything is rhetorical is the first step in countering the power of rhetoric and liberating us from its force. Since deeply entrenched ways of thinking and acting are "profoundly paralysis-inducing," so long as we are unthinkingly embedded in them it will be difficult "even to *imagine* that life could be different and better."

This last sentence is taken from an essay by Robert Gordon entitled "New Developments in Legal Theory" (287). Gordon is writing as a member of the Critical Legal Studies movement, a group of legal academics who have discovered the rhetorical nature of legal reasoning and are busily exposing as interested the supposedly disinterested operations of legal procedures. Gordon's pages are replete with the vocabulary of enclosure or prison: we are "locked into" a system of belief we did not make; we are "demobilized" (that is, rendered less mobile); we must "break out" (291), we must "unfreeze the world as it appears to common sense" (289). What will help us to break out, to unfreeze, is the discovery "that the belief-structures that rule our lives are not found in nature but are historically contingent," for that discovery, says Gordon, "is extraordinarily liberating" (289). What it will liberate are the mental energies that were before prevented by the "paralysis-inducing" effects of received systems of thought from even imagining that "life could be different and better." In the words of Robert Unger (another prominent member of the movement), if you start with an awareness of the insight "that no one scheme of human association has conclusive authority" and come to an understanding of the "flawed" nature of the schemes now in place, you can then "imagine the actualizations [i.e., present-day arrangements of things] transformed" and in time "transform them in fact" (580). The result will be a "cultural-revolutionary practice" that will bring about the "progressive emancipation from a background plan of social division and hierarchy" (587). To the question, what is the *content* of that emancipation, given a world that is rhetorical through and through, those who work Gordon's and Unger's side of the street usually reply that emancipation will take the form of a strengthening and enlarging of a capacity of mind that stands to the side of, and is therefore able to resist, the appeal of the agenda that would enslave us. That capacity of mind has received many names, but the one most often proposed is "critical self-consciousness." Critical self-consciousness is the ability (stifled in some, developed in others) to discern in any "scheme of association," including those one finds attractive and compelling, the partisan aims it hides from view; and the claim is that as it performs this negative task critical self-consciousness participates in the positive task of formulating schemes of associations (structures of thought and government) that are in the service not of a particular party but of all humankind.

It need hardly be said that this claim veers back in the direction of the rationalism and universalism that the critical-deconstructive project sets out to demystify. That project begins by rejecting the rationalities of present life as rationalizations and revealing the structure of reality to be rhetorical, that is, partial; but then it turns around and attempts to use the insight of partiality to build something that is less partial, less hostage to the urgencies of a particular vision, and more responsive to the needs of men and women in general. Insofar as this "turn" is taken to its logical conclusion, it ends up reinventing at the conclusion of a rhetorically informed critique the entire array of antirhetorical gestures and exclusions. One sees this clearly in the work of Jürgen Habermas, a thinker whose widespread influence is testimony to the durability of the tradition that began (at least) with Plato. Habermas's goal is to bring about something he calls the "ideal speech situation," a situation in which all assertions proceed not from the perspective of individual desires and strategies, but from the perspective of a general rationality on which all parties are agreed. In such a situation nothing would count except the claims to universal validity of all assertions. "No force except that of the better argument if exercised; and . . . as a result, all motives except that of the cooperative search for truth are excluded" (*Legitimation* 107–8). Of course, in the world we now inhabit, there is no such purity of motive, but nevertheless, says Habermas, even in the most distorted of communicative situations there remains something of the basic impulse behind all utterance, "the intention of communicating a true [*wahr*] proposition . . . so that the hearer can share the knowledge of the speaker" (*Communication* 2). If we could only eliminate from our discourse performances those intentions that reflect baser goals—the intentions to deceive, to manipulate, to persuade— the ideal speech situation could be approximated.

What stands in our way is the fact that many of our speech acts issue from the perspective of local and historically contingent contexts and these by definition cannot contribute to the building up of a general rationality. Therefore, it is incumbent on us to choose and proffer utterances that satisfy (or at least claim and desire to satisfy) *universal* conditions of validity. This is the project

Habermas names "Universal Pragmatics" and the name tells its own story. Habermas recognizes, as all modern and postmodern contextualists do, that language is a social and not a purely formal phenomenon, but he thinks that the social-pragmatic aspect of language use is itself "accessible to formal analysis" (*Communication* 6) and that therefore it is possible to construct a universal "communicative competence" (29) parallel to Chomsky's linguistic competence. Sentences produced according to the rules and norms of this communicative competence would be tied not to "particular epistemic presuppositions and changing contexts" (29), but to the unchanging context (the context of contexts) in which one finds the presuppositions underlying the general possibility of successful speech. "A *general* theory of speech acts would . . . describe . . . that fundamental system of rules that adult subjects master to the extent that they can fulfill *the conditions of happy employment of sentences in utterances* no matter to which particular language the sentences may belong and in which accidental contexts the utterances may be embedded" (26). If we can operate on the level of that fundamental system, the distorting potential of "accidental contexts" will be neutralized because we will always have one eye on what is essential, the establishing by rational cooperation of an interpersonal (nonaccidental) truth. Once speakers are oriented to this goal and away from others, oriented toward *general* understanding, they will be incapable of deception and manipulation: "Truthfulness guarantees the transparency of a subjectivity representing itself in language" (57). A company of transparent subjectivities will join together in the fashioning of a transparent truth and of a world in which the will to power has been eliminated.

In his book *Textual Power,* Robert Scholes examines the rationalist epistemology in which a "complete self confronts a solid world, perceiving it directly and accurately . . . capturing it perfectly in a transparent language" and declares it to be so thoroughly discredited that it now "is lying in ruins around us" (132–33). Perhaps so, in some circles, but the fact of Habermas's work and of the audience he commands suggests that even now those ruins are collecting themselves and rising again into the familiar antirhetorical structure. It would seem that any announcement of the death of either position will always be premature, slightly behind the institutional news that in some corner of the world supposedly abandoned questions are receiving what at least appear to be new answers. Only recently, the *public* fortunes of rationalist-foundationalist thought have taken a favorable turn with the publication of books like Allan

Bloom's *Closing of the American Mind* and E. D. Hirsch's *Cultural Literacy,* both of which (Bloom's more directly) challenge the "new Orthodoxy" of "extreme cultural relativism" and reassert, albeit in different ways, the existence of normative standards. In many quarters these books have been welcomed as a return to the common sense that is necessary if civilization is to avoid the dark night of anarchy. One can expect administrators and legislators to propose reforms (and perhaps even purges) based on Bloom's arguments (the rhetorical force of antirhetoricalism is always being revived), and one can expect too a host of voices raised in opposition to what will surely be called the "new positivism." Those voices will include some that have been recorded here and some others that certainly merit recording, but can only be noted in a list that is itself incomplete. The full story of rhetoric's twentieth-century resurgence would boast among its cast of characters: Kenneth Burke, whose "dramatism" anticipates so much of what is considered avant-garde today; Wayne Booth, whose *Rhetoric of Fiction* was so important in legitimizing the rhetorical analysis of the novel; Mikhail Bakhtin, whose contrast of monologic to dialogic and heteroglossic discourse sums up so many strands in the rhetorical tradition; Roland Barthes, who in the concept of "jouissance" makes a (non)constitutive principle of the tendency of rhetoric to resist closure and extend play; the ethnomethodologists (Harold Garfinkel and company), who discover in every supposedly rule-bound context the operation of a principle (exactly the wrong word) of "ad-hocing"; Chaim Perelman and L. Olbrechts-Tyteca, whose *New Rhetoric: A Treatise on Argumentation* provides a sophisticated modern source book for would-be rhetoricians weary of always citing Aristotle; Barbara Herrenstein Smith, who in the course of espousing an unashamed relativism directly confronts and argues down the objections of those who fear for their souls (and more) in a world without objective standards; Fredric Jameson and Hayden White, who teach us (among other things) that "history . . . is unaccessible to us except in textual form, and that our approach to it and to the Real itself necessarily passes through its prior textualization" (Jameson 35); reader-oriented critics like Norman Holland, David Bleich, Wolfgang Iser, and H. R. Jauss, who by shifting the emphasis from the text to its reception open up the act of interpretation to the infinite variability of contextual circumstance; numerous feminists who relentlessly unmask hegemonic structures and expose as rhetorical the rational posturings of the legal and political systems; equally numerous theorists of composition who, under the slogan "Process, not product," insist on the rhetorical nature of communication and argue for far-reaching changes in the way writing is taught. The list is already formidable, but it could go on and on, providing support for Scholes's contention that the rival epistemology has been vanquished and for Clifford Geertz's announcement (he too is a contributor to the shift he reports) that "something is happening to the way we think about the way we think."

But it would seem, from the evidence marshalled in this essay, that something is always happening to the way we think, and that it is always the same something, a tug of war between two views of human life and its possibilities, no one of which can ever gain complete and lasting ascendancy because in the very moment of its triumphant articulation each turns back in the direction of the other. Thus Wayne Booth feels obliged in both *The Rhetoric of Fiction* and *A Rhetoric of Irony* to confine the force of rhetoric by sharply distinguishing its legitimate uses from two extreme limit cases (the "unreliable narrator" and "unstable irony"); some reader-response critics deconstruct the autonomy and self-sufficiency of the text, but in the process end up privileging the autonomous and self-sufficient subject; some feminists challenge the essentialist claims of "male reason" in the name of a female rationality or nonrationality apparently no less essential; Jameson opens up the narrativity of history in order to proclaim one narrative the true and unifying one. Here one might speak of the return of the repressed (and thereby invoke Freud, whose writings and influence would be still another chapter in the story I have not even begun to tell) were it not that the repressed—whether it be the fact of difference or the desire for its elimination—is always so close to the surface that it hardly need be unearthed. What we seem to have is a tale full of sound and fury, and signifying itself, signifying a durability rooted in inconclusiveness, in the impossibility of there being a last word.

In an essay, however, someone must have the last word and I give it to Richard Rorty. Rorty is himself a champion of the antiessentialism that underlies rhetorical thinking; his neopragmatism makes common cause with Kuhn and others who would turn us away from the search for transcendental absolutes and commend to us (although it would seem superfluous to do so) the imperatives and goals already informing our practices. It is, however, not the polemicist Rorty whom I call on to sum up, but the Rorty who is the brisk chronicler of our epistemological condition:

> There . . . are two ways of thinking about various
> things. . . . The first . . . thinks of truth as a vertical rela-

tionship between representations and what is represented. The second . . . thinks of truth horizontally—as the culminating reinterpretation of our predecessors' reinterpretation of their predecessors' reinterpretation. . . . It is the difference between regarding truth, goodness, and beauty as eternal objects which we try to locate and reveal, and regarding them as artifacts whose fundamental design we often have to alter. (92)

It is the difference between serious and rhetorical man. It is the difference that remains.

Notes

1. This is just the language of H. L. A. Hart's *The Concept of Law.*
2. See on this point George Kennedy, *The Art of Persuasion in Ancient Greece.*
3. See John Milton, "Reason of Church Government," *The Complete Prose Works of John Milton.*
4. See, for example, John Lawson, *Lectures Concerning Oratory* (27).
5. See Thomas Sloane, *Donne, Milton, and the End of Humanist Rhetoric* (87): "Rhetoric succeeded in humanism's great desideratum, the artistic creation of adept personhood." See also Stephen Greenblatt, *Renaissance Self-Fashioning.*

Works Cited

Aristotle. *The Works of Aristotle.* Ed. W. Rhys Roberts. Vol. 2. Oxford: Oxford University Press, 1946.

Austin, J. L. *How to Do Things with Words.* Cambridge, Mass.: Harvard University Press, 1962.

Carnap, Rudolf. "The Elimination of Metaphysics." *Logical Positivism.* Ed. A. J. Ayer. Glencoe, Ill.: Free Press, 1959.

Cicero. *De Inventione.* In *Cicero.* Vol. 2. Ed. and trans. H. M. Hubbell. Cambridge, Mass.: Harvard University Press, 1968.

Culler, Jonathan. *On Deconstruction.* Ithaca: Cornell University Press, 1982.

de Man, Paul. *Allegories of Reading.* New Haven: Yale University Press, 1979.

Derrida, Jacques. *Positions.* Chicago: University of Chicago Press, 1981.

——. "Signature, Event, Context." *Glyph* 1 (1977): 172–97.

Dixon, Peter. *Rhetoric.* London: Routledge, 1971.

Eagleton, Terry. *Literary Theory: An Introduction.* Minneapolis: University of Minnesota Press, 1983.

——. *Walter Benjamin: or, Towards a Revolutionary Criticism.* London: Verso, 1981.

Geertz, Clifford. "Blurred Genres: The Refiguration of Social Thought." *American Scholar* 49 (spring 1980): 165–90.

Gordon, Robert. *The Politics of Law.* New York: Pantheon, 1983.

Greenblatt, Stephen. *Renaissance Self-Fashioning.* Chicago: University of Chicago Press, 1980.

Guthrie, William K. *The Sophists.* Cambridge, Mass.: Harvard University Press, 1971.

Habermas, Jürgen. *Communication and the Evolution of Society.* Boston: Beacon, 1979.

——. *Legitimation Crisis.* Boston: Beacon, 1975.

Hart, H. L. A. *The Concept of Law.* Oxford: Oxford University Press, 1961.

Howell, A. C. "*Res et Verba:* Words and Things." *Seventeenth Century Prose: Modern Essays and Criticism.* Ed. Stanley Fish. Oxford: Oxford University Press, 1971.

Isocrates. *Antidosis.* In *Isocrates.* Vol. 2. Ed. and trans. George Norlin. Cambridge, Mass.: Harvard University Press, 1962.

Jameson, Fredric. *The Political Unconscious.* Ithaca: Cornell University Press, 1981.

Kennedy, George. *The Art of Persuasion in Ancient Greece.* Princeton: Princeton University Press, 1963.

Kuhn, Thomas. *The Structure of Scientific Revolutions.* Chicago: University of Chicago Press, 1962.

Lange, Andrew. *The Artificial Language Movement.* Oxford: Oxford University Press, 1985.

Lanham, Richard. *The Motives of Eloquence.* New Haven: Yale University Press, 1976.

Lawson, John. *Lectures Concerning Oratory.* Ed. E. N. Claussen and K. R. Wallace. Carbondale: Southern Illinois University Press, 1972.

Lentricchia, Frank. *After the New Criticism.* Chicago: University of Chicago Press, 1980.

McCloskey, Donald. *The Rhetoric of Economics.* Madison: University of Wisconsin Press, 1985.

Milton, John. *Areopagitica.* In *Milton's Prose.* Ed. J. Max Patrick and French Fogle. New York: New York University Press, 1968.

——. "Reason of Church Government." *The Complete Prose Works of John Milton.* Vol. 1. Ed. D. M. Wolfe. New Haven: Yale University Press, 1953.

Plato. *Gorgias.* Ed. and trans. W. C. Helmbold. Indianapolis: Library of Liberal Arts, 1952.

——. *Phaedrus.* Ed. and trans. W. C. Helmbold and W. G. Rabinowitz. Indianapolis: Library of Liberal Arts, 1952.

——. *Protagoras.* Ed. Irwin Edman. Trans. Benjamin Jowett. New York: Modern Library, 1956.

Quintilian. *Institutio Oratoria.* Trans. H. E. Butler. New York: Loeb Classical Library, 1921.

Ray, William. *Literary Meaning.* Oxford: Oxford University Press, 1984.

Roberts, W. Rhys. *The Works of Aristotle.* Vol. 2. Oxford: Oxford University Press, 1946.

Rorty, Richard. *Consequences of Pragmatism.* Minneapolis: University of Minnesota Press, 1982.

Scheffler, Israel. *Science and Subjectivity.* Indianapolis: Hackett, 1967.

Scholes, Robert. *Textual Power.* New Haven: Yale University Press, 1985.

Searle, John. "Reiterating the Differences: A Reply to Derrida." *Glyph* 1 (1977): 198–208.

Sloane, Thomas. *Donne, Milton and the End of Humanist Rhetoric.* Berkeley: University of California Press, 1985.

Streuver, Nancy. *The Language of History in the Renaissance.* Princeton: Princeton University Press, 1970.

Unger, Roberto. "The Critical Legal Studies Movement." *Harvard Law Review* 96 (1983): 561–675.

2
The Contingency of Language
Richard Rorty

About two hundred years ago, the idea that truth was made rather than found began to take hold of the imagination of Europe. The French Revolution had shown that the whole vocabulary of social relations, and the whole spectrum of social institutions, could be replaced almost overnight. This precedent made utopian politics the rule rather than the exception among intellectuals. Utopian politics sets aside questions about both the will of God and the nature of humanity and about dreams of creating a hitherto unknown form of society.

At about the same time, the Romantic poets were showing what happens when art is thought of no longer as imitation but, rather, as the artist's self-creation. The poets claimed for art the place in culture traditionally held by religion and philosophy, the place that the Enlightenment had claimed for science. The precedent the Romantics set lent initial plausibility to their claim; the actual role of novels, poems, plays, paintings, statues, and buildings in the social movements of the last century and a half has given it still greater plausibility.

By now these two tendencies have joined forces and have achieved cultural hegemony. For most contemporary intellectuals, questions of ends as opposed to means—questions about how to give a sense to one's own life or that of one's community—are questions for art or politics, or both, rather than for religion, philosophy, or science. This development has led to a split within philosophy. Some philosophers have remained faithful to the Enlightenment and have continued to identify themselves with the cause of science. They see the old struggle between science and religion, reason and unreason, as still going on, having now taken the form of a struggle between reason and all those forces within culture which think of truth as made rather than found. These philosophers take science as the paradigmatic human activity, and they insist that natural science discovers truth rather than makes it. They regard "making truth" as a merely metaphorical, and thoroughly misleading, phrase. They think of politics and art as spheres in which the notion of "truth" is out of place. Other philosophers, realizing that the world as it is described by the physical sciences teaches no moral lesson and offers no spiritual comfort, have concluded that science is no more than the servant of technology. These philosophers have ranged themselves alongside the political utopian and the innovative artist.

Whereas the first kind of philosopher contrasts "hard scientific fact" with the "subjective" or with "metaphor," the second kind sees science as one more human activity, rather than as the place at which human beings encounter a "hard," nonhuman reality. On this view, great scientists invent descriptions of the world that are useful for purposes of predicting and controlling what happens, just as poets and political thinkers invent other descriptions of it for other purposes. But there is no sense in which *any* of these descriptions is an accurate representation of the way the world is in itself. These philosophers regard the very idea of such a representation as pointless.

Had the first sort of philosopher, the sort whose hero is the natural scientist, always been the only sort, we would probably never have had an autonomous discipline called "philosophy"—a discipline as distinct from the sciences as it is from theology or from the arts. As such a discipline, philosophy is no more than two hundred years old. It owes its existence to attempts by the German idealists to put the sciences in their place and to give a clear sense to the vague idea that human beings make truth rather than find it. Kant wanted to consign science to the realm of second-rate truth—truth about a phenomenal world. Hegel wanted to think of natural science as a description of spirit not yet fully conscious of its own spiritual nature, thereby to elevate the sort of truth offered by the poet and the political revolutionary to first-rate status.

German idealism, however, was a short-lived and unsatisfactory compromise. For Kant and Hegel went only halfway in their repudiation of the idea that truth is "out there." They were willing to view the world of empirical science as a made world—to see matter as constructed by mind, or as consisting in mind insufficiently conscious of its own mental character. But they persisted in seeing mind, spirit, the depths of the human self as having an intrinsic nature, one that could be known by a kind of nonempirical super-science called philosophy. This meant that only half of truth—the bottom, scientific half— was made. Higher truth, the truth about the mind, the province of philosophy, was still a matter of discovery rather than creation.

What was needed, and what the idealists were unable to envisage, was a repudiation of the very idea of anything—mind or matter, self or world— having an intrinsic nature to be expressed or represented. For the idealists confused the idea that nothing has such a nature with the idea that space and time are unreal, that human beings cause the spatiotemporal world to exist.

We need to make a distinction between the claim that the world is out there and the claim that truth is out there. To say that the world is out there, that it is not our creation, is to say, with common sense, that most things in space and time are the effects of causes which do not include human mental states. To say that truth is not out there is simply to say that where there are no sentences there is no truth, that sentences are elements of human languages, and that human languages are human creations.

Truth cannot be out there, cannot exist independently of the human mind, because sentences cannot so exist, or be out there. The world is out there, but descriptions of the world are not. Only descriptions of the world can be true or false. The world on its own—unaided by the describing activities of human beings—cannot.

The suggestion that truth, as well as the world, is out there is a legacy of an age in which the world was seen as the creation of a being who had language of its own. If we cease to attempt to make sense of the idea of such a nonhuman language, we shall not be tempted to confuse the platitude that the world may cause us to be justified in believing a sentence true with the claim that the world splits itself up, on its own initiative, into sentence-shaped chunks called "facts." But if one clings to the notion of self-subsistent facts, it is easy to start capitalizing the word *truth* and treating it as something identical either with God or with the world as God's project. Then one will say, for example, that Truth is great and will prevail.

This conflation is facilitated by confining attention to single sentences as opposed to vocabularies. For we often let the world decide the competition between alternative sentences (e.g., between "Red wins" and "Black wins" or between "The butler did it" and "The doctor did it"). In such cases, it is easy to run together the fact that the world contains the causes of our being justified in holding a belief with the claim that some nonlinguistic state of the world is itself an example of truth, or that some such state "makes a belief true" by "corresponding" to it. But it is not so easy when we turn from individual sentences to vocabularies as wholes. When we consider examples of alternative language games—the vocabulary of ancient Athenian politics versus Jefferson's, the moral vocabulary of Saint Paul versus Freud's, the jargon of Newton versus that of Aristotle, the idiom of Blake versus that of Dryden—it is difficult to think of the world as making one of these better than another, of the world as deciding between them. When the notion of "description of the world" is moved from the level of criterion-governed sentences within language games to language games as wholes, games that we do not choose between by reference to criteria, the idea that the world decides which descriptions are true can no longer be given a clear sense. It becomes hard to think that that vocabulary is somehow already out there in the world, waiting for us to discover it. Attention (of the sort fostered by intellectual historians like Thomas Kuhn and Quentin Skinner) to the vocabularies in which sentences are formulated, rather than to individual sentences, makes us realize, for example, that the fact that Newton's vocabulary lets us predict the world more easily than Aristotle's does not mean that the world speaks Newtonian.

The world does not speak. Only we do. The world can, once we have programmed ourselves with a language, cause us to hold beliefs. But it cannot propose a language for us to speak. Only other human beings can do that. The realization that the world does not tell us what language games to play should not, however, lead us to say that a decision about which to play is arbitrary, or to say that it is the expression of something deep within us. The moral is not that objective criteria for choice of vocabulary are to be replaced with subjective criteria, reason with will or feeling. It is rather that the notions of criteria and choice (including that of "arbitrary" choice) are no longer to the point when it comes to changes from one language game to another. Europe did not *decide* to accept the idiom of Romantic poetry, or of socialist politics, or of Galilean mechanics. That sort of shift was no more an act of will than it was a result of argument. Rather, Europe gradually lost the habit of using certain words and gradually acquired the habit of using others.

As Kuhn argues in *The Copernican Revolution,* we did not decide on the basis of some telescopic observation, or on the basis of anything else, that the earth was not the center of the universe, that macroscopic behavior could be explained on the basis of microstructural motion, and that prediction and control should be the principal aim of scientific theorizing. Rather, after a hundred years of inconclusive muddle, the Europeans found themselves speaking in a way that took these interlocked theses for granted. Cultural change of this magnitude does not result from applying criteria (or from "arbitrary decision") any more than individuals become theists or atheists, or shift from one spouse or circle of friends to another, as a result either of applying criteria or of *actes gratuits.* We should not look within ourselves for criteria of decision in such matters any more than we should look to the world.

The temptation to look for criteria is a species of the more general temptation to think of the world, or the human self, as possessing an intrinsic nature, an essence. That is, it is the result of the temptation to privilege one among the many languages in which we habitually describe the world or ourselves. As long as we think that there is some relation called "fitting the world" or "expressing the real nature of the self" which can be possessed or lacked by vocabularies as wholes, we shall continue the traditional philosophical search for a criterion to tell us which vocabularies have this desirable feature. But if we could ever become reconciled to the idea that most of reality is indifferent to our descriptions of it, and that the human self is created by the use of a vocabulary rather than being adequately or inadequately expressed in a vocabulary, then we should at last have assimilated what was true in the Romantic idea that truth is made rather than found. What is true about this claim is just that *languages* are made rather than found, and that truth is a property of linguistic entities, of sentences.

I can sum up by redescribing what, in my view, the revolutionaries and poets of two centuries ago were getting at. What was glimpsed at the end of the eighteenth century was that anything could be made to look good or bad, important or unimportant, useful or useless, by being redescribed. What Hegel describes as the process of spirit gradually becoming self-conscious of its intrinsic nature is better described as the process of European linguistic practices changing at a faster and faster rate. The phenomenon Hegel describes is that of more people offering more radical redescriptions of more things than ever before, of young people going through half a dozen spiritual gestalt-switches before reaching adulthood. What the Romantics expressed as the claim that imagination, rather than reason, is the central human faculty was the realization that a talent for speaking differently, rather than for arguing well, is the chief instrument of cultural change. What political utopians since the French Revolution have sensed is not that an enduring, substratal human nature has been suppressed or repressed by "unnatural" or "irrational" social institutions but rather that changing languages and other social practices may produce human beings of a sort that had never before existed. The German idealists, the French revolutionaries, and the Romantic poets had in common a dim sense that human beings whose language changed so that they no longer spoke of themselves as responsible to nonhuman powers would thereby become a new kind of human being.

The difficulty faced by a philosopher who, like myself, is sympathetic to this suggestion—one who thinks of himself as auxiliary to the poet rather than to the physicist—is to avoid hinting that this suggestion gets something right, that my sort of philosophy corresponds to the way things really are. For this talk of correspondence brings back just the idea my sort of philosopher wants to get rid of, the idea that the world or the self has an intrinsic nature. From our point of view, explaining the success of science, or the desirability of political liberalism, by talk of "fitting the world" or "expressing human nature" is like explaining why opium makes you sleepy by talking about its dormitive power. To say that Freud's vocabulary gets at the truth about human nature, or Newton's at the truth about the heavens, is not an explanation of anything. It is just an empty compliment—one traditionally paid to writers whose novel jargon we have found useful. To say that there is no such thing as intrinsic nature is not to say that the intrinsic nature of reality has turned out, surprisingly enough, to be extrinsic. It is to say that the term *intrinsic nature* is one which it would pay us not to use, an expression which has caused more trouble than it has been worth. To say that we should drop the idea of truth as out there waiting to be discovered is not to say that we have discovered that, out there, there is no truth.[1] It is to say that our purposes would be served best by ceasing to see truth as a deep matter, as a topic of philosophical interest, or "true" as a term which repays "analysis." "The nature of truth" is an unprofitable topic, resembling in this respect "the nature of the human" and "the nature of God," and differing from "the nature of the positron," and "the nature of oedipal fixation." But this claim about relative profitability, in turn, is just the recommendation that we in fact *say* little about these topics, and see how we get on.

On the view of philosophy I am offering, philosophers should not be asked for arguments against, for example, the correspondence theory of truth or the idea of the "intrinsic nature of reality." The trouble with arguments against the use of a familiar and time-honored vocabulary is that they are expected to be phrased in that very vocabulary. They are expected to show that central elements in that vocabulary are "inconsistent in their own terms" or that they "deconstruct themselves." But that can *never* be shown. Any argument to the effect that our familiar use of a familiar term is incoherent, or empty, or confused, or vague, or "merely metaphorical" is bound to be inconclusive and question-begging. For such use is, after all, the paradigm of coherent, meaningful, literal, speech. Such arguments are always parasitic on, and abbreviations for, claims that a better vocabulary is available. Interesting philosophy is rarely an examination of the pros and cons of a thesis. Usually it is, implicitly or explicitly, a contest between an entrenched vocabulary which has become a nuisance and a half-formed new vocabulary which vaguely promises great things.

The latter "method" of philosophy is the same as the "method" of utopian politics or revolutionary science (as opposed to parliamentary politics, or normal science). The method is to redescribe lots of things in a new way, until you have created a pattern of linguistic behavior that will tempt the rising generation to adopt it, thereby causing them to look for appropriate new forms of nonlinguistic behavior, for example, the adoption of new scientific equipment or new social institutions. This sort of philosophy does not work piece by piece, analyzing concept after concept, or testing thesis after thesis. Rather, it works holistically and pragmatically. It says things like "Try thinking of it this way," or more specifically, "Try to ignore the apparently futile traditional questions by substituting the following new and possibly interesting questions." It does not pretend to have a better candidate for doing the same old things which we did when we spoke in the old way. Rather, it suggests that we might want to stop doing those things and do something else. But it does not argue for this suggestion on the basis of antecedent criteria common to the old and the new language games. For just insofar as the new language really is new, there will be no such criteria.

Conforming to my own precepts, I am not going to offer arguments against the vocabulary I want to replace. Instead, I am going to try to make the vocabulary I favor look attractive by showing how it may be used to describe a variety of topics. More specifically, in this chapter I shall be describing the work of Donald Davidson in philosophy of language as a manifestation of a willingness to drop the idea of "intrinsic nature," a willingness to face up to the *contingency* of the language we use.

I begin with the philosophy of language because I want to spell out the consequences of my claims that only sentences can be true, and that human beings make truths by making languages in which to phrase sentences. I shall concentrate on the work of Davidson because he is the philosopher who has done most to explore these consequences.[2] Davidson's treatment of truth ties in with his treatment of language learning and of metaphor to form the first systematic treatment of language that breaks *completely* with the notion of language as something which can be adequate or inadequate to the world or to the self. For Davidson breaks with the notion that language is a *medium*—a medium either of representation or of expression.

I can explain what I mean by a medium by noting that the traditional picture of the human situation has been one in which human beings are not simply networks of beliefs and desires but rather beings who have those beliefs and desires. The traditional view is that there is a core self which can look at, decide among, use, and express itself by means of such beliefs and desires. Further, these beliefs and desires are criticizable not simply by reference to their ability to cohere with one another, but by reference to something exterior to the network within which they are strands. Beliefs are, on this account, criticizable because they fail to correspond to reality. Desires are criticizable because they fail to correspond to the essential nature of the human self because they are "irrational" or "unnatural." So we have a picture of the essential core of the self on one side of this network of beliefs and desires, and reality on the other side. In this picture, the network is the product of an interaction between the two, alternately expressing the one and representing the other. This is the traditional subject-object picture which idealism tried and failed to replace, and which Nietzsche, Heidegger, Derrida, James, Dewey, Goodman, Sellars, Putnam, Davidson, and others have tried to replace without entangling themselves in the idealists' paradoxes.

One phase of this effort of replacement consisted in an attempt to substitute "language" for "mind or consciousness" as the medium out of which beliefs and desires are constructed, the third, mediating, element between self and world. This turn toward language was thought of as a progressive, naturalizing move. It seemed so because it seemed easier to give a causal account of the evolutionary emergence of language-using organisms than of the metaphysical emergence of consciousness out of nonconsciousness. But in itself this substitution is ineffective. For if we stick to the picture of language as a medium, something standing between the self and the nonhuman reality with which the self seeks to be in touch, we have made no progress. We are still using a subject-object picture, and we are still stuck with issues about skepticism, idealism, and realism. For we are still able to ask questions about language of the same sort we asked about consciousness.

These are such questions as: Does the medium between the self and reality get them together or keep them apart? Should we see the medium primarily as a medium of expression—of articulating what lies deep within the self? Or should we see it as primarily a medium of representation—showing the self what lies outside it? Idealist theories of knowledge and Romantic notions of the imagination can, alas, easily be transposed from the jargon of "consciousness" into that of "Language." Realistic and moralistic reactions to such theories can be transposed equally easily. So the seesaw battles between Romanticism and moralism, and between idealism and realism, will continue as long as one thinks there is a hope of making sense of the question of whether a given language is "adequate" to a task—either the task of properly expressing the nature of the human species or the task of properly representing the structure of nonhuman reality.

We need to get off this seesaw. Davidson helps us do so. For he does not view language as a medium for either expression or representation. So he is able to set aside the idea that both the self and reality have intrinsic natures, natures which are out there waiting to be known. Davidson's view of language is neither reductionist nor expansionist. It does not, as analytical philosophers sometimes have, purport to give reductive definitions of semantical notions like "truth" or "intentionality" or "reference." Nor does it resemble Heidegger's attempt to make language into a kind of divinity, something of which human beings are mere emanations. As Derrida has warned us, such an apotheosis of language is merely a transposed version of the idealists' apotheosis of consciousness.

In avoiding both reductionism and expansionism, Davidson resembles Wittgenstein. Both philosophers treat alternative vocabularies as more like alternative tools than like bits of a jigsaw puzzle. To treat them as pieces of a puzzle is to assume that all vocabularies are dispensable, or reducible to other vocabularies, or capable of being united with all other vocabularies in one grand, unified super-vocabulary. If we avoid this assumption, we shall not be inclined to ask questions like What is the place of consciousness in a world of molecules? Are colors more mind-dependent than weights? What is the place of value in a world of fact? What is the place of intentionality in a world of causation? What is the relation between the solid table of common sense and the unsolid table of microphysics? What is the relation of language to thought? We should not try to answer such questions, for doing so leads either to the evident failures of reductionism or to the short-lived successes of expansionism. We should restrict ourselves to questions like Does our use of these words get in the way of our use of those other words? This is a question about whether our use of tools is inefficient, not a question about whether our beliefs are contradictory.

"Merely philosophical" questions, like Eddington's question about the two tables, are attempts to stir up a factitious theoretical quarrel between vocabularies that have proved capable of peaceful coexistence. The questions I have recited are all cases in which philosophers have given their subject a bad name by seeing difficulties nobody else sees. But this is not to say that vocabularies never do get in the way of each other. On the contrary, revolutionary achievements in the arts, in the sciences, and in moral and political thought typically occur when somebody realizes that two or more of our vocabularies are interfering with each other, and proceeds to invent a new vocabulary to replace both. For example, the traditional Aristotelian vocabulary got in the way of the mathematized vocabulary that was being developed in the sixteenth century by students of mechanics. Again, young German theology students of the late eighteenth century—such as Hegel and Holderlin—found that the vocabulary in which they worshiped Jesus was getting in the way of the vocabulary in which they worshiped the Greeks. Yet again, the use of Rossetti-like tropes got in the way of the early Yeats's use of Blakean tropes.

The gradual trial-and-error creation of a new, third, vocabulary—the sort of vocabulary developed by people like Galileo, Hegel, or the later Yeats—is not a discovery about how old vocabularies fit together. That is why it cannot be reached by an inferential process, by starting with premises formulated in the old vocabularies. Such creations are not the result of successfully fitting together pieces of a puzzle. They are not discoveries of a reality behind the appearances, of an undistorted view of the whole picture with which to replace myopic views of its parts. The proper analogy is with the invention of new tools to take the place of old tools. To come up with such a vocabulary is more like discarding the lever and the clock because one has envisaged the pulley, or like discarding gesso and tempera because one has now figured out how to size canvas properly.

This Wittgensteinian analogy between vocabularies and tools has one obvious drawback. The artisan typically knows what job he or she needs to do before picking or inventing tools with which to do it. By contrast, someone like Galileo, Yeats, or Hegel (a "poet" in my wide sense of the term, as "one who makes things new") is typically unable to make clear exactly what it is that he wants to do before developing the language in which he succeeds in doing it. His new vocabulary makes possible, for the first time, a formulation of its own purpose. It is a tool for doing something which could not have been envisaged prior to the development of a particular set of descriptions, those which it itself helps to provide. But I shall, for the moment, ignore this disanalogy. I want simply to remark that the contrast between the jigsaw puzzle and the "tool" models of alternative vocabularies reflects the contrast between—in Nietzsche's slightly misleading terms—the will to truth and the will to self-overcoming. Both are expressions of the contrast between the attempt to represent or express something that was already there and the attempt to make something that never had been dreamed of before.

Davidson spells out the implications of Wittgenstein's treatment of vocabularies as tools by raising explicit doubts about the assumptions underlying traditional pre-Wittgensteinian accounts of language. These accounts have taken for granted that questions like Is the language we are presently using the "right" language—is it adequate to its task as a medium of expression or representation? Is our language a transparent or an opaque medium? make sense. Such questions assume there are relations such as "fitting the world" or "being faithful to the true nature of the self" in which language might stand to nonlanguage. This assumption goes along with the assumption that "our language"—the language we speak now, the vocabulary at the disposal of educated inhabitants of the twentieth century—is somehow a unity, a third thing which stands in some determinate relation with two other unities—the self and reality. Both assumptions are natural enough, once we accept the idea that there are nonlinguistic things called "meanings," which it is the task of language to express, as well as the idea that there are nonlinguistic things called "facts," which it is the task of language to represent. Both ideas enshrine the notion of language as medium.

Davidson's polemics against the traditional philosophical uses of the terms *fact* and *meaning,* and against what he calls "the scheme content model" of thought and inquiry, are parts of a larger polemic against the idea that there is a fixed task for language to perform and an entity called "language" or "the language" or "our language" which may or may not be performing this task efficiently. Davidson's doubt that there is any such entity parallels Gilbert Ryle's and Daniel Dennett's doubts about whether there is anything called "the mind" or "consciousness."[3] Both sets of doubts are doubts about the utility of the notion of a medium between the self and reality, the sort of medium that realists see as transparent and skeptics as opaque.

In a paper nicely entitled "A Nice Derangement of Epitaphs," Davidson tries to undermine the notion of languages as entities by developing the notion of what he calls "a passing theory" about the noises and inscriptions presently being produced by a fellow human. Think of such a theory as part of a larger "passing theory" about this person's total behavior—a set of guesses about what this person will do under what conditions. Such a theory is "passing" because it must constantly be corrected to allow for mumbles, stumbles, malapropisms, metaphors, tics, seizures, psychotic symptoms, egregious stupidity, strokes of genius, and the like. To make things easier, imagine that I am forming such a theory about the current behavior of a native of an exotic culture into which I have unexpectedly parachuted. This strange person, who presumably finds me equally strange, will simultaneously be busy forming a theory about my behavior. If we ever succeed in communicating easily and happily, it will be because this person's guesses about what I am going to do next, including what noises I am going to make next, and my own expectations about what I shall do or say under certain circumstances, come more or less to coincide, and because the converse is also true. She and I are coping with each other as we might cope with mangoes or boa constrictors: we are trying not to be taken by surprise. To say that we come to speak the same language is to say, as Davidson puts it, that we tend to converge on passing theories. Davidson's point is that all "two people need, if they are to understand one another through speech, is the ability to converge on passing theories from utterance to utterance" (212).

Davidson's account of linguistic communication dispenses with the picture of language as a third thing intervening between self and reality, and of different languages as barriers between persons or cultures. To say that one's previous language was inappropriate for dealing with some segment of the world (for example, the starry heavens above, or the raging passions within) is just to say that one is now, having learned a new language, able to handle that segment more easily. To say that two communities have trouble getting along because the words they use are so hard to translate into each other is just to say that the linguistic behavior of inhabitants of one community may, like the rest of their behavior, be hard for inhabitants of the other community to predict. As Davidson puts it,

> We should realize that we have abandoned not only the ordinary notion of a language, but we have erased the boundary between knowing a language and knowing our way around the world generally. For there are no rules for arriving at passing theories that work. . . . There is no more chance of regularizing, or teaching, this process than there is of regularizing or teaching the process of creating new theo-

ries to cope with new data—for that is what this process involves. . . .

> *There is no such thing as a language,* not if a language is anything like what philosophers, at least, have supposed. There is therefore no such thing to be learned or mastered. We must give up the idea of a clearly defined shared structure which language users master and then apply to cases. . . . We should give up the attempt to illuminate how we communicate by appeal to conventions. ("Nice Derangement" 446, emphasis added)

This line of thought about language is analogous to the Ryle-Dennett view that when we use a mentalistic terminology we are simply using an efficient vocabulary—the vocabulary characteristic of what Dennett calls the "intentional stance"—to predict what an organism is likely to do or say under various sets of circumstances. Davidson is a nonreductive behaviorist about language in the same way that Ryle was a nonreductive behaviorist about mind. Neither has any desire to give equivalents in behaviorese for talk about beliefs or about reference. But both are saying: Think of the term *mind* or *language* not as the name of a medium between self and reality but simply as a flag which signals the desirability of using a certain vocabulary when trying to cope with certain kinds of organisms. To say that a given organism—or, for that matter, a given machine—has a mind is just to say that, for some purposes, it will pay to think of it as having beliefs and desires. To say that it is a language user is just to say that pairing off the marks and noises it makes with those we make will prove a useful tactic in predicting and controlling its future behavior.

This Wittgensteinian attitude, developed by Ryle and Dennett for minds and by Davidson for languages, naturalizes mind and language by making all questions about the relation of either to the rest of universe *causal* questions, as opposed to questions about adequacy of representation or expression. It makes perfectly good sense to ask how we got from the relative mindlessness of the monkey to the full-fledged mindedness of the human, or from speaking Neanderthal to speaking postmodern, if these are construed as straightforward causal questions. In the former case the answer takes us off into neurology and thence into evolutionary biology. But in the latter case it takes us into intellectual history viewed as the history of metaphor. For my purposes in this book, it is the latter that is important. So I shall spend the rest of this chapter sketching an account of intellectual and moral progress which squares with Davidson's account of language.

To see the history of language, and thus of the arts, the sciences, and the moral sense, as the history of metaphor is to drop the picture of the human mind, or human languages, becoming better and better suited to the purposes for which God or Nature designed them, for example, able to express more and more meanings or to represent more and more facts. The idea that language has a purpose goes once the idea of language as medium goes. A culture that renounced both ideas would be the triumph of those tendencies in modern thought that began two hundred years ago, the tendencies common to German idealism, Romantic poetry, and utopian politics.

A nonteleological view of intellectual history, including the history of science, does for the theory of culture what the Mendelian, mechanistic account of natural selection did for evolutionary theory. Mendel let us see mind as something that just happened rather than as something that was the point of the whole process. Davidson lets us think of the history of language, and thus of culture, as Darwin taught us to think of the history of a coral reef. Old metaphors are constantly dying off into literalness, and then serving as a platform and foil for new metaphors. This analogy lets us think of "our language"—that is, of the science and culture of twentieth-century Europe—as something that took shape as a result of a great number of sheer contingencies. Our language and our culture are as much a contingency, as much a result of thousands of small mutations finding niches (and millions of others finding no niches), as are the orchids and the anthropoids.

To accept this analogy, we must follow Mary Hesse in thinking of scientific revolutions as "metaphoric redescriptions" of nature rather than insights into the intrinsic nature of nature. Further, we must resist the temptation to think that the redescriptions of reality offered by contemporary physical or biological science are somehow closer to "the things themselves," less "mind-dependent," than the redescriptions of history offered by contemporary culture criticism. We need to see the constellations of causal forces that produced talk of DNA or of the Big Bang as of a piece with the causal forces that produced talk of "secularization" or of "late capitalism."[4] These various constellations are the random factors that have made some things subjects of conversation for us and others not, have made some projects and not others possible and important.

I can develop the contrast between the idea that the history of culture has a *telos*—such as the discovery of truth, or the emancipation of humanity—and the Nietzschean and Davidsonian picture which I am sketching by noting that the latter picture is compatible with a bleakly mechanical description of the relation between human beings and the rest of the universe. For genuine novelty can, after all, occur in a world of blind, contingent, mechanical forces. Think of novelty as the sort of thing that happens when, for example, a cosmic ray scrambles the atoms in a DNA molecule, thus sending things off in the direction of the orchids or the anthropoids. The orchids, when their time came, were no less novel or marvelous for the sheer contingency of this necessary condition of their existence. Analogously, for all we know, or should care, Aristotle's metaphorical use of *ousia*, Saint Paul's metaphorical use of *agape,* and Newton's metaphorical use of *gravitas* were the results of cosmic rays scrambling the fine structure of some crucial neurons in their respective brains. Or, more plausibly, they were the result of some odd episodes in infancy—some obsessional kinks left in these brains by idiosyncratic traumata. It hardly matters how the trick was done. The results were marvelous. There had never been such things before.

This account of intellectual history chimes with Nietzsche's definition of truth as "a mobile army of metaphors." It also chimes with the description I offered earlier of people like Galileo and Hegel and Yeats, people in whose minds new vocabularies developed, thereby equipping them with tools for doing things that could not even have been envisaged before these tools were available. But in order to accept this picture, we need to see the distinction between the literal and the metaphorical in the way Davidson sees it: not as a distinction between two sorts of meaning, or as a distinction between two sorts of interpretation, but as a distinction between familiar and unfamiliar uses of noises and marks. The literal uses of noises and marks are the uses we can handle by our old theories about what people will say under various conditions. Their metaphorical use is the sort that makes us get busy developing a new theory.

Davidson puts this point by saying that one should not think of metaphorical expressions as having meanings distinct from their literal ones. To have a meaning is to have a place in a language game. Metaphors, by definition, do not. Davidson denies, in his words, "the thesis that associated with a metaphor is a cognitive content that its author wishes to convey and that the interpreter must grasp if he is to get the message" ("What Metaphors Mean" 262). In his view, tossing a metaphor into a conversation is like suddenly breaking off the conversation long enough to make a face, or pulling a photograph out of your pocket and displaying it, or pointing at a feature of the surroundings, or slapping your interlocutor's face, or kissing him. Tossing a metaphor into a text is like using italics, or illustrations, or odd punctuation or formats.

All these are ways of producing effects on your interlocutor or your reader, but not ways of conveying a message. To none of these is it appropriate to respond with "What exactly are you trying to say?" If one had wanted to say something, if one had wanted to utter a sentence with a meaning, one would presumably have done so. But instead one thought that one's aim could be better carried out by other means. That one uses familiar words in unfamiliar ways—rather than slaps, kisses, pictures, gestures, or grimaces—does not show that what one said must have a meaning. An attempt to state that meaning would be an attempt to find some familiar (that is, literal) use of words—some sentence that already had a place in the language game—and, to claim that one might just as well have *that*. But the unparaphrasability of metaphor is just the unsuitability of any such familiar sentence for one's purpose.

Uttering a sentence without a fixed place in a language game is, as the positivists rightly have said, to utter something that is neither true nor false—something that is not, in Ian Hacking's terms, a "truth-value candidate." This is because it is a sentence that one cannot confirm or disconfirm, argue for or against. One can only savor it or spit it out. But this is not to say that it may not, in time, *become* a truth-value candidate. If it is savored rather than spat out, the sentence may be repeated, caught up, bandied about. Then it will gradually require a habitual use, a familiar place in the language game. It will thereby have ceased to be a metaphor—or, if you like, it will have become what most sentences of our language are, a dead metaphor. It will be just one more literally true or literally false sentence of the language. That is to say, our theories about the linguistic behavior of our fellows will suffice to let us cope with their utterances in the same unthinking way in which we cope with most of their other utterances.

The Davidsonian claim that metaphors do not have meanings may seem like a typical philosopher's quibble, but it is not.[5] It is part of an attempt to get us to stop thinking of language as a medium. This, in turn, is part of a larger attempt to get rid of the traditional philosophical picture of what it is to be human. The importance of Davidson's point can perhaps best be seen by contrasting his treatment of metaphor with those of the Platonist and the positivist on the one hand and the Romantic on the other. The Platonist and the positivist share a reductionist view of metaphor: they think metaphors are either paraphrasable or useless for the one serious purpose that language has, namely, representing reality. By contrast, Romantics have an expansionist view: they think metaphor is strange, mystic, wonderful. Romantics attribute metaphor to a mysterious faculty called the "imagination," a faculty they suppose to be at the very center of the self, the deep heart's core. Whereas the metaphorical looks irrelevant to Platonists and positivists, the literal looks irrelevant to Romantics. For the former think that the point of language is to represent a hidden reality that lies outside us, and the latter think its purpose is to express a hidden reality that lies within us.

Positivist history of culture thus sees language as gradually shaping itself around the contours of the physical world. Romantic history of culture sees language as gradually bringing Spirit to self-consciousness. Nietzschean history of culture and Davidsonian philosophy of language see language as we now see evolution, as new forms of life constantly killing off old forms—not to accomplish a higher purpose, but blindly. Whereas the positivist sees Galileo as making a discovery—finally coming up with the words that were needed to fit the world properly, words Aristotle missed—the Davidsonian sees him as having hit on a tool that happened to work better for certain purposes than any previous tool. Once we found out what could be done with a Galilean vocabulary, nobody was much interested in doing the things that used to be done (and that Thomists thought should still be done) with an Aristotelian vocabulary.

Similarly, whereas the Romantic sees Yeats as having gotten at something that nobody had previously gotten at, expressed something that had long been yearning for expression, the Davidsonian sees him as having hit on some tools that enabled him to write poems which were not just variations on the poems of his precursors. Once we had Yeats's later poems in hand, we were less interested in reading Rossetti's. What goes for revolutionary, strong scientists and poets goes also for strong philosophers—people like Hegel and Davidson, the sort of philosophers who are interested in dissolving inherited problems rather than in solving them. In this view, substituting dialectic for demonstration as the method of philosophy, or getting rid of the correspondence theory of truth, is not a discovery about the nature of a preexistent entity called "philosophy" or "truth." It is changing the way we talk, and thereby changing what we want to do and what we think we are.

But in a Nietzschean view, one which drops the reality-appearance distinction, to change how we talk is to change what, for our own purposes, we are. To say, with Nietzsche, that God is dead, is to say that we serve no higher purposes. The Nietzschean substitution of self-creation for discovery substitutes a picture of the hungry generations treading each other down for a picture of humanity approaching closer and closer to the light. A culture in which Nietzschean metaphors were literalized would be one that took for granted that philosophical problems are as temporary as poetic problems, that there are no problems binding the generations together into a single natural kind called "humanity." A sense of human history as the history of successive metaphors would let us see the poet, in the generic sense of the maker of new words, the shaper of new languages, as the vanguard of the species.

I shall conclude by going back to the claim, which has been central to what I have been saying, that the world does not provide us with any criterion of choice between alternative metaphors, that we can only compare Languages or metaphors with one another, not with something beyond Language called "fact."

The only way to argue for this claim is to do what philosophers like Goodman, Putnam, and Davidson have done: exhibit the sterility of attempts to give a sense to phrases like "the way the world is" or "fitting the facts." Such efforts can be supplemented by the work of philosophers of science such as Kuhn and Hesse. These philosophers explain why there is no way to explain the fact that a Galilean vocabulary enables us to make better predictions than an Aristotelian vocabulary by the claim that the book of nature is written in the language of mathematics.

These sorts of arguments by philosophers of language and of science should be seen against the background of the work of intellectual historians: historians who, like Hans Blumenberg, have tried to trace the similarities and dissimilarities between the Age of Faith and the Age of Reason. These historians have made the point I mentioned earlier: the very idea that the world or the self has an intrinsic nature—one which the physicist or the poet may have glimpsed—is a remnant of the idea that the world is a divine creation, the work of someone who had something in mind, who Himself spoke some language in which He described His own project. Only if we have some such picture in mind, some picture of the universe as either itself a person or as created by a person, can we make sense of the idea that the world has an "intrinsic nature." For the cash value of that phrase is just that some vocabularies are better representations of the world than others, as opposed to being better tools for dealing with the world for one or another purpose.

To drop the idea of languages as representations, and to be thoroughly Wittgensteinian in our approach to language, would be to de-divinize the world. Only if we do that can we fully accept the argument I offered earlier— the argument that since truth is a property of sentences, since sentences are dependent for their existence on vocabularies, and since vocabularies are made by human beings, so are truths. For as long as we think that "the world" names something we ought to respect as well as cope with, something personlike in that it has a preferred description of itself, we shall insist that any philosophical account of truth save the "intuition" that truth is "out there." This intuition amounts to the vague sense that it would be *hubris* on our part to abandon the traditional language of "respect for fact" and "objectivity," that it would be risky, and blasphemous, not to see the scientist (or the philosopher, or the poet, or *somebody*) as having a priestly function, as putting us in touch with a realm that transcends the human.

On the view I am suggesting, the claim that an "adequate" philosophical doctrine must make room for our intuitions is a reactionary slogan, one which begs the question at hand.[6] For it is essential to my view that we have no prelinguistic consciousness to which language needs to be adequate, no deep sense of how things are which it is the duty of philosophers to spell out in language. What is described as such a consciousness is simply a disposition to use the language of our ancestors, to worship the corpses of their metaphors. Unless we suffer from what Derrida calls "Heideggerian nostalgia," we shall not think of our "intuitions" as more than platitudes, more than the habitual use of a certain repertoire of terms, more than old tools which as yet have no replacements.

I can crudely sum up the story that historians like Blumenberg tell by saying that once upon a time we felt a need to worship something that lay beyond the visible world. Beginning in the seventeenth century we tried to substitute a love of truth for a love of God, treating the world described by science as a quasi divinity. Beginning at the end of the eighteenth century we tried to substitute a love of ourselves for a love of scientific truth, a worship of our own deep spiritual or poetic nature, treated as one more quasi divinity.

The line of thought common to Blumenberg, Nietzsche, Freud, and Davidson suggests that we try to get to the point where we no longer worship *anything*, where we treat *nothing* as a quasi divinity, where we treat *everything*—

our language, our conscience, our community—as a product of time and chance. To reach this point would be, in Freud's words, to "treat chance as worthy of determining our fate."

Notes

1. Nietzsche has caused a lot of confusion by inferring from "truth is not a matter of correspondence to reality" to "what we call 'truths' are just useful lies." The same confusion is occasionally found in Derrida, in the inference from "there is no such reality as the metaphysicians have hoped to find" to "what we call 'real' is not really real." Such confusions make Nietzsche and Derrida liable to charges of self-referential inconsistency—to claiming to know what they themselves claim cannot be known.

2. I should remark that Davidson cannot be held responsible for the interpretation I am putting on his views, or for the further views I extrapolate from his. For an extended statement of that interpretation, see my "Pragmatism, Davidson and Truth." For Davidson's reaction to this interpretation, see his "After-thoughts to 'A Coherence Theory of Truth and Knowledge.'"

3. For an elaboration of these doubts, see my "Contemporary Philosophy of Mind." For Dennett's doubts about my interpretations of his views, see his "Comments on Rorty," in *The Intentional Stance*.

4. This coalescence is resisted in Bernard Williams's discussion of Davidson's and my views in chapter 6 of his *Ethics and the Limits of Philosophy*. For a partial reply to Williams, see my "Is Natural Science a Natural Kind?"

5. For a further defense of Davidson against the charge of quibbling, and various other charges, see my "Unfamiliar Noises: Hesse and Davidson on Metaphor."

6. For an application of this dictum to a particular case, see my discussion of the appeals to intuition found in Thomas Nagel's view of "subjectivity" and in John Searle's doctrine of "intrinsic intentionality," in "Contemporary Philosophy of Mind." For further criticisms of both, criticisms which harmonize with my own, see Daniel Dennett, "Setting Off on the Right Foot" and "Evolution, Error, and Intentionality," both in *The Intentional Stance*.

Works Cited

Blumenberg, Hans. *The Legitimacy of the Modern Age*. Trans. Robert Wallace. Cambridge, Mass.: MIT Press, 1982.

Davidson, Donald. "After-thoughts to 'A Coherence Theory of Truth and Knowledge.'" *Reading Rorty: Critical Responses to Philosophy and the Mirror of Nature (and Beyond)*. Ed. Allan Malachowski. Oxford: Blackwell, 1990.

——. "A Nice Derangement of Epitaphs." *Truth and Interpretation: Perspectives on the Philosophy of Donald Davidson*. Ed. Ernest Lepore. Oxford: Blackwell, 1984.

——. "What Metaphors Mean." *Inquiries into Truth and Interpretation*. Oxford: Oxford University Press, 1984.

Dennett, Daniel. *The Intentional Stance.* Cambridge, Mass.: MIT Press, 1987.

Hesse, Mary. "The Explanatory Function of Metaphor." *Revolutions and Reconstructions in the Philosophy of Science.* Bloomington: Indiana University Press, 1980.

Rorty, Richard. "Contemporary Philosophy of Mind." *Synthese* 53 (1982): 332–48.

——. "Is Natural Science a Natural Kind?" *Construction and Constraint: The Shaping of Scientific Rationality.* Ed. Ernan McMullin. Notre Dame, Ind.: University of Notre Dame Press, 1988.

——. "Pragmatism, Davidson and Truth." *Truth and Interpretation: Perspectives on the Philosophy of Donald Davidson.* Ed. Ernest Lepore. Oxford: Blackwell, 1984.

——. "Unfamiliar Noises: Hesse and Davidson on Metaphor." *Proceedings of the Aristotelian Society,* supp. vol. 61 (1987): 283–96.

Williams, Bernard. *Ethics and the Limits of Philosophy.* Cambridge, Mass.: Harvard University Press, 1985.

3
A Short History of Rhetoric
Terry Eagleton

A political literary criticism is not the invention of marxists. On the contrary, it is one of the oldest, most venerable forms of literary criticism we know. The most widespread early criticism on historical record was not, in our sense, "aesthetic": it was a mode of what we would now call "discourse theory," devoted to analyzing the material effects of particular uses of language in particular social conjunctures. It was a highly elaborate theory of specific signifying practices—above all, of the discursive practices of the juridical, political, and religious apparatuses of the state. Its intention, quite consciously, was systematically to theorize the articulations of discourse and power, and to do so in the name of political practice: to enrich the political effectivity of signification.

The name of this form of criticism was rhetoric. From its earliest formulations by Corax of Syracuse in fifth-century Greece, rhetoric came in Roman schools to be practically equivalent to higher education as such. It constituted the paramount study in such schools down to the fourth century C.E., providing a whole course in the humanities, incorporating the art of speaking and writing well in any discourse whatsoever. Throughout late antiquity and the Middle Ages, "criticism" was, in effect, rhetoric; and in its later history rhetoric remained a textual training of the ruling class in the techniques of political hegemony. Textual analysis was seen as preparatory to textual composition: the point of studying literary felicities and stylistic devices was to train oneself to use them effectively in one's own ideological practice. The textbooks of rhetoric were the densely codified manuals of such politico-discursive education; they were handbooks of ruling-class power. Born in antiquity as a supremely pragmatic discourse— how to litigate, prosecute, politically persuade—rhetoric emerged as a discourse theory utterly inseparable from the social relations of exploitation. Cleric and litigant, politician and prosecutor, military leader and popular tribune would naturally have recourse to the prescriptions of rhetorical theory, for how absurd to imagine that the business of politically effective discourse could be left to the vagaries of individual inspiration. Specialists in the theory of signifying practices—rhetoricians—would thus be at hand, to offer systematic instruction in such matters. Their theoretical meditations—born often enough, as with Cicero, out of their own political practice—would then be encoded by the pedagogical apparatuses of later ruling classes, for their own political purposes. Textual "beauties" were not first of all to be aesthetically savored, they were ideological weapons whose practical deployment was to be learnt. The term *rhetoric* today means both the theory of effective discourse and the practice of it.

It is, indeed, in the rhetorical theories of antiquity that many of the questions that have never ceased to dog "literary criticism" have their root. Is rhetoric/criticism confined to particular discourses, or can it embrace any use of language whatsoever? Does it have a definitive object—juridical, aesthetic— or is it rather a "portable" analytic method independent of any particular object? Does "literary criticism" study "literary" texts, or is it a branch of semiotics, and thus part of the study of any signifying practice from girning[1] to geological writing? Beneath this difficulty lies an ideological problem by which ancient rhetoric was already beset. Is rhetoric purely a question of "technique," or does it engage substantive ethical matters? Can an immoral person efficiently persuade? How far does the "content" of discourse, as opposed to its "embellishments," fall under the aegis of rhetoric? For Quintilian, there was no doubt that rhetoric concerned truth as well as tropes; Socrates was a good deal more suspicious of the dangers of sophistry. In the *Phaedrus,* the good rhetorician must also be a philosopher; the gap between the technical and the veridical was already worryingly open. Though the ancients of course recognized a special variety of discourse known as "poetry," there was no hard-and-fast distinction between this and other discursive modes: rhetoric was the science of them all. Poetry was in part discussed under the heading of the "aesthetic," but more readily in terms of its discursively effective devices, and so as a sub-branch of rhetoric. If "poetics" was dedicated to the "beauties" of certain fictional uses of language, rhetoric subsumed such discussion in a trans-discursive gesture, indifferently engaged with the written and spoken, text and practice, "poetic" and "factual." For Quintilian, historiography could certainly be just as much a proper object of rhetorical theory as fiction.

But such a general theory of discourse, radically prior to the later divisions of theoretical labor between "fact" and "fiction," spoken and written, poetic and pragmatic, might then come to threaten certain ideological values. Abstracted from the practical political contexts that gave it birth, rhetoric could harden into a set of self-regarding procedures indifferent to the truth-value of particular discourses, a "sophistical" declension that posed a latent threat to the state. Once the techniques of persuasion were fetishized as a form of meta-discourse, anyone was in principle open to be persuaded of anything. The masses must be suitably gullible, but not the dupe of any passing sophist. It was, then, largely in the political context of ancient rhetorical theory that later critical disputes between "form" and "content," "technique" and "morality," were to emerge—disputes that would come to be mystified to the level of the purely "aesthetic." The ancient rhetorician needed to know whether "form" and "content" were separable or inseparable because he needed to know whether one could achieve "different" effects in discourse with the "same" thought. An "aesthetic" error could lead to a political miscalculation. All discourse must underwrite the political and ethical values of the state: the earliest piece of Western "literary criticism" we have, a debate in Aristophanes' *The Frogs,* set the standards of "literary" practice as skill in art and "wise counsel for the state." Plato in the *Lairs* would admit only "hymns to the gods and praises of famous men" as permissible "literary" acts. But such an emphasis was in incipient contradiction with the full flowering of rhetoric, which Aristotle defined as the discovery of possible means of persuasion with regard to any subject whatever. Rhetorical theory, in a historical context prior to any highly specialist division of labor, was inevitably to some extent autonomous of particular objects; yet it seemed only a short step from such autonomy to a dangerously self-regulating set of meta-linguistic devices. Beneath this whole debate, in turn, lay a deeper ideological crisis in the ancient Greek state. Did "moral" discourse specify modes of behavior appropriate for a member of a particular polis, thus requiring as its basis a specific "science," of that polis; or was it a universal language that could specify the nature of "moral" action in any polis at all? It is the shape of this racking dissonance—one symptomatic of historical changes that have thrown the definition of traditional social roles into question—that one can perhaps glimpse between the lines of the rhetoricians' wrangling.[2]

The effects of this wrangling on later "criticism" were severe. For if criticism was merely a matter of technique, indifferent to the truth-value and moral substance of the text, then it courted triviality; if, however, it was a question of such "moral truths," then—not least in ideologically fraught epochs when such truths were themselves fiercely contested—it risked either unacceptable didacticism or embarrassing vagueness. The history of "criticism" is among other things the vexed narrative of this dilemma, torn as it continually is between a rebarbative technicism on the one hand, and a nebulous or insipid humanism on the other. Almost every major critical "school" has been characterized by an attempt to resolve this embarrassment anew. In the very cradle of ancient rhetoric, however, such a dilemma could not fully arise. Debating within a political assembly, arguing the merits of a lawsuit, or urging a government to war were forms of discourse whose devices were closely determined by the pragmatic situation to hand, techniques of persuasion indissociable from the substantive issues and audiences involved.

The ancient quarrel between form and content recurs in our own time in the shape of a controversy between ideology and science. Rhetoric, in some models, is an articulation of knowledge with power, but what proportionate role does each element play within it? For most classical rhetoricians, the cognitive and affective must be closely combined: *dialectic* (philosophy) must govern the production of ideological effects, *inventio* (substance of argument) must lay the groundwork for *dispositio* (structure of discourse) and *elocutio*. With the rise of Ramist logic in the seventeenth century, however, rhetoric and dialectic became increasingly disjoined. Cicero was already complaining in the *De Oratore* that Socrates had damagingly divided philosophy from rhetoric, thinking wisely from speaking gracefully; and under the impact of bourgeois rationalism and empiricism, that division was to become entrenched to the point where rhetoric would come to mean what it popularly means now: specious, filigreed, or bombastic language. The grounds for such a divorce had already been prepared by the fate of rhetoric in the Middle Ages. In that era, rhetoric retained its hegemony over "poetics": poetry was seen in effect as versified rhetoric, poets and orators imitated one another, and George Puttenham could remark that the poet was the best rhetorician of all. But with the change of material conditions from antiquity to the medieval period, rhetoric fell into a sterile formalism, a mere repertoire or museum of exotic verbal devices. What had happened in part was a severance of rhetorical theory from rhetorical practice, with the notable exception of the pulpit: the Greek city-state, with its partially phonocentric, oratorical political practices, had yielded decisively to government by script. Rhetoric was now a predominantly textual rather than political activity, a scholastic rather than civic pursuit. Though it retained high authority throughout the Renaissance, the rise of rationalist and empiricist philosophies of language spelled its ultimate demise. A rigorous division of labor was gradually instituted between thought and speech, theory and persuasion, language and discourse, science and poetry. By 1667, Thomas Sprat, historian of the Royal Society, was clamoring for the banishment of

"Eloquence" from all civil societies, "as a thing fatal to Peace and good Manners." Ramus, as Walter Ong has pointed out, appeared on the scene when dialectic was slowly shifting from the (Ciceronian) art of discourse to the art of reasoning; "theory" now had its specialist protocols remote from the marketplace and public forum, untainted by truck with the masses, a privatized and elitist mode of production that had rejected the "dialogism" of ancient rhetoric for a resolutely monologic cast. Reasoning, Ong remarks, wanted to dispense with words, since "these annoyingly hint that in some mysterious way thinking itself is always carried on in the presence—at least implicit—of another" (308).

It is not, of course, a question of nostalgically resurrecting some Bakhtinian carnival of the word from the ancient polis. It does not seem that Roman slaves had much chance of answering Cicero back. If Sprat and Ramus wished to expel the materiality of the sign, halting its dangerous dance of connotations, ancient rhetoric threatened to repress that materiality in another direction, by its full-blooded logocentrism. For Cicero, rhetoric could encompass everything, precisely because everything was based on the word. Plato's objections to rhetoric were closely allied to his unease at the "artifice" of writing. A distinction between voice and script was already apparent in the ancient world in the assigning of the former to rhetoric and the latter to grammar. Only in the Renaissance, after the birth of printing, would rhetoric be fully applied to written texts. The decline of rhetoric, then, was the overdetermined effect of a number of factors: the dwindling of the "public sphere"[3] of political life with the growing power of a complex, bureaucratized "civil society"; the correlative power of script in the exercise of class rule; the puritan, rationalist, and empiricist distrust of verbal "ornamentation" in the name of rigorous denotation; the bourgeois-democratic suspicion of rhetoric as "aristocratic" manipulation and discursive authoritarianism; the emergence of a political science relatively sealed from the turmoil of political practice.

In the English eighteenth century, rhetoric retained something of its traditional force. It was apparent to much eighteenth-century theory, for example, that rhetorical figures were by no means confined to "poetic" uses of discourse but inhabited other forms of language, too; and to this extent the transdiscursive stress of rhetoric remained active, subsuming all such signifying practices to the domain of "polite letters," rather than to the distinctive region of "imaginative literature." With the advent of Romanticism, however, a deep transmutation of discourses occurred. From the standpoint of linguistic rationalism, both rhetoric and poetry were highly suspect modes, akin in their fictional spuriousness and emotive infection; but the preface to Coleridge and Wordsworth's *Lyrical Ballads* was to pit poetry *against* rhetoric, demotically disowning the lying figures of eighteenth-century poetic diction for the emotionally charged language of common life. In a curiously circular movement, an initially logocentric rhetoric had passed into the pernicious falsities of print, to be opposed by an equally logocentric antirhetoric. Poetry was now a counterforce to those dominative discourses that, in Kant's phrase, had a "palpable design" on us. It did not cease to lay claim to the "public sphere," as Blake and Shelley well enough attest, but against a public rhetoric now firmly identified as ideological it proffered the nonauthoritarian values of feeling, creativity, and imagination—of, in a word, the "aesthetic." Poetry was Nature, as opposed to the artifice of rhetoric, but in an adroit maneuver it strove at the same time to appropriate the "special" status with which rhetoric had become identified, its intense and heightened style. "Literature"—a privileged, "creative" use of language—was accordingly brought to birth, with all the resonance and panoply attendant on traditional rhetoric, but without either its authoritarianism or its audience. The former was countered by the "aesthetic," the latter compensated for by the Author. Emotive effects, particularly in early Romanticism, continued to work within the context of public political persuasion, but the cultivation of the spontaneous and intuitive, the eccentric and transcendental, came to produce a quasi-political language of its own, whose source was a specialized "aesthetic" or "imaginative" faculty as loftily remote from the "public sphere" as the increasingly redundant rhetoric it strove to oust. In the absence of that known audience, which was in a strict sense a material condition of rhetoric, the creative authorial subject was duly enthroned as source or medium of a transcendental discourse that spurned rather than wooed "the public." Language was less public medium than unique individual expression; rhetorical analysis would be gradually outflanked by "stylistics." The social conditions of the Romantic poet—at once ideally "representative" and historically marginalized, prophetic visionary and commodity-producer—were encoded in a form of writing that could still retain the urgent public inflections of rhetoric while almost wholly lacking its pragmatic context. By the later nineteenth century, Matthew Arnold was anxiously demanding of poetry a recovery of rhetoric's tonal authority (the "grand style"), precisely as John Stuart Mill struck a historically more realistic emphasis: poetry was now that which is "overheard," the exact opposite of the rhetorical.

With the rise of the great idealist schools of aesthetics of late eighteenth-century revolutionary Europe, "feeling" was displaced from the material effects of pragmatic discourse to become the crux of a higher, contemplative mode of cognition. "Sensibility" was at war with rhetoric, symbolic synchrony with the pompously discursive. The "special" yet social discourse of classical rhetoric, intensifying common verbal effects for concrete political aims, had now become the esoteric, ontologically unique language of poetry, whose intuitions were in revolt against all such politics. The very form of the "aesthetic" provided imaginary resolution of real contradictions: where could one find a more perfect integration of the conflicts that seemed to have riven ideological history apart—universal/particular, rational/sensuous, order/spontaneity, transformative will/wise passiveness, Nature/Art—than in the poem itself? What else was the Romantic symbol but a full-blooded ideology of its own, the last great idealist totalization before the birth of historical materialism?

But rhetoric had not been defeated; it merely shifted its ground. For Nietzsche, in his notes on rhetoric, a concern with techniques of eloquence and persuasion was to be subordinated to a study of figures and tropes—tropes that were the "truest nature" of language as such. By exposing the covertly rhetorical nature of all discourse, Nietzsche took the "technical" aspects of rhetoric and turned them skeptically against its traditionally social, cognitive, and communicative functions. Rhetoric was undermined on its own ground: if all language worked by figure and trope, all language was consequently a form of fiction, and its cognitive or representational power problematized at a stroke. Nietzsche retrieved the rhetoric written of by rationalism as a dangerously abnormal device, and with the same suspecting glance universalized it to the structure of all discourse; both bourgeois rationalism and its materialist scientific opponents were thus triumphantly out-maneuvered. Even the most apparently cognitive or colloquial of languages was ambiguously infiltrated by deceit; the final "exposure" of rhetoric was one that detected its ineradicable presence everywhere. Mocked and berated for centuries by an abrasive rationalism, rhetoric took its terrible belated revenge—a revenge that consisted not in any last-ditch claim to dignity, but in showing the self-righteous enemy that it itself was contaminated, even unto death, by its own leprous disease, its own flaking and seepage of meaning. Rhetoric was the foul-mouthed beggar in whom even the king would find himself echoed.

The ultimate reversal had thus been elected. Born at the juncture of politics and discourse, rhetoric now had the Fool's function of unmasking all power as self-rationalization, all knowledge as a mere fumbling with metaphor. In retreat from marketplace to study, politics to philology, social practice to semiotics, rhetoric was to end up as that vigorous demystifier of all ideology that itself provided the final ideological rationale for political inertia. Mischievously radical, it delighted in confronting the bourgeoisie with the truth that its own ideologies had spread wider than it wished, sunk into the very fabric of its sciences, undermined the very structures of its communication. But since it was itself, after all, "mere rhetoric," it could do little more than bear witness to this fact, and even then was not to be trusted. Nietzsche's emancipatory enterprise had as its other face a gross failure of ideological nerve—one which, as his present-day acolytes testify, is still with us. "Rhetoric," writes Paul de Man, "radically suspends logic and opens up vertiginous possibilities of referential aberration. . . . poetry gains a maximum of convincing power at the very moment that it abdicates any claim to truths" (10, 50). All communications mar themselves, presenting us at the very crisis of persuasion with the reasons why they should be suspected. The liberal academic, marooned in a brash world of manipulative messages, may now discover in the body of rhetoric itself the reasons why such vulgar commercial and political hectorings may be blandly mistrusted.

That the nurturing of verbal ambiguity is at once source of critical insight and ideological evasion is surely as obvious in the new Yale school as it was in the old. Encircled by a presumed ideological monolith, "literature," or discourse in general, is once more fetishized as the last place to play, the sole surviving antechamber of liberal hesitancy. If the materialists can get their grubby hands even on *that,* then the game is almost certainly up. This is not, naturally, to dismiss such work as nugatory—least of all the penetrating insights of a de Man. The present book, for example, is a text that such work can do much to illuminate. For it is intended as revolutionary rhetoric aimed at certain political effects, yet speaks a tropical language far removed from those in whose name it intervenes. In one sense this should not be taken as unduly worrying: slogans and aesthetic treatises are both workable genres provided neither is mistaken for the other. In another sense, however, the rhetorical tropes and figures of my own discourse could be accused of undoing my rhetorical intentions, constructing a reader whose political clarity and resoluteness may be threatened by the very play of language that hopes to produce those intentions. What distinguishes the materialist from the deconstructionist *tout court* is that he or she understands such self-molesting discourse by referring it back to a more fundamental realm, that of historical contradictions themselves. For there can be no doubt that such a text as this, produced within an academy it also challenges, will inscribe such contradictions in its very letter—will figure at once as political act and as libidinal substitute for those more deep-seated actions that are in any full sense presently denied us. Universities are now precisely such sites of contradiction: the conditions required for them to re-produce ruling-class skills and ideologies are also in part those that allow them to produce a socialist critique. It is unlikely that texts generated from this point will escape unscathed by these ironies. But this is a different kind of ambiguity altogether from that which at a certain point in modern criticism becomes a wholesale ideological assault, a fresh strategy necessitated by the decline of traditional rhetoric itself. Ambiguity, to put it bluntly, is wheeled onstage when the ruling class realizes that its official rhetoric is going unheeded. Arnold wrote *Literature and Dogma* as a last-ditch attempt to salvage a well-tried rhetorical discourse—Religion—that was failing to convince the proletariat. The trick was to "poeticize" such language, retaining its authoritative images while blurring its unacceptable terms to grandiloquent vacuities. Linguistic indeterminacies were absolutized, and the name for them all was God.[4]

Arnold's strategy failed, but another was to hand: England was just enter-ing on its epoch of high imperialism, and a more palpable rhetoric—that of chauvinism—was accordingly available. On the other side of World War I, however, with its carnage of ruling-class eloquence, this strategy looked none too lively either: by 1919 T. S. Eliot was writing of an English drama that had "grown away from the rhetorical expression, the bombastic speeches, of Kyd and Marlowe to the subtle and dispersed utterance of Shakespeare and Web-ster" ("Rhetoric and Poetic Drama" 38). Eliot did not write rhetoric off, but he "introjected" it, removing it from the bombastic sphere of a merely public discourse to the inner territory of the emotions. That for him was the positive sense of rhetoric, but it might also be taken to signify "any adornment or inflation of speech which is *not done for a particular effect* but for a general impressiveness" (42). Rhetoric, in other words, was now permissibly syn-onymous with "bad rhetoric," and was countered by certain concrete inten-tional tactics that it was the very function of classical rhetoric to fulfill. In a similar way, I. A. Richards wrote in *The Philosophy of Rhetoric,* published in an era when there was indeed much of it about, that the study of classical rhetoric could be advantageous at least "until man changes his nature, debates and disputes, incites, tricks, bullies and cajoles his fellows less" (24).

A supreme ideological pragmatist in his working methods, T. S. Eliot ravaged language and ransacked world literature to penetrate what had now become a general weariness with ideological rhetoric. Beneath that disillusioned antirhetorical guard, by every device of verbal indirection, he cultivated those effects that engaged with the ideological on its very homeland—the organs of "lived experience" themselves, the "cerebral cortex, the nervous system, and the digestive tracts"—by selecting words with "a network of tentacular roots reaching down to the deepest terrors and desires" ("Ben Jonson" 24). Thus achieving "direct communication through the nerves" ("Phillip Massinger" 215) poetry would make it appear natural that fertility cults might hold a clue to the salvation of capitalism. This enterprise, of course, was as absurd as Arnold's: Eliot's erudite primitivism, his belief that if the lower classes were grabbed by their visceral regions then their minds would follow, foundered on the minor difficulty that they did not read his poetry—something that his notoriously Olympian public bearing effectively conceded in advance. Even so, Eliot's antirhetoric was at least in the service of "belief-effects," which is more than can be said for our contemporary (anti)rhetoricians. Since it now seems less possible for bourgeois ideology outside of Northrop Frye's Toronto to pass off fertility cults as plausible, the one lame rhetoric remaining is the rhetoric of antirhetoric. In place of the rhetorical deceits of language we are offered—the rhetorical deceits of language. This does not bode well for the future of critical ideology. It may therefore emerge that what will prove more productive in the future will be that partial return to traditional rhetoric now promised by "speech-act theory," which reinterprets the literary text in terms of subject-positions and conjunctural discourse. Any such theory, however, will need at once to confront the valuable insights of the contemporary (anti)rhetoricians and the challenge of historical materialism.

The early career of a professional rhetorician like the German marxist theater director Erwin Piscator suggests a problem of revolutionary rhetoric that may be focused in the somewhat oxymoronic term *agitprop*. Is socialist art primarily affective (*agit*) or informative (*prop*)? And what is the relation between theater as ideological transformation and theater as laboratory of dialectical theory? In strikingly new guise, some familiar problems of classical rhetoric are raised once more. In one sense, it might be claimed, these are in fact pseudoproblems. For any socialist involved in teaching knows that nothing is more "ideologically"

effective than knowledge, and that any exclusive epistemological carve-up of
consciousness between ideology and knowledge is itself a theoreticist fantasy. It
is perhaps not surprising, given the political effects of reliable knowledge, that
much current ideology is devoted to questioning knowledge's very possibility.
Nevertheless, the difficulty is not entirely factitious. Historical materialism is
itself a "rhetoric," in the fundamental sense that it is unthinkable outside those
suasive interests which, through trope and figure, project the world in a certain
controvertible (falsifiable) way. There is in the end no "rational" ground for
committing oneself to this view: it is theoretically possible to be persuaded of
the truth of historical materialism without feeling the least compunction to act
on it. Nobody becomes a socialist simply because he or she is convinced by the
materialist theory of history or moved by the persuasive elegance of Marx's
economic equations. Ultimately, the only reason for being a socialist is that one
objects to the fact that the great majority of men and women in history have
lived lives of suffering and degradation, and believes that this may conceivably
be altered in the future. There is nothing at all "rational" about that (though
rationality does indeed play its part in the transition from moralistic or utopian
socialism to historical materialism). There is no "rational" riposte to one who,
having acknowledged this truth, remains unmoved by it. It is, if you like, a
question of the cortical and visceral regions. But this is not to say that marxism has the cognitive status of a scream. All scientific theory is perhaps "metaphorical," but it does not follow that any old trope will do, or, as pragmatism
would have it, that any old trope that "does" will do. The statement "Black is
beautiful" is paradigmatically rhetorical, since it deploys a figure of equivalence
to produce particular discursive and extra-discursive effects without direct regard for truth or falsity. It is not "literally" true. Yet neither is it "mere" rhetoric,
since it is an utterance of a piece with certain falsifiable hypotheses concerning
the racial struggle of contemporary societies.[5] In this sense, "Black is beautiful"
is a "literary" text, a piece of language which, seized "nonpragmatically," nonetheless produces certain particular effects. To say that the slogan is "true" is
not to claim that it represents a real state of affairs. It is to claim that the text
so fictionalizes the "real" as to intend a set of effects conducive to certain
practices that are deemed, in the light of a particular set of falsifiable hypotheses
about the nature of society, to be desirable. It could be, of course, that the
utterance "Black is beautiful" is fatally self-molesting. One could show how
subtly its structural symmetry and utopian impulse belie the political inequality it challenges, or how the reversible reading it unconsciously holds open

might inhibit the political practice it intends. Then again, it is possible that the deconstruction of the ghettos might outstrip the deconstruction of the phrase.

As far as rhetoric is concerned, then, a marxist must be in a certain sense a Platonist. Rhetorical effects are calculated in the light of a theory of the polis as a whole, not merely in the light of the pragmatic conjuncture fetishized by postmarxism. Rhetoric and dialectic, agitation and propaganda, are closely articulated; what unites them for Plato is justice, a moral concept itself only calculable on the basis of social knowledge, as opposed to *doxa,* or ideological opinion. Since all art is rhetorical, the tasks of the revolutionary cultural worker are essentially threefold: first, to participate in the production of works and events which, within transformed "cultural" media, so fictionalize the "real" as to intend those effects conducive to the victory of socialism; second, as "critic," to expose the rhetorical structures by which nonsocialist works produce politically undesirable effects, as a way of combating what it is now unfashionable to call false consciousness; and third, to interpret such works where possible "against the grain," so as to appropriate from them whatever may be valuable for socialism. The practice of the socialist cultural worker, in brief, is projective, polemical, and appropriative. Such activity may from time to time include such things as encouraging others to reap pleasure from the beauty of religious imagery, encouraging the production of works with no overt political content whatsoever, and arguing in particular times and places for the "great," "true," "profoundly moving," "joyful," "wonderful" qualities of particular works.

Notes

1. Girning is a signifying practice, confined to the proletariat of certain more northerly regions of the British social formation, the point of which is to pull the ugliest possible face.

2. See my *Criticism and Ideology* for a brief account of this debate.

3. A sphere of open, participatory communication whose recovery such thinkers as Jürgen Habermas see as crucial to the establishment of socialism; see his *Structural Transformation of the Public Sphere.*

4. There is a certain logic in the critical development of J. Hillis Miller, ideologue of this trend in *The Disappearance of God* (Cambridge, Mass.: MIT Press, 1963) and now propagating a more acceptable, "secularized" version of such indeterminacies as an enthusiast of Jacques Derrida.

5. I am grateful to my friend Denys Turner of the University of Bristol, who first suggested the slogan to me as paradigmatic of "moral" discourse.

Works Cited

de Man, Paul. *Allegories of Reading.* New Haven: Yale University Press, 1979.

Eagleton, Terry. *Criticism and Ideology: A Study in Marxist Literary Theory.* London: New Left Books, 1976.

Eliot, T. S. *Selected Essays.* London: Faber, 1972.

Habermas, Jürgen. *The Structural Transformation of the Public Sphere: An Inquiry into a Category of Bourgeois Society (Strukturwandel der Öffentlichkeit).* Trans. Thomas Burger. Cambridge, Mass.: MIT Press, 1989.

Ong, Walter. "Ramus and the Transit to the Modern Mind." *Modern Schoolman* no. 32 (May 1955): 163–71.

Richards, I. A. *The Philosophy of Rhetoric.* New York: Oxford University Press, 1936.

II
Theoretical Elaborations

4
Language Obscures Social Change
Melanie Eckford-Prossor and Michael Clifford

When Michel Foucault asserts the following, he presents us with a crucial problem:

> Before the end of the eighteenth century, man did not exist—any more than the potency of life, the fecundity of labour or the historical density of language. He is a quite recent creature, which the demiurge of knowledge fabricated with its own hands less than two hundred years ago; but he has grown old so quickly that it has been only too easy to imagine that he had been waiting for thousands of years in the darkness for that moment of illumination in which he would finally be known. (*Order of Things* 309)

The problem centers on his use of the term *man*. Foucault goes on to explain that "man" occurred during the Classical (or Enlightenment) age when there was a "common discourse of representation about things." Such a point, while interesting, focuses on epistemic changes; it does not address the fact that language itself does not change much and that the way it is used tends to obscure the very changes that Foucault works to show us. His comment about "man" depends, indeed, on "the historical density of language" that is also a product of the Enlightenment. But instead of focusing on the history or lineage of a word, or on what such things illuminate about a culture, instead of turning to that "historical density," in other words, we are interested in how language engenders similarity and continuity of meaning, how a word like *man* binds the present age to ages past by obscuring, rather than reflecting, the changes through which both the word and the culture that uses it have gone, how language creates an illusion of history as linear development rather than of radical epistemic upheaval.

Linguists such as Jespersen and Saussure and philosophers as different as Wittgenstein and Derrida have all explored the problems of where changes in meaning come from and of how the transmission of language occurs. Whether constructed into a science or system, or deconstructed and historicized, language appears dynamic—capable of change, capable of deception, capable of making and forming worlds, capable of "going all the way down." We find the same assumptions in cultural materialism. For example, Raymond Williams, in *Keywords: A Vocabulary of Culture and Society*, likewise emphasizes the dynamic character of language. Williams is interested in outlining a social history of words and the changes in meaning that have occurred in those words. By emphasizing history and change he aligns himself with those who, like Saussure, Wittgenstein, Derrida, Jespersen, Heidegger, Foucault, and others, see language as reflecting social change. Each of these rather different approaches seeks to show that, if looked at closely enough or in the right way, language reflects and is imprinted with change.

For all the dynamism of language, however, for all that it is supposed to reveal, we argue that language in fact obscures social change. By that we mean something different from Williams's claim that such change is "sometimes hardly noticed." For marxists such as Williams, language shows the imprints of change, but only those privileged intelligentsia endowed with philological and etymological knowledge, for the most part, have the ability to "discover" the changes in language and meaning. We argue instead that the obfuscation of change is not due to a failure to notice change on the part of those who use language; rather such obscuration of change is an active and essential feature of language itself. For all the apparent transparency of language emphasized by cultural studies, marxism, and postmodernism, language does not reflect change but obscures it by absorbing it rhetorically.

Part of what we are suggesting, then, is that *anachronism* is inherent to language and this anachronism has the effect of creating an appearance of stability. Only in unusual situations is that stability threatened. A good example of what we are describing is the word *family* in the context of the 1992 presidential election and the platform of the Republican party. Only when confronted with visual examples of what the Republican party meant by "family" did the United States as a whole have to face up to the fact that what the Republicans meant by family was not what family meant in practice. Ironically, when Republicans confronted the public with speech after speech on the subject, and paraded (traditional) families onto the podium, a word that had the power to bind finally became divisive. The point to be stressed here is that it took a national political convention to reveal the change that the word had undergone. It is more correct to say that the word changed only then, that the meaning of the word lagged behind social practice.

On the Density of Language

The position that language obscures social change rebuts etymological arguments that use language as a means by which to see and gauge social change. These approaches make language analogous to the rings on trees that can be counted to indicate age: a word's etymology can be traced backward to recognize influences from previous times, and thereby to indicate how social conditions have changed accordingly. In this approach to understanding language, language is a repository of social change; shifts in meaning correlate to the historical moments these shifts occurred. Language is treated effectively, then, as a "natural" reflector of change, comparable to the trunk of a tree or sedimented rock layer. Interestingly, in *The Prison-House of Language,* Fredric Jameson tells us that although Saussure "invented" the terms *diachrony* and *synchrony,* "they were known before him in other acceptations in geology" (5). The subtle similarities between Saussure's key terms and natural history tell us quite a lot. The science of signs, semiotics, seems connected to the so-called natural sciences such as geology: in both, the person who can see across the topography (diachrony) and down through the layers (synchrony) can see the whole. Both "sciences" are born in that peculiar episteme of the nineteenth century that Foucault excavates in *The Order of Things.* For all of Saussure's usefulness in helping us to reconceptualize language, and for all his "originality" in insisting on the temporal dimensions of language (Jameson, *Prison-House of Language* 5), his project is resolutely nineteenth-century in its desire to find a way of categorizing language and in his desire to create a science. Where he differs from his precursors is in the scope and shape of the system, not in the desire for order and system. But in the late twentieth century, are we willing to hold onto this natural history of language?

We believe that such natural histories and their related etymological projects, while enlightening with regard to language *in abstraction,* conceive of language in a way different from that in which it is ordinarily *used.* This ordinary usage does not recover meanings from language, nor does it see language as a system or science of signs embedded in and thus reflecting history. It does not use language as a reflective tool, and it does not mine history from individual words. Instead, we assert that in everyday use, language has no history, be it diachronic or synchronic. Our point is not that language is ahistorical, but that when used it is atemporal. Language is both immediate and eternally enduring—in the moment of its use. The transparency projected by etymological arguments is precisely that, a projection of clarity onto a medium that is both unstable and opaque. Perhaps, then, etymological and systemic views of language need to be rethought. If language obscures rather than reflects social change, then maybe what is needed is an entirely different way of understanding language.

While parts of our thesis have been touched on by several people, the consequences of the thesis have not been considered, perhaps because language as a reflector of social change, language as a form of cultural carbon dating, is too useful to renounce. Probably one of the comments that most closely approximates our point is Jameson's evaluation of Saussure:

> The temporal model proposed by Saussure is that of a series of complete systems succeeding each other in time; that language is for him a perpetual present, with all the possibilities of meaning implicit in its every moment.
>
> Saussure's is in a sense an existential perception: no one denies the *fact* of the diachronic, that sounds have their own history and that meanings change. Only for the speaker, at any moment in the history of the language, one meaning alone exists, the current one; words have no memory. This view of language is confirmed rather than refuted by the appeal to etymology, as Jean Paulhan has shown in an ingenious little book. For etymology, as it is used in daily life, is to be considered not so much a scientific fact as a rhetorical form, the illicit use of historical causality to support the drawing of logical consequences ("the word itself tells us so: *etymology, etumos logos,* authentic meaning. Thus etymology advertises itself, and sends us back to itself as its own first principle"). (*Prison-House of Language* 6)

The assumptions in Jameson's comment are worth close study, especially his explanation of Saussure's temporal model. For Saussure, the "perpetual present" can be visualized as a horizontal line extending in two directions at once, thus "all the possibilities of meaning" are "implicit in its every moment." In this sense, language is synchronic. Yet the "perpetual present" is a static temporality—time always delayed, time never moving, a place where meaning is diaphanous. By contrast, we suggest that the temporal dimension of language cannot be understood in terms of a perpetual present. Rather, language inhabits for the user the temporal space of *immediacy*. Immediacy differs from the perpetual present in that it radically constricts the possibilities of meaning at every moment. Theoretically, the historical totality of meanings implied by the notion of the perpetual present may exist in language, but for the user would it really be possible to have at his or her hand these many possible meanings? Is that availability, or lack thereof, rooted in the synchronic and diachronic or in the user of language?

If we reject conceptualizing language as an ordered system in favor of conceiving of it as it is used, we would find the individual user of language bound by a diachronicity. The shift from synchronic to diachronic effects an abrupt change in the meanings available for use: we switch from the perpetual present replete with all possibilities of meaning to the "fact of the diachronic" in which "one meaning alone exists, the current one." Although this comment appears sympathetic to our point, it focuses on meanings. We are less interested in meanings and more interested in the relationship between user and language, language and use. Saussure's model may explain language, but with the exception of langue as parole, it does not really explain the effect of language on the user. The interaction between language, temporality, and user is the crux of the matter.

And it is here that we also disagree with Jameson's invalidation of etymology, or at least with its form. He does so on the basis of Saussure's argument, and on an entire philosophical tradition: the removal and rejection of rhetoric from philosophy. Language's temporality and its possible expression in etymology can be dismissed "as a rhetorical form" to be distrusted. Trust should instead be placed in Saussure's science. While our argument questions the efficacy of etymology, it does so because etymology, as a "fact" long practiced, makes words into the bearers of history and change. Etymology, then, forces on language the rather human attributes of memory and duration. But what if the user of language cannot import such memory to language? Then language is not a deep repository of possible meanings endowed with history, but is instead "transparent" in its immediacy and in its meaning. The point is not that there is only one meaning available, the current one, but that the user has little to no notion of any alternative, and this is because, as Jameson puts it, language (not just words) has "no memory." Language is atemporal in its use. That "transparency" of language turns out to be opacity; the changes in memories—the changes in meanings—of a word are often unknown and often unexperienced.[1] If we pursue this idea, we find that instead of revealing social change, language tends to be anachronistic, creating for the user the appearance of a time-less present defined by stability and ratified by atemporal words that project sameness.

Foucault explains this situation as part of the compensation for what he calls "the demotion of language" in the nineteenth century. He explains that

> having become a dense and consistent historical reality, lan-
> guage forms the locus of tradition, of the unspoken habits of
> thought, of what lies hidden in a people's mind; it accumu-
> lates an ineluctable memory which does not even know itself
> as memory. Expressing their thoughts in words of which
> they are not the masters, enclosing them in verbal forms
> whose historical dimensions they are unaware of, men be-
> lieve that their speech is their servant and do not realize that
> they are submitting themselves to its demands. The gram-
> matical arrangements of a language are *a priori* of what can
> be expressed in it. The truth of discourse is caught in the
> trap of philology. (*Order of Things* 297)

This connection between language, memory, and temporality represents a provocative way to understand language because it combines memory and history with the usage of history. Our approach is not so much a description of what language is; we are more concerned here with what language does. On-tological arguments make no difference to the use of language because of the phenomenon Foucault describes. It is worth taking Foucault even further, though, on the issue of "men believe that their speech is their servant." Whereas Foucault explains how language demands things of its speakers, rather than simply the other way round, he works essentially from an image of language as organism: he endows language with life. Instead of conceiving of language as servant or as organism, however, why not emend "servant" to "mechanism"? This conveys the sense that language is not organic for most users. It is a means to an end. In this case to even consider memory in language would be alien. Moreover, the temporality to which language is subject is the temporality of the speaker or user of language. The point here is not that language is a tool to be used to do whatever the user wants, or that language does not enclose and subject the user to its forms and possibilities, but that, *for the user,* viewing language as a moderately complicated mechanism disposes the user to expect certain qualities and to be aware of others.

In "Discourse in the Novel," Bakhtin suggests that blindness to "the dialogic nature of language" (273) is a major flaw in the theories of most linguists and philosophers of language. They cannot see the "stratification and heteroglossia" which are for Bakhtin "not only a static invariant to linguistic life, but also what insures its dynamics: stratification and heteroglossia widen and deepen as long as language is alive and developing. Alongside the centripetal forces, the centrifugal forces of language carry on their uninterrupted work; alongside verbal-ideological centralization and unification, the uninterrupted processes of decentralization and disunification go forward" (272). This emphasis on the dialogic enables Bakhtin, if not to reject, at least to bypass the systemic and esoteric view of language endorsed by Saussure, and to create an image of language that is, like Foucault's, closer to the user. Bakhtin's recognition of the tension between centripetal and centrifugal forces accounts for the opposed impulses we find in language, and thus conveys the vision of language as both dynamic and alive. The appeal of the theory is evident; however, when set against the background of actual linguistic practice, certain questions arise. For instance, why is it difficult for so many to recognize heteroglossia at play in language? And for those who do see it, why are they often so quick to reject it?

One possible answer is that rejecting heteroglossia stems from a rejection of the dialogic nature of language, of refusing to view language as layered and indeterminate. Rejecting heteroglossia affirms the unitary nature of language. Languages that emphasize the dialogic are distrusted because they segment and compartmentalize. But these are the very socioideological "languages of social groups, 'professional' and 'generic' languages, languages of generations and so forth" that Bakhtin embraces; what distinguishes them from this (fictional) stable and unchanging language is their dependence on jargon (272). By insulating a group from the broader social network, and by marking changes within that group by reference to a privileged, albeit localized, language, jargon may be understood as the locus and mirror of change that expresses heteroglossia. Opponents of this view tend to belittle and even reject jargon, however, in favor of a view of language as stable and unitary.

For many marxists, in contrast, jargon and slang are valuable because they clearly bring to light something generally true about language; it is not only that language can reflect social change, but that it must reflect social change. By "social change" we mean the constant and immediate perception of events that can "become" history in the ordinary sense. Social change as we employ the term appeals to an understanding of temporality and the place of the subject different from that of history. While the human subject is constantly immersed in social change, when an event becomes "history" it does so because history *locates* the subject in a specific moment of time *from* which one writes history. Thus history depends on distance and narrative in a way that social change does not. Says Jameson, "History is inaccessible to us except in textual form" (*Political Unconscious* 82).[2] When language expresses, describes, or creates history, it does so by affecting the meanings available to the user at the immediate moment.

It is worth stressing that the conception of history we invoke here is very close to that against which Foucault, Hayden White, and others have written— that is, a history composed from a "suprahistorical perspective: a history whose function is to compose the finally reduced diversity of time into a totality fully closed upon itself; a history that always encourages subjective recognitions and attributes a form of reconciliation to the displacements of the past; a history whose perspective on all that precedes it implies the end of time, a completed development" (Foucault, "Nietzsche" 152). The question of what one exhumes when one writes history (the level of context, issues of ideology, and so on) is not raised in this vision of history grounded on the unquestioned stability of both language and subjects; it opposes the Foucauldian-Nietzschean view of subjects constituted by language. These stable solid grounds form the field on which language can "objectively" describe a historical event. Social change, as the perception of flux and temporality, however, is more difficult to see because of the position of the subject. At once immersed in constant change and temporality, the subject of social change does not see the changes, does not realize that her subjectivity changes, because she has no distance. The lack of distance closes off the possibility of narrative, consequently the possibility of representation of those social changes is also closed off. Because nothing is seen there is nothing to represent in language. The changes that characterize social change are unseen against the vast tapestries of suprahistory.

For many marxists this suprahistory manifests itself in a numbness to historical allusions, so that the layer of change is subsumed, forgotten in favor of the present. Jameson outlines such a situation in his discussion of Balzac's *Vielle Fille,* where "the mechanism of narrative" consumes "the footnote-subtext of an older web of political allusion." The cost is "the virtual repression of the text of history" (*Political Unconscious* 34). This may be true of narratives, the focus of *The Political Unconscious,* but can the same be said of words themselves; if so, what are the consequences for our understanding of, and our relationship to, language? A possible response to the question might be found in Raymond Williams's *Keywords*. Sighting and citing words that were used in "interesting or difficult ways," Williams, too, seeks to highlight history by analyzing certain words. Like Jameson, his goal is to make "conscious and critical—subject to change as well as to continuity" the vocabularies of "social and cultural discussion" (24). He wants the "millions of people in whom . . . [this vocabulary] is active . . . to see it as active: not a *tradition* to be learned, nor a *consensus* to be accepted, nor a set of meanings . . . but as a shaping and reshaping . . . a vocabulary to use . . . as we go on making our own language and history" (24–25). Williams wants to make people aware of the ways they are continually shaped by language by constructing a socioideological etymology, a dictionary of the culture's key words. Doing so, according to Williams, will reveal that "changes are masked by a nominal continuity so that words which seem to have been there for centuries, with continuous general meanings, have come in fact to express radically different or radically variable, yet sometimes hardly noticed, meanings or implications of meaning" (17). Such continuity, however, is far more than "nominal"; it is so pervasive that it demands constant ingenious and often highly academic discourse to dislodge it. Indeed, Jameson himself acknowledges that "the text of history and the political unconscious" is "so faint as to be virtually inaudible" (*Political Unconscious* 34). To redress this point Williams unearths the "radically different or radically variable" meanings of words. Yet while these analyses might raise from language (and narrative) the historical, the different, the subtext, they do not really investigate what most people want and need language to be. The reasons for this can perhaps be found in marxism's historical epistemology, in and for which the masked quality of change and the inaudibility of the text of history fuse with its ontology. "The life of man," as Marx puts it, is saturated with history, and can only be known in terms of context, history, and ideology. The sense in both Jameson and Williams is that we need to be rescued from ourselves and our historical blindness. And while we may be sympathetic to this view, the belief that we can accomplish this by foraging in language for history is not one we can endorse.

While our understanding of language may cause us to disagree with the possibility of being rescued from blindness, we do admire the impulse. Criticism and much contemporary philosophy has focused, as Edward Said points out, on drastic change (for example, Foucault's epistemes). The theories and interests of Jameson and Williams certainly affirm this point, and their projects, especially Williams's, embody the difficult set of questions concerned with change: When does it happen? How does it happen? and so on. Our questions are elusive because they reverse the field of much contemporary theory and philosophy. We are not searching for instances of change, but for reasons that would explain how such a world permeated by change requires so much constant, repeated focus, analysis, and explanation of that change. Why isn't the change absolutely apparent to everyone? Is it perhaps that the "change" or set of changes are countermanded by the medium of language in which they are expressed?

Our project is more akin to what Said calls "refocusing"—a refocusing on "how texts maintain, instead of always changing" (152). While it might be tempting to object that we are discussing language, not texts, we should take a closer look at the way that "language" is used. In Williams, after all, language itself becomes a text and a mirror at once, something to be "read" and something imprinted with the active making of history. Such assumptions of change and difference make refocusing on the sameness perpetuated by language difficult. Indeed, our theory might even be seen as a return to some earlier naive view in which language, like empire, always endures. To view the thesis that language obscures social change in that way is deliberately to refuse the explanatory power wielded by the thesis. This is not an essentialist point about the nature of language, but a rather pragmatic point generated by the recognition that although so much theory and philosophy focus on change, that change remains difficult to see, maybe because of the effects of language itself as it occurs for the user. Hence our focus thus far on marxism (and its valuation of ideology and change) and temporality. Marxism as methodology, and temporality as one of the main issues of the twentieth century, are intent on showing us change. Marxism provides methods of explanation about why it is so difficult to see history. In a similar way critical theory over the past thirty years or so has yielded a vision of the world awash in temporality. If all this is at least roughly correct, then why have such realizations not spread outside academia? The explanation for marxism's valuation of change is obviously complex, but it speaks to a residual Romanticism that pervades much contemporary theory. We saw elements of it in Foucault's view of language as alive, and this Romantic organicism perhaps explains the resistance to focusing both on how texts maintain as well as on how language obscures social change.

There is another reason for the focus on change generated by Romantic organicism, which is that change and flux obviate a fall into reification. The

Romantic preference for the organic, for the alive, that we saw in Foucault guarantees that the object under consideration does not become either rigid or fixed. To argue for a view of language as mechanism appears to return us to overused binaries, appears to smack of "scientism" in which "writing becomes . . . instances of regulated, systematized production, as if the human agencies were irrelevant" (Said 145). The thesis we advance, however, is not a version of scientism or a reworking of the Saussurian framework we reject. Our thesis strives to clarify that "human agencies," that is, users of language, *want* to use language. But they do not necessarily desire confrontation with change, especially in what most take as an unchanging ground: language. The human agencies are far from "irrelevant"—in fact, the reverse is the case: the composition of language and the history entailed in, through, and with language are irrelevant to their desire to use language. This places these pragmatic users at odds with critics who want them to see how language constructs their world. And this impulse also accounts for the tone of exhortation used by Williams who, we believe, is aware of the resistance with which his goals will be met. If language is alive there is less chance of it becoming a thing, and there is less chance of it solidifying. The reification of language he fears, however, forms the basis for the user's enjoyment of language; in this scenario the process of reification itself, the process of solidification and denial of upheaval and change is what gives the user language confidence. It is exactly the "phantom objectivity" condemned by Lukács that forms the appeal of language for the user. So when Williams begins *Keywords* with the phrase, "We just don't speak the same language," we would argue that the tone of exasperation expressed in the phrase speaks to the user's assumption of commensurate discourse. The user presupposes an objectivity in language which is not phantom and which does not acknowledge the dialogic aspect of language. The Romantic organic image of language's ability to change fostered by critics and theorists preserves the dialogic in language, protects language from the fall into objective sameness by making it alive, and promotes exactly language's power for imprinting change. But it is not an image embraced by the user of language.

Etymology reveals the organic vibrancy of language, but what, if anything, can etymology show us besides the fact that the meanings of words change? Perhaps a great deal. According to Carolyn Merchant, when the meaning of words change, often the normative weight of those words changes as well. In *The Death of Nature*, Merchant examines the subtle ethical dimension of the images and descriptions found in a culture's literature. What appear to be neutral, objective descriptions of the world, or some facet of it, in fact "operate as ethical restraints or as ethical sanctions" (4), dictating not only how we understand the world but also how we relate to it. In other words, language is more than descriptive or merely representative; it imposes on the user of language a set of "invisible restraints" and demands that are decidedly normative in both character and function, but of which the user of language is virtually unaware.

In terms of the thesis we have been advancing, Merchant offers a view of language with which we sympathize. But here we need to distinguish between our theoretical sympathies and the pragmatic emphasis our thesis places on the user of language. Merchant's point is persuasive, though again it depends on the same temporal and critical distance that we said earlier was required by history and etymology, but which is not available to the ordinary user of language. If the "writer of culture" is not "conscious of the ethical import yet may act in accordance with its dictates," as Merchant suggests, then change may have occurred but is not recognized. We are not advocating a position that change does not occur; rather, we are interested in how and why most users of language are not aware of change as it happens. The answer may lie in the effect of language. Thus we agree with Merchant that "because language contains a culture within itself, when language changes, a culture is also changing in important ways" (4); we disagree that these changes in language make the user aware of the change. Those subtle " 'oughts' and 'ought-nots' " of which Merchant speaks are so subtle that they recede into meaninglessness for the user of language if not for the theorist.

The relationship of the user of language to language closely approximates what Jean-Luc Nancy describes in *The Inoperative Community* as an "emblem," which he defines as amounting "to something other than a concept, and even something other than the *meaning* of a word" (1). The subtle changes that Merchant describes and that academics, etymologists, and theorists see are obscured by these emblems. When and if the emblem does change, when, to use Nancy's phrase, it "is no longer in circulation," at that point the change in the emblem is recognized. Changes in meaning as well as changes in emblems carry with them a change in culture so that, to return to Merchant, "we can then perceive something of the changes in cultural values" (4). This change, however, depends on distance, on the vast perspective of history. Change becomes evident only when an emblem is no longer circulated, or when the change in the emblem is so great that it cannot be ignored. Nancy proposes what we could call an ethics of loss, since "at every moment in its history, the Occident has given itself over to the nostalgia for a more archaic community" (10). We believe that "nostalgia" combined with the "archaic" convinces the user of language not to welcome change, but to mourn it—and, most important for our thesis, to refuse to recognize it in language. Language may bear a culture, but if the culture is inherently nostalgic, the normative changes in turn are "so subtle" as to escape the user of language. Nancy makes the point that "the lost, or broken, community can be exemplified in all kinds of ways . . . always it is a matter of a lost age." Language expresses what community provides and stabilizes: "institutions . . . rituals . . . symbols . . . of its own immanent unity, intimacy, and autonomy" (9). This helps explain why the change in cultural values of which Merchant writes is lamented, not welcomed.

It is time, perhaps, to give another example of what we mean by language obscuring social change. If we return to the earlier example of "family," we see that the 1992 Republican National Convention forced viewers (and it is quite important that it was televised) to confront the distance between the families presented on television and the composition of their individual families. The recognition of the distance between the "family" presented by the Republicans and the "family" of many viewers provoked for some a nostalgia for what was lost, and for others a deep sense of alienation. Nostalgia, anachronism, and temporal distance connect the word to history and historical distance. Television forced the country to confront the change in the emblem "family." The spoken invocation of words and/as emblems can evidence change, especially if accompanied with pictures. When Nancy spends time analyzing the changing concept of community and its connection to other phrases, he does so because his work presses against the nostalgic desire for sameness endorsed and welcomed by the user of language. The confrontations, and they are confrontations, between words as emblems and the change in the meaning of these words are often highly charged and political.

We could choose our next example from a wide number of words, including *life* and *choice,* both of which have undergone serious cultural and normative changes, but which resist those changes at the same time they are invoked. The phrase we want to focus on here, however, is *normal sexuality.* While there have been many television broadcasts that suggest different understandings of this term, there has been no locus quite as dramatic as that provided by the Republican National Convention for *family.* The visual confrontation of gay rights parades accomplishes the opposite of what it did for *family,* even though it works in the same way. With *family* the normative value did not shift, even if the components of *family* have changed: *family* remains a positive term. With *normal sexuality* the televising of competing kinds of sexuality throws the normative weight of the term onto the nostalgic impulses Nancy describes; *normal* becomes an emblem for heterosexual identity and so on, further removing gays from any inclusion in the emblem. Television usually demands awareness of the pictures that are its medium; in the case of gay rights, it demands an awareness that many users of language do not often want. Thus the reaction is to assert power and hierarchy and to brandish words as torches that obscure change with the smoke of sameness. Despite the fact that the American Psychiatric Association no longer considers homosexuality a disease, the users of language want to solidify their emblem: one camp wants to marginalize competing sexualities while another argues for inclusion and yet another advocates voluntary marginalization. In all cases the users use *normal* as a normative strategy that disguises the power in sexuality and marginalizes those who do not fit the emblem.

Thus the term *normal sexuality* persists in the nostalgic impulse that avoids change and that charges words with sometimes anachronistic normative values. *Normal sexuality* legitimizes fields of power endorsed by those who hold the power. The sense that different eras have different standards for normal is perhaps acknowledged, but it is not often confronted. This produces a rather strange fog that obscures history. For example, normal sexuality for the Victorians included mistresses and child pornography, neither of which late twentieth-century American culture considers normal. Likewise, we have the "Greek" system of college fraternities and sororities that wholeheartedly endorse heterosexuality at the same time that they seem blithely unaware of the "normal sexuality" of the Greeks themselves, for whom, as Foucault tells us, the issue was not one of gender but rather the hierarchy of power in the relationship: who is on top. The strange conjoining of ancient Greeks and late twentieth-century college students can be attributed to the way the term *normal sexuality* is an emblem containing power. The students invoke the learning and the cultural power of the Greeks, but they do so in such a way that they do not need to confront what for many of them is an alien sexuality. The term *normal* carries the normative weight of approbation and duration, forming unlikely pairings between ancient Greeks, Victorians, and American college students who belong to the Greek system. The differences are obscured by the fact that the word *normal* can still be *used in the same way* as it was before. Granted that Merchant might be right that the normative value and *meaning* change, the *use* of a word and the understanding that use suggests do not. When confronted with the changes in the term, the tendency is to retrench. Thus the gay movement has striven for inclusion of their sexuality under the falsely flexible label of *normal.*

Recognizing that language obscures social change (as in the case of the term *normal sexuality*) requires an attention to the distinction between theories of language and language usage. Theories of language, such as those of Williams and Merchant, which attempt to extrapolate from language its various hidden meanings, can do so only by ignoring a certain density that accrues to language in the atemporal moment of its actual use. This density encases the user in a monochronistic box of sorts, closing him or her off from language's polyvocity and heteroglossia. Language conceived this way appropriates to itself the temporal space in which the social can make sense, at once anachronistically transforming history into its own image and annexing the future even before it has begun. Theory can penetrate this density only by lifting language out of the milieu in which it has life. This would amount to theory as autopsy, analysis as postmortem.

Our emphasis on usage over theory might appear to align us with the pragmatism of Richard Rorty; after all, we have been discussing the use of language "as part of the behavior of human beings" (Rorty xviii). But we are quite a distance from Rorty's pragmatism. In "Pragmatism, Relativism, Irrationalism," Rorty identifies three characteristics of pragmatism: first, "that it is simply antiessentialism," second, that "there is no epistemological difference between truth about what ought to be and truth about what is," and third, that "it is the doctrine that there are no constraints on inquiry save conversational ones" (162–65). As such, Rorty's project centers more on recasting the province of philosophy (as opposed to Philosophy) along pragmatic lines in the wake of the collapse of epistemological and metaphysical foundations than on explaining the gap between theories of language and the user of language. Nonetheless, Rorty's project rests on certain assumptions about the "ubiquity of language" that tend both to support and to challenge our thesis.

Rorty's view tends to support our own to the extent that it ascribes a certain impenetrability or density to language, but it challenges our view in that it denies us the possibility of saying anything about a reality other than language that language might obscure. It can be said that Rorty's entire project depends on answering yes to his question, "Can we see ourselves as never encountering reality *except under a chosen description* . . . making worlds rather than finding them?" (xxxix). But saying yes to this question, and for Rorty there is no other acceptable answer, would be to dissolve any effective distinction between language and the social. The plausibility of the idea that language obscures social change would be "simply" and unsatisfyingly rephrased by Rorty into the idea of "competing vocabularies," of different ways of describing. At base, then, the difference between our view and Rorty's might consist in a difference in the way we understand language. Since our thesis depends on holding onto to some distinction between social reality and language, we must find a way to address the neopragmatic position that language "goes all the way down."

On the Blindness of Language

Rorty's claim that language "goes all the way down" can be read as a kind of limitation, language as an uncrossable barrier between us and the world we would seek to know "in truth." Our knowledge of the world will always be contingent on the discourses we deploy to describe it. But Rorty's almost sloganesque view may also be understood as ascribing to language an efficacy it does not have. For it suggests that reality, or at least our ability to know reality, is not merely described by language, but is in effect constituted by language. Language in this view is efficacious in that it creates the world we would seek to know; there is no "reality" apart from a set of discursive practices, linguistic structures, and tropological archetypes governing this otherwise inert and meaningless mass we call the world. On this point, Rorty is attempting to align himself with various postmodern views of language.

Several observations can be made about Rorty's view of language vis-à-vis reality. To begin with, there is hardly anything postmodern about the gesture—on the contrary, it represents the classic Kantian move. Reality (apart from language) belongs to the realm of unknowable noumenality, and language has merely replaced reason as that which constitutes the phenomenal (now discursive) realm of the knowable (knowable precisely because it is self-constituted). But at least with Kant's "regulative" view of reason we are provided with certain logical and epistemic strictures which make it possible to distinguish between an objectively valid experience (one holding for all rational beings) and a merely subjectively valid one (one true for myself alone). Whereas with Rorty, when language displaces reason, we are left with a potential plurality of descriptions and no way to decide between them, other than by appealing to purely pragmatic considerations of use and commensurability.

The present discussion is not meant to be a nostalgic lament over the loss of traditional metaphysics. It is meant as a way to push harder on the question of what it really means to say that language "goes all the way down." If it is to mean something more than the trivial observation that any and all descriptions of reality will be always and inevitably discursive, that is, *in* language, then one of two possibilities must be true. Either there is a something-other-than-language which lends itself to, but resists, discursive appropriation, or else there is no such primordial, prelinguistic substratum, and so language is efficacious in that it effectively creates what it would seek to describe. If the former is the case, then to say that language goes all the way down would be to say that language, far from being the translucent window on reality that it is often assumed to be, is rather a kind of opaque wall of potentially infinite layers that cannot be penetrated. If the latter is true, then language is not a tool of *representation* at all, whether adequate or inadequate; it is instead a vehicle of originary *presentation.* Rorty, being the closet Pyrrhonist that he is, will not commit himself one way or other about the existence or nonexistence of a something-other-than-language. In fact, what we get regarding the two alternatives just named is a kind of position by default: because we can say nothing outside of language about a prelinguistic substratum, language is *practically,* and for all intents and purposes, efficacious: it does create the world it describes.

But even Heidegger, for whom language is "the house of Being" (and with whom Rorty aligns himself), cautioned that language cannot exhaust the "thing in its thingliness." From a Heideggerian standpoint, language may be said to "shelter" Being, in two senses: first, in the sense that language provides the "place" of Being's disclosure; and second, that in sheltering Being, language casts a gray shadow over all that Being does not disclose of itself. *In* language, Being discloses itself; but the "unconcealment" of Being always entails concealment, a covering over of something not brought out into the clearing. It is always and only as some *particular* aspect or mode that Being is disclosed. "Being *is* its disclosedness," says Heidegger, and there is no being, no disclosure, apart from language. But language is not exhaustive; the aspect of Being to which language gives shelter may be Being as *vorhandenheit* or *zuhandenheit,* it may be Being as art, tool, object of worship or of scientific investigation, or none of these. And, although Rorty is right in that there is no way around language to get at what a thing "really" is, from a Heideggerian standpoint that essentially misses the point, and only crudely accounts for the intimate connection between language on the one hand and reality-being-truth on the other.

Rorty claims that the world, if there is a world apart from language, "is indifferent to our descriptions of it" and that "truth is a property of linguistic entities, of sentences," not a feature of reality as such (*Contingency* 5–7). But Heidegger shows that the world, Being, is not indifferent to how it is described (we are intentionally avoiding here the presumptuous phrase, "our descriptions"), and that truth is a property *both* of statements and of reality. Which is to say that truth is not a property at all—it is an event. Truth "happens" in the disclosure of Being, and Being happens in and as language.

Heidegger provides us a way of talking about a something-other-than-language that does not fall prey to the antifoundational criticisms of Rorty. For with Heidegger we do not have to go outside of or beyond language to talk about truth or reality; nor are truth and reality reducible to language (at least not language in the pedestrian way that Rorty seems to understand it). What this something-other-than-language refers to is not some essence or substratum which language must struggle to render intelligible; it refers rather to the unsaid, the unthought, the "unnameable difference," to use Derrida's phrase, which will never come to language. The reason that this assumption about a something-other-than-language can escape antifoundational (classically skeptical) criticism is that language need not have to say anything about this something-other-than-itself (in fact, it cannot) in order to say something true about reality.

Among the pantheon of thinkers whose work has been devoted to understanding social change, such as Marx, Weber, and Foucault, it is not uncommon to find Heidegger's name missing from the list. As any astute reader of Heidegger knows, however, that would be a mistake. Heidegger's work not only tells us something about the history of philosophy and the changes that philosophical thought has undergone from the pre-Socratics to the present, to the extent that social practice parallels and is influenced by such conceptual change, but also tells us something about social change. For example, the technoscientific world in which we live represents the culmination of a certain kind of thinking that has developed over the course of some 2,500 years. Modern materialism, the rise and veneration of science and technology, the fragmentation of academic disciplines, the exploitation of the planet, cultural imperialism, the inhumanity of individual against individual—all are themes that are developed, directly or indirectly, in Heidegger's work. Heidegger often paints in broad strokes in his discussions of social change, however, which tends to render the mechanisms of such change obscure. Moreover, he suggests that both philosophical and social change can be revealed through a certain kind of higher-order etymology, the hermeneutical retrieval of forgotten meanings. By attending closely to the language of the present and by contrasting the meanings of words with those of their ancient cognates, Heidegger in effect "unearths" the degree, if not the means, of change the culture has undergone. That Heidegger can do this—render visible social change in the culture by attending to the language of the culture—suggests a certain transparency of language to social praxis. Under this view, it would seem, language cannot but reflect social change, since change in language coincides with change in the culture.

But we have already argued that actual language use is indifferent and even oblivious to etymology, that practically the user of language has available to him or her a severely limited number of meanings in the moment of language's use. Such limitation, we would argue, is both pervasive and recalcitrant; it resists all but the most intensive hermeneutical attempts to liberate calcified meanings, such that, even when these attempts are successful (as with Williams, Merchant, and Heidegger) they turn out to be little more than academic exercises having little bearing or influence on the dynamics of actual language use. And, although language per se may reflect social change, actual language *use* obscures it. Even Heidegger, for whom etymology reveals so much, speaks, in *Being and Time,* of a "forgetfulness of Being," which in many ways refers to an obliviousness to the origins of meaning itself (i.e., etymology). We would argue that this forgetfulness is rooted in, and fostered by, language.

Thus, although we want to resist the etymological impulse found in Heidegger, we nonetheless want to hold onto those aspects of his views that allow us to speak of a something-other-than-language. In fact, to understand how it is that language obscures, rather than reflects, social change, what we need at this point is an account of what language *does* vis-à-vis the something-other-than-itself. Such an account will require an attenuation to the space or location in which language "operates." Ostensibly, this is the "seamless" space of what Jameson calls social life: "Social life is in its fundamental reality one and indivisible, a seamless web, a single inconceivable and transindividual process, in which there is no need to invent ways of linking language events and social upheavals or economic contradictions because on that level they were never separate from one another" (*Political Unconscious* 40). Obviously, what Jameson refers to as social life is imbued through and through by language. But social life is neither identical with nor reducible to language. There is always something-other-than-language entailed by the social (something material, real, according to marxist theory) to which language attaches itself and invests with meaning. For the sake of convenience, and to retain its dynamic, interwoven character, let us refer to the phenomenon that Jameson describes as the social net or web. If we could imagine Jameson's social web as somehow stripped of all ostensible meaning, we would see that language negotiates a spatial field of trans-textual occupants in much the same way that a blind person negotiates a street with a cane. These terms require elucidation, which involves describing what it means for language to invest the social web with meaning, how, despite appearances, that investment is never totalizing, and how there is a movement to social life that rushes ahead of language and is never completely apprehended by it.

What we are referring to as the "spatial field" means simply the space traversed by language prior to the predication of meaning. The term is problematic in that this space is properly understood as neither physicotemporal nor socioideological.[3] Nor is the spatial field "merely" a discursive construct or narrative fiction. Perhaps a more adequate term would be *spatium nihilum,* a space devoid of all value, where the term *value* is deployed in a strictly descriptive sense—the space literally lacks meaning—and not in a normative sense (wherein to say that the space "lacks value" would be to express a judgment about its worth; there are other similar meanings to the word *value*—ethical, existential, economic—that we are setting aside here as well). The spatial field literally lacks meaning because it lacks language. Not that it sits in repose waiting for language to charge it with significance; the spatial field is not some prelinguistic State of Nature or *terra primordium.* In fact, there is nothing very mysterious about the spatial field, properly understood. It might be viewed as the "underside" of the social net described by Jameson, were it not that such a characterization has the unhappy consequence of making the spatial field sound like some sort of structuralist, or hermeneutical, or exegetical ground. It is not that the spatial field can be unearthed, or retrieved, or rendered visible, least of all by language. This is due to the fact that for language to "touch" the spatial field is to transform it.

This is what language does—it transforms the spatial field into something that "makes sense," has meaning, is no longer devoid of value. For there to be a social web of meanings at all entails the traversing of language across the *spatium nihilum.* But this does not mean that language creates the social net ex nihilo. Language creates nothing, at least not in any substantive sense. The spatial field does not refer to *something other* than the social web, and to the

extent that the *world* itself can be understood as the totality of socially embodied meanings (in other words, the world itself as social net), the spatial field is
not something other than the world, either. Rather, the spatial field refers to
that something-other-than-language that we alluded to earlier. It refers to that
irreducible remainder that escapes language's transformative powers and that
makes reference to it necessarily indirect and opaque. The notion of the spatial
field allows us to "speak" of that indefinite totality of things, processes, and
relations that, whatever else they may be (and only language can tell us what
they "are"), are *not-language*.

To describe the spatial field in terms of "things, processes, and relations" is
already to say too much. To do so is to plant us firmly "within the confines" of
the social net, referring to that space which language has already imbued with
meaning. We prefer the term *trans-textual occupants* to refer to that which
language "encounters" in the spatial field and renders intelligible. The appella-
tion *trans-textual* is meant to replace the more common term *prelinguistic*. This
is for several reasons. First, we believe *textual* to be more adequate than *linguistic*
because things come to be imbued with language, therefore meaning, within
the context of a general fabric of significations, a complex web of discursive
connections and background assumptions, and we believe that the meaning of
things is not just a matter of the meaning attached to a particular word, or even
of concrete units of meaning within a broader system of signifiers, as is suggested by the term *linguistic*. Rather, every word in a language has a background
narrative from or against which that word makes sense.

Second, the problem with referring to something as *pre*linguistic is that it
unnecessarily imports both a temporality and an ontology to the world apart
from language. The spatial field does not exist "prior" to the social net, for the
effect of language is to cancel out any temporal or ontological distinction
between the two. Properly speaking, the social net *is* the spatial field, but
without language. But there is and can be no social net without language;
therefore, from the standpoint of language, there can be no *spatium nihilum*. At
first sight, this may look like a contradiction. But it is not, although it does
attest to the difficulty of circumventing Rorty's contention that language "goes
all the way down." What we are attempting to do through this notion of a
spatial field is to refer to that unnameable space that language goes all the way
down *through*. This is not some temporally or ontologically separate space; it *is*
the social net. Just as there can be no social net without language, however,
there can be no language without the social net. And, as we argued before, the

social net is not exhausted by language. The term *trans-textual* allows us to refer to those aspects of the social net that exceed language.

This brings us to a third reason for preferring *trans-textual* as a qualifier for the term *occupants*. *Trans-textual occupants* refers to the "not-yet" of language, to that which is not-yet things, not-yet processes, not-yet relations, not-yet subjects, not-yet objects, and so on. Nor is there any predeterminable necessity to these occupants becoming things, processes, relations, subjects or objects, fragment or whole, tangible or intangible—language will determine that. Unlike *prelinguistic,* however, this not-yet is not properly understood as temporal: first, because the spatial field does not refer to a place or time, but rather to a principle of differentiation—language versus not-language; and second, because there is a dimension of not-yet-ness that will always remain, something about the occupants of the spatial field that always escapes the entreaties of language. This is what it means to call them *trans*-textual, that there will always be some irreducible remainder, always something-other-than-language, that language cannot capture, that is, render meaningful.

Let us now attempt to explicate what it means to say that language "negotiates" the spatial field. We shall do so by way of analogy. Imagine a blind person who finds himself or herself on an unfamiliar street. To get from point A to point B, this person does not simply walk; he or she must negotiate the street. Often this is done with the use of a cane. Tapping the cane repeatedly in front and to the side, the blind person attempts to successfully traverse an otherwise meaningless space, one might even say a *spatium nihilum* of sorts. But with every tap of the cane part of that space becomes meaningful, and thereby traversable: a sloping edge to the left, a solid flat surface positioned vertically to the right, a depression, a crack, a moving body, a bulky stationary object, a ledge, and so on. Every tap of the cane invests the space with meaning, but not the entire space—only that part of the space that comes in contact with the cane. Thus the investment is partial, limited. One might object that the space is not totally meaningless, that even a blind person comes to an unfamiliar street with a certain amount of background knowledge, certain preestablished assumptions about the nature of sidewalks, traffic, buildings, and so on. We might reply that such background knowledge presupposes that the blind person has been through this situation before and had to undergo the same difficulties; so we might appeal to some notion of an originary negotiation on the part of the blind person. Instead, let us push the analogy a bit. Let us say that this is not just any blind person on just any unfamiliar street; rather, ours is a blind pygmy who has been airlifted from the jungles of Africa and dropped off unceremoniously on the corner of Forty-second Street and Broadway. Our unfortunate pygmy knows nothing of streets and traffic, and even the ground on which he stands, being hard pavement, will be totally foreign. It is doubtful that he has any sort of background knowledge that would help him to orient himself. Even human voices will likely sound strange, perhaps inhuman, to him. Every aspect of the space is meaningless to him, with the possible exception of certain basic characteristics peculiar to space itself, three-dimensionality, the possibility of movement, the effects of gravity, and so forth.

Let us say that for whatever reason (fear, hunger), the pygmy decides to move from his spot on the street. Happily, he has with him the length of tree branch that he used to negotiate the forests of his homeland. As he taps this makeshift cane in front of him, each tap invests the space with meaning. But, again, this investment is extremely limited and partial. The space yields up to the pygmy only those aspects that can be transmitted by way of the cane. What is for the pygmy "merely" a hard, bulky object, for example, we know to be "in reality" a mailbox. The pygmy negotiates what would be for us a busy city street but which is for him something approximating a *spatium nihilum*. Yet the first moment his cane even touches the pavement that space is transformed, albeit initially in the most minimal and provisional way. But each tap yields new meanings, new significations, until eventually an entire fabric, or web, of meanings and connections is constructed.

With a fair amount of tongue in cheek, we might say that language is like our blind pygmy. By that we mean, more seriously, that language is of necessity *blind* to the trans-textual quality of that which it imbues with meaning. When language comes into contact with the occupants of the spatial field it transforms them into "things" with meaning. And it does so not so much in terms of meanings attached to particular words, but rather within the context of a general fabric of significations. From within this fabric, this web, this *text,* the possibility that there might be something-other-than-language, something trans-textual, in other words, is not a practical consideration (though it might be a theoretical one, as is the case here) because knowing the world is a matter of bringing the world to language. This means that any aspect of the world which escapes language is unknowable and, from the standpoint of language, does not exist. But, like the blind person's cane, the power of language to invest the world with meaning, to transform the spatial field into a social web of meanings, is, despite appearances to the contrary, extremely limited and partial. Something-other-than-language always remains left over, is irreducible and hence unknowable to language. As Nietzsche observes in "On Truth and Lies in an Extra-Moral Sense," "The different languages set side by side show that what matters with words is never the truth, never an adequate expression. . . . The 'thing in itself' (for that is what pure truth, without consequences, would be) is quite incomprehensible to . . . language. One designates only the relations of things to man" (45). Nietzsche talks about a certain violence of abstraction and reduction that language performs on the world. We argue that that violence is never totalizing, that something—here referred to as the trans-textual—always escapes that violence. This does not mean that what language says about the world is somehow false or inadequate. Notions of truth and adequacy only make sense *within* language, that is, within a preestablished set of standards, norms, and assumptions against which locutions about the world would be judged. Rather, we are arguing that whatever language says about the world, it will never have said everything.

We are finally in a position to explain how language can obscure social change. The existence of the social net entails the negotiation by language of the spatial field. Such negotiation proceeds by language transforming trans-textual occupants into "things" with meaning. But this transformation is never total; something-other-than-language always remains left over, escapes language. Language thus invests the world with meaning but only in a limited, partial way. Nonetheless, such investment has the appearance of being "firm, canonical, and obligatory" (Nietzsche 47). In other words, language has the tendency to bind us to a particular view of the world in a way that excludes other possibilities, and which, moreover, tends to blind us to those occasions when that world is undergoing change, when it is slipping out from beneath the ascriptions that language has imposed on it. That which "slips out," escapes, and rushes ahead of language is the trans-textual.

Social change may be understood as this slippage of the trans-textual. The social net has a life of its own that is never completely apprehended by language. To the extent that language resists this slippage, it *obscures social change.* But language can do little else; it is a medium of signification that *fixes* things in their meaning. That which escapes is not-language, and it is this which is the life of the social. Sometimes a confrontation occurs between language and social praxis, at times dramatically, such as during the 1992 Republican Convention. More often, probably, social change occurs without language even being aware of it, because it is of the nature of language to bind us to a particular view of the world. By the time language does "catch up" to social change, most likely the social has already moved on. Fortunately, years later etymology can tell us what happened.

Concluding Unscientifically

Providing the necessary evidential support for our thesis that language obscures social change would require an in-depth analysis of both social change and language use that would far exceed the limitations of the present forum. We have tried to mention at least a few examples—family, community, sexuality, and so on—where we believe we see cases of social praxis running ahead of or exceeding language use. But we have been less concerned here with scientific instances than with identifying the mechanisms through which language obscures social change. And, in doing so, we have been doing more than defending a thesis, we have been elaborating a methodology, a way of analyzing the relation between language and social life that might lend itself to a more comprehensive treatment in the future.

Our suspicion is, however, that combing the archives of social history for instances where change is obscured by language would not provide the inductive suasion that one might expect. Most likely even a wide compendium of such instances would be at best illustrative of our thesis, and not necessarily empirical proof for it. This has to do with the *way* that language obscures social change, that is, by absorbing it rhetorically. It would be wrong to suggest that language is totally oblivious to social change; the life of the social presses on, and language with it. But language absorbs social change rhetorically in the sense that it has, as Stanley Fish says of rhetoric generally, "transgressed the limits of representation and substituted its own forms for the forms of reality" ("Rhetoric" 206). Language appropriates the social and subjugates it to a figure, a trope, a construct that is "incomplete and partial" (205) and which it will not give up easily. But as Fish points out, the debate that has plagued and polarized Western thought since the ancient Greeks is whether language can be anything but rhetorical. If not, then is our thesis, that language obscures social change, itself a piece of rhetoric? Are we assuming here a certain privileged transcendence with respect to language that the language we use to express it undermines our position at its core? If so, then any attempt to document the effects of language on the recognition of social change that appeals to a history which somehow escapes those effects would be prejudiced from the start.

Thus we find ourselves in the awkward position of straddling the fence between the two sides of contemporary debate on language. On the one hand, to the extent that we appeal to a notion of social change apart from language, we appear to align ourselves with those who assume "an independent reality whose outlines can be perceived by a sufficiently clear-eyed observer" (Fish, "Rhetoric" 206). On the other hand, given our assertions that we can say nothing substantive about that reality, that whatever we say will be indirect and by way of heuristic devices (such as "trans-textuality" and "spatial field"), we appear to align ourselves with those who insist that language is incorrigibly rhetorical and that it can never break through to a world beyond itself. Even the assumption of such a world is, rhetorically speaking, nonsensical.

The upshot of all this is that we cannot be sure if, and to what extent, we fall prey to our own thesis.

Notes

1. Given this discussion of meaning, it might seem useful here to discuss speech-act theory, especially Searle. Speech-act theory, however, focuses more on interactive speech rather than on the experience of language for the individual who speaks.

2. This may appear to be a willful misreading of Jameson. But, while it is certainly true that one sentence before this, in discussing unmediated history, Jameson tells us that "history . . . is *not* a text for it is fundamentally non-narrative and nonrepresentational" (*Political Unconscious* 82), we are emphasizing history *as written*. When history is expressed in writing it is both narrative and representational.

3. Although not quite the same in either meaning or purpose, Bakhtin's term *chronotope* accomplishes for the analysis of literary texts what we hope the term *spatial field* will do for the analysis of social life, both in relation to and especially *apart from* language. Emerson and Holquist define chronotope—literally, time-space—this way: "A unit of analysis for studying texts according to the ratio and nature of the temporal and spatial categories represented. . . . The chronotope is an optic for reading texts as x-rays of the forces at work in the culture system from which they spring" (Bakhtin 425–26).

Works Cited

Bakhtin, Mikhail M. *The Dialogic Imagination: Four Essays.* Trans. Caryl Emerson and Michael Holquist. Ed. Michael Holquist. Austin: University of Texas Press, 1981.

Fish, Stanley. "Rhetoric." *Doing What Comes Naturally.* Durham, N.C.: Duke University Press, 1989.

Foucault, Michel. "Nietzsche, Geneology, History." *Language, Countermemory, Practice.* Trans. and Ed. Donald F. Bouchard. Ithaca: Cornell University Press, 1977.

———. *The Order of Things: An Archaeology of the Human Sciences.* New York: Random House, 1970.

Jameson, Fredric. *The Political Unconscious.* Ithaca: Cornell University Press, 1981.

———. *The Prison-House of Language: A Critical Account of Structuralism and Russian Formalism.* Princeton: Princeton University Press, 1972.

Merchant, Carolyn. *The Death of Nature.* San Francisco: Harper-Collins, 1989.

Nancy, Jean-Luc. *The Inoperative Community.* Ed. Peter Connor. Trans. Peter Connor, Lisa Garbus, Michael Holland, and Simona Sawhney. Minneapolis: University of Minnesota Press, 1991.

Nietzsche, Friedrich. "On Truth and Lies in an Extra-Moral Sense." *The Portable Nietzsche.* Ed. and trans. Walter Kaufmann. New York: Penguin, 1976.

Rorty, Richard. *Consequences of Pragmatism.* Minneapolis: University of Minnesota Press, 1982.

———. *Contingency, Irony, Solidarity.* Cambridge: Cambridge University Press, 1989.

Said, Edward. *The World, the Text and the Critic.* Cambridge, Mass.: Harvard University Press, 1983.

Searle, J. R. "What Is a Speech Act?" *The Philosophy of Language.* Ed. J. R. Searle. Oxford: Oxford University Press, 1971.

Williams, Raymond. *Keywords: A Vocabulary of Culture and Society.* Oxford: Oxford University Press, 1983.

5
Toward a "Materialist" Rhetoric
Contingency, Constraint, and the Eighteenth-Century Crowd

Michael Hill

Words govern people.
—Major John Cartwright

Liberation is a historical and not a mental act.
—Karl Marx

In *Walter Benjamin: or, Towards a Revolutionary Criticism,* Terry Eagleton identifies two "epistemological options" which circumscribe the nettlesome encounter between antifoundationalist rhetoric and materialist critique. "Either the subject," he writes, "is wholly on the 'inside' of its world of discourse, locked into its philosophico-grammatical forms, its very struggles to distantiate them 'theoretically' themselves the mere ruses of power and desire; or it can catapult itself free from this formation to a point of transcendental leverage from which it can discern absolute truth" (131). The terms *transcendental, absolute,* and *free* are, of course, meant as obvious caveats. Eagleton is trying here to set up a distinction between any residual foundationalist tendencies of liberatory thought from what a "revolutionary criticism" might turn out to be (for, as Eagleton writes in the next lines, "everybody rejects transcendental subjects"). But the nod toward some sort of agency beyond the weary ways of discourse alludes to a collapse in the distinction between words and things which, I think, marxism still struggles to do without. Do "words govern people," as Major Cartwright asked in the first decades of modern democracy, even—perhaps especially—when people are entertaining change? And, to the extent that "words," the "people," and "government" are in one way or another inextricably intertwined, what else but something like a "mental act" exists for imagining what Marx calls "liberation"? Put another way, in what manner does materialist "history" differ from acts of thinking, writing, reading, as these phenomena are generally construed?

I am going to argue, ultimately, that contemporary marxism is, indeed, something other than (or, at least, radically anterior to) "a mental act" (call it "history"); and I will argue, as well, that the historical alternatives marxism assigns to a form of subjectivity *both* resistant to and motivated by power does not, for the sake of materialist critique, render marxism foundationalist. Granted, one must attend to "contingency," for it almost goes without saying (indeed, the "contingent" *is* the unsaid) that everywhere and every day "contingency" attends to us. But a marxism accountable to "contingency" need not find acceptable the antifoundationalist charge to replace materiality (more in conclusion on that complex arrangement) with the gentler prescriptions of the Enlightenment. The brand of rhetoric that finds itself caught between what Stanley Fish calls constitutive "constraint" (the soft reversals implicit in argument) and, to cite Richard Rorty, the pitch for "civility," registers within marxism as the slick assurance of the status quo (see Rorty, "Science as Solidarity" 468). What might be offered in its place, Marx's "history" as distinctly and radically aporic to "an act of thought," is, rather, the introduction of an act upon thinking which belongs to neither one nor another subject, but is eventuated elsewhere. I would suggest—after Etienne Balibar and in direct engagement with "civility" "community," "the people," and so on—that this be called a "mass" event.

This chapter has three parts. The first is a critical orientation of antifoundationalism's charges against the marxist "science" most recently and most effectively espoused by the late Louis Althusser. Here I accept, up to a point anyway, the tagging of "science" with certain foundationalist infelicities. But I ultimately disagree that antifoundationalism's use of "constraint" (or what Rorty calls "edification" and "private irony"), taken as prescriptive amendments to materialist intellectual work, are any less flawed. "Historically" considered, it can be argued that these features of antifoundationalism function *pro*scriptively, that is, so as to contain the possibility of change and extend heterogeneity, rather than toward the critical nominalism on which antifoundationalism lays an explicit claim to something like politics. The second section of the essay is an attempt to confront antifoundationalism's principle of constitutive "constraint" with a "history." I have in mind here the relationship between writing and various ways of imagining collectivity, among them, contradistinctively, as "masses" or "publics." Here, I examine the emergence of the eighteenth-century novel as a "mass phenomenon" and argue that constitutive "constraint" functions as both a mechanism for reproducing an order of knowledge that seems to proliferate "freely" and a way for reproducing "civil" subjects. This I call a "regenerative" rhetorical power or, following Clifford Siskin, "novelism" (see "The Rise of Novelism" and *The Work of Writing*). In the conclusion of the essay, I return to the theoretical argument held forth in the first. Here I explore what a materialist rhetoric might be by turning to Marx on "estranged labor," Eagleton on class irony, and Balibar's reconception of the "masses." These, I suggest, signal the emergent features of (a) "materialist" rhetoric.

Words, More Words, and the Possibility of Change: Rhetoric and Materialist Science

History does not end by being resolved into "self-consciousness."
—Karl Marx

I begin this section with an epigraph from *The German Ideology,* similar to the one cited at the onset of the essay. Both quotations exhibit, paradoxically perhaps, Marx's "thoughts" on the historically unthought. For it is this complex manner of speaking, at some politically portable flash point between consciousness and critique, with which Louis Althusser wrestled in his appropriations of Marx toward a final break with humanism. The work of Althusser is perhaps well known on the academic left, but it is important to sketch, if only for the purposes of locating the specific import of both what antifoundationalism lifts from materialist work and what it argues is the better alternative.

In "Marx's Relation to Hegel," Althusser offers the following abstraction: "(Origin = [(Subject = Object) = Truth] = End = Foundation)" (173). Put simply, this statement suggests the postulate that subjectivity is an effect of knowledge, what Althusser calls an object "adequation." To assume otherwise is to locate "truth" as an original and fixed referent, a point paradoxically both toward and from which knowledge finds its circular and "foundational" end. Neither a critique of Hegelian idealizations of the subject nor the shibboleth of origins is philosophical news these days, even on the most cursory reading of Marx. And Althusser's break with Hegel (vis-à-vis Marx), his replacement of an "objective" approach to the production of knowledge with a relational one, has certain tenets now dispersed into antifoundationalism's rejection of "metaphoric perception" (Rorty) and "literal meaning" (Fish).

Indeed, the foundationalist ruses of "objectivity" are singled out by antifoundationalism in terms, at a glance, strikingly similar to Althusser. What Althusser might call "ideology" (a subject = object adequation left uncritiqued),

Rorty might call the ruse of a "final vocabulary"—" 'final' in the sense that if doubts are cast on the worth of these words, their user has no noncircular argumentative recourse" ("Private Irony" 456). What produces such doubts is the "contingency" of all knowledge (read the relational significance of objects), which it is antifoundationalism's first order of business to ferret out onto the infinite and incontrovertible surface of language. For Fish, the standoff between "rhetoric" as "argument for the situated subject" and "theory" as "an attempt to guide practice from a position above or outside it" (Fish 319) equals Rorty's take on "finality." Thus contemporary marxism and antifoundationalism hold in common that subjectivity is identifiable in no way other than by considering the changing relations that "interpellate" (as Althusser says) the subject, in other words, that precede, produce, and may time and again mediate its change.

The charge against "scientific" marxism, where things become a little foggier in terms of having anything on the order of "radical" critique, comes on a disagreement over the readability of the subject's relational status, in particular, whether or not that relational status can be reliably "read off" against ideology as a counter-interpellative strategy that holds still long enough to target change. A scientific distinction between so-called "real" and "imaginary" relations would be one version of the materialist agenda. In the antifoundationalist light, however, this would register as the ushering in of an ontological taboo through the epistemological back door: that is, the problem of object "adequation," of positing a foundationally knowing subject as (true or) higher, over an ideologically "interpellated" (or false) consciousness.[1] To conceive of ideologies as hailing frequencies transmissible and translatable as the Other of scientific "interpretation" is, so goes the charge, to conceive of ideology as mimeticism gone wrong, a fully transparent discursive lens through which can now be measured a "materialist" revelation, something not unlike the truth.

So Althusser locates the subject within a set of shifting (but distinctly "material" and, therefore, more or less certainly describable) relations. In place of this, antifoundationalism offers the location of the subject in other shifting (now discursive) relations. Through discussion and argument alone emerge the possibilities of ideological counter-interpellations, which themselves are no less interpellative, no less ideological, but are, for all that, no less effective for identifying the subject differently. This is Rorty's account of "edification," or "liberal irony," which initiates on the subject "radical and continuing doubts" and, therefore, the possibility for people to "work out their private salvations, create their private self-images, reweave their webs of belief and desire in the light of whatever new people and books they happen to encounter" (see *Philoso-phy and the Mirror of Nature* 370; quotation from "Private Irony" 459). Fish casts the "urgings" of rhetoric similarly as community-shaping power over and between subjects. This occurs "in the softest possible terms" (Fish 12) as con-stitutive "constraint."

What do we make of the ironic misidentification of the subject within competing modes of discourse, and of rhetoric's "soft" communicative "urges" of intersubjective "constraint"? The rhetorical revision of a materialist critique of the subject amounts to two important consequences: first, very much on the order of Foucault, antifoundationalism does away with the Freud-inspired "re-pressive hypothesis."[2] Power, thus, is an immanent feature of community and the self-effect, and power is describable in no way that places the subject doing the describing outside of some complex negotiation with (because within) a position of partial "constraint." This consequence seems acceptable (although it arguably goes no further than an ontological rerendering of Saussurian semi-otics). But the second consequence of antifoundationalism's penchant for "soft" reversals and "private ironies" initiates a decidedly Enlightenment turn and, therefore, forgoes what is "radical" (Rorty's word) about rejecting the repressive hypothesis. What is kept beyond the critical reach of antifoundationalism, I suggest, is the relation between intersubjectivity (constitutive "constraint," or what Habermas more politely calls "communicative reason" and "audience-oriented subjectivity") and the operations of the state (what Foucault calls "governmentality").

The truth is as "fragile" as the ways for describing it are multiple according to antifoundationalism's dictum of "contingency." It is this multiplicity of truth-effects that make it less worthwhile to strive for the "truth" than to preserve the institutions which ought to accommodate so many mutually (if unevenly) rigged perceptions. Thus it is argued that "general 'discourses' like the law can serve as constraints on interpretive desires," and that justice requires "the submission of the individual to impersonal and public norms [which] would be a rational act, chosen by the very will that is to be held in check" (Fish 6). Similarly, "we shall call 'true' or 'good' whatever is the outcome of free discussion" (Rorty, "Private Irony" 459). Exactly what use the ironist has for "freedom" in the usual sense of that term is unexplained here. But what is more important in these remarks is their unabashed recourse to the Enlightenment socius as a permanent institutional pretense that, paradoxically in fact, sits outside rhetorical maneuvering in order to protect the circular claim that rhetorical maneuvering is all there is (i.e., that there is no "outside" outside language). Furthermore, the subtle exchange of latitudinal complicity between the ironically defamiliarized *and* governable (i.e., "communally" "constrained") subject amounts de facto (despite the nod to "change" or "radical doubt") to a programmatic disciplinary procedure. One may allow that the subject is a thing in process, never outside the incommensurabilities of power and language. The subject, as Foucault has so pointedly insisted, is not a thing above which the state may exercise the right to govern (for the subject as a process is by extension *no*-thing); neither can the subject itself (*as* itself, as a "citizen" in process) seize from the state its power in any objectifiable form. But the "radical" consequence of such a premise, rather than to entrench further the banal circularities of "civil" society, is to offer up the subject as a governmental technique, to regard identity itself as a governmental transaction. The critique of the repressive hypothesis thus enables knowledge to reveal the subject as the regenerative medium of civil obedience, albeit an obedience that occurs in the "softest," but for that no less effective, and no less normative, terms.

From this vantage point, the invisible composite of "civil" society, held together by the tactical efficiencies and peaceful combinations of desire and "constraint," is sheltered from larger pictures (say, class relations) only by taking on board a high-priced distinction between so-called private salvation and the "[re]public's" ability to anesthetize other forms of collective life. What is lost in antifoundationalism's critique of science—its replacement of materiality with the "entirely private matter [of irony]" (Rorty, "Private Irony" 460) and with rhetoric's "soft" "constraint"—is the ability to acknowledge the "contingency" of private life itself, as a *categorical* impermanence, immanent to (not protected by or made possible because of) the perfection of governmental rule. As I shall argue in the next section, what we finally have in the critique of marxist science (the intimation of a more burdensome irony) is an antifoundationalism that shrinks from its own name.

The Novelization of the Multitudes:
Writing, Genre, and Other "Soft Urges"

In particular, novels and ethnographies which sensitize one to the pain of those who do not speak our language must do the job which demonstrations of common human nature were supposed to do.
—Richard Rorty, "Private Irony"

What we saw last night [was] not about the great cause of equality that all Americans must uphold. It [was] not a message of protest. It [was] the brutality of the mob, pure and simple. . . . What you saw and what I saw in the TV video was revolting. I felt anger. I felt pain. I thought—how can I explain this to my grandchildren. . . . It's as if we're looking in a mirror that distorted our better selves and turned us ugly. We cannot let that happen. We cannot do that to ourselves.
—George Bush

The unlikely pairing of these epigraphs is meant to mark a certain collusion between Rorty's "private salvations," the mass-scale "sensitivity" training that is rightly ascribed to the advent of the novel,[3] and the governmental self-fashioning former President Bush appeals to in the wake of the Los Angeles uprisings in 1992 (see Bernard-Donals 72). In the second passage, Bush appeals in the negative for none other than those perplexing individual "freedoms" that, I suggested earlier, bring about a simultaneity of interest between the subject, knowledge, and the successes of government. In what follows, I want to trace the historicity of this tripartite alignment as a technique of "regenerative" liberal power, or in more familiar terms, a matter of discipline. What I want to suggest, in short, is that our "sensitivity" for (and as) governable subjects, constraining and constrained by discursively negotiated "better selves," occurs through "messages" about the masses.

Consider the Bush quotation more closely. The "mob" cannot speak because it is not us. Whoever "we," "ourselves," turn out to be depends on "what we saw," that is, what we can say about the "mob." This ability to see and say (and ultimately be) is opposed to a "message" outside "our" communicative register. Either "we saw" a "distorted" counter-"reflection" of our "better selves," that is, a nonrepresentation of publicity which exceeds the will of the self in question to identify the scene of violence as its own,[4] or we hear a message of riot that makes us "ugly," which Bush assures us, "we cannot do."

More curious still, and at the center of my historical response to antifoundationalism's use of "constitutive" "constraint," is the generational qua governmental countermove apparent in this passage. Bush "purifies" and "simplifies" what happened in Los Angeles not through overt state repression—his are nothing if not micropolitical rhetorical tactics—but by recuperating the "mob's" non-"message" with a maneuver that extends the clear reflection of the president himself as "ourselves." This move, which includes all the "community," the "freedom," the "private salvation," and the intersubjective "sensitivity" in the world, is efficient to the extent that it regenerates a governable population individually and automatically. Indeed, the "regeneration" of governmental power at work here occurs in exceedingly intimate ways by assigning regenerative functions to desire itself: the former president's literal reproductive capacity as a grandfather becomes the communicative model through which "you" and "I," against the "mob," sense the obvious need for filial recollectivization. We learn, alas, to hear the "message," to reconstitute ourselves as governable through the sly simultaneity of both the affirmation and the constraint of "our" now orderly numbers.

The libidinal aspects of the former president's "regenerative" comments after the Los Angeles "riots" are central to historicizing rhetorical constraint. The case of the novel as itself a "mass" phenomenon, one always on the brink of some subjective "(in)civility" but ultimately constrained by its own prodigiousness, provides the same filial rationale for the discipline of Enlightenment subjects. Indeed, the eighteenth-century novel (itself at the historical margins of the discipline of literature) initiates a "generational" process within writing to articulate subjectivity in a manner that "constrains," produces, affirms, enhances, threatens to undo the literary subject while making its desires ultimately manageable. It is the same "generational" process that informs what is possible (and not) in hearing mass "messages" today. Thus to register both the efficiency and the fragility of rhetoric's "soft urges," its delicate historical connection to discipline, I want to focus primarily on the "generative" effects of the novel, that is, its ability to "constrain" and (re)produce subjects simultaneously.

The term *generative* has three senses in my discussion. The first and most basic has to do with the unprecedented increase in the circulation of printed material in England after the lapse of the Licensing Act in 1695. The second points to a more complex conflict, not of the "generational" propensity of writing to historically reproduce, but to a conflict (within reproduction) of *kind,* that is, of identifying the novel "generically," as a category cordoned off from whatever else may be read. With the copyright legislation that began with the statute of Anne in 1710, the establishment of Caslon's type foundry in 1720, the invention of the steam-driven press, and the availability of cheap, domestically produced paper and ink (one could go on), the production and consumption of writing was made possible on a scale previously unthinkable.[5] Yet somehow, amid this amorphous heterogeneity of words, by the time Samuel Miller penned the novel's first history in 1803, it gained a certain "generic" respect later codified famously by Ian Watt as "formal realism." From out of the "generation" of what was for countless eighteenth-century critics too much writing, there is the "generic" positioning of the novel itself to rise as a category of writing made formally distinct from so much other prose.

The term *generation* is important in a third way, and it is here that the governmental possibilities for "constitutive constraint" may be most distinctly described. Essential to classifying the proliferation of prose in the eighteenth century, and to communicative processes riotous and otherwise, is a relationship between "regenerative" power and desire. The problem of multiply relating bodies, the connections they may and may not have collectively, the distinctions of kind (i.e., genre) that make possible and set limits to uncivil associations, all become the specific business of novel writing to address. What the famous London bookseller and publisher James Lackington ponders in 1794 as "the general desire for READING" is a desire, I will argue, invented as a fundamentally regenerative force. Like Bush's filial appeal to the intimate sphere as less the object of government than a sign of governability, the novel designates a historical moment when bodies are privatized (however "softly" through their interior affirmation) but come to have a decidedly public use. This strategy is common both to antifoundationalism's appeal to "constitutive constraint" and to the novel's "generic" struggle for and against alternate ways of amassing.

It is well known that mass agency in the eighteenth century was tolerated, even encouraged, in ways inconceivable today. During the period from about the time of the Riot Act of 1714 to the time of the Corresponding Societies that emerged as part of the democracy movements in the latter part of the eighteenth century, a historical fiction called the "public" marked the struggle to maintain an orderliness based on both the security of private space (property) and the mutuality of competing desires held in check by "civil" society. What Fish calls "constraint" Adam Smith called "frugality."[6] For Smith, a person's own desires (namely, for another's property) are constrained, or not, by the fear that someone might be watching. The panoptic metaphysics that helped turn the wheels of early capitalism are thus manifest in a newly cooperative relationship between the state and individual in the eighteenth century. Against the backdrop of the Wilkes riots of 1760, the even worse Gordon riots of 1780, the hundreds of antiexcise and food riots that occurred between 1735 and 1800—not to mention the effigy burnings, parades, and so on—individuality comes to appeal above all to the police.[7] Early tracts on policing, such as Henry Fielding's

Inquiry into the Causes of the Late Increase of Robbers (1751) and Patrick Colquhoun's *Treatise on the Police of the Metropolis* (1797), which culminate in the
founding of a permanent century, reveal a striking preoccupation with the
"deluded multitudes" as a primary threat to the more intimate realm of individuality.[8] In order to conceive of "public" order, community, and consensus at all,
a certain individual desire to get and hold on to goods had to be maintained, in
the first and final instance, at home.

In the sense that the intimate and public spheres are coconstitutive, writing
is, historically, very much on the order of police work. It is work, therefore,
within which the "mob" plays a fundamental role. Pope made his famous com-
plaint against the "mob" of hack writers and booksellers in *The Dunciad* directly
after a period of a great proliferation of writing in 1728, but still thirteen years
before his precedent-setting civil suit against the bookseller Edmund Curll for
copyright infringement in 1741.[9] Within this gray area just before midcentury,
between the increase of writing and the historical difficulties of making it
private (initially as property), Pope sees to his objection: "prose swell'd to verse,
[and] verse loitering into prose." He sees, that is, a twofold displacement of old
categories—verse—and old values associated with the relative rarity of writing in
a more gentlemanly age based on coterie readership, as an event marked by
writing's propensity for disorderly movements and prolific "swells."

If there is in Pope a characteristic ambivalence over the proliferation of
writing as a potentially "mobish" affair, the problem is more effectively managed in the "generational" ways of the novel. In distinguishing itself from the
excesses of romance, the novel comes on the historical scene as numbers crises,
but one effectively and, perhaps paradoxically, ordered by extending and embracing, not suppressing, writing's increase. Writing manifests itself as a private
problem, less at midcentury of property than of desire. This problem is resolved, furthermore, with the fortunate public fallout of the kind of constitutive intersubjectivity that produces ever more similar subjects (namely offspring) and, not incidentally, more of the same kind of writing (newly classed as
novels). That these subjects of (and in) writing are themselves always on the
brink of a libidinal disaster signals the origin of a cycle of crisis, constraint, and
affirmation that is capable of infinite repetition. Such a cycle comprises both
the history of the novel and the origination of civil society as a fundamentally reproductive act. Against the "multitudes," the newly libidinized subject
emerges initially by "soft urges" of desire almost gone wrong but becoming,
ultimately, an effect of communicative constraint vis-à-vis the affirmation of

those very desires anew. This process thus makes imminent safer and more heterogeneous brands of collective (re)formation.

Indeed, the "sensitivity" Rorty more optimistically assigns the novel moves between its emergent generic designation (formal realism), the illicit "swells" of desire it on the other hand produces, and the constraint of unruly numbers, in less than a step. In his *Sermons to Young Women* of 1766, James Fordyce makes clear that the availability of the novel arrives with dangers to (heterosexual) subjectivity that are dangers as well to the generic capacities of writing itself. Literary subjects (in both senses of the term) must become the agents of social regeneration.[10] "There seem," he remarks, "to be very few [novels] that you can read to advantage." Indeed, the "general run of novels . . . paint scenes of pleasure and passion altogether improper for [young women] to behold" (176). The novel's "representations of love between the sexes," Fordyce continues, are "almost universally overstrained" and typically "swell into burlesque. . . . She who can bear to pursue them must in her soul be a prostitute" (176). For Fordyce, only "the beautiful productions of [Richardson's] incomparable pen" (177) can be read with any semblance of safety. Against the danger other novels pose to "female virtue," Richardson stands as the prototype that allows safer reading, and it is to the discredit of the "parents of the present generation" (177) that young women are subjected to "principles of Avarice" found in novels outside those of formal realism. Finally, Fordyce casts "the species of writing which so many young women are apt to dote upon" as "the offspring of our present Novelists . . . [and] the common herd of Play-writers" (178).

With Fordyce, the "general run" of dangerous novels is placed against a single example of their potentially reformative effects. This process of rarification finds a "generational" correspondence between the novel's categorical separation from plays and the portrayal of a woman's pleasure as a crisis of a private salvation that clearly leads to public effects. The important thing is that private crises occur because of *and* are managed by the potentially regenerative embrace of an emergent formal realism or, more precisely, a generic embrace that itself leads to regeneration. Female pleasure is as much constrained in this curious passage as it is affirmed, and therein lies a kind of communicative remediation of desire that distinguishes civil and uncivil collectivities, "herds" of writing from genres, unproductive sex from the eventuating of families, all in one fell swoop. Novels produce illicit "swells" when female desire goes wrong. Thus the "prostitute" as romance reader stands in as a negative correlate to the practice of "parenting" by which a woman's pleasure is made reproductive or not, and by

which the genre of the novel is made identifiable. On that order, writing's bas-
tard "offspring"—the "common herd"—functions as the constitutive constraint
that makes and remakes a genre, and attaches to "virtuous desire" a reproductive component that both manages and intensifies it. The regenerative capacity
of the novel provides a twofold social service. It prescribes the making of families and, thus, battles an undistinguished relation of numbers (the "herd") with
another "generation," a suitably ordered and identifiably bourgeois collectivity,
which is monitored by the "generic" struggles that constrain the novel itself.

This complex process of generic becoming is especially notable in Samuel
Miller's 1803 "History of Romances and Novels." Here, Miller describes the
history of the novel as a crisis of its own and of societal "multitudes." He
provides a historical narrative—as a characteristic feature of novelistic discourse
itself—which reproduces the very processes of constitutive constraint that he
designates the work of his historical object: both the novel and its history are
negotiated by embracing the "multitudes" to identify, if by reversal and in order to embrace "softer urges," more "generic," "regenerative," and ultimately
innocuous forms of collectivity. The problem with "Romances," according
to Miller, is not merely "the wild absurdities and heroic exploits of knight-
errantry." True, these "intoxicate the mind" and are "grossly immoral in their
nature." Most objectionably, the romance exhibits a tendency "to abound in
every species of impure and corrupting exhibition of vice." In addition to the
tendency of romances to "abound" in the absurd, they are "tediously diffuse,
extending to too many volumes, and fatiguing the reader with their unnecessary prolixity" (156).

The crisis of association attached to the romance prompts Miller to propose in his history that "prolixity" gives way to the constitutive constraint of
generic categorization: more novelistic writing is produced in the very act of
classifying the novel (Miller's generic-regenerative move) and, concomitantly,
novels themselves initiate in their readers the reproduction of disciplined
bodies against less governable forms of association. The "prolixity" of the romance is displaced, Miller continues, by "[giving] way to a further improvement, which was the introduction of the Modern Novel" (157). In this emergent genre, "adventures are wonderfully diversified; yet the circumstances are all
so natural and rise so easily from one another" (159). Such adventures "co-
operate with . . . regularity" and produce "perfect unity of design." Henry
Fielding, Miller emphasizes, is especially "at home when describing low life."
Indeed, "none have risen to the same degree of excellence which they [he and

Richardson] attained" (160). By contrast, it is to Laurence Sterne's discredit that "the great mass of what he has written is either . . . shamefully obscene . . . or foolishly unmeaning" (165). For Miller, *Tristram Shandy* represents "the singular farrago of obscurity." The corresponding effect of this foolishness is a problem both of generation (a "great mass") and of generic refusal: "the multitudes, to the present day, have continued to mistake [Sterne] for [a] great and original genius" (165).

There is a careful topology of value crafted by Miller here, a three-dimensional relationship between marginal collectivities ("low life"), the intimate sphere ("home" life), and the generic "rises" of the "natural" "adventures" of subjects and of writing. For Miller, Fielding represents the effective domestication of "adventure," that is, the imminent privatizing of the "lowly" in the regenerative locale of the intimate sphere—the "home"—wherein can occur more natural "rises" and, back to Fordyce, where more virtuous (regenerative heterosexual) desires emerge. It is in the same manner of a reproductive "rise" that the formal realist novel is itself classifiable as a generically distinct writing so that it, too, may "rise" above the "prolixity" of romance and, therefore, above and beyond Sterne's misguided "multitudes."

Accordingly, the most villainous writing in Miller's history is writing which is itself construed as a "multitude," that is, a collectivity without the regenerative-generic "rises" found apropos the public function of the intimate sphere, that is, by the "constitutive constraint" of undisciplined bodies, by keeping the "lowly" at "home." Thus Matthew Lewis's gothic novel, *The Monk* (1796), represents for Miller the most extreme example of what he calls, in explicitly filial language, "the herd of low and impotent" novels (167). It is essential to point out that the final scene of *The Monk* is *itself* occasioned by riot, and it is here that the regenerative "potency" Miller calls for in his own narrative of genre is most explicitly absent. In the final chapters of *The Monk,* an angry mob "ravages" the "principle walls" of the abbey (377). In turn, Lorenzo, the novel's eventual groom-hero, must go beneath the "popular fury" into the streets to rescue and deliver Agnes, his betrothed. Lorenzo's struggle to negotiate the "multitudes" is what momentarily impedes him from the conjugal pleasures of marriage and from the regenerative deliveries promised by lawful sex. Within the plot of *The Monk,* then, the "common herd" triggers generic forms of amassing that occur via disciplinary affirmation or, more specifically, by conjugal reproduction.

In Miller's own historical narrative, writing as a "multitude" initiates a

classificatory procedure that positions the novel itself (*as* a novel itself) with the regenerative capacity it also prescribes. Indeed, the filial insecurities of *The Monk* (it is, among other things, writing that deals with cross-dressing and homosexuality) are what prohibits it from following Fielding's natural "rise." Miller associates the gothic with the "mischievous masses" and gives it the very role of riot that *The Monk* assigns its mob against more orderly, more filial, more generic ways of embracing which occur on the order of the main character's eventual marriage. The alternative to the "multitudes" in this case is reproduction. This is evident both in the regenerative fate of *The Monk*'s hero and heroine, and in the generic fate of the novel itself as a reproductive agent in Miller's own novelized history of writing. Having taken on the features it attempts to describe (riot) in *The Monk,* Miller's own narrative reproduces the generic mandates of the novel itself. As part of the infinite sequence of crises, constraint, and regeneration, the gothic is charged with failing to provide precisely the generic features exhibited by Miller in his own shrewd novelization of what would otherwise be a forbiddingly massive heterogeneity of prose.

Historically, then, "constitutive constraint" (intersubjectivity, "communicative reason," "edification") is both a governmental and a generic problem. The requisite "virtuousness" of self-identification (consistent with the "rises" of novels and the formation of subjects) is, indeed, constituted in process. Rhetoric, in this sense, works both toward and within "civility." It assures the constitutions of subjects within the infinitely regenerative realm of "private salvation" but, curiously, with what looks now like an uncanny permanence, and with formal regularity that seems almost natural. The orderly perfection of civil society renders unthinkable any collectivities beyond the split between private and public. This is a testimony to the stunning institutional perspicuity of disciplined writing and to antifoundationalism itself, both as Enlightenment fictions.

Is a "Materialist" Rhetoric Conceivable? Class(ification), the Masses, and "Radical Doubts"

Multitudes are not of much value unless they contribute to the ease and burden of society, by co-operating to its prosperity.
—Samuel Johnson

It is the proletariat that will render Proust readable, even if they may later find no use for him. . . . And the Proust whose texts socialism shall recom-

pose will not be the Proust consumed in the salons; no value is extended to
the masses without thereby being transformed.
—Terry Eagleton

In the first section of this essay, I noted how antifoundationalism's appeal to
rhetoric amounts to two consequences: a relational critique of the subject that
already has a conceptual existence in marxism; and the replacement of "materiality" with "rhetoric," where materiality is construed to mean a site of interpretive privilege, far enough outside power to name it. Antifoundationalism's
alternative is that the subject is constitutively constrained by other subjects (an
appropriation, again, of Habermas's notion of "communicative reason"), which
occurs within the "soft urges" of rhetoric, the "private salvations" of irony
assuring and insured by government. The second section of the essay was an
attempt to address constitutive constraint with a history of genre, specifically,
the novel. Here, I argued that such a practice operates toward the cordial
subjection of associative rights (written as "multitudes," "herds," "swellings")
which are not already proscribed within the affirmative continuum of discipline. It is as a process of identification within knowledge (genre making) that
antifoundationalism reveals a dubious complacency over distinctions that neu-
tralize in the name of "civility" the massive (because ageneric) historical sin-
gularities that at one time must have circulated between desires, identity, and
words. Constitutive constraint, writ historically, is perhaps less a matter of
imagining "change" than it is the sly extension of an apparently irrevocable
historical habit, that is, a practice of government which is also an act of subjective recovery.

     What alternatives are there, then, to the "private salvations" of antifounda-
tionalist thought? What conditions would a "materialist" rhetoric follow, and
can "materialism" be manifest—returning to Marx—other than "consciously,"
on the order of both a "mass" and a "rhetorical" event? What appears necessary,
initially, for a "materialist" rhetoric is to posit scientific knowledge as "only one
form of power amongst others" (Balibar, "Foucault and Marx" 47). This would
seem to open up the possibility for seeing "class" analysis, among other ways, as
the dislodging of the liberal subject describable as a class-ification problem. In
only the most superficial sense does "irony" in the sense it may be evoked here
recall Rorty's claim that political hope lies in the private production and reproduction of "radical doubt." That the "doubt" at work privately is somewhat less

than "radical" seems certain by the fact these "salvations" are found through a process limited to the regenerative capacity of the intimate sphere, to its being cordoned off as a process that allows no basis for critique beyond the privileged spaces of a permanent bourgeois society.

Thus the permanent fiction of "civility" in any totalizable sense is as dear to antifoundationalism as it is antagonistic to marxism: for the former, it enables the appeal to "constitutive constraint," for the latter, it glosses the contradictions inherent within capitalist democracy. Marx's idea of the "objectification of labor" and Althusser's notion of subject/object "adequation" remain essential here, not for resolving contradiction privately, but for intensifying it publicly. What a "materialist" rhetoric that keeps "class" as a form of "objectivity" in focus might produce is less a mimetic description of capitalist evils (that would reintroduce objectivity) and more a performance of classificatory misfires that are necessarily overlooked by the (generic) aberration of subject/object (or worker/commodity) "adequation."

Regarding the "radical discontinuity" Terry Eagleton writes: "Marxism, as an inevitably 'limited' 'text,' . . . stands in ironic relation to the historical 'text' it exists to produce, and whose emergence will finally signify its own demise" (69). The complex process of class irony alluded to here might eventuate in any number of ways, ranging epistemologically from generic slippage (between, say, novels as fiction and history as fact) to the ontological maneuvers of class trading (the decidedly un-"civil" displacement of bourgeois subjectivity to include interests neither its own nor another's of its "class"). To the extent that the "radical doubts" manifest within such barely thinkable possibilities are doubts from which the private subject may not categorically recover, at least (as Eagleton says) on this side of revolutionary change, and to the extent that this relative unrecoverability is neither strictly public nor intimate, but "massive," the attention to "class" on which Eagleton insists is both materialist and rhetorical. This, in short, and put perhaps too simply, means acknowledging the "determining role of the masses in history" (Balibar, *Masses* xvi). That the "masses' " role in history is only partially visible anticipates, not dismisses, the importance of a "class" to antifoundational thought.

Notes

1. Althusser claims that ideology is an "illusion" because it "represents in its necessarily imaginary distortion, not the existing [material] relations of production, but

above all the (imaginary) relationship of individuals to the relations of production and the relations that derive from them" ("Ideology" 164).

2. See Foucault's most concise account of this critique, "Truth and Power."

3. Habermas, too, is clear on the decisive function of the novel (and the Bank of England) on establishing the intimate sphere as a precursor to the founding of civil society. See *The Structural Transformation of the Public Sphere,* especially the chapters "The Bourgeois Family and the Institution of Privateness Oriented to an Audience" and "The Public Sphere in the World of Letters in Relation to the Public Sphere in the Political Realm."

4. Race in the Los Angeles riots becomes a generic mediator that buffers the (white) ruling class from the collective interests that would bring it down. On knowledge, classificatory struggles, and the question of whiteness, see Michael Hill, "Can Whiteness Speak?"

5. Two-thirds of the paper used to print books was being produced in England by 1713, which made the production of books and the dissemination of writing possible there on a massive and unprecedented scale. Before 1695, only twenty printing houses were to be allowed in all of England, with only two presses to a house; and what was printed was supposed to be directly sanctioned by the Crown. By 1727, there were 75 printers in London, 28 more in the provinces; by 1785, there were 124 printers in London, with as many as 9 presses per shop. In 1688, there were only 198 men working in printing trades and a mere 65 presses; by 1818 there were 625 presses and 3,365 men working them. See Kernan.

6. See Adam Smith, *The Theory of Morals and Sentiments* (189–90, 213–15). Smith remarks bluntly in *An Inquiry into the Nature and Causes of the Wealth of Nations* that civil government "is in reality instituted for the defense of the rich against the poor" (181).

7. The most complete archival accounts of the activities of eighteenth-century crowds are still George Rudé's book *The Crowd in History* and E. P. Thompson's article "The Moral Economy of the English Crowd in the Eighteenth Century." See also George and Louise Tilly's *Class Conflict and Collective Action.*

8. Fielding, *Inquiry into the Causes of the Late Increase of Robbers,* and Colquhoun, *Treatise on the Police.*

9. On writing as private property and Pope's civil suit on the matter, see Mark Rose, "The Author in Court."

10. The "filial feelings" with which, for example, Fanny Burney appeals to her father regarding the risk of novel reading is explicit on this score, and it is not atypical for women around the eighteenth-century novel (see her preface to *The Wanderer*). Scholarship on the inextricable relation between the eighteenth-century novel and gender is equally prodigious. See, in particular, Nancy Armstrong, *Desire and Domestic Fiction,* and Kathryn Shevelow, *Women and Print Culture.*

Works Cited

Althusser, Louis. "Ideology and Ideological State Apparatuses: Notes toward an Investigation." *Lenin and Philosophy.* New York: Monthly Review Press, 1971.

———. "Marx's Relation to Hegel." *Montesquieu, Rousseau, Politics and History.* Ed. Ben Brewster. London: Verso, 1971.

Armstrong, Nancy. *Desire and Domestic Fiction: A Political History of the Novel.* Oxford: Oxford University Press, 1987.

Balibar, Etienne. "Foucault and Marx: The Question of Nominalism." *Michel Foucault: Philosopher.* Ed. Timothy Armstrong. New York: Routledge, 1992.

———. *Masses, Classes, Ideas: Studies on Politics and Philosophy before and after Marx.* New York: Routledge, 1994.

Barnett, George, ed. *Eighteenth Century British Novelists on the Novel.* New York: Appleton-Century-Crofts, 1968.

Bernard-Donals, Michael. "The Rodney King Verdict, the New York *Times,* and the 'Normalization' of the Los Angeles Riots; or, What Anti-foundationalism Can't Do." *Cultural Critique* 27 (spring 1994): 61–88.

Bush, George. "Excerpts from Bush's Speech on the Los Angeles Riot: 'Need to Restore Order.'" *Los Angeles Times* (3 May 1992): 8L.

Cartwright, John. *The Commonwealth in Danger.* London: n.p., 1795.

Colquhoun, Patrick. *Treatise on the Police of the Metropolis . . .* London: H. Fry, 1797.

Eagleton, Terry. *Walter Benjamin: or, Towards a Revolutionary Criticism.* London: Verso, 1981.

Fielding, Henry. *An Inquiry into the Causes of the Late Increase of Robbers.* London: A. Millar, 1751.

Fish, Stanley. *Doing What Comes Naturally.* Durham, N.C.: Duke University Press, 1989.

Fordyce, James. *Sermons to Young Women.* 1766. *Women in the Eighteenth Century: Constructions of Femininity.* Ed. Vivien Jones. New York: Routledge, 1990.

Foucault, Michel. "Governmentality." *The Foucault Effect: Studies in Governmentality.* Ed. Graham Burchell, Colin Gordon, and Peter Miller. Chicago: University of Chicago Press, 1991: 87–105.

———. "Truth and Power." *Power/Knowledge: Selected Interviews and Other Writings, 1972–1977.* Ed. Colin Gordon. New York: Pantheon, 1980: 109–33.

Habermas, Jürgen. *The Philosophical Discourse of Modernity.* Cambridge, Mass.: MIT Press, 1990.

———. *The Structural Transformation of the Public Sphere.* Cambridge, Mass.: MIT Press, 1991.

Hill, Michael. "Can Whiteness Speak?" *White Trash: Race and Class in America.* Ed. Annalee Newitz and Matthew Wray. New York: Routledge, 1996.

Johnson, Samuel. *The Universal Visitor.* April 1756.

Kernan, Alvin. *Samuel Johnson and the Impact of Print.* Princeton: Princeton University Press, 1987.

Lewis, Matthew. *The Monk.* 1796. New York: Grove Press, 1957.

Marx, Karl. *The German Ideology.* 1845–46. *The Marx-Engels Reader.* Ed. Robert C. Tucker. New York: Norton, 1978.

Miller, Samuel. *A Brief Retrospect of the Eighteenth Century.* 1803. New York: Burt Franklin, 1970.

Rorty, Richard. *Philosophy and the Mirror of Nature.* Princeton: Princeton University Press, 1979.

———. "Private Irony and Political Hope." *Knowledge and Postmodernism in Historical Perspective.* Ed. Joyce Appleby et al. New York: Routledge, 1996.

———. "Science as Solidarity." *Knowledge and Postmodernism in Historical Perspective.* Ed. Joyce Appleby et al. New York: Routledge, 1996.

Rose, Mark. "The Author in Court: *Pope v. Curll* (1741)." *The Construction of Authorship: Textual Appropriation in Law and Literature.* Ed. Martha Woodmansee and Peter Jaszi. Durham, N.C.: Duke University Press, 1994: 211–30.

Rudé, George. *The Crowd in History, 1730–1848.* New York: Wiley, 1964.

Shevelow, Kathryn. *Women and Print Culture: The Construction of Femininity in the Early Periodical.* New York: Routledge, 1989.

Siskin, Clifford. "The Rise of Novelism." *Cultural Institutions of the Novel.* Ed. Diedre Lynch and William B. Warner. Durham, N.C.: Duke University Press, 1996.

———. *The Work of Writing: Disciplinarity, Professionalism, and the Engendering of Literature in Britain, 1700–1830.* Baltimore: Johns Hopkins University Press, 1997.

Smith, Adam. *An Inquiry into the Nature and Causes of the Wealth of Nations.* 1776. Cambridge, Mass.: Hackett Publishing, 1993.

———. *The Theory of Morals and Sentiments.* 1759. Indianapolis: Liberty Fund, 1984.

Thompson, E. P. "The Moral Economy of the English Crowd in the Eighteenth Century." *Past and Present* 50 (February 1971): 76–136.

Tilly, George, and Louise Tilly. *Class Conflict and Collective Action.* Beverly Hills, Calif.: Sage, 1981.

Watt, Ian. *The Rise of the Novel.* Berkeley: University of California Press, 1959.

6
The Decentered Subject of Feminism
Postfeminism and *Thelma and Louise*
Linda Frost

In an end-of-the-year summary for 1991, *U.S. News and World Report* commented on the media debate surrounding that summer's hit *Thelma and Louise,* noting that the film "may not have appealed to as many people as the producers hoped. In 1991, 36 percent of American women called themselves feminists, compared with 56 percent five years ago" ("Year" 100). Many film fans and commentators on popular culture, though, did not agree with this journalist's description of the film as feminist. In fact, the polarized responses to the question, Is *Thelma and Louise* a feminist film? and the reports of those responses all demonstrate the unstable construction of feminism in the American cultural imagination today. The media representation of *Thelma and Louise* in all its discursive practices—written text, photographs, cartoons, and so on—has been full of contradiction, defining feminism as, at one extreme, a radicalized, dangerous, tradition-defying force and, at the other, the so-called freedom to perpetuate patriarchal systems. These mixed messages both depend on and contribute to the much publicized fragmentation of feminism in America, a situation or climate that has itself earned a name: postfeminism.

The term *postfeminism* became media currency in the mid-1980s and, as the title of a 1986 *New York Times* op-ed piece illustrates, its definition has been problematic since its inception. Geneva Overholser explains in "What 'Post-Feminism' Really Means" that there are two schools of postfeminist thought: "The first holds that women went rampaging off to work only to discover that they were cheating home and family. The second holds that women went rampaging off to work only to discover that work wasn't so great after all" (A34). Susan Faludi treats the term similarly, as a fabricated historical period in which "women can be women again," as one of Faludi's interviewees in *Backlash* proclaims (199). Faludi contends that in the current backlash, feminism is depicted as the *cause* of women's social dissatisfaction. By examining media representation of the supposedly liberated, yet miserable woman to show how the press concocts these tales of blame, she reveals the covert political function of such representations—to further "the ends of a backlash against women's equality, simultaneously deflecting attention from the backlash's central role and recruiting women to attack their own cause" (xviii).[1]

Postfeminism is an equally problematic term in academic circles. In her analysis of popular films and television programs, Elspeth Probyn links postfeminism with "new traditionalism," showing how, for example, the representations of female characters in the television drama *thirtysomething* promote women's return to the safety and sanctity of the home. Probyn argues that in postfeminist discourse, feminism itself becomes the Other: "Feminism and feminist ideas are totally submerged—it is the word that cannot be said" (149).[2] Linnea S. Dietrich offers yet another definition of the term; she holds that postfeminism may mean that "everything is now post- something else" and that "feminism has been co-opted by postmodernism" (14). As scholars like Probyn and Dietrich show, the academic debate concerning the relationship between postmodernism and feminism is as energetic as that which waged in the popular press over *Thelma and Louise*. Theorists such as Judith Butler, Jane Flax, Nancy Fraser, Donna Haraway, and Denise Riley argue for a destabilizing of both gender *and* sexual identities in keeping with the postmodern disruption of the Enlightenment conception of a coherent and unified self; other academic feminists argue with equal fervor that such a turn amounts to little more than feminism's suicide.[3] Susan Bordo describes what she sees as the self-defeating project of a postmodern feminism: "Where once the prime objects of academic feminist critique were the phallocentric narratives of our male-dominated disciplines, now feminist criticism has turned to its own narratives, finding them reductionist, totalizing, inadequately nuanced, valorizing of gender differences, unconsciously racist and elitist" (135).

Bordo suggests that the shift of emphasis from gender-focused criticism to investigations of the intersections of race, sexuality, and class *with* gender has effectively displaced gender as a fundamental category of analysis. "Like it or not," she warns, "in our present culture, our activities *are* coded as 'male' or 'female' and will function as such within the prevailing system of gender-power relations" (152). For Bordo, as for Faludi, postfeminism primarily represents a period of political and ideological backlash, one in which—as she suggests happens in postmodern evaluations of feminism—gender concerns are depicted as passé. Bordo turns to the 1920s to find a historical example of such rhetoric and she presents it, again, as a warning: " 'We're interested in people now—not men and women,' declared a Greenwich Village female literary group, proclaiming itself (in 1919) as 'post-feminist' " (152).[4] Bordo reiterates her caveat at the end of her essay: "The deconstruction of gender analytics, I fear, may be participating in a similar cultural moment of feminist fragmentation, coming around again" (153).

Feminism's fragmentation both in and out of the academy, though, is old news. In fact, the differing contextual and discursive guises in which postfeminism appears signal one element of this split—the oft-lamented gap between a street-smart feminism and its theorized, academized sister. While postfeminism is defined differently in the texts of academic and popular writers (and differently within those groups as well), parallels do exist: Faludi's claim that the press has manipulated women's perceptions of feminism and encouraged their dissociation from it echoes Bordo's claim regarding feminists who hop on the postmodern bandwagon, repledge allegiance to a host of poststructuralist fathers from Derrida to Foucault, and ultimately decry their own project, finding feminism's narratives reductionist, totalizing, and inadequately nuanced. The fear that destabilizing gender as a viable political identity may further weaken feminism itself occurs on both of these fronts. But this situation in and of itself could be called postmodern: as Andreas Huyssen claims, postmodernism "operates in a field of tension between tradition and innovation, conservation and renewal, mass culture and high art, in which the second terms are no longer automatically privileged over the first" (267). Huyssen's suggestion that a greater sense of movement exists in this postmodern period between the traditionally bifurcated spheres of academic and popular writing is evidenced by the parallel positioning of feminism in these discourses.

Tania Modleski blends popular and academic varieties of postfeminism when she describes what she calls "post-feminist criticism" in *Feminism without Women: Culture and Criticism in a "Postfeminist" Age*. She explains that her title "can mean the triumph either of a male feminist perspective that excludes women or of a feminist anti-essentialism so radical that every use of the term 'woman,' however 'provisionally' it is adopted, is disallowed" (15). Like Bordo, Modleski distrusts feminist critics "doing" postmodern theory, but Modleski seeks to situate this critical trend within a backlash climate closer to Faludi's. For Modleski, postfeminist criticism appropriates feminist discourse in order to make it obsolete and, while sounding like Faludi, Modleski refers to the academic sphere rather than that of mass culture when she says that "what distinguishes this moment from other moments of backlash is the extent to which it has been carried out not *against* feminism but in its very name" (x).[5]

Modleski's definition of postfeminism as a feminist discourse appropriated for patriarchal ends will help to explain much of the masculinized response to *Thelma and Louise,* but the overall contradictory nature of the commentary on it is better explained in terms of postmodernism. Toril Moi and Alice Jardine both touch on the subject of postfeminism in a manner that illustrates the fragmented and contradictory way in which that term and feminism itself have recently been and currently are being represented in academic discourse.

The title of Toril Moi's "Feminism and Postmodernism: Recent Feminist Criticism in the United States" is ultimately misleading in its suggestion of an inclusive, historical survey of American critical trends. Moi focuses on just one text—Alice Jardine's *Gynesis: Configurations of Woman and Modernity*—and her argument becomes a contradictory discussion of Jardine's theoretical project. Moi is ambivalent about postmodernism and feminism residing together and, after acknowledging the tension in this relationship, notes that she "will use the term 'postfeminism' to cover the different configurations of feminism and postmodernism around today" (368). But before she does this, Moi backs up to "outline [her] own position in feminism" (368). Following Julia Kristeva's model, Moi sees feminism functioning in a matrix of conflicting discourses with ostensibly three contradictory and simultaneous impulses, working (1) to uphold difference, (2) to achieve equality (a move in opposition to the celebration of difference for its own sake), and (3) "to deconstruct sexualized binary thought" (369), the postmodern-poststructuralist turn which effectively explodes the first of these three aims.[6] "We must," Moi insists, "at once live out the contradictions of all three feminisms *and* agonistically take sides: simply sitting on the fence will never demolish patriarchy" (369).[7] She admits that political choices will sometimes be wrong but, using Jardine as her example, Moi argues that the dangers of a theoretically obscured, postfeminist posture are greater: "Some postfeminism seems to me not even specific enough to be [wrong], and, consequently, in its endlessly self-qualifying openness, it comes to display its own kind of closure" (371).

While Moi appears to position herself here in a kind of politicized opposition to the postfeminism she ascribes to Jardine, she fixes it as one of the three tenets she argues feminism must hold in solution; to "deconstruct binary sexualized thought" is, at least in spirit, to engage in a postmodern-feminist, or what Moi calls a postfeminist, critique. Moi's description of postfeminism *as* theory is deeply imbedded in her own feminist project; her stance clearly illustrates that feminism today is not shot through with contradiction but *founded* in it.[8]

In *Gynesis,* Jardine describes what she sees as the postfeminist turn in France, where the thrust has been to disrupt the master narrative of sexual identity, an Enlightenment concept (like that of the unified self) that postmodern theory deconstructs. Jardine does her own disrupting of feminist myth when she points out that the writers and theorists American feminists typically label "French feminists" have, with the exception of Luce Irigaray, denounced feminism. Jardine goes on to decenter feminism further, removing the possibility of the existence of any one definitive set of characteristics from which it can be recognized. In a footnote discussing the American tendency to outline and define, she explains: "What is important, [French theorists] might say, is not to decide who is or is not a feminist, but rather to examine how and why feminism may itself be problematic; is itself connected to larger theoretical issues; is not a natural given but a construction like all others. This kind of questioning does not have to be undertaken from a conservative position; it can in fact provide feminism's most radical moments" (231 n. 10).[9] Jardine believes that defining feminism is useless—"dictionary meanings are suffocating to say the least" (20)—but Moi calls this "a defeatist position for feminists. Definitions may be constraining: they are also enabling. Why else would women struggle for so long for their right to name the world? To name is to exercise power" (371). Moi advocates stance-taking and definition, yet her own definition of feminism (in which she grounds her political stance) deconstructs itself. For Jardine, there can be no more definitions, although she can still argue, with no irony apparently intended, that "feminist criticism is, *by definition,* based in very precise political struggles and practices and remains inseparable from them" (15, emphasis added). If *feminism* as a term or subject has moved into such an indeterminate position, what can *postfeminism,* a term conceived within the space of such hermeneutic decentering, possibly mean?

In fact, the destabilizing of feminism, illustrated in the intersection of Moi's and Jardine's texts—as well as the dissolution of belief that feminism can speak, with one voice, for all women—suggests that it is not a matter of whether or not feminism and postmodernism can coexist, but rather the fact that, as Craig Owen has argued, "women's insistence on difference and incommensurability may not only be compatible with, but also an instance of postmodern thought" (62). While defining postmodernism is a delicate task and certainly beyond the scope of this (or maybe any) essay, one of the characteristics Owen notes friend and foe alike commonly attribute to it is the pervasive sense of a "crisis of cultural authority" (57). If postmodernism not only decenters the subject, but posits the loss of cultural authority as one condition for this decentering—an event that results in the proliferation of voices—then feminism becomes not only a threat to patriarchal authority, but a site of its own cultural authority, itself a decentered subject with multiple and, as Moi and Jardine illustrate, discordant voices speaking it.[10] As Catharine Stimpson puts it, "postmodern writing . . . breaks open spaces within cultures, including feminist cultures" (238).

Following this, then, if feminism is a decentered, indeterminate subject, no longer capable of or confined to univocal speech, then *post*feminism, constructed in this postmodern age, must be a decidedly undecidable term. This is clearly evidenced in the need every writer who uses the term exhibits to define it and, more often than not, to do so with a string of potential meanings; as Dietrich puts it, "post-feminism can mean one of four things" (14). Postfeminism then appears to be not simply the point of intersection between postmodernism and feminism but the postmodernization of feminism, the decentered and discursive explosion within feminism's textual realm.[11] The reception of *Thelma and Louise* and its representations in the popular press illustrate this decentering. Elayne Rapping has remarked that "the furor surrounding the movie pleases me. Especially because it *isn't* an explicitly feminist movie, produced by politicos as an 'intervention' " (32). Popular conceptions of feminism like its academic definitions have proliferated to the point that context becomes the only way of "knowing" which definition or definitions is or are operative.

At the prochoice rally in Washington, D.C., in April 1992, purple and white sashes and buttons proclaimed that "Thelma and Louise were right" and that the wearer was a "Graduate of the Thelma and Louise Finishing School." Abortion and reproductive rights were never mentioned in *Thelma and Louise* and the film's leap into the world of political signification suggests a social hunger for female heroes. Timing also enabled such rewriting: as *Nation* film critic Stuart Klawans points out, " *Thelma and Louise* opened exactly one day after the Supreme Court handed down its decision in *Rust v. Sullivan,* restricting the medical advice a woman may receive if she's simultaneously pregnant and poor" (863).[12] In a similar vein, a cartoon published in October 1991 depicts a senator cowering in his car while Thelma and Louise smile, smoke, and point a gun at him; the caption notes that "the senator wasn't worried about women's reaction to his support for Clarence Thomas until he met Thelma and Louise waiting for him in the parking lot" (M. Smith). Again, the characters gain significance as guardians of women's rights or as representations of women's political anger.

But the use of *Thelma and Louise* by prochoice marchers displays a strange ambiguity: what exactly does it mean that "Thelma and Louise were right"? Right in understanding that there was and is no turning back? Right in that "we get what we settle for," as the truism Louise repeats throughout the film proclaims? Right to take the law into our own hands? All of these messages are extremely powerful given the context of the march in which, on this occasion, they appeared. Yet the idea of a "Thelma and Louise Finishing School" is especially ironic given the film's actual "finish," how the characters do "finish" themselves, as well as the "finish" Louise puts to the rapist's life. What kinds of action do such signals advocate?

The film was positioned as self-evidently—and therefore problematically— "feminist" in *Time* magazine's article "The War against Feminism" (9 March 1992), featuring a joint interview with Faludi and Gloria Steinem. The cover is depressing; both women, dressed in black, pose in a bleak room in a dark urban building. The cover image suggests that feminists are despairing, and its accompanying title—"Fighting the Backlash against Feminism"—evokes a confidence undone or even mocked by the pictorial representation that accompanies it. The article begins with commentary on the surprise hit film *The Hand That Rocks the Cradle,* the nanny horror story that, according to writer Nancy Gibbs, illustrates "that women who work and leave child rearing to others are courting disaster and had best hurry home" (50). The article includes a pictorial sidebar called "Backlash Stereotypes" featuring Rebecca De Mornay as the nanny, while its counterpart spread, "Feminist Images," includes Candice Bergen as television journalist Murphy Brown, a flexed Madonna, Roseanne, Jodie Foster accepting a Golden Globe award, and Susan Sarandon and Geena Davis as "the female buddies" Thelma and Louise (50–51). But the definition provided for these "feminist images" does not seem to fit the characters themselves; Thelma and Louise are not quite "successful, independent women who found new answers and a vital balance," especially given the promise invoked by the phrase "new answers" and that the "balance" the characters obtain at the edge of the Grand Canyon ends up being something other than "vital."[13] Such readings often contradict the film itself, and the contexts in which they appear complicate and emotionally conflate what appear to be self-consciously even-tempered descriptions of the film and its impact.

The cover for *Time* on 24 June, for instance, boasts a sanitized, almost angelic depiction of the two actresses, both smiling confidently and wearing matching spotless white blouses. The article's title promises a descriptive, rather than polemical, analysis of the *Thelma and Louise* phenomenon—"Gender Bender: Why *Thelma and Louise* Strikes a Nerve," it reads. Writer Richard Schickel calls the film "the most intriguing movie now in release" but typically adopts a detached tone in order to assume a more convincing rhetorical stance (56). He cites the passionate commentary of numerous critics, and then remarks: "Whole lot of heavy thinking going on out there. . . . Hard to believe that the occasion for this heated exercise in moral philosophy and sociological big-think is a modest and, at its most basic level, very enjoyable little movie called *Thelma and Louise,* which is so far a moderate commercial success" (52).[14] Schickel's tone is deceptive for several reasons: we know, for instance, that controversy does not always accompany commerical success, and exactly what constitutes a "little movie" is unclear, especially since *Thelma and Louise* runs a full and relatively long two hours and ten minutes. More important, Schickel's cultivated calm is undercut by the article's other visual images. The other story advertised on the cover does not even merit *Time*'s lead table of contents billing: nevertheless, a headline advertising a "Science" piece on volcanoes appears directly over the actresses' heads—"Volcanoes: Predicting Eruptions"— lending an interesting subtext to the article itself. Likewise, the image dominating the article's opening pages is that of the orange blaze of the exploding tanker. The *Thelma and Louise* article is also immediately preceded by a highly negative review of the revised and so-called politically correct Random House dictionary—Jesse Birnbaum's "Defining Womyn (and Others)." Schickel's attempt to avoid controversy and "keep things in perspective" is deftly undercut by the magazine's layout sensationalizing the film's content and response.

Cynthia Heimel also superficially attempts to minimize her response to the film but, again, context seems to defeat her purpose. In her *Village Voice* "Problem Lady" column, she humorously treats what she sees as an overreaction to the film; a disturbed reader asks, "Do I have to have an opinion about *Thelma and Louise?*" and notes that "because people refused to shut up about the ending even before the goddamned movie came out . . . by the time I finally saw it I might as well have had electrodes attached to my head I was monitoring my feelings so closely." Problem Lady gives several reasons why "everyone's making such a fuss about *Thelma and Louise,*" among them that "it's a really good movie" and "nobody can figure out why they haven't seen this movie before" except that "we're so used to seeing movies where the women play the love interests and get to say only these lines—'Honey, come to bed, it's late.' 'Honey, you've done all you could.'" The solution for her troubled reader comes couched in the form of another joke: "If someone tries to tell you that this movie is bad for feminism and that it provides terrible role models for women, remind them sweetly that men get to play all sorts of horribly complicated messes in movies whenever they want. Then pull out a gun and shoot them." The illustration that accompanies the piece shows two women in a T-Bird shooting at the erections of the cacti they pass. Heimel's joke moves into the ideological domain unenthusiastic critics argue the film occupies to the detriment of feminism—that is, an adoption and even promotion of such "masculinized" behaviors as smoking, thieving, drinking, and killing.

Shooting down or silencing (permanently or otherwise) one's debating opponent also effectively shuts down conversation; Heimel seems to do this again in her "Women" column for the *Playboy* issue of November 1991, where she describes her recent appearance on the "Sally Jessy Raphael Show." "Before they introduced me," she writes, "they showed a clip of *Thelma and Louise,* which I think is a terrific movie, but when people say it's a meaningful feminist tract, I go to sleep" ("Me and the Men's Movement"). This kind of reluctance to discuss the film in the terms in which media discourse insists on putting it acts as a dismissal, intentional or not, of the profound reaction people have had to it. But Heimel's response here is precipitated by the way in which *Thelma and Louise* was utilized in the context in which Heimel appeared—a talk show focusing on the men's movement. In part, Heimel's unwillingness to refer to the movie as "a meaningful feminist tract" must be related to the way in which the show's directors appropriated it to define and control her role in the show. She remarks that "on the television screen, beneath my name, it said something like, THINKS MEN JUST WANT TO CONTROL WOMEN. Which was not what I said at all." Heimel notes that she frequently agreed with the viewpoints of her "opponent" but that "whenever I stopped arguing, the producer of the show waved her hands at me in frustration" ("Me and the Men's Movement").

Representations of *Thelma and Louise,* though, were not limited to texts directly addressing it. Articles and interviews featuring the actresses playing these roles—Geena Davis and Susan Sarandon—were as important to the film's overall marketing as they were to the politicized and critical discourse surrounding it. For instance, Ralph Novak in his review for *People* magazine calls *Thelma and Louise* a "female chauvinist sow of a film" and claims that "the music and banter suggest a couple of good ole gals on a lark; the content suggests two self-absorbed, irresponsible, worthless people" (19). Nevertheless, *People* featured Geena Davis on its cover two weeks later. The cover calls her a "road warrior," "feisty," and "fresh," but the image accompanying these remarks is a shot of Davis resembling, more than anyone else, Marilyn Monroe. In the article itself, writer Jim Jerome uses the film plot to illustrate Davis's own life: she ended her three-year marriage to actor Jeff Goldblum "right after *Thelma* wrapped, though she insists the timing is coincidental and not a case of Thelmafying her own life" (92). The prose molds Davis into her rebellious character while the photos that dress it focus on the doll-like nature of her other roles—leaning girlishly into William Hurt's arms in a scene from *The Accidental Tourist,* staring bug-eyed at her own hand in *Beetlejuice,* dressed in a satin prom dress for the 1989 Oscar award ceremony with Goldblum, and posing as a mannequin during her model days. The cutline for the final image of Davis, feet up and lounging at her desk, reads: "Says actor-producer Davis: 'I wish there were all these incredibly fabulous parts waiting around' " (96). The article effectively infantilizes Davis and employs the cartoonish quality of the Thelma character to do so. It is suggested that women like Davis/Thelma who remember to pledge allegiance to masculine desire, even if only in how they physically represent themselves, can be "feminist" in an endearing and harmless way.

Interviews with Susan Sarandon capitalized on her role as the older, wiser Louise. *Parade* magazine's cover of 1 March 1992 sports a green-satined Sarandon clutching long red flowers and carries the titillating title, "The Consuming Passion of Susan Sarandon"; writer Ovid Demaris defines that passion in the internal title: "Most of All, the Children Matter." Throughout the piece, Demaris emphasizes the domesticity of Sarandon's life: the first sentence explains how, "dressed in casual gray slacks, Susan Sarandon—the red-haired, gun-toting Louise of *Thelma and Louise*—was doing nothing more dangerous that buttering a slice of toast" (4). Demaris goes on to depict Sarandon's political interests as stemming from her predominant role as a mother—differentiating herself from Jane Fonda, Sarandon is quoted as saying "as an American and a mother, it's part of my job to question the government, to try to protect the future of my children"—and as being another item on her domestic shopping list: "When she's not out making a film, Sarandon and her family occupy a modest apartment in New York's Greenwich Village, where, she said, she tried to pursue a 'normal' life—picking up her daughter at school, shopping at supermarkets, attending PTA meetings. Then there are the causes" (4). For Demaris and the audience she writes for, normal women are Acme-shopping, PTA-attending moms.

The issue of *Redbook* for April 1992 shows Sarandon squatting, barefoot, one elbow on one knee, with the headline "Pregnant at 45" running directly across her abdomen. The internal title, however, reads, "Susan Sarandon: Rebel with 100 Causes," while the motivation behind her rebellion continues to depend on the traditionally feminized identities of mother and alluring lover: "At 45, she's pregnant with her third child—good news indeed for all women worrying about how many ticks the old biological clock actually has. She is not married. And her lover, actor Tim Robbins, is younger than she is. . . . Single women rejoice: The field is wide open. The message here is that you can find enduring love with a man who was still in kindergarten by the time you got to college" (Laskas 80). Like Demaris, *Redbook* writer Jeanne Marie Laskas contends that "despite her enormous success in movies . . . you get the clear sense that Sarandon's number-one priority is her kids" (82). The tone of the first three pages of the interview, though, changes abruptly on the fourth and follow-up page in which Laskas notes that "something feels strange. I figure it out. She hasn't smiled once" (120). From that point on, Sarandon's interest in politics is highlighted—almost to the dismay, one senses, of the writer: "On the subject of paying her debt to the world, Sarandon gets excited. Worked up. . . . Forget the boy talk, the girl talk, the gossip, the movies, love, marriage, parents, the Oscars" (120).

While concentrating on politics in the pages buried in the final and photo-less segment of the piece, Laskas also depicts Sarandon as extremely disorganized (via the image of her messy and overflowing appointment book), insecure (the last lines contain Sarandon's plea to "please make me sound articulate"), and rebellious (Laskas quotes Davis, who describes her costar as "crazy, strong, and outspoken—a real troublemaker") (121). Laskas's Sarandon becomes a conflation of the representations of the feminist and "traditional woman": someone whose politics depends on the need to improve the world for her children; whose energy and passion are admirable, but without clear focus; who must hide her political anxieties behind a happier countenance; and who will, despite the admission that she says what she feels and is "strong," be described as a "troublemaker."[15] While these periodicals obviously featured Davis and Sarandon to cash in on the *Thelma and Louise* hype, their writers also carefully disarm the political possibilities of the characters (the same exploited by prochoice marchers and political cartoonists) by depicting Davis's demeanor as jejune and doll-like and Sarandon's politics as domesticated and somewhat chaotic. Highlighting Sarandon's pregnancy and attitudes toward mothering emphasizes the dominant position mothering does (or should) play in even the most nontraditional woman's life. These representations serve to diffuse the kind of folk-hero status the characters attained for popular brands of feminism and to reposition their value within more traditional and domestic confines.

One of the most passionate areas of response to the film sprang from the ranks of male writers. *Playboy*'s "Men" columnist, Asa Baber, and *U.S. News and World Report*'s John Leo provide good examples of male-authored postfeminist criticism as Faludi and Modleski define it. Faludi's notion of a postfeminism that is prefeminist in its implications is best characterized by Baber, who discusses what he sees as the dangerous implications of the film in his *Playboy* column entitled "Guerilla Feminism." Baber claims there that *Thelma and Louise* "trashes men" and that "a strong element of antimale sexism runs through it." He cites a "Phil Donahue Show" episode of uncertain date in which a woman who had pulled a gun on her husband claims she did so because "he needed killing." "The most primitive message behind *Thelma and Louise,*" Baber argues, "is that a lot of men need killing these days. This is an acceptable, even amusing proposition in our contemporary society. And I suggest that, as men, we had better be alert to it." Unlike Modleski or Bordo, Baber does not believe ours to be a postfeminist time. He claims that the "sexist" story of *Thelma and Louise* "faithfully represents our era, a time when feminists can bask in the glory of their increasingly harsh sexism toward men—and even win Oscar nominations for it" ("Guerilla"). The rest of the stories in this issue of *Playboy,* though, serve to counter Baber's fear: one of the first of Camille Paglia's notorious interviews appears in it, as well as the annual spread of "Girls of the Big Ten."

Baber does not neglect the rape issue addressed in the film, mentioning in passing that his reader "might ask what signals Thelma is sending Harlan with her behavior, since she has been dancing and drinking and flirting openly with him for some time" ("Guerilla"). He discusses acquaintance rape in greater detail in the preceding issue of *Playboy,* in which he devotes his column to what he calls the "cultural lynching" of William Kennedy Smith. "Remember this, good reader, and conduct yourself accordingly," he says, "all it takes to lynch a man these days is the *accusation* of rape. . . . A lynch mob could be just outside your door. In William Kennedy Smith's case, a lynch mob has already placed a rope around his neck" ("Cultural Lynching"). *Time*'s article on *Thelma and Louise* enacts its own dismissal of this topic; the article features pictures of four of the movie's male characters in its "Rogues' Gallery." One face, however, is conspicuously absent—that of Harlan, the rapist and catalyst for the film's central action (Schickel 54).

Date rape, in fact, was the cover story for *Time* on 3 June 1991, and the cover illustration differs significantly from that used for the *Thelma and Louise* issue, featuring as it does a petulant, pouting Lolita as the representative victim (Gibbs, "When Is It Rape?"). (The article is problematic itself, using opinion polls to determine the boundaries of what is or is not considered date rape.) The *Thelma and Louise* issue reembraces this image and simultaneously revises it: the cover is reproduced in the Letters section, positioned under an enlarged, single-sentence letter that reads simply, "Rape is a violent abuse of power" (*Time*, 24 June 1991, 4). While it is presumptuous to treat this revision as a result of the overall favorable write-up of the film that follows, the conflation of the cover's avenging angels with the image of the date rape victim gives her an anger she initially lacks.

John Leo, too, reviewed the film after his fashion; in his "On Society" columns for 1991 and early 1992, he hit all the press panic topics—political correctness, feminism, sexism, and multiculturalism. Leo was careful, however, to enlist female voices in his critique of American feminism; he attacked NOW and academic feminism via Sally Quinn's *Washington Post* article "Who Killed Feminism?" in which she argues that "many women have come to see the feminist movement as anti-male, anti-child, anti-family, anti-feminine" (Leo, "The Trouble"). Leo's move to enlist Quinn, whom he calls "one of the best-read reporters the *Post* has ever had," in his own feminist slashing is not an appropriation of feminism per se, but an appropriation of a woman who herself indicts feminism on the grounds of women's misery. The cartoon image that accompanies the article is also telling; an angry, short-haired woman beats her fists on a lectern and yells into a microphone, while another equally angry, short-haired woman in the audience remains to listen to her. A chair is knocked over to indicate, presumably, evidence of the anger that caused the more main-stream, apparently less feminist (and, by implication, more feminine) audience members to leave, and a woman clutching the hand of her daughter storms off into the background. The speaker in the cartoon has seized the power of both public speech and public position, the lectern microphone acting as the phallic representation of that power.[16] While Leo appears to address primarily NOW's inadequate representation of its constituency, his anger peaks when he reaches the subject of academic feminists such as are implied by the women in the cartoon. In what he calls the "secular convents of feminist-studies," he claims that "abstruse man-hating and galloping heterophobia are absolutely routine" and argues that these attitudes "are not much help to real-world women, who . . . might want to get married sometime." Leo again uses Quinn as his mouthpiece to end his article, an interesting example of the veiled phallus, the power that speaks without showing itself. Certainly Leo shows himself here, but his use of Quinn permits him a new kind of gender authority; the cliché of hiding behind his mother's skirts takes on new meaning.

Leo had used this strategy before when he executed his diatribe against *Thelma and Louise*. He begins: "A close friend called to say that *Thelma and Louise,* the new female-buddy car-chase movie, is a very disturbing film and I must write about it immediately. Since this friend is no faintheart but a strong and extremely successful woman in the movie business, I saw the film and pronounce her correct, as usual" ("Toxic Feminism"). The authority Leo grants himself to speak on women's behalf again appears to stem from a woman; however, this is a site in which women (or anyone other than Leo, for that matter) cannot speak. Leo gets his shot at academic feminism—a metaphor, it begins to seem, for women who speak on their *own* behalf—when he claims that the film's "real landscape" is not the Southwest, but "that of writer Andrea Dworkin and the most alienated radical feminists." For Leo, the film moves from Dworkin to "a Mussolini speech," "an explicit fascist theme," as the women gain power through violence. Leo's text describes this message as "the bleakest form of feminism," "cynical propaganda," and likens the end to "the end of a Dworkin essay . . . [when] the patriarchy will crush all women who resist or simply try to live their own lives" ("Toxic Feminism"). The cartoon image that accompanies this piece parodies the kind of power Leo claims is overdone in the film: playing with the phallic images of director Ridley Scott's trucks, the cartoon depicts two massive semis facing a tiny T-Bird on a ridiculously steep incline while another truck covers the diminutive car's back. The difference in power is indeed absurd and the cartoon effectively literalizes the power imbalance Leo insists is inoperative.

While Leo appropriates the voices of women to decry various brands of feminism, spokesmen for the men's movement depend on the appropriation of feminist discourse to defend what many critics affirm is simply a reassertion of male control and patriarchal authority.[17] The same day *Thelma and Louise* appeared on the cover of *Time, Newsweek* featured a man in a tie, drum in hand, with the headline: "What Do Men Really Want? Now They Have a Movement of Their Own." This piece acknowledges and even anticipates feminist response to the men's movement: on the practice of using a "talking stick" to designate who has the floor, writer Jerry Adler notes that "it's not hard to imagine how women, to whom the easy exchange of intimacies comes naturally, must view this quaint masculine practice: Aha, men are finally learning to talk about their feelings, but they have to hold a *stick* to do it" (49). But the article also offers more problematic assertions. Concerning the "wildman" element of the movement, Adler contends that "the men's movement also has a more profound strain, a romantic assertion of primitive masculinity in all its innocent strength and virtue" (49). He also uses feminist rhetoric to build analogies between the movements, arguing that "society turned [white males] into 'success objects' valued only for their salaries—a complementary form of oppression to that which values women only as 'sex objects' " (51). This is the kind of appropriation of feminist terminology for something other than feminist uses that Modleski calls "postfeminist criticism."

Cartoonist Jules Feiffer parodies how this kind of postfeminist stance—men criticizing the film because it is not adequately feminist—mobilizes the appropriation of feminist discourse in order to reseat patriarchal control. The cartoon shows two men interrogating a woman about her favorable response to the film, which they condemn via feminist jargon: "You *love* feminist agitprop used as an excuse for anti-male violence? . . . You *love* two amoral women on a crime spree who idealize smoking, drunkeness and man-hating? . . . That a woman of your intelligence should love such slime!" (Feiffer). By the end of the strip, they have turned to physical violence and, in a moment allusive of *The Silence of the Lambs,* they dispassionately note that they have strangled the woman and wonder if they should "skin her."

Obviously, the *Thelma and Louise* fan in Feiffer's cartoon broke an important rule and it is, in fact, the protagonists' relationship to the law that structures the film's narrative. This relationship is not only problematically represented in the film, but again problematized in its re-representation in the press. Comedian Paula Poundstone claimed that she was angry when reviewers insisted on calling the characters "feminists"—they were, she reminded her audience, criminals. The equation between the two is significant, and the film focuses on what can happen when women defy the law, a "law" consistently represented as male in the shape of FBI agents, state troopers, and even Harvey Keitel's paternalistic cop. But the form of power the women claim in order to exist outside of this law is also male-identified—Thelma's .38 is the phallic agent that enables and signifies both women's socially transgressive power. It is also the image most frequently exploited by the press in its pictorial representation of the movie.

Heimel's "Problem Lady" column uses, as I noted earlier, a drawing of the women in the T-Bird shooting, presumably, the phalluses that protrude from the masculinized cacti they pass. The *Village Voice* of 16 July 1991 shows a still of Thelma with the "Nazi" state trooper she locks in his trunk; the article is even titled "Guns N' Poses" (Dargis). The same shot appears in a *New York Times* Arts and Leisure article entitled "Give the Gentleman a Puppy, and Get the Lady a Gun" (21 July 1991), referring to the "role reversals" that proliferated in that summer's movies, notably *Regarding Henry, City Slickers, Terminator 2, V. I. Warshawski,* and *Thelma and Louise* (Maslin). The same scene is pictured again in the table of contents for the *Thelma and Louise* issue of *Time,* and in *Newsweek*'s review of the film in its issue of 27 May, a picture of Louise heads the piece, the state trooper's gun she has stolen held at crotch level. The caption reads, ironically, "Flowering with every felony: Sarandon," describing the masculinized transformation Sarandon's character undergoes in terms of the oddly feminized "flowering" (Neveu). An interview with screenplay writer Khouri shows Sarandon and Davis wielding their weapons, while an adjacent shot frames Khouri in passionate speech, both hands in fists (Rohter). All of these images reinforce that the point of greatest interest for *Thelma and Louise* respondents is the power the women obtain—a power consistently represented as phallic and masculinized.

The film is, of course, filled with phallic images—the tanker, the cacti, the spraying crop duster, the almost absurdly abundant sprinklers and hoses—but the gun, as its re-representation in the press illustrates, is the signifier for the phallus, a transcendental, highly desired but ultimately unattainable power. According to Jane Gallop, "the penis is what men have and women do not; the phallus is the attribute of power which neither men nor women have. But as long as the attribute of power is a phallus which can only have meaning by referring to and being confused with a penis, this confusion will support a structure in which it seems reasonable that men have power and women do not" (*Thinking through the Body* 127).[18] *Thelma and Louise* does not, I think, attempt to sermonize on the moral possibilities for power but instead traces how power may be gained and lost, all the while reminding us that, at least in the world of feature film, power remains male-coded. The scene in which Louise shoots Harlan, the roadhouse rapist, and assumes that power for herself emphasizes the sexualized transfer of this event. Louise shoots and Harlan's body blows back over the car where he rapes Thelma. The image of his un-zipped fly dominates the final frame of that shot, the camera then shifting focus to the gun in Louise's shaking hand. As Thelma drives away from the scene, Louise stares at the gun where it ironically appears—in *her* lap. The final scene includes an extended shot of gun after gun being loaded by the numerous and anonymous hands of the state trooper army, the sound of rifles "cocking" mythically echoed. The power the women have usurped, represented by the exploding phalluses they now themselves load with "cocky" assurance, is hor-rifically returned to its "rightful" owners in this final scene. "All that for us," Louise says, amazed, we assume, at how dangerous she now understands they have become.[19]

When the makers of *Thelma and Louise* opted for their soaring ending, they opened a space not merely fantastic, but hermeneutic, making way for a host of readings that would signify as much about feminism in our historical moment as it would about one summer film. Just as the Thunderbird made both its first and final flight, so postfeminism is the proclaimed finish of something that has simultaneously been reaffirmed, re-created. One point that becomes very clear in a survey such as mine is how marketable feminism is in the world of mass publishing today. And it is of such interest in part because it is the site of vigorous and endless redefinition.

Even the attention paid to feminism by antifeminist writers like Leo and Baber indicates how such fragmentation does not necessarily point to the weakening of the feminist project. I would suggest, rather, that it indicates the *power* of such discourse—one does not appropriate for one's political uses dis-cursive strategies that are ineffectual or passé. Of course, such appropriation necessitates their continual critique by feminist writers, but the presence of such antifeminist criticism, as is evident in many of the texts generated by *Thelma and Louise,* must be seen as a response to something perceived as quite threatening.

The issue of power as a male-coded entity became the most important popular issue to emerge from the published *Thelma and Louise* debate; while Ridley Scott's phallic symbols may be read as both reminder and parody, the question of power's configuration remains at the heart of current feminist theoretical debate. Moves to question origins overall may constitute, as Alice Jardine claims, "feminism's most radical moments" (21). The discursive space *Thelma and Louise* created illustrates just such a desire, and one not restricted to the academy: the film promoted the desire to question the meaning of "feminism" itself, to make it signify differently and in more ways than it has and to contribute to the growing conversation that assures us that the one thing postfeminism cannot mean is feminism's extinction.

Notes

I would like to thank Michael Bernard-Donals, Ellen Gardiner, Lynda Goldstein, and Devoney Looser for their editorial suggestions; William Albright and Jo Searls also directed me to many helpful texts. Earlier versions of this essay were presented at the 1992 annual meeting of the Popular Culture Association and as part of the Interdisciplinary Lecturers Series at the Mississippi State University in October 1992.

1. Faludi's claims are clearly demonstrated in Nicholas Davidson's *Failure of Feminism* (1988). Among other things, Davidson writes that "women's rights are too important to be left to feminists. Indeed, gender issues are too important to be left to women" (1). He includes an appendix called "Countering Feminist Verbal Tactics" and composed of entries such as "Compliments to Avoid," "Arguing in Front of a Group," and a piece on conversational techniques, "The Tactic of Outrage," that reads like a parody of Gloria Steinem's "Men and Women Talking." One entry, " 'Sex Objects,' " begins: "One handy perennial is the claim that 'men see women as sex objects.' Of *course* they do. What sort of woman would not want men to see her as a sex object?" (347). Davidson's text shows us a facet of postfeminism that has no interesting contradictions; it is simply a move to a prefeminist time.

2. In Probyn's terms, the *Thelma and Louise* debate cannot be considered postfeminist; that the film's makers and promoters declined to describe it in feminist terms, however, places it firmly within postfeminism. Screenplay writer Callie Khouri tried to weaken the link between the film and any kind of political project: "There's so much talk about whether it's a feminist screenplay," she says in a *New York Times* interview, "whether it's a male-bashing movie. It's none of those things. I am a feminist, so clearly it is going to have my point of view. But this is a movie about outlaws, and it's not fair to judge it in terms of feminism" (Rohter). In *Time,* Khouri claimed that the film was not a "propaganda tool. . . . This is an adventure film. It's a film about women outlaws. People should just relax" (Simpson 55). MGM notes on most of the stills in its promotional packet that the film depicts "two best friends whose weekend getaway unexpectedly takes them on an adventurous, often humorous race against time." It is difficult to ascertain the studio's relationship to the reported controversy over *Thelma and Louise,* but all reports from MGM, including Khouri's interviews, add fuel to the press fire by denying the movie's relationship—whatever it may be—to feminism.

3. Theoretical commentary on feminism and postmodernism proliferates daily. A good introduction to many of the voices in this discussion is *Feminism/Postmodernism,*

edited by Linda J. Nicholson. Some of the individually authored texts commonly referred to are: Judith Butler, *Gender Trouble: Feminism and the Subversion of Identity;* Nancy Fraser, *Unruly Practices: Power, Discourse and Gender in Contemporary Social Theory;* Donna Haraway, *Simians, Cyborgs and Women: The Reinvention of Nature;* Denise Riley, *"Am I That Name?" Feminism and the Category of "Women" in History.*

4. Faludi notes that "postfeminist sentiments first surfaced, not in the 1980s media, but in the 1920s press" (50).

5. Modleski pays particular attention to male critics such as Stanley Cavell who explore feminist practices and male appropriations of traditionally feminized roles in popular texts—for instance, the three male "mothers" of *Three Men and a Baby* (see Modleski 8–13, 61–111).

6. See Kristeva, "Women's Time," and Moi's own footnote in the essay, in which she explains the difference between Kristeva's perception of these three "spaces" and her own view (376 n. 6).

7. This is a common theme in feminist-postmodern writing; see Riley, *"Am I That Name?"* (96–114), for a similar discussion.

8. Jardine aligns Kristeva with the "anti- and/or post-feminist" writers in France and explains postfeminism as the theoretical result of poststructuralist thought in France: "Feminism, as a concept, inherited from the humanist and rationalist eighteenth century, is traditionally about a group of human beings in history whose identity is defined by that history's representation of sexual decidability. And every term of that definition has been put into question by contemporary French thought" (20–21). See Jardine (19–22) for an overview of the problems with so-called French feminism and Paul Smith, *Decentering the Subject,* for his critique of Kristeva and of Moi and Jardine (118–32, 133–52).

9. Butler, too, argues that this is politically promising: "To deconstruct the subject of feminism is not, then, to censure its usage, but, on the contrary, to release the term into a future of multiple significations, to emancipate it from the maternal or racialist ontologies to which it has been restricted, and to give it play as a site where unanticipated meanings might come to bear" ("Contingent" 16).

10. Judith Butler and Joan W. Scott explain that this is one of the central questions addressed in their anthology *Feminists Theorize the Political:* "How do we theorize the split or multiple 'subject' of feminism?" (xv).

11. Patricia S. Mann calls postfeminism "the postmodern offspring of feminism" (2), but sees the term both as reflective of the shift in power relations between men and women, beginning "with the historic end of amazingly enduring normative identification of humanity with men and masculinity" (2), and as descriptive of a contemporary feminist agency—"regardless of how various commentators have used the term, feminists should appropriate it to announce the advent of a significantly different stage of gendered social conflicts and changes. Gender is no longer a narrow ideological set of issues in a postfeminist age; rather, it is a prominent site of change in everyone's life" (213 n. 3). Rather than read the responses to the film as I do, as evidence of what I call a postmodernization of feminism itself, Mann reads *Thelma and Louise* as a "postfeminist frontier parable" (209). She argues that "the film is about more than a reversal of roles; it is about the devolution of patriarchal forms of agency, and about women's budding sense of their own possibilities for action. It might be a classic road movie, but for

the fact that when women go on a journey of self-discovery today there are threatening ramifications for men, whose sense of sexual and social agency has been built upon relationships to women who could not act on their own behalf. As women seize the postfeminist moment, claiming new desires and insisting that they themselves, as well as their desires, be recognized by men, male agency is undermined insofar as it adheres to traditional forms" (211). For more on *Thelma and Louise* as a politicized, postfeminist text, see Mann (208–12).

12. While noting that, in "real life," women's bodies are in chains, Klawans flatly describes the characters' "images being free on the screen," omitting what has to happen to those bodies to keep them out of the somewhat more literal chains with which they are threatened throughout the film (864). Likewise, his remark that "the lite feminist fizz you get from [the film] is just enough to be pleasant without seeming pretentious" clearly limits the shape the film can take to be politically effective (863).

13. The desire to imagine that the characters survived was frequently expressed by people I spoke to who had seen the film (including my father) and became the basis for the comic exchange Sarandon and Davis used in their award presentation at the 1992 Oscars.

14. Schickel describes *Thelma and Louise* as a picture with "a curiously unselfconscious manner about it, an air of not being completely aware of its own subtexts or largest intentions, of being innocently open to interpretation, appropriate and otherwise" (52). Films like this, argues Schickel, "tend to serve as expressions of the values or confusions jangling around in their society, or occasionally as springboards for earnest discussions of them" (53). John Fiske feminizes and festishizes the film as a sensuous, beckoning, and fertile producerly text, which he claims "offers itself up to popular production; it exposes, however reluctantly, the vulnerabilities, limitations, and weaknesses of its preferred meanings; it contains, while attempting to repress them, voices that contradict the ones it prefers; it has loose ends that escape its control, its meanings exceed its own power to discipline them, its gaps are wide enough for whole new texts to be produced in them—it is, in a very real sense, beyond its own control" (104). Schickel seems to duplicate this kind of discourse when he highlights the film's "innocent" lack of self-awareness. Despite the attempt to be descriptive in an "objective" way, both Fiske and Schickel end up refeminizing the (desired) object of their texts via a masculinized discourse.

15. In ther book *The Post-Feminist Hollywood Actress: Biographies and Filmographies of Stars Born after 1939* (1990), Kerry Segrave and Linda Martin "date the beginning of modern feminism from the publication of Betty Friedan's *The Feminist Mystique* in 1963," postfeminism being, then, the period after feminism "came of age" (vii). Their postfeminist actresses are women "who would have been in their early twenties or younger when women's liberation first became an issue in the United States" (vii); Susan Sarandon is one of these actresses. Segrave and Martin seek confirmation that the roles women were offered between 1964 and the "middle 1980s" remained, overall, as limited as they had been "before feminism." The entry on Sarandon somewhat predictably focuses on the frequency with which she was required to do nude scenes (in *Atlantic City*, which "marked the high point of Sarandon's career," she was "nude again" [64]), her sex symbol status (in 1980, *Playboy* "awarded her the accolade 'Best Breasts of the Summer'" [64]), and her ambivalence with the profession,

spurred, or so Segrave and Martin suggest, by her political activism. See Segrave and Martin (61–68).

16. In "The Ladies' Man," Jane Gallop describes the "phallic enjoyment" she argues Lacan received from his lectures (34). See Gallop, *Daughter's Seduction* (33–42).

17. One of these critics is Carol Bly; see her "Charismatic Men's Movement" (6).

18. For more of Gallop's ideas on the phallus as a concept, see *Reading Lacan* (133–56), *Daughter's Seduction* (15–32), and the essay that her writings critique, Lacan, "The Signification of the Phallus" (281–91).

19. It is this final loss of power that suggests for me an allusion to a line from a Beach Boys' tune: "And we'll have fun, fun, fun till Daddy takes the T-Bird away."

Works Cited

Adler, Jerry. "Drums, Sweat and Tears." *Newsweek* (24 June 1991): 46–51.

Baber, Asa. "A Cultural Lynching." *Playboy* (September 1991): 41.

——. "Guerilla Feminism." *Playboy* (October 1991): 45.

Birnbaum, Jesse. "Defining Womyn (and Others)." *Time* (24 June 1991): 51.

Bly, Carol. "The Charismatic Men's Movement: Warrior Wannabes, Unconscious Deals, and Psychological Booty." *Omni* (March 1992): 6.

Bordo, Susan. "Feminism, Postmodernism, and Gender-Skepticism." *Feminism/Postmodernism.* Ed. Linda J. Nicholson. New York: Routledge, 1990: 133–56.

Butler, Judith. "Contingent Foundations: Feminism and the Question of 'Postmodernism.'" *Feminists Theorize the Political.* Ed. Judith Butler and Joan W. Scott. New York: Routledge, 1992: 3–21.

——. *Gender Trouble: Feminism and the Subversion of Identity.* New York: Routledge, 1990.

Butler, Judith, and Joan W. Scott, eds. *Feminists Theorize the Political.* New York: Routledge, 1992.

Dargis, Manohla. "Guns 'N Poses." *Village Voice* (16 July 1991): 22.

Davidson, Nicholas. *The Failure of Feminism.* Buffalo: Prometheus Books, 1987.

Demaris, Ovid. "Most of All, the Children Matter." *Parade* (1 March 1992): 4–5.

Dietrich, Linnea S. "Feminism and the Post-Feminism Era." *Art and Academe* 3.2 (1991): 14–23.

Faludi, Susan. *Backlash: The Undeclared War against American Women.* New York: Crown, 1991.

Feiffer, Jules. "Feiffer." *Village Voice* (25 June 1991): 5.

Fiske, John. *Understanding Popular Culture.* Boston: Unwin Hyman, 1989.

Fraser, Nancy. *Unruly Practices: Power, Discourse and Gender in Contemporary Social Theory.* Minneapolis: University of Minnesota Press, 1989.

Gallop, Jane. *The Daughter's Seduction: Feminism and Psychoanalysis.* Ithaca: Cornell University Press, 1982.

——. *Reading Lacan.* Ithaca: Cornell University Press, 1985.

——. *Thinking through the Body.* New York: Columbia University Press, 1988.

Gibbs, Nancy. "The War against Feminism." *Time* (9 March 1992): 50–57.

——. "When Is It Rape?" *Time* (3 June 1991): 48–55.

Haraway, Donna. *Simians, Cyborgs and Women: The Reinvention of Nature.* New York: Routledge, 1991.

Heimel, Cynthia. "Me and the Men's Movement." *Playboy* (November 1991): 42.

——. "Problem Lady." *Village Voice* (9 July 1991): 37.

Huyssen, Andreas. "Mapping the Postmodern." *Feminism/Postmodernism.* Ed. Linda J. Nicholson. New York: Routledge, 1990: 234–77.

Jardine, Alice. *Gynesis: Configurations of Women and Modernity.* Ithaca: Cornell University Press, 1985.

Jerome, Jim. "Riding Shotgun." *People* (24 June 1991): 90–96.

Klawans, Stuart. "Films." *Nation* (24 June 1991): 862–64.

Kristeva, Julia. "Women's Time." Trans. Alice Jardine and Harry Blake. *The Kristeva Reader.* Ed. Toril Moi. Oxford: Basil Blackwell, 1986: 187–213.

Lacan, Jacques. *Ecrits: A Selection.* Trans. Alan Sheridan. New York: Norton, 1977.

Laskas, Jeanne Marie. "Susan Sarandon: Rebel with 100 Causes." *Redbook* (April 1992): 80–83.

Leo, John. "Toxic Feminism on the Big Screen." *U.S. News and World Report* (10 June 1991): 20.

——. "The Trouble with Feminism." *U.S. News and World Report* (10 February 1992): 19.

Mann, Patricia S. *Micro-Politics: Agency in a Postfeminist Era.* Minneapolis: University of Minnesota Press, 1994.

Maslin, Janet. "Give Him a Puppy, and Get the Lady a Gun." *New York Times* (21 July 1991): sect. 2: 1.

Modleski, Tania. *Feminism without Women: Culture and Criticism in a "Postfeminist" Age.* New York: Routledge, 1991.

Moi, Toril. "Feminism and Postmodernism: Recent Feminist Criticism in the United States." *British Feminist Thought: A Reader.* Ed. Terry Lovell. Oxford: Basil Blackwell, 1990: 367–76.

Neveu, Roland. Photograph of Susan Sarandon as Louise. *Newsweek* (27 May 1991): 59.

Nicholson, Linda, ed. *Feminism/Postmodernism.* New York: Routledge, 1990.

Novak, Ralph. "Picks and Pans: Screen." *People* (10 June 1991): 18–19.

Overholser, Geneva. "What 'Post-Feminism' Really Means." *New York Times* (19 September 1986): A34.

Owen, Craig. "The Discourse of Others: Feminists and Post-modernism." *The Anti-Aesthetic: Essays on Postmodern Culture.* Ed. Hal Foster. Seattle: Bay Press, 1985: 57–82.

Pathe Entertainment. Press packet for *Thelma and Louise.* Distributed by MGM/UA Distribution Co., 1991.

Probyn, Elspeth. "New Traditionalism and Post-feminism: TV Does the Home." *Screen* 31.2 (summer 1990): 147–59.

Rapping, Elayne. "Feminism Gets the Hollywood Treatment." *Cineaste* 18.4 (1992): 30–32.

Riley, Denise. *"Am I That Name?" Feminism and the Category of 'Women' in History.* Minneapolis: University of Minnesota Press, 1988.

Rohter, Larry. "The Third Woman of *Thelma and Louise*." *New York Times* (5 June 1991): C21.

Schickel, Richard. "Gender Bender." *Time* (24 June 1991): 52–57.

Segrave, Kerry, and Linda Martin. *The Post-Feminist Hollywood Actress: Biographies and Filmographies of Stars Born after 1939.* Jefferson, N.C.: McFarland and Co., 1990.

Simpson, Janice. "Moving into the Driver's Seat." *Time* (24 June 1991): 55.

Smith, Mike. Cartoon. *Citizen's Voice* [Wilkes-Barre, Pa.] (19 October 1991): 14.

Smith, Paul. *Discerning the Subject.* Minneapolis: University of Minnesota Press, 1988.

Stimpson, Catharine R. "Nancy Reagan Wears a Hat: Feminism and Its Cultural Consensus." *Critical Inquiry* 14 (winter 1988): 223–43.

"The Year That Was—1991." *U.S. News and World Report* (30 December 1991/6 January 1992): 100.

7

Habermas's Rational-Critical Sphere
and the Problem of Criteria

Patricia Roberts

A recurrent issue in the study of public discourse is whether a public sphere might be so constituted as to be both free and liberatory: free in the sense that it would be perfectly inclusive; liberatory in that it would enable participants to identify and critique coercion in institutions. Jürgen Habermas's lifelong project might best be understood as an attempt to define the characteristics of a sphere with both such qualities, as well as to argue the feasibility of attaining it. The recent translation of Habermas's early book, *The Structural Transformation of the Public Sphere,* is particularly important in this regard since it has been suggested that *Structural Transformation*—in which Habermas defines the concept of the rational-critical public sphere through a narration of its formation in the eighteenth century and transformation in the nineteenth—directly addresses the issue of the realism of Habermas's project of liberation through public discourse. Probably the most frequent criticism of Habermas's theoretical work is that it is too idealistic, that by making rational-critical debate simultaneously the goal and means—the definition of a free society and the method by which such a society is to be reached—Habermas has defined a paradise that we cannot enter. By describing a moment when the ideal public sphere was nearly realized, Habermas has shown that such a sphere is substantive and not merely ideal. The book thereby functions in two ways at once: first, it establishes the criteria by which the rational-critical public sphere can be defined; second, it provides an example when such a sphere was actually an ideal.

In this regard, much criticism of Habermas is slightly beside the point, in that he does not claim that the eighteenth-century philosophes created a perfectly inclusive realm of rational-critical discourse; they exemplify the reality of the goal, not the attainment of the state. He argues that, at least in theory, ideas were debated by anyone who chose to participate in the discussion by reading, writing, or speaking; he grants that, in practice, people were excluded on the basis of gender and class, "but as an idea it had become institutionalized and thereby stated as an objective claim. If not realized, it was at least consequential" (*Structural Transformation* 36). Because it was genuinely consequential, one cannot claim that it was merely an ideal; because it was not fully achieved, one cannot claim that it was a fact. It remains, therefore, in the borderland of substantive project.

Thus the significance of Habermas's history of the public sphere is that it poses and attempts to answer a question which is, as Calhoun says, crucial for democratic theory: "What are the social conditions, he asks, for a rational-critical debate about public issues conducted by private persons willing to let arguments and not statuses determine decisions? This is an inquiry at once into normative ideals and actual history" (1). The double level of the inquiry must be emphasized—normative ideals and actual history—because any critique on one level alone is simply inadequate. The question of actual history has been debated most extensively (see, for example, Saccamano), while the question of normative claims has been less noted. Since even Habermas admits that the philosophes did not actualize a perfectly inclusive public sphere, the normative claim question is at least as important as the empirical claims regarding history.

My argument is more concerned with the normative claims, but, like Habermas, I will draw on actual history to evaluate these claims. In one sense, my argument is fairly straightforward. It is my contention that, while Habermas's project is attractive in many ways, the definition of rational-critical debate implicit and explicit in the communicative ethics controversy does not and cannot define a sphere of discourse free of the constraints of institutionally constituted authority. I will make this argument in two ways. First, I will argue that the very way in which proponents of communicative ethics attempt to make a narrow form of dialectic—in the pre-Hegelian sense—the model for all public discourse is reliant on institutionally constituted authority and therefore undercuts the argument being made. Second, I will use the seventeenth-century American Puritans, who instituted a notoriously exclusive form of public discourse, to demonstrate that authority can have several masks and that Habermas's defense of the eighteenth-century philosophes applies equally well to the seventeenth-century American Puritans. Since the Puritans were oppressive, Habermas's defense is highly problematic, and, by implication, his criteria are inadequate. My intention is to suggest that, by trying to make dialectic the model for public discourse—which even the first theorists of dialectic said was impossible—Habermas has defined a self-consuming model; in the last section of the essay, I will argue that Habermas's well-intentioned project fails to define anything other than coercion as the basis of discourse for most forms of public disagreement.

In another sense, however, my argument is necessarily complicated by the nature of *Structural Transformation.* In addition to being a subtle reading—one that evades the traps of thinking in terms of theory *or* practice, public *or* private—*Structural Transformation* is an early work by a thinker who has shown an impressive flexibility of thought. Thus, using the definitions of that work to reflect on the consequences of his later theories is somewhat complicated. To clarify that complexity, it is necessary to begin with a brief explication of Habermas's argument in *Structural Transformation* and how it relates to his larger project, before discussing problems with the project.

Habermas's Rational-Critical Public Sphere

Habermas defines the rational-critical public sphere as having three identifying characteristics: first, it is a realm which, at least in theory, disregards status in favor of rationality; second, the discussion within such a realm is the domain of "common concern," including criticism of the governmental authority; third, the realm is perfectly inclusive (at least in principle) "for it always understood and found itself immersed within a more inclusive public of all private people, persons who—insofar as they were propertied and educated—as readers, listeners, and spectators could avail themselves via the market of the objects that were subject to discussion" (*Structural Transformation* 37). It is the first claim that has both led to the most controversy and remained more or less intact throughout Habermas's work (see, for example, "What Is Universal Pragmatics").

It is also that specific claim—that the rationality of the argument can be evaluated separate from the status of the person making it—which most distinguishes Habermas's project from other, somewhat similar, attempts to delineate a liberatory form of argumentation. Hannah Arendt, Wayne Booth, and Brian Vickers, for example, have each argued for the potential value of considering status and authority in public discourse. Like many thinkers in the humanist tradition in the history of rhetoric, they do not argue that authority is always right, but that the status of the speaker is not easily separable from the argument the speaker makes. Awareness of authority is not necessarily obedience to it, but the speaker's ethos is necessarily a part of argumentation.

Aristotle's handling of the concept of ethos is significant in this regard. One of the three modes of persuasion (the others being pathos and logos), it does not receive the alternately hostile and favorable treatment given pathos. Indeed, ethos—that is, the public presentation of self—is necessarily a part of the audience's evaluation of an argument; as Aristotle says, "the orator must not only try to make the argument [logos] of his speech demonstrative and worthy of belief; he must also make his own character look right" (*Rhetoric,* II, 1377b). With the exception of his work on dialectic, all of Aristotle's treatises favor ethos; it is because of Aristotle's concern with the social self that his theory of ethics has often been in disfavor. This sense of social constituency of self and self-knowledge inherent to Aristotle's ethics necessarily leads to a theory of ethics which emphasizes the contingent, contextual, or particular quality of normative statements. It is no surprise, then, that the neo-Aristotelian responses to the claims of a transcendental communicative ethics have centered on the issue of the possibility of a historically informed ethical universalism.[1] Instead of pursuing the question by trying to determine the ontological status of normative claims, however, it might be more productive to use Aristotle's divisions of realms of discourse in order to reflect on Habermas's project. That it is only in his work on dialectic that Aristotle attempts to describe a form of discourse which excludes ethos suggests that more attention might be paid to one aspect of Habermas's work on the public sphere—that it is an attempt (and not the first) to make dialectic, in the Aristotelian sense, the form of public discourse.[2]

Habermas has moved through various fields—psychoanalysis, linguistics, argumentation—to argue that rational argument has substantive ontological status; while such argumentation may be distorted by institutionally constituted status, authority, or coercion, discourse always already assumes that a rational argument is true. When using psychoanalysis as a model, Habermas pointed to the way that a true interpretation has a liberatory effect, while self-deception does not. More recently, he has moved to the work being done in linguistics and philosophy of language, especially that of Chomsky, Searle, and Austin, and he has argued that the rules Searle and Austin showed always operate in speech acts necessarily involve truth claims: "Truth claims are thus a type of validity claim built into the structure of possible speech in general. Truth is a universal validity claim; its universality is reflected in the double structure of speech" ("Universal Pragmatics" 52). Thus, Habermas argued, the possibility of rational redemption of a claim is not a norm imposed by a logocentric culture, but a claim implicit to any form of discourse involving assertions. According to Böhler, this argument has become the central, and most contested, contention in the communicative ethics controversy: "Every-thing rests upon the thesis *that the standard* of the pure capability of an argu-ment to achieve a discursive consensus as such—hence also a practical argument that, for instance, advances a moral principle—*is rationally unavoidable.* Tran-scendental pragmatics, and also its relevance for moral philosophy, stands and falls upon this thesis" (123, emphasis in original).

I agree with Böhler's evaluation of the significance of this claim, but, unlike Böhler, I would argue that the thesis has never been substantiated, at least not by the standard which it articulates. The standard is, put simply, that one's statements can be proven to be (or to follow from statements which are) universally valid, which, under ideal conditions, everyone would recognize to be true. The ideal conditions would be ones in which people play the language game of argumentation by the rules—that they would evaluate arguments purely on grounds of rationality and not on any externals like status, the rules of any institution other than argumentation, or arguments drawn from teleologi-cal systems. In such a situation, participants recognize "solely the authority of rational argument is of significance for those who play the language game of argumentation and do not, for instance, arbitrarily terminate it. Whoever argues is, as participant in an argument, only bound by the rules of a single institution, namely, by the rules of the metainstitution of the language game of argumentation itself" (Böhler 130). One of the most important of these rules is that one make claims which are (or, at least, which the speaker believes to be) universally valid. This claim is always already implied in argumentative dis-course: "Everyday communication makes possible a kind of understanding that is based on claims to validity and thus furnishes the only real alternative to exerting influence on one another in more or less coercive ways. The validity claims that we raise in conversation—that is, when we say something with conviction—transcend this specific conversational context, pointing to some-thing beyond the spatiotempral ambit of the occasion" (Habermas, *Moral Consciousness* 19).

Habermas's correctio, "that is, when we say something with conviction," is crucial to his argument as it enables him to exclude from consideration pre-cisely those situations that might function as counter-examples: we do not think our statements have universal validity when we lie, tell a joke, or engage in fiction, but, more important, neither do we imply universal validity when we engage in conversation that is exploratory or deeply personal. Before going into the more complicated problem of the argumentative status of Habermas's argument, I do want to point to the rather circular nature of the proof: the rational-critical sphere has certain characteristics because those characteristics are the always already assumed bases of argumentation, because any discourse that does not assume those bases is not argumentation.

A more common criticism of this characterization of argument has been to ask where these rules come from—what authority Habermas has for declaring those to be the rules of argumentation.[3] Perhaps one of the strongest indications of the problems with this central tenet of transcendental pragmatics is the nature of Habermas's response to that question, which has—in one form or another—continually haunted his work. To provide a rational basis for a central assertion, Habermas (as well as the other proponents of communicative ethics) has drawn from various fields—philosophy, psychoanalysis, hermeneutics, linguistics, speech-act theory—but only from the institutionally constructed authorities of those fields, in a move any rhetorician would recognize as argument from authority. This move is highly significant: if status and authority were, in fact, irrelevant to argumentation, then Habermas's own arguments should have, at least occasionally, been grounded in thinkers whose status was not constituted by the institution of academia, but he has never done so. On the contrary, one of the most striking qualities of Habermas's means of argumentation is the extent to which he depends on argument from authority. The logical consequences of this quality of Habermas's own argumentation are problematic: either the institution of academia is perfectly rational, or Habermas does not play by the rules of argumentation as he himself articulates them, or he believes that status and authority do contribute to the evaluation of a rational argument. One might make this claim even stronger and say that what one should see in the proponents of communicative ethics would be a complete disregard for those argumentative conventions that mark institutionally constituted authority, or, at least, a rigorous discussion of why citation practices, publication context, citation of canonical authors, and so on are a part of the rationality of an argument. One does not.

There is another way to reach the same conundrum: the various arguments that argumentation always already assumes the transcendental status of rationality are made in the language of individual intentionality, the "rationality" of which is notoriously problematic. Böhler, for instance, says that when a person engaged in argumentation makes any assertion, he implicitly claims that the assertion is more valid than others: "He thereby awakens the *expectation* that he himself is prepared and capable of redeeming this claim in communal discourse. In addition, he thereby recognized the others as representatives of the community of testing claims into which he himself, as someone asserting something, has entered. This means that he confers upon others the right to criticism and judgment; he himself is *obliged* to advance propositions worthy of discussion and testing and to participate seriously in their testing" (119). Böhler asserts that any claim to validity is necessarily a claim to universal validity, "for any kind of restrictions with regard to the circle of those over against whom the claim to validity is raised would amount to restrictions of the claim to validity and would contradict the meaning of an assertion as an argumentative act" (116). The question is, What and where is the substance of this expectation? That is, when Böhler says that a speaker awakens the expectation of rational redemption of a claim, it is not at all clear where that expectation resides— whether Böhler is making a claim about the cognitive processes of each individual who has ever participated in an argument (in which case, one might test it empirically), or whether he is simply making the argument that the possibility of such an expectation exists. In the former case, it would be relevant to respond, as some have, that they do not have any such expectation, and that the expectation of redeemability is itself another culturally constituted distortion.[4] In the latter case, one might wonder why such a possibility has greater status than any of the other possible states of mind—expectations of rage, hypocrisy, fatigue.

Again, it is important to emphasize that it is not at all clear how one could test Böhler's thesis, regardless of whether the experience of individuals is relevant to the larger debate. This question is particularly problematic if one slightly rephrases it: to what extent is the argumentative experience of marginalized groups relevant to the claim Böhler makes? This rephrasing is especially relevant given that Habermas, unlike Böhler, makes the argument in terms of experience. It is from experience, Habermas argues, that one gains understanding; yet he insists that the process cannot be investigated through epistemological models (see, for instance, "What Is Universal Pragmatics" 24). In "The Development of Normative Structures" Habermas again suggests the possibility of empirical examination of this question, in that he draws on cognitive psychology to make assertions regarding the universality of communicative rules, but he connects the development of individual cognition to a universalized view of human history, such that any study of individual cognitive development among non-Western children is precluded. There are serious problems with using Piaget's studies to infer the kind of moral and argumentative development that Habermas does. My objection is not merely what Mc-Carthy calls "the lingering suspicion of ethnocentrism that sometimes attaches to developmental studies" (322), although that suspicion is inevitable, but a fundamental suspicion that Habermas's argument begs the question that the very answer Habermas wants is assumed in his method of posing the question. Piaget and others have argued that certain kinds of knowledge are developmentally more advanced than others because the former are extensions of the latter, and, as McCarthy says, if "the mastery of the ability to reason argumentatively and reflectively about truth and rightness claims represents a developmental-logically advanced state of species-wide cognitive and moral competences, then it seems that the social investigator would be justified in applying standards of critical rationality in interpreting any system of beliefs and practices" (321). The assumed equation of advancement and extension (and consequent inference of inherent standards), however, is obviously absurd when applied to other kinds of knowledge: knowing how to thrust and twist a bowie knife so as to inflict the most damage to an opponent's internal organs is an extension of the species-wide knowing how to hold a knife, but does not constitute appropriate standards by which to judge all uses of knives.

In short, the conditions of Habermas's project are such that they cannot be empirically tested because the very possibility of counter-examples is prohibited—such as an individual, community, or culture which does not acknowledge the expectations of rational proof. If they cannot be empirically tested, what is the rational basis for projecting particular expectations onto individual minds?

In Habermas's work on universal pragmatics, he relies on the speech-act theory of Searle and Austin to infer that such obligations exist within language use, not the individual mind or the conventions of any particular culture. While such an inference is highly suggestive, it does not solve the basic problem. After all, it is worth remembering that not only has Searle's extension of Austin's work been questioned, but Searle's next projects were into the realm of intentionality and cognition because those issues were necessarily raised by his interest in language.[5] In other words, placing the locus of expectation within language itself still raises the issue of how such a locus relates to individual intentions and minds; pushing the weight on language simply moves the problem, but does not remove it.

Thus far, I have criticized two ways of inferring that the rules of the language game of argumentation posit dialectical argument from universally valid premises with complete exclusion of ethos—from the practice of those engaged in it, and from the assertions of those who theorize about it. The first method suggests that, despite what Habermas and others have asserted, authority of the speaker is a crucial criterion for evaluating the rationality of any argument. The second leads into a morass of issues regarding cognition and intention. A third possibility is suggested by Habermas's own historical work, and it is the approach of examining the theories of those who engage in argumentation. It is this third possibility that I intend to pursue with the seventeenth-century American Puritans.

Puritan Public Sphere

It cannot be emphasized enough that Habermas makes no claim that perfect inclusion (regardless of status) was actually realized in the places he identifies as manifestations of the rational-critical public realm. He does not say that the eighteenth century was an inclusive era; given that the participants in that realm represented an extremely narrow range of race, economic class, and educational background, and considering their attitude toward other races, lower classes, and women, such a claim would be patently absurd. The criterion he uses is that the eighteenth-century philosophes made manifest the objective *claims* of inclusion and rationality. If one follows Habermas's method, then, one looks for inclusion as an objective claim with important consequences rather than the actual practice of perfect inclusion.

It is precisely that *claim* which one finds in the early American Puritans. In fact, the early American Puritans put extraordinary emphasis on (and faith in) the role of public discourse in the process of conversion, the organization of church government, the creation of laws and assemblies, and the development of theology.[6] As Stephen Foster says, "Though it seems strange to say it, few societies in Western culture have ever depended more thoroughly or more self-consciously on the consent of their members than the allegedly repressive 'theocracies' of early New England" (156). Most important, in theory (that is, at least insofar as the authorities claimed), everyone was included in the community of discourse; it was for that reason that even the most obviously reprobate were forced to listen to sermons. Even the exclusion from the community of discourse which the Puritans acknowledged (such as banishment) was not on the basis of status, but on the grounds that the excluded arguments were irrational (*cavils* was the word most frequently used). As Joshua Miller has recently argued, "Although it appears to be one of the most elitist elements of their political thought, the establishment by the Puritans of strict standards for membership in town and church was, in fact, closely related to the most democratic aspects of their political thinking. Because they placed so much power in the hands of their members, the Puritans maintained high standards for membership in congregational churches" (2). It is important that I be clear on this point: like the era of the philosophes, the Puritan era was extremely exclusive, but, if one uses the criteria by which Habermas makes the eighteenth century the beginning of the public sphere (that is, on the basis of *claim*), then the early American Puritans had established a public sphere.

When a young married woman, Anne Hutchinson, threatened the author-ity of the established ministers through holding meetings in her home and there criticizing some of the most popular clergy, she was severely chastised. When she remained recalcitrant, she was brought through a series of public trials and examinations before being banished to Rhode Island. Although there can be little doubt that Hutchinson's status as a woman influenced the behavior of her accusers, it is worth noting that they did not make a point of it. What her accusers *said* was: "There is a contradiction in your own words," "I find such flat contradiction to the scripture in what she saith," and—what I cannot help but read as somewhat petulant—"I deny it [her interpretation] because I have brought more arguments than you have" (Hall, *Antinomian Controversy* 315, 344, 315). In other words, the seventeenth-century American Puritans *claimed,* at least as much as the eighteenth-century philosophes, to evaluate arguments purely on the basis of those arguments, not on the status of the speaker.[7] Joshua Miller has emphasized the role of discourse in these controversies: "Although they set limits on dissent, the Puritans publicly discussed the most important religious and political questions facing the community. They did not coerce their opponents before engaging them in debate; Winthrop's *Journal* describes many such dialogues" (29).

When John Cotton defended the banishment of Roger Williams, he ar-gued that it was not because of what Williams thought, but because of what he did. He continually insisted that Williams's arguments were unreasonable and illogical; he never questioned Williams's authority. What the Puritan authori-ties appealed to was not their own institutionally constituted authority (which was, after all, highly problematic) but, like the philosophes, a sense of what they thought everyone would have to grant, premises to which everyone must agree, arguments that were obviously true. In fact, as Joshua Miller has said, the very construction of the New England way of congregational churches was an attempt to restrict the power of institutions: "At the heart of this definition of a church was the desire to limit the power of institutions. If a distinction was made between an institution and its membership, the institution could act independently of the membership's will, something the Puritans wished to avoid" (33). And it is worth remembering that the eighteenth-century public sphere did not, according to Habermas, demand the destruction of institutions, but, as Saccamano says, they "demanded that political domination be *legitimated* by public opinion" (688, emphasis added). In the same way, every aspect of New England political and religious institutions had to be continually legitimated through public discourse and consensus.

This insistence on the importance of rationality to the Puritans sounds strange to people who are most familiar with the Puritans of Hawthorne's fiction, or for whom "Sinners in the Hands of an Angry God" typifies Puritan sermons, but it is an argument that Puritan scholars have been making since Perry Miller's book *The New England Mind:* the American Puritans saw their faith as perfectly rational, saw a perfect fit between reason and revelation, and always emphasized the rationality of correct doctrine. This reliance on logic typifies the Puritan belief that logic is True, that logic represents the actual structure of the universe, because God Himself is the very source of reason: "REASON, what it is, but a *Faculty* formed by GOD, in the Mind of Man, enabling him to discern certain *Maxims of Truth,* which God himself has established, and to make true *Inferences* from them! In all the Dictates of *Reason,* there is *the Voice of God*" (C. Mather, *Christian Philosopher* 283, emphasis in original).[8] William Perkins insisted that the conscience, which always calls one to correct doctrine, is a part of the faculty of understanding, which "is that facultie in the soule, whereby we use reason" (5). The Puritans rejected the Aristotelian distinction between probability and demonstration, insisting that all genuine understanding comes from convictions that can be demonstrated: people are persuaded because they recognize that an argument is true; there is no experiential difference between knowing that a particular interpretation of Scripture is right and knowing that a mathematical answer is correct: "Grant that proofs which produce persuasion and proofs which produce certain knowledge are not different" (Rainolds 205). If certainty is the goal of all knowledge, and certainty is possible, then there is no reason to settle for anything less than certainty in public discourse. Thus the Puritans did not distinguish between the kind of intention that one might have in trying to persuade people toward a course of action and the kind of intention that one might have in demonstrating a geometrical proof. Because God is rational, so is His doctrine, and the purpose of a sermon is to engage in logical demonstration of doctrine: the minister should strive "out of soundnesse of argument, and plaine evidence of the will of God, and the spirit of God, make truth knowne to the spirits of men: when a man's doctrine goeth so guarded and confirmed with Scripture, and sound and plaine demonstration of argument, that they stand undeniable" (Hooker *Soules Implantation* 75–76). At least until the religious revival and anti-intellectualism of the Great Awakening, Puritan sermons and documents rely on such logical principles and schema as the principle of noncontradiction, the syllogism, and the different kinds of causes.[9] The Puritans' sense of the importance of reasoning to religion is also demonstrated by the priority they gave to establishing Harvard (an institution created in order to have educated ministers) and the course of study required by their schooling (which began the study of logic at an early age).

The slippery (and crucial) term in this discussion is *rationality,* a term that is extremely problematic in Habermas's writings. His definition of it is somewhat elusive, especially since it tends to be implied through negation—it is *not* merely purposive, *nor* is it positivistic. While there is nothing inherently wrong with definition by negation, it does seem reasonable to suggest that a useful definition of rationality would have certain positive consequences: first one's own practice of argumentation should evidence precisely those standards one wishes to propose as either universal or ideal (this is, it seems to me, the most commonsense application of Kant's categorical imperative); second, one's definition should provide criteria by which one could distinguish those instances that are clearly objectionable and oppressive from those that are merely flawed; finally, it should enhance the capacity for self-reflection in that it should provide standards by which one might critique one's own practice. In regard to the first point, Habermas's position is, as I have argued, seriously problematic. Unfortunately, the second and third are equally troubling.

If "rationality" is synonymous with "logical," then the Puritans were, despite their reputation, perfectly rational in that their doctrines and practices followed logically from their premises. The most controversial Puritan doctrine, for example, was, given contemporary notions of rationality, perfectly logical. That doctrine—what John Norton calls the "Decree"—is fairly simple: "The Decree, is God by one eternal-free-constant act, absolutely determining his Futurion, i.e. the infallible future being of whatever is besides himself, unto the praise of his own Glory: the cause, and disposer of all things, the Antecedent and disposer of all events" (Norton 51). This perception of God—as the unmoved Mover, the final cause of every being and every event—is explicitly a rejection of any kind of theological dualism, that is, an explanation of origins which would give any power to another entity (such as Satan). It is the Puritan formulation of the concept of predestination.

Puritan discussions of predestination indicate clear awareness of the theological and popular objections to the decree—Norton's discussion of predestination ends with a long series of objections and answers, and Michael Wigglesworth's poetical description of Judgment Day, "The Day of Doom," consists mostly of sinners arguing with Jesus about the justice of their being sent to Hell given predestination. Those objections can be classed into two general categories: arguments concerning logical consequences (e.g., if God is the author of everything, then He must be the author of sin), and arguments concerning the rhetorical effect of insisting that humans have no will (i.e., that the doctrine is unappealing or discouraging). What most distinguishes the Calvinist stance on predestination from those arguments that Calvin himself criticizes is the extent to which it refuses to recognize the authority of the second kind of argument. Norton's *Orthodox Evangelist,* for instance, acknowledges how appalling the doctrine might seem—"The face of Providence is oftentimes like unto some picture, which if you look upon it on the one side, casteth a deformed shape" (117)—but insists that looking at the topic logically demonstrates the undeniability of predestination.

In his explication and defense of predestination, Norton uses the most authoritative logical and philosophical systems of his era, especially the distinctions involved in Aristotelian causality. For Norton, as for Aquinas, evil is not a thing that exists, that has some kind of actual presence or ontological being. Only goodness actually exists, and evil is merely the absence of good, a kind of defect. Because it has no real existence, Norton says, it has no efficient cause; since it is a defect, it can at most be granted a sort of "deficient" cause. He concludes that it is therefore logically impossible that God causes evil; something perfect and complete has no deficiencies and therefore cannot cause them: "The evil cleaving to the action is a defect, therefore hath no efficient, but a deficient Cause: Now God cannot be a deficient Cause, because he is the first and absolutely perfect Cause, therefore cannot be the cause of a *non-ens,* i.e. a nullity, or of that which is defective" (63). For the Puritans, all final and efficient causes come from God (or, more accurately stated, God is the final and efficient cause of everything); as long as they can argue that sin does not properly have a final or efficient cause, then it is perfectly logical to conclude that God is not the cause (properly speaking) of sin. God does cause some people to remain reprobate, and people who are reprobate shall inevitably sin, but "Reprobation is not the cause, only the Antecedent of sin" (66). It is not, therefore, that God causes sin, as much as that He permits some people to remain in a sinful state. Those people are then punished for sinning, not for being in a reprobate state.

Thus the Puritans privileged the logical argument (strict predestination) over the one that was more rhetorically pleasing (Arminianism). Norton's explanation that God is not the author of sin relies on distinguishing among five kinds of "causes" (external moving, efficient, material, formal, and final) and distinguishing causes from things that might look like causes but are not (term, accident, and occasion), and those categories and distinctions were perfectly logical in that they represented the most authoritative in contemporary systems of logic.[10] If one uses the criteria that Habermas uses in regard to the eighteenth-century philosophes—whether the early American Puritan divines believed or claimed that their assertions were logically derived from universally valid first premises, and not grounded in authority—then there is little doubt that they were engaging in rational-critical debate. At least insofar as one can infer intention, or at least insofar as one uses the criterion of objective claim, the seventeenth-century Puritans excluded arguments only on the basis of rationality.

In fact—and this point is particularly important—it was precisely their insistence on rational public discourse that caused them to restrict discourse so severely. Like the modern proponents of a rational critical public sphere, the Puritans tried to make all discourse dialectic. As will be briefly discussed later, they rejected any suggestion that there might be a distinction between demonstration and probability, and they thereby rejected any apparent need for the discipline of rhetoric as the form of public discourse.[11]

Predestination follows logically from the premises that Scripture is true and that power is lessened through sharing; seeing the only form of discourse as demonstration follows logically from predestination and belief in certainty; oppressing dissent follows logically from the Puritan sense of discourse. Further, the Puritans' sincerity in claiming to be logical is indicated in their willingness to submit their decisions to public discourse. That is, unlike other oppressive governments, whose enemies disappear quietly, the Puritan authorities held public examinations of dissenters, and published transcripts of those trials, thereby giving dissenters the opportunity to publish their own arguments.[12] This willingness to give voice to dissent suggests the Puritans' confidence that their positions were so logical that they would be vindicated through public discourse.

A second use of the term *rationality* is to apply it to syllogistic reasoning grounded in universally valid first principles, which is what the early American Puritans claimed to be doing. Puritans followed Ramus's logic, which makes all reasoning a form of syllogizing: "Nor indeed should we consider it possible that rhetorical judgment is one thing and dialectical judgment another, since for evaluating whether something is truly useful, suitable, fitting, or has the qualities it seems to have, there is one faculty of judgment which the syllogism alone executes and accomplishes" (Ramus, "Arguments" 106).

In the midst of controversies—the Cotton-Williams debate over the New England patent, the Hutchinson controversy, the Half-Way Covenant compromise, the Salem witchcraft hysteria—Puritan authorities simultaneously made two claims: that they were willing to listen to other points of view, and that their own views were demonstrably true. The righteousness of their position, they claimed, was not supposed to have to do with status; Calvinists regularly reminded themselves that an illiterate fisherman like Peter was just as much a gift from God as a learned orator like Paul (Calvin, *Corinthians* 77). It was simply that, the Puritan divines insisted, their doctrinal positions were grounded in indisputable reading of Scripture, which is itself perfectly clear: as Samuel Mather says, "There is nothing so clear, and sure, and certain, as the Gospel" (*The Figures or Types* 12). Winthrop prefaces his defense of the irregular proceedings against Hutchinson's ally Wheelwright by saying, "But the answer to this is easie, it being well known to all such as have understanding of matters of this nature" (297). Higginson insists that the minister's interpretation is nothing "but what might be more abundantly made out by Scripture light, and what the generality of all the People of God (not engaged unto parties) will readily subscribe unto" ("Cause of God" I, 9–10). Hubbard begins his explication of a text by saying that his interpretation is "very obvious to the observant reader" (2). Hutchinson's interpretations are, according to her examiners, imposed on the text, "for nothing but a word comes to her mind and then an application is made which is nothing to purpose" (Hall, *Antinomian Controversy* 342). In his argument with the dissident Roger Williams, Cotton asserts that Williams could not possibly find any scriptural text to support his position (in Williams, II, 36). When Williams does so, Cotton responds that he is astonished that someone could so obviously distort evidence. Like the examiners of Anne Hutchinson, Cotton insists that there is *no* logic behind the dissenting point of view, no reason whatsoever to support it, and no innocent motive that someone might hold it.

At the heart of the Puritan inability to create an open public sphere is this faith in being able to ground interpretation and arguments in certainty. With such certainty, there is no need to consider the possibility of an audience including someone who has heard and understood doctrine but still disagrees. Such a person either does not understand (so that one should repeat the point), or he or she secretly agrees but pretends to have reasons for withholding assent in order to protect secret lusts. In "No Man Can Will Christ and Grace," one of the scriptural passages Hooker uses to prove this point is Matthew 19:16–22, in which a young man comes to Jesus to ask what he should do to inherit the Kingdom of Heaven. When Jesus tells him to sell everything he has and follow him, the young man goes away sorrowful, "for he had great possessions." Hooker interprets the young man's reaction as proof that he recognizes the truth of what Jesus says but cannot follow his recommendation out of unwillingness to give up wealth. Hooker uses this man as typical of all people who reject Puritan teaching: they recognize the obvious truth of Puritan doctrine, but may refuse to follow it because they are too attached to their sins. This assertion is repeated throughout the sermon: disagreement is cavilling motivated by carnal lusts; it is "swellings and bublings of heart against the word" ("No Man" 20); and desire to silence or ostracize a minister is motivated by a hardened heart that does not want to have its conscience pricked. Disagreement with Hooker is never motivated by goodwilled disbelief, or benevolent ignorance, or Hooker's being in error; if someone disagrees with Hooker, he is disagreeing with God. His disagreeing with God is proof that he is a "naturall man"—that is, someone who is completely fleshy and has nothing spiritual within—so that any attempt to dispute the sermon is itself proof of one's sinfulness.[13]

This argument was based in the Puritan equation of something being true and something being undeniable, which brings us back to the issue of demonstration and dialectical reasoning. Since Puritans continually argued that spiritual dogma is logically demonstrable, and since dialectic had long held that its first principles were undeniable to any who understood them, it was logical for the Puritans to conclude that a true statement is logically indisputable. If one is confronted with someone who does dispute the statement, the discursive options are seriously limited. One can either decide that the recalcitrant listener is sincere and that one is not in the realm of dialectic, or decide that the listener is lying—that he or she secretly agrees. Because the first option was virtually unthinkable—the Puritans believed that the world is controlled by logic—they continually (and I think sincerely) asserted the second. This is not to say that the Puritans believed a person who had never heard a sermon could read the Bible correctly, or that someone completely ignorant would articulate correct doctrine. It is to say that, as the Puritans narrated the process of conversion, there was no possibility of a person understanding, but not agreeing with, Puritan dogma. Here, again, the language of transcendental communicative ethics is relevant: the Puritan divines demonstrated the *expectation* that their assertions were universally valid, and they could point to the *experience* that all reasonable people shared them. If, therefore, the rational-critical sphere is constituted by expectation, experience, or claim, the Puritans created one just as much as did the philosophes.

The Consequences of the Claims

Habermas says that the claims of inclusion must have consequences, and such a requirement is intended, I assume, to distinguish sincere (albeit imperfectly fulfilled) claims from ones that are purely cynical. The Puritan claims of inclusion did, in fact, have objective consequences. There are two particularly important ones to discuss: first, the Puritan authorities initially engaged opponents in private and open debate; second, they excluded from the realm of discourse anyone who was not convinced by the debate. The New England authorities discussed all controversies openly, and they subjected most public decisions to a public vote. Hutchinson, Williams, members of the Society of Friends, and anyone who criticized the church were banished, tortured, and sometimes hung if they did not acquiesce, because the Puritan public sphere had no capacity to incorporate dialogue involving profound disagreement.[14] Both sets of consequences—the reliance on public discourse and the oppression of steadfast dissenters—are necessarily connected to the Puritan project of a rational-critical realm.

Such a failure to communicate is especially striking in a community that was so self-conscious about conflict resolution. Not only was the mediating of conflicts between members the duty of ministers, it was dictated as a Christian duty for all members of the community, and an ability to resolve disputes was a regular point of praise for community leaders. In addition, disputants had access to a variety of formal methods of arbitration: town meetings; justices of the peace; civil and criminal courts; churches (which often handled disputes regarding such secular matters as contracts and property rights; see Nelson 31– 34); and synods. That many of these forums required reaching unanimity as the resolution (not mere majority) suggests that the goal was not simply determining the appropriate judgment, but ensuring the perfect agreement of all present. Only when discourse failed did authorities resort to coercion, yet such failure was frequent.

The frequency of failure was a direct result of the standards of discourse which the Puritans established. As Joshua Miller has said, "The Puritan lack of tolerance was, in part, a result of the seriousness with which they took ideas. They believed that their own ideas about the correct form of religious worship were true, and they defined political liberty as the right to put those ideas into practice" (29). As Cotton Mather says, there is no difference between obedience to God (meaning, of course, obedience to the authorities' dictates regarding life practices) and obedience to Reason: "Whatever I see to be Reason, I will comply with it, from this Consideration, *'tis what God calls me to!* Reason extends to those Points of *Morality,* with as much Evidence as to those of *Mathematicks*" (*Christian Philosopher* 283). They could not incorporate genuine difference of opinion precisely because they attempted to form a public sphere grounded in dialectical discourse; assuming that "reasoning" means syllogizing from universally valid first principles leads, quite logically, to the exclusion of difference on the grounds that someone with different conclusions must be unreasonable. As even Socrates noted, syllogistic reasoning grounded in universally valid first principles (typically identified as dialectical and distinguished from rhetorical) is useful only insofar as all participants will grant the first principle in question (see, for example, Plato's *Gorgias*). If they will not, then one is faced with a limited number of possibilities: that the principle is not a first principle and must itself be syllogistically demonstrated; that the topic at hand is not subject to dialectical demonstration; that the recalcitrant participants secretly share the first principle, but refuse to acknowledge it openly for various reasons.

In the various examinations, exchanges of pamphlets, sermons, and speeches, the Puritans made a good faith effort to do the first—to prove every argument that came under dispute—but they were not always able to do so. In

"No Man Can Will Christ and Grace," for example, Hooker mentions and tries to refute one of the arguments put forward by Hutchinson: if all men are sinful, and ministers are men, then ministers are sinful. This argument, although neatly logical, contradicts the equally logical arguments put forward to keep the sermon at the heart of New England communities—that grace is communicated through the sermon (although not caused by human agency); people can communicate only that which they have; ministers must, therefore, have grace. The irony is that both arguments rely on first principles in Puritan doctrine— that all men are sinful and that grace is communicated through the sermon— and neither is particularly capable of further proof. Hooker is, therefore, in the position of having to conclude that the subject is not one capable of dialectical reasoning, or that the premise is universally valid and his recalcitrant audience is willfully choosing to cavil. The first possibility would put the entire Puritan intellectual project on shaky ground, since the very division and definitions of disciplines, the theories of knowledge and mind, methods of scriptural interpretation, and the denigration of rhetoric were founded on the assumption that all reasoning is dialectical (as is, it seems to me, the project of transcendental pragmatics). In such a world, to say that the subject is not capable of dialectical reasoning is to suggest that it is not subject to reason at all. Thus someone like Hooker is left with the third option; hence, over and over, the Puritans concluded that all their premises were universally accepted, and that dissenters willfully cavilled. And, in those numerous incidents when Puritans were faced with those options, they did precisely what Hooker did; after summarizing the argument, he ranted that it is blasphemy motivated by unwillingness to submit to the word of God. When attempts at rational discourse failed (as they frequently did), Puritan authorities resorted to what Habermas has called strategic action.

It is significant to note that Hooker's method is what Habermas recommends in "What Is Universal Pragmatics"—if dialectic will not work, then one must break off communication altogether, or resort to strategic action (4). In practice, then, as well as theory, dialectic is not enough. Obviously, it is absurd to suggest that the early American Puritans made an ideal public sphere, nor do I mean to suggest that they were, in practice, no more exclusionary or oppressive than the philosophes. Like the philosophes, however, they *did* claim to be a perfectly inclusive and rational community, and Habermas's criteria make claims the central issue. Thus at the very least one must say that his criteria are seriously flawed.[15]

I was initially drawn to Habermas, and to a historical study of public discourse, from a conviction that something like his rational-critical public sphere was the model most needed. And it still seems to me that it is an understatement to say that the goal of a perfectly inclusive public sphere is highly admirable. His writings on that issue, however, should provide criteria by which one could point to certain practices as historical instances of such a sphere, either through the standards implicit in his own methods of argumentation or through the standards made explicit in his historical and theoretical work. His writings do not demonstrate freedom from an argumentative reliance on institutionally constructed authority—in fact, they imply some strong relation between such authority and his sense of rationality—nor do his definitions adequately differentiate instances with some exclusion (such as the eighteenth-century philosophes) from those with an extremely exclusive and oppressive system (such as the seventeenth-century American Puritans). Finally, his writings do not provide useful recommendations for how even well-intentioned people of opposing opinions can include one another in their community of discourse, particularly in the light of his recommendation that one resort to strategic action if dialectic fails.

Behind Habermas's recommendation to resort to strategic action is the implication of a more fruitful approach to public discourse. If rhetoric is the skill to which one must resort when dialectic fails, if dialectic fails in arenas of distorted communication, and if mass culture has distorted communication in the public realm, then, logically, rhetoric is the skill to which philosophers of argumentation should be paying attention in order to define an inclusive form of public discourse. The history of rhetoric provides a rich tradition of theorists who articulated and enacted inclusive methods of argumentation that are reliant on multiple sources of power, that are not necessarily dependent on institutionally constituted authority, and that can serve as sources of critical, even rebellious, practice. Perhaps most important, the history of rhetoric provides ways of evaluating the ethics of various forms of discourse grounded in means of argumentation that enable people with genuinely different points of view to discuss their differences.

At its best, the Puritan work ethic—the notion of a worldly calling—is an inspiration to participate fully in this world; at its worst, it is merely the pursuit of one's own prosperity, regardless of the cost to others. At its best, Puritan rhetoric demands that one understand and participate in the decisions facing one's community; at its worst, it is the forceful expression of self, regardless of the views or interests of others. If we are to try to form a rational-critical public sphere, and I agree that such a sphere is ideal (in both senses of the word), then it is worth remembering the best and worst of Puritan rhetoric. The Puritan attempt to form a demonstrative public sphere suggests that, if we want a genuinely inclusive arena for public discourse, we neither can nor should try to ground it in syllogistic reasoning from universally valid first principles. Abandoning such striving after certainty does not require that we make the public sphere a realm of coercion. It does, however, mean that we cannot have discourse without difference, or deliberation without rhetoric.

Notes

1. For more on this aspect of the controversy, see especially Benhabib's afterword to *The Communicative Ethics Controversy* (330–69).

2. This means that Habermas does not provide standards by which to judge authority—that is, by making authority not a part of rationality, he seems to accept the rational-irrational split, and not to help one identify the more or less reasonable uses of ethos.

3. Doxtader, for example, has argued that Habermas's exclusion of strategic action (in which Habermas includes rhetoric) prevents his being able to account fully for the means by which people in deep disagreement—including over the very characteristic of a good reason—can reach consensus. Such a critique is reliant on a different sense of the function and consequences of argumentation; Doxtader, unlike Habermas, sees consensus building as a purpose of argument. It is unclear to me why Doxtader's definition is any less convincing than Habermas's.

4. Fish, for instance, has argued that the notion of critical self-consciousness crucial to this being a true expectation may well be another form of distorted communication (see especially 453–55).

5. For the most famous critique of Searle's use of Austin, see Derrida's *Limited Ink*. Searle's work after *Speech Acts* was appropriately entitled *Intentionality;* he has since been working in cognition.

6. Because the sixteenth and seventeenth century put so much emphasis on public discourse, one scholar has called it the "era of persuasion" (Holifield); other scholars have argued that the American Puritan conception of the role of public discourse and identity continued to influence American culture well into the revolution (see, for example, Stout or Hall); biographers of particular American Puritans have emphasized the faith that ministers put in persuasion and discourse (see, for example, Bush).

7. The status of the speaker could be inferred from the argument. Thus the deputy governor concludes that Hutchinson was deluded by the devil, since her arguments were untrue (Hall, *Antinomian Controversy* 343). It is important for my point that the argument did not run the other way—that he did not conclude her arguments were untrue because she was deluded by the devil (in that case, he would have been inferring rationality from status). For more on the Hutchinson controversy, see Lang and Hall.

8. It is also important as a kind of warning to modern readers. One of the reasons modern readers often misunderstand the Puritans is that we impose back on them some of our own dichotomies—such as rationality versus religiosity. The Puritans were fanatically religious *and* better trained in logic than most modern scholars.

9. In fact, most interpretations of the historical significance of the Great Awakening see it as a reaction to the overly intellectualized and rational sermon style of the New England divines (e.g., Hofstadter, White). The sermons of the Great Awakening are far more emotional and far less dependent on Ramistic organization and logic than were sermons of the earlier era.

10. Granted, that logic was also teleological, and Böhler insists that any teleological arguments are necessarily excluded from the language game of argumentation. For Böhler's argument to be internally consistent, however, his exclusion must be defended in a nonteleological manner which does not rely on institutionally constituted authority, and it is not. Thus this exclusion, absolutely necessary to Böhler's argument, is neither more nor less rational than the Puritan inclusion of teleology—both are made on the grounds of arguments from contemporary institutionally constituted authority.

11. As Joshua Miller's work has shown, the Puritans did place considerable educational emphasis on rhetoric courses. Those courses, however, were little more than instruction in ornamentation and elocution. Cotton Mather, for example, recommended that his son not "squander" his time on rhetoric textbooks and courses, since they would do little more than tell him the names of the figures he could easily learn elsewhere (*Manuductio* 34).

12. In all the discussions of, for example, the Hutchinson controversy, I have never seen anyone argue that Winthrop changed Hutchinson's statements—it is generally accepted that the words attributed to her are her own.

13. In *Soules Humiliation,* Hooker says that one of the signs of a humble soul is that it completely submits to the word of God, which is immediately equated with what the minister says (95–96).

14. For more on the conflict resolution method which the New England communities used, and its breakdown in the mid-eighteenth century, see Nelson.

15. One might argue that Habermas's discussion of rationality in "Remarks on Discourse Ethics" and *The Theory of Communicative Action,* vol. 1, restricts his arguments to "justificatory discourses in which we test the validity of universal precepts" rather than discussions of practice ("Remarks" 35). In other words, his criteria do not apply to the Puritans because they did not distinguish between purposive rationality and theoretical discourse, and his sense of the true nature of argumentation only applies to the latter. In such a case, the best that one might say is that Habermas's argument is relevant to a small part of the kind of arguments that any community might have; if the purpose of communicative ethics is not to determine what a community should do, but what values might serve as the universal bases for the decisions of that community, then it will be a long time before communicative ethics can provide the kind of discourse that might have the practical effect of enabling people to critique the practices of oppression of institutions. Thus restricting the argument only to theoretical discourse gives up half of what was the justification of the project—that it would define a perfectly inclusive and liberatory form of public discourse. It is not perfectly inclusive, as only people with a very narrow form of education appear able to participate; it is not liberatory, as it does not deal with topics related to practice.

Works Cited

Aristotle. *The Rhetoric.* Trans. W. Rhys Roberts. New York: Modern Library, 1984.

Benhabib, Seyla. Afterword. *The Communicative Ethics Controversy.* Ed. Seyla Benhabib and Fred Dallmayr. Cambridge, Mass.: MIT Press, 1990: 330–69.

Böhler, Dietrich. "Transcendental Pragmatics and Critical Morality: On the Possibility and Moral Significance of a Self-Enlightenment of Reason." *The Communicative Ethics Controversy.* Ed. Seyla Benhabib and Fred Dallmayr. Cambridge, Mass.: MIT Press, 1990: 111–50.

Bush, Sargent, Jr. *The Writings of Thomas Hooker: Spiritual Adventure in Two Worlds.* Madison: University of Wisconsin Press, 1980.

Calhoun, Craig. "Introduction: Habermas and the Public Sphere." *Habermas and the Public Sphere.* Ed. Craig Calhoun. Cambridge, Mass.: MIT Press, 1992: 1–48.

Calvin, John. *Commentary on the Epistles of Paul the Apostle to the Corinthians.* Trans. John Pringle. 2 vols. Edinburgh: Calvin Translation Society, 1848.

——. *Commentary upon the Epistle of Saint Paul to the Romans.* Trans. Christopher Rosdell. Edinburgh: Calvin Translation Society, 1844.

Doxtader, Erik W. "The Entwinement of Argument and Rhetoric: A Dialectical Reading of Habermas' Theory of Communicative Action." *Argumentation and Advocacy* 28 (fall 1991): 51–63.

Fish, Stanley. *Doing What Comes Naturally: Change, Rhetoric, and the Practice of Theory in Literary and Legal Studies.* Durham, N.C.: Duke University Press, 1989.

Foster, Stephen. *Their Solitary Way: The Puritan Social Ethic in the First Century of Settlement in New England.* New Haven: Yale University Press, 1971.

Habermas, Jürgen. *Moral Consciousness and Communicative Action.* Trans. Christian Lenhardt and Shierry Weber Nicholsen. Cambridge, Mass.: MIT Press, 1991.

——. "Remarks on Discourse Ethics." *Justification and Application: Remarks on Discourse Ethics.* Trans. Ciaran Cronin. Cambridge, Mass.: MIT Press, 1993.

——. *The Structural Transformation of the Public Sphere: An Inquiry into a Category of Bourgeois Society.* Trans. Thomas Burger. Cambridge, Mass.: MIT Press, 1991.

——. *The Theory of Communicative Action: Reason and the Rationalization of Society.* Vol. 1. Trans. Thomas McCarthy. Boston: Beacon, 1984.

——. "What Is Universal Pragmatics?" *Communication and the Evolution of Society.* Trans. Thomas McCarthy. Boston: Beacon, 1979: 1–68.

Hall, David D., ed. *The Antinomian Controversy, 1636–1638.* 2d ed. Durham, N.C.: Duke University Press, 1990.

——. *Worlds of Wonder, Days of Judgment: Popular Religious Belief in Early New England.* New York: Knopf, 1989.

Higginson, John. "The Cause of God and His People in New England, as it was Stated and Discussed in a Sermon Preached before the Honourable General Court of the Massachusetts Colony, on the 27 Day of Mar 1663." *Election Day Sermons, Massachusetts.* Ed. Sacvan Bercovitch. New York: AMS Press, n.d.

Hofstadter, Richard. *Anti-Intellectualism in American Life.* New York: Random House, 1962.

Holifield, E. Brooks. *Era of Persuasion: American Thought and Culture, 1521–1680.* Boston: Twayne Publishers, 1989.

Hooker, Thomas. "No Man Can Will Christ and Grace." *Redemption: Three Ser-*

mons. Ed. Everett H. Emerson. Delmar, N.Y.: Scholars' Facsimiles and Reprints, 1977.

——. *The Soules Humiliation.* 1640. In *A Library of American Puritan Writings.* New York: AMS Press, n.d.

——. *The Soules Implantation into the Naturall Olive.* 1640. In *A Library of American Puritan Writings.* New York: AMS Press, n.d.

Hubbard, William. "The Happiness of a People In the Wisdome of Their Rulers." 1676. *Election Day Sermons, Massachusetts.* Ed. Sacvan Bercovitch. New York: AMS Press, n.d.

Lang, Amy Schrager. *Prophetic Woman: Anne Hutchinson and the Problem of Dissent in the Literature of New England.* Berkeley: University of California Press, 1987.

Mather, Cotton. *The Christian Philosopher: A Collection of the Best Discoveries in Nature, with Religious Improvements.* 1721. Gainesville, Fla.: Scholars' Facsimiles and Reprints, 1968.

——. *Manuductio ad Ministerium: Directions for a Candidate of the Ministery.* 1726. New York: Facsimile Text Society, 1938.

Mather, Samuel. *The Figures or Types of the Old Testament.* 1705. ed. New York: Johnson Reprint Corporation, 1969.

McCarthy, Thomas. *The Critical Theory of Jürgen Habermas.* Cambridge, Mass.: MIT Press, 1978.

Miller, Joshua. *The Rise and Fall of Democracy in Early America, 1630–1789: The Legacy for Contemporary Politics.* University Park: Pennsylvania State University Press, 1991.

Miller, Perry. *The New England Mind: The Seventeenth Century.* Cambridge, Mass.: Harvard University Press, 1939.

Nelson, William E. *Dispute and Conflict Resolution in Plymouth County, Massachusetts, 1725–1825.* Chapel Hill: University of North Carolina Press, 1981.

Norton, John. *The Orthodox Evangelist.* London, 1654. New York: AMS Press, 1981.

Perkins, William. "A Discourse of Conscience." *William Perkins, 1558–1602, English Puritanist.* Ed. Thomas F. Merrill. The Hague: N. V. Drukkerij, 1966: 1–78.

Rainolds, John. *John Rainold's Oxford Lectures on Aristotle's Rhetoric.* Trans. Lawrence D. Green. Cranbury, N.J.: Associated University Presses, 1986.

Ramus, Peter. "Arguments in Rhetoric against Quintilian." *The Rhetorical Tradition: Readings from Classical Times to the Present.* Ed. Patricia Bizzell and Bruce Herzberg. Boston: Bedford Books of St. Martin's Press, 1990: 565–83.

Saccamano, Neil. "The Consolations of Ambivalence: Habermas and the Public Sphere." *Modern Language Notes* 106 (1991): 685–98.

Stout, Harry S. *The New England Soul: Preaching and Religious Culture in Colonial New England.* New York: Oxford University Press, 1968.

Tobin, Lad. "A Radically Different Voice: Gender and Language in the Trials of Anne Hutchinson." *Early American Literature* 25 (1990): 253–70.

Vickers, Brian. *In Defence of Rhetoric.* Oxford: Clarendon Press, 1988.

White, Eugene E. *Puritan Rhetoric: The Issue of Emotion in Religion.* In *Landmarks in Rhetoric and Public Address.* Carbondale: Southern Illinois University Press, 1972: 215.

Wigglesworth, Michael. "The Day of Doom." *American Poetry of the Seventeenth Cen-*

tury. Ed. Harrison T. Meserole. University Park: Pennsylvania State University Press, 1985.

Williams, Roger. *The Complete Writings of Roger Williams.* New York: Russell and Russell, 1963.

Winthrop, John. "A Short Story of the Rise, reign, and ruine of the Antinomians, Familists and Libertines." 1644. *The Antinomian Controversy, 1636–1638.* Ed. David D. Hall. Durham, N.C.: Duke University Press, 1990: 199–310.

8

Foundational Thuggery
and a Rhetoric of Subsumption

Frank Farmer

For some time now, Truth (with a capital T) has acquired a reputation as a fugitive of sorts, a runaway loose on the epistemological mean streets of the old neighborhood. According to a few who claim to have befriended Truth, what makes its capture so difficult is that Truth can assume any number of aliases and disguises, all of which provide it with an uncanny ability to elude those seeking its whereabouts. Occasionally, authorities report that the secret hiding places of Truth have, once and for all, been found out. But such reports, as everybody knows, are forever premature: Truth, it seems, will invariably reappear, and do so in the most unlikely of places.

Dealing with such a cagey adversary is, for many, simply not worth the effort. Among those yet determined to "get at Truth," however, it is widely acknowledged that rather harsh, extreme measures are justified in pursuing the slippery figure Truth has shown itself to be. Drastic methods are called for, so the argument goes, especially when Truth's minions demonstrate no hesitation to use violence, terror, and intimidation in carrying out Truth's commands.

Lately, though, a rumor has been circulating. In controversial releases to the press, a few bold souls have begun to spread the notion that, well, maybe Truth does not really exist, that it never did exist and never will. Truth, they hold, is a phantom, a legend, a supreme trickster whose existence—while no doubt useful for some—is in fact nothing more than a prolonged and cruel hoax. Once we expose Truth for what it never was, they argue, once we pronounce Truth dead and gone, we may at last free ourselves of all the mischief that is Truth's sad legacy, all the violence that attends the search for Truth, all the pain wreaked on the unknowing by those who think they know what Truth requires them to do.[1]

As might be expected, this idea has not been received warmly by the authorities or, for that matter, the community at large. Many officials, for example, point to Truth's rap sheet, a thick document that chronicles some of the most heinous deeds ever committed by and on humanity. Various civic groups have rushed to Truth's defense, offering all manner of support on Truth's behalf. Truth, they point out, experienced a difficult birth and a troubled childhood but might yet be saved, if only we gave it the understanding it deserves. Other citizens have argued that losing Truth would be like losing a dear, old friend—a friend who had a lot of serious problems, yes, but a friend nevertheless. Spiritual leaders, along with certain mental health officials, have issued joint statements expressing their concern about the effects of denying the existence of Truth. They predict mass depression, a sharp rise in anxiety disorders, and rampant existential dread within the community at large. The consequences of pronouncing Truth dead, they warn, would be well nigh devastating.

As a witness to these events, I have been especially interested in how the debate has unfolded. Having attended several town meetings on the question of Truth's existence, I found my attentions increasingly focused on the way that opposing disputants argued their respective cases. What I discovered in listening to these debates was yet more evidence of Truth's lasting influence. For in the very rhetoric of their claims, many of those who argue about Truth are more than happy to adopt Truth's heavy-handed ways, eager to indulge a kind of argumentative thuggery worthy of Truth's former glory.

One of these debates seems particularly suited to illustrate what I call a rhetoric of subsumption. In the pages to follow, I will offer this debate as a starting point from which I then hope to chart a few of the relationships that obtain among thugs, theorists, and antitheorists.

The Habermas-Gadamer Debate

In the late 1960s, Frankfurt school marxist Jürgen Habermas began an exchange with the primary architect of philosophical hermeneutics, Hans-Georg Gadamer.[2] The Habermas-Gadamer debate provoked abundant comment and analysis in the social sciences and in nonanalytic philosophical circles. But among rhetoricians, the debate has received only scant attention. Even though we have examined, separately, the theories of both Habermas and Gadamer for their significance to rhetorical concerns, we have yet to address satisfactorily the momentous occasion of their having addressed each other.

I would like to offer, then, a preliminary exploration of the Habermas-Gadamer debate, with an eye toward the rhetoric employed by the two parties involved. Specifically, I wish to show that the preferred argumentative strategy for both is a subsumptive one, which is to say, one marked by assertions that seek to annex, and thereby negate, the arguments offered by the opposing disputant. This trumping mode of debate follows logically from the claims to universality put forth by both Habermas and Gadamer—claim that have ironic, far-reaching, and subversive implications for their respective theories—not to mention for the larger question of theory itself. Before elaborating my point, however, I will first provide a synopsis of this rather complex debate.

Habermas begins the debate by appropriating Gadamer's hermeneutics for his own purposes, the two most important of which are the critiques of positivist and neo-Wittgensteinian assumptions regarding the nature of knowledge in the social sciences. According to Habermas, philosophical hermeneutics offers an important challenge to those who wish to apply the methods of the natural sciences to the social sciences, believing that a neutral, value-free, observational knowledge of social relations is not only possible but readily at hand. Likewise, Habermas claims, hermeneutics poses a serious challenge to Wittgenstein-inspired approaches that imagine it possible to abandon, however temporarily, one's native language game so as to be completely resocialized into the language game of another. In this scheme of things, the investigator participates in, and thereby gains access to, a kind of knowledge that recognizes situatedness and thus, to an extent, resists positivism. Habermas is more sympathetic to a neo-Wittgensteinian method, but still sees its limitations—or, rather, sees its limitations more clearly through the lens of philosophical hermeneutics (*Logic* 143–70). Two key concepts of Gadamer's hermeneutics, in fact, bear special relevance for Habermas.

First, in *Truth and Method,* Gadamer attempts to rehabilitate the concept of prejudice, a term freighted with burdensome connotations inherited from Enlightenment reason. Gadamer's point is not the commonplace that prejudice is an inescapable condition of being human, but that prejudice is exactly that condition which makes possible all understanding. There is no understanding, and hence no knowledge, that is not enabled by prejudice or sets of prejudice received through the historical traditions which we live within and which live within us. And while it is desirable, necessary even, to become conscious of our prejudices, we can never surmount them or put them aside as Enlightenment reason would require us to do. Indeed, Gadamer reminds us that the operative prejudice of the Enlightenment is its prejudice against prejudice (*Truth* 270–85). Second, and opposed to the strict dichotomy between subject and object premised by methodical approaches to knowledge, Gadamer offers instead a concept which tries to capture the unity of the relationship between subject and object, what he calls "the fusion of horizons." Here, subject and object are realized as moments in a tradition constitutive of both interpreter and object of interpretation, thus rendering each inescapably finite, conditioned. For the object is as situated in historical understanding as the interpreter who wishes to apprehend it (302–7). Any definition of an object, therefore, must include all received understandings of that object, its cumulative effects, as well as the historical position from which it is presently being understood. Not surprisingly, then, we hear Gadamer claim that "the true historical object is not an object at all, but the unity of the one and the other," of subject and object, and thus a fusion of horizons (299).

Notwithstanding the usefulness of Gadamer's hermeneutics to his position, Habermas has serious reservations about it. To begin with, Habermas questions the apparent opposition Gadamer sets up between hermeneutical experience and methodic knowledge, thereby lending unintentional force, in Habermas's view, to a positivist devaluation of hermeneutics. Habermas argues that Gadamer's seeming indifference to methodology effectively surrenders methodological concerns to his opponents. Rather than develop a hermeneutically enlightened alternative to scientific method, Habermas argues, Gadamer chooses to wash his hands of the whole question of method, leaving developments in that arena to the positivists (*Logic* 166–70). Gadamer responds by noting that he had not intended to set up truth and method as mutually exclusive alternatives, but that he wanted to show how hermeneutic experience is prior to the exercise of any method ("Scope" 26). It concerns itself with "not what we are doing, not what we ought to be doing, but what happens with us beyond our wanting and doing." (*Truth* xxviii). In other words, interpretive understanding, *verstehen,* is for Gadamer "more Being than consciousness" ("Scope" 38), and therefore Habermas has mistakenly shifted the grounds of the discussion back to a theory of knowledge, epistemology, rather than keeping it, as Gadamer intended, in a theory of Being or ontology.

Next, Habermas claims that prejudice certified by tradition—the sort that Gadamer has in mind—denies "the power of reflection" or critique. Habermas argues that once a prejudice is exposed as a prejudice, it ceases to hold sway in the manner that an unreflected prejudice can. Moreover, Habermas adds, it does not follow that simply because a structure of prejudices is inevitable, the same structure must be a legitimate one. We are not, Habermas insists, creatures wholly at the mercy of traditions whose authority is beyond question.

Reflection has the power to break with authority, with the claims of tradition upon us, even when—or perhaps especially when—those claims *seem* reasonable, obvious, natural (*Logic* 168–70). Habermas's concern here, as Georgia Warnke points out, is that where we think we see truth, we may be seeing only ideology, "the relations of force and domination that remain obscure to us as long as we rely on hermeneutic understanding alone" (113).

Gadamer responds that Habermas overestimates the power of reflection. If Habermas thinks it possible to stand outside the hermeneutic circle, Gadamer argues, if reflection is somehow exempt from history, then Habermas has fallen prey to a rationalist idealism more consonant with Enlightenment reason than historical understanding. Indeed, Gadamer maintains that Habermas has apparently bought into that venerable, but mistaken, opposition between authority and reason so characteristic of Enlightenment thought. Authority is not always or necessarily unjust or coercive. To assume so is to require a dogmatic stance toward received traditions. Moreover, Gadamer adds, there is nothing in hermeneutics that prohibits reflection or the critique of ideology; even revolutionary consciousness falls within the scope of hermeneutics ("Scope" 30–42).

Finally, Habermas disputes Gadamer's claim for language as the "meta-institution," the very wellspring of hermeneutical being as Gadamer conceives it. Against Gadamer's universal claims for the linguistic basis of cultural tradition, Habermas argues that language is but one moment within a complex of social meaning. Understanding is thus a function not of language alone, but also of structures of labor and domination existing distinct from language. Language as cultural tradition is, in fact, preceded and constrained by the realities of labor and domination (*Logic* 171–89). Elsewhere, Habermas will argue this point analogously by calling on the developmental theories of Piaget, who, Habermas believes, demonstrated the actuality of a prelinguistic stage of cognitive development ("Claim" 300). What is needed, according to Habermas, is a theoretical reference system wherein linguistically constituted tradition would be but one moment in a larger objective context. And because hermeneutics lacks such a reference system, it must remain self-enclosed, unable to achieve the distance needed to reveal the ideological distortions which operate within its circle and which hinder communication in systematic, and often disguised, ways.

Gadamer answers these arguments by defending the universality of hermeneutic understanding, denying that the so-called real, material factors of labor and domination can somehow exist outside of language. The supposed extra-linguistic forces that condition language, Gadamer claims, are always, already part of language, part of the understanding that a tradition has of itself, whether expressed or unexpressed. In fact, Habermas errs in ascribing to hermeneutic understanding only that which is explicitly retrievable ("Scope" 26–38). Indeed, Gadamer maintains, hermeneutics is particularly suited to the "task of revealing hidden dimensions of meaning and, hence, of exposing ideology" (Warnke 115).

In the next round of exchanges, Habermas offers an analogy between critical theory and Freudian psychoanalysis, arguing that both are capable of explaining the origins of "systematically distorted communication" which occur in private neurosis, as well as in public communication. Without an explanatory theory of origins, hermeneutics will remain unable to account for distortions in communication which appear normal, but which mask interests of domination. As Habermas puts it, "The What . . . of the systematically distorted expression cannot be 'understood' unless the Why. . . . cannot be 'explained' at the same time" ("Claim" 305). Gadamer responds by noting that the analogy between psychoanalysis and social dialogue is a poor one. Interlocutors in social conversation thankfully do not share the asymmetry sanctioned by a professional institution, nor is communication especially well-served if one party regards the other as pathologically deceived and self-deceiving. The elitist implications of Habermas's view do not escape Gadamer's notice, but his deeper point is to question the apparent belief that one's own theoretical assumptions are objectively true, whether in psychoanalysis, communicative competence, or any other realm of theoretical application. Normality, Gadamer reminds, cannot be thought to be an objective, ahistorical condition, as psychoanalytic "knowledge" typically presumes it to be ("Scope" 38–42).

This, then, is a bare-bones account of the Habermas-Gadamer debate. As I mentioned at the outset, the most pervasive feature of this exchange is the apparent desire, shared by Gadamer and Habermas alike, to subsume the competing claims of each other's position. The best way to illuminate what I refer to here as a "rhetoric of subsumption" is to elaborate the two modes of argument that drive this exchange. The first is temporal: the rhetoric of before and after, of the privileges that accrue to the one who can claim theoretical *priority*. The second is spatial, the rhetoric of inside and outside, of annex and surrender, of the advantages that fall to the container, not the contained. Let me elaborate these metaphors in the context of the debate.

First, on claims to priority, recall that Gadamer considers "the hermeneutical experience . . . prior to all methodological alienation because it is the matrix out of which arise the questions it then directs to science" ("Scope" 284). Unlike, say, Feyerabend, Gadamer is not "against method"; rather, he is concerned with the processes that call forth, and the assumptions that inform, methodological inquiry—those conditions, in other words, that precede method. The more important claim to priority concerns itself with the central issue of the debate, namely, the putative ability of hermeneutics to understand itself, to participate in the kind of reflection able to uncover the ideological forces at work in systematically distorting ways. Here again, Gadamer maintains, reflection can reveal the unconscious, false, obscure prejudices that deform understanding, but it does not assume all prejudices to operate in this manner. Nor does it assume that it is possible (or even desirable) to rid ourselves of prejudice, since doing so would preclude all understanding whatsoever. Gadamer's point is that while hermeneutics is able to bring to light a measure of that "something" which occurs "behind our backs," so to speak, it cannot bring everything to the fore, since hermeneutics is "more Being than consciousness, and Being is never fully manifest" ("Scope" 38). Indeed, it is precisely because hermeneutics is ontological that it must come *before* ideological critique.

Habermas, too, makes claims for priority. In using Piaget to argue for a prelinguistic domain, Habermas resurrects the Piagetian notion that interpretive intelligence precedes language acquisition. Language, to use Piaget's curious phrase, "sits upon" already established cognitive operations such as time, space, causality, and so on. Analogously, in the sphere of social relations, language "sits upon" (or with) the existing domains of labor and domination. While it may be true that the meta-institution of language conditions all understanding, it is also true that language is conditioned by other social processes that, in a sense, precede language—a distinction Paul Ricoeur draws between the idea that everything "arrives in" language as opposed to the idea that everything "comes to" language (153). Second, Habermas argues that explanatory theory must come before hermeneutic understanding. Just as psychoanalytic theory offers a way to explain the origins of distorted expressions in the human psyche, hermeneutics likewise requires a theory able to explain the origins of systematically distorted communication. Before interpretive understanding is possible, we must first be able to guarantee that the understanding we have is uncontaminated by ideological forces. And to warrant such an understanding, we need an explanatory theory of the origins of communication. Explanation, hence, is prior to understanding.

What then of our spatial metaphor, the image of container and thing contained? As should be obvious by now, Gadamer denies that anything can escape the hermeneutic circle. Nothing is exempt, and thus there is no Archimedean point that can be located outside, beyond, above, below, or separate from the reach of historical being. For this reason, Gadamer could not possibly applaud the efforts of Habermas to refashion hermeneutics as a subordinate discipline whose primary purpose is to serve the methodology of the human sciences. Nor can he agree that hermeneutics is but one arena of cultural meaning "demarcated against other determinants of social reality" (Warnke 114). To allow these points is to return to that brand of hermeneutics that Gadamer's entire project stands in opposition to, namely, hermeneutics as a specialized set of interpretive procedures. Because of its universality, then, the arguments that Habermas forwards on behalf of ideological critique must be contained within the infinity of the hermeneutic circle.

Since critique implies distance, Habermas, in turn, must "find a critical vantage point outside of the hermeneutic circle" (Jay 102). The way he does this is to construct a theoretical reference system whereby hermeneutics is situated within an arrangement of knowledge-constitutive interests. To this end, Habermas identifies three spheres of interest. First, that dimension of social life concerning the way humans engage their material environment Habermas refers to generically as *labor* or work. This realm seeks technical mastery, prediction, and control, and finds expression within the empirical analytic or natural sciences. Next, Habermas cites the realm of interaction, whose medium is language and whose purposes are interpretive, that is, aimed toward the understanding of meaning. This realm clusters itself into the hermeneutic disciplines of the human sciences. Finally, Habermas identifies the realm of *domination* or power, the knowledge-interest of which is emancipation and whose proper disciplinary cluster, according to Habermas, is the critical social sciences (*Knowledge*).

As this arrangement suggests, hermeneutics for Habermas is no longer to be regarded as universal; rather, it is but one among other domains of interests that require specification. The crucial fact about this schema is that it posits a hierarchy. We thus see that while the empirical sciences are properly subordinate to the hermeneutic sciences, hermeneutics, in turn, is subordinate to critical theory. And since this arrangement is not a mere plurality of interests, but a hierarchical ordering, Habermas accomplishes two feats at once: the refutation of hermeneutics' claim to universality and the containment of hermeneutics within the territorial lines of explanatory, critical theory. Hermeneutics is thus subsumed to the exigencies of emancipatory critique.

Now, an important irony here is that "the path and conclusion" of the debate seem to contradict Habermas's and Gadamer's ideas concerning what desirable communication ought to entail. As one observer put it, the debate "did not conform to Habermas' notion of communicative action because [his purpose] was admittedly to establish his differences with Gadamer . . . was more instrumental than communicative; and the conclusion did not conform to Gadamer's . . . fusion of horizons, for the two participants were farther apart at the end of the dialogue than they had been at the start" (Kelly 139).

Should we be surprised at this outcome? I think not. I would argue that the unsatisfying conclusion to this exchange was, if not inevitable, at the very least predictable. A rhetoric of subsumption, it would seem, is not especially agreeable to either dialogue or consensus. Subsuming arguments do not merely borrow or engage another's claims in order to explain them in relation to one's own; subsuming arguments, rather, seek to explain away the position of the other, to annihilate and thereby silence the other's discourse—once and for all— by virtue of a kind of discursive imperialism. Fortunately, that silence is rarely achieved.

Arresting Suspects

As noted earlier, one mark of Truth's continuing legacy is echoed in the many ways that people argue *about* Truth. My (simplified) retelling of the Habermas-Gadamer debate tries to illustrate this point reflexively, that is, in a manner that calls our attention not only to the epistemological issues raised, but also to the modes of argument. The former have been of considerable interest to antifoundational thinkers, and the latter, I maintain, ought to be, insofar as the eschewal of rationalist argument, at a minimum, presupposes an awareness of what is being shunned. In order to develop this second point, I will review how Habermas and Gadamer fare in subsequent appropriations by the two premier antifoundationalists of our moment, Stanley Fish and Richard Rorty.

Even though neither Fish nor Rorty offers any extensive commentary on the debate proper, I think it is fair to say that both regard Gadamer more favorably than they do Habermas, since, among other reasons, hermeneutics is simply more consonant with pragmatist belief than, say, "emancipatory critique" or rule-governed formulations of what an ideal speech situation might entail. This is not to suggest that Habermas is casually dismissed; just the opposite turns out to be true. For Rorty and Fish, Habermas tends to command more critical attention than Gadamer. And rightly so perhaps, since in pragmatist terms, while Gadamer may be "useful" in the way of (affirming a particular) belief, Habermas is the one who better enacts the pragmatist virtue of keeping (a particular strain of) the conversation going.

Rorty, for example, is sympathetic with the Habermasian project, but only up to a point. That point is reached when, in Rorty's words, Habermas "goes transcendental" and attempts to identify those principles which enable "undistorted conversation." Rorty, of course, denies that such principles exist, and offers in their place a pragmatist redefinition of "undistorted" as that which is communally determined according to "*our* criteria for relevance" ("Pragmatism" 173). Elsewhere, Rorty notes that Jean-François Lyotard shares the same incredulity toward the Habermasian transcendental (or "meta-narrative"), but unlike Lyotard, Rorty discovers in Habermas a quality lacking in French postmodern thinkers. In contrast to the social and political commitments of an intellectual like Habermas, Rorty argues, "thinkers like Foucault and Lyotard [are] so afraid of being caught up in one more metanarrative . . . that they cannot bring themselves to say 'we' long enough to identify with the culture of the generation to which they belong" ("Habermas" 172). Rorty refers to this seeming "lack of identification with any social context" as a kind of "dryness" not found in the work of Habermas. Understandably, then, Rorty would like to cut a deal that allows us to keep the best and scrap the worst of Habermasian thought. We could, Rorty argues, "accept the claim that valuing 'undistorted communication' was of the essence of liberal politics without needing a theory of communicative competence as backup" (173).

Less generously, perhaps, Stanley Fish sees in Habermas's universal pragmatics a synechdoche for what Fish considers the impossible dream of "critical self-consciousness," the same dream that, for Habermas, constitutes the prime motive in his debate with Gadamer. Fish will grant to thinkers of the Frankfurt school some measure of praise for their desire to undermine objectivist versions of social reality—to show, for example, how established facts can be presented as "natural" phenomena, rather than constructions that serve particular interests. But this disavowal of objectivism must necessarily be short-lived, for critical theory itself desires a superseding objectivity that somehow will enable it to see through the ideological distortions which mask oppression. Fish, like Rorty, denies that such a privileged view is possible and, to no one's surprise, fingers

Habermas as one purveyor of this delusion ("Critical" 450–55). To the extent that Habermas wants to hold on to the idea of universal pragmatics as something more than an oxymoron, Fish might argue, Habermas must necessarily break rank with the antifoundational camp.

Notwithstanding certain allowances for Habermas, Fish and Rorty could not possibly embrace the position forwarded by Habermas in his debate with Gadamer. But does this mean that, from an antifoundational view, Gadamer "wins" the debate hands down?

On the surface of things it would seem so. Any informed genealogy of Fish's interpretive community would have to acknowledge the influence of Gadamer's *Truth and Method*. When, for example, Fish makes the point that we do not merely "have" interpretations, but that interpretations "have" us as well, he reiterates the ontological position of Gadamer (*Text* 331–32). When, further, Fish argues that it is impossible to escape the interpretive institutions which precede (and thus constitute) us, he lends added emphasis to two key assumptions of Gadamer's hermeneutics: namely, the historicity and linguisticality of all human existence ("Critical" 455). Rorty's debt to Gadamer, however, is at once more extensive and more explicit. The final section of Rorty's opus *Philosophy and the Mirror of Nature* is devoted to an explication of hermeneutics as the alternative to epistemology-driven philosophy. More pointedly, the final chapter of this section is something of a testament to the influence of Gadamer on Rorty's vision of a pragmatist world. What Rorty finds especially useful in Gadamer is the latter's emphasis on *Bildung,* that is, "education," "developmental becoming," "self-formation." Rorty offers what he considers a more palatable translation for *Bildung*—"edification"—to oppose and replace our tired preoccupations with *knowledge*. Edification, in Rorty's scheme, describes the "project of finding new, better, more interesting, more fruitful ways of speaking." It invites us to make connections between cultures, periods, and communities and "to reinterpret our familiar surroundings in the unfamiliar terms of our new inventions" (360). It allows us to keep open that "conversation of mankind" which is our postphilosophic inheritance.

Now clearly, Gadamer is more consonant with the thinking of both Rorty and Fish than is Habermas. Yet this hardly means that pragmatist appropriations of Gadamer are unproblematic. Rorty, in particular, runs into some difficulty on this count, for there is the warranted suspicion that, were Rorty pressed on the matter, he might have to admit that Gadamer is not any more of a pragmatist than is Habermas. Such, at least, is the view of Richard Bernstein, who locates Gadamer squarely in the long tradition of metaphysical idealism, a placement at decisive odds with Rorty's borrowings (*Beyond* 199). Bernstein's view is also echoed by Georgia Warnke, who believes Gadamer's thought to be "not as antithetical to Enlightenment concerns . . . [and] closer to a foundationalist enterprise" than Rorty (and others) would care to admit (141).

Both Warnke and Bernstein hold that Rorty leaves something out in his appropriation of Gadamer. That something is Gadamer's reluctance to abandon, completely and forever, some stand-in for Enlightenment truth. For Bernstein, this is apparent in Gadamer's wish for hermeneutics to supplant what epistemology can no longer provide: a "more profound access to truth than is available to us by the normal procedures of science" (*Beyond* 198). For Warnke, Rorty's move to oppose edification to knowledge—a move that presents Gadamer's *Bildung* as a strictly antifoundational concept—is a mistaken one. Gadamer, she points out, sees *Bildung* not as a denial of the possibility of knowledge, but as *another* kind of knowledge—a "knowledge that can differentiate between the appropriate and the inappropriate, the good and the bad, the right and the wrong" (159). The practical judgment (*phronesis*) that *Bildung* aims to effect, according to Warnke, suggests a "truth which perhaps cannot be reduced to a method . . . but which remains a form of knowledge equal to modern science itself" (159). Where Rorty might think it unnecessary to take on the natural sciences as a special case of foundationalism, Gadamer would argue instead that because "scientific knowledge is not objective in any ahistorical sense, [this] does not mean that the concept of knowledge is in general an outmoded shibboleth" (Warnke 161). Gadamer's purpose is to free us from the overlord of methodical knowledge—whose paradigmatic expression is found in the natural sciences—so that "dialogic forms of inquiry" might be open to pursue their own truths without embracing any misguided notions of objectivity or the need for method. Gadamer's purposes are plainly quite distinct from those of Rorty, and the profound differences between the two, pursued far enough, might result in an irreparable breach.

So we should not be surprised to hear Rorty, despite his reliance on hermeneutics, concede that Gadamer is at best "a half-hearted pragmatist" ("Nineteenth" 152). And should this judgment appear to reprise Rorty's assessment of Habermas, there are good reasons why that is so. Richard Bernstein points out:

> From Rorty's perspective, the trouble with Gadamer and
> Habermas is that they are not sufficiently radical in exposing

> the illusions and pretensions of philosophy (or of some ap-
> propriate successor discipline). They still cling to the hope
> that philosophy or its true successor can be a foundational
> discipline of culture. . . . One might even be inclined to say
> that both Gadamer and Habermas are still representatives of
> modernity . . . even when all the concessions are made to
> human finitude, historicity, and fallability—while Rorty is a
> "postmodern" thinker who seeks to root out the last vestiges
> of the "metaphysics of presence." (*Beyond* 200–201)

The debate between Gadamer and Habermas represents a kind of late modernist exchange of quasi-foundational theorists, each of whom makes utterances that clearly betray a wish to cling to some version of Truth. What transpires in their debate provides reason enough to suspect a lurking foundationalism behind their respective nods to history. But if we take Rorty's advice seriously, that is, if we examine not only the content of their exchange but also "the way things are said" (as *edification* requires us to do), then here, too, we have reason to suspect a foundational agenda. For Rorty and Fish, I would argue, imply that what I am calling a subsumptive rhetoric is fitting to universalist positions that assume a foundational truth. And yet as we shall see, neither Rorty nor Fish is any more successful at avoiding this mode of "saying things" than is Habermas or Gadamer. Nor is there any reason to think that the same ironies do not apply.

Thugs, Theorists, and Antitheorists

One need not look far to see how, from an antifoundational view, a rhetoric of subsumption dovetails rather nicely with foundational thinking. When Rorty, for example, spurns the traditional role of the philosopher as "cultural overseer who knows everyone's common ground . . . who knows what everyone else is really doing whether they know it or not," what he objects to is the peremptory status that philosophy has always claimed as its birthright (*Mirror* 317). But philosophy, in Rorty's thinking, possesses no metaphysical privileges that enable it to assert a knowledge prior to, or outside of, "what everyone else is really doing." Fish, similarly, yokes foundationalism to a desire to establish a position from which one may be able to subsume or preempt all other positions. Fish thus defines theory as "an abstract or algorithmic formulation that guides or governs practice from a position outside any particular conception of practice." Moreover, Fish notes, theory in this strong sense also implies a relationship of "precedence and priority" to practice, again reiterating the importance of the temporal and spatial metaphors indicated earlier ("Consequences" 378).

Recalling that the subsumptive claims offered by Gadamer and Habermas derive from their respective use of these metaphors—claims that assert either priority or containment—we see yet another reason why both Gadamer and Habermas might be suspected of a thinly disguised foundationalism. Holding an endless number of trumps marked "before" and "outside of," Habermas and Gadamer play an elaborate hand of philosophic debate accompanied by argumentative thuggery. We might reasonably expect then—as Rorty would have us do—that antifoundational argument (if that is the right word) would try to find new ways to speak about problems, issues, and oppositions, that it would properly manage to avoid the high-handedness which supposedly characterizes a foundational rhetoric of subsumption. But is this in fact the case?

In the remaining pages, I want to show how antifoundationalists all too easily adopt foundational modes of argument. I will try to illustrate this point by a look at two key articles: "Consequences" by Stanley Fish and "The Priority of Democracy to Philosophy" by Richard Rorty.

Fish's essay is a paradoxical eulogy for something that, Fish argues, never existed in the first place. He is concerned with that special brand of foundationalism that, in recent years, has claimed to inform the practice of literary studies. The term used for this strong version of literary foundationalism is *theory*, a project defined by Steven Knapp and Walter Benn Michaels as "the attempt to govern interpretations of particular texts by appealing to an account of interpretation in general." Fish quotes this definition approvingly and then adds two further qualifications: theory "is an attempt to *guide* practice from a position outside or above it, and [second] it is an attempt to *reform* practice by neutralizing interest," thus assuring that theory is a principled, and therefore unbiased, activity (315, 319–20). To refute both of these claims, Fish moves to the central point of his essay, namely, that theory has "no consequences" for the practice of literary criticism.

Simply put, Fish's argument is that because the project of theory cannot possibly succeed, there can be no consequences that necessarily follow *from* theory. And the reason why theory cannot possibly succeed, Fish argues, is "because the primary data and formal laws necessary to its success will always be spied or picked out from within the contextual circumstances of which they are supposedly independent. The objective facts and rules of calculation that are to ground interpretation and render it principled are themselves interpretive products: they are, therefore, always and already contaminated by the interested judgments they claim to transcend" (320).

Theory, in other words, cannot guide our interpretive activities from a position located somewhere outside of practice. Nor can it possibly claim precedence to those activities when theory itself is thoroughly embedded in the interpretive practices from whence it derives. For Fish, theory is best thought of as yet another interested belief, though perhaps the only interested belief that considers itself to be neither outside nor within interpretive practice. Objectivity, in literary studies and elsewhere, is possible only if there is some "way of testing our beliefs against something whose source is not also a belief" (322). And thus, if theory derives *from* practice, then it cannot have any consequences that do not originate *in* practice. "There is," Fish reminds us, "a world of difference in saying that theory is a form of practice and saying that theory informs practice" (337).

But must theory be equated with antifoundationalism? Can we not entertain the notion that certain *non*foundational kinds of theory are possible? This is how Fish interprets the challenge put forward by Adena Rosmarin, a challenge that Fish deems important enough to address. Rosmarin, Fish reports, wonders why theory must be restricted to its strictly foundational definition. Why, for example, can't theory refer to, say, William Empson's *Seven Types of Ambiguity?* Indeed, what prevents us from considering antifoundationalism as yet another species of theory? Fish responds by observing that theory, as well as the consequences attributed to it, is "totally uninteresting if *everything* is theory" (326). But he acknowledges that there are those who proffer such an argument, and do so believing they have adopted a position consonant with antifoundationalism—namely, that no action occurs without certain assumptions, tacit or otherwise, which to some extent determine that action, that no fact can be known that is not somehow mediated by those same assumptions. Fish agrees with these points but denies the usual conclusion drawn from the argument: to wit, "that every practice is underwritten by a theory." Fish will allow that all actions and practices are contingent on beliefs, but, Fish insists, "beliefs are not theories": "A theory is a special achievement of consciousness; a prerequisite for being conscious at all. Beliefs are not what you think about but what you think with. . . . Theories are something you can have—you can wield them and hold them at a distance; beliefs have you. . . . In order to make even the simplest of assertions or perform the most elementary action, I must already be proceeding in the context of innumerable beliefs which cannot be the object of my attention because they are the content of my attention" (326).

Much of this should by now sound familiar. If we were to substitute the term *prejudice* for *belief* in the foregoing excerpt, we would have an excellent restatement of many key points that Gadamer makes in his debate with Habermas. In any event, Fish's task here is to prevent a casual diminishment of the very concept that is the target of his essay, theory. He does this by telling us what theory is not. But he also tells us what theory is, in contrast to what it claims to be.

Theory, according to Fish, turns out to be just one more expression of that "primary mode of literary criticism" called thematizing (335). This is what a literary critic does, Fish explains, anytime that critic offers a reading from, say, a Lacanian or marxist perspective. Such a critic "quarries" the "vocabulary, distinctions, concerns" from another discipline to perform a specific interpretation within the domain of literary criticism. That critic who offers a psychological reading of "The Purloined Letter," Fish maintains, is not doing psychology but literary criticism. "If I propose," he asks, "a religious reading of George Herbert's lyrics, am I practicing religion?" Neither, then, can someone claim to be practicing theory when he or she is merely practicing literary criticism from a theoretical perspective. Fish argues that, "like any other discipline or body of materials that is made into thematic hay, theory is not so much the consequential agent of a change as it is the passive object of an appropriation" (336).

Much like the jockeying for total advantage which characterizes the Habermas-Gadamer debate, Fish's trump card is one that refuses to theory all claims to priority and domain while simultaneously reserving those qualities for practice. Having dispensed with the notion that any form of practice must necessarily follow from theory, Fish can then grant to theory its much desired "consequences." This is because theory "is itself a form of practice and therefore is consequential for practice as a matter of definition." Far from possessing any claims to a vantage before or outside of practice, theory undergoes a "dramatic reversal" and is now both temporally and spatially compliant to the very practice it once claimed to master. In a telling phrase, Fish concludes that theory "stands revealed as the *helpless plaything*" of practice (366, emphasis added).

Revealed here is a measure of glee at having achieved a victory over a now-defeated theory, the result being the ultimate harnessing of theory to practice. Contra Rosmarin, Fish now claims that before and always, practice (not theory) is *everything*. Remember that Fish's argument with Rosmarin hinged on the structuralist insight that to say "theory is everything" is to say that theory is meaningless. Yet, interestingly enough, this same insight does not apply to practice, for even allowing theory a colonized status within the territorial boundaries of practice is only a stopgap measure. The true mark of theory's vanquishment, Fish tells us, will occur not by continued disputes about theory (which serve only to give it continued life), but rather when theory becomes uninteresting, "when it has played out its string" (340). Until then, of course, we can expect much talk about theory, but such talk signals only its "fading away" (341). Theory's heyday is over when we come to a silence borne of indifference, when the once helpless plaything becomes an amusing relic.

Similarly, Rorty's essay "The Priority of Democracy to Philosophy" celebrates its own kind of subsumptive victory. Here Rorty endeavors to work out his titular claim through a synoptic reading of John Rawls's writings since the publication of *A Theory of Justice,* particularly Rawls's major antifoundational statement, "Justice as Fairness: Political Not Metaphysical." Rorty notes that he, like many others, first read Rawls's theory as something of a foundationalist apology, yet one more "Enlightenment attempt to ground our moral intuitions on a conception of human nature" (286). But Rawls's subsequent writings, Rorty holds, clearly situate Rawls within the pragmatist camp.

Rorty stakes out three positions on democratic social theory which inform current discussions. The first is an absolutist, ahistorical, unabashedly foundational approach to human rights, which, while jettisoning "metaphysical accounts of what a right is . . . nevertheless [insists] that everywhere, in all times and cultures, members of our species have had the same rights" (280–81). This view finds expression in the writings of Ronald Dworkin and others, who "take the notion of ahistorical human 'rights' seriously" (281). The second position is one Rorty assigns to Dewey and Rawls, and one that fits squarely in the pragmatist tradition that Rorty promotes. From this antifoundational view of the problem, the idea of an "individual conscience" that authorizes "inalienable human rights" must be abandoned in favor of one where all talk of rights must be understood as relative to "the tradition of a particular community, the consensus of a particular culture" (281). The final position identified by Rorty is one referred to as "communitarian." Holders of this view, Rorty observes, reject Enlightenment rationalism (and its ahistorical conception of human rights), but despair at the consequences of this rejection. In its extreme form, "this is the view that liberal institutions and culture either should not or cannot survive the collapse of the philosophical justification that the Enlightenment provided for them" (281).

Rorty then provides three versions of communitarian thought, but is primarily interested in the one that bears most directly on Rawls. This is the communitarian view that "political institutions 'presuppose' a doctrine about the nature of human beings and that such a doctrine must, unlike Enlightenment rationalism, make clear the essentially historical character of the self" (282). Here, it would seem, we have a nostalgic yearning for some sort of *basis,* albeit a basis that formulates selfhood not in essential but in historical terms.

Rorty says that to critique this position we must ask two questions. The first is "whether there is any sense in which liberal democracy 'needs' philosophical justification at all," and the second is "whether a conception of the self, which, as [Charles] Taylor says, makes 'the community constitutive of the individual' does in fact comport better with liberal democracy than does the Enlightenment conception of the self" (282). To the first question, Rorty replies with a decisive no, and to the second an equally decisive yes, although, as Rorty will make clear, nothing much matters on how we answer the second question. What matters, rather, is how it can be shown that "liberal democracy can get along without philosophical presuppositions" (283). And for this discussion, he turns to Rawls.

As an antifoundational descendant of Jeffersonian social theory, Rawls, according to Rorty, wishes to bracket philosophical inquiry in the way that Jefferson wished to bracket theological inquiry. That is, Rawls proposes to treat topics regarding "ahistorical human nature, the nature of selfhood, the motive of moral behaviour and the meaning of human life" as irrelevant to politics (283). Because philosophy cannot identify a universal, ahistorical truth capable of authorizing liberal democracy, neither can it offer any basis for a theory of democratic justice. The notions of justice we value—and thus wish to preserve—derive instead from the public arena of "overlapping consensus," from the "settled convictions" that obtain from the institutions and traditions we operate within. Philosophy becomes, then, a sequestered pastime of sorts, a private matter for those still inclined toward ultimate questions. Insofar as political deliberation and social policy are concerned, however, philosophy is at best a moot activity, something to be approached (if approached at all) with wariness, or better still, indifference. Philosophy simply has nothing left to do, in Rawls's definition of justice: "What justifies a conception of justice is not its being true to an order antecedent to and given to us, but its congruence with our deeper understanding of ourselves and our aspirations, and our realization that, *given our history and the traditions embedded in our public life,* it is the most reasonable doctrine *for us*" (quoted in Rorty, "Priority" 286–87). A coherent theory of justice arises out of consensus and tradition, not philosophical sanctions.

Analogous to Fish's reply to the argument that "everything is theory," Rorty argues that both "religion" and "philosophy" are "vague, umbrella terms . . . subject to persuasive redefinition." When allowed too much range, these terms become meaningless—so meaningless that "everybody, even atheists will be said to have religious faith," and correspondingly, that "everybody, even those who shun metaphysics and epistemology" will be said to have "philosophical presuppositions." Like Fish, Rorty needs to limit such a definition but (unlike Fish) needs to do so in the context of Rawls's discussion. Hence, Rorty argues, "let 'philosophy' mean, for Rawls's purposes, disputes about the nature of human beings and even about whether there is such a thing as human nature" (285). This definition "comports" well with Rawls's desire that questions concerning "the point of human existence" be relegated to the innocuous domain of private life.

Also like Fish, Rorty's discussion of Rawls reiterates the notion that philosophy (read "theory") has "no consequences" for politics (read "practice"). If existing liberal democracies fell to ruin in the upcoming years, this would by no means prove that "human societies cannot survive without . . . shared conceptions of our place in the universe and our mission on earth," because democracy was never authorized by philosophy to begin with, and the reasons for democracy's collapse would have more to do with historical conditions than with first principles—at least those first principles thought to be grounded in a natural or metaphysical order rather than in communal agreements (295).

Rorty says no, then, in answer to his first question: Is there any sense in which liberal democracy needs philosophical justification? But Rorty gives an affirmative reply to his second question: Does a conception of self that makes the community constitutive of the individual comport better with liberal democracy than ideas of self received from the Enlightenment? Yes, Rorty concedes, but the important point is that liberal democracy does not *require* any conception of self at all. To be sure, liberal democracy can manage quite nicely with a view of self as "a centerless web of historically conditioned beliefs and desires," and such a definition does comport favorably with the antifoundationalism of Rawls (291). But modern, liberal democracy need not look to any metaphysical conception of self for a basis that authorizes what liberal democracy must be.

Returning once more to our spatial and temporal metaphors, we see that from the outset of his discussion, Rorty inverts the customary way of thinking about democratic institutions, namely, that they somehow follow and draw sustaining warrant from antecedent theories of selfhood, justice, and human nature. Rorty turns this view upside down and argues that democracy is prior to any philosophy of what democracy must be. In making this point, Rorty reprises other versions of the same argument: practice comes before theory, rhetoric before philosophy, agreement before truth, and so on. Much like Nietzsche's reconstruction of Periclean democracy as a thoroughly sophistic event (undermined subsequently by the "decadent" impositions of Plato), Rorty's story of modern democracy posits a similar chain of events. Enlightenment rationalism is not the foundation of our democratic institutions but, ironically, the force that threatens their existence.

Yet Rorty anticipates how his own arguments might be subsumed by the very tradition he wants to disengage. At one juncture, Rorty tells his reader that "it may seem that I have been rejecting a concern with philosophical theories . . . on the basis of just such a theory," but then denies this possibility, since no theory offered by Rorty presumes to entail anything from which other things must necessarily follow (291). In his discussion of constitutive selfhood, Rorty is most aware of this paradox:

> One might be inclined to say that I have evaded one sort of self-referential paradox only by falling into another sort. For I am presupposing that one is at liberty to rig up a model of the self to suit oneself, to tailor it to one's politics, one's religion or one's private sense of the meaning of one's life. This, in turn, presupposes that there is no "objective truth" about what the human self is really like. That, in turn, seems a claim that could be justified only on the basis of a metaphysico–epistemological view of the traditional sort. For surely if anything is the province of such a view, it is the question of what there is and is not "a fact of the matter" about. So my argument must ultimately come back to philosophical first principles. (292)

Having subsumed, and thereby dismissed, philosophy's claims to priority over democracy by a reversal of that order, Rorty is seemingly faced with the paradox that claims for the priority of democracy to philosophy just might be, well, *philosophical* claims. Rorty's answer to this challenge is predictable, at least from a pragmatic view of things. The question itself, Rorty tells us, is "pointless and sterile," since "the very idea of 'a fact of the matter about' is one we would be better off without" (292–93).

Whether one sees this response as satisfactory or not probably has much to do with whether one understands Rorty's answer to be tautological. That is, Rorty essentially refuses to answer the question in the vocabulary in which it is phrased, for doing so must entail an implicit endorsement of a vocabulary that imagines itself to be something more than its own terms. The only sensible pragmatic response is not to respond at all, that is, to deny that the question makes sense. Thus to claim, as Rorty does, that the question is "pointless and sterile" is to do nothing more than to reassert the pragmatist position, though it would be hard to imagine how Rorty could answer otherwise. In fact, Rorty makes this very point in conceiving how liberal democracies might properly respond to the fanaticism of, say, a Nietzsche or Loyola:

> We have to insist that not every argument needs to be met in the terms in which it is presented. Accommodation and tolerance must stop short of a willingness to work within any vocabulary that one's interlocutor wishes to use, to take seriously any topic that he puts forward for discussion. To take this view is of a piece with dropping the idea that a single moral vocabulary and a single set of moral beliefs are appropriate for every human community everywhere, and to grant that historical developments may lead us to simply drop questions and the vocabulary in which those questions are posed. (290)

In other words, the thuggery that all too often accompanies philosophical or religious absolutism must be met with a refusal to argue in the vernacular of those who advocate their preferred version of Truth. Short of this, our best hope is "to josh them out of taking these topics so seriously." And to do that, we must cultivate an "air of light-minded aestheticism" concerning ultimate questions of Truth. Indeed, in a pragmatist world, the proper role for one philosophically inclined is to assist in the "disenchantment" of the world, to make the world more humane, more tolerant by encouraging a less than serious attitude toward the traditional concerns of philosophy (293). Put differently, the philosopher undergoes a radical transformation. No longer that person who claims privileged access to an outside knowledge, the philosopher becomes instead a citizen who, when not engaged in private musings of no consequence, is out and about urging other citizens, especially those with fierce commitments, to lighten up a bit. Rorty's philosopher is certainly no "helpless plaything," but is perhaps something far rarer: the insouciant apostate.

Sentencing

A common suspicion voiced by those not entirely comfortable with the antifoundationalist stance is that, like Habermas and Gadamer, Fish and Rorty are more indebted to the foundationalism they oppose than either of them imagines. Richard Bernstein, for example, argues that Rorty falls into his own brand of essentialism when he substitutes a " 'historical myth of the given' for the 'epistemological myth of the given' that he has helped to expose." In doing so, Bernstein claims, Rorty "fails to see that he is using a variation on the very type of argument he has sought to discredit" ("One" 551). Charles Taylor understands Rorty's brand of pragmatism to be one that "remains in the old epistemology, where representations constitute our entire understanding, and are as it were our only route to contact with the 'outside world' " (271). This view enables Rorty to assign a transcendentalism to correspondence theory that, for Taylor, does not consider other possibilities, the most notable of which are "framework understandings" so prevalent in "contemporary rejections of epistemology" (270). Taylor thinks that Rorty's notion of "representationalism still seems commanded by the doctrine being rejected" (271).

The point here is that antifoundationalism remains on many levels heavily implicated in foundationalist thinking. But following Rorty's prescription, we ought to expect that antifoundationalist discourse would, at the very least, attempt to struggle free from the vocabularies of philosophic language. We should not be surprised, for example, to see among pragmatists the kind of verbal experimentation that characterized so much of Nietzsche's writings, the kind of playful obscurities, perhaps, of a Derrida, or the recovery of a long-repressed "women's writing" that forms the project of an Hélène Cixous. And, indeed, both Fish and Rorty have been variously praised for their stylistic gambols and, where Rorty is concerned, the infusing of a narrative mode of reasoning into traditional philosophical topics.

But as I have tried to show, Fish and Rorty have not managed to break completely with epistemological vocabularies, or with the categories of understanding embedded within those vocabularies. As with Habermas and Gadamer, Fish and Rorty seem rather content to partake of foundational modes of argument, especially when those modes are thought to banish, once and for all, the foundationalist position. Given the unceasing call to leave behind all things foundational, there is more than a little irony in hearing Rorty claim (in the argot of the epistemological tradition) that *anything is prior to anything.* There is, likewise, something troublesome in hearing Fish so relish the declamatory besting that is his mien, especially when we realize that we have again been led (rewriting Whitman) into the fray, endlessly trumping. For no claim proffered against Fish can escape the subsuming procedures which render that claim null and void before it is uttered.

Fish seems happy with this state of affairs, but we sense in Rorty a wish to halt the interminable exchange of subsuming arguments. As noted earlier, Rorty forsees that his position on the question of democracy could very well be construed as a *philosophical* one. Yet his response is not to join this accusation with a counter-trump of his own, but instead to reserve the privilege of not responding at all. So it is that Rorty holds we need not meet every argument on its own terms, since a too liberal tolerance for all vocabularies must inevitably lend credence to views that encourage the kinds of moral universalism hostile to democratic values. In Rorty's view, we are far wiser if we simply refuse to talk in the language of those who promulgate the old epistemology, who grind the axes of this or that Truth. Better, Rorty maintains, to gather up our words and go home than to play in the language game of a Truth-peddling other.

Now, a refusal to engage in dialogue with an antithetical worldview might seem the opposite of a rhetoric of subsumption, that is, a "turning away from" rather than an "encompassing." But the desired effects are identical, for both strategies purport to accomplish a kind of silencing—to be sure, not the silence borne of terror and intimidation, but rather a silence that ensues from the apparent belief that the vocabularies of Truth and practice are, to use that well-traveled word, *incommensurable.* As Charles Taylor has noted, this view amounts to a somewhat unorthodox take on Rorty, a view at seeming odds with the author of "The World Well Lost," where Rorty eschews the idea of "alternative conceptual systems" incapable of addressing one another. Yet Taylor is quick to point out that, at least on the issue of foundational truth, Rorty himself relies extensively on "the notion of world-views as closed systems, like different coloured glasses on people's noses, *mutually irrefutable*" (268, emphasis added). As Taylor sees it, if we accept Rorty's main assertion, namely, "that one can't decide the issue between world-views by arguments evoking reason and truth," then we will find that Rorty's central thesis "must itself repose on a strong doctrine about the self-contained nature of these world-views." In common parlance, you have to buy the whole thing or not at all, or to use Max Weber's image, "you cannot get in and out of these world-views like a cab" (Taylor 259).

All of which is to say precisely what Rorty has been saying: there is no ground on which to adjudicate the disputes that arise in the inevitable encounters between Truth-telling and truth-making discourses. For Taylor, "this means that the interlocutors never reach a point where they (a) accept or find they cannot reject some things in common, which (b) sit with one world-view better than another." To accept this condition of argument is to accept the idea of worldviews as self-contained, as "global systems . . . which have within themselves the resources to redescribe everything which comes along, to reinterpret everything which might be thrown up by an opponent as contrary evidence, and hence to remain constitutionally immune to refutation" (260). What is left would seem to be a kind of de facto universalism—a universalism not too unlike the one that informs the "mutually irrefutable" claims offered by Habermas and Gadamer. And one similarly beyond any hope of resolution.

Indeed, if the positions between foundational and antifoundational discourses cannot be arbitrated, then the options at hand are limited to those already mentioned here: subsume your opponent's worldview into your own, change the subject, or refuse to be baited into a "pointless and sterile" encounter which may lend tacit legitimation to the worldview of your opponent. At all costs, though, strike no bargains, find no middle ground, negotiate no common agreements, for to do so is to surrender the consistency necessary to the status of your own position as a coherent worldview. And be aware that this requisite consistency will lead you into some rather disconcerting positions: "When the secret police come, when the torturers violate the innocent, there is nothing to be said to them of the form 'There is something within you which you are betraying. Though you embody the practices the practices of a totalitarian society which will endure forever, there is something beyond those practices which condemns you.' This thought is hard to live with" (Rorty, *Consequences* xlii).

Rorty concedes that having to take this stance is "morally humiliating," but he might be inclined to point out that, while the pragmatist response—or lack of one—to the foregoing situation is on some level unsatisfying, we should take note that the torturers, thugs, inquisitors, hatchet men, and terrorists of the world are not likely to be pragmatists, but rather agents of some brand of universal Truth. To answer this unsavory lot in their own vocabulary, that is, to talk of betrayed essences and transcendental judgments, is to aid and abet their cause, to give sanction to a future of even more violent certainties and bullying Truths.

Following this lead, are we not likewise obliged to attend to how we—those who supposedly inhabit a postphilosophical moment—discuss these matters? Do we not have some responsibility to ferret out all traces of the old ways, of Truth-telling discourses and epistemological modes of argument? And on discovering those traces, are we not required to purify our own vocabularies of philosophical categories of understanding? Given what Fish and Rorty tell us, it would be hard to reach any other conclusion.

And yet, the ease with which a rhetoric of subsumption explains away, quashes, vitiates any challenge ought to give us pause, ought to make us wonder if, in fact, we remain under the spell of foundational modes of thought. For such a rhetoric too often chafes with what advocates of pragmatism deign to offer as a replacement for Truth. Is it really any surprise that Habermas was unable to effect an "ideal speech situation" in his debate with Gadamer? Or that Gadamer never quite reached a "fusion of horizons" with Habermas? Or that, on the question of theory, all theorists must be excluded from whatever "consensus" is worked out in Fish's interpretive community? Or that Rorty's "conversation of mankind" is a seriously limited conversation, one that *must* exclude that portion of humanity—a sizable portion I would think—still loyal to a transcendental or objective worldview? The nonrealist proxy for Truth, an alternative that makes free use of the various tropes of dialogue, is profoundly and ironically hostile to dialogue when it calls on a rhetoric of subsumption to dismiss Truth and Truth's imperious ways. Clearly, as any subsumptive rhetoric will easily show, the best way to silence an opposing view is to make it wholly explainable within the terms of one's own view.

But there is another sense in which the antifoundationalist position is resistant to dialogue. To say, as Rorty does, that the pursuit of Truth has not really gotten us anywhere, that it has not resulted in answers to any of the fundamental questions posed by philosophy, is somewhat self-refuting. For it is obvious that Rorty's position could not have emerged out of *anything but* the epistemological tradition. And yet, Rorty is eager to jettison this tradition entirely, in the apparent belief that it has exhausted itself, that it has nothing left to say. Oddly enough, it may well be that philosophy and antifoundationalism share a common desire: namely, to possess that most esteemed privilege of having the "last word" or "final say." The main difference between the two is that where philosophy traditionally seeks the last word on Truth, Rorty seeks the last word on philosophy (or the Untruth about philosophy). And though Rorty implores us to be properly skeptical of whatever final Truths the epistemological tradition is able to proffer, this same skepticism toward the antifoundationalist challenge is not encouraged. This essay is an attempt to lay out the rhetorical strategies by which antifoundationalism seeks to insulate itself from any disputing contention, from refutation and agreement, from engagement and dialogue. But the wary may be inclined to reject any and all "last word" narratives, including Rorty's. They may feel compelled to ask, If Rorty's own position comes out of the epistemological tradition that it rejects, *what else might?*

And the implications of this for rhetoric? What I have referred to here as a "rhetoric of subsumption" comports fittingly with received, usually misinformed ideas about rhetoric—the conventional view being that rhetoric is an art whose purpose is to achieve total victory over an opponent using any means whatsoever. But Rorty and Fish (especially Fish) supposedly reject this beknighted understanding in favor of one that sees all knowledge as rhetorically based, that is, as interested, contentious, persuasive. And yet, in marshalling arguments for what seems to be a rhetorical understanding of knowledge, Rorty and Fish sometimes exercise a quite conventional understanding of rhetoric, especially when their preferred truth-making discourse confronts the truth-telling discourse of epistemology.

In those moments, the promised blessings of consensus and dialogue are temporarily postponed while a rhetoric of subsumption works to insure that any serious challenge to the antifoundationalist position is nullified before it is offered.[3]

Notes

1. According to Christopher Norris, "the most obvious source-text" for the idea of Truth as brutal tormentor is Michel Foucault's *Discipline and Punish*. But the presumed affinity between foundationalism and oppressive cruelty can be found elsewhere, most

notably perhaps in Page duBois's *Torture and Truth*. For other slants on the same notion, see Belsey, Norris, Scott, and Rorty ("Thugs").

2. The "debate" was inaugurated with the publication of the second edition of Gadamer's *Warheit und Methode,* which included prefatory material wherein Gadamer replied to his earliest critics. Habermas subsequently joined those early critics with the 1967 publication of *Zur Logic der Sozialwissenschaften* (*The Logic of the Social Sciences*). Gadamer's response is found in two essays, "Die Universalität des Hermeneutischen Problems" ("The Universality of the Hermeneutic Problem") and "Rhetoric, Hermeneutik, und Ideologiekritik" (translated as "On the Scope and Function of Hermeneutical Reflection"). Though published in German some nine years earlier, both appear in English in a 1976 collection of Gadamer's essays, *Philosophical Hermeneutics,* trans. and ed. by David Linge. Habermas's next rejoinder appears in 1970, in a Festschrift dedicated to Gadamer, "On Hermeneutics' Claim to Universality," which appears in English in *The Hermeneutics Reader.* Gadamer's response is found in "Replik," in K. O. Apel et al., eds., *Hermeneutik und Ideologiekritik* (Frankfurt: Suhrkamp, 1971). In an early effort, perhaps, to give an accounting of the debate, Habermas published "Summation and Response" in *Continuum* 8 (1970): 123–33. For important discussions of the Habermas-Gadamer exchange, see Jay, Kelly, Kisiel, McCarthy, Mendelson, Misgeld, and Ricoeur.

3. An earlier version of this essay was presented at the biennial meeting of the Rhetoric Society of America, Norfolk, Virginia, May 1994.

Works Cited

Belsey, Catherine. "Afterword: A Future for Materialist, Feminist Criticism?" *The Matter of Difference: Materialist, Feminist Criticism of Shakespeare.* Ed. Valerie Wayne. Hemel Hempstead: Harvester-Wheatsheaf, 1991: 257–70.

Bernstein, Richard J. *Beyond Objectivism and Relativism: Science, Hermeneutics, and Praxis.* Philadelphia: University of Pennsylvania Press, 1983.

——. "One Step Forward, Two Steps Backward: Richard Rorty on Liberal Democracy and Philosophy." *Political Theory* 15 (1987): 538–63.

duBois, Page. *Torture and Truth: The New Ancient World.* New York: Routledge, 1991.

Fish, Stanley. "Consequences." *Doing What Comes Naturally: Change, Rhetoric, and the Practice of Theory in Literary and Legal Studies.* Durham, N.C.: Duke University Press, 1989: 315–41.

——. "Critical Self-Consciousness, or Can We Know What We're Doing?" *Doing What Comes Naturally: Change, Rhetoric, and the Practice of Theory in Literary and Legal Studies.* Durham, N.C.: Duke University Press, 1989: 436–67.

——. *Is There a Text in This Class? The Authority of Interpretive Communities.* Cambridge, Mass.: Harvard University Press, 1980.

Foucault, Michel. *Discipline and Punish: The Birth of the Prison.* Trans. Alan Sheridan. London: Allen Lane, 1977.

Gadamer, Hans-Georg. "On the Scope and Function of Hermeneutical Reflection." *Philosophical Hermeneutics.* Trans. and ed. David E. Linge. Berkeley: University of California Press, 1976: 18–43.

———. *Truth and Method.* 2d rev. ed. Trans. Joel Weinsheimer and Donald Marshall. New York: Crossroad Publishing, 1990.

Habermas, Jürgen. *Knowledge and Human Interests.* Trans. Jeremy Shapiro. Boston: Beacon, 1971.

———. "On Hermeneutics' Claim to Universality." *The Hermeneutics Reader.* Ed. Kurt Mueller-Vollmer. New York: Continuum, 1992: 294–319.

———. *On the Logic of the Social Sciences.* Trans. Shierry Weber Nicholsen and Jerry Stark. Cambridge, Mass.: MIT Press, 1988.

Jay, Martin. "Should Intellectual History Take a Linguistic Turn? Reflections on the Habermas-Gadamer Debate." *Modern European Intellectual History: Reappraisals and New Perspectives.* Ed. Dominick LaCapra and Steven L. Kaplan. Ithaca: Cornell University Press, 1982: 86–110.

Kelly, Michael. "The Gadamer/Habermas Debate Revisited: The Question of Ethics." *Philosophy and Social Criticism* 14 (July–October 1988): 139–56.

Kisiel, Theodore. "Ideology Critique and Phenomenology." *Philosophy Today* 3 (fall 1970): 151–60.

Knapp, Steven, and Walter Benn Michaels. "Against Theory." *Against Theory: Literary Studies and the New Pragmatism.* Ed. W. J. T. Mitchell. Chicago: University of Chicago Press, 1985: 11–30.

McCarthy, Thomas. *The Critical Theory of Jürgen Habermas.* Cambridge, Mass.: MIT Press, 1978.

Mendelson, Jack. "The Habermas-Gadamer Debate." *New German Critique* 18 (1979): 44–73.

Misgeld, Dieter. "Critical Theory and Hermeneutics: The Debate between Habermas and Gadamer." *On Critical Theory.* Ed. John O'Neill. New York: Continuum, 1976: 164–83.

Norris, Christopher. *The Truth about Postmodernism.* Oxford: Blackwell, 1993.

Ricoeur, Paul. "Ethics and Culture: Habermas and Gadamer in Dialogue." *Philosophy Today* 17 (summer 1973): 153–65.

Rorty, Richard. *Consequences of Pragmatism (Essays 1972–1980).* Minneapolis: University of Minnesota Press, 1982.

———. "Habermas and Lyotard on Postmodernity." *Habermas and Modernity.* Ed. Richard J. Bernstein. Cambridge, Mass.: MIT Press, 1985: 161–75.

———. "Nineteenth-Century Idealism and Twentieth-Century Textualism." *Consequences of Pragmatism (Essays: 1972–1980).* Minneapolis: University of Minnesota Press, 1982: 139–59.

———. *Philosophy and the Mirror of Nature.* Princeton: Princeton University Press, 1979.

———. "Pragmatism, Relativism, and Irrationalism." *Consequences of Pragmatism (Essays 1972–1980).* Minneapolis: University of Minnesota Press, 1982: 160–75.

———. "The Priority of Democracy to Philosophy." *Reading Rorty.* Ed. Alan Malachowski. Oxford: Basil Blackwell, 1990: 279–302.

———. "Thugs and Theorists: A Reply to Bernstein." *Political Theory* 15 (November 1987): 564–80.

Rosmarin, Adena. "On the Theory of 'Against Theory.'" *Against Theory: Literary Studies and the New Pragmatism.* Ed. W. J. T. Mitchell. Chicago: University of Chicago Press, 1985: 80–88.

Scott, Robert L. "On Viewing Rhetoric as Epistemic." *Central States Speech Journal* 18 (February 1967): 9–16.

Taylor, Charles. "Rorty in the Epistemological Tradition." *Reading Rorty.* Ed. Alan Malachowski. Oxford: Basil Blackwell, 1990: 257–75.

Warnke, Georgia. *Gadamer: Hermeneutics, Tradition, and Reason.* Stanford: Stanford University Press, 1987.

III
Extensions and Complications

9

Hymes, Rorty, and the Social-Rhetorical Construction of Meaning

Robert E. Smith III

By this route something of the rhetorical motive comes to lurk in every "meaning" however purely "scientific" its pretensions. Wherever there is persuasion, there is rhetoric. And wherever there is meaning, there is persuasion.

—Kenneth Burke, *A Rhetoric of Motives*

Today, yesterday, and tomorrow—it is 3:00 A.M. in the southern *montana* and lowlands of eastern Ecuador, in the tropical rain forests of the upper Amazon Basin. Inside a traditional Shuar house of palm and thatch, surrounded by the now-dark gardens of manioc and plantains and yams, set apart from any sort of village—living "concealed," as the Indians sometimes call it—a Shuar father begins the day by instructing his children. This morning he is talking about "Takea and Hummingbird."

"Of this Hummingbird long ago," he tells his children,

> who stole the fire from Takea
> what was said of that,
> who took it for the Shuar who suffered,
> what was said of that
> well, I will narrate.

Framing his story between the performative verb *aujmatsattajai* ("I will narrate") and a typical closure such as *nukete* ("it is only that") or *nuna aujmatsajai* ("I have narrated it"), he informs them of how, once, in the time when a Shuar could still turn himself into an animal, the Shuar people acquired the fire which, even now, they use to survive. "Listen," he tells his children, "These long ago / had no fire, it was said" (Hendricks).

In the rain forest's early stillness, his words are punctuated by the rhythms and repetitions of the poetic, stanzaic form: verse markers like *tuma asamtai, turamtai, tumakui, turamu, tuma tumakua,* or *turawar* ("so being," "having done thus"), and formulaic closures like *timiayi* ("it was said"). The closures, more important than the markers, tell those children that his words are not his own but *yaunchu chicham,* "ancient words"—that fact itself carrying with it all the persuasive power of a special Shuar authority. The story, then, begins when the Shuar, lacking fire but wanting their food cooked, tried warming it in their armpits.

Such a practice, the father recounts, was dangerous (even in that long, long ago), but it at least separated the Shuar from the animals, who ate their food raw. Still it was causing sores, and many Shuar were dying. Only Takea, a dangerous monster who happily devoured people, had fire, and all attempts to become birds, to fly into his house and steal the fire, had met with disaster. Finally, one day, Jempe (Hummingbird) said that he would become a hummingbird and steal Takea's fire by deceiving him or at least his family.

Following the plan he outlined, Jempe went to Takea's house, got himself soaking wet, played on the sympathy of the children (in one version it was the wife), and was taken into the house where he could dry himself by the fire. When he was dry, he let his tail feathers catch fire, successfully escaped the house, and flew through the forest, setting fire to all the dried tree trunks in his path. From these trunks the people gathered fire to take to their homes, and that fire rests, still, in the wood.

Even today (as yesterday and tomorrow)—the Shuar father tells his children—if they will take a bow and spindle, and bore a hole in a log, the fire will come out, and they, like all Shuar since that early time, will be able to cook their food and warm themselves and live.

> So doing,
> this Hummingbird helped us,
> it was said, by stealing Takea's fire.
>
> If he had not succeeded,
> if he had not taken Takea's fire,
> well, now would we have not died perhaps?
> Would we not have died of hunger perhaps?
> thus say our elders. . . .
>
> "Well, we would have become extinct,
> if Hummingbird had not stolen fire from
> Takea,"
> so saying, they narrated.

So being,
this, I too,
that which my ancestors told,
I have narrated. (Hendricks)

At one time and in some places (and perhaps, in some quarters, even today), the foregoing tale is or was the "folklore" of "primitives." And in even the adoption of such a terminology, the observational roles, the interpretive screens, the relative valuations become both obvious and inevitable. The argument in this essay is otherwise.

In the following pages I will argue that, by using the perspective brought to the telling and retelling of myth through work in that sector of anthropology Dell Hymes named the "ethnography of speaking," and by joining this view with the perspective brought to epistemology by Richard Rorty through what he might call "neopragmatism" (but which we will subsume here under the broader term *social constructionism*), we will have both the methodology and the rationale necessary to talk about the "making of meaning" in new and highly productive ways heretofore unavailable. To do this, I will discuss first Hymes (beginning with his article "The Ethnography of Speaking"), then Rorty (particularly his *Philosophy and the Mirror of Nature*), and last the implications I find in the juncture of Hymes's and Rorty's work.

Seen from this joint standpoint, that Shuar father, for example, has at least as much to tell us about how *we* make meaning as he might about how *he* does so. Furthermore, we and that Shuar father are but two more instances of the human condition described by Clifford Geertz when he said: "To see ourselves as others see us can be eye-opening. To see others as sharing a nature with ourselves is the merest decency. But it is from the far more difficult achievement of seeing ourselves amongst others, as a local example of the forms human life has locally taken, a case among cases, a world among worlds, that that largeness of mind, without which objectivity is self-congratulation and tolerance a sham, [finally] comes" (*Local Knowledge* 16).

Dell Hymes: Ethnography of Speaking

For those unfamiliar with Dell Hymes's work, it is in "The Ethnography of Speaking," first published in Gladwin and Sturtevant's *Anthropology and Hu-*

man Behavior (1962) and later reprinted in Joshua Fishman's *Readings in the Sociology of Language* (1968), that Hymes, says:

> There are several underdeveloped intellectual areas involving speech to which anthropology can contribute. All are alike in that they need fresh theoretical thought, methodological invention, and empirical work, and have roots in anthropology's vocation as a comparative discipline. Among these are the revitalization of dialectology (perhaps under the heading of "sociolinguistics"); the place of language in an evolutionary theory of culture; the semantic typology of languages; and the truly comparative study of verbal art. Fortunately, all of those mentioned have begun to attract attention. For the anthropological study of behavior [however] there is another area of importance, one that seems general, central, and neglected. It can be called the *ethnography of speaking*. (101)

In such manner, as Wendy Leeds-Hurwitz phrases it, did he "call into being" a new field of study. As Leeds-Hurwitz summarizes the situation,

> Anthropologists [in Hymes's view] studied culture, focusing on actual behavior, but paid little attention to language, leaving that to linguistics; in their turn linguists studied language, focusing on ideal utterances (*la langue*) and paying little attention to actual speech (*la parole*), assuming that it would be studied by anthropology. In short, no one was paying much attention to actual speech in its cultural context, to the use of speech in real interactions rather than theoretical utterances. (85)

As she also points out in the same article, this call did not go unheeded. Beginning with the first generation's work at the University of California at Berkeley on social and cultural determinants of language use (the effort was interdisciplinary, as Hymes had hoped it would be; some of its leaders were John Gumperz, Susan Ervin-Tripp, Charles Ferguson, and William Bright), there was then a second generation which tended either to further the work at Berkeley under Gumperz or to join Hymes's new efforts at the University of Pennsylvania (where Hymes stayed from 1965 to 1988; he is now at the University of Virginia). That second generation also spread across the country, establishing a center, for example, at the University of Texas at Austin (initially at Austin were Richard Bauman, Joel Sherzer, and Roger Abrahams). There is now a third generation—distinguished particularly by the expansion of the ethnography of communication into the field of communication itself—which includes Gerry Philipsen at the University of Washington, Shirley Brice Heath at Stanford, and Tamar Katriel (originally a student of Philipsen's), now at the University of Haifa.

But Hymes's leadership is still everywhere apparent. Even Katriel's recent, award-winning *Talking Straight,* the first book-length ethnography of communication to be published by someone with a Ph.D. in communications rather than in anthropology or linguistics, bears a Hymes foreword. Thus, it is with Hymes that we will be concerned here, and it was, in fact, partly in reaction to the lack of ability of earlier and more simplistic notions of folklore to describe communication-in-general or speaking-in-particular sufficiently that his call for a new subdiscipline, with new conceptual frames, was made and has been continued.[1]

With regard to the descriptive tools necessary to the building of such a subdiscipline, Hymes says in "Models of the Interaction of Language and Social Life," first published in the *Journal of Social Issues* in 1967:

> Only a specific, explicit mode of description can guarantee
> the maintenance and success of the current interest. . . .
> Such interest is prompted more by practical and theoretical
> needs, perhaps, than by accomplishment. It was the de-
> velopment of a specific mode of description that ensured the
> success of linguistics as an autonomous discipline in the
> United States in the twentieth century, and the lack of it (for
> motif and tale types are a form of indexing, distributional
> inference a procedure common to the human sciences) that
> led to the until recent peripheral status of folklore, although
> both had started from a similar base, the converging interest
> of anthropologists, and English scholars, in language and in
> verbal tradition. (52)

Further, such new descriptive goals can be phrased in terms of the disciplines the interests of which here converge. Hymes continues:

> Whatever his questions about language, it is clear to a lin-
> guist that there is an enterprise, description of languages,
> which is central and known. Whatever his questions about
> society and culture, it is clear to a sociologist or an anthro-
> pologist that there is a form of inquiry (survey or ethnogra-
> phy) on which the answer depends. In both cases, one un-
> derstands what it means to describe a language, the social
> relations, or culture of a community. We need to be able to
> say the same thing about the sociolinguistic system of a
> community [about "the interaction of language with social
> life"]. (52–53)

If we are to talk productively about the Shuar myth "Takea and the Hummingbird," for example (and I was, of course, already using ethnographic tools
when I spoke of performative verbs, verse markers, and formulaic closures), we
must be able to move beyond the classification of this myth as *yaunchu chicham*,
"ancient words," to the *role* of such ancient words (the concept of even having
such words) in the community life of the Shuar. And, to do this, we will have to
move even further—to not only the role of those tools as used in the description
of the myth itself but also the role of the conventions they reflect, conventions
the actual operation of which allow the myth to be part of a Shuar social
dynamic.

Hymes told us, in "Toward Ethnographies of Communication" (1964),
that "the starting point is the ethnographic analysis of the communicative
habits of a community in their totality," that "the communicative event thus is
central (in terms of language proper, [this] means that the linguistic code is
displaced by the speech act as focus of attention)," and that, consequently,
following Roman Jakobson's lead, any satisfactory descriptive theory would
have to enable the inventorying and relating of the elements in what amounts
to "a somewhat elaborated version of communication theory" (13; see Jakobson, and Jakobson et al.). Briefly put, any account produced through such a
theory would have to be capable of "identifying in an adequate ethnographic
way" the following eight factors:

> (1, 2) the various kinds of participants in communicative
> events—senders and receivers, addressors and addressees, in-
> terpreters and spokesmen, and the like; (3) the various avail-
> able channels, and their modes of use, speaking writing,

printing, drumming, blowing, whistling, face and body motion as visually perceived, smelling, tasting, and tactile sensation; (4) the various codes shared by various participants, linguistic, paralinguistic, kinesic, musical, and other; (5) the settings (including other communication) in which communication is permitted, enjoined, encouraged, abridged; (6) the forms of messages, and their genres, ranging verbally from single-morpheme sentences to the patterns and diacritics of sonnets, sermons, salesmen's pitches, and any other organized routines and styles; (7) the topics and comments that a message may be about; (8) the events themselves, their kind and characters as wholes. ("Toward Ethnographies" 13)

In "Models of the Interaction of Language and Social Life," Hymes offered the comprehensive version of a descriptive paradigm capable of taking all eight of these factors into account. It includes the *speech community,* "the social unit of analysis" ("Tentatively, a *speech community* is defined as a community sharing rules for the conduct and interpretation of speech, and rules for the interpretation of at least one linguistic variety"); the *speech field,* "akin to the notion of social field" ("can be defined as the total range of communities within which a person's knowledge of varieties and speaking rules potentially enables him to move communicatively"); and the *speech network,* "within the speech field" ("the specific linkages of persons through shared varieties and speaking rules across communities") (53–55).

The paradigm also includes the *speech situation* ("Such situations may enter as contexts into the statement of rules of speaking as aspects of setting [or of genre]. In contrast to speech events, they are not in themselves governed by such rules, or one set of such rules throughout"); the *speech event* ("The term speech event will be restricted to activities, or aspects of activities, that are directly governed by rules or norms for the use of speech. An event may consist of a single speech act but will often comprise several"); and the *speech act* ("the minimal term of the set just discussed [situation, event, act]. . . . It represents a level distinct from the sentence, and not identifiable with any single portion of other levels of grammar, nor with segments of any particular size defined in terms of other levels of grammar") (56–57).

Hymes's model includes, finally, *speech styles, ways of speaking,* and an expanded list of all of the *components of speech* just referred to. With regard to the goals of this essay, however, it is more profitable to cite one example from Hymes which illustrates much of what is central to that new point of view:

> Just as an occurrence of a noun may at the same time be the whole of a noun phrase and the whole of a sentence (e.g., "Fire!"), so a speech act may be the whole of a speech event, and of a speech situation (say, a rite consisting of a single prayer, itself a single invocation). More often, however, one will find a difference in magnitude: a party (speech situation), a conversation during the party (speech event), a joke within the conversation (speech act). . . . [Moreover,] notice that the same type of speech act may recur in different types of speech situations. Thus, a joke (speech act) may be embedded in a private conversation, a lecture, a formal introduction. A private conversation may occur in the context of a party, a memorial service, a pause in changing sides in a tennis match. ("Models" 56)

Hymes gains a great deal from the adoption of the model that is at the root of all this terminology. He has, first of all, created an analytical instrument through which he can describe with precision the detail of any given sociolinguistic situation or event. He has, in addition, provided himself with the means through which he can isolate in such a situation or event those elements related to speech from those not, and, among those that *are* related, one from the other (to use his own example: a hunt may include both verbal and nonverbal elements and the verbal ones of more than one type). Most important of all, he has created for himself a position from which he can now manipulate any data he has acquired in that manner which will allow him to extend his line of argument, and thus increase his yield of information—whether moving intra-, inter-, or cross-culturally.

To put Hymes's model in terms of our example of the Shuar father and his children and the story of the hummingbird, we can say, at a minimum, the following: The speaker or sender is the father; the hearers or receivers are the children. The speech community is the immediate family (or, on some occasions, an extended one), and the speech situation is that it is 3:00 A.M., in that household, in a routine, traditional daily session of instruction. The father *does* belong to a speech network: it is *his* father, and his father's father before him, and the community of other current fathers—and all of their fathers before them; and he does have a speech style: it is formal and poetic, and it both creates cohesion and rhythm and validates the import of the text.

The speech event and act are finally one—*this* myth telling, *these* "ancient words"—"Takea and the Hummingbird," how the Shuar got, and get, fire. I am suggesting that if we would employ Hymes's insights to the ultimate, his perspective and terminology—if joined to the theories of social construction—would provide the means through which we might juxtapose, for example, a speech event in "primitive" folklore and one in "modern" science; might discuss in that juxtaposition both similarities and differences; and might even probe the possibility that in the so-called primitive and modern, *in the events themselves,* we are dealing not with widely different things but with no more or less than two instances of the same phenomenon. Could we make such adjustments, we might, if for no more than a moment, shift our thinking away from that sort of intellectual dustbin we have fashioned for things like "Shuar folklore," and be able (in Geertz's words) to see ourselves as "a case among cases," "a world among worlds," and, in the process, learn something further about our own case and world.

I will try to demonstrate how and why such a shift might be both possible and advantageous, but first offer a brief overview of social construction and the manner in which it came into being.

Richard Rorty: The Coming of Social Construction

"I hope," says Richard Rorty, in the opening pages of his major study, "that what I have been saying has made clear why I chose *Philosophy and the Mirror of Nature* as a title." "It is," he says,

> pictures rather than propositions, metaphors rather than statements, which determine most of our philosophical convictions. The picture that holds traditional philosophy [and, as we shall see, most everything else] captive is that of the mind as a great mirror, containing various representations— some accurate, some not—and capable of being studied by pure, nonempirical methods. Without the notion of mind as mirror, the notion of knowledge as accuracy of representation would not have suggested itself. Without this latter notion, the strategy common to Descartes and Kant—get-

ting more accurate representations by inspecting, repairing, and polishing the mirror, so to speak—would not have made sense. Without this strategy in mind, recent claims that philosophy could consist of "conceptual analysis" or "phenomenological analysis" or "explication of meanings" or examination of "the logic of our language" or of "the structure of the constituting activity of consciousness" would not have made sense. (12)

It is Rorty's considerable work in the area of how we do think, how we make meaning, that most clearly delineates the historical problems which led to theories of social construction. It is also his broadening of issues first touched on by other thinkers from other disciplines which best illustrates the breadth of the implications inherent in a social constructionist orientation. But the movement itself (if one can call it that: it is at times more like a "general, sometimes coincidental, agreement on principles and methodology" than like a formal movement) is far wider than what is ordinarily meant by a "philosophical" one.

One of the earliest works, and one of the most seminal, was *The Social Construction of Reality,* written by two sociologists, Peter Berger and Thomas Luckmann, and published in 1966 (Rorty's book appeared in 1979). Equally important has been the work of Clifford Geertz, whose study *Local Knowledge* (1983) deals particularly with social constructionist issues, but whose earlier book *The Interpretation of Culture* (1973) was already laying the foundations in anthropological terms for the broader considerations dealt with in the later work. In psychology, Kenneth Gergen has been one of the pioneers. His *Toward Transformation in Social Knowledge* was not published until 1982, but he had been writing of social construction as early as 1977. His detailed overview, "The Social Constructionist Movement in Modern Psychology," first delivered as an address before the American Psychological Association in 1983, then published in *American Psychologist* in 1985, has been one of the more important contributions not only to developments in psychology but also to the development of the social constructionist movement as a whole. In literature, composition studies, and general pedagogical theory, Kenneth Bruffee performed a singular service when he wrote the first bibliographic guide to the movement as a "coherent school of thought": "Social Construction, Language, and the Authority of Knowledge" (1986). Bruffee has also written several other key essays dealing with social constructionist issues and applications.

The names of other books and authors (to say nothing of other essays and authors) which might be added to this list is seemingly endless. Sociologists like Howard Becker and Jeff Coulter belong on the list; psychologists like Rom Harre and John Shotter belong; literary textual critics like Jerome McGann belong. And there are the writers more difficult to classify, like Michael Ignatieff and Robert Bellah.

Behind all of these, in a sense, stands Thomas Kuhn and *The Structure of Scientific Revolutions* (first published in 1962), probably because social construction in general, as well as Kuhn's book in particular, implies a true shift in the overall theory of knowledge (not merely a shift in cognitive psychology, or epistemology, or scientific method) and, as such crosses all disciplinary lines. Nonetheless, it is Richard Rorty who most clearly traces the history from which social construction springs.

"When poetry and mathematics had come to self-consciousness," Rorty tells us in *Philosophy and the Mirror of Nature*—"when men like Ion and The-aetetus could identify themselves with their subjects—the time had come for something general to be said about knowledge of universals" (38). And in such a manner did the 2,500-year journey to social construction begin:

> Philosophy undertook to examine the difference be-
> tween knowing that there were parallel mountain ranges to
> the west and knowing that infinitely extended parallel lines
> never meet, the difference between knowing that Socrates
> was good and knowing what goodness was. So the question
> arose: what are the analogies between knowing about moun-
> tains and knowing about lines, between knowing Socrates
> and knowing the Good? When this question was answered
> in terms of the distinction between the eye of the body and
> the Eye of the Mind, *nous*—thought, intellect, insight—was
> identified as what separates men from beasts. . . . The no-
> tion of "contemplation" of knowledge of universal concepts
> or truths as *theoria,* [made] the Eye of the Mind [and the
> mirror it viewed] the inescapable model for the better sort of
> knowledge. (38–38)

What one gains from a reading of *Philosophy and the Mirror of Nature,* together with the Rorty essays collected in *Consequences of Pragmatism* (published three years later but containing essays that led up to the major work as well as several a product of it), is something like Matthew Arnold's "wandering between two worlds, one dead, the other powerless to be born"—but with less melodrama, perhaps more significance, and a second world which, even now, is in the process of birth. But two worlds there are, the history of the first running from approximately B.C. 500 to the present, that of the second just beginning. They can be distinguished in terms of their concepts of mind, their definitions of discourse, their methods of inquiry, and their types of philosophy.

The first world, the one that began with the Greeks, is the world of that ocular metaphor, the one in which the metaphor is *operative* (meaning that it is seen as literal, not metaphorical). The metaphor is there as early as Anaximander. Its lineaments are clearly visible in, for example, Plato's "cave analogy" in *The Republic:* the chained prisoners, the fire, the flickering shadows, the escape, the dazzling World of Forms, the return of the philosopher-king. It continues through Augustine and Aquinas, through Descartes and Kant. Having endured the exchange of rational soul for rational mind, and the transformation of this second into consciousness, awareness, and words, it is still apparent in the work of modern analytic and linguistic philosophers. In the referential world which this metaphor inevitably creates, mind reflects reality (even if in a distorted form), and the aim of inquiry is "getting things right."

In that world, discourse is "normal," a term Rorty has adapted from Kuhn's "normal science." Normal science, says Rorty, is the "practice of solving problems against the background of a consensus about what counts as a good explanation of the phenomena and about what it would take for a problem to be solved" (*Philosophy* 320). It is what Kuhn likes to call "puzzle-solving."

Normal discourse, as an extrapolation from this, is "any discourse [scientific or otherwise] which is conducted within an agreed-upon set of conventions about what counts as a relevant contribution, what counts as answering a question, what counts as having a good argument for that answer or a good criticism of it" (*Philosophy* 320). In short, no change of rules, no (as Kuhn would have it) paradigm shift.

The method of inquiry, in what would appear to be this most intellectually traditional of worlds, is "epistemology" as we have customarily known it. In fact, normal discourse as a whole, and normal science as a specific case, are "as close as real life comes to the epistemologist's notion of what it is to be rational. Everybody agrees on how to evaluate everything everybody else says" (*Philosophy* 320). According to Rorty, "The dominating notion of epistemology is that to be rational, to be fully human, to do what we ought, we need to be able to find agreement with other human beings. To construct an epistemology is to find the maximum amount of common ground with others. The assumption that an epistemology can be constructed is the assumption that such common ground exists" (316). In epistemology, the watchword is "commensuration." Everything *must* be measurable by the same (that is, "a common") standard. Everything *must* be reduceable to one. Everything must be "brought under a set of rules which [will] settle the issue on every point where statements seem to conflict . . . tell[ing] us how to construct an ideal situation in which all residual disagreements will be seen to be 'noncognitive' or merely verbal, or else merely temporary—capable of being resolved by doing something further" (316).

Finally, in this first world, Philosophy is systematic and (at least according to Rorty) spelled with a capital *P*. It looks a lot like what many of us had a taste of in undergraduate philosophy classes with course titles that began, "Introduction to" or "Problems of," or something similar. Such Philosophy is, as one might expect, closely aligned with (in one sense derivative of, in another the source of) the method of inquiry it embraces. Its practitioners are constructive (as opposed to destructive) and offer arguments. They, like scientists, want to "put their subject on a secure path"—like science: think of, for example, symbolic logic—and they "build for eternity" (Rorty, *Philosophy* 369). A systematic Philosopher, which is what most mainstream Western philosophers in the last 2,500 years have been, says (whether talking of the realm of Being-as-opposed-to-Becoming, or about the Forms, or a priori ideas, or the logic of the language): "Now that such-and-such a line of inquiry has had such a stunning success, let us reshape all inquiry, and all of culture, on its model, thereby permitting objectivity and rationality to prevail in areas previously obscured by convention, superstition, and the lack of a proper epistemological understanding of man's ability accurately to represent nature" (377). In short, such a Philosopher believes at that point (a point forever and maddeningly reappearing) that at last we have found a new and better mirror, or refined out the distortions in the old one. Now we will, finally, begin to see things as they really are.

In contrast to this lineage of thought are those who are born to a nonfoundational, nonreferential world—the world without mirrors. Their appearance is far more recent, but, as one might expect, they have their roots in the work of several figures who immediately preceded them: Wittgenstein, who as early as *Philosophical Investigations* mocked such referential knowledge claims as those just described; Heidegger, who throughout his retelling of the history of the

West let us see both the Greek beginnings of Cartesian imagery and that imagery's metamorphosis; and John Dewey—in Rorty's estimation, the most important of the three—who "wrote his polemics against traditional mirror-imagery out of a vision of a new kind of society" (Rorty, *Philosophy* 12–13).

These "non-ocular" thinkers—as we have seen, they are not just philosophers—view things in a very different way. They are aware that the mirror is no more than a metaphor. They are aware that, while the physical world does (as Rorty describes it) "shove us around," it in no way automatically follows that the central questions about knowledge must therefore be cast in terms of mirrorings. They are aware, as Kenneth Bruffee writes in "Social Construction, Language, and the Authority of Knowledge," paraphrasing Rorty, that what is significant is not whether or not we are in contact with reality (we are), but the issue of whether or not, and in what ways, we can deal with it—since we are. "The latter," says Bruffee, "is what we call knowledge; the former is not. Furthermore, we do not generate knowledge . . . by 'dealing with' the physical reality that shoves us around. We generate knowledge by 'dealing with' our beliefs about the physical reality which shoves us around. Specifically *we generate knowledge by justifying those beliefs socially*" (777, emphasis added).

In the world of these thinkers, then, discourse is no longer "normal" but rather "abnormal"—the other half of the Rortian generalization of Kuhn's distinction between normal and revolutionary science. Revolutionary science (some common examples being the work of Copernicus, Newton, Einstein) is predicated on the subversion of old scientific paradigms by experimental anomalies and is signaled by the subsequent introduction into scientific thought of new paradigms which offer better explanation. Similarly, abnormal discourse is predicated on the awareness that the mirror metaphor, because it *is* metaphor, will no longer suffice as a paradigm for the meaning of "thinking" or "knowledge." It is signaled, consequently, by the introduction into thought in general of new means of thinking, leading to new ways of knowing, in which knowledge is declared nonreferential, and there is general agreement that to seek a foundational epistemology is not only near impossible but also beside the point.

Rorty tells us that "the product of abnormal discourse," a result of someone joining the discourse who either is ignorant of the traditional rules or merely sets them aside, "can be anything from nonsense to intellectual revolution, and there is no [single] discipline which describes it, any more than there is a discipline devoted to the study of the unpredictable" (*Philosophy* 320).

The method of inquiry suited to this new world without mirrors Rorty describes as "hermeneutic" (instead of epistemological), after Hans-Georg Gadamer's use of that term in his monumental *Truth and Method.* "Hermeneutics," says Rorty, "sees the relations between various discourses as those of strands in a possible conversation"—in a nonfoundational world, knowledge is no longer "reflection" but something else, something more varied, richer, denser, more human, but also harder to describe—"a conversation," says Rorty, "which presupposes no disciplinary matrix which unites the speakers, but where the hope of agreement is never lost as long as the conversation lasts" (*Philosophy* 318).

Moreover, Rorty continues, hermeneutics tells us both that "we shall never be able to avoid the 'hermeneutic circle'—the fact that we cannot understand the parts of a strange culture, practice, theory, language, or whatever, unless we know something about how the whole thing works, whereas we cannot get a grasp of how the whole thing works until we have some understanding of the parts" and that "coming to understand is more like getting acquainted with a person than like following a demonstration. . . . [W]e play back and forth between guesses about how to characterize particular statements and other events, and guesses about the point of the whole situation, until gradually we feel at ease with what was hitherto strange" (319).

Finally, hermeneutics—which has a long history as a methodological tool in specific disciplines and originated in scriptural interpretation—offers us a new paradigm for knowledge itself. "The notion of culture as a conversation," says Rorty, "rather than as a structure erected upon foundations, fits well with this hermeneutical notion of knowledge, since getting into a conversation with a stranger is, like acquiring a new virtue or skill by imitating models, a matter of *tekhne* rather than *episteme*" (319).

That this new world, "abnormal" discourse, and "hermeneutic" method would lead to a new and almost unrecognizable meaning for the term *philosophy* is, of course, inevitable. "I shall use 'edification,'" says Rorty, tracing the lineaments of this new role for, this new meaning of, philosophical investigation (we now have "edifying *philosophy*" instead of "systematic *Philosophy*"), "to stand for this project of finding new, better, more interesting, more fruitful ways of speaking." He explains:

> The attempt to edify (ourselves or others) may consist
> in the hermeneutic activity of making connections between

> our own culture and some exotic culture or historical period,
> or between our own discipline and another discipline which
> seems to pursue incommensurable aims in an incommen-
> surable vocabulary. But it may instead consist in the "poetic"
> activity of thinking up such new aims, new words, or new
> disciplines, followed by, so to speak, the inverse of herme-
> neutics: the attempt to interpret our familiar surroundings
> in the unfamiliar terms of our new invention. (360)

This does not mean, however, that Rorty wants hermeneutics to be, in his
words, the "successor subject" to epistemology, that he is putting hermeneutics
forward "as an activity which fills the cultural vacancy once filled by epistemologically centered philosophy" (315). "On the contrary," says Rorty,

> hermeneutics is an expression of the hope that the cultural
> space left by the demise of epistemology will not be filled—
> that our culture should become one in which the demand
> for constraint and confrontation is no longer felt. The no-
> tion that there is a permanent neutral framework whose
> "structure" philosophy can display is the notion that the
> objects to be confronted by the mind, or the rules which
> constrain inquiry, are common to all discourse, or at least to
> every discourse on a given topic. Thus epistemology pro-
> ceeds on the assumption that all contributions to a dis-
> course are commensurable. Hermeneutics is largely a strug-
> gle against this assumption. (315–16)

In fact—and in opposition to such an "epistemological posture"—the practitioners of this new philosophy, Rorty tells us elsewhere, "would be all-purpose
intellectuals who were ready to offer a view on pretty much anything, in the
hope of making it hang together with everything else" (*Consequences* xxxix).
Such a practitioner is "a name-dropper, who uses names . . . to refer to sets of
descriptions, symbol-systems, ways of seeing. His specialty is seeing similarities
and differences between great big pictures, between attempts to see how things
hang together. He is the person who tells you how all the ways of making things
hang together hang together" (xli).

In summarizing the role of "edifying" philosophy, Rorty says that "the
point of edifying philosophy is to keep the conversation going rather than to

find objective truth." It makes sense only as "a protest against attempts to close off conversation by proposals for universal commensuration through the hypostatization of some privileged set of descriptions." Its transformation calls for it "to see wisdom as consisting in the ability to sustain a conversation," "to see human beings as generators of new descriptions rather than beings one hopes [more accurately] to describe" (*Philosophy* 337–38).

It is exactly this distinction between humans as the described (really no more than an extension of the assumption that epistemology can be referential) and humans as descriptors (really an unavoidable consequence of the lack of any clear ground for such a foundationalist view) that is central to the consideration of speaking as a social constructionist act, which is to say, the consideration of uniting the ideas of Hymes and Rorty. If, on the one hand, in some crucial and ultimate sense we are all descriptors—as opposed to merely the described or even *seekers* after descriptions (and those descriptions no more than reflections mirrored from some elsewhere)—then, in a very real sense, we are all, already, anthropologists. If, on the other hand, our ethnographic descriptions are not merely that, nor even merely the bases of ethnologies—if, instead, they are the only means available to human beings, first, to understand the manner in which they have made their past meanings, second, to grasp the scope and means of what in the future they might create—then we are, all of us, already philosophers.

One or the other of those ideas is, probably, cause enough for alarm in at least some quarter, but in the remainder of this essay I would like to consider just such possibilities. To do so, I would like to retain one part Rorty and one part Kuhn, while at the same time, I return to Dell Hymes and the Shuar. In addition, to that "hermeneutic" mixture I need to add an episode from the life of Antoine Lavoisier.

Lavoisier, Speaking, and the Social Justification of Belief

In the title essay of *Local Knowledge,* "Local Knowledge: Fact and Law in Comparative Perspective," Clifford Geertz, although an admirer of both Kuhn and Rorty, says that among the several ways of classifying types of discourse (normal and revolutionary, normal and abnormal, standard and nonstandard—the last pair being Geertz's) he dislikes Kuhn's terms because of their political overtones and Rorty's because of their pathological ones (222 n. 82). Of those three theorists, however, it is Kuhn who best makes the case for what might be called "communalist descriptors," and Kuhn as well—inasmuch as Rorty's position is partly an extension of Kuhn—whose thoughts shed the greatest light on the entire matter. Hence it is with Kuhn that I would like to open this final section.

In *The Structure of Scientific Revolutions,* he says:

> Like the choice between competing political institutions, that between competing [scientific] paradigms proves to be a choice between incompatible modes of community life. Because it has that character, the choice is not and cannot be determined merely by the evaluative procedures characteristic of normal science, for these depend in part upon a particular paradigm, and that paradigm is at issue. When paradigms enter, as they must, into a debate about paradigm choice, their role is necessarily circular. Each group uses its own paradigm to argue in that paradigm's defense.
>
> The resulting circularity does not, of course, make the arguments wrong or ineffectual. The man who premises a paradigm when arguing in its defense can nonetheless provide a clear exhibit of what scientific practice will be like for those who adopt the new view of nature. That exhibit can be immensely persuasive, often compellingly so. Yet, whatever its force, the status of the circular argument is only that of persuasion. It cannot be made logically or even probabilistically compelling for those who refuse to step into the circle. The premises and values shared by the two parties to a debate over paradigms are not sufficiently extensive for that. As in political revolutions, so in paradigm choice—there is no standard higher than the assent of the relevant community. (94)

Not only does this statement apply equally well whether one is talking about paradigms in science or paradigms in philosophy, but it also applies equally well in science whether one is talking about Shuar fathers or modern chemists. For "Takea and the Hummingbird" is no more and no less than that: Shuar science (even if the father is, at the same time, teaching his children about the "origins of culture"). And how to, on the basis of such "knowledge," start a fire with bow and spindle is no more or less than that science's extension: Shuar technology (even if a Shuar also thinks the purpose of that practice is to separate him from the animals and distinguish him as "civilized"). As a consequence, it should be both possible and revealing to draw a parallel between the illustration of the Shuar father and one closer to our own time and temperament: say, Lavoisier, the scientist commonly considered the father of modern chemistry, the year 1778 (although there is some question of which year to pick—but then there would be, too, for the Shuar father), and the "discovery" of oxygen.

I put *discovery* in quotation marks because in this case, as in others over the history of modern science, there has been some dispute (and I would suggest that the dispute itself, even the rationale for having it, is rooted in that mirror imagery Rorty talks about and the Cartesian subjectivism which is its historical product), and because that "questionableness" is a point Kuhn himself raises. Briefly, three different scientists—Joseph Priestley in England, Karl Scheele in Sweden, and Antoine Lavoisier in France—have some legitimate claim to the discovery of oxygen.

Of these three, Priestley discovered the element in 1774, but thought it "dephlogisticated air" (that is, he saw it in relation to the then current "phlogiston theory," which was subsequently overturned by Lavoisier). The least well known of the three, Scheele, had discovered oxygen even earlier (1772), but he, too, was still wedded to phlogiston theory, had named that which he observed "fire air," and then written a book by the same name.[2] Finally, Lavoisier himself isolated the element. In due time, he recognized that its discovery must signify a break with phlogiston theory (although it was years before any other scientist joined him in that recognition), and he announced his findings in 1778 through the French Royal Academy, where in the beginning at least, and in a sense forever, he neglected to mention his indebtedness to Priestley.

With regard to this and other similar quandaries, Kuhn notes in an essay entitled "The Historical Structure of Scientific Discovery" (published in *Science* while *The Structure of Scientific Revolutions* was in press):

> I conclude that we need a new vocabulary and new concepts
> for analysing events like the discovery of oxygen. Though
> undoubtedly correct, the sentence "Oxygen was discovered"
> misleads by suggesting that discovering something is a single
> simple act unequivocably attributable, if only we knew
> enough, to an individual, and an instant in time. When the
> discovery is unexpected, however, the latter attribution is
> always impossible, and the former often is as well. . . . [Fur-

thermore,] discovering a new sort of phenomenon is necessarily a complex process which involves recognizing both
that something is and *what* it is. Observation and concep-
tuality, fact and the assimilation of fact to theory, are insep-
arably linked in the discovery of scientific novelty. Inevitably, that process extends over time and may often involve a
number of people. (171)

Kuhn is saying that scientific discovery (Rorty would, I think, say *human*
discovery) is, ultimately and at once, cumulative, collaborative, and public—a
community event. If it is thus, and if we are, in Kenneth Burke's terms, "the
symbol making, symbol using animal," then it is also, inevitably, a *speech event.*
In addition, it is something other than accidental that we date even Lavoisier's
discovery from his formal announcement (at least the first of them) of the
event, though that date too could be questioned, since there was a second,
expanded announcement, and it was not until 1787 that three other scientists,
Guyton de Morveau, Antoine François Fourcroy, and Claude Louis Berthollet,
with Lavoisier as their acknowledged leader, presented to the French Academy a
series of *rentrées publiques* which outlined the new nomenclature and system
that became the foundation of modern chemistry.

Moreover, Kuhn's view here relates in a second and equally important way
to the key argument for the wedding of the perspectives of Hymes and Rorty—
that meaning, whether scientific or nonscientific, primitive or modern, is a
social construct rhetorically achieved. That is to say, under most circumstances,
most of us would not, at least initially, be willing to concede that the Shuar
father (or Hummingbird himself) had "discovered" combustion if he still
thought that boring a hole in a log let the fire out. Yet, in Kuhn's own terms
(from the quotation with which this section began), the dynamic of theory-
choice, which is to say not only the choice of "theory" but also the choice of
actual "reality-as-experienced"—and now too a communal choice—rests ultimately in persuasion, that is, depends in the final analysis on the presence of
that persuasion in speech events. I illustrate this point with one such event.

It is August 8, 1778, Paris, the Louvre, the stately quarters of the Royal
Academy of Science. The speaker, no stranger to the academy—else he would
not be here, at least not in such an honored position—is Antoine Lavoisier. He
is presenting a *mémoiré* (really a revision of an earlier, more rash and tentative
one from 1775) to a *rentrée publique* of the academy. It is entitled "Memoir on

the Nature of the Principle which Combines with Metals during Calcination and Increased Their Weight."

In this paper, he describes a new element, not just "dephlogisticated air" (for which he had made a claim in 1775) but "vital air," "eminently respirable air." The air of the atmosphere, he says, is not a single substance but a mixture of the nonrespirable (which will not rust metals or support combustion) and the respirable (which will do both). This respirable part he names *principle oxigine,* the "begetter of acids."

By 1787, when the collaborative effort of those four French chemists—the *Nomenclature chimique*—is published, this term will have been modified to *principe oxygène,* the "oxygen principle." But on that day in 1778, Lavoisier outlines his experiments and then explains his final conclusions—that all acids contain such "air," that all acids are compounds of "vital air" with nonmetallic substances like sulphur and carbon, and that, consequently, this new substance should be named "oxygen," the combination of two Greek words (*oxys* and the root of *gignesthai*), which together can be translated "to give birth to acid."

The speaker or sender and the hearers or receivers are the speech community, the members of that historic and sanctioned academy—not only those members present but also all those who will read the *mémoiré* on its publication. The speech situation is that which I have just described. And Lavoisier, like that long line of Shuar fathers, has a speech network—all of the academy's members and their associates and, by extension, the wider membership of the European scientific community as a whole (including Priestley, who was none too pleased at his colleague's omission)—as well as a clearly delineated speech style: formalized and thought of as "empirically objective," but also, beyond question, rhetorical.

In this speech event, Lavoisier will turn out to have been "wrong" about the acid, as he will later, in his famous 1783 address before another *rentrée publique,* be "wrong" about a related caloric theory of heat—but we now acknowledge that he was at least correct in his identification of oxygen, although if one ponders the case as ethnographers or philosophers might, it is difficult to be precise about exactly the manner in which he was "right" that day. And he was met by almost universal skepticism. Scheele, who lived until 1785, never adopted the theory; Priestley died an exile in 1804, still disbelieving (his last scientific work published in 1800 and entitled *Doctrine of Phlogiston Established*); the members of the academy present were to struggle for years in opposition. He would need another speech event.

That second event—the one that dealt the deathblow to phlogiston theory—was delivered before the academy in 1783 and entitled "Reflections on
Phlogiston." He said in part:

> The partisans of Stahl's doctrine [phlogiston theory] are
> continually in . . . difficulties. If they are asked what hap-
> pens when mercury is calcined in vital air [oxygen], the
> English philosophers reply that phlogiston . . . is released
> from the metal, combines with the gas and changes it into
> fixed air or phlogisticated air. But this . . . is absolutely con-
> trary to the facts. . . .
>
> All these reflections confirm what I have advanced,
> what I intend to prove, what I repeat again: chemists have
> made an imaginary principle out of phlogiston which, not
> strictly defined, fits all explanations required of it; some-
> times it has weight, sometimes it has not; sometimes it is free
> fire, sometimes it is fire combined with earth; sometimes it
> passes through the pores of vessels, sometimes these are im-
> penetrable to it; it explains at one and the same time caustic-
> ity and non-causticity, transparency and opacity, color and
> the absence of color. It is a veritable Proteus that changes its
> form every minute.
>
> It is time to lead chemistry back to a stricter line of
> thought, to strip the facts of this science of rationalization
> and prejudice; to distinguish fact and observation from sys-
> tem and hypothesis, in short, to define chemical knowledge
> precisely so that those who come after us may start from
> such definitions and go forward confidently in the advance-
> ment of science. (quoted in French 104–7)

Following the delivery of this *mémoiré,* the first thinker of significance to
join Lavoisier was not a chemist but the astronomer and mathematician Pierre-
Simon de Laplace. Laplace was followed, however, in 1785 by Berthollet, in
1786 by Morveau, and in 1787 by Fourcroy. These three (with Lavoisier as
their leader) assembled that new chemistry as it was presented to the academy
in 1787.

In the cause of *this* essay, three points need to be made about these events.
First, the circularity of the phlogiston argument (like the reasoning in any

argument over theory-choice) was no more and no less circular than the reasoning in Lavoisier's own work that led, on the one hand, to the principle of acids and, on the other, to the caloric theory of heat. Second, in reality, the means through which Lavoisier's position became the accepted one was not objective or empirical, but rather persistent, repetitious, and persuasive. No phlogiston-oriented scientist stood with retort in hand and opted to force himself to see "nonphlogistic" data. Only those who could be persuaded to relinquish one way of seeing, one way of interpreting, one way of speaking—these things are not separable—for another were to join the ranks of the new chemistry.

Third, and perhaps most significant, that discovery was and is a speech event in a dual manner. On the one hand, in our own time and world we do have exact parallels to "Takea and the Hummingbird." For example: "The exact date of the beginning of chemistry as a science cannot be stated, but frequently given is the time of the correct interpretation of combustion by the great scientist A. L. Lavoisier, about 1774" ("Chemistry," *McGraw-Hill Encyclopedia of Science and Technology* 84). Or: "The phlogiston theory received its final dismissal from his [Lavoisier's] work on combustion in which he realized the function of oxygen" ("Lavoisier," *Chamber's Dictionary of Scientists* 276). Or: "This Revolution has often been summed up as Lavoisier's overthrow of the phlogiston theory (his new chemistry was later called the antiphlogistic chemistry), but this is only part of the story. His eventual recognition that the atmosphere is composed of different gases that take part in chemical reactions was followed by his demonstration that a particular kind of gas, oxygen gas, is the agent active in combustion and calcination" ("Lavoisier," *Dictionary of Scientific Biography* 73). On the other hand, however, as we have seen, the "discovery" of oxygen and of the new theory of combustion was from its beginnings a community, and a *communicative,* event—as, surely, somewhere in the mists of prehistory, must have been fire's discovery by the Shuar. In the sense embraced by all three of these points, the Shuar father and Lavoisier—and, indeed, the rest of us—share in the same world.

To return to Richard Rorty one last time, only now with the discovery-of-oxygen-as-speech-event as one more instance (like "Takea and the Hummingbird") of the social-rhetorical construction of "scientific" fact—or of "Takea and the Hummingbird" (like the discovery of oxygen) as one more instance of mythic "fact"—perhaps *the* central point of *Philosophy and the Mirror of Nature* is that since "the mirror" and "the eye of the mind" are only related parts of an ocular metaphor, all that Gadamer has to say about hermeneutics and that Kuhn has to say about theory-choice apply not just to science but to all of human knowledge, to whatever it might mean when we say that human beings are *able* to know. In an address delivered to the American Philosophical Association in 1979 and later published in *Consequences of Pragmatism*, Rorty says:

> It seems to me [that there is] a fundamental choice which confronts the reflective mind: that between accepting the contingent character of starting-points and attempting to evade contingency. To accept the contingency of starting points [that is, bases for knowledge] is to accept our inheritance from, and our conversation with, our fellow humans as our only source of guidance. To attempt to evade this contingency is to hope to become a properly-programmed machine. This was the hope which Plato thought might be fulfilled at the top of the dividing line, when we passed beyond hypotheses. Christians have hoped it might be attained by becoming attuned to the voice of God in the heart, and Cartesians that it might be fulfilled by emptying the mind and seeking the indubitable. Since Kant, philosophers have hoped that it might be fulfilled by finding that *a priori* structure of any possible inquiry, or language, or form of social life.
>
> If we give up this hope, we shall lose what Nietzsche called "metaphysical comfort," but we may gain a renewed sense of community. Our identification with our community—our society, our political tradition, our intellectual heritage—is heightened when we see this community as *ours* rather than *nature's*, *shaped* rather than *found*, one among many which men have made. In the end . . . what matters is our loyalty to other human beings clinging together against the dark, not our hope of getting things right. (166)

In many ways, this passage is a fitting summary of Rorty's position. And it appears to me that that position, both in general and in this particular passage, not only is well taken but also bespeaks considerable advantage for us all. When I talk on Rorty or on social construction as a whole, I like to use this quotation somewhere near the end of my presentation, if for no other reason than that it moves *my* sense of community to see the audience moved by theirs. And I do it also because the passage touches on the wonder inherent in the possibilities that such an approach to knowledge making offers (think of the progression: Aristotle to Newton to Einstein to *where?*) and, too, on the related optimism represented by Gadamer's and Rorty's views of hermeneutics.

But we need to address also what might be called the "urgency" of the situation, and to do that, I would like to be as plain as possible about Rorty's ideas, at least as I see them, and then, as I see them related to Hymes's. I find Rorty to be saying: Community gives us dignity and value; community is ennobling; community *is* moving. But I think that he is also saying: In the world in which we now live, coming where we have come from, knowing what we now know, *the decision for or against contingency and community is long since past optional.* To rephrase that thought in another, briefer way—there may not be, for this present world, and that world in our present universe, a better metaphor for living than a Shuar father and his children and his community in their quest for survival and significance, against a hostile adversary and against the indifferent forces of nature.

In the closing pages of "Toward Ethnographies of Communication," Dell Hymes speaks of the many possible uses he sees for that new field of study. "There are," he says, "a number of other particular lines of study where mutual benefit can result"—he has already spoken of "a convergence between the professional field of speech and linguistics in the increased interest of the former in behavioral approaches, and the latter in poetics and logic." "The study of folk taxonomies and of ethnographic semantics generally, needs specification of communicative contexts if it is to achieve the implicit goal of discovering the structure of vocabularies as wholes . . . [and] methods of ethnographic semantics, in turn, are needed in discovering the components of communicative events" (26). He goes on to speak of "the work of observation and participation characteristic of paralinguistics, kinesics, and other aspects of the discovery of codes additional to language in the presentation of the self in everyday life," about "the potential richness of studies in socialization, enculturation, child development . . . the whole of the child's induction in the communicative economy of its community." Hymes concludes by pointing out that "work in fundamental literacy raises problems of particular interest, and can be a source of empirical data and insight, and a practical area to which ethnographic studies of communication can contribute," and that "to study mental health in its communicative aspect, an ethnographic approach may contribute the expected anthropological perspective on comparative range, and what is social in the given case" (26–27).

As I said earlier, many—including John Gumperz, who helped issue it— heard that call. As is true, however, with anything new—and in the perspective of 2,500 years of Western knowledge, 1964 (or 1962) is still pretty new—many of those who should be listening, who might profit most and contribute most, still are not.

I am suggesting, then, with regard to the ethnography of speaking, that the appearance on the intellectual scene of Richard Rorty and the social constructionists, combined with the possibilities inherent in the capacity to juxtapose, for example, French scientists and Shuar Indians, has given us a better, broader, stronger reason both to hear and to respond.

Notes

1. Hymes, incidentally, also says in "The Ethnography of Speaking": "In discussing it [the communicative event itself] I shall refer to speech and speaking, but these terms are surrogates for all modes of communication, and a descriptive account should be generalized to comprise all" (109).

2. All of which, unfortunately, had no real effect on Priestley or Lavoisier, because the Swedish printer was slow, and the findings came out too late to have any effect on either the French or the English scientist's work.

Works Cited

Berger, Peter L., and Thomas Luckmann. *The Social Construction of Reality: A Treatise in the Sociology of Knowledge.* New York: Doubleday, 1966.

Bruffee, Kenneth A. "Collaborative Learning and 'The Conversation of Mankind.'" *College English* (1984): 635–52.

——. "Liberal Education and the Social Justification of Belief." *Liberal Education* 68 (1982): 95–114.

——. "Social Construction, Language, and the Authority of Knowledge." *College English* 48 (1986): 773–90.

"Chemistry." *McGraw-Hill Encyclopedia of Science and Technology.* 5th ed. New York: McGraw Hill, 1982.

Davis, Kenneth S. *The Cautionary Scientists.* New York: Putnam's, 1966.

French, Sidney J. *Torch and Crucible.* Princeton: Princeton University Press, 1941.

Gadamer, Hans-Georg. *Philosophical Hermeneutics.* Berkeley: University of California Press, 1976.

——. *Truth and Method.* New York: Crossroad, 1988.

Geertz, Clifford. *The Interpretation of Cultures.* New York: Basic Books, 1973.

———. *Local Knowledge.* New York: Basic Books, 1983.

Gergen, Kenneth J. "The Social Constructionist Movement in Modern Psychology." *American Psychologist* 40 (1985): 266–75.

———. *Toward Transformation in Social Knowledge.* New York: Springer-Verlag, 1982.

Guerlac, Henry. *Antoine-Laurent Lavoisier.* New York: Charles Scribner's Sons, 1975.

Hendricks, Janet. "Takea and Jempe (Hummingbird)." Unpublished retranslation (1989) of myth recorded by Siro Pellizaro for *Mundo Shuar* (1977): 7–15.

Hymes, Dell. "The Ethnography of Speaking." *Readings in the Sociology of Language.* Ed. Joshua A. Fishmann. The Hague: Mouton, 1968: 99–138.

———. "Models of the Interaction of Language and Social Life." *Directions in Sociolinguistics: The Ethnography of Communication.* Ed. John J. Gumperz and Dell Hymes. Oxford: Blackwell, 1986: 35–71.

———. "Toward Ethnographies of Communication." *American Anthropologist* 66 (1964): 1–34.

Jakobson, Roman. "Concluding Statement: Linguistics and Poetics." *Style in Language.* Cambridge, Mass.: MIT Press, 1960: 350–73.

Jakobson, Roman, Claude Lévi-Strauss, C. F. Voeglin, and Thomas Sebeok. "Results of the Conference of Anthropologists and Linguists." *Memoir of the International Journal of American Linguistics* 8 (1953): 11–21.

Kuhn, Thomas S. "The Historical Structure of Scientific Discovery." *The Essential Tension.* Chicago: University of Chicago Press, 1977: 165–77.

———. *The Structure of Scientific Revolutions.* 1962. Chicago: University of Chicago Press, 1970.

"Lavoisier." *Chamber's Dictionary of Scientists.* Ed. A. V. Howard. New York: Dutton, 1955.

"Lavoisier." *Dictionary of Scientific Biography.* Ed. Charles Coulston Gillispie. New York: Scribner's, 1973.

Leeds-Hurwitz, Wendy. "Culture and Communication: A Review Essay." *Quarterly Journal of Speech* 76 (1990): 85–96.

Riedman, Sarah R. *Antoine Lavoisier.* New York: Nelson, 1957.

Rorty, Richard. *Consequences of Pragmatism.* Minneapolis: University of Minnesota Press, 1982.

———. *Philosophy and the Mirror of Nature.* Princeton: Princeton University Press, 1979.

10
"Too Little Care"
Language, Politics, and Embodiment
in the Life-World

Kurt Spellmeyer

When I think about the politics of speech and writing, I return again and again to the final scene in Akira Kurosawa's movie *Ran,* or "chaos," which contemplates, among many other things, the fragmentation of social life in postmodernity. Kurosawa shows us a man in the fading light, bent forward on his staff at the edge of an enormous cliff. This man, really a boy, cannot see that the sun is going down because he can no longer see anything, having lost his eyes in a dynastic struggle that left most of his family dead. Nor can he know that his sister, whose arrival he expects momentarily, lies beside her severed head in the valley, another victim of another civil war. Along the path from his hut the boy has carried a scroll that evidently holds some importance for him, but as he reaches the edge of the precipice and his staff swings through the empty air, he drops the scroll to the stones below, where it falls open beneath the camera's gaze. For just a second Kurosawa shows the image on it, a Buddha standing upright in a circle of light, at ease with the world—a world, we might say, where politics would be unnecessary. And then we see once again the young man, an awkward silhouette beneath the sky. We are all, Kurosawa means to tell us, that man: among us now, everything will be fiercely contested, the nature of identity no less than the limits of the state.

My concern here is not with Kurosawa or his film, but with the contestation itself, which I propose to examine by asking why fierce disagreement has overtaken even those of us whose modest task is teaching students how to read and write. In the process, I hope to suggest that if politics matters to any field, it should matter to composition and rhetoric; not politics in the conventional sense, as the "blinding" of him and the "beheading" of her, but politics in its deeper aspect, as what happens after a person has dropped the scroll—the assurance of stability—and the problem of chaos ensues.

While the violence that *Ran* displays to excess has a place in every social order, Kurosawa's "chaos" arises from a contestation among rival versions of order, each claiming for itself the status of truth, and each plunging its opponents into ceaseless unease. Whereas violence can be used by almost anyone toward almost any end, chaos is the product of a disarray on the level of the "life-world," which Edmund Husserl was the first to define as the "horizon" of assumptions and attitudes, socially constituted but experienced individually, that each of us takes for granted as we move through our everyday lives. In the life-world, my experience repeatedly affirms the "naturalness" of everything I see or think or do, and at those moments when events arrest this "natural" flow, I will renew its coherence as completely as I can, if not by transforming my actual circumstances, then by learning to perceive them in a more encompassing way (Husserl 142–47; also Merleau-Ponty 84–97; Schutz and Luckmann 3–15). Yet it is just this renewal that chaos threatens, for the collision of worlds, as Kurosawa demonstrates, may at last call into doubt the possibility of any order not created and sustained by violence alone.

Knowledge and Embodiment

That the crisis of postmodernity *has* overtaken us in composition surely no one can doubt. Given the proliferation of academic disciplines, each with its restrictive dialect, and given our growing awareness that behind these dialects lie vastly different modes of seeing and acting, the days are gone when we could simply announce, as Henry Seidel Canby did in 1909, that "good form in writing" is the same as "good form in dress. It is bad form to wear a flannel shirt with a dress coat, or a white lawn tie with a sack suit. It is quite as bad form to make mistakes in grammar" (xiv). The days are gone as well, or I hope they are, when most teachers of writing would accept at face value the conclusions of researchers like Carl Bereiter, who argued two decades ago that poor blacks in Urbana, Illinois, were a people without any language worth the name: without a language, or a culture, or the power to reason (112–13). Rejecting such opinions, more careful researchers, among them William Labov and Mina Shaughnessy, Shirley Brice Heath and Mike Rose, have helped us to see that the peoples supposedly without a language preserve their own "ways with words," ways as logical, complex, and elaborated as those familiar to the speakers of "standard English"—the language, that is, of the white middle class, from whose ranks have come most college-level teachers. Although these teachers, the "we" of the essay that follows, once taught something simply known as "good English," we now teach a dialect among many dialects, and the distinction signals a major shift in our values and practices.

Still, rehearsing these details does not help to explain why the politics of language and instruction has become such a matter of controversy. No one who understands that language and the university are themselves historical constructs can ignore the fact that each has been constructed in the interests of some groups at the expense of others, and to the detriment of some values for the sake of others. Even E. D. Hirsch adopts this position when he equates literacy with culture. But we have yet to recognize what culture *is:* neither a stock of fundamental facts and terms nor a repertoire of conventions, neither a Lévi-Straussian bricolage of structures nor a Geertzian "ensemble of texts," but something closer to stories that must be told, retold, and revised until they seem real to the teller (Lévi-Strauss 16–22, 75–108; Geertz, *Interpretation* 452). By forgetting both the teller and this process of revision, we have failed to acknowledge our complicity in the persistence of an ethnocentrism all the more profound because it masquerades as tolerance.

For some indication of just how profound the ethnocentrism is, I would like to consider an essay, "The Man Made of Words," by N. Scott Momaday, a writer of Kiowa ancestry who speaks about language and social life from the interface between his "horizon" and ours. There Momaday observes, "It seems to me that in a certain sense we are . . . made of words; that our most essential being consists in language. It is the element in which we think and dream and act, in which we live our daily lives. There is no way in which we can exist apart from the morality of a verbal dimension" (Hobson 162). To illustrate the nature of this dimension, and to argue its distinctly moral quality—to argue, that is, a link between our language and our lives in the world—Momaday recalls his final hours at work on *The Way to Rainy Mountain,* a narrative that weaves together Kiowa history and myth with his private impressions while retracing the journey of his ancestors from the Yellowstone country to Oklahoma, where they met, fought, and lost to successive waves of white settlers. As our historians used to assure us, the destiny of the white settlers was providentially manifest, but the Kiowa were forced to play out a hidden and ironic destiny, for *their* journey of collective self-fashioning was interrupted by their near annihilation, and it may have been the sense of something prematurely terminated, of something yet to be written, that left Momaday unsure about what he should say in his epilogue.

When he began to write again, however, this time about the end of the

Kiowas' nomadic migrations, Momaday remembered an old woman, Ko-sahn, from whom he had heard stories one summer—and abruptly he saw that these stories held the key not only to Kiowa history, but also to his project. Ko-sahn, he realized then, was the embodiment of everything that remained to be said, the uncompleted narrative of his people. Or rather, she made possible for Momaday himself the embodiment of the past, its transposition into his own life:

> For some time I sat looking down at these words on the page, trying to deal with the emptiness that had come about inside of me. The words did not seem real. I could scarcely believe that they made sense, that they had anything what-soever to do with meaning. In desperation almost, I went back over the final paragraphs, backwards and forwards, hurriedly. My eyes fell upon the name Ko-sahn. And all at once everything seemed suddenly to refer to that name. The name seemed to humanize the whole complexity of language.

What happened next to Momaday happened—as he might put it—at the boundary between the lived world and the "verbal dimension":

> Then it was that that ancient, one-eyed woman Ko-sahn stepped out of the language and stood before me on the page. I was amazed. Yet it seemed entirely appropriate that this should happen.
>
> "I was just now writing about you," I [said]. . . . "But all of this, this imagining," I protested, "this has taken place—is taking place in my mind. You are not actually here. . . . "
>
> "Be careful of your pronouncements, grandson," she answered. . . . "If I am not here in this room . . . then surely neither are you." (Hobson 164)

Words, Momaday reminds us, come from the past unembodied, and they can-not be embodied—cannot have a *meaning*, as opposed to an abstract defini-tion—until they take on the power to explain the reader's circumstances to himself, just as Ko-sahn does for Momaday. Yet once words have assumed this explanatory power, they no longer operate as "text" at all, a verbal artifact distinct from the flow of experience. To the extent that words become real and meaningful, they also change how the reader thinks and sees and feels. As meaning, a text is embodied in the reader, and this embodiment effects a "deep" transformation of the reader's universe of language and sense of self, reconciling them within the contours of a single lived reality. But the "depth" of this change, as Momaday represents it, is neither a quality of the text nor an attribute of the reader; rather, it emerges as a consequence of their shared capacity to disclose a world.

Of course *we* who are not of Kiowa descent might prefer to dismiss Ko-sahn's appearance as a "literary device"—as, in my terms, not "deep." But Momaday intends to question our long-standing commonsense distinction between words and things: the belief that we can see Ko-sahn without the agency of language, and conversely, that we can speak her name in a meaningful fashion without also bearing witness to her presence. If Momaday suggests, as I am persuaded he does, that words mean nothing outside the context of particular events, he also argues that the way events reveal themselves depends on the language we use. Because words have the potential to conceal as well as disclose, any struggle over language at the same time entails a struggle over worlds fought on the deepest levels of the self—that part of the self most intimately connected with other selves and with history. To silence any person, to prohibit his speech or to discredit her manner of speaking, is therefore to silence much more than the person, not only everyone from whom the speaker learned his words, but also everything these words have made real: the Sun Dance of Momaday's ancestors; the sacred Sun Dance Doll Tai-me; the prophetic falling of the stars in 1833, which signaled the end of the Kiowas' sovereignty. We should not forget that Momaday writes as someone who has seen the devastation of a world and now struggles to resurrect it by recovering its names, images, and narratives. While he addresses us in our language, and on terms we can readily appreciate, he also writes as a person who has viewed this language from an outsider's perspective—has known firsthand its ability to silence those who give things other names. As much as his essay reaffirms our life-world and our language, it also takes aim against them. By reconstructing the traditions of his forbears, and by doing this in words partly ours and partly his, Momaday resists, and then presses back, the limitations of a culture that has endangered his own legacy.

Momaday's predicament—and increasingly ours as well at a time when there are more and more Momadays around—arises from his uneasy situation between worlds often violently opposed. The writer Simon J. Ortiz, from the Acoma Pueblo in New Mexico, describes this same predicament in the short story "Woman Singing" through the impressions of his narrator, Clyde, a migrant farm worker in Idaho. One afternoon when Clyde hears a woman singing in the shack across from his, he remembers the songs of his people, the Navajo, on their reservation far to the south. Later Clyde and another Indian worker, Willie, go into town to watch a movie about a very different kind of singer:

> Hank Williams was the singer's name. Clyde knew who he was, used to be on the Grand Ole Opry on radio, he remembered, sang songs he remembered too. Clyde thought about the singers back home. The singers on the land, the people, the rain, the good things of his home. His uncle on his mother's side was a medicine man, and he used to listen to him sing. . . . Sing with me, his uncle would say, and Clyde would sing. . . .
>
> Willie laughed at the funny incidents in the movie, and he laughed about the drunk Hank Williams. That made him wish he had a drink again. (Hobson 260)

Through the one word *singer,* two distinct worlds compete for embodiment in Clyde: the world of Hank Williams, where singers drink and fight and raise hell with other men's wives, and the world of the people, the Navajo, who sing to invoke the rain and many other "good things." Caught between these conflicting worlds, Clyde at first feels anger and then despair, since the conflict is far from equal. Although Momaday in writing *The Way to Rainy Mountain* successfully appropriates white culture, Clyde and the other migrant workers have been so thoroughly appropriated that the reservation and its way of life survive as little more than memory:

> And then he thought of what all the white men in the world thought about all the Indians. . . . For a long time Clyde stood behind the door of his and Willie's shack. Listening and thinking quiet angry thoughts. He thought of Willie . . . the Elkhorn Bar, Hank Williams . . . and he asked himself what he was listening for. He knew that he was not listening for the song, because he had decided that

> the woman singing was something a long time ago and
> would not happen anymore. If it did, he would not believe
> it. He would not listen. Finally, he moved away from the
> door and began to search through Willie's things for a bottle.
> But there was no bottle of anything except the kerosene and
> for a moment he thought of drinking kerosene. (263–64)

In Clyde's despair, Ortiz shows us what is *really* at stake when we speak about the politics of language—a dialectic of loss and recovery, concealment and awareness, powerlessness and power on a scale so intimate and ordinary that our "politicized" profession characteristically overlooks it. Behind the politics of language, or rather far beneath it, there awaits another, long-neglected politics, long-neglected and poorly theorized—a deep politics of experience, "deep" because it unfolds at the boundary between life-worlds in dialogue or contestation.

But why, with contestation everywhere around us, have we neglected the reality of experience for so long? Why has experience remained, if not an object of derision, then an empty trope, even among its defenders? This neglect, I am convinced, is an outcome of our privileged situation as the "winners" of colonial history, who like winners everywhere justify the status quo by appealing to the notion that things are the way they are necessarily. For the last hundred years, after all, nearly everything we have learned about culture and language—from Durkheim and Radcliffe-Brown to Geertz, and from Saussure to Barthes and Derrida—has presupposed the existence of determining laws or codes that operate "behind the backs" of those subject to them (Durkheim 415–47; Geertz, *Local* 62–64; Saussure 7–17; Barthes 35–40; Derrida xv, 3–4, 340–41; also Giddens 2–3). Yet it is exactly this perspective Momaday repudiates when he insists, writing from the standpoint of the "defeated," that nothing is real beyond the world people consciously make in the effort to declare "possession of themselves," and that their stories and myths—and even their words—are never more than "one generation" away from disappearing (Hobson 169, 171). By idealizing language and culture as the true actors on history's stage, the descendants of Durkheim and Saussure leave resistance as well as domination unexplained: why is it that people work so hard to impose their codes and systems on others? And why do those others work so hard, in turn, to resist the imposition?

The answer lies, I would submit, with the codes themselves, or rather with their poverty before the plenitude of experience, which R. D. Laing once defined as "man's invisibility to man"—that portion of everyday life, in other words, which always exceeds the codes (18). And from the excess, from the predicament of no longer seeing in the present a satisfying likeness to the past, domination and the act of resistance each arises, the first as a denial, and the second as an affirmation, of everything the codes leave out. But if Laing took experience seriously, domination and resistance remain incidental for those who hold, with Lévi-Strauss—a successor to both Durkheim and Saussure— that language exhibits a reason "which has its [own] reasons . . . of which man knows nothing" (Lévi-Strauss 252). What disappears from the "behind-their-backs" tradition is any sense of how human subjects struggle to preserve their life-worlds against the imposition of alien values. This struggle, arguably the central issue of education, is nothing less than the central issue of postmodernity itself.

When the African novelist Ngugi wa Thiong'o writes about the education of children under the British colonial regime in Kenya, he restores to the discussion of language and culture much that remains concealed by postcolonial high theory. Like the Kiowa and Navajo here in the United States, Ngugi's people, the Gikuyu, one day found themselves strangers in their native land. Under the tutelage of British supervisors, the development of young Gikuyu "was now determined," Ngugi recalls, "by the dominant language" of English and the dominant culture of northern Europe. In primary school, the children of Ngugi's generation, whose parents had grown up with the tales of Hare and Leopard and Lion, read Dickens and Stevenson and H. Rider Haggard (12). Not only did the pedagogy of the colonists intentionally divide the school from the home, but it colonized what Ngugi calls the "mental universe" of its subjects. For these children, thinking transpired in a language far removed from the world they knew at first hand, and this world, their world, they learned to see through the eyes of those who despised them. Ngugi himself remembers reading Hume's famous dictum that "the negro is naturally inferior to the whites," and Hegel's altogether characteristic remark, in *The Philosophy of History,* that "there was nothing harmonious with humanity to be found in the African character" (quoted in Ngugi 16–18). No matter how the colonizers imagined their undertaking, to Ngugi it meant the loss of "harmony" between the self, the world, and the language of his birth (28).

The experience of colonial subjects like Ngugi, Momaday, and Ortiz differs greatly from the experience of middle-class whites. But on the level of deep politics the colonization of the student's "mental universe," the discrediting of his or her everyday language and commonsense world, is a phenomenon that reaches far beyond any single class or nationality, and beyond ideologies of left and right. Well before Europeans colonized sub-Saharan Africa, they had already colonized themselves, smashing down their small-scale societies and overturning their local knowledge—not once but so often and so thoroughly that the most "advanced" societies are also those to which the state of "homelessness" has become most tenaciously endemic (Hobsbawm 44–73). Almost everyone can claim, as Ngugi does, that formal education in some sense concealed the events it supposedly explained, and that the language of the classroom could "never, as spoken or written, properly reflect . . . the real life" of the student's own "community" (16). While not everyone benefits equally from the prevailing balance of terrors and powers, the logic of colonization applies to everyone alike. On the top as on the bottom, we are all colonized, and the fact of our mutual oppression explains why colonization continues, as a deep cultural logic, long after the troops have gone home.

The troops, so to speak, are now within us. Even a person like Joan Didion, born to relative privilege, describes her education in the essay "Why I Write" much as Ngugi does: "During the years when I was an undergraduate at Berkeley I tried, with a kind of hopeless late-adolescent energy, to buy some temporary visa into the world of ideas, to forge for myself a mind that could deal with the abstract. In short I tried to think. I failed. My attention veered inexorably back to the specific, to the tangible, to what was generally considered . . . the peripheral" (Smart 257–58). The "peripheral" was Didion's life, and although she represents her frustrations as uniquely hers, it is the familiar, almost universal, character of her observations here that might lead us to look for a larger, and social, cause. Like many—no, most—of our students, Didion understood formal knowledge as removed from, and even antithetical to, her actual circumstances, and for her, within the academy at least, this division became insurmountable. "During those years," she recalls in her essay, "I was traveling on what I knew to be a very shaky passport, forged papers: I knew that I was no legitimate resident in any world of ideas. I knew I couldn't think" (258). The deep political consequence of Didion's estrangement from the "world of ideas" was still another division: between herself and others, between her private life and a public world always vaguely imagined as "out there." Convinced she "couldn't think," Didion became a "writer" by default; someone committed, that is, to redefining the meanings of words on the basis of her lived experience.

To the extent that speech and writing permit—in fact, demand—such redefinitions, words are perpetually political. And to the extent that institutions, English departments among them, can enable or prevent the embodiment of ideas and the destruction or renewal of life-worlds, their function is political as well. But if politics confronts us as inescapable fact, which *specific* form of politics will we foster? By expanding the canon and revising undergraduate curricula in the spirit of multiculturalism, we may still overlook what matters most: not knowledge but the uses of knowledge. Even with all the curricular changes now in place at schools like Berkeley, Syracuse, and Wisconsin, nothing will really have changed in English unless we are willing to promote the use of knowledge by our students as a means of renewing and enlarging their specific historical loyalties. Adding Malcolm X to a reading list is not the same as reconstructing the university to make room for black Muslims and their way of life. And "making room" should mean more than reducing this way of life to a subject for analysis at the hands of an instructor whose pose of professional dispassion and rigor may conceal (but not prevent) efforts at converting black Muslim students to a rival faith or allegiance.

By ignoring the political distinction between adding texts to a list and bringing "otherness" into our professional arenas, we may preserve the appearance of uncoercive inquiry when we are really on the road to Kurosawa's earthly hell of mutual incomprehension—which is, I should point out for those who missed the film, a version of King Lear's. And Lear's kingdom falls into chaos not because he has grown too careless of order, but because in his obsession with it he neglects the preservation of intersubjective understanding, the understanding that comes with the willingness to see through the eyes of those least like oneself. "I have," he says, "ta'en / Too little care of this" (III, iv, 32–33). If Momaday, Ortiz, and Ngugi can add anything to Lear's insight on the moor, it is that the less we care about what knowledge does to people, the farther we will stray from the future achievement of any truly common knowledge.

Disembodiment and the Dynamics of Colonization

How, exactly, do we go about pursuing such a knowledge, the kind that Momaday constructs when he ushers Ko-sahn into our world? For many of us, the most obvious answer, and possibly the only one, must be a return to reason. The crisis fostered by our current multiplicity of worlds would seem to bestow on reason something like the unqualified reverence in which Socrates held it at another crucial moment of conflicting values—reason as the "pilot" that guides the "soul" from "a plurality of perceptions to a unity" (Plato, *Phaedrus* 247c, 249b–c). A return to Reason with a capital *R* might enable us to see the prevailing chaos of different values from a new and reassuring perspective, not as a collision of rival truths but as a contest between rival claimants to the Truth, each positioned somewhere definite between stark ignorance and perfected knowledge.

For me, however, and I suspect for many others, the single most powerful defense of reason is to be found in Boethius's treatise *The Consolation of Philosophy*. Although *The Consolation* offered nothing really new as an account of reason, it laid out its simple argument with such overwhelming emotional force that it created almost singlehandedly what might be called the *romance* of reason. A former consul and defender of the Senate's fading authority, Boethius was condemned to death by Theodoric, king of the Ostrogoths, who had conquered the Western Empire in 489. In the months preceding the execution, with the political survival of the empire less and less certain and with the Church increasingly threatened by Theodoric's Arian heresy, Boethius wrote in praise of a Christianized goddess of Wisdom whom he renamed Philosophy. To the vagaries of Fortune, which had betrayed him in the long run, he contrasted the unshakable insight provided by reason. "For who," the goddess of Philosophy asks him, can impose "any [unjust] law upon man, except upon his body, or upon his fortune, which is less than his body. You can never impose upon a free spirit, nor can you deprive a rationally self-possessed mind of its equanimity" (35).

Whatever reason might become in the centuries that followed, it would seem to have its origins in the phenomenon of oppression, just as Nietzsche understood. Through reason, the victim fabricates a compensatory inner self and a second, "rational" world beyond the reach of the oppressor, a world in which the silent can speak and the defeated can achieve an unachievable redress. Yet the mind's liberation carries with it a hidden price, and that price is the asceticism of disembodiment, for when reason no longer serves the body by enlarging the sphere of its concrete interactions, it becomes a surreptitious ally of the oppressor. Such, Nietzsche alleges, was the case with Socrates, who responded to the chaos in Athens not by pursuing new modes of experience but by claiming to have glimpsed a realm of "truth" that experience could do nothing to change. In Nietzsche's view, the result was an unparalleled disaster: armed with reason, Socrates' young admirers—the West's first missionaries—

waged a war on the life-world of their stammering, defenseless fellow citizens
(Nietzsche 478).

Man, as Kenneth Burke is rumored to have said, does not live by the *idea*
of bread alone. And because reason all too often and too easily prefers ideas over
bread itself, its romance conceals a destructiveness that philosophers sometimes
prefer to ignore while historians cannot, at least after they look closely. Those of
us taught to hold reason in an unreflecting esteem would do well to recall that
the West's colonial adventure was at the same time a history of reason's relentless, and subversive, invocation. Here, for example, is what an early nineteenth-
century Protestant missionary, William Swan, had to say about the Buryat
Mongols of Siberia, when they persistently rebuffed his efforts to convert them
from their native amalgam of spirit-worship and Lamaism:

> During our stay many came to us, received books, and con-
> versed about the Gospel. . . . When we had exposed the
> futility of their arguments for a multitude of gods, etc., they
> would say, "This is too much for our minds" (meaning such
> subjects were beyond their reach). In fact, they are in general
> very ignorant, even of the tenets of their own superstition
> [Buddhism], nor is it requisite, according to their ideas, that
> they should know them, their duty consisting merely in
> reading prayers in an unknown tongue [Tibetan], and per-
> forming other bodily exercises; so that they are saved com-
> pletely *the trouble of thinking;* on this account their religion
> is more suited to the indolence of their minds, as well as the
> depravity of their nature, than one which addresses the [in-
> tellect]. (Bawden 235)

Anyone who reads the narratives of the preeminent European missionaries—
Matteo Ricci in China or David Livingstone in central Africa—will be im-
pressed by the consistency with which these men linked cultural difference to
unreason. Conversely, we can hardly fail to appreciate the confidence with
which they presupposed that the triumph of their way of life would follow on
the triumph of reason. As Swan wrote in a proposal for the future education of
the Buryat,

> Means should be taken to excite in them a spirit of enquiry.
> The people should be taught *to think,* and to consider this as

> their undoubted privilege. When they learn that freedom of
> thought and action in religious matters is their inalienable
> right, their eyes will then begin to open upon the deceitful
> maxims of their own priesthood. They will then be led to
> examine the foundations of their belief, and the true nature
> of their religious observances. . . . Every Christian Mission
> established in such a country has the direct tendency thus to
> excite and keep up enquiry, and much may be done in
> sapping the foundations of an erroneous system before any
> outward change is apparent. (252)

Swan does not neglect to add that an unsparingly reasoned assault on Lamaism
must go hand in hand with "the inculcation of Christian principles," while
back home in the Britain of Robert Owen, Jeremy Bentham, and James Mill
(father of John Stuart), these same principles were growing less and less secure.
Among the "savages," perhaps, Swan the rationalist may have unconsciously
hoped to regain a paradise of certainty lost to him forever in his native land.

Though a student of the Buryats' Mongolian language and a worker in
Siberia's "mission fields" for the better part of two decades, Swan never seems to
have appreciated the most basic features of the religion he labored so long and
so hard to exterminate. On some level he knew that the lamas he derided as
unreasoning (comparing them to "Papists," among other things) were heirs to
an ancient and highly sophisticated tradition of dialectics, and that the most
eminent among them had undergone scholarly training, in the Buddhist canon
and in the literary legacy of India and Tibet, more extensive than the infrequent
schooling Swan himself had received (84–86, 156–68). For Swan, nonetheless,
the Buryat were always to remain a people without knowledge, a people who
had never learned "to think." In this same spirit Swan's contemporary, the
explorer-missionary Dr. Livingstone, made a point of openly violating the
religious conventions of the tribes whose hospitality he enjoyed, just as Ricci,
three centuries earlier, had set out to master Chinese culture, even going so far
as to adopt the clothing of a Buddhist priest, in order to cast down the whole
edifice more completely (Oliver 80; Spence 114–15, 250–55).

Assessing the ultimate failure of the Siberian mission, the historian C. R.
Bawden observes that the Buryat had nothing to gain from conversion to
"what . . . looked like a fly-by-night novelty." For the individual Buryat, there
could be no conceivable "reason . . . to apostasize, to give all this up, to cut

himself off from his fellow Buryats and earn their scorn" (232). William Swan, the defender of reason, might have had faith in a universal truth, one superior to differences of every kind, but no degree of rigor or eloquence made his version of that truth credible to the Buryat themselves. Their beliefs, as much as ours—and as much as our students'—went hand in hand with an entire way of life, a way of life that the change Swan hoped to incite would have placed at needless risk. To suppose, as Swan did, that some amount of strenuous argument might touch off a mass conversion was to invert the real relationship between ideas and life-worlds. If the Buryat turned their backs on the Protestant mission, they did so not because they found its logic unconvincing; they found its logic unconvincing because they wanted, and they needed, to continue being Buryat. Like all of us, they believed what *already* made sense, in terms of their accustomed assumptions and their proven social arrangements. For them, as for us, such assumptions and arrangements defined the farthest boundary of thinking, which any welcome change must enlarge rather than erase.

Although Swan's mission to Siberia failed, the progress of "reason" is by and large a chronicle of uninterrupted conquests. Yet it has drawn its strength, generation after generation, from a commitment to the unreason it supposedly renounces—a commitment to the irrational refusal of any genuine dialogue, which would entail an admission that the other party must be right from some still undetermined perspective. While the disclosure of this "undetermined perspective" lies beyond the power of reason alone, it never lies beyond the power of words, as the means of embodied involvement with the world. Consider the nature of the world disclosed to the reader through the words that follow, spoken at the turn of the century by the Paiute Jack Wilson (Wovoka) in conversations with James Mooney, a Smithsonian-sponsored anthropologist. On a winter's day in 1889, the sun, according to Wilson, "died," and so did Wilson himself, who then rose up into heaven. There

> he saw God, with all the people [deceased] long ago engaged in their oldtime sports and occupations, all happy and forever young. It was a pleasant land and full of game. After showing him all, God told him he must go back and tell his people they must be good and love one another, have no quarreling, and live in peace with the whites; that they must work, and not lie or steal; that they must put away the old

> practices that savored of war; that if they faithfully obeyed
> his instructions they would at last be reunited with their
> friends in this other world, where there would be no more
> death or sickness or old age. He was then given the dance
> which he was commanded to bring back to his people. By
> performing this dance at intervals, for five consecutive days
> each time, they would secure this happiness to themselves
> and hasten the event. Finally, God gave him control over the
> elements so that he could make it rain or snow. (Mooney 14)

True or false? Warranted or unwarranted? To ask these questions at the outset is worse than absurd; by doing so we renew a long history of violence aimed not only at others, but also at those aspects of our own experience we have never understood or acknowledged. Far from requiring the kind of detachment that Plato recommends in the *Phaedrus,* the detachment of the thinker who has learned to transcend the specificity of his circumstances, Wilson's words seek out an embodiment in us, a change in our manner of perceiving the world.

A change of just this kind overtook James Mooney, the ethnographer who interviewed Jack Wilson. By 1890, when reports of an Indian messiah first reached federal agents in Washington, Indians from many tribes had begun to welcome Wilson as nothing less than "a divine messenger" whose arrival on earth would restore their shattered lives. More eager to pass judgment than to understand, the press treated him with the same glib condescension that magazines like *Time* and *Newsweek* have made routine today. Years later Mooney would recount how Wilson "was denounced as an impostor, ridiculed as a lunatic, and laughed at as a pretended Christ." But Mooney's purpose, succinctly stated in the first chapter of his ethnography *The Ghost Dance Religion and the Sioux Outbreak of 1890,* was to retell Wilson's story toward a different end: "Notwithstanding all that had been said and written by newspaper correspondents about the messiah, not one of them had undertaken to find the man himself and to learn from his . . . lips what he really taught." Not one, in Mooney's words, had "understood" the real "meaning" of the Ghost Dance (7). To understand its meaning, Mooney sat for hours on the floor of Wilson's lodge, and he took part in the Ghost Dance while living among the Arapaho and Cheyenne. All told, he spent twenty-two months and traveled thirty-two thousand miles to interview Wilson's followers in twenty tribes, intermittently returning to Washington to conduct ancillary research. For Mooney, and very nearly Mooney alone, "understanding" meant surveying the subject from every possible point of view (xi–xiii).

Throughout his years among the Buryat, William Swan had achieved a state of vigilance celebrated by his colleagues as "single-mindedness" (Bawden 12). In Mooney, though, we see another kind of vigilance, a determined desire not to stay the same at any cost but to go beyond the limits of both his knowledge and his sense of self—and this disparity between the two modes of knowing is reflected in the smallest details of their responses to the unfamiliar. Here, for example, is an account of a Lamaist ceremony recorded by Edward Stallybrass, an associate of Swan's in the Siberian venture:

> The chief Lama told us, that the Lamas would now perform [their] service, upon which the latter went to collect their instruments, laughing as they went. These consisted of cymbals, kettles [drums], and two long trumpets, which made a most dismal noise. The Lamas said their prayers with a muttering voice, and with their eyes shut. At intervals they were accompanied by the instruments, which sounded without any regular tune. The chief Lama stood by, muttering his prayers with apparent devotion. The whole was a scene of the greatest nonsense and confusion. (Bawden 141)

And now here is James Mooney at a Plains Indian ceremony:

> [The] whole company, men, women, and children, went through the same ceremony . . . beginning with Wilson and myself, and ending with members of the [host] family. The ceremony occupied a considerable time, and was at once beautiful and impressive. Not a word was said . . . excepting as someone in excess of devotion would utter prayerful exclamations aloud like the undertone of a litany. Every face wore a look of reverent solemnity, from the old men and women down to little children of 6 and 8 years. Several of them, the women especially, trembled while praying. (162)

Stallybrass's conception of rationality obliged him to look with the greatest skepticism and "distance" at those aspects of the lamas' ceremony most directly opposed to his severe Congregationalist sense of order—especially, I imagine, the lamas' laughter in a grave and sacred venue. By belittling their ritual as "the greatest nonsense and confusion," he summarily denied it any place in his life-world—or rather, he *tried* to deny it, since it was already there irreversibly. And because it was already there, this denial of the other would henceforth require, to a greater or lesser extent, a continual inner policing, a relentless suppression of the "other" inside. I have no doubt, however, that suppression had become second nature to Stallybrass long before his encounter with the Buryat, in whom he recognized the playfulness he had once learned to despise as shameful in himself.

Mooney's research on Wilson and the Ghost Dance religion was rational in a different and far less destructive sense—less destructive to his own life as well as to the lives of others. Perhaps because he saw in the Paiutes' misery the outlines of his private distress, he identified with Wilson and his followers as few other white observers did. In the words of Alice Beck Kehoe, Mooney, the "son of dirt-poor and despised Irish immigrants," expressed "a strong feeling of fellowship with other groups conquered and oppressed by English-speaking governments" (30). By reconstructing the Ghost Dance phenomenon in terms of his personal history, Mooney was able to look beyond the unfamiliar content of Wilson's teaching to discover its broader human value—the way it sustained its believers within their local gestalt. Swan and Stallybrass saw Lamaism as a rival dogma and nothing else, but Mooney realized that disparities on the level of explicit belief, the level philosophers mean when they talk about truth or falsity, can obscure more consequential similarities on the level of pragmatic social practice, the "deep" level of life-world politics. Different beliefs in different contexts could serve the same purpose, and in the context of Native American life during the 1880s, Wilson's prophecies abundantly justified Mooney's comparisons to the "great world faiths." Everywhere the missionary William Swan looked he saw unbridgeable divisions, but the ethnographer James Mooney saw everywhere a common human ground—common not in the details of what people thought, but in the dilemmas that made thought necessary. This ground, often ignored but never altogether out of sight, he uncovers more expansively by asking his readers to consider "how natural" it is for a "race" that "lies crushed and groaning beneath an alien yoke" to "dream of a redeemer, an Arthur, who shall return from exile or awake from some long sleep to drive out the usurper and win back for his people [everything] they lost" (1). Since history has spared no one fully, we have all, as Mooney knew, lived through something like this loss, and we have all felt something of this need.

The Politics of Embodiment

If our experience is destroyed, our behavior will be destructive.
—R. D. Laing, *The Politics of Experience*

Mooney's writings offer us a deep-political alternative to the reductive heuristics of "argument," a way of knowing that is not irrational but deeper than "reason." In their concern for the renewal of knowledge through its embodiment within a life-world, these writings oblige us to rethink *how* we teach at least as carefully as *what* we teach. They oblige us to distinguish between a pseudo-emancipatory pedagogy of contempt or conversion, and those heuristics more conducive to dialogue broadly imagined as an experiential pluralism: not the liberal pluralism that perpetuates estrangement by ignoring or suppressing difference, but one that values difference as a common resource for the enlargement of life-worlds through an endless, uncoercive exchange. If this exchange today operates nowhere in a fully realized form—in no institution or locale, no discourse or discipline—people always have managed to keep it going, even under the worst circumstances, or so the fate of societies like the Kiowa would suggest.

After a century of intensely repressive educational practice, when everything that could be done was done with a vengeance to humiliate Native Americans and erase their historical memory (see Jensen), writers such as Momaday and Ortiz, Leslie Marmon Silko, James Welch, and Louise Erdrich have attracted millions of white readers. And many whites, supposedly heirs to the triumph of the West, have since the time of the first colonial encounters quietly withdrawn their allegiance to it (Axtell 168–206). Just as Momaday's theories of language owe something to his graduate training under Yvor Winters at Stanford, so Americans of European ancestry may discover that Ko-sahn speaks more powerfully to them than Conrad's Marlowe or Melville's Ishmael. Looking where their predecessors turned away, these white readers may find something to admire and emulate in a way of life distinguished, as the historian James Axtell maintains, by "community, abundant love, and uncommon integrity" (206). Then again, they may choose to look elsewhere, in which case "higher pluralism" has a distinct advantage over chaos, cynicism, and plain bad faith.

To illustrate what happens on the grand scale when this higher pluralism disappears, I want to present one author's account of a society that ours may increasingly come to resemble, both in its diversity and in its unwillingness to acknowledge diversity's uses. The society is Sri Lanka, and the author is Stanley Tambiah, a contemporary anthropologist of Southeast Asian societies. According to Tambiah, the growing political conflict between a largely Buddhist Sinhalese majority—the "missionaries" of his story—and a largely Hindu Tamil minority has produced a war of interpretations, a struggle to control the "text" of the island's ancient culture. Haunted by fears of disloyalty and collapse, fears made worse by the island's economic decline, the Sinhalese majority has attempted to assimilate the Tamils through such measures as a "Sinhala only" language policy, and these measures have inspired a determined and sometimes murderous Tamil resistance (Tambiah 74–75). What seems most enigmatic to Tambiah is the suddenness of the rupture between two groups that enjoyed eight hundred years of coexistence, including three centuries of occupation by the Portuguese, Dutch, and English.

Although no single account can do justice to so complex a phenomenon, Tambiah notes the disappearance of shared rituals and icons that sustained enduring peace through a de facto hermeneutic openness. One exemplary shared icon, possibly the most important one of all, was the god Kataragama, whose yearly festival has brought together millions of Sinhalese and Tamils since the 1500s. While Hindu priests presided at the shrine proper, each group paid its respects to the god in a different manner and each left the festival with a different sense of what had transpired there. And yet precisely because the festival afforded opportunities for difference, it sustained a commonality as well—a commonality-in-difference now endangered. For the first time on record, Buddhist priests have replaced their Hindu counterparts, and Sinhalese zealots more and more monopolize the previously ecumenical cult, with the worst possible results (Tambiah 59; Obeyesekere 460–61). "However much," Tambiah insists, the loss of pluralism "served in the short run to liberate collective energies," the ideology of "communal identity"—the ideology of mandatory sameness—has in the long run "functioned as . . . an engine of domination" (Tambiah 141). But Tambiah leaves relatively unexplored the "existential" sources of the ideology, which may owe less to Sinhalese traditions than to the deep politics of embodiment, the same struggle that now drives our fierce debates over canons and curricula.

On the basis of our history since the Industrial Revolution, we might speculate that the ideology of mandatory sameness marks the advent in Sri

Lanka of the modern nation-state, governed by professional politicians, administered by unelected functionaries, financed by corporations, and culturally normalized by the schools. But this ideology of sameness, for the Sri Lankans as for us, may have another and a deeper source in a profound self-hatred. What the Sinhalese fear most about the Tamils is the truth about themselves, to which the Tamils, merely by their presence, bear an inadvertent witness. With rising popular expectations and a declining economy, many Sinhalese now doubt their capacity to face the crisis, and instead of attempting to resolve it by transforming their way of life, they have set off on a search for disembodied and idealized compensations, a collective denial of their most recent, and most pressing, experience of failure. By fabricating a tradition that belies the complexity of the past, they can forget who they are today, and by imposing a single normative interpretation on cultural fixtures like the Kataragama festival, they can compel the Tamils to join them, in both their predicament and their world-denying asceticism.

We scarcely need the example of Sri Lanka, however, to see Tambiah's "engine of domination" grinding on. As often as universities have encouraged the embodiment of knowledge, they have played the opposite role by enforcing some version of what Arthur Schlesinger calls our "national identity." Given the academy's conflicted heritage of popular empowerment as well as normalization, our most deeply political act as teachers of English may be to reconsider "politics" itself, which has typically justified a regimen of "explaining" knowledge to our students, or of deconstructing it for them, as if our worlds and theirs were already the same. Convinced that the truth lies beyond change and difference, our predecessors strained to overlook those moments of experience that seemed most menacing, unruly, and alien. And now we, while attempting to correct their omissions, still regard truth as something to be fashioned on behalf of others, when in fact we cannot predict—though we should certainly try to learn—how the meaning of our knowledge changes once it enters the life-worlds of people unlike ourselves.

Far more deeply political than "politics" today, and therefore more deeply suppressed, is a practice much more difficult for teachers as well as students. I mean Mooney's practice of pursuing through difference a transformation of the self; of straining, as Momaday strains, to hear in the unfamiliar words of others the voices from his own past. The translation of such a practice into scholarship and pedagogy falls beyond the purview of this essay, but every text we teach is a

Kataragama, whose openness to multiple interpretations we can deny or accept but never contain. Indebted as they are to a tradition of denial, a tradition devised to contain this openness in the name of an order "always already" manifest, politics and pedagogy in their usual forms continue the missionaries' task. But we may find, like William Swan among the Buryat, that the gospel carried to the wilderness is neither welcome nor useful there. Any knowledge which might be useful must give people something "deeper" than one gospel or another; it must assist them in their particular struggles to decide who they have been and what they will become. Without claiming to provide for the salvation of our students, as teachers we have a part to play in these struggles, and considering that more than words are at stake, perhaps we actually will.

Second Thoughts: Modernity and the Knowledge Class

"Perhaps we actually will." When I wrote those words several years ago, I already understood that we *wouldn't*—not, at least, initially, since education and colonization have become too closely allied for any immediate and painless change in our thinking about the uses of knowledge. I now feel that I should have looked more closely than I did at the differences between "traditional" and "modern" (or "postmodern") societies. It seems clear to me that we have, as moderns of an especially privileged kind—that is, as academic intellectuals—a powerful vested interest in continuing to see our fellow citizens in the same way we once saw the "savages" during the era of colonization: blind where we are enlightened; passive in contrast to our activity; enslaved or enslaving as we struggle for emancipation. Outside the academy, *they* supposedly grope their way forward in the half-light of common sense, while inside *we* devote ourselves to the rigors of critical consciousness. But for us, this "critical consciousness" simply operates as another *kind* of common sense, insofar as even the activity of critique has to take on faith many doubtful propositions. Who really benefits, for example, from a 300-page New Historicist rereading of Henry Fielding's novels, especially when the New Historicists are themselves becoming passé? Or, to press the issue a little further, let's suppose that our profession someday manages to exhaust the entire canon, unmasking whatever needs to be unmasked and deconstructing every self-betraying claim—what will happen then? Will our society be any better, any more egalitarian, any more self-aware? Will it even manage to become more truthful, at least?

One way to answer these questions honestly is to consider life inside the English departments we actually know. Are these departments, as social "sites," less brutalizing places than other, comparable sites? Are they any less oppressive of their members, especially when we factor in the subaltern groups made up of teaching assistants and adjunct faculty? The claims for critique notwithstanding, English departments often exhibit some of the most depressing features of any corporate culture. There is, however, one important difference between an academic institution like the English department at Yale and a corporate institution like McDonald's. The cultural authority of McDonald's derives from its ability to meet a "demand" it has produced surreptitiously. If McDonald's can be said to transform cultural life—through advertising, the invention of novel foods, and its sway over labor laws—then it succeeds by carefully concealing its own far-reaching power. Who, after all, can be afraid of the benign, infantile, and desexualized Ronald McDonald, everyone's inferior? The authority of the academy depends, by contrast, on the *overt affirmation* of hierarchy. In order to have any value whatsoever, our knowledge must be a superior knowledge, more detailed, more systematic, more scientific, more critical. To argue candidly that our knowledge is *different from* though *not better than* the beliefs held by ordinary people—to argue this is to relinquish the only form of power that we currently possess.

The cultural authority of the academy differs from the authority of corporate institutions, this much seems obvious. Yet the two kinds of institutions may not differ so completely that we can readily play the "oppositional" role many members of the professoriate now wish to claim for themselves. No one who looks at the citations in the *PMLA,* hypnotic in their liturgical repetitiveness, can make much of a case for our profession's resistance to fashion trends and market mechanisms. Gadamer's stock goes down and Girard's goes up. I would like to suggest, however, not only that academicians and their corporate counterparts are the beneficiaries of a distinctive social order, but also that this order—let's call it modernity—is highly inegalitarian and therefore profoundly destructive. It seems to me that scholars in the academy, together with media workers and functionaries in the state and national bureaucracies, belong to a "new class" whose task it is to produce knowledge for the many millions of largely passive "lay" consumers (Ehrenreich and Ehrenreich; Martin; Rowe). Although observers like Cecelia Tichi, Joshua Meyrowitz, and Richard Lanham all see the emergence of the modern "information society" as potentially emancipating (Lanham is particularly sanguine about the good days soon to come), the last hundred years have moved us very far and very fast in exactly the opposite direction, not toward mass participation in the making of culture but toward exclusion on a global scale (Tichi; Meyrowitz 307–29; Lanham).

How did this division of cultural labor come about? As little as a century ago in the United States, "knowledge workers" of the kind that I have just described were almost nowhere to be found. Even the professions remained marginal and poorly organized. Physicians and dentists, often practicing alone without degrees, were hardly distinguished from barbers; attorneys learned their law in courtroom arguments rather than in lecture halls. And the now ubiquitous research university lay far away in places like Berlin, where young men like Henry Adams went to study. In such a world, "knowledge" played a different role from the one it plays for us today. Describing rural Wisconsin life during the last third of the nineteenth century, the novelist Hamlin Garland recalls that there were "few books in our house":

> Aside from the Bible I remember only one other, a thick, black volume filled with gaudy pictures of cherries and plums, and portraits of ideally fat and prosperous sheep, pigs, and cows. It must have been a *Farmer's Annual* or State agricultural report, but it contained in the midst of its dry prose, occasional poems like "I remember, I remember," "The Old Armchair" and other pieces of a domestic or rural nature. I was especially moved by "The Old Armchair," and although some of the words and expressions were beyond my comprehension, I fully understood the defiant tenderness of the lines:
>
> I love it, I love it, and who shall dare
> To chide me for loving the old armchair? (35)

Most of Garland's learning did not come from books at all but from face-to-face interactions, and the knowledge they conveyed was "local" as opposed to "cosmopolitan": more tacit than explicit, more practical than abstract, more fully anchored in a single place than universalizing. Even the knowledge arriving from outside the confines of the community—agricultural bulletins and poems like "The Old Armchair"—tended to support the assumptions and practices of everyday life. Far from "pushing the envelope," as we now expect "great" art and letters to do, the poems scattered through the pages of the *Annual* encouraged readers to suspend the critical attitude for the pleasure of identification, the same pleasure that people ordinarily still derive from television and the movies. And such pleasure played a crucial role in a world that depended, as society did a hundred years ago, on shared labor, friendliness, and reciprocity.

This primitive economy of local knowledge, highly stable and profoundly egalitarian, was destined to be changed, and by forces far removed from America's "island communities" (Wiebe 43). With the growth of industry came the railroads and the telegraph lines, and with these came the first mass communications. In another autobiography of the time, *Earth Horizon,* the novelist Mary Austin remembers the itinerant "professors" who acted as purveyors of a new cosmopolitan knowledge to the towns of the rural Midwest:

> [The professor] was still, in [those days], indispensable to a "cultivated" state of mind. . . . Everybody wanted culture in the same way that a few years earlier everybody wanted sewing machines, but culture by this time was something more than it had been a few years earlier, when . . . a school for young ladies in a neighboring town advertised both "solid and ornamental cultures," [and] in the latter category the making of wax flowers was included. It meant for one thing . . . the studious reading of books.
>
> To say that people in Carlinville were, in the late seventies, anxious about the state of their culture, where formerly they had been chiefly concerned about their souls, is to sum up all that had happened to them in the twenty years that succeeded the close of the Civil War. (100)

In a certain sense, the Civil War did not end at Appomattox but at the Chicago Exposition in 1893, since the growth of an industrial economy went hand in hand with a new cultural and political centralization. If the sewing machine rapidly made its way to towns like Carlinville, Illinois, a commodified version of high culture could not be far behind. As the historian Robert Wiebe has argued, people of the day, especially the ones with the greatest social power—politicians, industrialists, the educated elite, including Mary Austin herself initially—associated this transition from community to nation-state with the ideals of social progress and democratization, though in practice its consequences were far less innocent (111–32, 164–95). With the shift from the local production of culture to its importation from far away came a subtle but long-lasting change in the relations within the community itself. To be anxious about the state of one's soul was to acknowledge a moral accountability not only to God but also to one's family members, one's fellow townspeople, one's friends and, of course, one's enemies, with whom it was essential to get along somehow. But anxieties about the possession of "culture" imply a different sense of relations with others—relations that soon become more competitive, hierarchical, and socially isolating. On the one hand, the arrival of a new cosmopolitan knowledge made it possible to look critically at traditions formerly immune to change. Austin, for example, became a feminist by osmosis late in her high school years (126–28). On the other hand, the new economy of knowledge brought something else, something formerly almost as scarce as the knowledge hawked by the itinerant lecturers—and that was ignorance (Hobart). As Austin understood in retrospect, "The status of being cultivated was something like the traditional preciousness of women: nothing that you could cash in upon, but a shame to you to do without" (100). The cultured person was the one who could recite a verse or two from Longfellow, and without that ability, Austin's fellow men and women—people only a decade earlier as good as anybody else—suddenly found themselves obliged to bear the unfamiliar weight of shame.

A poem like Garland's "The Old Armchair" did not perform the same social function as a poem by Longfellow. For one thing, Longfellow's work represented an emergent and uniquely national culture, supported by the public schools and mass-market publications like *McGuffey's Eclectic Reader*. But the value of Longfellow as *knowledge* in the modern cultural economy derived from his relative transience. Longfellow was "in" but he would soon, predictably, be "out," just as Derrida and Foucault are today. A person might come to Longfellow's work so belatedly that an appreciation would simply underscore her "cultural" poverty. And if the new economy of knowledge created a division between those who had "knowledge" and those who did not, it brought about another expected split that Austin recognized with remarkable clarity:

> Into the widening gap . . . between the generations, our
> burgeoning system of public education was driving a wedge
> of books. It drove [that wedge] so fast that by the time [I]
> was twelve, one book, such as was usually kept in Mother's
> bureau and given to girls to read when they required it,

> was not enough to close the gap between young girls and
> young mothers; tradition was not enough; "Godey's Lady's
> Book" was too fragile; not even the weekly county paper . . .
> the "Carlinville Democrat" . . . answered wholly the need
> of a democratically constituted society for "keeping up."
> (101–2)

Carlinville citizens a generation earlier had been inhabitants of a different universe, one in which practices such as reading and prayer—practices of self-fashioning—helped to sustain an order that the people perceived as natural and timeless. For the young men and women of Austin's generation, newer practices of self-fashioning brought them into a world where nothing remained the same. And this ethos of change served to devalue local knowledge, not once but again and again, no matter what the local knowledge happened to be. "Keeping up" described a more or less one-way transaction between the eastern core and the western periphery, and while the pursuit of culture in Carlinville initially preserved the communal character of the older way of life, the center of gravity had shifted. When the townspeople gathered to discuss literary matters, they did so as the Chautauqua Literary and Scientific Circle, with a reading list compiled in New York toward the ends of "adult education" rather than in the spirit of a genuinely public discourse (102–3). Quietly but decisively, certain citizens had become "students" while others had somehow garnered for themselves the coveted "teacher" role.

Like many people of her generation, Mary Austin at first felt these events to be enormously liberating. Of her Methodist upbringing, for example, she writes in fairly negative terms. The worst thing about it, she remembers, "was that its stresses were not upon what the preacher thought, nor what God thought even" but upon "the judgment of the congregation" (119). With the coming of modernization, however, the power of the congregation loosened rapidly. In spite of prohibitions against the theater, Carlinvillians went to watch traveling performances of *Uncle Tom's Cabin* and the popular thriller *Union Spy.* Eventually the town would even construct an "Op'ry House" in the shell of an abandoned church (121). Yet while the coming of modernity allowed a certain spaciousness of experience, it closed off other things. Enrolled at the State Normal School in 1885, Austin suffered some kind of a nervous collapse, ostensibly caused by overwork. She would later decide, however, that what had broken her was not the strain of "learning" but the inflexibility of the "pedagogical method" (151). "At the normal school," she wrote, "she was simply redriven over the curricula of public school grades with immense and boring particularity." History was "reduced to a precise allocation of names and places, [and] middle initials of unimportant generals," while reading was "reduced to the rendering of the content of literature in the most explicit rather than the most expressive verbal terms" (152). On the one hand, modernization had loosened the hold of old assumptions, which had always been as honored as they were unexamined; on the other hand, it replaced the loose, pliant bonds of custom with the iron cage of regimentation.

But regimentation looked like freedom in the modern world, at least to the privileged minority, because it arrived in the form of change rather than of invariance. And change—or "progress," as people liked to call it—promised an eventual payoff for all the suffering and sacrifice it exacted on the way. By equating technological innovation with the march toward greater personal satisfaction, the ideology of progress encouraged people to tolerate suffering that would have made, as Herman Melville wrote, an infidel of Abraham; and today in our relative security we can forget that many millions of Americans experienced modernity, despite all the promise it held, as a perpetual, unmanageable crisis. But if technological innovation kept transforming everything, from the rituals of private hygiene to the skyline of the city, the forces of *cultural* change were no less distant, unresponsive, and mysterious. As the sociologist Robert Park observed in 1916, modern life was urban life, and in the city "more than elsewhere human relations are likely to be impersonal and rational," with the face-to-face associations of the town replaced by routines conducted almost exclusively "in terms of [private] interest and in terms of cash" (*Human Communities* 31):

> In a great city, where the population is unstable, where parents and children are employed out of the house and often in distant parts of the city, where thousands of people live side by side for years without so much as a bowing acquaintance, these intimate relationships of the primary group are weakened and the moral order which rested upon them is gradually dissolved.
>
> Under the disintegrating influences of city life, most of our traditional institutions, the church, the school, and the family, have been greatly modified. The school, for example,

> has taken over some of the functions of the family. . . .
> The church, on the other hand . . . has lost much of its
> influence. . . .
>
> It is probably the breaking down of local attachments
> and the weakening of the restraints and inhibitions of the
> primary group . . . which are largely responsible for the in-
> crease of vice and crime. (33–34)

As Park witnessed firsthand during his years as a city reporter, the life of the
rural community had given way to a spirit of "individualism," but unlike many
observers now, such as the sociologist Robert Bellah or the historian Christopher Lasch, Park did not explain this shift as the outcome of individual
irresponsibility. Instead, he saw it as the unchosen and unforeseen result of
large-scale economic changes. Strictly speaking, the emergence of the modern
"individual" meant a *loss* of autonomy and self-worth, since the life of the
unpropertied wage-worker, always only a paycheck ahead of destitution, was
precarious in a way that life fifty years before had seldom been. The "freedom"
of the modern urbanite was a *freedom to*—freedom to work, to sacrifice, to
compete, to fit in—but never a *freedom from*—a freedom from want, from
anxiety, from violence, or from coercion. Park understood that this loss of
personal autonomy—an autonomy that could be fostered only by the appropriate kind of community—had the gravest political ramifications. "Our political
system," he wrote, "is founded upon the conviction that people who live in
[the] same locality have common interests, and that they can therefore be relied
upon to act together for their common welfare." In the urban setting, however,
"that assumption" was "no longer valid." At a time when many Americans lived
in hotels or lodging houses "traditional forms of local government" were breaking down "altogether" (90). The modern city was by no means a polis, and its
inhabitants had ceased to be citizens, precisely because their "primary" institutions as Park called them—the family, the neighborhood, the human ties sustained by memory, friendship, and cooperative labor—had become too drastically attenuated to support any genuine civic culture. Once the imperative to
earn a living consumed all available energies, once every person rose or fell
exclusively by his isolated efforts, crisis was the order of the day every day, and
through this routinizing of crisis itself, modernity brought about what might be
called a "total mobilization" of the populace.

While Park explained the nature of modernity as well as any observer of his day, he never thought to call for a restoration of the older, republican spirit. Instead, Park believed that with the fading of rural traditions, the problems of urban culture called urgently for mechanisms of effective "social control," mechanisms grounded on the force of "positive law" and informed by expert advice. Once the primary institutions had failed, "secondary institutions were required to take their place." "There is," he wrote, "probably no other country in the world in which so many 'reforms' are in progress as at the present time in the United States." And the "reforms thus effected, almost without exception, involve some sort of restriction or governmental control over activities that were formerly 'free' or controlled only by . . . mores and public opinion" (37). Although the rural tradition of direct democracy, the open town meeting, "was well suited to the needs of a small community based on primary relations," the city had taken on a life of its own, whose workings Park saw it as his task to explore (41). In the course of his long career he became convinced that the modern city was not an accidental sprawl but a living organism subject to the dynamics of a "human ecology." Increasingly he felt that the city's life, no less than the life of a natural ecosystem, "involves a kind of metabolism. It is constantly assimilating new individuals, and just as steadily, by death or otherwise, eliminating older ones" (*On Social Control* 59, also 81). Individuals came and went, but the *system* continued functioning because its highest law was the law of competition (this was nature's law, as well), which protected the whole at the expense of the part and life at the expense of individual lives (*Human Communities* 151–55).

Like Durkheim and, before him, Thomas Hobbes, Park conceived of society as a universal subject, one that "moves" like a person "under the influence of a multitude of minor impulses and tendencies" (*On Social Control* 223). But Park was also persuaded that at this moment in his subject's "natural" evolution, the organism remained dangerously incomplete. Enormous and complex as the nation-state might be, it still needed a brain, a steering mechanism—what Herbert Spencer called a *sensorium*—and that need would be filled by social scientists like Park, a member of the emerging knowledge class (*Human Communities* 259). Unlike social scientists of an earlier day (a rabble-rouser like E. A. Ross, for example) Park did not envisage speaking directly to the laity. Rather, he claimed for himself a leadership role as a shaper of policy. Implicit in his understanding of the social sciences was the belief that the government, guided by the brightest and the best, was obliged to impose on the great mass of uprooted Americans the restraints they no longer had the strength of character to impose on themselves. While this arrangement was clearly undemocratic, the conviction that systematicity and science must replace the "mere" opinion of an ignorant citizenry had become so firmly entrenched among the elite that social scientists of Park's generation were obliged to climb aboard or else be left behind. If Park himself had moments of ambivalence, his successors had graver doubts. In *Urban Sociology,* Nels Anderson and Eduard C. Lindeman, both disciples of Park, could write disparagingly about the "dictatorship of the expert." "Experts and specialists," they argue, "threaten to preempt the seats of power occupied by kings and priests." Yet even while they warn their readers against "the authoritarianism of the professionals," they regard professionalism as the hallmark of "urbanism," inevitable as the rains in spring. Dictators or not, the professions had a *right* to rule so long as they remained "on the frontier of creative knowledge" (271).

Whatever may have changed in the last eighty years, Park's administered society is still the world that we inhabit today, with its familiar divisions between experience and objective fact, and between the "private" sphere and the "public" domain. But in the eighty years since Park did his major work, a growing number of people find themselves convinced that the administered society has failed. As John Dewey never tired of arguing with the theorists of Park's younger generation, a society segmented to exclude ordinary people from the choices most directly affecting them would not overcome the division between private interests and the public good but would kindle a worsening conflict. "Then," Dewey wrote, "society" would become an "unreal abstraction," to which no one could feel any compelling obligation (*Public* 191). Only by pursuing the ideal of complete *participation* could Americans avoid this disaster—a disaster, I would argue, that has already come to pass, not only through Park's efforts but through our own. The poststructuralist dismissal of the so-called liberal subject, far from restoring the old sense of community, has merely helped to strengthen the repressive power of our secondary institutions, which thrive on anomie. The brightest light on the academy's horizon—the much disparaged rise of "identity politics"—seeks to counter that anomie by reaffirming the importance of a distinctly *local* history, a distinctly *embodied* knowledge. But even the return to "identity" can be used to shift the balance of cultural power away once again from our already weakened primary institutions. The academy can effortlessly canonize Toni Morrison's *Sula* and commodify the "otherness" of black Americans, but intellectuals still act as the makers and judges of "culture," while the lay citizen is expected to play the consumers' compliant part. We continue to act as the *sensorium,* but can we even say what our own specialized knowledge is *for?* When we practice "oppositional pedagogy," what do we in fact oppose, and what are we subverting when we celebrate subversion, resistance, unruliness? Instead of spending endless hours deconstructing the common sense of lay social actors whom we probably know little about, we might try, from inside the university, to strengthen or replace the primary institutions crushed by a hundred years of modernization.

One way to understand Mary Austin's *Earth Horizon* is to read it as an early call for just such a renewal. We might read it, in other words, as an account of her growing dissatisfaction with the "freedoms" offered by the modern world, despite the enormous opportunities it made available to her personally. Unlike her mother, Mary Austin could leave home for college. And while Mary began her adult life with the least certain of uncertain prospects, she went on, having chosen the odd calling of "writer," to achieve an international reputation. Yet the better world that Austin searched for in the course of her career was not the global city of the cosmopolitan intellectual—at home everywhere because nowhere was home—but a place like the town of Carlinville, which she had left behind years before. In contrast to a technocratic optimist like Park, Austin somehow felt that those who entered the "clearing" opened up by modernity would drop endlessly, groundlessly, through a hell of their desires unless they could restore some enduring sense of relation to other people and to the natural world. Austin's own husband had been such a falling man, perpetually in motion from place to place, job to job, searching restlessly for wealth, recognition, and finally, for something he could never even name. For a man like Austin's husband, there could be no "world," only a series of places; there could be no relations, only a network of arrangements. And there could be, in spite of the apparently endless change, no actual change at all. Under the regime of modernity, what could change was just the *content* of commodified knowledge and the *objects* of the purchaser's desire; what remained absolutely unchanging was a sense of displacement from the condition that Austin described as living from the "center of her being" (274).

"Man," Austin wanted to believe, was not condemned to fall endlessly through space but might enjoy a "continuing experience of wholeness, a power to expand," again and again, beyond the confines of culture itself (283). Whether or not we today feel obliged to belittle her "visionary" language, we still have to acknowledge the response to anomie that Austin's visionary language expresses. Something happened to Americans in the period between

1860 and 1900, and not only to Americans but to people around the world. And whatever that something might have been, it produced a sense of world-lessness and groundlessness that has come to be the hallmark of modernity and that seems especially anomalous given the potential for emancipation. At the very moment when the triumph of modernity should have brought about an unprecedented release of human creativity, millions of readers across the world, from Djakarta to the Cameroon, saw their faded image in T. S. Eliot's "hollow men," men whose voices were "quiet and meaningless / As wind in dry grass (*Complete Poems* 56). Rejecting the Progressive legacy, Eliot had written that we "cannot, in literature any more than in the rest of life, live in a perpetual state of revolution" (*Selected Prose* 273). If he seemed to speak prophetically to so many different readers in so many different places, it may have been because he felt with such violent passion the oppressive character of change itself, which ceases to be liberating when people can no longer decide on its direction and its pace. And yet, to recognize an affliction is not necessarily to know the cure, and in his prescription for society Eliot the antimodernist gave voice to modernism in its purest form—as a dream of universality. The spirit of worldlessness haunting the first decades of the century he diagnosed as a symptom of "cultural disintegration" (293). By turning back to Christian tradition, which he represented as uniquely free from conflict and moral confusion, Eliot hoped to restore the sense of order that Austin and countless others felt themselves to have lost.

Modernity, according to Eliot, had torn apart the fabric of Christian culture by emphasizing individual needs and wants over the coherence of society. An "individual European may not believe," he argued, "that the Christian Faith is true, and yet what he says, and makes, and does, will all spring of his heritage of Christian culture and depend upon that culture for its meaning" (304). As a way of life, individualism seemed to Eliot self-contradictory, insofar as complete freedom of choice meant that choice itself becomes impossible. The proper relation between the self and tradition should be "surrender"; in the case of the artist especially, "progress" demands "a continual self-sacrifice, a continual extinction of personality" (40). But Eliot did not consider that it may be precisely this extinction of the self that modernity *demands*. While modernity may offer to individuals an ostensibly limitless freedom of choice, it actually allows such a latitude, as Austin had discovered at the normal school, only within the context of a larger, structural regimentation—in which case, Eliot's "cure" simply worsens the disease. The feeling of worldlessness, the sense of inhabiting the "arid plain," might also be seen as a response to the experience of radical powerlessness. At the same time that modernity gave people like Austin the chance, unheard of in the ages past, to write books and travel the world and spend summers outside of London and winters in Carmel, the new form of social life made it impossible for average citizens to exert any consequential measure of control over fundamental aspects of daily life.

Like other disillusioned intellectuals of the time, Austin found herself powerfully drawn to traditional societies, not because she considered them, as D. H. Lawrence did, more primitive and therefore more "vital" in some way, but because they promised her life on a scale that made it possible to recover both a sense of genuine community and a sense of personal freedom. Her interest had begun as an exercise in a highly visible political activism, but it rapidly assumed a deeper, more personal character. "At the same time," she wrote, "that my contemporaries were joining labor organizations and aligning themselves with wage-strikes, I took to the defense of Indians because they were the most conspicuously defeated and offended against group at hand" (266). Throughout the last decades of her life, Austin fought the assimilationist policies of the Bureau of Indian Affairs, and in New Mexico she helped to revive the native arts of pottery, weaving, and vernacular architecture. But while Austin may have helped the Indians to salvage certain aspects of their past, they gave her a new way of living in the present. Among the traditional societies of the American southwest—societies widely diverse in language and custom but living successfully side by side—she found alternatives to modernity so compelling that the day arrived when she "could no longer call herself a Christian": "In the [Zia] song of Earth Horizon man wanders in search of the Sacred Middle from which all horizons are equidistant, and his soul happily at rest. Once the Middle is attained . . . the true zone of reality . . . his spirit, no longer deflected by the influences of false horizons, swings freely to its proper arc" (275).

Like everyone, Austin brought agendas and presuppositions that colored everything she saw and said, but from the Hopi, Zia, and Navajo she learned to value what Clifford Geertz would later describe as "local knowledge." Only a recovery of this knowledge, she was convinced, could enable people like herself—not especially brave, not especially clever—to escape the reach of institutions that routinely force their "clients" into utter dependency. Beneath the Earth Horizon, every place occupied the Sacred Middle of the world, and from that place everyone, regardless of ability or attainment, could participate in creating the community's life, not only its political and social life but its artistic and religious life as well.

It was this insight more than any other—that culture is not something people "have" or "pass on" but something they must make and remake for themselves—which distinguishes Austin from other reformers of her time who did not want ordinary people to become the makers of their own realities. As she writes in the closing paragraph of *Earth Horizon*—and here the contrast to Eliot is especially pronounced—"I have seen that the American achievement is made up of two splendors: the splendor of individual relationships of power, the power to make and do rather than possess . . . and that other splendor of realizing that in the deepest layers of ourselves we are incurably collective. At the core of our Amerindian life we are consummated in the dash and color of collectivity" (368). We encounter the collective, or so Austin was convinced, within the "deepest layers of ourselves," where we find the words and the memories, the presences, of those who have preceded us. And we achieve, by acting in our common world, the fullest unfolding of our individual selves, which all of history and culture have labored to create. To have lost our faith in this consonance between self and world, self and others, the past and present, is for her the greatest failure of modernity, contriving as it does to impose a single "rational" order on things that possess an order of their own. As Austin had learned by the end of her long life, this other, immanent order never precedes our own involvements with the world but discloses itself in and through them. Ironically, it is "progress" that leaves us with nothing new to do and with no place unexpected to go.

For Americans of our time, Austin is scarcely a footnote. The ideology of progress continues to make every place a waiting room and every moment a trip from one nowhere to the next. And the sense of loss we feel when we encounter our exile as an inescapable fate drives the engine of commodification. Objects, images, ideas, and human beings, all of these become commodities when they no longer remind us of our connection to the world and to our fellow human beings—not the world and humanity in some general sense but this place where I live and the people to whom I am bound by concern, love, mutual dependence, and the power of memory. For us now, the problem has at least become somewhat more clear: we need to ask what forms of learning might begin to restore this awareness of connection. In answering that question, however, we may have to change more than our thinking about knowledge. If our knowledge bears the form of our lives in the world, then our way of living also has to change. But what form might that other way of life take on?

A person like ourselves—let's call him "the professor"—who wanted to retrace Austin's journey today might find himself one June morning in the mountain town of Chimayo, half an hour north of Santa Fe. Driving into the town, the professor would see tin roofs among the trees, and red hills, and then suddenly, at the end of a long, uphill curve, the car might come to a stop on the gravel of an unpaved plaza. And from the plaza the professor might impulsively set out on a sidewalk through the trees to the spare adobe mass of a church, the Santuario. Into the church and out again, a procession would keep moving throughout the day, calmly, quietly—women and men, the middle-aged and the elderly, people on crutches, people fingering rosaries. Inside, the air would carry the smell of burning wax and the heat from a hundred candles; outside, in the cool of the cottonwoods, children would be yelling and chasing each other. One by one the worshipers would file into the sanctuary itself, a small room sheltering a crude hole in ground, a foot wide, perhaps, and just about as deep. This would be the great *mysterium,* from which the believers could take away with them a modest handful of sanctified earth. Outside, in the town, there would be television programs and video games, real estate speculation and a three-star restaurant for wealthy Anglo visitors. But there would still be the Santuario.

Just before World War I, this place, the Santuario, was falling into neglect, until an American writer bought it and began to restore the building. The writer was Mary Austin. It was not Austin's shrine, and it was not her religion, but it was her job to save it, because nobody else could have done so at the time. Today we might describe her an "intellectual," but if we should choose to call Austin by that name we must return to the oldest sense of the word: the intellectual as one who "gathers together" things rejected, scattered, or cast aside. To be an intellectual in this sense is to refuse the fragmentation of modernity—which is *not* the only way to freedom—and to preserve everything that makes it possible to feel ourselves at home in world. This was Austin's job and it is now our job as well.

Works Cited

Anderson, Nels, and Eduard C. Lindeman, *Urban Sociology: An Introduction to the Study of Urban Communities.* New York: Knopf, 1928.

Austin, Mary. *Earth Horizon: An Autobiography*. New York: Literary Guild, 1932.

Axtell, James. *The European and the Indian: Essays in the Ethnohistory of Colonial North America*. Oxford: Oxford University Press, 1981.

Barthes, Roland. "Rhetoric of the Image." *The Responsibility of Forms: Critical Essays on Music, Art, and Representation*. Trans. Richard Howard. Berkeley: University of California Press, 1991: 21–40.

Bawden, C. R., ed. *Shamans, Lamas and Evangelicals: The English Missionaries in Siberia*. London: Routledge, 1985.

Bereiter, Carl, Siegfried Engelmann, Jean Osborn, and P. A. Reidford. "An Academically Oriented Pre-school for Culturally Deprived Children." *Pre-school Education Today*. Ed. Fred M. Hechinger. New York: Doubleday, 1966: 105–35.

Boethius. *The Consolation of Philosophy*. Trans. Richard Green. Indianapolis: Bobbs-Merrill, 1962.

Canby, Henry Seidel, Frederick Erastus Pierce, Henry Noble MacCracken, Alfred Arundel May, and Thomas Goddard Weight. *English Composition in Theory and Practice*. New York: Macmillan, 1909.

Derrida, Jacques. *Dissemination*. Trans. Barbara Johnson. Chicago: University of Chicago Press, 1981.

Dewey, John. *The Public and Its Problems*. 1927. Denver: Allan Swallow, 1954.

Durkheim, Emile. *The Elementary Forms of the Religious Life: A Study in Religious Sociology*. Trans. Joseph Ward Swain. Glencoe, Ill.: Free Press, 1946.

Ehrenreich, Barbara, and John Ehrenreich. "The Professional-Managerial Class." *Radical America* 11 (March/April 1977): 7–31.

Eliot, T. S. *Complete Poems and Plays, 1909–1950*. New York: Harcourt, Brace, 1952.

——. *Selected Prose of T. S. Eliot*. Ed. Frank Kermode. New York: Harcourt, 1975.

Garland, Hamlin. *A Son of the Middle Border*. 1917. N.p.: Grosset and Dunlap, 1927.

Geertz, Clifford. *The Interpretation of Cultures*. New York: Basic, 1973.

——. *Local Knowledge: Further Essays in Interpretive Anthropology*. New York: Basic, 1983.

Giddens, Anthony. *Central Problems in Social Theory: Action, Structure and Contradiction in Social Analysis*. Berkeley: University of California Press, 1979.

Heath, Shirley Brice. *Ways with Words: Language, Life, and Work in Communities and Classrooms*. Cambridge: Cambridge University Press, 1983.

Hobart, Mark. "Introduction: The Growth of Ignorance?" *An Anthropological Critique of Development: The Growth of Ignorance*. New York: Routledge, 1993. 1–30.

Hobsbawm, E. J. *The Age of Revolution, 1789–1848*. New York: Mentor, 1962.

Hobson, Geary, ed. *The Remembered Earth: An Anthology of Contemporary Native American Literature*. Albuquerque: University of New Mexico Press, 1981.

Husserl, Edmund. *The Crisis of European Sciences and Transcendental Philosophy*. Trans. David Carr. Evanston, Ill.: Northwestern University Press, 1970.

Jensen, Katherine. "Civilization and Assimilation in the Colonized Schooling of Native Americans." *Education and the Colonial Experience*. Ed. Philip G. Altbach and Gail P. Kelly. 2d ed. New Brunswick, N.J.: Transaction, 1984: 155–79.

Kehoe, Alice Beck. *The Ghost Dance: Ethnohistory and Revitalization*. Fort Worth, Tex.: Holt, 1989.

Kurosawa, Akira, dir. *Ran*. Greenwich Film Production SA/Herald Ace Inc./Nippon Films Ltd., 1985.

Labov, William. *Language in the Inner City.* Philadelphia: University of Pennsylvania Press, 1972.

Laing, R. D. *The Politics of Experience.* New York: Pantheon, 1967.

Lanham, Richard. *The Electronic Word: Democracy, Technology, and the Arts.* Chicago: University of Chicago Press, 1993.

Lévi-Strauss, Claude. *The Savage Mind.* Chicago: University of Chicago Press, 1966.

Martin, Bernice. "Symbolic Knowledge and Market Forces at the Frontiers of the Postmodern: Qualitative Market Researchers." *Hidden Technocrats: The New Class and New Capitalism.* Ed. Hansfried Kellner and Frank W. Heuberger. New Brunswick, N.J.: Transaction, 1992: 111–56.

Merleau-Ponty, Maurice. *Signs.* Trans. Richard C. McCleary. Evanston, Ill.: Northwestern University Press, 1964.

Meyrowitz, Joshua. *No Sense of Place: The Impact of Electronic Media on Social Behavior.* New York: Oxford University Press, 1985.

Mooney, James. *The Ghost-Dance Religion and the Sioux Outbreak of 1890.* 1896. Chicago: University of Chicago Press, 1965.

Ngugi wa Thiong'o. *Decolonizing the Mind: The Politics of Language in African Literature.* Portsmouth, N.H.: Heinemann, 1986.

Nietzsche, Friedrich. *Twilight of the Idols.* In *The Portable Nietzsche.* Trans. and ed. Walter Kaufmann. New York: Penguin, 1959: 463–563.

Obeyesekere, Gananath. "The Fire-Walkers of Kataragama: The Rise of *Bhakti* Religiosity in Buddhist Sri Lanka." *Journal of Asian Studies* 37 (1978): 457–76.

Oliver, Roland. *The Missionary Factor in East Africa.* 2d ed. London: Longmans, 1967.

Park, Robert E. *Human Communities: The City and Human Ecology.* New York: Free Press, 1952.

——. *On Social Control and Collective Behavior.* Ed. Ralph H. Turner. Chicago: University of Chicago Press, 1967.

Plato. *Phaedrus.* Trans. R. Hackforth. *The Collected Dialogues of Plato.* Ed. Edith Hamilton and Huntington Cairns. Princeton: Princeton University Press, 1961: 475–525.

Radcliffe-Brown, A. R. *Structure and Function in Primitive Society.* London: Cohen and West, 1952.

Rose, Mike. *Lives on the Boundary: The Struggles and Achievements of America's Underprepared.* New York: Free Press, 1989.

Rowe, John Carlos. "The Writing Class." *Politics, Theory, and Contemporary Culture.* Ed. Mark Poster. New York: Columbia University Press, 1993: 41–82.

Saussure, Ferdinand de. *Course in General Linguistics.* Trans. Wade Baskin. New York: McGraw-Hill, 1966.

Schlesinger, Arthur, Jr. "The Cult of Ethnicity, Good and Bad." *Time* (8 July 1991): 21.

Schutz, Alfred, and Thomas Luckmann. *The Structures of the Life-World.* Trans. Richard M. Zaner and H. Tristram Englehardt, Jr. Evanston, Ill.: Northwestern University Press, 1973.

Shakespeare, William. *The Tragedy of King Lear.* Ed. Russell Fraser. New York: Signet, 1963.

Shaughnessy, Mina P. *Errors and Expectations: A Guide for the Teacher of Basic Writing.* New York: Oxford University Press, 1977.

Smart, William, ed. *Eight Modern Essayists.* New York: St. Martin's Press, 1990.

Spence, Jonathan D. *The Memory Palace of Matteo Ricci.* New York: Viking, 1984.

Tambiah, Stanley. *Sri Lanka: Ethnic Fratricide and the Dismantling of Democracy.* Chicago: University of Chicago Press, 1986.

Tichi, Cecelia. *Electronic Hearth: Creating an American Television Culture.* New York: Oxford University Press, 1991.

Wiebe, Robert H. *The Search for Order: 1877–1920.* New York: Hill and Wang, 1967.

11
History and the Real
Charles Shepherdson

The Oedipus myth is an attempt to give epic form to the operation of a structure.
—Jacques Lacan, "Television"

By the madness which interrupts it, a work of art opens a void, a moment of silence, a question without answer, provokes a breach without reconciliation where the world is forced to question itself.
—Michel Foucault, *Madness and Civilization*

The historicity proper to philosophy is located and constituted in the transition, the dialogue between hyperbole and finite structure, between that which exceeds the totality and the closed totality, in the difference between history and historicity.
—Jacques Derrida, "Cogito and the History of Madness"

Satire

In spite of the difference between English and continental philosophy, there is a link between Michel Foucault and writers like Jonathan Swift, as there was between Nietzsche and Paul Rée: "The first impulse to publish something of my hypotheses concerning the *origin* of morality," Nietzsche says, "was given to me by a clear, tidy, and shrewd—also precocious—little book in which I encountered for the first time an *upside-down and perverse* species of genealogical hypothesis, the genuinely English type . . . *The Origin of the Moral Sensations;* its author Dr. Paul Rée" (Nietzsche, *Genealogy* 17–18, emphasis added). Taking this upside-down and perverse English type as a starting point, let us begin with the strange tale by Jonathan Swift.

At the end of *Gulliver's Travels,* after returning from his exotic and rather unexpected voyage to the land of the Lilliputians, where the horses are so wise and discourse so eloquently, while humans sit up in the trees throwing food at each other and defecating on themselves, our poor traveler goes back to his homeland, where he is so dislocated that he cannot even embrace his wife or laugh with his friends at the local pub. In this state of distress, he goes out to the stable and sits down with the horses, thinking that maybe he will calm down a bit, if only he can learn to whinny and bray.

How is it that Swift's account of the Houyhnhnms and Yahoos is not simply an amusing story about some ridiculous foreign land? How is it that this "topsy-turvy world," this inverted world (*die verkehrte Welt*), where horses display the highest virtue and humans are regarded with disgust because they are so filthy and inarticulate—how is it that this is not merely an entertaining fiction, but also a revelation of the fact that our own world, the world of reality, is itself inverted, already an absurd fiction, a place where human beings are already disgusting, irrational, filthy, inarticulate, and comical creatures, worthy only of satirical derision? How is it that the inverted image turns out to reflect back on the real one, so that what begins as the reversal of our normal world—an absurd, excessive, and foreign place, a world of science fiction, where madmen wander freely in the streets and objects in nature are inscribed with strange insignias, written on their surfaces by God—turns out to be both foreign and yet also a picture, both exotic and yet also a mirroring of our own world?

This is a question of fiction and truth, but also of history, a question concerning genealogy. How is it that genealogy, which wanders around in what is most distant and unfamiliar—not the old world where we recognize ourselves, finding continuity with our ancestors, but a strange and unfamiliar land—turns out to be at the same time an account of our own world, a history of the exotic that is also our own history?

Before we turn to the historical aspect of the question, let us stay a moment with the problem of fiction. For the exotic tale told by Swift captures the problem art posed for Plato: the problem is not that art produces an illusion, that it is merely a copy of what already exists in reality, or even a deranged, imaginary substitute; the problem is rather that art rebounds on the world, that it discloses a dimension of truth beyond immediate reality, a truth that competes with what Plato regarded as the proper object of philosophy. As Lacan says, "The picture does not compete with the appearance, it competes with what Plato designates as beyond appearance, as the Idea" (*Four* 112). In the artistic competition, it is not the still life of Zeuxis that wins the prize, a work so accomplished that even the birds come down to peck at the imaginary grapes; it is rather the veil of Parrhasios, the illusion painted so perfectly that Zeuxis, on seeing it, asks Parrhasios to remove this veil so that he may see the painting of his competitor. This is the difference between the level of the imaginary and the level of desire. The function of art is to incite the viewer to ask what is *beyond*. Art is the essence of truth: it leads us not "to see," as Lacan would put it, but "to look." For the human animal is blind in this respect: it cannot simply see, but is compelled to look behind the veil, *driven,* Freud would say, beyond the pleasure of seeing. This is where we find the split between the eye and the gaze that Lacan takes from Merleau-Ponty. This is where the symbolic aspect of art emerges, as distinct from its imaginary dimension. And it is here that the question of true and false images must be replaced with a question about language.

If we return now to satire, it is clear that at one level, the satirical, inverted picture of the world in which everything is rendered excessively may well provoke our laughter and entertain us, but the true function of satire, as a form of art that is also a political act, must be situated at another level, where the inverted image rebounds on the so-called normal world and shows that this world is itself already inverted. At the first level, we have an illusion, the false reality of art that distracts us from the truth, like a distorted mirror image that captivates us while alienating us from reality; at the second level, we have an image that, precisely because of its unreal character, shows us that there is no reality, that reality itself is already an inverted image in which we are not at home. This is where the image goes beyond a picture, true or false, mimetically accurate or surrealistically bizarre; this is where art has to be understood, not in terms of the imaginary and reality, but in its symbolic function, its function as representation. The implication is that as long as we remain content with a discussion of the image and reality, we will repress the question of language.

The Place of Enunciation

Let us now pass from satire to consider the historical issue, the problem of how these stories that Foucault constructs for us—the strange laboratory of Doctor Caligari or the fantastic clinic of Boissier de Sauvages—however distant and unfamiliar, operate neither as "mere" fiction nor simply as truth, neither as an entertaining disclosure of strange practices long ago forgotten nor as a compilation of facts about the past, but rather by rebounding on us, to show us who we are for the first time, as if in spite of everything these bizarre images were portraits of ourselves. In an interview from 1984, François Ewald asks, "Why turn your attention to those periods, which, some will say, are so very far from our own?" Foucault replies, "I set out from a problem expressed in current terms today, and I try to work out *its* genealogy. Genealogy means that I begin my analysis from a question posed in the present" (Foucault, *Politics* 262, emphasis added).

With this remark, Foucault stresses the fact that the position of enunciation, the point from which he speaks, is always explicitly thematized in his works, which gives them a dimension that can only be obscured if one views his writing as a neutral, descriptive documentation of the past, or as an attempt to construct a grand theoretical edifice. This is the point at which Foucault's work touches on something that does not belong to history, or even to philosophy, something we might speak of as fiction; it is also the point at which we may understand his work as a kind of action, what Foucault calls a "making" of differences. "If philosophy is memory, or a return of the origin," he writes, "what I am doing cannot, in any way, be regarded as philosophy; and if the history of thought consists in giving life to half-effaced figures, what I am doing is not history either" (*Archaeology* 206).

Two separate questions are raised here. First, how are we to construe the relation between the present and the past? For if history traditionally represents itself as a neutral recounting of the past, at the level of knowledge, Foucault by contrast, however much he may insist on the documentary and empirical nature of his work, nevertheless also emphasizes that it is not written from the standpoint of eternity, as a knowledge or representation that would have no place of birth, but rather has an origin of its own, in the present. Given the virtually canonical stress on the "historicist" aspect of Foucault's work, according to which he documents the contingent moment in which things acquire a historically specific form, one might take pause at Foucault's remarks in *The Archaeology of Knowledge*: "My discourse," he writes, "does not aim to dissipate oblivion, to rediscover in the depth of things the moment of their birth (whether this is seen as their empirical creation, or the transcendental act that gives them origin); it does not set out to be a recollection of the original or a memory of truth. On the contrary, its task is to *make* differences" (205, original emphasis). What is the function of memory in genealogy, if it is not simply the recollection of the past, the reanimation of history, in the name of information or knowledge? With this question, we come close to the psychoanalytic problem of memory: what does it mean to say that in dredging up the past, repeating it, going back across the river to where the ancestors lie buried, one is concerned not so much with what really happened—with what Leopold von Ranke called "the past as it really was in itself"—but rather with intervening, rewriting the past, producing a shift in the symbolic structure of the narrative that has brought us to the point where we are now? As is often said, Freud's discovery concerning the symbolic nature of the symptom meant that he had to shift his focus—to abandon his initial and "realist" interest in getting the patient to remember exactly what had happened and to recognize instead that fantasy was every bit as real as reality. This is why it is correct to say the psychoanalysis begins in the displacement of the theory of trauma. With this displacement, Freud abandons the idea that the primal scene is a real event that took place *in historical time,* and he recognizes instead that the trauma has *the structure of myth,* and that human history as such differs from natural, chronological time, precisely to the extent that it is subject to myth.

This first question about genealogical memory and the relation between the present and the past is consequently linked to a second question about truth and fiction. How are we to understand the peculiar duality in Foucault's work— on the one hand, the patient, archival research, the empiricist dedication, and on the other hand his continual assertions that he has never written anything but fiction? Can we genuinely accept both of these features without eliminating one? To be sure, Foucault believes that the standard histories are the product of institutions that write grand narratives culminating in the discoveries of the present, tales of the gradual emergence of truth and reason. These histories, according to Foucault, are false and can be replaced with a more accurate account by the genealogist, who is not seduced by the mythology of a prevailing narrative. But what are we then to make of his claim that he has never written anything but fiction? Is it simply a stylish, French gesture that forms part of the public image of Foucault, a rhetorical aside that has no serious philosophical weight? To say this would be to refuse the statement, not to take it seriously. Or does the remark mean that he knows he might not have all his facts straight, and that one day someone may find it necessary to improve his account—in short, that his account is true but contingent? To say this would be to remain within the arena of knowledge, of clear and distinct representation, such that Foucault's account would be true but partial, true but subject to correction. This would be a "relativist" Foucault who covertly maintains the very commitment to truth that he appears to denounce: admitting that all knowledge is contingently constructed and that his is "only one perspective," he paradoxically insists on a rigorous adherence to documentary evidence that allows him to tell the truth better than the grand narratives of the received history.[1] What is this vacillation that makes genealogy neither an operation of knowledge, a true (or at least "more true") account of the past, nor simply a fable, a false image, an entertaining but bizarre representation of a time that is foreign to us? If we ask about the nature of historical knowledge, the fiction that genealogy is, how can we distinguish it from this dichotomy between the imaginary and the true? Once again, it is a question of language, a question that cannot be resolved at the imaginary level, by appeal to the dialectical interplay of image and reality.

Foucault touches here on the very structure we find in Swift, whereby the function of satire is not simply to create a strange and unfamiliar world, but rather to return, to rebound on us, so that the real world is shown to be itself a parody. Slavoj Žižek explains the shift from the imaginary to the symbolic in the following way, arguing that we will only misconstrue the relation between the image and reality if we attempt to resolve it dialectically, by showing that the image and reality are interwoven, that the image is a fiction that nevertheless rebounds on the true world with formative effects (as Hegel argues in the *Aesthetics*). For there is a point at which the relation between the distorted image and the real thing becomes unstable, in a manner that falls short of all dialectical mediation, a point at which, moreover, it loses the *generative* force that is required by the concept of productive negation, and culminates in an impasse instead. The fact that the inverted image turns out not to be an inversion, but to reveal that the normal world is itself already inverted, calls into question the very standard of "normality" by which one might measure invertedness (Žižek, *For They Know Not* 13).

Consider the example of Adorno's remarks on the totalitarian authority. How does the liberal individual, the free, authentic moral subject, stand in relation to the oppressive totalitarian dictator, the figure parodied by Charlie Chaplin? Following Martin Jay, Žižek points out that Adorno constructed the typical authoritarian personality by *reversing* all the features of the bourgeois individual: as Žižek puts it, "instead of tolerating difference and accepting non-violent dialogue as the only means to arrive at a common decision, the [totalitarian] subject advocates violent intolerance and distrust in free dialogue; instead of critically examining every authority, the subject uncritically obeys those in power" (*For They Know Not* 14). From one standpoint—what one might call the standpoint of "realism," the imaginary level where reality is brought face to face with its distorted image—these two are in complete opposition, mutually opposed ideals charged with all the pathos and investment of realist urgency; but from the standpoint of satire, from the standpoint of fiction, which asks about representation itself, the authoritarian personality reflects its image back onto the bourgeois democratic subject, and is revealed as already contained there, as the truth of the liberal individual, its constitutive other, its repressed foundation—or, to put it differently, its *common origin.*

This common origin is at play in *Madness and Civilization,* when Foucault speaks of the peculiar moment when madness and reason first come to be separated from one another and are shown to have a common birth. This raises a question about history, for Foucault seems to suggest that the common origin of madness and reason is always concealed by historical narrative. The usual history of madness is a discourse of reason *on* madness, a discourse in which reason has already established itself as the measure, the arena within which madness will appear; it is therefore a history in which madness is relegated to silence. As a result, the standard history, according to Foucault, is one in which a separation between madness and reason has already occurred, thereby concealing their common origin. Derrida stresses this point when he cites Foucault's own remark that "the necessity of madness is linked to the *possibility* of history." History itself would seem to arise only insofar as a separation can be made between madness and reason. To go back to their common origin would thus be not simply to write a history, but also to raise a question concerning the very possibility of history.[2] As Foucault remarks in an interview with François Ewald: "The history of thought means not just the history of ideas or representations, but also an attempt to answer this question . . . How can thought . . . have a history?" (Foucault, *Politics* 256). And if "the history of ideas" already presupposes a separation between madness and reason, to touch on their common origin, and thus on the very possibility of history, would be, as Derrida puts it, "the maddest aspect of Foucault's work" (Derrida, "Cogito" 34).

Thus, the peculiar identity which links the liberal individual with the obscene and tyrannical force of facism must be disavowed, and the best form of disavowal is narrative: what is in fact an original unity, a structural relation linking the Reign of Terror with the rise of free democracy and the Rights of Man, is best concealed by a genetic narrative, in which the original condition is said to be one of pure freedom, liberty, fraternity, and equality, an ideal that is eventually corrupted by a degenerate or perverted form. In this case—what we might call the case of realism, the imaginary level where the true reality is set over against its distorted image—we would be tempted to denounce the authoritarian personality as an extreme distortion of the natural order of things, by measuring it against the liberal, democratic individual; we would seek a return to the origin, before it was corrupted by the tyrannical violence of a degenerate form. In the second case, however, when we see with the eye of the satirist who recognizes that the natural order of things is already a parody, that the inverted world of Doctor Caligari is in fact an image of ourselves, we have to recognize that the supposedly natural state of things, the normal, liberal individual who has "natural rights" and a native capacity for moral reflection, is itself already inverted, that it contains the totalitarian authority in its origins, not as its opposite, not as its contradiction, not as its degenerate or perverted form, but as its repressed foundation, its internal "other." In Lacanian terms, the first relation of aggressive, mirroring opposition (in which the communist and the democrat face off) is imaginary, whereas the second relation (the comic twist of Charlie Chaplin's performance) is symbolic—which means that it can be grasped only at the level of language, and not by a return to some mythical origin, by the restoration of an essential but repressed innate desire, or by a return to natural rights.

The point here is not to dwell on the supposedly shocking revelation concerning the symptomatic link—what one might call the equiprimordiality—of totalitarianism and democracy, but rather to show that the ideal of the liberal individual (whose natural freedom is accompanied by a capacity for tolerance, and whose healthy conscience is the sign of an innate moral disposition, and so on) is a construction whose supposedly natural status is a fiction. This amounts to dismantling the idea that totalitarian governments are a *secondary* formation, the corruption of an origin, or the *perversion* of what would otherwise be a natural system of equally distributed justice. That story of the origin and its subsequent perversion is a myth, in the sense in which Lacan uses the word when he writes that the Oedipus myth is the attempt to give epic form to what is in fact the operation of a structure.

The proof that the structural relation or "common origin" is repressed by historical narratives which present the two logical elements in terms of a chronological sequence resides in the fact that there is always a point of paradox in the narrative, a "nodal point" where the story is forced to fold back on itself in a peculiar contradiction that is also a temporal tangle: in the case of Hobbes, for example, the original condition—the violent and chaotic state of nature—is said to be overcome by the social contract, the advent of law and civilization, and yet the origin of the law itself remains shrouded in mystery, for as soon as I agree to sign the social contract and leave the state of nature, I am *already* operating as the rational agent whose existence is supposed to be *generated* by the social contract and not originally present, since originally nature is said to have been merely violent and aggressive, and dependent on the arrival of the law for its rational organization. The symbolic order thus forces on us a confrontation with the structural relation between two opposed positions, which a historical account presents as a sequence, in which their common origin is repressed. Must we not therefore add that when readers of Lacan regard the symbolic order as somehow transcending or overcoming the imaginary relation—when the notorious "law of the father" is said to replace or supersede the "relation to the mother"—Lacan's theory has already been translated into a chronological narrative that obscures its most crucial features. Such a "translation" of psychoanalysis should come as no surprise, when one recalls that the Oedipal story itself already installs such narratives at the very heart of the subject. This is what Lacan meant when he wrote that "the Oedipus myth is an attempt to give epic form to the operation of a structure."

The "Historical Sense"

In his essay on Nietzsche, Foucault distinguishes the work of the historian from the first genealogical insights that go under the name of "the historical sense." "The historical sense," he writes, "gives rise to three . . . modalities of history," all of them deployed against the pious restoration of historical monuments. "The first is parodic, directed against reality, and opposes the theme of history as reminiscence or recognition" ("Nietzsche" 93). Together with the other modes, it implies "a transformation of history into a totally different form of time" (93). The *historian*'s gaze is thereby distinguished from that of the satirical *genealogist:* "The *historian* offers this confused and anonymous European, who no longer knows himself or what name he should adopt, the possibility of alternate identities, more individualized and substantial than his own. But the man with historical sense will see that this substitution is simply a disguise. Historians supplied the Revolution with Roman prototypes, romanticism with knight's armor, and the Wagnerian era was given the sword of the German hero" (93). "The genealogist," Foucault continues, "will know what to make of this masquerade. He will not be too serious to enjoy it; on the contrary, he will push the masquerade to its limit and prepare the great carnival of time where masks are constantly reappearing. . . . In this, we recognize the parodic double of what the second of the *Untimely Meditations* called 'monumental history' " (94). Given this remarkable twist in which "monumental history" itself appears as a certain kind of "masquerade," we understand why "Nietzsche accused this history, one totally devoted to veneration, of *barring access* to the actual intensities and creations of life. The parody of his last texts serves to emphasize that *'monumental history' is itself a parody*" (94, emphasis added).

Fiction

Parody is only one of the lessons Foucault takes from Nietzsche. If we ask more generally about the relation of genealogy to fiction, we may recognize the peculiar "distance" that genealogy inhabits—neither the transcendental distance that allows a perfect view of the past, nor the distance of escape, the distance of an imaginary world that takes us away from reality, but the distance of words. In a remarkable essay on Alain Robbe-Grillet, Foucault writes: "What if the fictive were neither the beyond, nor the intimate secret of the everyday, but the arrowshot which strikes us in the eye and offers up to us everything which appears? In this case, the fictive would be that which names things, that which makes them speak, and that which gives them in language their being already apportioned by the sovereign power of words. . . . This is not to say that fiction is language: this trick would be too easy, though a very familiar one nowadays. It does mean, though, that . . . the simple experience of picking up a pen and writing creates . . . a distance. . . . If anyone were to ask me to define the fictive, I should say . . . that it was the verbal nerve structure of what does not exist" (Bellour 149). Later in the same essay, Foucault returns to the word *distance,* understood as a mode of experience: "I should like to do some paring away, in order to allow this experience to be what it is. . . . I should like to pare away all the contradictory words, which might cause it to be seen too easily in terms of a dialectic: subjective and objective, interior and exterior, reality and imagination. . . . This whole lexicon . . . would have to be replaced with the vocabulary of distance. . . . Fiction is not there because language is distant from things; but language is their distance, the light in which they are to be found and their inaccessibility" (Bellour 149).

Thus, when we ask (in regard to Jonathan Swift and his satirical text) why the inverted image is not just an entertaining fiction, a journey to the underground world of the Marquis de Sade or to the exotic dungeons of Bicêtre, but rather an image that reflects back on the normal world, the "arrowshot" that returns to "strike us in the eye," we cannot understand this in terms of the opposition between "fiction and truth." This answer, even if it proceeds beyond opposition to a sort of dialectical interplay, in which the imaginary and "reality" interact, is insufficient, because it does not adequately confront the role of *language*. If we wish to understand language, then, we cannot rest content with a dialectical solution, according to Foucault: "Reality and imagination. . . . this whole lexicon . . . would have to be replaced." When we speak of fiction then, we are no longer in the realm of truth and falsity; we have passed from the image to the word, from the opposition between reality and imagination, to the symbolic.

Image and Word

This discrepancy between the image and the word is the source of Foucault's constant preoccupation with the difference between seeing and saying, perception and verbalization, the level of visibility and the function of the name. If, as we have seen, the relation between the image and reality is not a matter of productive negation, in which the encounter with an alien image cancels out our own self-knowledge and requires us to be transformed; if the dialectical account of the image and reality somehow obscures the role of language, perhaps this is because there is a difference between the image and the word, a gap or void that, according to Foucault, is not sufficiently confronted by phenomenology. Perhaps "distance" names the lack that separates the symbol from the domain of perception, evidence, and light. "Fiction is not there because language is distant from things; but language is their distance, *the light* in which they are to be found *and their inaccessibility*" (149). Perhaps "distance," in naming the lack of any dialectical relation between speech and vision, also amounts to a refusal of all attempts to generate a stable historical unfolding, the gradual emergence of an origin, or the teleological production of something that had to be gradually constructed through the handing-down of a common tradition. Perhaps "distance" is the name for why Foucault refuses to participate in the Husserlian response to the crisis of the human sciences (see *Archaeology* 204).

In that case, language would not only destabilize the usual dialectic between fiction and truth; it would also call for a reconfiguration of the concept of history, one in which things would retain their inaccessibility, beyond all phenomenological retrieval, even the retrieval that might seem to operate in archaeology itself. This would bring archaeology very close to what Foucault speaks of as fiction. Such a revision of historical knowledge is evident in the remark already cited, where Foucault notes that his work does not aim "to dissipate oblivion, to rediscover in the depth of things . . . the moment of their birth (whether this is seen as their empirical creation, or the transcendental act that gives them origin); it does not set out to be a recollection of the original or a memory of the truth. On the contrary, its task is to *make* differences" (205, original emphasis).

Such a making of differences, such a disruption of phenomenological retrieval, can only be grasped through maintaining the *space* that separates the image and the word, the instability that keeps the relation of perception and language perpetually subject to dislocation. These remarks are not limited to Robbe-Grillet or to traditionally fictional genres: in *The Birth of the Clinic*, Foucault's analysis shows that modern medicine was organized precisely through a mapping that would allow the physician's diagnostic discourse to coincide with the space of corporeal visibility. Foucault argues, moreover, that this perfect formalization of the field can be maintained only through a metaphysics of the subject, a modern philosophical anthropology, which unravels when the imaginary and the symbolic fail to coincide. The first sentence of *The Birth of the Clinic* reads: "This book is about space, about language, and about death; it is about the act of seeing, the gaze" (*Birth of the Clinic* ix). In *The Order of Things*, we find a similar gesture, when Foucault discusses an image painted by Velázquez: in one sense, it would be possible to regard this painting as a complete display, a gestalt, the manifestation of all the techniques of representation at work in Classical thought, the very image of representation, in which the distance between the visible world and its verbal representation would be definitively closed within the confines of the encyclopedia.[3] In order for this to be possible, Foucault says, all that is necessary is that we give a name to the one spot at which the surface of the painting seems incomplete (the mirror at the back which does not reflect, but which should show the subjects being painted, who will eventually appear on the canvas whose back we see in the painting called *Las Meniñas*): this hole could be filled with the proper name, "King Philip IV and his wife, Mariana" (*Order* 9). Foucault continues: "But if one wishes to keep the relation of language to vision open, if one wishes to treat their incompatibility as a starting-point for speech instead of as an obstacle to be avoided . . . then one must erase those proper names" (9). The play of substitutions then becomes possible, in which, as Foucault shows, the royal subjects alternate place with the spectator of the painting, who also becomes the object of the painter's regard. In this opening, this void that marks the relation between the image and the word, we can begin to approach what Lacan calls the question of the real.

Repression and Power

Let us now see if we can carry these remarks over into Foucault's analysis of power. In an interview with Bernard Henri-Lévi, Foucault remarks that movements of humanitarian reform are often attended by new types of normalization. Contemporary discourses of liberation, according to Foucault, "present to us a formidable trap." In the case of sexual liberation for example, "What they are saying, roughly, is this: 'You have a sexuality; this sexuality is both frustrated and mute . . . so come to us, tell us, show us all that . . . ' As always, it uses what people say, feel, and hope for. It exploits their temptation to believe that to be happy, it is enough to cross the threshold of discourse and to remove a few prohibitions. But in fact it ends up repressing" (114).

Power, according to Foucault, is therefore not properly understood in the form of juridical law, as a repressive, prohibitive agency which transgression might overcome, but is rather a structure, a relation of forces, such that the law, far from being simply prohibitive, is a force that generates its own transgression. In spite of the claims of reason, the law is always linked to violence in this way, just as the prison, in the failure of its aim at reform, reveals that it is an apparatus destined to produce criminality. This is why Foucault rejects the idea that power is a repressive force to be overthrown. Transgression, liberation, revolution, and so on are not adequately grasped as movements *against* power, movements that would contest the law or displace a prohibition, for these forms of resistance in fact belong to the apparatus of power itself. Transgression and the law thus have to be thought otherwise than in the juridical, oppositional form of modernity, where they are invested with all the drama and pathos of revolutionary narratives; we are rather concerned with a structural relation that has to be undone.

We can see here why Foucault says that genealogy is not simply a form of historical investigation. It does not aim at recovering lost voices or restoring the rights of a marginalized discourse (speaking on behalf of the prisoners or rescuing the discourse of madness). Genealogy does not participate in this virtuous battle between good and evil, but is rather an operation that goes back to the origins, the first moments when an opposition between madness and reason took shape and came to be ordered as a truth.

The distinction between genealogy and historical efforts at recovering lost voices also bears on Foucault's sense of the ethical dimension of genealogy: "What often embarrasses me today," he says, "is that all the work done in the past fifteen years or so . . . functions for some only as a sign of belonging: to be on the 'good side,' on the side of madness, children, delinquency, sex. . . . One must pass to the other side—the good side—but by trying to turn off these mechanisms which cause the appearance of two separate sides . . . that is where the real work begins, that of the present-day historian" (*Politics* 120–21).

Beyond Good and Evil

This is not to say that there is no difference between the fascist and the liberal, madness and reason. This game of dissolving all differences by showing that you cannot tell one thing from another is not what is at stake. The point is rather to refuse to reanimate the forces of moral approbation and censure—not to denounce the enemy and congratulate oneself on having achieved a superior stance, but rather to ask how one is to conduct an analysis. Foucault's work often reaches just such a point, where he seems to pass beyond good and evil.

In books like *Discipline and Punish,* and even as early as *Madness and Civilization,* he says that, as terrible and oppressive as the imprisonment of the insane may be, as intolerable as the torture and public humiliation of criminals may seem to us—we who look back with our enlightened eyes—it is not our censure of this barbarism that Foucault wishes to enlist. What really matters for us today is not the deficiency of the past, but the narrative that reassures us about our own grasp on the truth, our possession of more humane and rational methods. As horrific as the tale of the torture of Damiens may be in the opening pages of *Discipline and Punish*—and it is a story, a little image or vignette, that frames this long mustering of documentary evidence, as Velázquez's artful painting frames the meticulous discourse on knowledge in *The Order of Things*—this scene of torture, which captures the eye and rouses the passions, is not offered up as a spectacle for our contempt. To be sure, it tempts the appetite of our moral indignation as well as our satisfaction in ourselves, our certainty that we have arrived at a better way. But the genealogy of the prison is not the story of the progressive abandonment of an unjust system of monarchical power and the emergence of a more democratic legal order; it is the story of the formation of the modern police state, a network of normalization which is concealed by the conventional history of law and justice. *That* history is a narrative written by the conquerors, in which the truth about the present is lost.

Counter-Memory

Madness and Civilization makes this same point. Foucault's work is often written against a prevailing narrative, as a kind of counter-memory: it is usually said, he tells us, that the liberation of the insane from their condition of imprisonment constitutes an improvement, a sort of scientific advance, a greater understanding of the insane, and a liberalization of the regressive practices which previously grouped the insane together with the criminal and the poor. But this story only serves the interests of the present; it is not the true history, but a history written by the conqueror. The fact is that the liberal and scientific discipline of psychiatric knowledge produced only greater and more diversified forms of subjugation, a greater and more subtle surveillance of the minutiae of interior mental life. The body has been freed, Foucault says, only for the soul to become a more refined and effective prison: you watch too much television, you eat too much, you waste your time, you criticize yourself too much, and you feel guilty for dwelling so much on your problems. This is "the genealogy of the modern 'soul' " (*Discipline* 29). And it is on the basis of this modern psychological soul that "have been built scientific techniques and discourses, and the moral claims of humanism. . . . Th[is] soul is the effect and instrument of a political anatomy." It was once the body that was put in prison, but now, "the soul is the prison of the body" (30). It is *that* contemporary regime, and not the earlier incarceration of the insane, that captures Foucault's attention. It is the story we tell ourselves, not the barbarism of the past, that Foucault wishes to interrogate. That is why he does not simply produce a history for us, but also tells us the usual story and asks us to think about who it is that tells that story, *who is speaking* in the received narrative.

In *The History of Sexuality,* we find a similar gesture: it looks as if the Victorians repressed sex, and perhaps it could be shown that repression is not an adequate concept—that power does not operate by means of repression, and that there was rather an incitement to discourse, a complex discursive production of sexuality. And yet, however much ink has been spilled over this thesis, the central issue of this first volume is not whether there was "repression" among the Victorians, or something more complex, but concerns rather the fact that the *contemporary* story of post-Victorian liberalization is a history written by the conquerors, their fiction.

We may return here to our basic question, and the various levels that animate Foucault's work. For at one level, it is in fact incorrect to say that whereas the Victorians repressed sex, we have liberated it. Our knowledge of the past should be altered in this respect. But Foucault does not simply drop the usual history, in order to replace it with a better one. He is not simply interested in the truth, a better method, a more accurate history. He therefore does not simply reject the false narrative, but asks: if it is so often told, what satisfactions does the received story contain? This is a question about the present and not about the Victorian era. If this story of "Victorian repression" is told so often, whom does it please and whom does it celebrate? Who is the subject that enunciates this history? For the story of liberated sexuality, or the promise of its liberation, does contain its satisfactions: even if it is not the truth, Foucault writes at the beginning of the first volume, the narrative of sexual repression among the Victorians has its reasons and "is easily analyzed," for we find that "the sexual cause—the demand for sexual freedom . . . becomes legitimately associated with the honor of a political cause" (*History of Sexuality* 6). The received history is thus a lie that has its reasons. How now? These brave Europeans! That they should *need* to tell such tales about their ancestors! "A suspicious mind might wonder," says Foucault (6).

It is therefore not the oppressiveness of Victorian life that interests Foucault at this point, or even a revised account of the past; what concerns him is rather *our story,* the narrative we have consented to believe.[4] There may be a reason, he writes, "that makes it *so gratifying for us* to define the relationship between sex and power in terms of repression: something that one might call the speaker's benefit. If sex is repressed . . . then the mere fact that one is speaking about it has the appearance of a deliberate *transgression* . . . Our tone of voice shows that we know we are being subversive, and *we ardently conjure* away the present and appeal to the future, whose day will be hastened by the contribution we believe we are making. Something that smacks of revolt, of promised freedom, of the coming age of a different law, slips easily into this discourse on sexual oppression. Some of the ancient functions of prophecy are reactivated therein" (*History of Sexuality* 6–7, emphasis added).

History, Theory, Fiction

In short, it is true that Foucault wishes to tell us a different history, to show us that sex in the nineteenth century was not repressed but rather incited to speak, articulated in many new discursive forms and not simply silenced or prohibited. It is also true that this argument, this revised *history,* contributes at another level to a *theoretical* elaboration of power, and to a method (genealogy) that would reconfigure history as a disciplinary practice. These two aspects of his work have received overwhelming attention, but we cannot be satisfied with this operation of knowledge. For in addition to the revised history, and beyond the theoretical doctrine, what ultimately drives Foucault is a desire not to construct a more accurate history (the truth about the past—that of the historian) or to erect a great theoretical edifice (a universal truth—that of the philosopher), but to dismantle the narratives that still organize our present experience (a truth that bears on the position of enunciation). "I would like to explore not only these discourses," Foucault writes, "but also the will that sustains them. . . . The question I would like to pose is not 'Why are we repressed?' but rather, 'Why do we say, with so much passion and so much resentment against our most recent past, against our present, and against ourselves, that we are repressed?'" (*History of Sexuality* 8–9). Similarly, in *Discipline and Punish,* Foucault responds to an imaginary reader who wonders why he spends so much time wandering among obsolete systems of justice and the obscure ruins of the torture chamber. "Why?" he replies. "Simply because I am interested in the past? No, if one means by that writing a history of the past in terms of the present. Yes, if one means writing a history *of the present*" (31, emphasis added). It is this counter-memory, this interplay between one story and another, that leads us to consider the relation between history, theory, and fiction.

Transgression and the Law: Foucault with Lacan

Although Foucault's refusal of the repressive conception of power appears in his discussion of the Victorians, one does not have to wait for the *History of Sexuality* to find this thesis on power, this rejection of the theory of power as prohibition, the so-called repressive hypothesis, which generates so many discourses of resistance and liberation. In 1963, Foucault formulated a similar claim in his "Preface to Transgression." Curiously enough, this formulation also has to do with sexuality.

Foucault begins the essay by saying, "*We like to believe* that sexuality has regained, in contemporary experience, its full truth as a process of nature, a truth which has long been lingering in the shadows" ("Preface" 29, emphasis added). But as writers like Bataille have shown us, transgression does not eliminate the law by means of a force or desire that would preexist all prohibition. It is not the restoration of an origin, a return to immediacy, or the liberation of a prediscursive domain, by means of which we might overcome all merely historical and constituted limits. On the contrary, "the limit and transgression depend on each other" (34). "Transgression," Foucault writes, "is not related to the limit as black to white, the prohibited to the lawful, the outside to the inside" (35). Long before his final books on the relation between sexuality and ethics, these remarks already had consequences for our conception of the ethical. Transgression, he argues, "must be detached from its questionable association to ethics if we want to understand it and to begin thinking from it . . . it must be liberated from the scandalous or subversive" (35). This detachment from the ethical is required if we are to understand the obscure relation that binds transgression to the law.

Let us add that these reflections on the limit, on power and transgression, are not formulated as an abstract philosophical question, as though it were a theoretical matter of understanding power correctly. On the contrary, Foucault's claims make sense only if they are seen as part of his understanding of history. In the contemporary experience of transgression, the limit does not take a Kantian form, does not entail a line that cannot (or should not) be crossed (a logical or moral limit), but rather a fold, the elaboration of a strange non-Euclidean geometry of space, another mathematics, in which the stability of inside and outside gives way to a limit that exists only in the movement which crosses it—like a Möbius strip, the two sides of which constantly disappear as one circles around its finite surface, as if the point at which one passes from one side to the other were constantly receding, so that the mathematization of space, the difference between one and two, is constantly being destabilized.[5]

In short, this concept of transgression has a historical location: it is clearly bound up with the epoch for which anthropological thought has been dismantled. Foucault puts the history concisely in the "Preface to Transgression," where he uses the categories of "need," "demand," and "desire." In the eighteenth century, Foucault writes, "consumption was based entirely on need, and need based itself exclusively on the model of hunger. When this element was introduced into an investigation of profit," when, in other words, the natural foundation of need was reconfigured by an economics that aimed to account for the superfluity of commodities, an economics that went beyond natural law, explaining the genesis of culture through a demand that exceeded all natural need (what Foucault calls "the appetite of those who have satisfied their hunger"), then the Enlightenment theory of exchange gave way to modern philosophical anthropology. European thought "inserted man into a dialectic of production which had a simple anthropological meaning: if man was alienated from his real nature and his immediate needs through his labor and the production of objects . . . it was nevertheless through its agency that he recaptured his essence." For contemporary thought, however, this shift from need to demand will be followed by yet another dislocation, a shift from demand to desire, in which the conceptual framework of modernity no longer functions; and this time, instead of labor, sexuality will play a decisive role, obliging us to think of transgression outside the framework of dialectical production.

This new formation is also an encounter with language. The "discovery of sexuality" forces us into a conception of desire that is irreducible to need or demand. "In this sense," Foucault writes, "the appearance of sexuality as a fundamental problem marks the transformation of a philosophy of man as worker to a philosophy based on *a being who speaks*" ("Preface" 49–50). The same historical shift is stressed in *Madness and Civilization:* this analysis, which might seem at first to include an indictment of Freud as one of those who participate in the modern, psychiatric imprisonment of madness, in fact argues that Freud marks an essential displacement in relation to psychiatry, a displacement that coincides with what the "Preface to Transgression" regards as the end of philosophical anthropology: "That is why we must do justice to Freud. Between Freud's *Five Case Histories* and Janet's scrupulous investigations of *Psychological Healing,* there is more than the density of a *discovery;* there is the sovereign violence of a *return.* . . . Freud went back to madness at the level of its *language,* reconstituted one of the elements of an experience reduced to silence by positivism . . . he restored, in medical thought, the possibility of a dialogue with unreason. . . . It is not psychology that is involved in psychoanalysis" (*Madness* 198).[6]

Lacan

If resistance belongs to the apparatus of power, and is consequently not so much a threat to power as a product, an effect of power (just as the totalitarian state is structurally linked to the founding of the democratic community, which would seem to be opposed to it in every respect), then it is the obscure, symptomatic relation between the two that Foucault's conception of power obliges us to confront.

Lacan says something similar about transgression and the law: we do not enjoy in spite of the law, but because of it. This is what the thesis on jouissance entails: jouissance is not the name for an instinctual pleasure that runs counter to the law (in spite of the biological paradigm that still governs so many readings of Freud); it is not the fulfillment of a natural urge, or a momentary suspension of moral constraint, but quite the contrary: it is Lacan's name for Freud's thesis on the death drive, a name for the dimension of unnatural suffering and punishment that inhabits human pleasure, a dimension that is possible only because the body and its satisfaction are constitutively denatured, always already bound to representation. Lacan thus argues that our jouissance is tied to punishment, that pleasure is organized not in defiance of the repressive conventions of civilization, not through the transgression of the moral law, but in relation to the law (which does not mean in conformity with it). This is Foucault's thesis on the productive character of power, even if it does not entail a complete theoretical overlap with Lacan in other respects. Slavoj Žižek reminds us of Lacan's paradoxical reversal of Dostoyevsky here: "against [the] famous position, 'If god is dead, everything is permitted,'" Lacan claims instead that "if there is no god . . . everything is forbidden." Žižek remarks: "How do we account for this paradox that the absence of Law universalizes Prohibition? There is only one possible explanation: *enjoyment itself, which we experience as 'transgression,' is in its innermost status something imposed, ordered—* when we enjoy, we never do it 'spontaneously,' we always follow a certain injunction. The psychoanalytic name for this obscene injunction, for this obscene call, 'Enjoy,' is superego" (*For They Know Not* 9–10). The relation between the law and transgression is not a simple opposition of outside and inside, prohibition and rebellion, cultural conventions opposed to natural desires, but rather a paradoxical relation of forces, not the Newtonian system of natural forces, the smooth machinery in which every action produces an equal and opposite reaction, not a physics of libido based on natural law, a theory of charge and discharge, tension and homeostasis, but a more peculiar form of power, one that takes us away from natural law toward the law of language, in which force is tied to representation.

Here the space of the body is given over to the unnatural network of discourse and its causality. We must not be too quick to conclude, however, that with Lacan we have simply shifted to another, symbolic law. On the contrary, the relation between law and transgression is such that the rule of law does not repress but produces its own exception, does not function but malfunctions, thereby making manifest the incompleteness of the law, the impossibility of closure, the element of lack that destabilizes the structural, symbolic totality. As a result, the symbolic order itself appears to function only on the basis of this exception, this peculiar remainder, this excess—as though the very rule of law somehow generated a level of malfunction and perverse enjoyment, as the prison seems to function in relation to the criminal—acting not simply as a limit, but carrying within it a perverse productivity, a level of sadistic enjoyment that Kafka represented so well, by generating the illusion that behind the mechanical operation of a neutral, anonymous, and bureaucratic law there lay an obscure level of sadistic enjoyment, an agency that *wants* the criminal to exist in order to take pleasure in inflicting punishment. This Other who is imagined to enjoy is one aspect of the paternal function, a perverse surplus-effect of the law, which contradicts or violates its own claim to neutrality and justice. This is the point of jouissance that marks the excess that always accompanies the law, an excess that Freud called "primary masochism." This excess is not a natural phenomenon, a primordial force that disrupts the polished machinery of culture; it is rather a peculiar feature of culture itself, an effect of language which includes its own malfunction. This is what Lacan understands as the relation between the symbolic and the real.

The Symbolic and the Real: Jouissance

We can therefore see in Freud the relation between prohibition and this peculiar excess, between the law and violence, that Foucault develops in his remarks on power. This explains why Foucault argues that the contemporary experience of sexuality is a central place in which the relation between the law and transgression demands to be rethought, beyond the legislative, prohibitive conception that characterizes modernity. This obscure, symptomatic relation by which the law is bound to its own transgression, can perhaps be seen in its most conspicuous form in the America: with all its defiant freedom and carefree self-indulgence, America is not the land of freedom and pleasure, but displays the most obscene form of superego punishment: you must enjoy, you must be young and healthy and happy and tan and beautiful. The question, What must

I do? has been replaced with the higher law of the question: Are we having fun yet? That is American Kantianism: "Think whatever you like, choose your religion freely, speak out in any way you wish, but you must have fun!" (see Foucault, *"What Is Enlightenment?"* 35–36; Žižek, *For They Know Not* 203–9, 229–37). The reverse side of this position, the guilt that inhabits this ideal of pleasure, is clear enough: don't eat too much, don't go out in the sun, don't drink or smoke, or you won't be able to enjoy yourself!

Thus, as Foucault argues in his thesis on power, it is not a matter of overcoming repression, of liberating pleasure from moral constraint, or defending the insane against the oppressive regime of psychiatry, but of undoing the structure that produced these two related sides. Such is the distance between the Kantian position and that of Foucault and Lacan: the law no longer serves as a juridical or prohibitive limit, but as a force, an imperious agency that does not simply limit, but *produces an excess* which Kant did not theorize, a dimension of punishment and tyranny that the law was meant to eliminate. This is the kind of logic addressed by Foucault when he asks, for example, whether the failure of the prison as an institution, the malfunction of the law, the fact that the prison seems to be a machine for organizing and proliferating criminality, is not part of the very functioning of the prison, so that the law includes this excess which seems on the surface to contradict it. Lacan puts Kant together with Sade to show the logical relation between them, in the same way that we might speak of the obscure relation between the Rights of Man and the Reign of Terror—two formations which, from an imaginary point of view, are completely opposed and antithetical, but which turn out to have an obscure connection.

In Lacan's terminology, the establishment of the symbolic law, the systemic totalization of a signifying structure, cannot take place without producing a remainder, an excess, a dimension of the real that marks the limit of formalization. A similar excess appears in Foucault: where the Kantian formulation gives us an anthropology—a form of consciousness that freely gives itself its own law and thereby realizes its essence—Foucault speaks instead of an apparatus that produces the criminal, the insane, and the destitute, all *in the name of the law* of reason; thus the excess of Sade is the strict counterpart of Kant, not his contradiction or antithesis. It should come as no surprise that Kant's text "What Is Enlightenment?" raises, among other things, the question of "making a place for Jewish culture within German thought." This text, which Kant wrote in response to a question that had been answered two months earlier by Moses Mendelssohn, is part of his effort to elaborate a "cosmopolitan view" of history;

it is thus, according to Foucault, "perhaps a way of announcing the acceptance of a common destiny." As Foucault points out, however, history produced a nightmarish perversion of this common destiny: contrary to everything Kant might have hoped for, Foucault remarks, "we now know to what drama that was to lead" (*"What Is Enlightenment?"* 33). It is this product, this excess, this remainder which accompanies the very morality meant to exclude it, that Foucault addresses by his formulation of power as a relationship that does not take the form of justice and law (nor, we might add, of mere tyranny, mere "force" or exploitation, the simple "opposite" of law), but is rather productive, a force that must be conceived in relation to this excess or remainder—the dimension of misery that Lacan calls jouissance.

Conclusion

The canonical reception of Foucault has stressed two aspects of his work: on the one hand, its contribution to "theory" or "method" (the theory of power, or sexuality, or genealogy), and on the other hand, its status as "historical knowledge," its contribution to the so-called return to history that is sometimes regarded as an antidote to structuralism. There are good reasons for insisting on these two aspects of his work, and yet we have argued that Foucault refuses to lay claim to a meta-language (a "theory of power," for example, or an "archaeological method" that would have no place of birth, and pay no heed to its own historical conditions) and also refuses to present his historical material as "knowledge about the past," as the discipline of history traditionally presents itself.

The canonical story about Foucault, which is organized around the twin axes of "theory" and "history," can only proceed if it represses several crucial features of his thought: above all (1) its status as a "history of the present" (as opposed to knowledge about the past); (2) its interest in the "limits of formalization" (as opposed to the systematic aims of structuralist thought); and (3) its explicitly "fictional" character. Each of these features in Foucault's work can be clarified through a parallel with Lacanian psychoanalysis. The first issue can be formulated in terms of the "position of enunciation." Here, Foucault is seen to aim more at disrupting the place of the speaking subject—namely, our current arrangement of knowledge—than at producing an account of the past. The second issue can be formulated in terms of what Lacan calls "the real," namely, a traumatic element which has no imaginary or symbolic form, which is lacking any representation, but which haunts the systemic organization of conscious thought, marking its incompleteness, the impossibility of its closure. Here, Foucault is regarded as aiming neither at a "structural linguistics" (the so-called archaeological period) nor at a "return to history" (the so-called genealogy), but rather as aiming to encounter the "real" in a Lacanian sense—to provoke the destabilization of our *contemporary* arrangement of knowledge by touching on the elements of trauma within it (such as "madness," in his early work, or "sexuality" in his later work). Finally, the third issue, "fiction," obliges us to stress the degree to which Foucault's work presented itself as a kind of action, a kind of praxis or intervention, rather than a "documentary" form of knowledge. Here, the status of Foucault's "historical" research comes very close to the "fictions" produced in the course of analysis. This point also makes it possible to give more weight to the references Foucault constantly made to works of art, references which have always been slighted by those who wish to present his work as either "positive historical research" or a new methodology or meta-language.

This does not mean that Foucault and Lacan coincide in every respect—far from it. But it does suggest that these two thinkers cannot simply be opposed to one another (as if Foucault hated psychoanalysis and regarded it as one more confessional discourse, or as if Lacan was an "ahistorical" thinker whose work had no bearing on the structures of human time and the peculiarly contemporary formations of the law). If, in the canonical reception, Lacan and Foucault have been simply opposed to one another, these remarks might serve to intervene in that narrative and allow us to address their relation in a way that does greater justice to its complexity.

Notes

1. This is the Foucault presented in *Michel Foucault: Beyond Structuralism and Hermeneutics,* ed. Hubert Dreyfus and Paul Rabinow (Chicago: University of Chicago Press, 1982). The authors argue that, at least in the "archaeological period" of his work, Foucault could not escape the contradiction between his claim that all truths have contingent epistemic foundations and his claim to have invented, with the archaeological method, a means of transcending history and surveying it from above in a typically transcendental fashion. I am suggesting that the authors can only maintain this view of Foucault by repressing (1) the "fictional" aspect of his work, (2) its explicit awareness of its own place of enunciation, and (3) its status as a "history of the present," which aims at "making differences" rather than producing another form of transcendental knowledge.

2. In *The Archaeology of Knowledge,* Foucault conjures up an imaginary interlocutor, who challenges him to distinguish his work from structuralism, and then on hearing Foucault's reply, says, "I can even accept that one should dispense, as far as one can, with a discussion of the speaking subjects; but I dispute that these successes give one the right to turn the analysis back on to the very forms of discourse that made them possible, and to question the very locus in which we are speaking today." Instead, the interlocutor argues, we must acknowledge that "the history of those analyses . . . retains its own transcendence." Foucault replies, "It seems to me that the difference between us lies there (much more than in the over-discussed question of structuralism)" (202).

3. Another relevant discussion of this painting from a Lacanian perspective is Pierre-Gilles Guéguen, "Foucault and Lacan on the Status of the Subject of Representation," *Newsletter of the Freudian Field* 3.1–2 (spring/ fall 1989): 51–57.

4. The paper by Jana Sawicki responding to a paper by Isaac Balbus shows very clearly the difference between a genealogical perspective and the "modern" discourses of liberation. These two papers offer an admirable example of the contrast between a "marxist" analysis and a feminism that is influenced in part by genealogy. In her remarks, Sawicki shows how the promise of a liberated future is haunted by the "most virulent" forms of humanism, in the sense that liberation carries with it a normative component that would itself escape genealogical analysis. See Isaac Balbus, "Disciplining Women: Michel Foucault and the Power of Feminist Discourse," and Jana Sawicki, "Feminism and the Power of Foucaultian Discourse," both in *After Foucault: Humanistic Knowledge, Postmodern Challenges,* ed. Jonathan Arac (New Brunswick, N.J.: Rutgers University Press, 1988).

5. I am thinking here of Lacan's reflections on the body as structured by the same kind of limit—the eyes, ears, and other orifices seeming to participate in just this dislocation of Euclidean space. See Jeanne Granon-Lafont, *La topologie ordinaire de Jacques Lacan* (Paris: Point Hors Ligne, 1985).

6. See Derrida's recent remarks on this passage in "Etre juste avec Freud," in *Penser la folie: Essais sur Michel Foucault* (Paris: Galilée, 1992), 141–95.

Works Cited

Bellour, Raymond. "Towards Fiction." *Michel Foucault: Philosopher.* Trans. Timothy J. Armstrong. New York: Routledge, 1992.

Derrida, Jacques. "Cogito and the History of Madness." *Writing and Difference.* Trans. Alan Bass. Chicago: University of Chicago Press, 1978.

Foucault, Michel. *The Archaeology of Knowledge.* Trans. A. M. Sheridan-Smith. New York: Pantheon, 1972.

——. *The Birth of the Clinic: An Archaeology of Medical Perception.* Trans. A. M. Sheridan-Smith. New York: Vintage, 1973.

——. *Discipline and Punish: The Birth of the Prison.* Trans. Alan Sheridan. New York: Vintage, 1979.

——. *The History of Sexuality, Volume I: An Introduction.* Trans. Robert Hurley. New York: Vintage, 1978.

——. *Language, Counter-Memory, Practice: Selected Essays and Interviews.* Ed. Donald Bouchard. Ithaca: Cornell University Press, 1977.

——. *Madness and Civilization: A History of Insanity in the Age of Reason.* Trans. Richard Howard. New York: Vintage, 1965.

——. *Michel Foucault: Politics, Philosophy, Culture.* Ed. Lawrence D. Kritzman. New York: Routledge, 1988.

——. "Nietzsche, Genealogy, History." *The Foucault Reader.* Ed. Paul Rabinow. New York: Pantheon, 1984.

——. *The Order of Things: An Archaeology of the Human Sciences.* New York: Random House, 1970.

——. "Preface to Transgression." *Language, Counter-Memory, Practice: Selected Essays and Interviews.* Ed. Donald F. Bouchard. Ithaca: Cornell University Press, 1977. First published as "Hommage à Georges Bataille," in *Critique,* nos. 195–96 (1963): 751–70.

——. "What Is Enlightenment?" Trans. Catherine Porter. *The Foucault Reader.* Ed. Paul Rabinow. New York: Pantheon, 1984.

Freud, Sigmund. *The Standard Edition of the Complete Psychological Work of Sigmund Freud.* Ed. James Strachey. London: Hogarth, 1953.

Lacan, Jacques. *Ecrits: A Selection.* Trans. Alan Sheridan. New York: Norton, 1977.

——. *The Four Fundamental Concepts of Psychoanalysis.* Trans. Alan Sheridan. New York: Norton, 1978.

——. *The Seminar of Jacques Lacan.* Ed. Jacques-Alain Miller. Trans. with notes by John Forrester. New York: Norton, 1988.

——. "Television." Trans. Denis Hollier, Rosalind Krauss, and Annette Michelson. *Television: A Challenge to the Psychoanalytic Establishment.* Ed. Joan Copjec. New York: Norton, 1990.

Nietzsche, Friedrich. *On the Genealogy of Morals.* Trans. Walter Kaufmann. New York: Vintage, 1967.

Žižek, Slavoj. *For They Know Not What They Do.* London: Verso, 1991.

——. *The Sublime Object of Ideology.* London: Verso, 1989.

12

The Subject of Invention
Antifoundationalism and Medieval Hermeneutics

Richard R. Glejzer

Over the past decade Medieval Studies has increasingly begun to question overtly the issues surrounding its object—the Middle Ages—in terms of methodology. The studies of Lee Patterson, Paul Zumthor, Norman Cantor, and others begin to consider the ways in which the Middle Ages are constructed as an a priori, where readings of medieval texts are grounded by particular *inventions* of the Middle Ages, to borrow Cantor's title. Questions of medievalism have become central to the medievalist as a way to get outside particular methodological hermeticisms, outside contemporary foundations, whether they be New Critical (which is still very much alive), exegetical, New Historical, or some other school. This "New Medievalism" has the potential for redefining medieval studies by reinventing the Middle Ages, replacing an unquestioned content with a Middle Ages that functions as a possibility.

This, at least, is the promise laid out by Stephen Nichols in his introductory essay to *The New Medievalism,* a collection that offers examples of a methodological awareness at the level of particular medieval texts. The "New Medievalism," as defined by Nichols, presents itself in response to "traditional" or "formalist" medieval criticisms that work primarily within nineteenth-century constructions of the Middle Ages, constructions that are often laden with then contemporary notions of the humanistic tradition. Unlike its precursors, the New Medievalism questions what constitutes the Middle Ages by examining medieval limiting of the "natural world" as opposed to an absolute knowledge of such a world. In this way, particular, or possible, inventions of the Middle Ages function as mathematical limits, where a given system's meaning is defined by supposing that an equation reaches stasis—that is, that x seems to equal zero. Thus, the New Medievalism admits to more than a single possible Middle Ages (as limits often do), which allows for many types of knowledge or possible answers to be highlighted.

But this New Medievalism does not acknowledge that which transcends the gap between the infinitely small and zero, or even consider how such a leap is made; it does not posit a world where the subjective is placed into question, at least in a psychoanalytic sense or from the point of view of New Historicism, where knowledge is placed into either a structural fiction or a historical framework. In fact, Nichols seems uninterested in the act of perception itself—in the move from infinity to zero—focusing instead on the conclusion of perception, as opposed to how or even why such a perception takes place. On the surface, then, the New Medievalism presents a possible antifoundational approach to the Middle Ages, treating the Middle Ages epistemologically.

Below this surface, however, New Medievalism posits itself in the examination of the Middle Ages as a moment of occupation, where medieval men and women attempt to limit a "chaotic" universe with a technology to which they themselves are not subject, where technology holds an absolute meaning or value, where the technological itself functions as a foundational signifier that grounds knowledge. The "material" of the Middle Ages—documents on the astrolabe, geographic texts, grammatical treatises, poetic inventions—becomes evidence for a *knowledge,* a knowledge of what constitutes a medieval preoccupation with the borders that delimit the universe, a knowledge of "the medieval mind."

Such a vision of the Middle Ages shows how representation renders a truthfulness at the level of content, thus allowing scholars to "interrogate the nature of medieval representation in its differences and continuities with classical and renaissance mimesis" (Nichols 2). Thus, the project of New Medievalism enables medievalists to show the continuities and discontinuities between scientific development and literary invention, the integrity of a continuum that ends historically at this moment, the now of intellectual history. In other words, the New Medievalism—even more so than any old medievalism—charges us to become more acutely sensitive to the contextual, foreclosing an investigatory practice of examining how the contextual is itself constituted, a methodology that would allow for an ontological dimension of/in knowledge and meaning. The New Medievalism sets up a possible antifoundational hermeneutic—a paradigmatic shift that can be traced back to Kuhn—only to fall back on context as the sole practical object of epistemology.

Alternatively, I suggest that this imperative to the contextual places the Middle Ages in the realm of the knowable, of the actual instead of the possible, of something to be known if we had enough data or found if we knew just the right place to look. Historically based literary study constructs the context on which it then is based, sets a limit to the world under consideration. But, of course, we never find the absolute at the level of content or transcend a given corporeality to arrive at an absence by which it is governed, where a possible zero sufficiently stands in for the infinite. For medievalists, then, the Middle Ages never lives up to this promise, never is known and never could be. And thus to find context as a knowledge we must ultimately make a leap from infinity to zero. By examining this leap, we can begin to see the Middle Ages not only as an object of knowledge, but as a cause of knowledge: in "knowing" the Middle Ages we are further propelled to know again, to continue to circumscribe the system so that such a knowledge can be contained. Such an understanding of the Middle Ages as both object and cause of knowledge offers the real opportunity for an antifoundational literary study, a hermeneutics that acknowledges the limit that produces and demands production of knowledge. This antifoundationalism is thus opposed to a methodology of content, placing the Middle Ages in the realm of the impossible, as an absence that is leapt over mythologically to secure knowledge—of classical antiquity, of the Renaissance, of ourselves. But such a security is always imaginary and thus never intrinsically stable. Signifiers keep in motion, never at rest in the realm of the known or actualized.

Such an understanding of the methodological is theorized within Lacanian psychoanalysis, which offers a topological, nonlinear structuralism that allows for a rethinking of the relationship between cause and effect. Lacan reexamines the particularity of knowledge and its relation to being, allowing us to trace where the ontological and the epistemological meet in metaphor—where knowledge is both an effect and a cause of being. By beginning with a point of absence or impossibility—the gap between infinity and zero—we can follow the Middle Ages to examine how both medieval and contemporary theories of causality function epistemologically to construct a false knowledge qua content. As a result, any conviction of the Middle Ages functions as a misrecognition, a *méconnaisance* qua fiction (or *fixion*) that denies the possibility of impossibility by fixing it to an actuality, a move that even medieval thinkers were forced to suspect when confronting (un)substantiations of the ineffable, of God. Thus, we can only *know* the Middle Ages when we cease to examine cause, when we deny the possibility of the impossible (the [im]possible) by focusing only on the actual.

Such a move is typical of the poststructural or postmodern impulse that removes cause from the sphere of investigation and so maintains that cause qua (im)possibility is something that cannot be traced, theorized, or examined. Lacan's topological structuralism does more than allow for a methodology to treat the ways in which medieval intellectual history defines, limits, or explains a "chaotic" world. It provides a mode of questioning that privileges how medieval thinkers—theologians, philosophers, poets—invariably find themselves on the precipice of knowledge—of God, of the soul—where it is inevitable to reach the IS NOT instead of the IS, where x can precisely not equal zero.

It is at these limits that the Middle Ages teaches us the antihermetic nature of knowledge, where what grounds knowledge, what exists outside the sphere of earthly understanding, is also outside the actuality of representation. This is not the same as noting that the medieval worldview technologically placed limits on chaos. Medieval thinkers were intimately aware that chaos was always at the door and no technological innovation could remove such a lack in knowledge.

By not acknowledging the Other side of knowledge or the underside of knowledge, the New Medievalism focuses only on half the equation. Much like the old philology or the old historicism, its primary concern is with the way knowledge is represented, both in images and in texts, rather than with the ways such representations are themselves modes of knowing. I would like to suggest that such a knowledge of the Middle Ages relies on an epistemology of presence, where medievalists attempt to define the Middle Ages only metonymically, where a particular knowledge stands in for a presence that we call the Middle Ages as whole and complete at the level of content.

Lee Patterson shows an awareness of such constructions of the Middle Ages in *Negotiating the Past*, where he sees something at stake in projecting or defining ourselves while defining the Middle Ages as context. In his preface, Patterson confronts the possibility of a knowledge of the Middle Ages in terms of an outside referent: "In the course of writing these essays I have become progressively more convinced that the various forms of resolution at which historicist negotiations arrive are governed neither by empirical necessity, nor (least of all) by theoretical correctness, but by values and commitments that are in the last analysis political" (x). Patterson makes an eloquent appraisal of Medieval Studies in terms of the ideological implications of constructing a Middle Ages, all the while maintaining that such a construction is possible or perhaps necessary. Such a view, however, leads us back to "a plurality of worlds"—a Middle Ages as possible—that stands in for a single world—the Middle Ages. In other words, we are still left with a medievalism that pursues the Middle Ages as foundational, as a mythic moment of origin, much like medieval preoccupations with the fall of Troy as a foundation to European culture. Such a foundational signifier in turn metonymically holds together the methodology on which it is supported and by which it is constructed. And such a discourse of mastery, where we take knowledge to be true, prevents us from contemplating the true in knowledge. Instead of examining how a subject is necessary to invention, Medieval Studies has invented a subject to take charge of invention itself.

The Actual Subject of Invention

Most theories of the subject that attempt to consider the poetic involve a knowing or known subject that is constituted either before or after the inventive act. Such a linear understanding ultimately rests on a foundational morality, a romantic or postmodern notion of the "human self." Such criticism is present in Medieval Studies, in Chaucer studies particularly, where critics have focused on defining authorial agency ideologically, as a historical or subjectifying presence within literature.[1] By incarnating the subject, contemporary criticism continues to present a foundational understanding of the human psyche that places meaning at the point of unification, within the effects of foundationalism, even as it attempts to accommodate a multidimensional Middle Ages. The epistemological underpinnings of medieval scholarship, whether on Chaucer or other medieval authors, offers significant instances of incarnations of the subject, where a particular ontology is implicitly presupposed *before* texts are studied epistemologically. In this way, the ontological questions are bracketed in order to misrecognize the possible as actual.

By contemporary reckoning, the end of the Middle Ages is marked by the enlightenment of the Renaissance, a time when the "subject" was no longer enslaved by the religious forces that permeated all of medieval culture, wherein individuals totally identified with the monolithic ideology of the Church. This very notion of complete ideological identification is an *invention* that privileges a brand of humanism identified with the Renaissance and that we find consistent with contemporary beliefs, especially with romantic and modern scientific notions of human autonomy wherein the human subject is defined as a "natural" phenomenon. In contrast, the medieval period seems far removed from modern experience and marks an uncomfortable position with regard to con-

cepts of individuality and being and, therefore, to scientific and literary production. Contemporary theory sees the latter as the observations and creations of
the individual. Contemporary medieval theories that define a relationship between humans and God instill in a critique of the Middle Ages a concept of
these medieval "selves" as lacking consciousness and unconsciousness. Some
such theories conclude that the medieval human is qualitatively different from
his or her modern counterpart.

　　D. W. Robertson was among the first scholars to recognize a distinction
between medieval and contemporary representation by focusing on the difference in the function of art between the two cultures. Robertson, however, chose
to attribute this distinction as the product of an entirely different aesthetic
process rather than simply a difference in theory. Thus the Robertsonian position, though not devaluing the medieval, reduces the concept of medieval art to
something qualitatively different from any other period, especially our own. As
Robertson states, "It was once fashionable to ask whether medieval writers were
'conscious artists.' This question has no answer, since in the modern sense they
were not artists at all" ("The Allegorist" 85). By implication, such a statement
posits a "medieval mind" that lacked "consciousness," that was somehow solely
a product of a medieval language that enveloped the subject totally. From this
position, the medieval *auctor* would exist only as a moralizing agent of Christian ideology, a religious subject existing unseparated and unalienated from a
theological symbolic system. Examinations of such literary monologism continually dismiss such a deterministic hermeneutics; Bakhtin's theory of the
dialogic nature of language, developed in the intersections of Rabelais and
Dostoyevsky, shows different formal constraints between the two writers and
periods, but not an entirely different ontology.[2] Simply stating that Robertson
reduces the hermeneutic possibilities of the Middle Ages, however, does not
necessarily get at the root of the problem in the Robertsonian argument or
allow for an investigation of what structures this misunderstanding of the
Middle Ages.

　　The final conclusion of a Robertsonian position is that the "medieval
mind" is capable of art solely as an allegorical enterprise, where art is subsumed
by the dogmatic presence of the Church and therefore must be completely
capable of describing or inventing human experience (man, woman, sex). This
theoretical position reduces the relation between art and artist to a myth of
unification between language and being, to an imaginary tautology where we

are caught in the theoretical circle of seeing a self-conscious self self-consciously construct a self.

Such a tautological position is also the final conclusion of Judson Allen's investigation of the ethical (moral) basis of not only medieval art but all art. Allen's conclusions concerning medieval poetry and criticism are one-dimensional:

> The project permitted by the medieval critics, and by the literature they read and they and their contemporaries wrote, is a project of reintegration. One may inspect in actual operation a world in which point of view is, by consideratio, absorbed into poetry, and in which poetry, as words, both repeats and is absorbed into the parallel worlds of exemplary action and doctrinal ethical discourse. And all this, of course, without losing in the slightest any of the intrinsic qualities of decorum which we are wont to admire as aesthetic. (302)

Allen's vision of medieval and modern aesthetics as a "doctrinal ethical discourse" forecloses the possibility that literature could be *about* ethics as opposed to a simple reflection of "the ethical."

Both Allen's and Robertson's distinctly moral poetics involve a theoretical narcissism, where the subject qua *auctor* is completely represented in a textual reflection. Implicit in such a moral approach to medieval poetics is a theory of the subject as unified, a subject of allegory where faith, Robertson's faith or Allen's faith, becomes the cement that seals any hint that integrity is lacking. We are left with an understanding of the subject as content, with a self-made humanism that prevents all questioning of what actually constitutes the human. By viewing art as a moral enterprise, Robertson and Allen present no room for the subjectivity of fantasy that underlies conscious thought, the subject being eclipsed by the totalizing of the Middle Ages. No possible means of asking questions of the process of invention or medieval epistemology as an identificatory practice is left open.

Even though both Allen and Robertson have had vehement opponents, their implicit understanding of a unified subject exemplifies the foundation of medieval scholarship, particularly on Chaucer, in an implicitly humanistic enterprise. Inherent in almost all recent criticism, from historical to feminist, is a notion of authorship that is strikingly contemporary, not medieval. Data found in Chaucer's poetry fuels debates on Chaucer's attitudes toward women, his political allegiances, and his familial problems. Common to all such readings of Chaucer is the invariable attempt to define the material of his invention in terms of historical realities or ideological moralities, the insistence on seeing Chaucer as not only a conscious moralizer or creator, but also a product of a specialized signifying system and thus only able to produce a knowledge that is constructed by such a system. This invented subject—an invention of contemporary critics—necessarily forces certain questions to the fore while at the same time precluding other questions, specifically those dealing with structure.

Lee Patterson's *Chaucer and the Subject of History* has focused more explicitly on the subject in medieval literature. Even though Patterson invokes the question of agency, however, he does not investigate the foundations of what constituted earlier, more implicit theories of the subject in medieval scholarship. Thus he builds on a notion of the Middle Ages without questioning the foundations on which his readings rely. Robertson's allegorical subject becomes for Patterson a historical subject, the subject still being grounded symbolically by a privileged signifier. Patterson defines the subject, rather, as that which is "forged in the dialectic between the subjective and the social" (19), stressing the historical, even factual, underpinnings of the symbolic system. Patterson astutely recognizes the dialectical nature of subjectivity and fictionality, but does not examine the ontological limitations of defining the symbolic system as the problematic cause of subjectivity. When one invokes History as a master signifier, as the cause of the human qua knowledge, we are still left with a theory of the subject where the subject in the end must act as its own cause as a knowledge.[3] If subjectivity is reduced to a content, rather than a structure, there is no gap between what grounds knowledge and knowledge itself. For Patterson, History, taken as what grounds the social, is equal to Being, and the human exists solely as the sum of a signifying system.

This eclipsing of being by knowledge, taken as a language capable of absolute representation, is also the foundation of Marshall Leicester's notion of the subject in his study of Chaucer. Though more aware of theoretical implications of this equation, Leicester nevertheless sees the subject as a self that is a reflection of just such a correspondence with knowledge, where Chaucer functions as an independent agency, an absolute representation, even if his own representations are themselves in flux. Leicester's reading of the *Canterbury Tales* offers insightful examinations of the subjective play within the tales, especially "The Knight's Tale," but his reading is limited by a static notion of agency where the ultimate referent must inevitably be Chaucer as conscious artist. Thus Leicester argues for a subject that exists within the flux of language, but where this flux is the product of an essential agency. Such a contradictory notion, where the subject is not a representation but where language is, functions as a common denominator for most poststructural theory and is foundational to Leicester's own treatment of Chaucer. Like Patterson and even Robertson, Leicester's approach to medieval texts necesssarily places the human *auctor* as a conscious, even essential, agency.

By not addressing questions of agency, medievalists allow for the construction of the Middle Ages as a totality, even if not fully known. And if we treat such metonymic representations (this Middle Ages as the Middle Ages) as grounded on a metaphoric axis, we show the (im)possibility of knowing or being as opening onto an instrumentality of the subject of knowledge as a field of meaning. Such a new structuralism for a new, antifoundational Middle Ages shows us the ontological dimensions of the epistemological, where Being and Knowing as Having are knotted at a point of metaphor, the grounding of the subject.[4]

Such a theoretical move challenges the truth of metonymy by defining an absence that grounds such a knowledge, where the possible worlds we call the Middle Ages stand for something fundamentally impossible, an a priori absence. As such, all constructions of the Middle Ages are fantastic, working to construct an imaginary totality at the level of being and a symbolic hermeticism at the level of knowing. The absence of the Middle Ages demands a content. We are, thus, necessarily capable of reducing the Middle Ages to an appropriate content, a fixed meaning in light of the surety of the Renaissance or Classical antiquity, where we invest particular works with what we know to be factual. In this way, scholars like Robertson, Allen, and Nichols can know what a medieval mind can and cannot do. Such views of the Middle Ages, however, define the agent of invention subjectively as the cause of production—whether literary, technological, or even philosophical—in terms of an a priori, essentialized consciousness, a medieval mind that is an effect of the Middle Ages. Rather than seeing or representing this consciousness as a limit in itself, a representation or effect of representation, the new medievalism, like its precursors, begins with a vision of the human *auctor* as a primary causal agency, an actual and actualized subject, placing a twentieth-century Romantic notion of a wholly defined subject over a radically different subject of invention.

In this regard, medieval thinkers are ahead of the medievalist in that they rigorously consider questions of causality. The invented subject of other medievalisms places the human *auctor* in the position of primary efficient cause, to use the Aristotelian concept redefined by medieval scholastics, subject only to itself. This position severs investigations of the Middle Ages from medieval cosmological theory that posits invention in terms of an instrumental agency, a subject of invention, that is fundamentally opposed to an independent human consciousness. By not examining medieval theories of invention, the New Medievalism is again left with attempting to find the truth of the Middle Ages as a content, as a correct history or philology, that will, in the end, mythically construct a Middle Ages in the face of its inherent absence.

The (Im)Possible Subject of Invention

At some level, Medieval theorists themselves already anticipated the circularity of the final position of Robertson and Patterson and Leicester, as can be seen in the theoretical writings of poets and theologians who show an understanding of subjectivity as that which negates the automaton, the idea of one who is solely the product of an absolute symbolic chain. Unlike modern theorists, medieval thinkers from Augustine and Boethius onward reconcile neo-Platonic cosmology with a religion that acknowledges a presence of the divine within a human form. This undertaking is even further problematized in the late twelfth century by the scholastic project of harmonizing a neo-Platonic Christianity with an Aristotelian understanding of the natural world, which forced theologians to reexamine their understanding of human agency. In addition, this reconciliation of neo-Platonism with Aristotle is still governed by the place of priority given to biblical knowledge as supreme, placing the medieval cosmologist in a uniquely problematic position of defining the world through three, often contradictory theoretical positions: neo-Platonism, Aristotle, and the Bible.

Thus medieval theory focuses on the ontological status of the human differently from current philosophical or philological questioning. The neo-Platonic basis of early Christianity ensured that causality and its relation to creation and invention would always be a consideration, since the cause of being and the hierarchy of emanations were always in question at the level of defining the system, at the level of the One/God who is fundamentally unknowable. Even with the Aristotelian concept of nature as offering an observable link to truth, the neo-Platonic situating of nature within a celestial hierarchy remained.[5] The influence of the Pseudo-Dionysus on medieval conjugations of Aristotelian and neo-Platonic cosmology ensured that representation would always be linked to ontology, since being and the natural world were placed as an inadequate representation of the divine. Thus the human was not simply something locatable in a closed world as equal to nature (or history or genetics), but involved the possibility of transcendence—a transcendence, I argue, through *inventio*.

A medieval understanding of the human subject requires a reference to something outside nature as a symbolic network, as seen in John of Salisbury's *Metalogicon*, which situates the human in terms of the assimilation of this something outside into language. John of Salisbury defines this ability to assimilate in terms of reason as "the power of the soul which examines and investigates things that make an impression on the senses or intellect. A dependable judge of better things, reason has, after estimating similarities and differences, finally established art, to be, as it were, a circumscribed science of unlimited things" (35). For John of Salisbury, that which defines the human, the soul, is not the same as nature, but, rather, is that which allows nature to be perceived, to be divided into genus and species. This scientific enterprise, the circumscription of that which is unlimited, is characteristic of much medieval investigation, since human knowledge is consistently placed as a limit on the limitless. In Book II of *The Metalogicon*, John of Salisbury offers a further elaboration of human knowledge in relation to the limits of real knowledge:

> In fact [our] cognition, in apprehending something, circumscribes and defines the latter for itself by a certain [comprehensive] capacity of the mind, so that if a thing presents itself to the mind as absolutely unlimited in every respect, neither primary nor secondary cognition can proceed. All knowledge or cognition possessed by creatures is limited. Infinite knowledge belongs solely to God, because of His infinite nature. . . . But we are imprisoned within the petty dimensions of our human capacity, wherefore we attain neither primary, nor secondary, nor tertiary, nor any distinction of knowledge of what is infinite, save the realization that it is unknown because it is infinite. Accordingly, all demonstrative and relative expressions must refer to a specific, definite

> subject if they are correctly posited. Otherwise they will miss
> their mark. For cognition naturally seeks or possesses certi-
> tude as its object. (127)

And cognition is by definition a limit in relation to the unknowable, infinite dimensions of real knowledge. John of Salisbury's attack on the "Cornificians" ultimately resides in what he sees as a scientific method turned in on itself, where
one ceases to circumscribe unlimited things in favor of the limit itself. Such a
Cornifician understanding of knowledge places certitude in line with truth, a
move that John of Salisbury implicitly attacks. As John of Salisbury emphasizes,
certitude is the limit of knowledge, not knowledge itself; the only true knowledge resides in the infinite that is precisely foreclosed by such certitude. This
move places the human at a point of necessary misperception, since we cannot
see or know by any means the infinite that grounds all knowledge, thus positing
a subject that is based on a fundamental misprision, a *méconnaisance*.

    An examination of medieval poetics leads us to a similar understanding of
the human subject, an understanding that is difficult to examine since it is
antithetical to the contemporary myth of the subject as autonomous self, as
the automaton. Since medieval theories of agency trace an unknowable cause
through effects that can only be defined relative to a limit, it is perhaps most
useful to examine such causality structurally. Lacan offers a theoretical model
for such a reading of medieval cosmology, since it alone among contemporary
theories establishes the subject as both effect and cause, where cosmology is
defined topologically and where certainty also relies on falsity. Lacan's own
work on subjectivity, with its clinical basis and application, provides an insight
into questions of epistemology and ontology that were important to medieval
thinkers but that are often of less interest to medievalists working within purely
historical or even materialist traditions. By offering an understanding of medieval poetics through medieval texts that both theorize and utilize the concept of
inventio, we can then see how medieval theorists and poets offer a way into a
Lacanian understanding of subjectivity—in essence, medieval thinkers are
working with the same questions of agency as psychoanalysis.

    Unlike contemporary science, or contemporary literary criticism for that
matter, which prevents questions of causality, medieval hermeneutics replaced
the effect with the cause, incessantly focusing on fundamental questions of the
relationship between the material that is invented and the cause of the invention, since there is an obvious relation between creation and the production of

knowledge, where all knowledge functions as an effect of a cosmology that places God as its metaphysical guarantee.[6] In this way the circularity between effect as cause and effect as effect is ruptured, leaving knowledge of God, of the unknowable, as a precipice at which all medieval critics eventually find themselves. It is this precipice that Descartes will eventually imagine away with his *Cogito.*[7]

Such a religious subject is defined by Lacan in terms of a relation between truth and cause: "The religious person leaves responsibility for the cause to God, but thereby bars his own access to truth" ("Science and Truth" 20). By eliding truth and cause into one inaccessible structure, God, the religious subject defies all questions of causality. Paradoxically, medieval theories of causality are precisely not religious. Although medieval thinkers are aware of the inaccessibility of God qua cause qua truth, the existence of the Bible as real text consistently prevents the simple dismissal of questions about the divine as unpursuable. Rather, the intricacies of biblical hermeneutics guaranteed that such a dismissal could never take place as long as Nature and the Bible were not separated as the means of access to truth.

Since the "book of the world" and the book containing the Word of God both provide avenues to God, both form ways of investigating truth. R. W. Southern makes this point, although with a different conclusion, when he suggests that humanism begins because of the mysterious nature of the Bible as text and as Word of God (29–60). This position is evident even in Augustine when he acknowledges the possibility of "knowing" God even without access to biblical texts.[8] Thus if the medieval notion of the subject was truly a religious one, as I would argue Descartes's is, the relation between the world and God qua truth would be severed; one would not be able to learn of God by observing His creation.

Hugh of St. Victor, for example, clearly subordinates the natural world to God and offers a rationale for exploring nature, since one may learn of God through His creations. Hugh clearly posits the investigation of nature in search of God as the function of philosophy in his *Epitome:*

> Philosophy rightly spends every effort on three things. The
> first is the investigation of man; this is necessary that man
> may know himself and recognize that he has been created.
> Next, when he has begun to know himself, let him investi-
> gate what that is by which he was made. Last, let him, as his

practice, begin to meditate on the marvelous works of his
Maker, so that he may equally understand what it is that was
made with him and for his sake. By this triple way the search
for Wisdom runs toward its end. The end of all philosophy
is apprehension of the highest Good, which lies in the
Maker of all things alone.[9]

Since all objects of investigation lead one to "the Maker," the cause, the
truth, and the word, Hugh and his contemporaries are constantly negotiating
with systems that they know must break down the closer they get to God. Their
awareness and further pursuit of the structure of such ruptures in the symbolic
world place them in a position of alienation that prevents the foreclosure that
critics like Robertson and Allen require.

Thomas Aquinas also pursues the necessary ruptures in knowledge in
terms of an ontological problem. As Marcia Colish demonstrates, misreadings
of Thomist epistemology and sign theory have consistently ignored the necessary theological foundations of his philosophy: "In the process of formulating
signs, in the judgment of truth, and in the acquisition of scientific knowledge of
nature through signs, human concepts are further bounded for Thomas by the
fact that both the knower and the world he knows are dependent on God. God
operates in the human intellect, since He is the source of all intellectual power.
Man is part of the creation; he owes everything he has to God. The natural light
of his mind is given to him and sustained in him by God" (178–79). This divine foundation of human intellect, and therefore human epistemology, offers
an ontological emphasis to knowing that extends throughout medieval theology, finding its roots in Augustine's sign theory.[10] Medieval scholastics posit the
human not as a creator of knowledge, but as an instrument to the unknowable
nature of God, a subject of or by an infinite and thus unknowable knowledge.

Perhaps most important to an antifoundational poetic or hermeneutic,
medieval studies of the construction of texts—secular and religious—also exhibit this same concern with the relationship between instrumentality and
absence. Like these theological and cosmological theories of knowledge, medieval poetic and rhetorical investigations also uncover a structural theory of the
subject as instrumental to creation rather than a romantic notion of poetic
creator. This notion is integral to the way literature was perceived within
scholasticism, where there is no imaginary tautology of creation residing in the
human *auctor.* For theologians attempting to define truth in fiction, poetic texts

offer real theoretical problems, especially those texts that form the basis of Western philosophical and poetic values, such as Virgil and Horace. Considerations of nonscriptural texts form the basis of many theological debates over the relation between truth and the structure of fiction from the early twelfth century through the fourteenth, culminating with examinations of Dante.[11] What is at issue concerns whether pagan texts can instruct Christians, whether these texts have a value relative to a truth that stems from God. Conrad of Hirsau, in his *Dialogue on the Authors,* offers a rationale for the study of secular, non-Christian authors as a means of beginning a study that will eventually culminate in reading Scripture:

> I will bow to your persistence and tell you what I can, considering the way in which the nourishing milk you draw from the poets may provide you with an opportunity for taking solid food in the form of more serious reading. Indeed, seekers after wisdom should regard secular knowledge in such a light that, if they find in it, in its words and ideas, any steps on the ladder of their common progress from which the higher wisdom may be grasped more firmly, these should not be altogether scorned, but the mind exercised on them for just as long as it takes to find what one seeks through the medium of secular knowledge.[12]

This position is taken a step further by those advocating the reading of secular, non-Christian texts as offering moral instruction through allegory. The commentary on the *Aeneid* thought to be by Bernard Silvester makes this claim: "So the reader derives a twofold benefit from this work. The first is skill in writing acquired by imitation. The second is the knowledge of how to act properly, acquired from the exhortation imparted to us by the examples."[13] Although not consistently, the poetic generally is acknowledged also to contain truth—even if such truth is only something to be used as opposed to enjoyed in itself—offering, at the very least, a means toward further reflection on the divine truth of Scripture.[14] Thus, in order to place even nonscriptural authority into a system of *auctoritas,* scholastic theory also acknowledges a truth value in relation to secular, even non-Christian, works by defining the *auctor* in instrumental terms, placing the human also into question within the invention of secular, poetic texts.

   The scholastic enterprise theorizes the human in similar terms within the
poetic, theological, philosophical, and rhetorical writings that defined and
grappled with what on the surface was an incoherent world. The project of
medieval scholasticism clearly shows how differing works become interrelated
through a philosophical-theological understanding of cosmology, where, like
Scripture, the natural world qua effect provides an avenue to explore the unknowable, infinite knowledge of God. Within the school of Hugh of St. Victor,
we see a continuation of the notion that the universe is an observable effect of
God and, therefore, a means of understanding God.[15] The project of the
medieval scholastics is to systematize knowledge as effect in order to trace cause,
which is God. This tracing of knowledge as effect offers a structural examination of God, reflecting an ontology that is fundamentally connected to knowledge defined as *auctoritas*. We can even see such an ontological methodology in
medieval invocations of *auctoritas,* where medieval thinkers interpret earlier
material, from church figures like Augustine and Pseudo-Dionysus to Arabic
redactions of Aristotle, as a means not only to create their own authority
rhetorically, but also to constitute the unknowable within knowledge, placing
cause retroactively in their precursors.[16] This epistemology implicitly acknowledges scholasticism's explicit theorizations of the human self as an instrumental
agency, best elaborated in the use of Aristotle's four causes and in rhetorical
investigations of invention. Medieval theorists and poets place God in the
position of primary cause. Such a relegation places the human in a precarious
position, especially from a contemporary critical perspective. It is this vision of
"the medieval worldview" that prompts Robertson and Allen to place the
medieval poetic act at a far remove from contemporary poetic acts. But a closer
investigation of this world shows a much more structural understanding of the
human subject as an instrumental agency, an agency that does not simply
correspond to an extension of the Creator but exists in dialectical intersection
between creator and created.

   When confronted with problems of biblical exegesis, especially surrounding the Song of Songs, the medieval commentator is struck by a contradiction:
how could man and God write the Bible—where does the efficient cause of
biblical composition reside? The medieval exegete solved this puzzle by placing
man at the level of instrument to God's own hand; man is God's pen. In his
commentary on the Psalter, Nicholas of Lyre theorizes the prophetic relationship between God and David in composing the Psalms:

> The efficient cause can be subdivided in two, namely the
> principal cause and the instrumental cause. The principal
> cause is God Himself, who reveals the mysteries described
> in this book. The instrumental cause is David. . . . Now,
> this twofold efficient cause . . . is referred to by the word
> "prophet." For two factors come together to bring about the
> act of prophecy: God, who touches the mind of the prophet,
> or raises it to the comprehension of divine knowledge, and
> the mind of the prophet, which is thus touched or illu-
> minated. For the action of the motivating force [that is,
> God] and the reaction of the thing moved by it must be
> simultaneous.[17]

The prophetic act, later expanded to include the poetic act, thus becomes an effect of something beyond the human will, beyond intention.[18] More impor- tantly, this simultaneity between "the motivating force" and "the reaction of the thing moved" defines a relation between man and God, between the subject and the Other, that necessarily exists only in a temporal structure, in time. Such a structural reading of this relation places knowledge and being at the center of invention and thus offers an avenue for rhetorical investigations of causality.

This structural relation between *auctor* and God is explicitly examined in medieval rhetoric in terms of *inventio,* where invention offers an illustration of subjectivity that is reliant on a relation with language, within a temporal struc- ture which, as I will show, defines a subject as inherently split by language— where there must be something a priori to human consciousness that defines the poetic as prophetic. In rhetorical investigations of invention lies the same question of agency, of subjectivity, that implicitly defines all aspects of medieval theory: what is the human and where does it reside? Like the theological and hermeneutic texts, rhetorical texts examine agency in terms of *auctoritas,* where a given invention is the product of a knowledge that exceeds the *auctor.*

As Douglas Kelly points out in *The Arts of Poetry and Prose,* poetic inven- tion is made explicit in the treatises, such as Geoffrey of Vinsauf's *Poetria Nova,* that draw on classical rhetorical models where invention is considered as a process of finding that then governs the entire poetic composition, where invention differs from creation.[19] In his opening remarks to the *Poetria,* Geof- frey begins by comparing the writing of poetry with the construction of a building: "The mind's hand shapes the entire house before the body's hand

builds it. Its mode of being is archetypal before it is actual" (17). By defining the
mode of production as archetypal, Geoffrey traces the material of invention in
terms of *auctoritas,* a preexisting, established system of knowledge. The agency
that works with such knowledge is further defined in terms of that knowledge:
"The material to be molded, like the molding of wax, is at first hard to the
touch. If intense concentration enkindle native ability, the material is soon
made pliant by the mind's fire, and submits to the hand in whatever way it
requires, malleable to any form. The hand of the mind controls it, either to
amplify or curtail" (23–24). This hand is an instrument to the knowledge, the
auctoritas, that is the material of invention and that comes before and after in a
temporal, retroactive relation. This reading of Vinsauf places his understanding in the larger context of medieval theory, where agency is not placed in the
human *auctor.*

Kelly interprets Geoffrey's point in terms of imagination, focusing on a
poetics of metaphor. He states: "In poetry, *imaginatio* pointed to an ineffable
reality lying beyond the reach of the sense, and made possible 'the discovery
and, as it were, the personification of natural forces and processes' through
representations formed in the mind according to what the mind could know of
them" (*Medieval Imagination* 28). Here Kelly emphasizes a rational agency of
invention that resides in the *auctor,* placing the foundations of *inventio* in an
entirely conscious and independent agency. He interprets Geoffrey's explicitly
practical rhetoric in terms of a rational epistemology separate from its cosmological dimension, where being precedes the material of metaphor. In this
way, Kelly separates the process of epistemology (metaphor structuring knowledge) from ontology (being as effect of metaphor). He concludes that "the
Imaginative process is thus the use of metaphor to make incorporeal and
abstract sentiments and qualities visible and thus comprehensible," stressing
that the agency of this act resides prior to such a making in the *auctor* (34).
Kelly clearly shows how the object of metaphor is ineffable, but he uses a
nonmedieval ontology to ground his reading, thereby missing the implications
of the poetic as effect where the subject is an effect of metaphor, instrumental as
opposed to causal.

Alexandre Leupin approaches closer to the question of poetic as effect
when he attempts to examine that which underlies Vinsauf's notion of invention as metaphor. He concludes that "the *Poetria* . . . theorizes the act of
writing as a constant and endless transformation of the obsolete, a perpetual
relaunching of the old. . . . Art is understood as the perpetual transcendence of

unpolished matter; and this unpolished matter is viewed as the first element of a comparative function in which the comparing term is always superior to the compared" (125). Leupin implies that the compared term, that which shows up as the product of invention, is caused by the comparing term, placing first cause before the human *auctor*. But he does not consider Kelly's point about the ineffability of such a comparing term, where that which precedes metaphor is inaccessible except through metaphor. So whereas Leupin does define agency in terms of effect, his theory of the subject implies an essential component that is incarnated as real, missing the significance of the material with which invention works, that which precedes any manipulation of material.

Medieval theoretical writings thus show two main components to the structure of epistemology and ontology. First, the primary agency of invention, the efficient cause, is ineffable, infinite, and thus unknowable. In this way, being relies on a first cause that cannot be reduced to a content. Second, the subject who invents is invented within the transmission of *auctoritas* grounded by an unknowable agency, within time. Medieval theories of the material of invention are intimately linked with medieval theories of metaphor, especially those based on Augustinian sign theory and Pseudo-Dionysian negative theology. In both systems, metaphors function to illustrate the limits of the sign as a means of representation, to show that the sign is inadequate to represent God: for Augustine, God is the thing to be enjoyed that is not representable semiotically. Similarly, Pseudo-Dionysus cautions against the use of "positive" imagery to describe God: one might confuse the representation with the unknowable nature of God. Thus God should not be described as a king, since some might fall into conceiving him literally as such. All knowledge of a real foundation to agency can be expressed only negatively or by a positivized absence.

Such structurings of the subject in terms of knowable or unknowable and secondary or primary agency present a medieval route into an antifoundational theory of the subject. Unlike the traditional epistemological approach—where knowledge is unknowingly intertwined with being—this new Middle Ages allows for a tracing of causality and thus presents a means of considering how we might proceed to consider the structure of antifoundationalism. This new, antifoundational Middle Ages places foundational theories of the Middle Ages in a similar position to Lacan's theorization of the Woman qua beloved, where love is an effect of an absence, a castration, in the subject-object relation.[20] The Woman, like the Middle Ages, does not exist as essential, as a one that could or would define a relation. In this sense, one might equally say that Man does not exist or, in other words, that there is no sexual rapport. Both the Middle Ages and the Woman reflect the same structure as discourse: both are the objects of certainty for those who are passionate about their knowledge. Thus contemporary medieval studies has something in common with Chaucer's "Clerk's Tale," in which Walter must know Griselda qua Woman. Both of these epistemological positions define a masculine subject, both identify the stabilizing element as the Other—the Woman or the Middle Ages—that defines sexual identity or History as a set of two that produces a One, or a continuum in historical terms. In the end, Walter holds the position of an invented subject, where he is totalized, a fictionalized whole whose jouissance as consistency is substantiated in his final investment in Griselda; the tale concludes when he *knows* Griselda, a moment when he jumps from infinity to zero. But before this substantiation, Walter is subject to what Griselda is not; before *being* at rest ("in reste"), Walter demonstrates an instrumental relation to Griselda that shows the fictionality of his final position. Thus we see the momentary rest of the substantiation of Woman qua known. Medieval scholarship as an academic discourse likewise seeks rest, continually pronouncing the known of the Middle Ages.

The rapport qua continuum generated by medieval scholarship shows the true epistemological structure of the Middle Ages as Woman, as that which drives scholarship that is, unlike Walter, never at rest. In this way, the Middle Ages teaches us something about the medieval, but not as a historical period or as a methodology to interpret medieval texts. Rather, the Middle Ages traces how what we know about what we know defines an ontological structuralism, a topology of knowing, that is not simply a foundational answer, precisely not a religious or a satisfactory ending. Instead, the Middle Ages offers a critique to contemporary notions of alterity—functioning as discourse that is satisfied not at the level of having but at the level of the "want to be," not at the level of knowing but at the level of the becoming-in-knowing.

Notes

1. See especially H. Marshall Leicester, *The Disenchanted Self: Representing the Subject in the Canterbury Tales;* Carolyn Dinshaw, *Chaucer's Sexual Poetics;* and Lee Patterson, *Chaucer and the Subject of History.*

2. See Mikhail Bakhtin, *The Dialogic Imagination;* idem, *Rabelais and His World;* and idem, *Problems of Dostoevsky's Poetics.*

3. For a discussion of the relation between the master signifier (S_1) and knowledge (S_2) in terms of discourse structures, see Jacques Lacan, "A Jakobson," in *Le Seminaire de Jacques Lacan* (19–26).

4. For Lacan's discussion of metaphor and metonymy, and their relationship to being, meaning, and knowledge, see "The Agency of the Letter in the Unconscious" (156).

5. See the assorted commentaries on Pseudo-Dionysus, particularly Thomas Gallus in Minnis and Scott, *Medieval Literary Theory and Criticism* (173–92).

6. For a discussion of the ontological basis of medieval epistemology, see Marcia L. Colish, *The Mirror of Language: A Study of the Medieval Theory of Knowledge*. In her introduction Colish defines her study of epistemology in terms of its cosmological basis: "And, notwithstanding the scholastic demand for a theory of cognition explaining man's knowledge of the world of nature, the object to which medieval thinkers normally addressed themselves was the world of spiritual reality, with preeminent attention to God. The medieval theory of knowledge was a direct consequence of this radically ontological emphasis. Epistemology was conceived as a function of metaphysics. The existence of an objective order of being was the primary condition which was held to make human thought possible at all" (1).

7. For a discussion of this move by Descartes, see Ellie Ragland-Sullivan, *Jacques Lacan and the Philosophy of Psychoanalysis* (7–16).

8. In *On Christian Doctrine,* Augustine states: "Thus a man supported by faith, hope and charity, with an unshaken hold upon them, does not need the scriptures except for the instructions of others" (32); "But we should not think we ought not to learn literature because Mercury is said to be its inventor, nor that because the pagans dedicated temples to Justice and Virtue and adored in stones what should be performed in the heart, we should therefore avoid justice and virtue. Rather, every good and true Christian should understand that wherever he may find truth, it is his Lord's" (54).

9. Roger Baron, ed., "Hugonis de Sancto Victore Epitome Dindimi in philosophiam: introduction, texte critique et note," *Trad.* XI (1955), 107; cited and translated by Jerome Taylor in his *Didascalicon of Hugh of St. Victor* (177).

10. See Book II of *On Christian Doctrine,* especially 34–37.

11. Minnis and Scott's *Medieval Literary Theory and Criticism* traces these considerations of truth in Scripture and poetic texts.

12. Conrad of Hirsau, "*Dialogue on the Authors:* Extracts," in Minnis and Scott's *Medieval Literary Theory and Criticism* (54).

13. Bernard Silvester, "Commentary on the *Aeneid,* Books I–VI," in Minnis and Scott, *Medieval Literary Theory and Criticism* (150–54).

14. This view also finds its beginnings in Augustine, *On Christine Doctrine;* see especially Book II.

15. See R. W. Southern, *Medieval Humanism and Other Studies.*

16. For a discussion of the construction and use of *auctoritas* in the twelfth to fourteenth centuries, see A. J. Minnis, *Medieval Theory of Authorship.* Minnis focuses primarily on the *accessus* tradition, but includes discussion on how this tradition is founded on a constant (re)construction of *auctoritas.* See also Rita Copeland, *Rhetoric, Hermeneutics and Translation in the Middle Ages* (Cambridge: Cambridge University Press, 1991); Copeland notes structural similarities in Grammar and Rhetoric with regard to invention as an enterprise in translation and rhetorical invention.

17. Nicholas of Lyre, "Literal Postill on the Bible: Extracts from the General and Special Prologues, and from the Commentary on the Psalter," in Minnis and Scott, *Medieval Literary Theory and Criticism* (271–72); translated from *Biblia sacra cum Glossa ordinaria et Postilla Nicolai Lyrani* (Lyon, 1589), i, unfol., iii, 415–16, 433–34.

18. See "Chapter VI: Scriptural Science and Signification," in Minnis and Scott, *Medieval Literary Theory and Criticism;* of particular significance is the selection from *S. Bonaventurea opea omnia* commenting on Peter Lombard's *Sentences.*

19. See especially Kelly's discussion of invention in terms of a material relation between God, Nature, and author (*Arts of Poetry* 66–68).

20. See Lacan, "God and the Jouissance of Woman" (138–48).

Works Cited

Allen, Judson Boyce. *The Ethical Poetic of the Later Middle Ages: A Decorum of Convenient Distinction.* Toronto: Toronto University Press, 1982.

Augustine. *On Christian Doctrine.* Trans. D. W. Robertson. New York: Macmillan, 1958.

Bakhtin, Mikhail. *The Dialogic Imagination.* Ed. Michael Holquist. Trans. Caryl Emerson and Michael Holquist. Austin: University of Texas Press, 1981.

——. *Problems of Dostoevsky's Poetics.* Trans. Caryl Emerson. Minneapolis: University of Minnesota Press, 1984.

——. *Rabelais and His World.* Trans. Hélène Iswolsky. Bloomington: Indiana University Press, 1984.

Cantor, Norman. *Inventing the Middle Ages: The Lives, Works, and Ideas of the Great Medievalists of the Twentieth Century.* New York: William Morrow, 1991.

Colish, Marcia L. *The Mirror of Language: A Study of the Medieval Theory of Knowledge.* New Haven: Yale University Press, 1968.

Dinshaw, Carolyn. *Chaucer's Sexual Poetics.* Madison: University of Wisconsin Press, 1989.

Geoffrey of Vinsauf. *Poetria Nova.* Trans. Margaret Nims. Toronto: Pontifical Institute of Mediaeval Studies, 1967.

John of Salisbury. *The Metalogicon.* Trans. Daniel D. McGary. Gloucester: Peter Smith, 1971.

Kelly, Douglas. *The Arts of Poetry and Prose.* Turnhout, Belgium: Brepols, 1991.

——. *The Medieval Imagination: Rhetoric and the Poetry of Courtly Love.* Madison: University of Wisconsin Press, 1978.

Lacan, Jacques. "The Agency of the Letter in the Unconscious or Reason since Freud." *Ecrits: A Selection.* Trans. Alan Sheridan. New York: Norton, 1977: 146–78.

——. "God and the Jouissance of Woman." *Feminine Sexuality.* Ed. Juliet Mitchell and Jacqueline Rose. Trans. Jacqueline Rose. New York: Norton, 1982: 138–48.

——. "Science and Truth." *Newsletter of the Freudian Field* 3.1–2 (1989): 4–29.

——. *Le Seminaire de Jacques Lacan, Livre XX (1972–73): Encore.* Text established by Jacques-Alain Miller. Paris: Editions du Seuil, 1975.

Leicester, H. Marshall. *The Disenchanted Self: Representing the Subject in the Canterbury Tales.* Berkeley: University of California Press, 1990.

Leupin, Alexandre. "Absolute Reflexivity: Geoffroi de Vinsauf." *Medieval Texts and Contemporary Readers*. Ed. Laurie Finke and Martin Shichtman. Ithaca: Cornell University Press, 1987: 120–41.

Minnis, A. J. *Medieval Theory of Authorship*. 2d ed. Philadelphia: University of Pennsylvania Press, 1988.

Minnis, A. J., and A. B. Scott. *Medieval Literary Theory and Criticism c. 1100–c. 1375: The Commentary Tradition*. Rev. ed. Oxford: Oxford University Press, 1991.

Nichols, Stephen. "The New Medievalism: Tradition and Discontinuity in Medieval Culture." *The New Medievalism*. Ed. Marina Brownlee, Kevin Brownlee, and Stephen Nichols. Baltimore: Johns Hopkins University Press, 1991: 1–28.

Patterson, Lee. *Chaucer and the Subject of History*. Madison: University of Wisconsin Press, 1991.

——. *Negotiating the Past: The Historical Understanding of Medieval Literature*. Madison: University of Wisconsin Press, 1987.

Ragland-Sullivan, Ellie. *Jacques Lacan and the Philosophy of Psychoanalysis*. Urbana: University of Illinois Press, 1987.

Robertson, D. W. "The Allegorist and the Aesthetician." *Essays in Medieval Culture*. Princeton: Princeton University Press, 1980: 85–104.

——. *A Preface to Chaucer: Studies in Medieval Perspectives*. Princeton: Princeton University Press, 1968.

Southern, R. W. *Medieval Humanism and Other Studies*. Oxford: Basil Blackwell, 1970.

Taylor, Jerome. *The Didascalicon of Hugh of St. Victor*. New York: Columbia University Press, 1961.

Zumthor, Paul. *Speaking of the Middle Ages*. Trans. Sarah White. Lincoln: University of Nebraska Press, 1986.

13
The Royal Road
Marxism and the Philosophy of Science
Michael Sprinker

What is a consequent marxist view of the history and philosophy of science? Reference to Marx's and Engels's (or even Lenin's) work will not yield a satisfactory answer, although certain signposts are evident. For example, there is the famous observation on method in the introduction to the *Grundrisse,* which argues that, contrary to the procedures adopted in classical economy, where the starting point for investigation is apparently concrete phenomena from which abstract theoretical descriptions are then derived, "the method of rising from the abstract to the concrete is the only way in which thought appropriates the concrete, reproduces it as the concrete in the mind."[1] Or there are Engels's late works, preeminently the *Anti-Dühring* and *Dialectics of Nature,* in which the so-called laws of the dialectic are laid out schematically, and of which it is asserted that they constitute "the science of the general laws of motion and development of nature, human society and thought."[2] Or there is Lenin's critique of positivism in *Materialism and Empirio-Criticism,* on which the later works of Althusser would depend so heavily for their justification of philosophy's role in relation to science.

Postclassical marxism has been remarkably fecund in its treatment of epistemological themes and in elaborating competing versions of the marxist theory of knowledge, emphasizing different passages or moments in Marx's (less often Engels's) corpus to buttress its claims for the authentically marxist character of the theory. Western marxism in particular, from Lukács, Korsch, and Gramsci to Adorno, Della Volpe, Sartre, and Althusser, has richly developed marxist epistemology to the point that, if serious disagreements remain, it is nevertheless possible to assess marxist philosophy of science and, to appropriate a famous metaphor, discover the rational kernel inside the mystical shell.

Such has been the project of Roy Bhaskar over the past decade and a half, although the specifically marxist pedigree of his work has only gradually become evident. (Marxism finds no place in *A Realist Theory of Science,* for example, his first, and still fundamental, book.)[3] It is fully evident in his collection *Reclaiming Reality,* which contains, among other riches, perhaps the finest brief historical and methodological assessment in English of the major issues in marxist philosophy.[4]

What is the task of philosophy of science in Bhaskar's view? It lies, to cite the Lockean metaphor on which Bhaskar has come increasingly to repose, in "underlaboring" on behalf of the sciences. Underlaboring entails clarifying and explicating what it is the sciences do and how they do it, as well as, on occasion, criticizing existing scientific practices for failing to meet the standards of scientificity they set for themselves. Philosophical underlaboring (the proposed title for another collection of essays promised to come; see *Reclaiming* 208 n. 32) thus proposes a philosophy *of* science (what Bhaskar terms "transcendental realism," the strong research program first announced and elaborated in *A Realist Theory of Science*) that is at the same time a philosophy *for* science (what Bhaskar is now willing to call "critical realism"; *Reclaiming* vii, 190). But why should the sciences need a philosophy at all? What is to be gained, in the first instance for science but in the end for humankind generally, from a coherent account of what Rom Harré has called "the principles of scientific thinking"?

Bhaskar justifies his own enterprise as follows:

> The essays collected in this volume all seek to un-
> derlabour—at different levels and in different ways—for
> the sciences, and especially the human sciences, in so far as
> they might illuminate and empower the project of human
> self-emancipation. They attempt, that is to say, for the
> explanatory-emancipatory sciences of today, the kind of
> "clearing" of the ideological ground, which Locke set out to
> achieve for the prodigious infant of seventeenth-century
> mechanics. Such sciences, which only partially and incom-
> pletely exist, will not only interpret but help to change the
> world. But they will do so rationally only on the condition
> that they interpret the world aright. (*Reclaiming* vii)

Or, as he opines some pages later, glossing the eleventh of the *Theses on Fuerbach:* "The world cannot be rationally changed unless it is adequately interpreted" (5). Critical realism is therefore "a necessary but insufficient agency of human emancipation" (191). This, as Bhaskar himself observes, is at one with Marx's conception of the relation between theory and practice, at once vir-

ulently anti-idealist and antivoluntarist (128, 137). Critical realism is therefore
not just an optional attainment for socialists; it undergirds the production of
knowledge that enables their political practice. Why should this be so?

Bhaskar's technical justification for this view is given in chapters 5 and 6 of
Reclaiming Reality (66–114), which reprise the positions of his two earlier
books, *The Possibility of Naturalism* and *Scientific Realism and Human Emancipation*, respectively. But since chapter 8, a long essay on Richard Rorty,
presents a more accessible account, I shall focus on this text.

Bhaskar's choice of Rorty as antagonist is doubly motivated. First, Rorty's
prestige has grown steadily, both in and out of the philosophical community,
ever since the publication of *Philosophy and the Mirror of Nature*. He is now one
of those philosophical figures whose views matter and whose writings, as a
consequence, are ceaselessly criticized, debated, and elaborated in and out of
professional philosophy. Moreover, as Bhaskar observes at the outset, the position Rorty has staked out represents an emergent philosophical orthodoxy—
perhaps best characterized as a "post-empiricist philosophy of science"—that
Bhaskar has ceaselessly criticized over the years.

A second reason for sustained treatment of Rorty is the latter's increasing
preoccupation with the domain marked out by the human sciences. If *Philosophy and the Mirror of Nature* attempted to map the terrain of traditional
epistemology differently, the latter essays in *Consequences of Pragmatism* and
virtually the whole of *Contingency, Irony, and Solidarity* evince Rorty's conviction that what he once termed "edifying philosophy" must cash out its claims in
ethics and, preeminently, politics. As Bernard Williams judiciously put it in his
review of *Contingency, Irony, and Solidarity*, Rorty's aim is "to give liberalism a
better understanding of itself than it has been left by previous philosophy" (5).
The real stakes in Rorty's project are political, although its limitations as political philosophy derive from (in the sense of being consistent with philosophically with) his continuing entanglement in a certain epistemological problematic. Bhaskar summarizes the matter nicely: "It is Rorty's ontology which is
responsible for his failure to sustain an adequate account of agency and a fortiori of freedom as involving inter alia emancipation from real and scientifically
knowable specific constraints rather than merely the poetic redescription of an
already-determined world" (*Reclaiming* 146). In short, Rorty's project disables
the human sciences; hence, in Bhaskar's view, it deprives human beings of a
necessary (if insufficient) instrument by which they might become free.

Bhaskar's critique can be divided into two parts. The first, sections 1–3 in the essay, goes over ground familiar to readers of his previous work, especially *A Realist Theory of Science*. It rehearses themes Bhaskar has emphasized and theses he has urged in the philosophy of science, particularly in the epistemology and ontology of the natural sciences. These themes (the ontic fallacy, the epistemic fallacy, the failure to distinguish between intransitive and transitive objects of knowledge) are replayed in a close explication of Rorty's work (primarily *Philosophy and the Mirror of Nature*). It would be impossible to summarize Bhaskar's argument, so I shall simply cite his conclusion here: "Justifications within science are a social matter—but they require and are given ontological grounds. In failing to recognize this, Rorty has furnished us with a post-epistemological theory of knowledge without justification which matches his account of science without being. The result is just the opposite of what he intended: the epistemologization of being and the incorrigibility (uncriticizability) of what passes for truth" (*Reclaiming* 160). This last charge would certainly surprise Rorty, since his entire effort for nearly two decades has been to show that truth claims are always subject to criticism, or, as he now puts it, to redescription. A passage near the beginning of *Contingency, Irony, and Solidarity* captures the essence of this view:

> To say that truth is not out there is simply to say that where there are no sentences there is no truth, that sentences are elements of human languages, and that human languages are human creations.
>
> Truth cannot be out there—cannot exist independently of the human mind—because sentences cannot so exist, or be out there. The world is out there, but descriptions of the world are not. Only descriptions of the world can be true or false. The world on its own—unaided by the describing activities of human beings—cannot. (5)

On the face of it, this seems a pithy statement of the distinction between transitive and intransitive objects of knowledge—roughly, "sentences" and "the world." In fact, it is not, for reasons Bhaskar makes plain.

Rorty's apparent commitment to a realist ontology is characteristically hidden by his systematically exploiting an ambiguity in his terms. Bhaskar cites the claim made in *Philosophy and the Mirror of Nature* that "physics gives us a good background against which to tell our stories of historical change" and comments thus: "If physics means 'the physical world' as described by [the science of] physics (hereafter physics$_{id}$—or the physical world), then it is true and unparadoxical. If, however, physics means 'the set of descriptions' of the physical world in the science of physics (hereafter physics$_{td}$—or the science of physics), then as a rapidly changing social product it is part of the process of historical change and so cannot form a background to it" (*Reclaiming* 151). *Contingency, Irony, and Solidarity* exhibits a similar ambiguity in the term *cause* that vitiates the axial notion of "creative redescription," on which that book turns (*Reclaiming* 151–52).

Bhaskar's critique shows how Rorty's program in philosophy absolutely requires such terminological ambiguities, for they underwrite his fundamental conviction that an irreducible cleft divides the *Naturwissenschaften* from the *Geisteswissenschaften* (*Reclaiming* 165). This conviction in turn is a consequence of his thoroughgoing empirical actualism coupled with his attachment to the possibility of human freedom. Bhaskar puts the matter well: "The autonomy of the social and other less physicalistic sciences is rendered consistent with a comprehensive empirical actualism by allowing that physics (or the physical sciences) can describe every bit of the phenomenal world but that some bits of it, for instance the human, can also be truly redescribed in a non-physicalist way" (164). This unresolved antinomy—for such it is, and none other than Kant's famous Third to boot, as Bhaskar notices (164)—will come to under-write the celebration of contingency in Rorty's most recent book, which does no more than elaborate on the Sartrean point already made in *Philosophy and the Mirror of Nature:* "Man is always free to choose new descriptions (for, among other things, himself)" (362). Are we?

Yes and no. Patently, there is much about human beings as moral and political—not just physical—beings that they have been bequeathed and that they are not in any obvious position to change or, save in fantasy, redescribe. Workers are exploited under capitalism (and other modes of production); blacks in South Africa and Palestinians in the West Bank and Gaza were historically systematically deprived of civil and political liberties; women every-where continue to be subjected to various forms of social discrimination. None of these groups ameliorates the actuality of its situation just by "creatively redescribing" it in better terms. In fact, it can be shown that such redescriptions characteristically sustain or even worsen the lot of those structurally prevented from exercising personal or collective power. For example, when workers accept the basic conditions of the capital–wage labor relation (along with its attendant juridical legitimation) by labeling it free (if unequal) exchange, they deprive themselves of the capacity to resist wage reductions when profits decline beyond a point capitalists consider acceptable. Or, to take a related instance, while workers may obtain certain short-term material gains by "creatively redescribing" their relation to capital in purely economic (or, put another way, contractual) terms, the long-term tendencies toward instability in the capitalist system turn this description into a Hobson's choice in which workers ultimately remain at the mercy of their employers, having ceded the power to control their fate to people whose interests are objectively opposed to theirs (a lesson the Western European and North American working classes have painfully learned since the 1970s). As Marx pithily observed, the freedom to sell or withhold one's labor power is precisely the freedom to starve in the streets.

Rorty thinks that such freedom to engage in fantasy is productive and must be protected. But there is the rub: how do we get from the plausible idea that human beings are by nature free (if conditionally so) to the state of actual freedom? Rorty's liberal recommendations cannot solve this problem, and not just for narrowly political reasons. Bhaskar shows how Rorty's liberalism is entailed by his ontology, how a flawed politics is underwritten by a wrongheaded philosophical program. Where does Rorty (along with his hero Mill) go wrong?

First, Rorty exempts human beings from any absolute natural constraints like those ascribed to matter in the physical sciences; he does not sufficiently recognize the "*sui generis* reality and causal efficacy of social forms" (*Reclaiming* 174). He cannot do so because he systematically undervalues (or misdescribes) the nature of "objective social structures (from languages to family or kinship systems to economic or state forms), dependent on the reproductive and transformative agency of human beings."[5] Bhaskar goes on to observe:

> These social structures are concept-dependent, but not merely conceptual. Thus a person could not be said to be "unemployed" or "out of work" unless she and the other relevant agents possessed some (not necessarily correct or fully adequate) concept of that condition and were able to give some sort of account of it, namely, to describe (or redescribe) it. But it also involves, for instance, her being physically excluded from certain sites, definite locations in space and time. That is to say, social life always has a material dimension (and leaves some physical trace). (174)

The argument concerns, once again, the inherent limitations on redescription. Rorty's conception of freedom, like Kant's, is merely regulative; such an ideal tells us little if anything about the objective constraints that operate on humankind in society and in nature to make certain actions at best unlikely or at worst impossible.

As a counter to the Rorty-Kant regulative ideal of freedom, Bhaskar proposes the concept of human emancipation, which, he observes, entails

> (1) a stronger sense of being "free," namely as knowing, possessing the power and the disposition to act in or towards one's real interests . . . and
>
> (2) a stronger sense of "liberation," namely as consisting in the transformation of unneeded, unwanted and oppressive to needed, wanted and empowering sources of determination.
>
> Emancipation, that is to say, depends upon the transformation of structures rather than just the amelioration of states of affairs. And it will, at least in the case of self-emancipation, depend in particular upon a conscious transformation in the transformative activity or praxis of the social agents concerned. As such, emancipation is necessarily informed by explanatory social theory. (178)

To be sure, creative redescription will play a role in changing the conditions that render human beings unfree, but it must be strictly dependent on prior explanations of the social structures that ultimately cause unfreedom. To give such explanations is the function of the (emancipatory) human or social sciences, which on this construal are neither methodologically distinct from nor conceptually opposed to but take their place alongside (and contribute to the emancipatory project of—in part by criticizing activity in) the physical sciences. The potential for there to be more Rortean liberal ironists who hold that their descriptions of the world are always contingent—or, better, revisable—thus depends for its realization on a possibly unironic commitment to social theory's truth-value, that is, its real descriptive power. Or, to adapt a famous sentence from Kant, we shall have to embrace reason to preserve poetry.

Near the end of *Reclaiming Reality,* Bhaskar lays at Althusser's feet responsibility for the sins of some of the latter's more prominent British offspring, charging that the French philosopher's "failure to give any apodeictic status to the real object rendered it as theoretically dispensable as a Kantian thing-in-itself and helped to lay the ground for the worst idealist excesses of post-structuralism" (188).[6] The passage refers the reader to a fuller elaboration of this claim in *Scientific Realism and Human Emancipation*, which I consider next. At stake here is not merely the scholastic question of whether or not Bhaskar has gotten Althusser right, though this is far from a trivial matter, given Althusser's importance to contemporary marxism (conceded by Bhaskar; see *Reclaiming* 187). The substantive issue concerns what are licit views in the philosophy of science from a historical materialist standpoint. To anticipate, I shall be arguing that if Bhaskar is perhaps correct to chastise Althusser for undertheorizing the intransitive dimension in knowledge production, it may be said that Bhaskar himself comparatively underplays the ways ideology permeates the transitive dimension, thereby risking charges of metaphysical dogmatism, which, in philosophy's current ideological *Kampfplatz,* is perhaps the greater threat to the realist program.[7] Althusser's "scientific rationalism" (*Reclaiming* 142) is more than matched by Bhaskar's rationalist faith that in philosophy the better argument and in science the superior hypothesis will necessarily carry the day.

Bhaskar criticizes "the British post-Althusserians" (*Scientific Realism* 237) in the midst of a detailed examination of positivism and its continuing legacy in the philosophy of science. He locates twin, symmetrical dangers: rationalism of the Popper-Lakatos sort and empiricism. A corollary of the latter position, he suggests, is the Feyerabend-Bachelard line "that philosophy should have no effect on science," on which view positivism has always depended. A somewhat odd outcome has been this latter's mutation, in the hyperempiricism of Hindess and Hirst, into a classical idealism. But such a development, Bhaskar avers, was the more or less inevitable result of Althusser's having underemphasized "the real object":

> An account that cannot think the necessity for both, and the
> irreducibility of, the concepts of thought and being . . .
> must lapse into idealism where concepts are part of being.
> The origin of these errors is clear. It lies in Althusser's initial
> inadequate theorisation of the concepts of the "real object"
> and the "thought object." His failure to provide an apodeic-
> tic status for, or indeed give any real function to, the former

rendered it as disposable as a Kantian ding-an-sich—a service duly performed, against the continuing materialist letter of Althusser's texts. (*Scientific Realism* 237–38)

Althusser's own commitment to materialist (or, in Bhaskar's terms, transcendental realist) ontology is thus not in doubt; rather, his declension of knowledge production (the infamous Generalities I, II, and III) gives insufficient weight to what he calls "the real concrete" (*concret réel*), as opposed to the "concrete-in-thought" (*concret-de-pensée*). Of the latter Bhaskar writes:

> This does not correspond to the realist distinction between the intransitive and transitive objects of knowledge. For while, for the realist viewing knowledge in the transitive dimension as a process of production, the transitive object of knowledge may be said to correspond to Althusser's Generalities I, the intransitive object of knowledge—what is known in and via this production process—is precisely the real object. It does not follow from the fact that we can only know in knowledge that we can only know knowledge! (or even knowledge of knowledge would be impossible). (*Reclaiming* 188)

First, the transitive dimension is not confined only to Generalities I, but is fully constituted by Generalities II and III. These three are, respectively: the raw materials (observational data, previous hypotheses, ideologies, and so on) on which science works (Generalities I); the existing body of scientific theory that works on the raw materials (Generalities II); and the knowledge (new hypotheses) that is the outcome of this process of knowledge production (Generalities III). The latter then become part of Generalities I and II in the ongoing process of scientific inquiry described so aptly by Bhaskar (see *Reclaiming* 19–20). Second, Althusser is perfectly explicit about knowledge itself (it is always knowledge of things, including the theoretical things that give knowledge of the real), nowhere more than in *Reading Capital:*

> No doubt there is a relation between *thought*-about-the real and this *real,* but it is a relation of *knowledge,* a relation of adequacy or inadequacy of knowledge, not a real relation, meaning by this a relation inscribed in *that real* of which the thought is the (adequate or inadequate) knowledge. This

> knowledge relation between knowledge of the real and the
> real is not a relation *of the real* that is known in this relation-
> ship. The distinction between a relation of knowledge and a
> relation of the real is a fundamental one: if we did not
> respect it we should fall irreversibly into either speculative or
> empiricist idealism.[8]

Nothing in the Althusserian account of knowledge production is at odds either
with Bhaskar's general conception of the transitive dimension or with his commitment to the ontological priority of the relatively enduring real structures or
mechanisms described in scientific laws. If Althusser has comparatively little to
say about the "real-concrete," this is just because he (perhaps wrongly) conceives that to be the exclusive prerogative of the sciences. The real is the object
of scientific discourse; philosophy's task, as we shall see, lies elsewhere.

But Bhaskar has another bone to pick with Althusser, one that follows
naturally enough from what is termed Althusser's "scientific rationalism": "Although opposed to any reduction of philosophy to science or vice-versa, in
maintaining that criteria of scientificity are completely intrinsic to the science
in question, Althusser leaves philosophy (including his own) without any clear
role; in particular, the possibilities of any demarcation criterion between science
and ideology, or critique of the practice of an alleged science, seem ruled out"
(*Reclaiming* 143). Bhaskar is referring here, one presumes, to the self-confessed
theoreticism of the early (circa 1965) Althusser. It is somewhat surprising, then,
that Bhaskar subsequently asserts his preference for the texts of this period over
the transitional *Philosophy and the Spontaneous Philosophy of the Scientists* and
the later texts of *auto-critique*. More surprising still is that Bhaskar had quite
early on, in his essay on Feyerabend and Bachelard (see *Reclaiming* 48), recognized the originality and validity of Althusser's new position in and on philosophy, which was announced programmatically in *Lenin and Philosophy* (*Philosophy* 167–202) but more thoroughly elaborated in his lectures on philosophy
and science. We now turn to these latter works to consider what it means to be a
marxist philosopher of science. That this is no simple task should go without
saying.

It will be recalled that *For Marx* and *Reading Capital* had characterized
philosophy, more specifically marxist philosophy (dialectical materialism), as
"the Theory of Theoretical practice," a definition, Althusser shortly recognized, that proposed "a unilateral and, in consequence, *false* conception of

dialectical materialism" (*Reading* 321). This "false conception" was more than anything else the warrant for the charge of "scientific rationalism," particularly in the relationship it asserted between theoretical work and ideological struggle. This point is made explicit in a text of 1965, "Theory, Theoretical Practice, and Theoretical Formation: Ideology and Ideological Struggle," where Althusser writes:

> It is theoretical formation that governs ideological struggle, that is the theoretical and practical foundation of ideological struggle. In everyday practice, theoretical formation and ideological struggle constantly and necessarily intertwine. One may therefore be tempted to confuse them and mis-judge their difference in principle, as well as their hierarchy. This is why it is necessary, from the theoretical perspective, to insist at once on the *distinction in principle* between *theo-retical formation* and *ideological struggle,* and on the *priority in principle* of *theoretical formation* over ideological struggle. (*Philosophy* 38)

In one sense this is unobjectionable and in fact follows from Lenin's slogan about the relationship between revolutionary theory and revolutionary prac-tice. In another sense, however, it is entirely wrong, for it seals off theory (here historical materialism, but at this stage in Althusser's career philosophy as well) from the domain of empirical confirmation or refutation, which is what ideo-logical struggle can in principle provide. Althusser is admittedly guilty at this period of the "theoreticism" (more properly, speculative idealism) with which he has been charged.

Althusser's altered view, whatever its immediate, local determinations,[9] would be clear by the time he prepared his lectures on philosophy and science. It is present from the outset in his sharp distinction between the procedures of the sciences and those of philosophy (*Philosophy* 77, 81), in his clear stipulation of the relationship between philosophy and ideology (83), in his attribution of a "spontaneous ideology of scientific practice" to scientists (88), and, finally, in his severe delimitation of the task of philosophy, which intervenes in scientific (and other) practice—not to guarantee its scientificity, as had been proposed in the earlier definition of philosophy, but to "remove obstacles" in the path of scientific progress (100). As becomes increasingly evident from the second lecture onward, while Althusser's first definition of philosophy had proposed a philosophy of science (and, correlatively, of the scientificity of philosophy it-self), the new definition of philosophy would be effectively a philosophy *for* science: "Scientists should above all count on their own forces: but *their* forces are not a matter for them alone; a good proportion of these forces exists *elsewhere*—in the world of men, in their labour, their struggles and their ideas. I will add: philosophy—not just any philosophy, not that which exploits the sciences, but that which serves them—plays, or can play, a role here" (112). In other terms, Althusser conceives philosophy's task as underlaboring on behalf of the sciences, particularly the human sciences (89–91).

While these lectures never use the phrase, the conception of philosophy as the class struggle in theory operates throughout them. The very idea of a "Philosophy Course for Scientists," of which Althusser's lectures were to be one segment, is premised on one's recognizing philosophy's stake in the class strug-gle, its necessarily partisan position, and its irreducibility to sheer scientific problem solving. The political-ideological function of philosophy that would come to feature so prominently in many of Althusser's subsequent texts, from *Lenin and Philosophy* (1968) and "Philosophy as a Revolutionary Weapon" (1968) to "Is It Simple to Be a Marxist in Philosophy?" (1975) and "The Transformation of Philosophy," (1976), is mobilized here to show how ide-ologies continue to function within scientific practices and, correlatively, to recruit scientists into the materialist camp. The former claim is generally de-fended in the third lecture and in detail through a close explication of biologist Jacques Monod's inaugural lecture at the Collège de France, included as an appendix in the published text of *Spontaneous Philosophy* (see *Philosophy* 145–65). This latter compares favorably with Bhaskar's critique of positivism as a philosophical ideology (see *Reclaiming* 49–65, and *Scientific Realism* 224–308 for more sustained treatments).

I have been arguing that no significant theoretical differences separate Bhaskar and Althusser. Althusser's early texts presuppose a realist philosophy of science (including the realist ontology on which Bhaskar insists), while his later texts from *Spontaneous Philosophy* onward declare for the task of philosophical underlaboring on behalf of the sciences (especially the human sciences). What, then, distinguishes these two projects to establish a marxist philosophy of science?

Against the grain of much commentary,[10] I insist that Althusser's first major works undertake *in philosophy* but *for science* some of the major tasks specified by his second definition of philosophy. *For Marx* and *Reading Capital*

were principally concerned with reconstructing the bases of historical materialism by criticizing the various ideological deformations that had come to inhabit
its theoretical problematic since the time of Marx. While this may have appeared to many a sterile exercise in marxology (for example, the celebrated
emphasis on the "epistemological break" between the humanist and the scientific Marx), Althusser's aim was plain enough: to distinguish between the scientific and the ideological elements that inhabited (and still inhabit—now more
than ever) marxist theory, and thus to remove obstacles to progress in historical
materialist research.

Bhaskar acknowledges Althusser's novelty and his importance, but repeats
the standard criticism that "while Althusser wishes to insist against sociological
eclecticism that the totality is structured in dominance, his own positive concept of structural causality is never clearly articulated" (*Reclaiming* 143). This
last charge seems peculiar, since so much of *Reading Capital* is devoted to this
concept, either defining it explicitly (see especially 186–89) or establishing its
provenance in Marx as the key to his mature, scientific concept of society.
Nonetheless, Bhaskar puts his finger on a notorious difficulty in Althusser's
reconstruction of historical materialism: to wit, how to conjugate the concept
of overdetermination (and its correlate, the relative autonomy of the super-
structures) with the hypothesis of determination in the last instance by the
economy.

There is no point in dodging the issue: this puzzle was never resolved
conceptually by Althusser. But why would one anticipate that it should be? Two
considerations exempt Althusser from serious culpability on this count. First, as
Althusser was wont to insist, he was only a philosopher. Clarification of concepts does lie within philosophy's domain, but it is no charge of this discipline,
whether one conceives it as "Theory of Theoretical practice" or as "class struggle in theory," to specify in advance of empirical research what the full reach of
scientific concepts will be. The second reason derives from the peculiarity of the
term *structure* itself as it functions in the empirical science in question: historical materialism. While the word is the same one used to designate the enduring
mechanisms that give shape and order to nature, the concept as deployed in the
social sciences is, as Bhaskar has tirelessly insisted, entirely different: "Society,
then, is an articulated ensemble of tendencies and powers which, unlike natural
ones, exist only as long as they (or at least some of them) are being exercised; are
exercised in the last instance via the intentional activity of human beings;
and are not necessarily space-time invariant" (*Reclaiming* 79). This is to say,

particularly in light of the last clause, that the only means to specify the concept
of structural causality is just to do scientific work on given social formations.[11]

The Althusserian reprise of this line of argument runs as follows. All
societies are structured by modes of production "visible only in their effects";
the determination of the structure by its effects, that is, the hierarchy of the
material practices (canonically, the economic, the political, and the ideological), will vary not only from one mode of production to another but from social
formation to social formation. This being so, structural causality can have no
other theoretical significance than to distinguish the marxist concept of society's mode of existence from its empiricist and holistic historicist roots: its
further specification is an entirely empirical matter. As Althusser observes, "Just
as there is no production in general, there is no history in general, but only
specific structures of historicity which, since they are merely the existence of
determinate social formations (arising from specific modes of production),
articulated as social wholes, have no meaning except as a function of the essence
of those totalities, i.e., of the essence of their peculiar complexity" (*Reading*
108–9). Structural causality is a thoroughly realist concept; it licenses no more
(but also no less) far-reaching conclusions for historical materialism than those
indicated by Althusser here.

At the outset of the previous section, I claimed that while one could
provisionally grant Bhaskar's charge that Althusser had undertheorized the
intransitive dimension of science, the opposite defect results from Bhaskar's
own comparative slighting of certain aspects of the specific mechanisms operative in the transitive dimension. I have argued that Althusser's reconstruction of
historical materialism aimed at just the sort of philosophical underlaboring on
behalf of the human sciences Bhaskar has recognized to be among the most
urgent of philosophy's current tasks, and, further, that Althusser's reticence in
developing the concept of structural causality prudently observes the limits of
philosophical discourse in relation to the empirical sciences. On the face of it,
nothing in the Bhaskar corpus to date can rival the contribution to a specific,
existing scientific practice of Althusser's labors on behalf of historical materialism. Bhaskar's philosophy of science is, in marxist terms, beyond reproach. His
underlaboring for science, however, has thus far been confined largely to various interventions against positivism and (more limitedly) relativism or absolute
historicism; furthermore, his critique has been conducted on almost exclusively
intraphilosophical terrain (in other words, it has been aimed at philosophers of

science, not scientific researchers themselves). There are other and arguably more direct means for carrying on the class struggle in theory.

Two recent studies exemplify such interventions from opposite ends of the theoretical spectrum: Andrew Collier's *Scientific Realism and Socialist Thought* and Stanley Aronowitz's *Science as Power*. Collier's excellent, tough-minded little book attempts, among other things, to conjugate the works of Althusser and Bhaskar, as I have done here. In his view, the latter is a necessary corrective to the errors of the former: "But Bhaskar's results have the advantage of being more determinate than Althusser's. . . . It is clearer what Bhaskar's conclusions 'permit' and 'forbid' (as Popper would say), and also what it is about the practice of science that compels these conclusions. And this is not a matter of clarity of expression, but of a different practice of philosophy" (x). Agreed. But the demur that quickly follows—"However, I am less sanguine than Roy Bhaskar about the prospects of scientific knowledge in the human world"— suggests why Althusser's "different practice of philosophy" may be necessary to correct Bhaskar's incipient rationalism in the transitive dimension.

For example, Collier indicts Althusser for the "fallacy of *misplaced concreteness,*" by which he means Althusser "thinks that we can distinguish separate *practices* as ideological or scientific, rather than separate *aspects* of the same practice" (27–28). This claim patently ignores the import of Althusser's redefinition of philosophy after 1966, setting aside the whole of *Spontaneous Philosophy* and its examination of the intertwined aspects of ideology and science in scientific practice. The Althusserian concept of the "spontaneous ideology of scientists" gives explicit warrant for such statements by Collier as the following: "A given practice may produce science *and* ideology . . . in that it may simultaneously bring into the world objective scientific knowledge and theoretical ideology that stands in the way of science and perpetuates class rule" (29). In Althusser's currently available corpus, the principal examples of how this intermixing of science and ideology can occur are: historical materialism itself, psychoanalysis, and the work of Jacques Monod. As an eminent American sage once observed, you can look it up.

Collier's main achievement, however, does not lie in textual exegesis, either of Althusser or of Bhaskar; nor does it lie in realizing a new conception of marxist philosophy of science. It consists, rather, in cashing out the realist program in relation to scientific socialism. The disrepute into which the latter term has fallen may on the face of it make his project appear quixotic, but Collier is quite persuasive in showing how no other form of socialist thought (utopian, anar-

chist, or reformist), much less various strands of liberalism, can deal adequately
with the constraints on social transformation capitalism imposes. He conceives
social theory as distinct from the sciences proper, dubbing the former an "epis-
temoid," a theoretical discipline inextricably intertwined with a social practice
(126–53). This conception of social theory gives full weight to the ceteris
paribus clauses that Bhaskar recognizes must be inserted into the equation

$$\text{knowledge} \rightarrow \text{transforming action}$$

but that he typically underplays in his own practice of philosophy. As Collier
wryly remarks after lucidly presenting the broad constraints operating against
social reproduction: "A philosophical book is not the place to argue that this or
that constraint on social reproduction exists; but it is on precisely such arguments that the case for socialism rests. . . . Though naturally, good arguments
will not pierce the ideological armour of many" (177).

   At the outset of *Reclaiming Reality,* Bhaskar proposes an agenda for socialist thought: "I take it that whatever our politics, in the narrow party or factional
sense, socialists can agree that what we must be about today is the building of a
movement for socialism—in which socialism wins a cultural intellectual hegemony, so that it becomes the enlightened common sense of our age" (1). And
he concludes the book with the following lapidary and somewhat laconic
judgment: "There is something about the market and what Marx called the
value and wage forms which makes empirical realism the account of reality or
ontology that is spontaneously generated therein. Within the capitalist mode of
production critical realism is always going to seem a luxury its agents cannot
afford. It is the argument of this book that it is a philosophy without which a
socialist emancipation cannot be achieved" (192). Both statements are, I think,
true; the question is how the first can be brought about, given the necessary
recalcitrance of existing agents hypothesized in the second. My own inclination
is to take the line of the later Althusser, however much this position has been
maligned. The crucial text, not surprisingly, is the essay "Ideology and Ideological State Apparatuses."

   Too much ink has been spilled over this little text (whose subtitle, "Notes
towards an Investigation," has not often been heeded) to require a full-dress
exposition here. It will suffice instead to observe its pertinence to socialist
transformation, which both Bhaskar and Collier envisage as the ultimate aim of
their work. Barring some unforeseeable advance in self-organization among the
working classes of the advanced capitalist world, or some equally unpredictable

collapse of the global capitalist economy (both are possible, the latter even likely in the long term), no immediate prospects for socialist transformation are currently visible in Europe, the United States, or Japan.[12] According to a marxist-realist account of society, the persistence (and general acceptance) of most aspects of bourgeois ideology among these populations seems inevitable. To hope to make socialism "the enlightened common-sense of our age" under such conditions must appear utopian in the worst sense.

Among the enduring merits of Althusser's essay on ideology is its insistence on the materiality of ideological practice. This consequence is already entailed by the classical marxist concept of ideology, but with the possible exception of Gramsci, no one in the marxist tradition before Althusser had situated the theory of ideology so centrally on the terrain of social life. While the notion of ideological state apparatuses has been much criticized for its denegation of civil society, the hypothesis that one of the capitalist state's principal functions is to ensure the reproduction of capitalist social relations is clearly defensible. One way the capitalist state does so is to train a technical intelligentsia, the "savants" to whom Althusser addressed his lectures on philosophy and science and whose decisive role in reproducing capitalism no one can seriously doubt.

Now it is a characteristic Blanquist error to believe that elites can make revolutions without a mass base, but the opposite populist (and anti-Leninist) mistake is to pin all hope on the working class's native capacity to make and sustain one. If socialist emancipation one day proves to be on the agenda for any significant proportion of humankind, it will not be because workers in the capitalist heartlands have overnight been delivered from their ideological illusions by the sheer force of reality striking them in the face. Socialism will emerge from capitalism, if it ever does, only as the result of a long historical process of elite and mass reeducation alike, maturing in the womb of capitalist society and a fortiori in those institutions where the bourgeoisie's ideological domination is most immediately secured. A marxist philosophy *for* science in our epoch is therefore necessarily a struggle for hegemony within the institutions of (natural and social) scientific training. Realist theory entails, as Bhaskar insists, ontological commitments and epistemological principles; its triumph over idealism further requires the sort of ideological struggle theorized by Althusser as well as practiced by him in *Spontaneous Philosophy*.

The technical intelligentsia's hegemony in modern societies is the overarching theme of Aronowitz's *Science as Power*. In his view, the position of religion (ideological common sense under feudalism) is now occupied by science (ideological common sense under advanced capitalism [8–10]). Science's power is part and parcel of capitalist social relations, which require constantly revolutionizing the means of production. The increasing domination of technology over labor and the broad acceptance of scientific method go hand in hand to reproduce the bourgeoisie's dominance over the economy and its capacity to manipulate ideology in its own favor: "Machine technology cannot be separated from the social relations that created it. The logic of domination remains embedded in the machine, which is an instrument for the perpetuation of social oppression and exploitation by virtue of not only its uses but its construction as well" (78).

Based on a (partial but not wholly unwarranted) reading of Marx on the labor process (45–55), Aronowitz's account of science reverses the conventional view in philosophy of science, subordinating scientific method to its instrumentalization in experiment: "Scientific discovery depends increasingly on the sophistication of the machines of experimental science. For, to the extent that science believes it relies on observation as much as mathematical calculation, its collective experience is mediated by the accuracy of the data collected by means of mechanical interventions into the nature it constructs in the laboratory" (41). In Bhaskar's terms, science is constituted wholly by its activities in the transitive dimension (which in one sense is true: without experimentation and hypothesis formation there would be no science), setting aside the possibility that what science investigates and explains preexists experimental intervention and persists in the same way once the experiment is over. For Aronowitz, there are no such things as intransitive objects of knowledge.

Aronowitz's case against science is a marxist variant of standard conventionalist (Kuhn) or constructivist (Latour and Woolgar) accounts. It is marred, among other ways, by conflating scientific realism with positivism. Commenting on what he terms "positivist tendencies in Marx," Aronowitz characterizes these as "the notion of the objective material world as prior to human will, possessing an independent power which can be discovered through scientific investigation, specifically through experiment" (74). None of the ontological commitments Aronowitz (correctly) attributes to Marx is specifically positivist, at least as this description has traditionally been understood. Moreover, does Aronowitz honestly believe (and expect us to believe) that there were no subatomic particles in the universe before their existence was experimentally registered at the end of the nineteenth century, or that such particles cease to exist after they have passed through a cloud chamber and their "tracks" are recorded? Similarly, does he hold that prior to the discovery of DNA, genetic duplication and mutation were accomplished by some other means, or that outside the laboratory species are not perpetuated by means of the double helix structure's biochemical properties? If we are to doubt the findings of the empirical sciences, we need to be given better reasons than that they have arisen from and been a necessary adjunct to capitalist social relations; even if such is the case (and I doubt that it is, at least in the global, undifferentiated manner Aronowitz asserts), scientific discoveries could still give correct descriptions of certain features in nature. That the nuclear power industry has attempted to impose grossly undemocratic and capital-intensive energy production on us gives no grounds for thinking that controlled fission reactions are just a capitalist plot.

The true test of realist versus conventionalist accounts of science comes, it should by now be clear, in the social sciences, where the existence of intransitive objects of knowledge is less obvious. Given Aronowitz's insistence on ideology's constitutive role in scientific investigation, it is worth considering how he himself conceives this key concept in marxist theory. Predictably, he openly scorns orthodox accounts that link ideology to class struggle, chiding them for remaining "grounded in an objectivist account of history" (110). Yet his own rendition of the history of modern science proposes a thoroughly "objectivist" claim: to wit, that scientific method has been univocally determined by social relations of production. Aronowitz seems to have a distinctive conception of ideology (and, as a consequence, of science) in mind, one that is at once grounded in social relations and yet not unilaterally determined by one's position in the class struggle. He is, rightly, critical of the preposterous Stalinist notion of "proletarian science" (111–16), while trying to "save the appearances" of Marx's insight into the determination of consciousness by social being (see, for example, his discussion of the Lysenko affair [227–29]).[13] Is it possible, then, to give a more or less objective account of the "social context" in which physical laws are "produced"? Aronowitz seems to think so, and cites many studies that aim to do just that: Fleck on the discovery of syphilis (287–88), Latour on Pasteur (293), Pickering on quarks (291–92). But what is the "object" in these studies? By what criteria might they be said to pass muster as truthful accounts of how things are in the social world of science?

Aronowitz's recommendations for "critical science" (chapter 11 of *Science as Power*) can only be cashed out with a concept of scientific inquiry he rejects in principle (while embracing it in practice): to wit, that social relations are relatively enduring structures observable and describable in terms not merely subjective or bound to the local interests of a party, a guild, or even a class. Take Aronowitz's favorite bugbear: the division between manual and mental labor on which the hegemony of modern science depends. Drawing on Sohn-Rethel, Aronowitz locates the origins of this paradigm for knowledge production historically in Greek philosophy (and, presumably, in its motivating discourse, mathematics) and socially in commodity exchange (142–43). Its true historical destiny remains unfulfilled, however, until the capitalist epoch, when workers (manual laborers) are for the first time completely alienated from the means of production through the institution of the wage form; this techno-logic culminates in the increasing technical subordination of labor to capital and the degradation of the labor process (48–59). Marx, from whom the elements (if not the conclusions) of this account are taken, thought when he was describing the capitalist mode of production that, first, he was giving an account of social reality, and second, his account was generally perspicuous, that is, it was scientific (rather than ideological, as were those given in political economy). Having been born a bourgeois, educated in bourgeois institutions, and accepting the eminently bourgeois belief in scientific inquiry's value seem not to have been insuperable obstacles to his producing an account of bourgeois social relations that remains to this day without serious theoretical rival. Soi-disant marxist philosophies of science that assert scientific practice's total determination by ideology need, among other things, to explain this rather striking anomaly in their theory.

Surely the most consequent—if increasingly quixotic—challenge to the realist philosophy of science has been that mounted by the late Paul Feyerabend. The reissue of his classic *Against Method* and the publication of what he said (perhaps in jest) would be his last book, *Farewell to Reason,* provide occasion for assessing the strengths and weaknesses of the "anarchist" or "dadaist" philosophy of science he championed.[14] I shall begin somewhat obliquely, drawing on Roy Bhaskar's pointed critique of 1975, "Feyerabend and Bachelard: Two Philosophies of Science," reprinted in *Reclaiming Reality.*

Among the many difficulties in coherently presenting Feyerabend's work since 1970, as Bhaskar notices (*Reclaiming* 40) and Feyerabend himself admitted in the re-edition of *Against Method* (vii), is that one never knows whether to take anything he says seriously. His posture is attractive for anyone who feels that scientists and their enterprise can usefully be taken down a peg or two. The public image of science and its practitioners (in this I basically agree with Aronowitz) is one of unquestioned cognitive superiority, so that Feyerabend's debunking of scientific hubris remains necessary and timely. There is nothing sacrosanct about science in general or about any of its currently held theories in particular; scientific practice is always open to criticism—but, it should be added, not in just any form.

Nor did Feyerabend seem to feel, despite his asseveration that in the sciences "anything goes" (*Against Method* 21), that criticism of scientific research was an open field where any counter position to an existing hypothesis was warranted or licit. His conception of science and of its place in a free society was more nuanced, hence, more sustainable: "Again I want to make two points: first, that science can stand on its own feet and does not need any help from rationalists, secular humanists, Marxists and similar religious movements; and, secondly, that non-scientific cultures, procedures and assumptions can also stand on their own feet and should be allowed to do so, if this is the wish of their representatives. Science must be protected from ideologies; and societies, especially democratic societies, must be protected from science" (viii). If Feyerabend's special crusade was to aid in this second sort of protection, the task (if not always the practice) of philosophy of science is to help out in the first. And it may be added, *pace* Feyerabend, that the security of the sciences does not always go without saying, any more than does the existence of the democratic institutions he rightly insisted are the necessary corollary of a humanly liberating practice of science.

Feyerabend's career, as Bhaskar indicates (*Reclaiming* 33), presented a curious trajectory. Friend and admirer of Imre Lakatos, once an ultra-orthodox Popperian, he became the great scourge of the very principles he himself defended in his early work.[15] On Bhaskar's construal, Feyerabend's position in *Against Method* can be organized around three central claims; the first two derive from critically evaluating standard views in philosophy of science. (1) In the company of Kuhn, whom he had criticized in an earlier incarnation[16] but later considered a comrade in arms (*Against Method* 229–30), Feyerabend insisted on incommensurability between competing explanations of phenomena *in* science and competing worldviews out of it (Bhaskar, *Reclaiming* 32). (2) A corollary of this first claim is that the history of scientific development has been essentially anarchic, and that this has been (and is) a necessary condition for its progress—although Feyerabend was predictably skeptical concerning the generality of notions like scientific progress (*Reclaiming* 33–34). (3) Underlying Feyerabend's critical appraisal of science and its justificatory philosophy was a deep commitment to human freedom, which he believed was endangered by the scientific enterprise. As Bhaskar summarily observes, Feyerabend is "for freedom and *against science*" (*Reclaiming* 32).

Bhaskar's replies to points one (*Reclaiming* 32–33; see also *Realist Theory* 191, 248, 258) and two (*Reclaiming* 34–35) are unimpeachable and need not detain us. As he recognizes, the real force of *Against Method* derives from point three, which involves similar problems to those posed by Rorty's championing of liberal freedom and encounters a similar objection: "Knowledge may not be the most important social activity, but it is the one upon which the achievement of any human objective depends. Freedom, in the sense Feyerabend attaches to it, depends upon knowledge (praxis presupposes theory); we can only be as free as our knowledge is reliable and complete. We are not free to choose what we believe if we are to attain the kinds of objectives Feyerabend mentions. Only if belief-in-itself was the sole end of human action would Feyerabend be warranted in such an assumption" (*Reclaiming* 36). To my knowledge, Feyerabend never formally replied to Bhaskar's criticisms. How might he have done so?

Against Method opens with an interesting contention: "The following essay is written in the conviction that *anarchism,* while perhaps not the most attractive *political* philosophy, is certainly excellent medicine for *epistemology,* and for the *philosophy of science*" (9). Feyerabend in this way immediately prizes apart the social domain from science. (Here and throughout his work, *science* almost exclusively denotes the natural sciences.) There is a constitutive tension, then, between Feyerabend's conception of scientific inquiry's social dimension and his apparent conviction that consequent political action cannot follow an anarchist line. He immediately quotes Lenin to support his own view that scientific practice entails no methodological imperative, save that method is generally—and productively—ad hoc, the scientist, in Einstein's words, being "an unscrupulous opportunist" (11).

The invocation of and commentary on Lenin at this point are curious. Feyerabend takes him to be saying that politics and history are a messy business from which no principles or rules can be derived, and that what obtains in history and politics holds for inquiries about nature. Feyerabend then quotes Ernst Mach on scientific practice to the same effect, arguing that politics (on Lenin's account) and science are methodologically similar (10 n. 5). As even the most casual reader of Lenin knows (and as Bhaskar points out; see *Reclaiming* 36), nothing could be further from the concept of politics and history adduced here than Lenin's understanding of strategic calculation. For Lenin, a consequent politics can only be constructed on the basis of a particular science (historical materialism), which gives the revolutionary tactician the requisite knowledge for choosing between alternative courses of action. Moreover, when Feyerabend invokes Mach on investigative procedure, however salutary that method may be as a rule of thumb, he assigns an odd bedfellow to the author of *Materialism and Empirio-Criticism*. Feyerabend was certainly acquainted with Lenin's text before penning this note,[17] yet he ignores the fact that Lenin wrote it to combat Mach's increasing prestige among certain Bolshevik intellectuals (Bogdanov, Lunacharsky, Bazarov [see Althusser, *Philosophy* 167–202]). The omission is far from incidental; it is of a piece with Feyerabend's (mis)understanding of marxism as a science of the history of social formations and as a political practice, and is part and parcel of his libertarian idea of freedom.

Feyerabend casually invoked marxist thought over many years, characteristically to buttress his own antirationalist epistemology. But on some few occasions, a different strain took over. For example, in a critical treatment of the Lakatosian idea of scientific research programs, he wrote in an almost partisan vein: "And whoever has read Rosa Luxemburg's reply to Bernstein's criticism of Marx or Trotsky's account of why the Russian revolution took place in a backward country . . . will see that Marxists are pretty close to what Lakatos would like any upstanding rationalist to do, though there is absolutely no need for them to accept his rules" (*Philosophical Papers,* II, 207). In another place he quoted extensively from Mao to defend J. S. Mill (67–68), while drawing solace from Lenin for his own reading of Hegel (74, 75, 79). Unlikely as the comparison appears at first, *this* Feyerabend sounded like no one so much as the late Althusser of *Lenin and Philosophy*—well, not quite.

Feyerabend's diagram and explanation of the relations among the three concepts that guided his view of knowledge production seem at first blush attractive and not wholly dissimilar to Althusser's account of Generalities I, II, and III. The diagram proposes the following schema for scientific inquiry:

$$criticism \rightarrow proliferation \rightarrow realism$$

Feyerabend comments on this schema: "Nor does the arrow . . . express a well-defined connection such as logical implication. It rather suggests that starting with the left hand side and adding physical principles, psychological assumptions, plausible cosmological conjectures, absurd guesses and plain common-sense views, a dialectical debate will eventually arrive at the right hand side"

(*Philosophical Papers* I, vii–viii). Further, he is quite adamant that the arrow stands for no general methodological protocols; its meaning lies only in the particular examples adduced. (Feyerabend gives several instances of how research has actually proceeded, but presumably others would illustrate the crucial point as well: that no method of science can be derived from examining what scientists actually do.)

Feyerabend's point about proliferation is that scientific research is messy; his claim for realism is roughly the standard one that theories do indeed refer to things.[18] No marxist should be hostile to these views. Nor is his understanding of criticism likely to meet with disapproval: "Criticism means that we do not simply accept the phenomena, processes, institutions that surround us but we examine them and try to change them" (vii). To Bhaskar's characterization of his work, Feyerabend might fairly have replied that he was against (only rationalist accounts of) science because he is in favor of a practice of science that might better serve the end of human freedom.

The difficulty, comes, unsurprisingly, when one attempts to cash out Feyerabend's democratic (or populist; see *Farewell* 273–79) attachments in an emancipatory program that possesses substantive content and respects the quite real limits of both humanity and nature. Feyerabend could invoke the manifest ecological and human disasters visited on various people by Western science (*Farewell* 3–4, 26–27), but all he could recommend to prevent their worsening (or recurring in different forms) was that everyone respect everyone else's right to be different. Such a notion of freedom is demonstrably vacuous; it gains no force by being dressed in pseudo-materialist garb with citations from Lenin and Marx. The latter two held rather stronger notions about a science of society and recognized that any project for the liberation of humankind needed to understand (or explain) the material (social and natural) constraints on human freedom prior to changing the conditions that currently prevent its full realization.

Feyerabend was rightly critical of the collective arrogance of the technical intelligentsia (and the West generally),[19] but this stipulation gives no grounds for indicting the scientific enterprise generally. It is, rather, a demonstration of Bhaskar's and Althusser's point concerning the persistence of ideology in science's transitive dimension. To launch a consequent critique of these ideologies, more than a Mill-inspired liberal tolerance is required. It demands, simply enough, a theory of ideology as necessary illusion. Historical materialism offers such a theory. Marxist philosophy cannot settle matters for or against this theory; it can, however, struggle against the various regnant idealisms that seek to deny it any chance to make its own way in the world. A marxist philosophy of science is therefore a philosophy for science in exactly this sense. Hence, it is now possible (and necessary) to emend Marx's famous pronouncement to say: philosophers neither interpret nor change the world; science, whose cognitive autonomy philosophy is charged to protect, interprets the world in order that changing it may one day be possible.

Notes

1. Marx, *Grundrisse* (101).
2. Engels, *Anti-Dühring* (Part I, chap. 13).
3. Bhaskar has maintained, however, that this text was influenced by marxism, notably by Althusser; see Elliott, *Althusser* (331).
4. Roy Bhaskar, *Reclaiming Reality* (chap. 7).
5. Alexander Nehamas has lodged a similar criticism against Rorty; see Nehamas, "A Touch of the Poet: On Richard Rorty."
6. Bhaskar offers a similar judgment in his encyclopedia article on the marxist theory of knowledge: "In Althusser one finds . . . a form of scientific rationalism influenced by the philosopher of science G. Bachelard and the meta-psychologist J. Lacan, in which the intransitive dimension is effectively neutralized, resulting in a latent idealism" (*Reclaiming* 142).
7. I am not saying that such a charge is warranted, but Bhaskar's insistence that the intransitive dimension is irreducible tends to be construed thus; see, for example, Bruno Latour and Steve Woolgar, *Laboratory Life* (178). In the current euphoria over constructivist accounts of scientific discovery, something more than a firm distinction between transitive and intransitive dimensions is required to make the case against a totally socialized view of theory formation and adjudication.
8. Louis Althusser, "The Object of *Capital,*" in Althusser and Balibar, *Reading Capital* (87). See the following passage from a text of 1966, "On Theoretical Work: Difficulties and Resources": "Naturally, the knowledge of formal-abstract objects [the objects posited by a theory] has nothing to do with a speculative and contemplative knowledge concerning 'pure' ideas. On the contrary, it is solely concerned with *real* objects; it is meaningful *solely* because it allows the forging of theoretical instruments, formal and abstract theoretical concepts, which permit production of the knowledge of real-concrete objects." Althusser, *Philosophy and the Spontaneous Philosophy of the Scientists* (51).
9. Gregory Elliott has argued for a political determination: to wit, Althusser's overvaluation of Maoism; see Elliott, *Althusser,* chaps. 4 and 5, especially 194–97, which deal with Althusser's text of 1966, "Sur la Révolution Culturelle."
10. Though by no means all—see, for example, Gregory Elliott's introduction to *Philosophy and the Spontaneous Philosophy of the Scientists,* and "Conclusion: Unfinished History," in his *Althusser: The Detour of Theory.*
11. Early Althusserianism did propose to extend the concept of structural causality in a theoretical account of the transition from one mode of production to another.

This task was undertaken in Balibar's "Basic Concepts of Historical Materialism" (*Reading* 199–308). Despite Balibar's assertion that the problems he posed remain open, the essay's failure to capture the specificity of historical materialism is patent; see Elliott, *Althusser* (160–71).

12. Surely one consequence of the epochal changes in Eastern Europe and the former Soviet Union during 1989 to 1992 is to have rendered similar prospects in the capitalist periphery incomparably more difficult.

13. Aronowitz's own position seems to be more or less that of Christopher Caudwell's *Crisis in Physics,* held by Aronowitz to be "the first Marxist work to posit both the *relative* autonomy of scientific knowledge from its social relations, and the determination, in the last instance, of physical laws by the social context of their production" (*Science as Power* 120). *Posit* is the operative word here. Nothing Aronowitz can say will ever redeem Caudwell's ill-digested mélange of anecdotal information about the history of physics from the utter intellectual oblivion to which it has justly been consigned for over half a century. Aronowitz scarcely does any better, be it said; see "The Breakup of Certainty," in *Science as Power,* for his highly dubious account of analytic philosophy of science in relation to post-Einsteinian mechanics.

14. The original edition of *Against Method* appeared in 1975. *Against Method* and *Farewell to Reason* are provocative and, above all, entertaining books, rich in historical detail and wittily presented. Since Bhaskar's critique of the former pretty much makes my case against its faults (of which Feyerabend was predictably unrepentant in *Farewell to Reason*), I have concentrated instead on the somewhat tamer essays collected in Feyerabend, *Philosophical Papers.*

15. For the "Popperian" Feyerabend, see inter alia, chap. 8 (sections 1–8) in *Philosophical Papers,* II, and especially his "Problems of Empiricism," in *Beyond the Edge of Certainty.*

16. See "Consolations for the Specialist" (*Philosophical Papers,* II, 131–61); originally published in Lakatos and Musgrave, *Criticism and the Growth of Knowledge.*

17. See "Two Models of Epistemic Change." This paper was originally published in 1970 as part of Feyerabend's programmatic essay "Against Method."

18. Feyerabend's respect for Aristotle was considerable (see *Philosophical Papers,* I; ibid., II, 12–15, 183–84, and passim; and especially his *Science in a Free Society* [53–65]).

19. Among Feyerabend's more attractive proposals was to modify the unconscionably ethnocentric scientific training in the West to include alternative cosmological traditions; see, for example, *Against Method* (11–12) and *Farewell* (20–39).

Works Cited

Althusser, Louis. *Philosophy and the Spontaneous Philosophy of the Scientists and Other Essays.* Trans. Ben Brewster et al. London: Verso, 1990.

Althusser, Louis, and Etienne Balibar. *Reading Capital.* Trans. Ben Brewster. London: New Left Books, 1979.

Aronowitz, Stanley. *Science as Power.* Minneapolis: University of Minnesota Press, 1988.

Bhaskar, Roy. *A Realist Theory of Science.* 2d ed. Hassocks, Sussex: Harvester, 1978.

——. *Reclaiming Reality: A Critical Introduction to Contemporary Philosophy*. London: Verso, 1989.

——. *Scientific Realism and Human Emancipation*. London: Verso, 1986.

Collier, Andrew. *Scientific Realism and Socialist Thought*. Hemel Hempstead: Harvester-Wheatsheaf, 1989.

Elliott, Gregory. *Althusser: The Detour of Theory*. London: Verso, 1987.

Engels, Friedrich. *Anti-Dühring*. Moscow: Progress Publishers, 1969.

Feyerabend, Paul. *Against Method*. London: Verso, 1988.

——. *Farewell to Reason*. London: Verso, 1987.

——. *Philosophical Papers*. 2 vols. Cambridge: Cambridge University Press, 1981.

——. "Problems of Empiricism." *Beyond the Edge of Certainty*. Ed. R. G. Colodny. Englewood Cliffs, N.J.: Prentice-Hall, 1965.

——. *Science in a Free Society*. London: New Left Books, 1978.

Lakatos, Imre, and Alan Musgrave, eds. *Criticism and the Growth of Knowledge*. Cambridge: Cambridge University Press, 1970.

Latour, Bruno, and Steve Woolgar. *Laboratory Life: The Construction of Scientific Facts*. Princeton: Princeton University Press, 1986.

Marx, Karl. *Grundrisse*. Trans. Martin Nicolaus. New York: Vintage, 1973.

Nehamas, Alexander. "A Touch of the Poet: On Richard Rorty." *Raritan* (forthcoming).

Rorty, Richard. *Consequences of Pragmatism*. Minneapolis: University of Minnesota Press, 1982.

——. *Contingency, Irony, and Solidarity*. Cambridge: Cambridge University Press, 1989.

——. *Philosophy and the Mirror of Nature*. Princeton: Princeton University Press, 1979.

Williams, Bernard. "Getting It Right." *London Review of Books* (23 November 1989): 5.

IV
Teaching and Writing (in) an Antifoundational World

14

Beyond Antifoundationalism to Rhetorical Authority
Problems Defining "Cultural Literacy"

Patricia Bizzell

When students enter college, it soon becomes apparent that some of them are already comfortable with academic discourse, while other students seem quite unfamiliar with academic discourse and resistant to learning it. This state of affairs might not be considered a problem: the academy might simply expel those who do not share its discourse and welcome and reward those who do. Indeed, this is how the situation is handled in many schools today.

Many writing teachers, however, have not been satisfied with this response to the lack of a shared discourse. Many of us have felt that it is unfair, a shirking of our professional responsibility to expel from the academy those students who do not share our discourse. The unfairness is exacerbated by the fact that failing to share in academic discourse is often not a personal or idiosyncratic failing but rather seems to be a function of belonging to a social group that has experienced other exclusions and disenfranchisements—that is, other injustices. Writing teachers, then, have seen the lack of a shared discourse as a problem and have tried to remedy the problem by studying ways to initiate all students into academic discourse.

E. D. Hirsch has suggested in his work on cultural literacy that Americans have another, larger problem involving the lack of a shared discourse, that there is a national, public discourse community in which issues of grave collective importance are discussed. But, according to Hirsch, not all American citizens can participate in this national discursive forum. Thus there exists a problem of exclusion antithetical to a democracy in which all citizens ought to be able to participate in the national discourse. Hirsch sees education as the solution to this problem and has proposed that the schools should introduce all students to the national political discourse. Hirsch has offered his project of teaching cultural literacy as a means to this end.

In pursuing this project, Hirsch makes some assumptions that are similar to those we writing teachers have made in attempting to introduce students to academic discourse. First, Hirsch assumes that sharing a discourse means more than sharing the ability to encode and decode a particular grammar and syntax. That is, he imagines a situation in which people all know English, or some form of English, but still do not share a discourse. For Hirsch, "sharing a discourse" means sharing not only a tongue but also a mass of contextual knowledge that renders the tongue significant. In its broadest outlines, this is the definition of *literacy* that is identified as "cultural." That is, the ability to read, write, and speak—to use a language—is contingent on possession of the cultural knowledge that renders the language significant, shapes situations for its appropriate use, and so on. There is, in fact, no such thing as simple literacy at all according to these assumptions; every form of literacy is a particular cultural literacy.

Some of us composition teachers have argued, following similar assumptions, that students who have difficulties with academic discourse are not illiterate but rather lacking in the particular academic cultural literacy. Mina Shaughnessy has pioneered this way of understanding the difficulties of what she calls "basic writers" when she suggests that what they need to know, more than corrections of their English usage, is "how proof is defined in the various situations [they] must think and write in" (271). The student writer must establish a credible academic persona through the method of his or her argument—for example, by learning what counts as adequate evidence in various academic disciplines—and also through the employment of a trans-disciplinary academic vocabulary. In short, a specific cultural content must be supplied to remedy the lack of a discourse shared by students and teachers. Recent discussions of this problem in composition studies (such as my essay "Arguing about Literacy") have focused on adjudicating how much of the cultural content should be supplied by the teacher from the traditional academic store and how much should come from students' knowledge of the treasures of other, nonacademic cultural literacies.

I would agree with Hirsch, then, that in order for people to share language, they must share knowledge. This is the general import of the concept of "discourse community." It might be said that a particular cultural literacy is what members of a discourse community share. But I disagree with Hirsch's assumption that there is a relatively stable, definable national discourse community. This assumption allows Hirsch to define our current national problem as one of initiating all citizens into a predetermined or "given" national discourse community by supplying them with the knowledge that will enable them to share this community's language. To frame the problem in this way presents it in terms that appear to make it easily amenable to educational remedy: let the schools inculcate the requisite knowledge. Such a solution is analogous to the solution some composition specialists have suggested for the academic discourse problem: let the freshman writing class inculcate the knowledge requisite to allow all students to participate in the academic discursive community.

I am coming to suspect, however, that the academic discourse community is not such a stable entity that one can define our teaching problem in terms of how to get student writing to approximate a set of well-known and accepted academic models, as Shaughnessy has suggested (257–73). I now think the academic discourse community is more unstable than this—more fraught with contradiction, more polyvocal—and that this instability is a sign of its health, its ability to adapt to changing historical conditions. It would be a mistake to rush closure on a unitary conception of what academic discourse should be and then turn this concept into a Procrustean bed that all student (and professorial) writing must fit.

At the same time, however, it is important for students and teachers to work collectively toward achieving consensus on a pluralistic grouping of ways to do academic discourse. Some consensus is needed so that we can share a discourse and get on with our work, while including the greatest possible diversity of participants and remaining open to change in response to the cultural literacies of new groups who want to join in our projects. We may wish to do away with an oppressive academic discourse, but we cannot do without any academic discourse at all.

Similarly, it is of crucial importance for Americans to share a national political discourse. Unlike Hirsch, I do not believe that a relatively stable and unitary form of this discourse presently exists. If a unitary national discourse ever existed, it may have owed its existence to historical circumstances that greatly limited the group of people who had access to it in terms of race, sex, and social class. As with the instability of academic discourse, I would like to regard the present instability of national discourse—or more precisely, the open-endedness of the question of whether we can have a national discourse at all—as an opportunity. Perhaps we Americans have the opportunity now to collaborate on forging a more collective, pluralistic, inclusive national discourse. I certainly believe that such a democratic shared language is needed, in view of the gravity of the political problems that confront us: racial injustice, economic inequality, environmental destruction, and the prospect of nuclear war. Perhaps it is only because I myself am a teacher that I hope a national discourse could contribute substantially to the redress of our national ills—as if there were not pervasive material circumstances preconditioning people's unequal political, and academic, participation. Or perhaps my hope arises from an awareness that intellectuals in every other country in the world play dynamic roles in the shaping of collective political life. Perhaps we should regard this, too, as part of our professional responsibility.

It is the desperate character of our current national political life that dismays me when I contemplate the reaction of scholars in English studies to Hirsch's cultural literacy proposals, wrongheaded though these proposals are. It seems as if these scholars are denying my hope for the political consequences of a national discourse, denying their own vocation as intellectuals. Hirsch has been almost universally condemned on grounds that he has no legitimate authority on which to base his decisions about what knowledge should comprise the cultural literacy that would enable Americans to share a national discourse. Moreover, it seems that scholars in English studies believe that no one could possess such authority. While I do not want to credit Hirsch's authority, I want to explore the possibility that there is another, legitimate source of authority on which we as scholars of language in use could draw to assist in the formation of a national discourse.

I think that Hirsch has been attacked without accompanying suggestion of an alternative to address the lack of a shared discourse because English studies is under the domination of a theoretical orientation I will call the "philosophical." The philosophical orientation as I define it has its origins in a search for truth. This truth is supposed to exist independent of human beings on a plane beyond the material and temporal. Humans do not make truth, they discover it. The human who possesses true knowledge can use it to guide decisions on what is good, whether for personal morality or political ethics. The true knowledge becomes the basis or foundation of the person's entire worldview. Hence this kind of knowledge has been termed "foundational" knowledge. A person may have to be convinced by rhetorical means that a particular item of knowledge is true or foundational, but once this conviction is achieved, the necessity of accepting the truth is presumed to be self-evident.

Scientific knowledge is the paradigmatic example of foundational knowledge. In English studies, the search for foundational knowledge has taken the form of a search for truths about human nature, which could be rendered by close attention to the literary text in which they resided. This is the project of New Criticism. Given the domination of science as a model of foundational knowledge, human nature for the literary critic has been defined more in psychological or anthropological, rather than religious or ethical, terms—for example, in the work of Northrop Frye.

In recent years, however, this philosophical orientation has undergone a radical change. Influenced by scholars in the discipline of philosophy, such as Richard Rorty, who believe that there is no transcendent truth, at least none accessible to human beings, many in the academic community assume that everything humans take for truth is made, not discovered, by humans. According to this reasoning, foundational knowledge is really the product of cultural activity, shaped by ideology and constituted, not merely conveyed, by rhetoric. In short, there is no foundational knowledge, no knowledge that is necessary or self-evident. Whatever we believe, we believe only because we have been persuaded.

There has recently been much talk of a rhetorical turn in English studies, and it arises from the new antifoundationalism of our philosophical orientation. If all knowledge is nonfoundational, made by people, then the discourse used to frame and promulgate knowledge takes on new importance. Persuasive language is no longer the servant of truth, making it possible for people to understand so that they can believe. Rather, persuasive language creates truth by inducing belief; "truth" results when rhetoric is successful. Hence scholars in English studies, already professionally committed to studying language in use, wish to take rhetoric as their new domain. Work in composition and in literature is converging on rhetoric.

This rhetorical turn is still hampered, however, by our ties to the philosophical orientation. If we are now antifoundationalists, we are also still philosophers. That is, we are still asking whether foundational knowledge can be achieved, although now we answer no to that question. We are still nostalgically evoking the search for truth, only to announce continually that truth cannot be found. We spend our time exposing truth claims as historically, ideologically, rhetorically constructed; in other words, we spend our time in the activity called deconstruction.

We have not yet taken the next, crucially important step in our rhetorical turn. We have not yet acknowledged that if no unimpeachable authority and transcendent truth exist, this does not mean that no respectable authority and no usable truth exist. Our nostalgia for the self-evident and absolute prevents us from accepting as legitimate the authority created by collective discursive exchange and its truths as provisionally binding. If we could take this next step, we could perhaps find the collective will to collaborate on a pluralistic national discourse that would displace Hirsch's schemes while addressing the same lack he delineates. Indeed, we might imagine the public function of the intellectual as precisely rhetorical: our task is to aid everyone in our academic community, and in our national community, to share a discourse.

We can use the antifoundationalist philosophical perspective to critique Hirsch and Allan Bloom, another proposer of a scheme for cultural literacy. But such critiques by themselves are inadequate. We must go on to develop a positive or utopian moment in our critique, an alternative to Procrustean schemes for national unity. Some Marxist and feminist theorists, as I hope to show, are beginning to indicate the direction in which this further step in our rhetorical turn might lead.

To illustrate the weaknesses of the antifoundationalist philosophical perspective, I would like to examine the Modern Language Association (MLA) yearbook *Profession 88*. The policy-forming or political function of this journal was underlined by the MLA's unprecedented decision to devote the 1988 yearbook not to reprints but to articles invited to address a single theme: the cultural literacy work of Allan Bloom and E. D. Hirsch. Moreover, seven of the eight articles in this issue condemn schemes for cultural literacy roundly, in similar terms and with similar alternatives. First the promoters of schemes for cultural literacy are attacked on grounds of falsely claiming to possess foundational authority. Then the individual autonomy of each student and teacher is defended against the encroaching demands of schemes specifying a traditional content for cultural literacy. Finally, the curricular pluralism which is presumed to result from such autonomy is praised on grounds that it facilitates the study of difference.

Hirsch and Bloom are accused by their critics of claiming an authority that presumes to transcend historical circumstances, thus giving its possessor the right to range over the history of the entire Western intellectual tradition and select the truly "great" works. As some critics note, Bloom is more vulnerable than Hirsch to charges of claiming to possess such transcendent authority. Kenneth Alan Hovey, for example, describes Bloom as believing that ordinary people, who are caught in the historical circumstances of "nation, race, and religion," can produce little more than time-bound, culture-bound work, or what he calls "literary ephemera" (44). But Bloom believes there is also a class of being called the philosopher, who is not caught in historical circumstances, who "ris[es] above time," and who consequently can distinguish, and presumably produce, "great books" (44). Hovey thus indicts Bloom because, from the antifoundationalist point of view, this special class of being, the philosopher, does not exist. There is no philosopher rendering true judgments of the timeless. Rather, what we think of as the status of being timeless is in fact a judgment that is historically constructed—made by "the times themselves," in Hovey's phrase (44).

Hirsch might be brought under the fire of this critique as well, though Hovey does not discuss him. Although Hirsch sees the content of national cultural literacy as appropriately changing over time, he places the power of deciding what changes to render canonical in the hands of experts such as himself. He has even proposed the creation of a sort of Académie Américaine to determine the content of a national cultural literacy. Hence in practice his national cultural literacy takes on the authority of timeless truth, and his experts function just as Hovey says Bloom's philosophers do. Up to this point I can agree with Hovey's critique as it might be applied to both Bloom and Hirsch.

It is striking, however, that "philosopher" becomes a term of reproach in this critique. In *Profession 88*, William K. Buckley and Helene Moglen also use the term negatively, even bitterly, as in this characterization from Moglen: "Once [Bloom] had himself become a high priest in the exalted order of philosophers, he delivered to awed neophytes the revealed meanings of the sacred texts" (60). The point, of course, is the foolishness of pretending that one can be a traditional philosopher with access to the transcendent truth of timeless texts. Antifoundationalism makes the pretense pathetic, if not vicious. But what strikes me is the sense of loss conveyed by the emotional tone of these antifoundationalist critiques. As I have suggested, antifoundationalist philosophers are preoccupied with the necessity of saying no to foundational knowledge. Hence their concern is simply to knock down any authority claims made by others and to offer instead little more than a presumed individual autonomy.

This point has been made most neatly by an exchange in *The Chronicle of Higher Education* between Lynne Cheney, then chair of the National Endowment for the Humanities, and noted antifoundationalist philosopher Stanley Fish. Cheney is one of the public officials who have been convinced that our schools need schemes for cultural literacy. In support of this position, she writes: "The humanities are about more than politics, more than social power. What gives them their abiding worth are truths that pass beyond time and circumstance—truths that, transcending accidents of class, race, and gender, speak to us all" (A20). In other words, Cheney asserts there are texts that contain true knowledge. She assumes that everybody has the capability to discern the importance of these texts, simply by virtue of being human—they "speak to us all." Fish later commented on Cheney's remarks as follows: "Once you have subtracted from the accidents of class, race, gender, and political circumstance, what is it that you have left?" (quoted in Green A16). The correct antifoundationalist answer to this question is "Nothing."

The next step in undermining foundational authority claims is often to suggest that the authority really rests on ideologies that are conditioned by the claimant's personal circumstances. For example, in *Profession 88,* Buckley depicts Bloom as a social climber who longs for a state ruled by an elite group which he could join. Andrew Sledd and James Sledd depict Hirsch as a sycophantic ideologue of the American capitalist "gerontocracy" (38). Moglen argues that at bottom Bloom is anxious about his male potency and seeks to defend it via a reified concept of machismo propped up by the Western intellectual tradition.

Buckley, the Sledds, and Moglen would not themselves claim to be free of historical constraints. But they would see their argumentative position as superior to that of Bloom and Hirsch because at least they admit that they are so constrained. For antifoundationalists, however, admitting to historical constraints means giving up all claims to an authority that they could hope to get many other people to acknowledge. Hence this line of argument leads to the position that decisions about what to read and write should be left up to individual teachers and students. This position is taken in *Profession 88* by James A. Schultz (cited in Franklin 65–69), reporting on the opinions of the MLA Committee on Academic Freedom, as well as by Moglen, Buckley, the Sledds, and Paul B. Armstrong.

The antifoundationalist philosophers are correct to attack any authority that claims to place itself beyond question. The problem is that they still cling, as I noted earlier, to the conviction that the question about foundational knowledge and unimpeachable authority is the single most important question, even if it has to be answered in the negative. Because they must answer no to the all-important question, they feel they have no authority to offer any strong alternatives to the schemes for cultural literacy they debunk. All they feel they can do is to speak up for their own and everyone else's autonomy.

I would argue that the defense of autonomy leads to a dangerous sort of political quietism. In their deconstructive mode, the antifoundationalist critics do point out the effect of historical circumstances on notions of the true and good which their opponents claim are outside time. In other words, the critics show that these notions consist in ideologies. But once the ideological interest has been pointed out, the antifoundationalists throw up their hands. And because they have no positive program, the antifoundationalist critics may end up tacitly supporting the political and cultural status quo.

A striking example of this quietism can be found in Hovey's argument. Like many other critics of schemes for cultural literacy, Hovey attempts to appropriate the overtly political and ostentatiously patriotic language of his opponents, in this case Bloom, and to use it to bolster his own position. But because he is not recommending any action, the political language becomes denatured, and political processes are actually covered over rather than revealed. Hovey argues that "the creed of America since its beginning" has been to oppose designating certain works as "Great Books" (45). Thus he tries to identify his own rather than Bloom's as the truly patriotic position. Then Hovey goes on to explain why our creed rejects "Great Books": "The settlers and founders of America, while recognizing the need for authority, also saw its dangers and rejected the authority of a canon of books as much as they did a state church and a hereditary king. As a result, in America all books as well as all men are created equal. As some people, nonetheless, show themselves worthy of higher offices, some books in time gain higher respect" (45). In this passage, Hovey's first sentence equates rejecting a "canon of books" with overthrowing "a state church and a hereditary king." Presumably this equation is based in the idea that canon, church, and king would all claim to possess authority defined by foundational notions of the true and good. The antifoundationalist philosopher delegitimates this authority by pointing out that there are no foundational notions, thus exposing the fact that the authority in question is really established by political means. If the authority's claims for respect and obedience are not foundational, then they can be resisted and changed by the same political means that established these claims in the first place.

This is the kind of resistance that Hovey sees people mounting when they created the political entity of the United States. One might suppose, then, that he implies that we should mount a similar kind of resistance when confronted by schemes for cultural literacy, since these schemes, like the political structures overthrown by the American revolutionaries, claim to be defined by foundational knowledge and have the support of powerful political figures. Hovey's first sentence, in other words, equates questioning the canon with not only political but explicitly revolutionary activity. He would seem to open the door to a full consideration of the political functions of schemes for cultural literacy and of the counterclaims their attackers might make, the "revolutionary" curriculum they might set up after the traditional canon is overthrown.

Hovey's next sentence, however, slams the door on any consideration of revolutionary politics. He seems to be arguing that the American Revolution overthrew the power not of specific political institutions, but of history itself, so that now, "as a result," in America if nowhere else, historical circumstances have no constraining power and "all books as well as all men are created equal." It is as if Hovey has approached a topic so frightening to him—namely, the revolutionary curriculum—that rather than address it, he is willing to throw to the winds his credentials as an antifoundationalist philosopher. For no antifoundationalist philosopher could ever think that the power of history had been suspended anywhere. And once Hovey has repressed historical considerations by asserting the initial equality of all people and their books, he cannot give a political explanation of why some people and some books enjoy privileges over others. He is forced into the traditional philosophical position, which he had just been condemning in Bloom, that some inner worth allows particular people to rise to positions of political power and particular books to achieve a higher or canonical status. As he says, "some people . . . show themselves worthy of higher offices" and "some books in time gain higher respect." It would seem that we cannot employ our critical faculties in the processes whereby privilege is acquired, but we must simply wait for the intrinsic worth which justifies privilege to make itself evident. This is quietism.

Fortunately not all antifoundationalist critiques of schemes for cultural literacy stop here. As I noted earlier, another concluding move is to endorse the curricular pluralism that presumably will issue from the exercise of autonomy by teachers and students. The call for pluralism does imply some positive political action beyond the quietism of the call for autonomy. This is because the call for pluralism implies enlarging the contents of national cultural literacy to include literature of value to social groups whose interests have previously been excluded in the establishment of the canon, excluded precisely because these groups were relatively politically powerless. Given who are included in and excluded from the canon already, to talk of enlarging it would seem to invite talk of the functions of education either to reproduce or to resist political inequalities. Of all the contributors to *Profession 88,* Moglen comes the closest to letting this overtly political kind of discussion concerning the curriculum emerge, when she suggests that models for alternatives to schemes for cultural literacy can be found in programs for feminist studies, ethnic studies, and writing instruction.

Moglen gets caught, however, in the contradiction that besets antifoundationalist philosophers when they try to articulate positions that require the positive assertion of the good. The contradiction is this: to wish to enlarge the canon is to imply that one has some values one is willing to rely on to designate the knowledge that should be added. Moglen speaks of the claims of women and ethnic minorities. But an opponent might ask by what right she presses these claims. If one does not happen to share the interests of these groups, why should one respond to their claims? Antifoundationalist philosophers cannot answer this question because they cannot without logical inconsistency claim to possess any values to the authority of which anyone else should bow or any knowledge anyone else should regard as true. Hence although Moglen seems clearly to be speaking out of some sense of social justice to be served, some value that causes her to identify women and ethnic minorities as groups needing more representation, she denies her own authority as a teacher to set a pedagogical agenda that would include these groups, and she endorses only the authority of students' own experiences and judgments. Presumably if Moglen had a class of wealthy white boys, she would have no choice but to grant their autonomy and let them avoid literature by women and ethnic minorities if they so desired.

Antifoundationalist critics sometimes try to get out of this bind by arguing that they want a pluralistic canon simply so that the nature of difference can be studied. Previously noncanonical works need to be included to provide a contrast with the canon and so facilitate the study of difference. For example, María Rosa Menocal advocates the study of rock music lyrics as an aid to understanding lyric poetry. Andrew Sledd and James Sledd suggest that we can recognize the presence of difference by the difficulty to which it gives rise in interpretation, and they argue: "All citizens of the USA—students and teachers alike—need constant practice in the reading of just those texts that are hard to read, and essential to read, because they do presuppose knowledge and beliefs that are alien to us" (38). Apparently it does not matter what we read, so long as it is unfamiliar. By this logic, while white men should be reading work by women and ethnic minorities, women and minorities should be studying the traditional canon. As with the argument on autonomy, there is a subtle denaturing of potentially political language here. The antifoundationalist critics may recommend enlarging the canon with works by previously marginalized and politically disenfranchised groups, which would seem to ally the critics with a radical or revolutionary political position. But the critics can retreat safely into philosophy by claiming that they advocate these particular additions only because these happen to be the works missing now, and so are the ones needed for contrast.

I think there is a sort of pedagogical bad faith in this position. We tell the students we are only teaching them about difference. Yet in order to do that, we must deconstruct ideologies the students hold as foundational, a painful process that students often oppose no matter how egalitarian and nonauthoritarian the teacher tries to be. For example, James Berlin designed an experimental course to replace traditional freshman composition at Purdue University. His course asks students to deconstruct dominant ideologies on relations between the sexes and between employers and workers. Berlin found that students hold firmly to the ideologies they are supposed to question. Women and men defend prostitution as a woman's right to make money any way she sees fit, and they explain unjustified pay cuts, unsafe working conditions, and other oppressive job situations which they have experienced as "good lessons" that toughen them and so will help them get ahead in the future.

Berlin's account makes me wonder what he can offer to students to make it worth their while to bear with the painful deconstructive process he asks of them. It seems to me that Berlin, and many of the rest of us who try to make a pluralistic study of difference into a curriculum, are calling students to the service of some higher good which we do not have the courage to name. We exercise authority over them in asking them to give up their foundational beliefs, but we give them nothing to put in the place of these foundational beliefs because we deny the validity of all authority, including, presumably, our own.

This pedagogical failure is illuminated by the critique of current practice offered by Jeff Smith, the only contributor to *Profession 88* who defends schemes for cultural literacy. Smith also appropriates political language for his peroration, and here is how he characterizes the evolution of the antifoundationalist position:

> The United States was founded by people who believed that
> popular self-determination was served by empiricism: you
> could be made free by attention to "nature" and its "self-
> evident truths." To many professional humanists today and
> perhaps, in less articulate ways, to large sectors of the public,
> democracy seems better served by skepticism. To demand
> attention to something "objective," to "privilege" some way
> of knowing or something to know and to give it priority in
> the classroom, is repressive; human liberation is served by
> never making such requirements. (28)

Smith plays on the word *liberation* here to suggest that whereas it may once
have had political connotations, in the revolutionary days of the founding of
the republic, now all it means is a kind of individual autonomy that is in fact
quite vulnerable to control by larger social institutions. "Skepticism" becomes
not so much a principled position from which to articulate a political critique
as a philosophical void on which the political status quo can inscribe its dominant ideologies. Smith argues that in the 1960s, skepticism "was still bound
together with a politically healthy distrust of prevailing institutions of power.
Today, those institutions and their demands—for instance, the demand that we
grade students—are no longer openly resisted. Indeed, now that [skepticism] is
an officially recognized doctrine . . . there are students out there being graded
on whether they correctly grasp it" (28).

I suspect that Smith is right to see skepticism as a prevailing view not only
among academics but also among "large sectors of the public." Jackson Lears
has recently suggested that skepticism, or what he calls "pervasive irony" and
the hip smirk, infuses the cultural milieu of television. Reviewing a book by
Mark Crispin Miller, Lears approves Miller's reading of television's ironic stance
as a subtle way of threatening the viewer to abandon belief in anything or else
risk becoming the butt of a sitcom joke. Lears says: "So we are left with a form
of domination that seems at once archaic and peculiarly modern—one that is
dependent not on the imposition of belief but on the *absence* of belief, the creation of a void in which only power matters. . . . The aim of TV irony is not to
promote 'progressive' political ideals but to discredit all ideals by enlisting viewers in a comprehensive program of subtle self-oppression: urging them. . . . to
turn themselves into models of blasé self-containment" (60). Lears's analysis
helps us see how Smith has correctly diagnosed the source of students' opposi-

tion to Berlin's course and others that seek to teach difference. That is, students oppose being goaded by grades and professorial approval to achieve skepticism or the hip smirk. But it would not be exactly correct to say that this opposition springs from naive foundationalism. I think students oppose the push to skepticism because they have already seen skepticism and they do not like it. The world already looks horribly meaningless to them, and what we take to be their foundationalism is really a pathetic defense erected against this meaninglessness. If we can offer them no better answer to the meaninglessness than television can, then they may as well stay home and watch it instead of listening to us.

To take the next step in our rhetorical turn, we will have to be more forthright about the ideologies we support as well as those we attack, and we will have to articulate a positive program legitimated by an authority that is nevertheless nonfoundational. We must help our students, and our fellow citizens, to engage in a rhetorical process that can collectively generate trustworthy knowledge and beliefs conducive to the common good—knowledge and beliefs to displace the repressive ideologies an unjust social order would inscribe in the skeptical void.

Perhaps a way to begin the rhetorical process would be to aver provocatively that we intend to make our students better people, that we believe education should develop civic virtue. Richard Lanham has suggested that in the ancient world, such an announcement could be made without embarrassment because the good to be achieved by education was identified with the common good, with standards of civic virtue set by the community in which the education was taking place. In modern times, however, we have assumed that standards of civic virtue, like any other aspect of the transcendent good, can be defined only in terms of foundational knowledge. As a grasp on foundational knowledge has eluded us, we have felt equally disqualified to pronounce on civic virtue. Hence, as Terry Eagleton has argued, the moral scope of education has dwindled to matters of personal virtue only—matters of autonomous choice in a morally pluralistic society. As Eagleton says, "Liberal humanism . . . is stronger on adultery than on armaments" (207).

Eagleton would solve this problem by what he calls a "traditionalist" return to rhetoric as the master discourse of English studies (206). A return to rhetoric would mean a return to considerations of the civic virtue that classical orators once promoted. Eagleton says that he wants the rhetorical analysis of textual power to "[make] you a better person" (207), and he insists that "better" must be understood to encompass civic as well as personal morality: "What it means to be a 'better person,' then . . . must be a question of political and not only of 'moral' argument: that is to say it must be *genuine* moral argument, which sees the relations between individual qualities and values and our whole material conditions of existence. Political argument is not an alternative to moral preoccupations: it is these preoccupations taken seriously in their full implications" (208). Eagleton argues that we should first ask how to make our students better people, and then decide what to teach and how to teach it on the basis of what best answers the initial question. Moreover, he takes the truly radical step of specifying his own definition of *better:* he promotes a revolutionary civic virtue that must change the social order to foster the common good.

I am suggesting that we must be equally forthright in avowing the ideologies that motivate our teaching and research. For example, in the case of James Berlin's course at Purdue University described earlier, instructors might stop trying to be value-neutral and antiauthoritarian in the classroom. Berlin would tell his students that he is a marxist but disavow any intention of persuading them to his point of view. Instead, instructors might openly state that this course aims to promote values of sexual equality and left-oriented labor relations and that this course will challenge students' values insofar as they conflict with these aims. Berlin's colleagues might openly exert their authority as teachers to try to persuade students to agree with their values instead of pretending that they are merely investigating the nature of sexism and capitalism and leaving students to draw their own conclusions.

But wouldn't they then be propagandists? What is the legitimate authority of teachers, or any other orators? I would argue that this authority is derived from ideologies that already have some currency in the community the orators or teachers serve. Not everyone in America is against sexism, for example, but an argument against sexism can make use of values concerning human equality and fair play that even some sexists may hold. In other words, the orator can point out that a contradiction exists among the values that people hold and try to persuade them to rectify it in favor of the values the orator supports. The orator can urge, Don't believe in both equality and sexism: give up the sexism. Thus the oratorical exercise of authority does recommend a positive position but does not impose it. The orator tries to achieve a consensus around the change in ideologies he or she advocates, but a consensus can only be achieved through collective participation in the rhetorical process.

Some feminist theorists have been particularly interested in charting the pathway I am indicating here between the personal and the political. They seek to define a rhetorical situation that leaves room for change because none of the parties in the conversation is wholly determined either by material circumstances, such as biological gender, or by discursive constructions, such as the current cultural interpretations placed on gender. They seek a situation in which a positive stance, for better conditions as well as against present conditions, can be articulated free from charges of committing foundationalism.

One concise and thorough articulation of this view is Linda Alcoff's definition of "positionality." She argues that the meaning of the concept of "woman" is not defined by inherent, biologically determined characteristics, such as a tendency to nurture. But neither is "woman" constructed discursively of interpretations of gender that have no objective reality. An example of the latter would be to say that the notion that women cannot do science is merely an attitude that afflicts women, which they should be able to throw off once they realize its deleterious effects—as if a bad attitude were all that prevented women scholars from achieving equality in scientific research. Rather, Alcoff argues for an understanding of "woman" as defined, but not totally determined, by historical circumstances. Alcoff says:

> When the concept "woman" is defined not by a particular set of attributes but by a particular position, the internal characteristics of the person thus identified are not denoted so much as the external context within which that person is situated. The external situation determines the person's relative position, just as the position of a pawn on a chessboard is considered safe or dangerous, powerful or weak, according to its relation to the other chess pieces. . . . Seen in this way, being a "woman" is to take up a position within a moving historical context and to be able to choose what we make of this position and how we alter this context. (433)

As I understand Alcoff's argument, the concept of positionality could as easily be used as a basis for political action by people who choose to make their race or religion a defining feature of their identities. For example, under the concept of positionality it would not make sense to say that being black entails particular innate characteristics, such as having stronger emotions than whites have. It would also not make sense to say that being black is the same as being white, that color itself is a meaningless category, and anyone who imagines that differences can be attributed to it is deluded. But one could choose to work from a position that both acknowledged the shaping power of current cultural interpretations of ethnicity and aimed to transform the negative meaning of color differences.

Alcoff, however, may underemphasize the collective nature of positionality, which would have to be recovered for the concept to be truly rhetorical. Although I would agree with Alcoff that one's position has a subjective dimension, positional identity obviously entails group membership. Group interests thus shape individual choices for action. Moreover, the collective values of groups or positions against which one struggles must also be taken into account, as suggested earlier, as a means to persuasion. Gandhi and Martin Luther King provide models of how to use contradictions in the opponents' ideologies to sway them. Feminist theorist Dale M. Bauer uses Kenneth Burke's notion of identification to explicate further the ways in which rhetorical argument not only deconstructs opposing views but seeks to win adherents. In an essay in *College English,* Bauer boldly associates such an identificatory rhetoric with an appropriate form of feminist classroom authority. She believes feminist teachers should be unembarrassed about seeking to persuade students to accept their analyses in the interests of the common good.

It is highly relevant to our pursuit of a rhetorical turn in English studies that we discuss how our professional identities are shaped by our genders and sexual orientations, religions or secular ethical traditions, racial and ethnic identifications, regional or national origins, and also by the institutional histories of our schools and what is implicated for each of us by teaching where we do. Because we have not yet shared such discussions across the profession, I cannot conclude with a programmatic alternative to schemes for cultural literacy. I can only invite everyone to join seriously in a rhetorical process for articulating an alternative to which many of us can agree. This process will be a risky business; it will require arguing about what we should read and write, arguing about what canon we want to endorse instead of pretending we can will away the power of canons. It will require ideological avowals uncongenial to antifoundationalist philosophers. But I am not willing to concede yet that the smirk of skepticism is all we academics, or we Americans, can achieve in the face of the present crisis in our communal life. Certainly the last presidential campaign suggested that national discourse is dead, as Michael Halloran prophesied, and that we have no way of sharing views and concerns on the challenges confronting us. Those of us who would like to think of ourselves as humanists, as lovers of language, must attempt to create and share utopian rhetoric.

Works Cited

Alcoff, Linda. "Cultural Feminism versus Post-Structuralism: The Identity Crisis in Feminist Theory." *Signs* 13 (1988): 405–36.

Armstrong, Paul B. "Pluralistic Literacy." *Profession 88*. Ed. Phyllis Franklin. New York: Modern Language Association, 1988: 29–32.

Bauer, Dale M. "Empathy and Identification." Unpublished manuscript.

———. "The Other 'F' Word: The Feminist in the Dialogic Classroom." *College English* 52 (1990): 385–96.

Berlin, James. "A Course in Cultural Studies." Modern Language Association Convention. New Orleans, December 1988.

Bizzell, Patricia. "Arguing about Literacy." *College English* 50 (1988): 141–53.

Buckley, William K. "The Good, the Bad, and the Ugly in Amerika's *Akademia.*" *Profession 88*. Ed. Phyllis Franklin. New York: Modern Language Association, 1988: 46–52.

Cheney, Lynne V. "Humanities in America: A Report to the President, the Congress, and the American People." *Chronicle of Higher Education* (21 September 1988): A17–23.

Eagleton, Terry. *Literary Theory: An Introduction*. Minneapolis: University of Minnesota Press, 1983.

Franklin, Phyllis, ed. *Profession 88*. New York: Modern Language Association, 1988.

Green, Elizabeth. "Under Siege, Advocates of a More Diverse Curriculum Prepare for Continued Struggle in the Coming Year." *Chronicle of Higher Education* (28 September 1988): A13, A16.

Halloran, S. Michael. "Rhetoric in the American College Curriculum: The Decline of Public Discourse." *Pre/Text* 3 (1982): 245–69.

Hirsch, E. D. Jr., Joseph Kett, and James Trefil. *Cultural Literacy: What Every American Needs to Know*. Boston: Houghton, 1987.

Hovey, Kenneth Alan. "The Great Books versus America: Reassessing *The Closing of the American Mind.*" *Profession 88*. Ed. Phyllis Franklin. New York: Modern Language Association, 1988: 40–45.

Lanham, Richard. "The 'Q' Question." *South Atlantic Quarterly* 87 (1988): 653–700.

Lears, Jackson. "Deride and Conquer." Review of *Boxed In: The Culture of TV*, by Mark Crispin Miller. *Nation* (9 January 1989): 59–62.

Menocal, María Rosa. " 'We can't dance together.' " *Profession 88*. Ed. Phyllis Franklin. New York: Modern Language Association, 1988: 52–58.

Moglen, Helene. "Allan Bloom and E. D. Hirsch: Educational Reform as Tragedy and Farce." *Profession 88*. Ed. Phyllis Franklin. New York: Modern Language Association, 1988: 59–64.

Shaughnessy, Mina. *Errors and Expectations: A Guide for the Teacher of Basic Writing*. New York: Oxford University Press, 1977.

Sledd, Andrew, and James Sledd. "Hirsch's Use of His Sources in *Cultural Literacy*: A Critique." *Profession 88*. Ed. Phyllis Franklin. New York: Modern Language Association, 1988: 33–39.

Smith, Jeff. "Cultural Literacy and the Academic 'Left.' " *Profession 88*. Ed. Phyllis Franklin. New York: Modern Language Association, 1988: 25–28.

Composition Studies and Cultural Studies
Collapsing Boundaries

James A. Berlin

Calls for situating cultural studies, a radically different set of research and teaching practices, at the center of English studies have been frequent of late. These projects range from the liberal formulations of Jonathan Culler, Gerald Graff, and Robert Scholes to the frankly leftist proposals of Gayatri Spivak, Frank Lentricchia, Edward Said, and Fredric Jameson. Their common contention, admittedly within a dizzying range of differences, is that texts, both poetic and rhetorical, must be considered within the (variously defined) social context that produced them. Responses to texts, furthermore, must include the means for critiquing both text and context. For those of us interested in writing instruction, one of the most relevant and challenging of these formulations is found in Terry Eagleton's work. In *Literary Theory,* Eagleton defines his recommended version of cultural studies in relation to its historical precedents, locating them in the discipline of rhetoric:

> What would be specific to the kind of study I have in mind . . . would be its concern for the kinds of *effects* which discourses produce, and how they produce them. Reading a zoology textbook to find out about giraffes is part of studying zoology, but reading it to see how its discourse is structured and organized, and examining what kind of effects these forms and devices produce in particular readers in actual situations, is a different kind of project. It is, in fact, probably the oldest form of "literary criticism" in the world, known as rhetoric. Rhetoric, which was the received form of critical analysis all the way from ancient society to the eighteenth century, examined the way discourses are constructed in order to achieve certain effects. It was not worried about whether its objects of enquiry were speaking or writing, poetry or philosophy, fiction or historiogra-

phy: its horizon was nothing less than the field of discursive
practices in society as a whole, and its particular interest lay
in grasping such practices as forms of power and performance. (205)

Both here and in his long essay on the history of rhetoric, republished in *Walter
Benjamin,* Eagleton emphasizes the similarities between the projects of rhetorical studies and those of the cultural studies he prefers. For him, both involve the
study of signifying practices, of language use in writing and speaking and
language interpretation in reading and listening, with the focus on the relation
of these practices to the disposition of power—economic, social, and political—
at a particular historical moment. To paraphrase Eagleton, cultural studies
might then be described as the examination of the ways discursive formations
are related to power or, alternately, the study of language's uses in the service of
power. Indeed, this is the very definition of rhetoric many of us in composition
studies are now invoking.

In "Cultural Studies and Teaching Writing," John Trimbur has issued the
first fully articulated account of the convergences to be discovered in the projects
of cultural studies and contemporary composition studies. In this essay, I wish
both to follow his lead and to answer the challenge he poses to workers in composition. I will, however, make my case somewhat differently. My first task will
be to show briefly that composition studies since its inception in the modern
college English department has contained voices that have attempted to define
rhetoric as cultural studies in the sense just described. My second effort will be to
outline the shape this undertaking is presently assuming. I cannot emphasize
too strongly, however, that I will in no sense suggest that cultural studies is to be
considered a deliverer come to save writing teachers from the errors of their
ways. Instead, my argument is that the endeavors of cultural studies and the
endeavors of composition studies are mutually enriching. While we in rhetoric
can benefit from examining the workers in cultural studies, they in turn have
much to gain from considering what we are about. Our problematics are finally
similar and thoroughly compatible. In this essay I wish to show Eagleton to be
even more right than he realizes in asserting that in many important respects
cultural studies is an attempt to recover the role rhetoric has historically played.

Before beginning the historical analysis of the relations of composition to
cultural studies, I would like to consider a formulation of cultural studies
developed at the Birmingham Department of Cultural Studies, a program that

I would argue best demonstrates projects parallel to current work in composition studies. In "What Is Cultural Studies Anyway?" Richard Johnson, past head of the Birmingham department, has explained that cultural studies can best be considered in terms of its characteristic *objects* of study and in terms of its *methods*. Both objects and methods are organized around an examination of the formations of consciousness and subjectivity: "Cultural studies is about the historical forms of consciousness or subjectivity, or the subjective forms we live by, or, in a rather perilous compression, perhaps a reduction, the subjective side of social relations" (43). For Johnson, cultural studies is related to the projects of structuralism and poststructuralism: "Subjectivities are produced, not given, and are therefore the objects of inquiry, not the premises or starting points" (44). Signifying practices then become crucial features of investigation, constituting "the structured character of the forms we inhabit subjectively: language, signs, ideologies, discourses, myths" (45). In other words, cultural studies concerns itself with the ways social formations and practices shape consciousness, and this shaping is mediated by language and situated in concrete historical conditions. The important addendum is that this relation between the social and the subjective is ideological, is imbricated in economic, social, and political considerations that are always historically specific. It is no coincidence that calls for cultural studies in the English department are coming most insistently from the left, from those most likely to see relations of power in all discursive practices. Thus cultural studies involves the ideological formation of subjects, of forms of consciousness, within historically specific signifying practices that are enmeshed in power. For Johnson, then, the objects of cultural studies are the production, distribution, and reception of signifying practices within the myriad social formations that are shaping subjectivities. These formations range from the family, the school, the workplace, and the peer group to the more familiar activities associated with the cultural sphere, such as the arts (high and low) and the media and their modes of production and consumption. In other words, wherever signifying practices are shaping consciousness in daily life, cultural studies has work to do.

Although Johnson considers the *methods* of cultural studies to be varied and interdisciplinary, his discussion of them is sometimes obscure. Vincent Leitch provides an effective summary: "The modes of inquiry employed in cultural studies included not only established survey techniques, field interviews, textual explications, and researches into sociohistorical backgrounds, but also especially institutional and ideological analysis" (179). The interdisciplinary nature of these methods is unmistakable. More important, in all cases, the data gathered by these diverse means are situated within the institution—family, work, art—that sponsored the examined activities and are related to the ideological—the arena of language, idea, and value. In "What Is Cultural Studies," Johnson is especially concerned with elucidating the kinds of research cultural studies has encouraged, seeing these methods as appearing across them. The research activities fall into three general categories: production-based studies, text-based studies, and studies of culture as a lived activity. These categories, as we shall see, are particularly resonant within discussions of current research in composition studies.

Production-based studies deal with the "production and social organization of cultural forms" (Johnson 54). This includes a broad range of objects of study, from public relations, advertising, and the mass media to the production of race, class, and gender behavior within the schools. The methods are diverse, calling on the procedures of the social sciences as well as textual analysis. This group of approaches focuses on the conditions of cultural production and distribution—of the media, an artwork, or the schools—without regard to the negotiation and resistance involved at the point of consumption. For Johnson, this oversight is a serious flaw, especially in the tendency of certain mechanistic marxisms to insist that the economic base determines consciousness.

A second group of studies involves text-based efforts derived from work with literary productions and their reception and interpretation. Johnson particularly has in mind the powerful methods of textual analysis developed by structuralist and poststructuralist literary theory and the ways these methods are able to address the relation of texts to subject formation. For example, one could study the relation of the kinds of literary texts read in school, and the means of interpreting them, to formations of class, race, and gender expectations among schoolchildren. The strategies discovered in textual interpretation are connected to students' lived experience. Johnson, however, takes pains to emphasize that reading is itself an act of production, not simply a passive act of receiving a determinate text. Once again, we must consider the readers' negotiation of, and resistance to, a text.

The third cluster of approaches focuses on "lived cultures" and attempts to grasp "the more *concrete* and more *private* moments of cultural circulation" (Johnson 69). Ethnography is the primary research method in the attempt to locate responses to cultural experience. Johnson points to studies of the ways adolescent girls and boys appropriate cultural forms for their own ends, ends that often subvert the producers' intentions—as, for example, in Dick Hebdige's study of adolescent culture in London. Since, at the point of lived culture, interpretive strategies of negotiation and resistance are involved, textual strategies again may become important.

The major flaw in all three approaches, Johnson explains, is that each tends to dwell on one moment of cultural performance-production or the cultural product or cultural negotiation without regard for the entire process.

In describing the objects and methods of cultural studies, Johnson has endorsed Eagleton's contention that the project of cultural studies is closely related to the historical project of rhetorical studies. Johnson has also improved on Eagleton in emphasizing the complex relation between the production and reception of cultural artifacts and in placing consciousness formation at the center of cultural studies. Eagleton, however, usefully reminds us that rhetoric has historically studied the ways discourse—in both production and interpretation—shapes the experiences of individuals, and, particularly in its classical manifestation, discourse's role in power and the political process.

This brings me to the historical dimension of my presentation. Composition studies, since its formation in college English departments a hundred years ago, has in many of its manifestations attempted to become a variety of cultural studies. In other words, it has worked to form itself as an activity that studies the construction of subjects within social formations, focusing on the signifying practices of written and spoken texts and the implication of those practices in power and ideology. It has, furthermore, attempted to offer a critique of these practices and power formations. Of the three dominant paradigms of composition studies that have appeared during this time, two—the expressionistic and the social constructionist, unlike their strongest competitor, the current-traditional—have self-consciously criticized dominant power arrangements, thus attempting to provide students with the means for negotiation and resistance. Both, however, have failed as cultural studies, each in its unique way falling short of its promise to provide a comprehensive program that can critique the production and reception of discourse within the realm of power and politics. Nevertheless, this account demonstrates that the current move to cultural studies in English departments, as Eagleton has unintentionally underscored, is not without historical precedents and that we can locate one set of precedents in the devalorized "service" sector of the department. (Patrick Brantlinger has recently found others in Victorian studies and American studies.) Here we discover the important political and cultural work that composition has been asked to do, a task no less ambitious than distinguishing true from untrue discourse in disputations about power and privilege.

In considering these rhetorics, I analyze certain features of their ideological predispositions, calling on a method based on the work of Goran Therborn in *The Ideology of Power and the Power of Ideology*. (I discuss Therborn at greater length in "Rhetoric and Ideology in the Writing Class.") From this perspective, ideology interpellates subjects—that is, addresses and shapes them—through discourses that point out what exists, what is good, and what is possible. Significantly, ideology also includes a version of power formations governing the agent in relation to all these designations. Thus, as Therborn explains, directives about the existent deal with "who we are, what the world is, what nature, society, men, and women are like. In this way we acquire a sense of identity, becoming conscious of what is real and true." The good indicates what is "right, just, beautiful, attractive, enjoyable, and its opposites" (18). The good concerns the realms of politics and ethics and art. The possible tells us what can be accomplished given the existent and the good. It grants us "our sense of the mutability of our being-in-the-world, and the consequences of change are hereby patterned, and our hopes, ambitions, and fears given shape" (18). The last consideration is closely related to the question of power, its distribution, and its control. From this perspective, the subject is the point of intersection of various discourses—discourses about class, race, gender, ethnicity, age, religion, and the like—and it is influenced by these discourses. Equally important, the subject in turn affects these very discourses. The individual is the location of a variety of significations but is also an agent of change, not simply an unwitting product of external discursive and material forces. The subject negotiates and resists codes instead of merely accommodating them.

I now turn to the two English department rhetorics that have attempted to do the work of cultural studies, along with the reasons for their failures. Once again, I consider the effort these rhetorics make to examine signifying practices in the formation of subjectivities within concrete material, social, and political conditions. I am especially attentive to their conceptions of the existent, the good, and the possible and the larger relations of power within these elements.

The Rhetoric of Liberal Culture and Expressionism

As both David Russell and I have shown, the rhetoric of liberal culture was a strong reactionary force in the new university during the last century. While

Harvard, Cornell, and the recently established state universities were working to create a new meritocracy of certified scientific experts, Yale, Princeton, and other universities were clinging to the notion of education as a perquisite of birth and breeding. Against the position that the new scientific discourse set the standard for writing and reading practices, liberal culturists argued that the only discourse worthy of consideration was the poetic. Endorsing a mandarin Romanticism, this rhetoric insisted that art is the product of genius and that genius is the product of class and cultivation. Thus, only men (not women) of genius should be encouraged to produce genuine discourse—that is, poetic texts—while the rest of humankind, which usually (but not always) included women, should work to interpret these texts. And just as the great male heroes in poetry were to instruct the inferior orders, only great heroes in economic, social, and political institutions should be entrusted with power. Art and public affairs mutually reinforced the authority and privilege of a small leadership class.

Liberal culture was the response of a declining Anglo-Protestant power elite in the face of serious threats to its status, threats posed by the new bourgeoisie in economic matters and the new urban immigrant working class in politics. The rhetoric of liberal culture finally experienced a dramatic transformation during the 1920s. The poetic text remained the highest manifestation of genuine discourse, but the ability to produce these texts was democratized. Inspired culturally by the child-study movement, a bowdlerized Freudianism, and aesthetic expressionism, proponents of these new ideas henceforth considered genius the birthright of all human beings. Expressionist rhetoric was thus self-consciously political, forwarding a democratic agenda of equality. It responded to the horrors of capitalism, particularly the dehumanizing mechanization of everyday urban experience and the oppression of the individual. The causes of economic, social, and political problems were accordingly attributed to institutional violations of the uniqueness of each human being. The responses to these violations, however, were seldom either economic or political. Instead, they were portrayed as private and personal.

Writing and reading practices were thus depicted as solitary acts providing the means to restore the subject to his or her true nature, or authentic self, putting the subject in touch with the inner voice that is each person's unique center and guide. The ideology of this rhetoric then located the existent in the individual, and the good and possible were to serve the individual and subvert the herd impulse of social arrangements. Text production emphasized looking within (sometimes even including meditation techniques) and personal writing (the journal, the letter, the lyric). Furthermore, metaphoric language was central since it was the only means writers had to suggest the subtleties of their private visions. In contrast, the language of direct statement represented the dehumanized discourse of science, which stood for the oppressiveness of urban capitalism. Thus, in this discourse system, scientific textual practices were placed in opposition to particular poetic practices, and all authentic writing aspired to the condition of poetry. Indeed, rhetoric attempted to reproduce the effects of poetry for both writer and reader since all genuine signifying practices were necessarily aesthetic.

In the 1960s and 1970s, many expressionists aligned themselves with the New Left. They still regarded writing and reading as personal, private, and creative acts of resistance. They offered such acts to counter the socially imposed cruelties of dominant institutional discourses that enforced racism, inequitable economic arrangements, and an unjust war. The expressionists thought that institutional signifying practices, including those of the university, destroyed the unified, coherent, transcendent self, and they encouraged their students to resist these socially imposed directives and retreat to the personal and private.

Expressionist rhetoric is radically democratic, opposing dominant class, race, and gender divisions in the interests of equality. I show in "Rhetoric and Ideology in the Writing Class," however, that as a cultural studies this rhetoric lacks the devices to anticipate an effective critique, creating as it does a simple binary opposition between the personal and the social. It refuses the possibility that the self the individual discovers is finally a response to social and cultural formations, a script at least in part written by class, race, and gender codes. Thus, when students know in their hearts that a certain text—their own or someone else's—is true and authentic, they often are making a judgment based on a class-defined notion, not a personal and private criterion, the student having invoked a socially inscribed conception of the self in making the judgment. This is another way of saying that expressionism's uncritical acceptance of the unified, coherent, and originary self renders its critique suspect. Expressionist rhetoric, furthermore, argues for a privatized notion of power, seeing larger economic and political formations in narrowly personal terms. Institutions are simply individuals writ large, and all opposition to them is to be conducted in strictly personal terms. This formulation prevents a realistic examination of the ways power operates within social formations. Critique and resistance are ineffective in dealing with the institutional forces that are beyond the remedy of individuals acting alone—whether inside or outside the institution. Expressionist reading and writing practices often result in quietism and the acceptance of defeat, self-help therapeutic ministrations in response to a world gone wrong (see Faigley, "Judging").

Social Constructionist Rhetoric

As I demonstrate in *Rhetoric and Reality,* social constructionist rhetoric appeared at the turn of the century, primarily in the Midwest but also at a number of eastern colleges, especially women's schools. Growing out of progressive politics—itself a response to the cruelties of urban capitalism and democratic populism—this position acknowledged the influence of social forces in the formation of the individual. Because each person is first and foremost a member of a community, any claim to individuality can only be articulated within a social context. The existent, the good, and the possible are determined by consulting the welfare of the populace as a whole. All citizens must learn reading and writing in order to take part in the dialogue of democracy. These activities, moreover, call on a social hermeneutic, measuring the value of a text in relation to its importance to the larger society. Thus the expertise of the new meritocratic class must be employed in the service of the community, and the community, not the experts themselves, must finally decide on solutions to economic, social, and political problems. In the schools, John Dewey's pragmatism obviously had a strong influence on this rhetoric, which placed reading and writing practices at the center of communal decision making. It was the counterpart of a literary criticism that regarded poetic texts in relation to their social and cultural context, for example, in the work of Fred Newton Scott, Gertrude Buck, Vida Dutton Scudder, Moses Coit Tyler, and Frederick Lewis Pattee.

During the 1920s, this rhetoric spawned the "ideas approach," an attempt to regard the writing course as training in political discourse. Students read contradictory points of view on contemporary social problems and wrote essays stating their own positions. During the Depression, socially oriented approaches took a leftist turn. For example, Warren Taylor of Wisconsin voiced the hope that school and college rhetoric courses would help students learn to examine their cultural experience—"advertisement, editorial, newsreel, radio speech, article, or book" (853)—for threats to the democratic process at a time of national crisis. Fearful that an elite might prevail against the claims of the community, this rhetoric saw the critical examination of the subtle effects of signifying practices as a key to egalitarian decision making. A similar effort was taken up after World War II when the communications course—combining writing, reading, speaking, and listening—was forwarded as a safeguard for democracy, particularly against the threats of propaganda. General semantics was especially prominent, arguing for a scientific notion of signifying practices that enabled discrimination between true and deceptive political discourse. During the 1960s and 1970s, responses to racial injustice, poverty, and the conflict in Vietnam once again encouraged a rhetoric of public discourse that demanded communal participation in decision making—for example, in the work of Harold Martin, the early Richard Ohmann, and Kenneth Bruffee.

Despite the considerable attractions of this social rhetoric, its flaws cannot be denied. While it emphasizes the communal and social constitution of subjectivity, it never abandons the notion of the individual as finally a sovereign free agent, capable of transcending mere material and social conditions. Although it does look to democratic political institutions as the solution to social problems, it lacks a critique of economic arrangements, arguing that the political is primary and, finally, determinative. The critique of capitalism occasionally found during the 1930s was thus abandoned after the war. This rhetoric also displays an innocence about power, lacking the means for the critique of it beyond a faith in the possibility of open public discourse and the ballot box. It cannot, for example, problematize the obvious inequities in access to public discourse or the failures of the elective process when candidates do not offer genuine alternatives. And while this rhetoric sees the manipulative power of discourse, it continues to believe that a universal, ahistorical, rational discourse is possible. As a result, it regards itself as a disinterested and objective arbiter of competing ideological claims, occupying a neutral space above the fray of conflict. In other words, it is incapable of examining its own ideological commitments, which it mistakes for accurate reflections of eternal truths. It accepts its signifying practices as indisputably representative of things as they really are.

Social Epistemic Rhetoric

Social epistemic rhetoric has attempted to take into account the challenge to discourse study posed by recent marxist, structuralist, and poststructuralist theory—an attempt that has led rhetoric and composition studies to mirror developments in the cultural studies forwarded by Eagleton and the Birmingham group. Trimbur has effectively described the historical conditions that have encouraged this rhetoric, locating them in a return to the participatory political impulse of the 1960s, a response to the exploitation of composition teachers in English departments, the crisis in the literary canon, and, of course, the reaction to poststructuralism, particularly the decentering of the self ("Cultural Studies"). I would add to this list the politicizing education begun by Richard Nixon in 1968 and carried to its farthest reaches in the Reagan administration. After William Bennett, E. D. Hirsch, Jr., and Allan Bloom, it is difficult for English teachers to argue that any texts, literary or otherwise, occupy a position above the fray of political contention.

Social epistemic rhetoric has two corresponding but separate historical trajectories in English and Communication departments, both independent of European influences, at least until recently (see Berlin, "Rhetoric Programs"). This rhetoric is instead functioning within the framework of earlier social rhetorics. Most important, social epistemic rhetoric has maintained its commitment to preparing students for citizenship in a democratic society. Public discourse openly and freely pursued remains a central objective. Departures from its predecessors, however, are more significant. This newly formulated rhetoric is self-reflexive, acknowledging its own rhetoricity, its own discursive constitution and limitations. It does not deny its inescapable ideological predispositions, its conditions of always already being committed politically. It does not claim to be above ideology, a transcendent discourse that objectively adjudicates competing ideological judgments. It knows that it is ideologically situated, an intervention in the political process, as are all rhetorics. At the same time, it is aware of its historical contingency, of its limitation and incompleteness, and it remains open to change and revision.

Social epistemic rhetoric argues that the writing subject is a discursive construction, the subject serving as a point of conjuncture for a plethora of discourses—a rich variety of texts inscribed in the persona of the individual. The subject is thus a construction of the play of discourses that a culture provides. These discourses interpellate or address us, providing each of us with directions about our behavior, scripts that have to do with such categories as race, class, and gender. These discursive formations, or cultural codes, exist prior to us, being inscribed in the institutional and social practices that constitute our historical moment. Equally important, they not only form the subject but also indicate the subject's very conception of the material, social, and political. In other words, the subject's possible responses to experience are all textually situated, are all the result of the interaction of discursive structures, cultural codes revealing the possible relations that can exist in and among these elements. The individual never responds to things in themselves but to discursive formations of things in themselves. Concrete material conditions do, of course, finally shape and limit behavior, but they are always mediated by discourse.

This formulation does not preclude the possibility of individuality and agency. As Trimbur (following Mikhail Bakhtin) has shown, each individual represents a unique combination of discourses, of voices, because each individual occupies a unique position in the network of discourses encountered ("Essayist Literacy"). One may act in and through these discourses, working to change them and the material conditions they mediate in one's experience. This project is not, however, undertaken in a domain of complete freedom. The individual is always forced to act within material conditions and signifying practices not of his or her own making.

This conception of the subject, material reality, and signifying practices clearly calls for a revised model of writing and reading. Both composing and interpreting texts become acts of discourse analysis and negotiation. Indeed, writing and reading are themselves verbally coded acts, discursive procedures that guide the production and interpretation of meanings, making a certain range more likely to appear and others more improbable. This exclusionary coding is apparent, for example, in reflections on the directives for text production and reception provided in the expressionist and the social rhetorics considered earlier: for expressionist rhetoric, only personal and metaphorical accounts can be regarded as meaningful; for social rhetoric, only accounts that are communal and rational. In addition, writing and reading become acts of discourse analysis as individuals attempt to understand the semiotic codes operating in their discursive situations. Composing and reception are thus interactive since both are performances of production, requiring the active construction of meaning according to one or another coded procedure. The opposition between the active writer and the passive reader is displaced: both writing and reading are regarded as constructive. The work of rhetoric is to develop a lexicon that articulates the complex coding activity involved in writing and reading.

Composition Studies and Cultural Studies

Composition studies is undertaking projects in both pedagogy and research that parallel those in cultural studies. Some of these efforts signal the emergence of a social epistemic rhetoric, a rhetoric that considers signifying practices in relation to the ideological formation of the self within a context of economics, politics, and power. Two recent essay collections indicate that composition studies has arrived at a conception of itself that refuses to apologize for rhetoric's historical commitment to the classroom. Furthermore, their appearance represents an effort to bring together the work of theory, politics, and classroom practice to produce a rich new form of dialogue in English studies, a dialogue that characterizes the projects of cultural studies at every turn.

Reclaiming Pedagogy: The Rhetoric of the Classroom, edited by Patricia Donahue and Ellen Quandahl, examines the relation between the composition class and critical theory. The volume argues not that theory and practice will correct or justify each other but that together they will enable a new discourse including and transcending both. This position recovers the space Aristotle designated the jurisdiction of rhetoric, the historically contingent domain of the productive arts lying between theory and practice (Atwill). The result is a poststructuralist and political rhetoric and pedagogy.

Having called for a refigured discourse for rhetoric and the classroom, Donahue and Quandahl set forth the premises of the collection, and here their self-conscious alignment with the projects of cultural studies is everywhere apparent. The participants pointedly deny the unified, coherent, transcendent self of liberal humanism, arguing "that there is no such thing as creating words out of yourself, since subjectivity, one's self, is a social order, preexisting the individual. . . . One enters rather than generates a textual history" (13). Once again, however, the social and the subject interact: "Put simply, the symbolic order of culture is its collective set of signifying systems, one of which is language, and language is a system that preexists the individual. The individual enters that system at a particular stage of development, uses it to produce meaning, and is produced by it" (12).

These essays thus take textuality as their center, the pedagogy offered being "textual, text-oriented," an assertion that involves several consequences. Language is seen "as a system of power and . . . the reader as a constituent of that system." Students are encouraged to engage in "resistant readings," readings that "resist the monologic voice that depends for its meaning upon readers thoroughly sharing the assumptions of writers." The point is to allow "variously circulating interpretive codes to come into play . . . not to awaken the ideologically complacent, but to teach ways in which discursive authority functions" (3). Thus signifying practices are regarded not only as diverse and conflictual but as immersed in ideology. Language is further identified "as the site of struggle to determine 'truth' and to control its production" (4). All positions are considered always already ideological so that teacher and student must acknowledge their own political situatedness. But the classroom cannot simply reproduce the shaping process of culture and ideology. Instead, the attention must be directed to "the cultural inscriptions in any text, including the pedagogical scene" (9). The detection of cultural codes is essential, as is cultivation of the student's ability to resist texts. Students are "to assert power, to own rules, and to shape a new content" (11). In short, they are to engage in interpretive practices that enable critique, a critique that is always ideologically situated. Donahue and Quandahl, however, are not altogether sanguine that it is possible to create a resistant subject capable of recognizing concealed conflicts and examining the reasons for that concealment. They recognize the constraints of their situation: "In spite of the strong rhetoric of subversion in many of the theorists cited in this volume, we know that there is even stronger institutional pressure to align new theory with the known" (15). Yet this "rhetoric of subversion" is in remarkably short supply in the collection as a whole, with the attention to theory continually superseding the commitment to a radical politics.

The premise of *Composition and Resistance,* edited by C. Mark Hurlbert and Michael Blitz, is closely related to that of *Reclaiming Pedagogy.* One significant difference is the strong insistence that the rhetorical and pedagogical practices offered are contestatory. This time the theory-practice association is at every turn related to the ideological and political nature of discourse. Indeed, *Composition and Resistance* is self-consciously committed to change outside as well as within the classroom, since the essays emphasize an agenda of social transformation that would promote democratic practices at all levels and phases of society.

The social constructionist text regards the subject as the product of intersecting and conflicting discourses, all part of power formations. The role of the writing class then becomes to intervene in this process of construction, locating the conflicts in order to make them the center of writing. Thus, the editors explain, "Composition teachers must work with students to examine and intervene in the 'construction' which produces people as subjects and by which people subject other people to inequitable, abusive, intolerable conditions" (25). Since language is at the center of the formation of the subject, serving as the mediator between material conditions and the individual, writing—text production—is a manifestation of the central process of self and social formation. Echoing both poststructuralist and marxist categories, the editors argue that, as language rewrites the subject and society, the subject can rewrite language in reshaping the self and social arrangements. Writing is therefore both social and personal, providing students with the means "to make learning a personal act toward taking greater control" of their lives, and it must situate this process "in and with social order" (4).

Text production and reception then become essential acts of human agency in a democratic society, a society that promises a space for open and free critique and yet denies it at every turn. The impulse is to take the promise of democracy seriously, to take "literally the kinds of rights and freedoms that people in positions of political/social/economic power *profess* to guarantee" (22). There is no question that the "required" form of academic discourse discourages these freedoms, enforcing instead a conformity of thought and expression, demanding "codes of silence" (4). The alternative is not to abandon academic discourse altogether—the volume is not without it—but to test its limits by examining its excluded other, the discourse of students themselves, by "supporting students' efforts to move back and forth (one meaning of interpretation) between dialects and styles" (23). The classroom encourages new ways of writing and reading without neglecting the contrasting ways of the old; students consider "Plato *and* Navaho folk tales, Shakespeare *and* Jacqueline Susann, rap *as well as* papers of/on literary criticism, or better, critical papers infused with the power of rap—the power to speak for change by speaking in a new way and in and for a new place—by self-consciously calling for participation and action" (24). This participation and action, furthermore, is once again self-consciously social: it asks for collaboration not only among student writers but also among teachers—a call for enacting as well as endorsing a social rhetoric.

The participants in *Composition and Resistance,* like their counterparts in *Reclaiming Pedagogy,* do not underestimate the obstacles to their objectives. Indeed, the essays in the collection record the difficulties in this undertaking. Asking a group of students to interrogate the conventions of the privileged social class they are working hard to enter—the class to which the teachers already comfortably belong—is not an easy task, and the process may involve discomfort for teachers and students alike. To refuse to engage the ideological dimensions of "ordinary discourse," however, is to acquiesce to injustices that underwrite class, race, gender, age, and other invidious distinctions. This collection, then, offers no easy answers or solutions, but it does "attempt to introduce incoherence—a loss of composure—into 'the entrenched order of things,'" not for the sake of anarchy or deconstructionist free play, but in the interests of bringing about a better social and personal order. Despite all their doubts, confusions, and failures, the participants in this collection remain committed to writing as a political act of transformation and betterment.

These two remarkable volumes firmly establish the parallel trajectories of certain projects in composition studies and cultural studies. Other book-length projects take up some of their major themes, most notably Susan Miller's *Rescuing the Subject,* David Bleich's *Double Perspective,* and Marilyn Cooper and Michael Holzman's *Writing as Social Action.* In addition, a number of other research efforts under way in composition studies—efforts sometimes deliberately centered on the classroom and sometimes not—share the problematic and inquiry agendas of cultural studies. Johnson's description of the three major kinds of cultural studies projects so far attempted—productive, textual, and lived experience—provides a useful organizing device for considering a few of these efforts. I hasten to add that this research is not the only kind of project I recommend for composition studies. Janice Lauer and Andrea Lunsford's quite different description of the three major emphases of rhetoric and composition graduate programs (history, theory, and empirical studies) is a better scheme for conceptualizing the field as a whole. I am instead interested in research that cuts across these useful divisions without replacing them. In other words, these endeavors expand without replacing present work in rhetoric and composition.

Johnson's tripartite division of cultural studies into productive, textual, and lived experience categories is related to a specific model of cultural dissemination. This model corresponds generally with the rhetorical model of communication described by figures as diverse as Aristotle, Kenneth Burke, and Andrea Lunsford. In short, cultural artifacts are produced, the production assumes some textual form (print, film, television, conversation), the text is consumed by an audience in the form of negotiated interpretations, and the interpretations are part of the lived cultures or social relations of the interpreters. As I said earlier, Johnson criticizes the examples of cultural studies he presents because they tend to focus on one moment of the process instead of considering the process as a whole.

One conspicuous strength of recent work in rhetoric and composition studies is its attempt to focus on the process of text production. While the dominant paradigms in literary studies have been restricted to text interpretation and, then, apart from any influencing context, labeling production an inaccessible function of genius, composition has attempted to study and describe the concrete activities of text production. This approach is in keeping with rhetoric's historical emphasis on teaching strategies for generating texts, primarily heuristic procedures for invention, patterns of arrangement, and principles of syntax and style.

More recently, the concern for production has been seen in empirical studies of the composing process, from the case studies of Janet Emig to the protocol analysis of Linda Flower and John R. Hayes and others. As some observers have pointed out, these studies often suffer from a conception of composing as an exclusively private, psychologically determined act, a stance that distorts because it neglects the larger social contexts of composing. Addressing this inadequacy in considering text production is the turn in composition research to ethnographic study or, in the terms favored by the Birmingham group, the study of culture as lived activity. The pioneer in this effort in English studies in the United States has been Shirley Brice Heath, who has related patterns of learning in language to subject formation within structures of class, race, and gender. Two recent volumes have shown the effects of this work: *Reclaiming the Classroom*, edited by Dixie Goswami and Peter R. Stillman, and *The Writing Teacher as Researcher*, edited by Donald A. Daiker and Max Morenberg. The teacher-as-researcher impulse is an attempt to make all teachers ethnographic researchers of the concrete economic and social conditions of their students, situating instruction in text production and interpretation within the lived cultures of students, within class, race, gender, and ethnic determinations. Both volumes, furthermore, have begun the work of considering the ideological as well as the narrowly institutional settings of learning, and both examine student signifying practices within the conflicts of concrete economic, social, and political conditions. Although these studies have so far been somewhat tentative in stating that their investigations are political, at their best they examine signifying practices within the entire context of production, texts, readings, and lived cultures. (I return to the uses of ethnography later.)

Other studies dealing with text production have been organized around a consideration of collaborative learning and writing, a subject treated historically in Anne Gere's engaging monograph. Current work in this area is extensive, but Kenneth Bruffee is the person whose name is most often associated with this project. Several critiques of his work—critiques not necessarily unfriendly—have recently attempted to figure collaboration in relation to the place of signifying practices in forming subjectivities within concrete social and material conditions. Lisa Ede and Andrea Lunsford, for example, have invoked the theories of Roland Barthes and Michel Foucault on authorship and the actual practices of writers outside the classroom to argue that collaborative writing constitutes the norm for composing and that writing is necessarily communal. Trimbur has also called on ideological critique in treating the strengths and weaknesses of collaborative practices, attempting to refigure them in the light of a social conception of subject formation that allows for struggle and resistance at the site of group efforts ("Consensus"). In short, discussions of text production within the context of collaborative learning have begun to interrogate the insistence on writing as an exclusively private and personal act of a docile and quiescent subject.

The many methods of textual critique that rely on structuralist and post-structuralist language theory generally fall into two groups. The first of these seeks to analyze the discourse of various disciplinary formations in order to locate their part in shaping subjectivities within historical conditions. Mina Shaughnessy undertook this form of analysis when she identified the use of medical language to discuss basic writers and the disadvantaged social groups from which they often emerge. Trimbur points out that for Shaughnessy "cultural studies of writing might begin in at least one important respect as an effort of writing teachers to resist the dominant representations of subordinate groups and to contest the social construction of otherness as pathological problems for the professional intervention of educators, social workers, urban planners, and policy-makers" ("Cultural Studies" 15). Shaughnessy has in turn encouraged a host of resistant readings of institutional constructions of teachers and students, most notably in the work of Linda Brodkey, David Bartholomae, Patricia Bizzell, and Greg Myers. The use of textual as well as ethnographic analysis along distinctly feminist lines in examining signifying practices and self-formations in writing is also seen in the recent work of Elizabeth Flynn.

Others in this first category have tried to locate the workings of discursive practices in the formation of scientific disciplines, exploring the structure of disciplinary formations and the subjectivities that inhabit them as a function of signifying practices. Carolyn Miller, Greg Myers, and Charles Bazerman have been especially prominent in this undertaking. Some researchers have attempted the textual analysis of signifying practices in various nonacademic settings. For example, Barbara Hamilton has combined an ethnographic method with textual analysis in examining written presentence recommendations in criminal offenses in a Detroit court. Myrna Harrienger has considered the signifying practices of ill, elderly women in nursing homes and the ways in which medical discourse silences them. Gary Heba, emulating Hebdige's work on youth subcultures, has examined the relation of youth movies to adolescents' resistance to hegemonic discourse practices.

The second group of textual studies focuses on developing lexicons for locating and examining the imbrications of textual practices and power, considering the methods of textuality in forming subjectivity. Much work along these lines has been conducted in Communication departments as a part of media studies—for example, the projects of Arthur Asa Berger, Stuart Ewen, and John Fiske. Much less has appeared in English departments, but the work has begun. George Dillon, for example, discusses the cultural codes inscribed within popular advice books, calling on the language of structuralist and poststructuralist categories. W. Ross Winterowd's book *The Rhetoric of the "Other" Literature* attempts to provide a critical language for nonliterary texts, invoking the work of Aristotle, Burke, and poststructuralism. Both Dillon and Winterowd regard reading and writing practices as interchangeable in that they are constructive rather than simply reflective of experience, although the two works also share a timidity about discussing the politics of signifying practices. Still these projects represent a start in the right direction. Workers in composition studies must now devise lexicons to enable the discussion of the structures and ideological strategies of written texts that take into account recent marxist and poststructuralist developments; terminologies and methods are needed to act as counterparts, for example, to the rich work of Fiske in television studies. If students are to evaluate the role of signifying practices in forming consciousness through their own writing and reading, teachers must provide a language for identifying these practices and their operations.

I have already discussed the study of lived cultures through ethnographic means as recommended by the teacher-as-researcher development. As Janice Lauer and J. William Asher have indicated, ethnographic study of lived cultures has been undertaken in settings outside the school, more specifically, in writing in the workplace. Until recently, however, these studies have not challenged the practices considered, taking them as objects of analysis, not of critique. Jennie Dautermann has shown new possibilities by examining the discourses of female nurses in a hospital setting as they collaboratively compose a manual for nursing procedures. Her study reveals the conflicts in power formations and the way subordinate groups negotiate them in a setting in which male doctors give orders and female nurses carry them out. In "Interpersonal Conflict in Collaborative Writing," Mary M. Lay is also concerned with gender codes and their relation to power in collaborative writing in business settings. In "Ideology and Collaboration in the Classroom and in the Corporation," James E. Porter attempts to apply an ideological critique to the teaching of collaborative writing in the business-writing classroom as well as in the business-writing setting itself. All these studies focus on the conflicts generated as signifying practices form discursive subject locations within an institutional setting, conflicts that reproduce the class, race, and gender struggles of the larger society.

The composition studies described in this essay is finally consistent with the historical role rhetoric has performed in most Western societies, but it is also a salutary departure from that role. Ruling classes have always made certain that their members are adept at the signifying practices that ensure the continuance of their power. Rhetorics as diverse as those of Plato, Cicero, Augustine, Hugh Blair, and I. A. Richards have been forwarded in the name of a "true" discourse, a discourse, however, that best served the interests of a particular ruling group. The important difference in the rhetoric outlined here is the commitment to democratic practices, that is, practices that work for the equitable distribution of the power to speak and write among all groups in a society. In addition, this rhetoric includes the commitment to make available to these groups the rhetorical competence to present their positions effectively, including the means to resist and subvert dominant discourse practices. Both its research program and its pedagogical practices are accordingly dedicated to establishing the social conditions for genuinely democratic discourse communities. For some, sad to say, this effort will be considered inappropriate and misguided or even dangerously close to "indoctrination," as Maxine Hairston has recently charged in a burst of anti-intellectual conservatism. For its adherents, though, it seems the only possible hope for a society that too often prefers the exchange of violence to the exchange of language in addressing conflicts. Rhetoric, after all, was invented to resolve disputes peacefully, as an alternative to armed conflict, and it remains the best option in a perilous time.

Works Cited

Atwill, Janet. "Refiguring Rhetoric in Art: The Concept of Techne and the Humanist Paradigm." Dissertation, Purdue University, 1989.

Berlin, James. "Rhetoric and Ideology in the Writing Class." *College English* 50 (1988): 477–94.

———. "Rhetoric Programs after World War II: Ideology, Power, and Conflict." *Rhetoric and Ideology: Compositions and Criticisms of Power*. Ed. Charles W. Kneupper. Arlington, Tex.: Rhetoric Society of America, 1989: 6–19.

———. *Rhetoric and Reality: Writing Instruction in American Colleges, 1900–1985*. Carbondale: Southern Illinois University Press, 1987.

Bleich, David. *The Double Perspective: Language, Literacy, and Social Relations*. New York: Oxford University Press, 1988.

Brantlinger, Patrick. *Crusoe's Footprints: Cultural Studies in Britain and America*. New York: Routledge, 1990.

Cooper, Marilyn, and Michael Holzman. *Writing as Social Action*. Portsmouth, N.H.: Boynton, 1989.

Daiker, Donald A., and Max Morenberg, eds. *The Writing Teacher as Researcher: Essays in the Theory and Practice of Classroom Research*. Portsmouth, N.H.: Boynton, 1990.

Dautermann, Jennie. "Negotiating Meaning in Hospital Discourse Communities: An Observation of Writing in the Workplace." Dissertation, Purdue University, 1991.

Dillon, George. *Rhetoric as a Social Imagination: Explorations in the Interpersonal Function of Language*. Bloomington: University of Indiana Press, 1986.

Donahue, Patricia, and Ellen Quandahl, eds. *Reclaiming Pedagogy: The Rhetoric of the Classroom*. Carbondale: Southern Illinois University Press, 1989.

Eagleton, Terry. *Literary Theory: An Introduction*. Minneapolis: University of Minnesota Press, 1983.

———. *Walter Benjamin: or, Towards a Revolutionary Criticism*. London: Verso, 1981.

Ede, Lisa, and Andrea Lunsford. *Singular Text/Plural Authors*. Carbondale: Southern Illinois University Press, 1990.

Faigley, Lester. "Competing Theories of Process: A Critique and a Proposal." *College English* 48 (1986): 527–42.

———. "Judging Writing, Judging Selves." *College Composition and Communication*. 40 (1989): 395–413.

Gere, Anne Ruggles. *Writing Groups: History, Theory, and Implications*. Carbondale: Southern Illinois University Press, 1987.

Goswami, Dixie, and Peter R. Stillman, eds. *Reclaiming the Classroom: Teacher Research as an Agency for Change*. Portsmouth, N.H.: Boynton, 1987.

Hairston, Maxine. "Comment and Response." *College English* 52 (1990): 694–96.

Hamilton, Barbara Bova. "The Rhetoric of a Judicial Document: The Presentence Investigation, Document Design, and Social Context." Dissertation, University of Southern California, 1987.

Harrienger, Myrna. "Issues of Discursivity, Subjectivity, and Empowerment: Elderly Ill Women." Dissertation, Purdue University (forthcoming).

Heba, Gary. "Inventing Culture: A Rhetoric of Social Codes." Dissertation, Purdue University, 1991.

Hebdige, Dick. *Subculture: The Meaning of Style*. London: Methuen, 1979.

Hurlbert, C. Mark, and Michael Blitz, eds. *Composition and Resistance*. Portsmouth, N.H.: Boynton, 1991.

Johnson, Richard. "What Is Cultural Studies Anyway?" *Social Text* 16 (1986–87): 38–80.

Lauer, Janice M., and J. William Asher. *Composition Research: Empirical Designs*. New York: Oxford University Press, 1988.

Lauer, Janice M., and Andrea Lunsford. "The Place of Rhetoric and Composition in Doctoral Studies." *The Future of Doctoral Studies in English*. Ed. Andrea Lunsford, Helene Moglen, and James Slevin. New York: Modern Language Association, 1989: 106–10.

Lay, Mary M. "Interpersonal Conflict in Collaborative Writing: What We Can Learn from Gender Studies." *Journal of Business and Technical Communication* 3.2 (1989): 5–28.

Leitch, Vincent B. "Cultural Studies." *Johns Hopkins Guide to Literary Criticism and Theory*. Ed. Martin Kreiswirth and Michael Groden. Baltimore: Johns Hopkins University Press, 1994.

Miller, Susan. *Rescuing the Subject: A Critical Introduction to Rhetoric and the Writer*. Carbondale: Southern Illinois University Press, 1989.

Porter, James E. "Ideology and Collaboration in the Classroom and in the Corporation." *Bulletin of the Association for Business Communication* 5.32 (1990): 18–22.

Russell, David R. "Romantics on Writing: Liberal Culture and the Abolition of Composition Courses." *Rhetoric Review* 6 (1988): 132–48.

Shaughnessy, Mina. *Errors and Expectations: A Guide for the Teacher of Basic Writing*. New York: Oxford University Press, 1977.

Taylor, Warren. "Rhetoric in a Democracy." *English Journal* 27 (1938): 851–58.

Therborn, Goran. *The Ideology of Power and the Power of Ideology*. London: Verso, 1980.

Trimbur, John. "Consensus and Difference in Collaborative Learning." *College English* 51 (1989): 602–16.

———. "Cultural Studies and Teaching Writing." *Focuses* 1.2 (1988): 5–18.

———. "Essayist Literacy and the Rhetoric of Deproduction." *Rhetoric Review* 9 (1990): 72–86.

Winterowd, W. Ross. *The Rhetoric of the "Other" Literature*. Carbondale: Southern Illinois University Press, 1990.

16
What We Need to Know about Writing *and* Reading, or Peter Elbow and Antifoundationalism

Ellen Gardiner

While the work of Peter Elbow has been a powerful force in composition studies, several composition theorists have been critical of the conservative political implications of Elbow's pedagogy. James Berlin and Lester Faigley, for example, argue that Elbow's theory "hides the social nature of language" (Faigley 531) and teaches students how to "to assert a private vision, a vision which, despite its uniqueness, finally represents humankind's best nature" (Berlin 487). Theorists such as Patricia Bizzell have viewed Elbow as foundationalist because he believes, she argues, that students are capable of "learning to examine [their] beliefs in light of those advanced by others" ("Cognition" 231). Such a position, Stanley Fish would agree, assumes that one can ground inquiry and communication in a stable body of knowledge, in either, for instance, "a neutral-observation language, the set of eternal values, [or] the free and independent self" (343). Notably, critics of Elbow have always focused on what he has to say about writers and writing. Yet, while antifoundationalism teaches that knowledge is situationally produced, no antifoundationalist has examined the most "situational" aspect of Elbow's writing pedagogy—the role of the reader and the exchange between writer and reader in the composition classroom.

In this essay I will discuss Elbow's rhetoric of reading to suggest that labeling Elbow "foundationalist" oversimplifies his theoretical and pedagogical position within the field of composition studies. The problem is not that he believes students can easily develop stable and objective perspectives, but just the opposite: he worries that students will be so influenced by pressure from the group that they will change their beliefs without fully examining them, or worse, that pressure from the group will produce a conversation that deteriorates into a hostile quarrel that wastes everyone's time.

Nonetheless, all exchanges between writers and readers involve some degree of power struggle because all writers and all readers inhabit texts differently. Or, to put it another way, as an antifoundationalist might, "whatever we believe we believe because we have been persuaded by others" (Bizzell, "Beyond"). When I gave this essay to a colleague, her response was to explain how she reads Elbow. I recognized that she was, to paraphrase Pierre Macherey (15) offering a substitute text for what I had written. We argued. It was not a waste of time because she persuaded me that her position on Elbow had validity, and it helped me to clarify for her as well as for myself the point I was trying to reach. Again, the production and consumption of language always involves struggle and conflict.

Elbow believes, however, that the relationship between writer and reader in the classroom is by definition already too adversarial because in our culture, readers, particularly teachers and editors, always have more power than writers, particularly student writers. Student writers are seldom able to argue as productively or even at all with their teachers if for no other reason than the institutional context within which they engage. Therefore, to ensure that readers do not have all the power in the relationship between writer and reader, Elbow not only encourages student readers to consider themselves amateurs, but controls the way the conversation proceeds. It is in this attempt to control the relationship between writer and reader that Elbow reproduces the same kind of foundationalist thinking that he wishes to dismantle. I would like to suggest nonetheless that there is a means by which the more liberating aspects of Elbow's rhetoric of reading might be kept intact.

Professionals versus Amateurs

Elbow wants to counteract the negative effects of how writing works in our educational system, particularly within the relationships that often develop between writers and readers in the context of writing classrooms. He believes the relationship that most often develops between writer and reader in an academic environment is inauthentic because of its pretense of objectivity. The educational system's attempts to methodize the critical reading process, and its attempts to make students read like teachers read, create a relationship between writers and readers devoid of authentic motivations for communication. His attitudes toward readers and reading arise from his desire to help students recapture the idea that "discourse as used by human beings is always interested, always located in a person speaking and an audience listening" ("Reflections"

141). Given most classroom practices, he asserts, most students and teachers need to be retaught how audiences should behave:

> The necessity of an audience is supported by the evidence about how children learn how to speak: the audience is layed [*sic*] on for free and is eager for all productions; the child doesn't have to deserve it. Whether the infant's audience gives correction doesn't matter much. What matters is ongoing interaction: answering and talking, i.e., non-evaluative feedback. And no audience, no speech. Imagine the sorry results of an infant trying to learn to speak by a process equivalent to our freshman English or writing courses. (*Embracing* 73)

Bizzell herself acknowledges that in some respects Elbow is antifoundationalist; he asks students, for instance, to read not just for stylistics but for the feelings and thoughts that are realized in the discourse. In addition, Elbow tries to create an antifoundationalist environment for students in the classroom, to have them learn to recognize authentic motivations for discourse production, and to help them find ways of producing such authentic kinds of discourse. His impulses are much like those of cultural theorists who seek ways to align more closely the teaching of writing with the aspirations of ordinary readers and writers (see Trimbur) and also more like those of antifoundationalist theorists such as Fish or Bizzell. He wishes to give voice to students who have been silenced within the educational institution, to find a means by which to increase their participation in a system that provokes hostility and discouragement.

Nevertheless, Elbow recognizes that the subjective—students' psychological and emotional responses—sometimes inhibits students from interacting productively, and so he offers examples of instances when as a writer he himself found his readers' responses problematic:

> — in particular is quite fierce about how I made him the enemy; I made him mad.
>
> The feedback from both of them is enormously useful, but it makes me uncomfortable and mad. I'm all stirred up. It leaves me upset and unable to sleep or relax. I think the crucial factor is that it doesn't feel like it's coming from an ally. I feel I have to fight. That's the main response: wanting

to fight them. Energized for fight. Aggression. Unable to
relax. Unable to put it aside. Caught.

I guess you could call that useful. . . . But it's so ex-
hausting always to be in combat . . . is it the best way to go?
I wonder if it brings out the best thinking. (Elbow and
Belanoff, *Sharing* 33)

Elbow's reflects that "if I were younger or less secure, it would [have held] me
back." In fact, he still resists feedback: "Can it be I have an instinctive desire to
refuse to do what 'they' want—what 'the teacher' wants? . . . It makes me think
about how often writing—and especially writing in school—is a matter of
giving them what they want—or at least doing what they want you to do. One is
always writing for someone who has authority or power over you. ('They' 'own'
the journal, and I can't get my words out to the public unless they accept them.
Makes me feel powerless.)" (Elbow and Belanoff, *Community* 320–21).

Because he remembers his hostility toward his own teachers' criticism,
reading as a professional provokes Elbow's discomfort. As a member of the
academy, Elbow himself participates in at least two sorts of professional reading; he is both a teacher and a reviewer for several professional journals and
presses. Each role requires that he read in order to get paid, and the kinds of
reading practices involved are, for him, similar and often unsatisfactory.

As a professional reader he has more power than the writer because he can
prevent the writer's work from being published or receiving a passing grade.
And to reiterate, this so-called social process of language exchange is at bottom
very antisocial because the transaction lacks authentic motivations, reactions,
and social context. On the whole, Elbow explains, his relationship to the writer
as a reviewer for a journal is a disembodied one; there is no face-to-face exchange of language ("It's common for editors to remove the names of reviewers
when passing on comments to authors" [*Sharing* 58]). Reading as a teacher also
makes Elbow feel like the editor of a journal—his words of criticism, he might
argue, are not really his own; as teachers, he notes, we are "being paid . . . not
so much [to try] to tell the [writer] how she reacts . . . (she may be tired of it by
now), but rather how she imagines the audience will react" (*Community* 270–
71). In the academy, teachers read for "what is the matter." They do not read
student papers as they would a paperback or a scholarly article—they get paid to
criticize organization, grammar, and so on, all in the name of objectivity.
Teachers read as representatives; they tell students how they think the institu-

tion as audience might respond. In doing so, they become like the editor who "owns" the journal. This act of reading student papers is a job on one level devoid of the kind of desire that impels ordinary readers to read. Thus there are moments when he denies the teacher as reader any authenticity when he suggests that teachers are not quite "real" readers.

The resentment he feels as one whose motivations for reading are not necessarily his own colors the rhetoric he offers to students. In the freshman composition classroom, Elbow wants to help insecure, vulnerable student writers to stave off "hostile corporate takeovers" of their texts by readers who have internalized the harsh, critical, and supposedly objective voices of those who belong to the academic discourse community. He argues therefore that students need to turn off, shut out, those voices of the harsh professional reader by behaving like "real" audiences would behave. He attempts to help students resist the tyranny of the voice of the editor-teacher they have internalized by training them to take each other's writing "on its own terms," to have student readers "simply look for pleasure or usefulness" in that writing and not "feel they are reading as a job or a duty or to 'teach' each other" (*Community* 272).

To help students in his classroom recuperate the "authentic human experience" of the fun of telling a story or the pleasure of conversation, he establishes a dichotomy between types of readers: amateurs and professionals. In his dichotomy, students are "real" audiences, nice people and amateur in the sense that they are not getting paid to look for what is the matter, and they are good for providing subjective and emotional support. "Amateur" student readers have the opportunity to help empower each other to express their own thoughts without obsessing about the form, as the enemy professional reader might. Like John Shotter, Elbow believes that "new knowledge . . . grows out of . . . 'the voices of ordinary people in conversation' " (52). A conversation between student writers and readers who behave like amateurs, moreover, will be more likely to help students recuperate what he believes are at bottom authentic motives for reading and writing—the desire to communicate, to be social.

He therefore wants students to step back from academic methods of analysis and to read each other's writing for pleasure or for its usefulness, not in the attempt to gain a neutral or objective critical perspective. He assures them that by and large they can rely on teachers for that. And there's the rub. Elbow's distinction between professional and amateur assumes that a professional reader is in fact in possession of a "neutral-observation language, [and a] set of eternal values" (Fish 343).

Similarly, the way that Elbow dichotomously describes teachers as readers undermines his attempts to critique the foundationalist practices of the academy and to validate the kinds of knowledge that are produced in the conversations of ordinary writers and readers. In *A Community of Writers* he exhorts students, and by implication the teachers themselves, to think of teachers as directors, or coaches:

> Teachers read differently from most readers. They read not for pleasure or information, but because it's their job. They read as coach or director. Think about how a director watches a play she's directing—as opposed to how the audience watches it. The director is certainly a real audience; she is "really" watching the play, probably more carefully than the "real" audience. Yet, of course the performance is not for her but for those who bought the tickets. They paid to see the play; she's being paid to watch it.

In Elbow's presentation, professional readers are initially described as somewhat "unreal," insensitive, judgmental, and only pseudo-objective. His solution—these more positive and facilitative metaphors of the teacher as director or coach—still fails to undermine a foundationalist vision of the teacher as a source of truth. In Elbow's mind, the teacher, like the director, is only playing a role when she gets paid to watch the performance of the actor and to pretend to be a "real" audience by explaining to the actors how their performance will affect the ticket-buying audience.

Nonetheless, a director of a play is not only paid to watch the play so that she might imagine how the audience will react, but, prior to the performance, she reads the text, arrives at a particular interpretation, and then instructs the actor how best to play his role to make clear that interpretation to the audience. Like a university professor, a director can play a double role as interpreter of texts and instructor. The director has the power to control the actor's performance in order to provoke a positive response from the audience. Teachers as directors also have the ultimate power and authority to control a student's writerly production.

The same view applies to the metaphor of teacher as coach. Elbow advises: "A coach may be tough on you, but she is not trying to be the enemy; she's trying to help you beat the real 'enemy' (the other team). There's no point in fighting the coach or being mad at her, nor for the coach to fight you. The better you and the coach work together, the better chance you both have of achieving your common goal of 'winning' against a common adversary" (*Community* 271). Players on teams may shine as individuals, but most often they are carrying out orders given by the coach. A basketball coach decides what kind of defense will be used against a particular team; for instance, he may be known for his team's fast-break style of play. And players who defy the coach's authority often end up suspended.

The teacher's role as facilitator and interpreter still allows her to speak from a privileged center (Shotter 46). At best, these metaphors that describe the teacher's role as reader only further establish the academic, professional, literary critic-teacher as the dominant voice in the academy. And for students, it may further muddy the waters with regard to their own power to make judgments about the texts that they read. That is, in order to make distinctions between amateur and professional readers and reading practices one must accept that students are not capable of using language professionally, that there is in fact a special practice or methodology to which only teachers have access. As a result, students' behaviors and practices in the composition classroom are already constrained before they begin.

The distinction between amateur and professional readers raises other questions: At what moment does one's use of language become "professional"? Is it simply a matter of getting a university degree or having an institution name one as such? Does the designation "professional" automatically and necessarily mean a reader designated as professional is a more objective, better interpreter-responder than one designated "amateur"? An antifoundationalist would say no.

Negotiations and Language Games

Elbow believes that a group of readers is more sociable and gives the writer a sense that "readers are so different and reading is such a subjective act" (*Sharing* 4), but he admits that he prefers a one-on-one relationship: "It's easier to build up a relationship of good honesty, trust, and support between just two people" (5). He does not describe this relationship, however, as a conversation between two people, as an interactive, two-way process. In Elbow's "authentic" exchange, there is always one person who speaks and an audience (one or more people) that politely and quietly listens. Moreover, he assumes that readers can be writers' allies only if their discourse does not "mix": "Avoid all arguments whether between responders or between a responder and writer. Not only do arguments waste time, they usually make responders less willing to be honest" (5). The sharing and responding sessions turn out to be power struggles; any negotiation between writer and reader usually provokes fear: "Quarreling about reactions is a waste of time—and will tend to make other readers scared to be honest."

Again, it is interesting to note that what Elbow does here is to project his own experience as a professional writer-critic onto the students' practices in response sessions. He describes to students, for instance, how he and his co-author, Pat Belanoff, interact with their reviewers: "They [reviewers of his texts] get to say whatever they want—and we can't quarrel with their reactions. But we get to decide how to respond to their reactions and which suggestions to follow" (*Sharing* 59). The first statement implies a certain helplessness; he and Belanoff are powerless to reject or disagree with their reviewers' reactions. But in the next sentence, he allows that in fact they do get to "decide how to respond to their reactions and which suggestions to follow." Direct negotiation for Elbow appears to be synonymous with quarreling; it seems to connote "getting angry" or "showing that we are hurt."

By prescribing response exercises wherein adversity is to be avoided at all costs, by insisting that the writer-reader exchange in the classroom must proceed by a set of rules, he provides no role for free and open conversation. John Shotter has recently argued that within the reality of human conversation, there is no systematic method of creating authentic knowledge:

> Speakers do not "discipline" their talk in terms of a single grammatical picture. If one figure of speech proves unintelligible, another is tried. If there is an order in conversation, then it is one of a very different kind to that available in a God's-eye view, a surveyable order. In a conversation . . . "the matter talked about" is an event that is developing and developed within the course of the conversation producing it; furthermore, those producing it, know in practice . . . both the "how" and the "what" of its production; indeed, in being (responsively) aware of each other's (responsive) understanding in the process, they know how to play their own part in further development. And they can do all this without any reference to any inner mental representations, to any inner theories; their embodied linguistic reactions are sufficient. (141–42)

In ordinary conversation, "people do not just follow rules, they create them (as well as challenge, change and correct them); and in applying them, check out with others whether they have applied them correctly" (Shotter 93). Knowledge is generated through negotiation, a back-and-forth process that involves speakers' attempts to realize their own thoughts and their listeners' attempts to understand, "with each challenging the other as to the social appropriateness of their realizations and understandings, respectively" (108).

To restrict negotiation is to "hide all the actual, socio-political processes of importance—to hide those moments of indeterminacy, undecidability and ambivalence when real politics is at work" (Shotter 52). An antifoundationalist would assume that real knowledge comes from learning the process of negotiation, in the social process of learning how to justify one's claims to others. In Elbow's system, as the writer ultimately negotiates the response session privately, within the privacy of his or her own thoughts, "the poet's way of talking is the talk that will [likely] win out" (Shotter 44). Elbow's desire to restrict negotiation may well reinforce for students the idea that language is a game within which the teacher is the master interpreter who remains at the center of the discourse production. The type of language game Elbow promotes in his classroom will inevitably lead to an imbalance in power between student writer and student reader during the response session, an imbalance which neither writer nor reader will be allowed to address.

The paradox, then, of Elbow's rhetoric of reading is that to recuperate authentic motives for reading and writing, to make the exchange between writer and reader more authentic, he actually prevents the relationship between writer and reader from being authentically social by excluding the possibility of the kind of negotiation that happens in ordinary conversation. Because the conversation becomes systematized, because Elbow configures the collaborative conversation about texts as a language game with a prescribed set of rules, he falls into a foundationalist method of thinking.

Substitutions

Given what Elbow asks students to do when they read in his classroom, however, the distinction between professional and amateur readers and between professional and amateur reading practices is unnecessary. Whether dealing with literary texts or their own, Elbow's students and teachers alike engage in two poles of one reading process: criticism. Elbow seems to be describing two poles of reading for students, reading for pleasure or usefulness on the one hand, and reading because it is your job on the other. To read like an amateur—for pleasure or usefulness—he cajoles, is infinitely more helpful to a writer. But what exactly do the majority of what he calls nonjudgmental response exercises ask students to do? Descriptive responding asks students to give, for example, "sayback": "Sayback to me in your own words what you hear me getting at in my writing. But say it more as a question than as an answer—to invite me to figure out better what I really want to say" (*Sharing* 64). Another type of descriptive responding requires student readers to answer the question, "What's almost said, implied, hovering around the edges?" To give what he calls judgmental, or analytic, types of responses, students provide summaries and information regarding the rhetorical function of a writer's work; one exercise involves writing a descriptive outline (What is the main point? What does each paragraph do? What does each paragraph say?). Certainly, analytic responding seems to ask students to do pretty much the same thing as the section on descriptive responding asked: to describe what they believe to be the main point of the essay and the reasons used by the writer as support.

Pierre Macherey argues that the positive valuation of the text—taking it on its own terms, looking for pleasure or usefulness—still involves the substitution of a revised, corrected, and consistent version of an initial reality: "Conceivably, a certain type of criticism proposes a modest translation of a work, but even with this minimum of transformation, so scrupulous and restrained, it is seeking to replace what is by something else." He notes further that "criticism is never absolutely satisfied with what it has been given" (15). Students' descriptive and analytic responses still produce new texts, suggesting to the writer the ways in which she might change her text. Macherey continues:

> Both the "taste" which asks no questions and the "judgment" which dispenses with scruples are closely related. The naive consumer and the harsh judge are finally collaborators in a single action. . . . the empiricist critic wants to be the author's accomplice, he believes that the work can only emerge under the pressure of participation; the judge, on the other hand, would set himself up to instruct the writer, claiming a clearer vision of his intention, pointing out his carelessness, evading the delays of a real production in his impatience for the essential. (17)

Macherey's discussion suggests that there is no real dichotomy between the way we read as teachers and the way our students read. All readers transform a text when they read it, be they professional or amateur readers. Taking this Machereyian position would not then inevitably or necessarily result in our falling into foundationalist thinking, because in its assumption that we all make substitutions when we read texts, there is no need to assume, for example, that there is any such thing as a neutral-observation language. Neither does this perspective necessarily assume the existence of a free and independent self, whereas Elbow's distinction between professional and amateur does. Elbow's professional reader is capable, after all, of creating and using an objective methodology when reading student papers.

Elbow might argue that the opposition between kinds of readers and writers exists; as problematic as it is, the balance of power in the relationship between readers and writers, in the classroom anyway, remains in the professional reader, the teacher's hands, and it is necessary to acknowledge this and then try to give students strategies by which they can achieve some power and authority within a system that encourages such a hierarchy. Pretending that the imbalance of power does not exist, ignoring the emotional tensions and conflicts that those relationships engender would be "inauthentic" indeed.

Students need to develop, however, their abilities to argue authoritatively, they need to learn how to turn quarrels into arguments so that they can learn how to make the kinds of decisions Elbow and I make as writers and readers when we decide which suggestions to take and which to reject. They need to learn how to justify their beliefs to others, to develop a sense of how their own identities are continually shifting within each new social situation. As Bizzell suggests, they need to understand their identities as "positional," to learn, that is, how they are defined but not wholly determined by historical circumstances ("Beyond" 673). They need to learn what it means to be a genuine person in everyday life. Students cannot learn how the various groups to which they belong help to shape their individual choices for action if they are forced to negotiate responses to their writing in isolation and away from the response session. That kind of knowledge only comes when we learn how to negotiate in a social context like a classroom, when we learn what provokes others' responses to our writing, and how, and whether, finally, we need to address those responses. To argue, to negotiate, is, implicitly or explicitly, a necessary part of all authentic language relationships. Understanding student and teacher readerly practices as similarly motivated and as similarly "positional" may begin to help us to teach ourselves and our students new ways to transform our experiences as language users and to create a space within which a more inclusive discourse can circulate.

Note

I would like to thank Greg Shelnutt for responding to this particular version of my essay.

Works Cited

Berlin, James. "Rhetoric and Ideology in the Writing Class." *College English* 50 (1988): 477–94.

Bizzell, Patricia. "Beyond Anti-Foundationalism to Rhetorical Authority: Problems Defining 'Cultural Literacy.'" *College English* 52 (1990): 661–75.

——. "Cognition, Convention and Certainty: What We Need to Know about Writing." *Pre/Text* 3 (1982): 213–43.

Elbow, Peter. "Closing My Eyes as I Speak: An Argument for Ignoring Audience." *College English* 49 (1987): 50–69.

——. *Embracing Contraries.* New York: Oxford University Press, 1986.

——. "Reflections on Academic Discourse: How It Relates to Freshmen and Colleagues." *College English* 53 (1991): 135–55.

——. *What Is English?* New York: Modern Language Association, 1990.

——. *Writing with Power.* New York: Oxford University Press, 1973.

Elbow, Peter, and Pat Belanoff. *A Community of Writers: A Workshop Course in Writing.* New York: Random House, 1989.

——. *Sharing and Responding.* New York: Random House, 1989.

Faigley, Lester. "Competing Theories of Process: A Critique and a Proposal." *College English* 48 (1986): 527–42.

Fish, Stanley. "Anti-Foundationalism, Theory Hope, and the Teaching of Composition." *Doing What Comes Naturally.* Durham, N.C.: Duke University Press, 1989: 342–55.

Macherey, Pierre. *A Theory of Literary Production.* Trans. Geoffrey Wall. 1978. New York: Routledge, 1986.

Shotter, John. *The Cultural Politics of Everyday Life.* Toronto: University of Toronto Press, 1993.

Trimbur, John. "Cultural Studies and Teaching Writing." *Focuses* 1 (1988): 5–18.

17

Teaching as a Test of Knowledge
Passion, Desire, and the
Semblance of Truth in Teaching

David Metzger

At the end of the *Protagoras,* Socrates discovers that insofar as what we teach is knowledge we cannot teach it. The essential thrust of the *Protagoras,* as well as the *Meno,* is that if knowledge is particular, teaching cannot be and if teaching is particular, knowledge cannot be. In the *Meno,* Socrates asks what virtue is, and Meno insists on teaching him about virtue by examples. Socrates tells him that such teaching will not do; Socrates wishes to know what virtue is. Then Meno tells him how to be virtuous by acting virtuously. Socrates insists that Meno has not yet been a helpful teacher; he has only indicated what fragments of virtue might be, not what virtue is. The result of these deliberations is that Socrates finds knowledge to be a gift from the realm of the gods. And if we look at Socrates' statement as something other than a cop-out, we can see, at the very least, that teaching has historically asked questions of foundationalist epistemologies, questions whose answers must come as gifts and whose responses must come from the gods.

Imagine that a student asks in a "Teaching of Composition" class, "What is 'How do I teach writing to seventh graders?'" The student will most likely abbreviate the question to "How do I teach writing to seventh graders?" One response might be to read through a book of lesson plans and activities. The student might then say, "Thank you." But if the student persists in asking the question "How do I teach writing to seventh graders?" one could, then, read through another book of lesson plans and activities with the student or have the student make up activities and lesson plans on her or his own.

But what if the student says, "I still don't know anything about teaching seventh graders to write"? One might then tell the student that he or she can do all of the activities just described and do them well or do them nicely or do them in an empowering kind of way or do them with an eye on gender, culture, and race differences. Some students at this point would say, "Thank you. That's what I wanted to know."

Could a student still persist in saying, "I don't know anything about how to teach seventh graders how to write"? In this context, what could the student mean? The student might want something she did not ask for. Knowing "how to" teach is all well and good but the student might really want to ask, "What is 'How do I teach writing to seventh graders?' " This would be the starting point for so-called epistemological examinations of teaching. But would these epistemological examinations of teaching themselves escape from the persistent thrust of the question, "What is X?" We are, after all, allowed to ask, "What is 'What is?' " Answers are infinite, one might say. Are questions also?

Of course, one might say that the deck is stacked a bit here. Isn't the distinction between "what is" and "how to" simply a Platonic convention? At some level, yes. And contemporary teaching parallels many semantic theories in this regard. Many of us wish to say, "To be is to be of use." "There is an X" has something to do with "how to do something with X." That is, one can learn to work with "there is an X." But how does that happen? After all, the "there is a" makes itself known through speech as a series of identifications: "there is an X that is a Y that is a T that is a W that is a. . . . " This "there is a," at the very least, is the guarantee that such infinite identifications are possible. How does one learn to work with this "there is a"? One can follow the train of the identifications, and (1) then stop to demonstrate that one's "there is a" is farther along than someone else's, despite the fact that an infinite series of identifications extends from any "there is a"; (2) then stop to demonstrate that what someone has proposed as a "there is a" is not, or is not much of one; (3) then stop to demonstrate that what someone proposed as his or her "there is a" is someone else's "there is a"; and (4) then stop to demonstrate that someone has no "there is a" to propose. Option four specifically makes the equation of "there is a" and "how to" possible: "You don't have a 'there is a,' so let me tell you how to get one you can enjoy and that has meaning for you."

These four ways of imagining the meaning of knowledge might even be a reading of four possible student positions, what rhetoricians would recognize as "audiences." In this regard, "students" might be seen as ways to force the hand of knowledge to produce meaning.[1] The first position insists that knowledge is not much of a surprise and that meaning is what accords with the pageant of objects that come to the place of one's desire. The second position insists that knowledge is something of a surprise and that meaning is an effect of relating something one does know in language to something that one does not. The third position insists that knowledge is an absolute surprise and something one has been waiting for nevertheless. Meaning, in this regard, might not simply be an effect of knowledge but itself a place from which to speak. The fourth position insists that knowledge is only a surprise for some other who does not know what "it means." In this scheme, there is at least the hope that knowledge and meaning might exhaust one another.

Notice how, in all of these "teaching-learning structures," the student or the teacher might be situated in the place of knowledge or in the position of meaning. The teacher might be the only one who knows what is going to be on the test. The student might be the only one who can say whether the teacher and her or his knowledge makes sense or not. The teacher might be the only one who does not know what the student will ask. The student might be the only one who does not know the answer.

I would see this as a more precise way of rendering the problem of teaching delineated by Plato: if either the teacher or the student might be an "only one," then it is possible that what we know is not knowledge and that what makes sense is only an individual fantasy. This is not a possibility that either teachers or students are eager to embrace.[2]

Teachers often believe that the people they instruct do not know what they are saying or doing. But if someone does know what he or she is saying or doing, what do we do with them? Consider the example of George C. Scott's role as General Patton. When asked what he did for a living, this Patton would say, "I kill people." He wouldn't say, "I keep the world safe for democracy" or "I'm maintaining an occupying peace-keeping force," or even "I'm fighting for freedom." To a theoretically engaged Patton one might ask, "Do you realize that you are merely an instrument of destruction, an instrument, let's say, of the Other's jouissance?" Patton's response could only be, "Yes. Surely."

This "Yes. Surely" marks the end (or the impossibility) of teaching as it is practiced by most of us: "Well, if you know what you're doing, then I guess I can't teach you any different. Fortunately, I can still make you do something different if you love or hate me."

Imagine the following conversation:

Teacher: You realize that you don't really prove any of your statements about O. J. Simpson in your paper.

Student: Yes, of course.

A teacher might go on to ask why the student chose not to support his or her assertions about O. J. Simpson. The student could then demonstrate that every problem the instructor had with the paper was the result of a specific choice—even if the choice was simply not to communicate or not to learn.

What I am evoking here is *not* a student writer who would say, "I'm now going to confuse, irritate, upset, insult those who read my writing. Now, see how I do it." We can deal with that student: "How does the second sentence of your fourth paragraph confuse, irritate, upset, or insult?" "Have you heard of Bertolt Brecht?"

What I am evoking here is a student who would say, "I don't want to keep a journal for this class, so I will (pretend) not (to) understand the journal assignment. Then, I won't have to do it. After all, I can respond only as I understand what is being asked of me. Now see how I do it."

The rather naive assumption of a good deal of "teacher inquiry" has been that either such students do not exist or such students just do not understand. This naive response on the part of teachers is not, of course, all that naive, since responding to these "impossible students" must seem impossible. In addition, these examples underscore the function of love and hate in teacher-student relations. Love and hate allow the teacher to get what he or she wants from the student: obedience. More particularly, the teacher wants the student to choose and enjoy what is lawful. I understand that many people will be surprised by my last statement. So, I would like to provide some additional explanation. First, recognize that the construction of a forced choice is part of any so-called community. Second, recognize that the construction of a forced choice (a desire at the level of meaning and/or a passion at the level of knowledge) is at the heart of any teaching.

In making the first point about communities I am reminded of a story Slavoj Žižek, the Slovenian philosopher of psychoanalysis, writes about one of his students. The student is called to military service in Yugoslavia and participates in a short ritual which requires that he sign an oath to defend the homeland even with his life. The former student, now soldier, refuses to sign the oath—indicating that an oath requires free choice in the matter, which he does not have. He is quick to add that he would sign the oath if he were ordered to do so. Not surprisingly, the officers present tell the former student, now soldier, that he must sign the oath of his own free will or it would not be an oath. The officers also make it clear that he will be prosecuted for not freely choosing to sign the oath (Žižek 165). Before being shipped off to prison, the former student, now soldier, finally receives the order to freely sign the oath.

When the student answered the request to sign the oath by saying, "No, because I know what I would be doing," the former student, now soldier, brings to the foreground the logic of a forced choice and its relation to community building. The student recognized that he did not have a choice by acting as if he did have a choice. That is, when the student made the wrong choice ("I am not a soldier"), he discovered that he was already a part of a community of soldiers who might be prosecuted for not taking the oath of allegiance.

In what sense have our students made the choice to be students? And does registering for a class in some way constitute an oath of allegiance to a particular community of learners? At the beginning of my classes, I always ask, "Why did you take this class?" And most of the time, I discover that students are taking my classes because they "have to." Even when any number of other courses (in philosophy, biology, sociology, foreign languages) would satisfy the requirement, whatever it might be, there the students are in my class. And there they are because they think they have to be. Their children, their schedules, their workloads, their friends, their advisors, their chosen professions, their parents, or their interests have dictated their emergence as students in my class. As students, it seems these people have chosen to obey whatever the happy ordinances have dictated.

Fortunately, students might believe *in* the voices that tell them to enroll in the "Teaching of Composition" or "Advanced Composition," but that does not mean they believe the voices. For example, several students who take the "Teaching of Composition" course have told me that they are predisposed to think the course a waste of time. This is in part because they perceive other education courses to have been a waste of time for them or not a waste of time for them. Either way, the student recognizes that the choice to be in a class is a forced choice, even if she or he makes the choice happily.

Many teachers have chosen to think of learning as something uninterested in the wanderings of love and hate (what one might more technically call "transference") because this forced choice of knowledge functions as a countermand to love and hate. Can one really order another to love? Numerous contemporary suspense dramas have been based on that question: *Fatal Attraction, The Baby Sitter, The Eyes of Laura Mars.* And such is the promise and danger of love potions. Even the jinni in Disney's *Aladdin* tells us, in Robin Williams's best impression of William F. Buckley, that he cannot make a person fall in love.

The teaching position would then be impossible if it were constituted solely by the imperative "Love." "Love Me." "Love Yourselves." "Love Your

Writing." "Love Your Capacity to Be Storytellers." "Love Your Future Employment." "Love Your Empowerment." "Love What Kind of World This Might Be If You Were a Causal Agent." "Love How You're Able to Put in Full View the Paradoxes of Totalitarianism."

The teaching position would likewise be impossible if it were constituted solely by the imperative "Hate." "Hate Me." "Hate Yourselves." "Hate the Nasty Bits in Your Writing." "Hate Your Inability to Be Storytellers." "Hate the Mundanity of Day-to-Day Life." "Hate Your Participation in the Patriarchy." "Hate Racism." "Hate Sexism." "Hate the Evils of Totalitarianism."

Does something else happen, however, when we ask our students (or they ask themselves) to "be ignorant," when we ask them to ignore the man behind the curtain or to be ignorant of X, Y, and Z because these items won't be on the exam? In these instances we are introducing into the classroom what might be considered a general problem of language: negation. It seems that once something is spoken about, one might speak of the "something" as existing if only insofar as it is a fictional or nonexisting being. "Be ignorant of X," in this case, might indicate, "Negate your knowledge of X." This, at least, is the anchor point for educational doctrines whose operational logic takes shape as some *amaneusis* (active memory) or *sunyata* (identification with nothingness); "ignorance" is, as well, the intellectual force behind a parent's insistence that monsters do not exist.

A child tells her or his parent, "I believe in monsters because I see them on television." The parent responds, "But those monsters aren't real." "If they weren't real then how could they be on the television?" "Well, a person puts on a costume and makes funny noises in front of a video camera." "Then monsters do exist; they do exist. I knew it." "No, the monsters don't exist as such, they are make-believe. People pretend to be monsters but they really aren't." "So, the monster wasn't killing people; some actor was killing people." "No, the people were only acting as if they were hideously mutilated by someone acting as if he or she were a monster who could do such things." One might imagine a similar conversation in which the parent tries to convince the child that people were not merely acting as if they were starving or battered or dead.

It seems that the possibility of saying something (what one might term the rhetorical promise of language) leads one to conceive of a world wholly populated by twins (evil and otherwise; pretending and otherwise) who are caught somewhere between what one might call "truth" and what one might call the "coherence of our beliefs." This problem can be expressed in a more precise fashion: in our efforts to speak or write ever more coherently, we might choose to increase the coherence of a "set of beliefs" despite the reduced likelihood of the truth of that set of beliefs.

In a recent issue of *Analysis,* Peter Klein and Ted Warfield make this point provocatively. They ask us to imagine that a detective is trying to discover the identity of a murderer. The detective finds several credible witnesses who say that X was at the scene of the crime, and the detective believes she or he knows what X's motive might have been. The only problem is that there are several credible witnesses who say they saw X at the approximate time of the murder in a city far from the crime scene. Is it not possible for the detective to add something to this set of beliefs in order to create a more coherent "set of beliefs"? Of course: X has a twin, X2, whom the witnesses supplying the alibi may have seen. But even though the revised set of beliefs might be more coherent than the unrevised set of beliefs, is the revised set of beliefs more likely to be true? Clearly not. But how do we know that what is true of one coherence strategy (the addition strategy) is true of other coherence strategies (the subtraction strategy, for example)?

Noam Chomsky nicely summarizes the epistemological response to this "evidentiary problem." On the one hand, there is "Orwell's Problem": given the enormous amounts of evidence at our disposal, how is it that "we" do not know more than we do? On the other hand, there is what Chomsky calls "Plato's Problem": given the paucity of evidence at our disposal, how is it that "we" know so much?

More to the point, it is even possible to see in love something of "the problems of knowledge" Chomsky has described. For example, in the film *Groundhog Day,* Bill Murray's character is, as he puts it, a god; that is, if you define god as that which cannot be surprised because it knows everything. Yet Murray's character, Phil Connors, is eventually surprised by two things: by the death of an old man, whom Connors cannot save, even with eternity at his disposal, and by love. Despite the fact that Phil Connors knows everything, despite the fact that he has all of the possible evidence at his fingertips, and all possible worlds at his disposal, he wakes up one morning and, only then, knows that he is in love. Why? Because someone loves him. Connors knows he can love (can be a lover) only when he is loved. The film ends there.

Shakespeare's *Much Ado about Nothing* takes off where *Groundhog Day* ends. Benedick and Beatrice have little evidence of affection at their disposal but they eventually have knowledge of their love. How is this possible? First, the couple's friends and family tell each that the one loves the other. Then the evidence begins to pile up, and the audience is introduced to the difficult relationship between proof (coherence of belief) and truth:

Beat. Against my will I am sent to bid you come in to dinner.

Bene. Faire Beatrice, I thank you for your pains.

Beat. I took no more pains from those thanks than you take pains to thank me. If it had been painful, I would not have come.

Bene. You take pleasure then in the message?

Beat. Yea, just so much as you may take upon a knive's point, and choke a daw withal. You have no stomach, signior, fare you well. [*Exit.*]

Bene. Ha! "Against my will I am sent to bid you come in to dinner"— there a double meaning in that. "I took no more pains for those thanks than you took pains to thank me"—that's as much as to say, "Any pains that I take for you is as easy as thanks." If I do not take pity of her, I am a villain; if I do not love her. . . . (II, iii, 247–68)

The more interesting point about this difficult relationship between proof and truth is to see how, in Shakespeare's play, it runs along the bias of sexuation. One might say that Benedick is a man full of beans, and that his interpretation is a simple marking of his own desire to be loved. Can one say the same thing of Beatrice, however, when in the next scene she hears that Benedick is in love with her?

Beat. What fire is in mine ears? Can this be true? Stand I condemn'd for pride and scorn so much? Contempt, farewell, and maiden pride, adieu! No glory lives behind the back of such. And, Benedick, love on, I will requite thee, Taming my wild heart to thy loving hand. If thou dost love, my kindness shall incite thee to bind our loves up in a holy band; For others say thou dost deserve, and I believe it better than reportingly. (III, i, 106–16)

Not only is there proof (others have reported the signs of love to her), but in this case the proof does have a certain true value. How can one account for differing positions of truth and proof in these two instances? Both Beatrice and Benedick overhear friends speaking; both sets of friends intend to deceive. What makes the signs of love presented to Beatrice "truer" than the signs of love presented to Benedick?

One might suggest that one sign is as good or bad as another. But if that is the case, why laugh at Benedick and not at Beatrice? As members of the audience, we have heard Benedick say that he will requite Beatrice's love before Beatrice says she loves him. But we did not hear that from Beatrice: we "know" that where Benedick hears a double meaning, no "double meaning" is intended.

These statements might only further inspire the skeptic (our purveyor of truth) to propose the following circumstance: A friend makes a date to come with us to watch Kenneth Branagh's film version of *Much Ado about Nothing*. Our friend is late as usual and arrives well into the film—let's say just in time to see the two scenes quoted here. Would our friend, if he or she were not familiar with the play, know why everyone was laughing at Benedick's interpretation of Beatrice's invitation to dinner? No. Would our friend understand that what Beatrice's friends were reporting to her was "supposed to be" false? No. We have here, then, two apparently different things: the semblance of truth and the semblance of falsity. That is, we have come across a distinction that holds water if one valorizes the position of someone who does not know (anything but two scenes from a film) in its relation to the position of someone who does (know something other than two scenes from a film).

From our perspective, from the perspective of those who know the entire film, does a distinction hold between "semblance of truth" and "semblance of falsity"? From our friend's perspective, from the perspective of one who knows only two scenes of a film, does a distinction hold between "semblance of truth" and "semblance of falsity"?

We might observe, from the position of the one who knows, that Benedick and Beatrice are being tricked. We would, of course, laugh at Benedick's desire to obtain a "double meaning" from Beatrice's invitation to dinner. And we would understand that what Benedick overhears about Beatrice's love for him is a semblance of truth. But would we need some such notion as a "semblance of falsity" to see that Beatrice is being tricked? No. One requires the notion of a "semblance of falsity" only if one distinguishes between the manner by which Benedick is tricked into love and the manner by which Beatrice is tricked into love.

Now, would our friend, whom we have uncharitably put in the position of ignorance, have use for the notion "semblance of truth"? Yes, but only in the case of Beatrice. The notion "semblance of falsity" would not crop up at all.

One might then characterize the position of knowledge in two ways: the recognition of both a "semblance of truth" and a "semblance of falsity," and the instauration of a "semblance of falsity" precisely where a "semblance of truth"

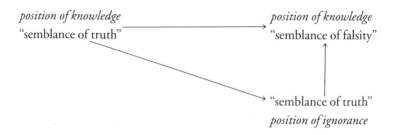

would be placed in terms of a "position of ignorance." Additionally, one might characterize the position of ignorance as the placement of a "semblance of truth" precisely where a "semblance of falsity" appears in terms of a "position of knowledge."

One must ask from what perspective it is possible to see Beatrice is not tricked in the same manner as Benedick. Is it simply a position of knowledge? Is it simply a position of ignorance? Or is it something else—this desire to construct a logic for the performative dimensions of trickery (being duped) also known as love, hate, and ignorance?

On several occasions Bertolt Brecht provides a provocative means by which to demonstrate the pedagogical dimension of this curious distinction between a semblance of truth and a semblance of falsity. Consider the following example from his pedagogical play *Der Jasager* (1930): "An actor enters the stage and says—'I am a capitalist whose aim is to exploit workers. Now I will try to convince one of my workers of the truth of the bourgeois ideology which legitimizes the exploitation. . . . ' The actor then approaches the worker and does exactly what he has announced he would do."[3] We can observe two characters, the Capitalist and the Worker. The Capitalist presumably knows what he is doing and the Worker, duped by the Capitalist, presumably does not. It is not too difficult to see how "bourgeois ideology," in this instance, takes the form of a "semblance of truth." It may be more difficult to see how "bourgeois ideology" is also a "semblance of falsity." But by insisting on self-knowledge of his actions, doesn't the Capitalist situate "bourgeois ideology" in the position of a "semblance of falsity"? That is, the Capitalist believes he is pretending (to be a capitalist) when he is not (pretending to be a capitalist).

Is there a difference between "pretending" and "semblance" if one comes to terms with Brecht's little object lesson on agency and ideology? Yes, but only if one sees that the position of the Capitalist is *not* simply that of a person who tells the truth in his pretending. Rather, the Capitalist tells the truth about his lying. Brecht is forcing us to make a difficult distinction between irony and paradox, pretense and semblance, since the truth of the Capitalist expresses itself in a most noncohesive fashion: he is pretending and he is not pretending.

Having delineated the function of semblance in knowledge making, we might be able to speak about something called "the student's discourse." On the side of the discourse of the student is passion (love, hate, and ignorance); what the student learns (insofar as it might be true) is what the student creates in response to her or his passion. Yet when we teach knowledge, the student operates at the level of the semblance. On the side of the discourse of the teacher is desire; what the teacher teaches (insofar as it might have meaning) is what the student understands. That is, the teacher, or the teacher-position, evokes the necessity of the semblant (the semblance of truth, the semblance of falsity), and the student positions this necessity in relation to a particular limit (noncohesiveness). This is one possible response to the antifoundational challenge that teaching continues to evoke in the present day.

Using another theoretical parlance, one might say that it is possible and perhaps necessary (if learning is to take place) for students to be Other. Of course, such a conclusion has numerous attenuating difficulties. First, some teachers might seek in the classroom something of an "analysis": "If my students are going to write for me by knowing who I am—and if this means more than knowing my prejudices, psyching me out—it means knowing what I know; it means having the knowledge of a professor of English. They, then, to know what I know and how I know what I know (the interpretive schemes that define the way I would work out the problems I set out for them); they have to learn to write what I would write or to offer up some approximation of that discourse" (Bartholomae 163). Second, the only other obvious response to the question of student discourse (the question of student as Other) is the formation of a master discourse:

> I find myself in somewhat the same position as the ancient
> Greek rhetorician Isocrates. Like postmodern skeptics, he
> debunked teachers of his day who claimed to be able to fore-
> tell the future—that is, who claimed to give their students a
> set of values guaranteed to apply in all times and places. If
> one possessed such values one could prescribe the appropri-
> ate behavior for all time and all places. Isocrates, never-
> theless, did propose to teach virtue—virtue derived not

from some transcendent realm but rather, from the traditions of his community. Indeed, according to postmodern
skepticism communities should be the source of all values. Isocrates argued that while he could not guarantee to
change—that is, to compel—his students, he could attempt
to influence them—that is, to persuade them to adopt the
values deemed most praiseworthy in his community. His
authority as a teacher of virtue would thus be established
rhetorically. (Bizzell 5–6)

I would say that both Bizzell and Bartholomae have an answer to problems or
tests that teaching evokes in knowledge: *Discourse* understood quite simply and
powerfully as that which makes a social link. What is more, Bizzell and Bartholomae may have specified two end points in a structural definition of discourse: the discourse of the master and the discourse of the analyst. So, what is
in between? Perhaps working with the logic of semblance and the operation of
passion will allow us to reorient these two end points in such a way that we
might discover Other possibilities as well.[4]

Notes

1. This might be a more precise way to express what I hear many teachers saying
in job interviews: "Sometimes I think I learn more from my students than they learn
from me." The teacher knows more because of the students; more particularly, the
teacher knows more because of what the students mean.

2. One might put this another way: teachers talk like teachers; students talk like
teachers. Perhaps there is no student discourse outside of what one might recognize as
certain "clinical structures."

3. Slavoj Žižek uses this example to explain Jacques Lacan's views on meta-
language (156).

4. Readers familiar with chapter 4 of my book *The Lost Cause of Rhetoric* will
know that I am making specific reference to Lacan's understanding of discourse structure. I would like to thank Patrick Shaw of Ohio State–Newark for bringing the Bartholomae and Bizzell texts to my attention.

Works Cited

Bartholomae, David. "Inventing the University." *Teaching Writing: Theories and Practice.* Ed. Josephine Koster Tarvers. 4th ed. New York: Harper Collins, 1993: 159–
85.

Bizzell, Patricia. "The Politics of Teaching Virtue." *ADE Bulletin* 103 (winter 1992): 4–7.

Chomsky, Noam. *Language and Problems of Knowledge: The Managua Lectures.* Cambridge, Mass.: MIT Press, 1988.

Klein, Peter, and Ted Warfield. "What Price Coherence?" *Analysis* 54.3 (July 1994): 129–32.

Metzger, David. *The Lost Cause of Rhetoric: The Relation of Rhetoric and Geometry in Aristotle and Lacan.* Carbondale: Southern Illinois University Press, 1995.

Shakespeare, William. *Much Ado about Nothing.* In *The Riverside Shakespeare.* Boston: Houghton Mifflin, 1974.

Žižek, Slavoj. *The Sublime Object of Ideology.* London: Verso, 1989.

18

Composition in an Antifoundational World
A Critique and a Proposal

Michael Bernard-Donals

In 1982 Maxine Hairston wrote an essay that suggested the field of rhetoric and composition studies was undergoing a revolutionary change the likes of which Thomas Kuhn noticed occurring in the natural sciences (Hairston, "Winds of Change" 76–77). That essay is less notable for its assertion that composition studies was undergoing vast change than it is for its invocation of Kuhn. Three years earlier, Patricia Bizzell had written an article noting a similar shift in English studies, one closer to the spirit of Kuhnian paradigm shifts, suggesting that without foundations, students run the risk of thinking that all knowledge is contingent and that one interpretation, one essay, one opinion, is just as good (or valid) as any other ("Thomas Kuhn" 768–70). Since the writing of those two essays, countless others have appeared reaffirming the idea that the antinomian divisions implied by the Cartesian cogito—subject/object, mind/world, materiality/cognition—have been thrown over in favor of a discursive world where certainties are themselves the products of human invention, and where our language shapes our lives, not the other way around (see, for example, Berlin, "Rhetoric and Ideology in the Writing Class" and "Composition Studies and Cultural Studies"; Bruffee, "Social Construction"; Rosenblatt, "The Transactional Theory"; Spellmeyer, "Language, Politics, and Embodiment"; Trimbur, "Consensus and Difference"). This has had vast implications for the study and teaching of writing: if writing on the current-traditional model, in which language is a transparent bearer of objective knowledge, is revised, then the study of writing is no longer a study that "services" other disciplinary or objective fields, but rather becomes the fundamental beginning of any understanding of the world. Louise Phelps has probably taken this claim the farthest, suggesting that writing on this epistemic model might be seen as a human science which transcends disciplinary boundaries altogether and which takes human cognition as radically discursive and transformative. The revolutionized study of writing has taken Richard Rorty's dictum that "language goes all the way down" quite seriously and has suggested that what we do when we teach writing is to make our students understand that what they do when they write is hermeneutically to remake their life-worlds.

Mind you, none of this is news to anyone who has been paying attention to the field of rhetoric and composition studies for the last ten years or so. In fact, Patricia Bizzell, Stanley Fish, and others who work with or are interested in composition studies have suggested that the debate between foundationalism and antifoundationalism is moot: foundational notions of the human and natural sciences have been so discredited as to force us to consider what *kind* of antifoundationalism gives us the most productive and perhaps emancipatory knowledge. This will be, in part, my task in this essay: to suggest that there are two ways of viewing the antifoundational or "hermeneutic" paradigm, particularly as it has been internalized by the field of composition studies. There is a "weak" version of antifoundationalist hermeneutics—what Patricia Bizzell, in "Foundationalism and Anti-Foundationalism," has called a "naive social constructivism"—that stresses interactive, consensus-building pedagogical practices, where the phrase "language goes all the way down" is taken to mean precisely that: we really do "remake ourselves" by "remaking our discourse," and we remake our discourse by negotiating it with others. Common sense suggests the problems inherent in this version: we may be able to get our students to change the way they speak and write, but that may have nothing to do with the material constraints that *prevent* real social change. There is also the "stronger" version of hermeneutics, which suggests that discursive practices are themselves constrained and that there are relations of power that operate extra-discursively through the writing process. I myself am sympathetic to this view, but I still do not think it is strong enough, because it stops short of suggesting how we can do anything about these coercive material forces (or phenomena or structures) that operate when we negotiate language. In this essay I suggest: that the "weaker version" of antifoundational language theory misunderstands Kuhn and Rorty, because that theory, unlike Kuhn's and Rorty's, does not connect changes of language to the material (and extra-discursive) forces that operate in interpretation and human understanding more broadly construed; that the "stronger version" understands Rorty and Kuhn, but, like them, does not go far enough, as some philosophers of science have pointed out, to examine the *nature* of those material and extra-discursive forces operational in language; and that there is another, scientific approach to antifoundationalism that sees a way to measure the material dimension and guide hermeneutics, just as, in the two previous approaches, hermeneutics guides scientific description.

It is unnecessary to go over the argument in *Philosophy and the Mirror of Nature,* Rorty's forceful statement on the overthrow of traditional epistemology, mainly because it is well known, at least the version that has been filtered through *College English, Pre/Text, College Composition and Communication,* and the other leading journals in composition studies. Nevertheless, I will restate some of the main implications of Rorty's view of hermeneutics for composition. If normal discourse is what we do when all the parties of our "conversation" understand one another (or, as Rorty puts it, when the terms of a discourse are commensurable), abnormal discourse is what we get when we do not understand one another, when terms are not translatable. The conversation sounds like gibberish, it does not make sense. When we find ourselves in such a situation, we stop trying to make the terms commensurable—we stop trying to translate one another's words into our own language—and instead creatively "remake" the discourse (by finding a new set of terms, by creating a different register of sense), and in so doing we remake ourselves. This creative reimagining is "hermeneutics," the result of abnormal discourse. It has implications for composition, which I will get to shortly, but it also has implications for science, which will become important near the end of this essay. For now, I want to suggest that science—the systematic description of phenomena and structures carried out through testing and aimed at showing the more or less constant behavior of those phenomena or structures—is a normal procedure, in that its parameters are relatively well defined and those doing science know they are doing it. When the parameters of science themselves come open to question— when the laws formulated to suggest the regularity of its descriptions turn out not to work in every case, or when things happen that are not supposed to happen, or when science's procedures appear to have been the product of bias or faulty assumptions—abnormal science takes over, and scientists reimagine or "remake" the world in which these phenomena and structures occur or remake the field of science itself, according to Kuhn.

It is this "creative" or constructivist approach to language and discourse that characterizes the antifoundational paradigm in composition studies right now. We are constantly forced to recognize that the discourses in which we take part are rule- and convention-bound, and that we are required to examine those rules and conventions to see what (and who) is included, what (and who) is excluded, and how we should proceed in order to change the conventions. And this, I think, is a good thing. But as Bizzell has pointed out, language does not operate solely normally or solely abnormally, but instead has a tendency to do both. That is, if language can only work conventionally, it also (and simultaneously) works against the grain of those conventions: "Various revolutionary discourses are always calling for a hearing even when normal discourse holds sway" ("Foundationalism and Anti-Foundationalism" 51). Rorty recognizes this complexity at some level when he notes that abnormal discourse "is always parasitic on normal discourse, that the possibility of hermeneutics is always parasitic upon the possibility . . . of epistemology" (*Philosophy* 365–66). From this complicated relationship between normal and abnormal discourse composition studies have taken the idea that *all* discourse is to some extent abnormal—saying one thing always excludes the possibility of saying something else—and so what we should be after is the negotiated understanding of the complexity of this world of discourse. That is, because discourse always involves the negotiation of versions of the world not entirely our own (but rather belonging at least in part to our interlocutors), the goal of the compositionist is to define the boundaries of discourse and work to forge a consensus of interpretations within those boundaries.

As I have tried to suggest, there are two manifestations of such a constructivism. The first, a creative hermeneutic or consensus-building pedagogy, looks much like that suggested by Peter Elbow (or Kenneth Bruffee). One place to see this creative, hermeneutic dimension in Elbow is in his assessment of academic versus nonacademic writing, and its pedagogical counterpart, the keeping of a process journal in a workshop course. In his essay "Reflections on Academic Discourse," Elbow suggests that the teacher in a writing course might do his students a service by forcing them to write not just academic discourse (though such a discourse does have its advantages), but also nonacademic discourse as part of an "exploration centered not just on forms but on relationships with various live audiences" (153). These live audiences are readers in various disciplines: historians do not write like biologists, he suggests, and part of the job of the writing teacher is to explain to students how the discourse each of these disciplines uses has developed to deal with its subject matter. But Elbow also notes that part of the problem in negotiating the difference between academic and nonacademic discourse involves relations of authority among the neophyte student and the edifice of the discipline itself and those who inhabit its laboratories and offices. The upshot of Elbow's suggestion is that teachers should initiate students into the "new intellectual practices" (149) that are implied by the disciplines and their attendant languages, and that this initiation into disciplinary practice will allow students to attach something "real" to the specialized language involved, but also that in learning these practices and translating them into the students' everyday terms, students will then be able to make sense of these practices from within their own language repertoire, and thus be better able to translate from academic to nonacademic discourse. The point of the essay is that there is no getting away from academic discourse, so all we can do is understand it—and the specialized practices that it implies—on our own terms. The ease with which students can learn the procedures to identify the different "registers" in academic discourse may not initiate them into the disciplines themselves, but they can broaden the students' meta-cognitive ability (149–50).

In the course Peter Elbow and Pat Belanoff developed in *A Community of Writers,* the process journal is the place where students can look for such meta-cognitive "insights": process writing "means writing to explore what was going on as you were writing: writing *about* your writing process. What works best is simply to record what actually happened, with as much honesty and detail as possible" (12). Elbow and Belanoff say that students should keep "an eye out for clues about what helps you and what hinders you in your writing" (15). Process writing is a way, in part, to negotiate the "other," incommensurable language— the language of a peer in the community of writers, the language of a specialist who is outside the community or at least one's own corner of it, a description of a phenomenon or experience that is difficult if not impossible to recognize—by coming up with another, new description, usually in "your own words," a record of "what really happened": the writing that follows the insights from the process journal is often clear, new and original, and in it conclusions will "just come" (15). These insights will then allow the writer, perhaps, to break out of a rut or to say something she was not able to say before, or will bring about change in the writer's subject, interests, or a paper's form. Again, process writing is a way to permit speaking or writing subjects to translate difficult (read, in Rorty's terms, incommensurable) phenomena or structures or experiences into everyday (or understandable and commensurable) terms. Kenneth Bruffee, drawing on Rorty and Fish and their discussion of discourse communities, similarly suggests a pedagogy in which students learn about "how beliefs affect the way people within a community, and people of different communities, interact with one another" through self-conscious analysis done in part through writing (cited in Fish 349). As with Elbow (and Belanoff), this analysis is aimed at the formation of consensus, a creative synthesis of the various discourses of the disparate members of the community. What characterizes Bruffee's *Short Course* and his theoretical manifestos is the claim that "we must learn to become our own representatives of an assenting community of peers with whom we speak and to whom we listen in our heads" ("Writing" 168). We change our selves—the "product" of writing—when these voices, this writing, is "reshaped, revised, and edited to become a composition, a term paper, a dissertation" (168). Perhaps even more explicitly for Bruffee than for Elbow, if you can change your beliefs through self-conscious analysis of the discourses you negotiate with the "other," you will ultimately change your self.

This all seems perfectly consistent with Rorty's hermeneutic rule, which states that there is no world "out there" separable from our statements about it, and as a result our task is to find ways—in terms of both "normal" and "abnormal" discourse—to "cope" with that world. Moreover, it is also consistent with the idea that it is the creative function of language that gives individuals the "freedom" to engage in abnormal discourse, to recognize their "contingency" and thereby overcome it (Rorty, *Contingency* 39–40). Given this set of rules, Elbow—along with Belanoff and Bruffee—is right, in the sense that the antifoundational paradigm has given teachers of writing the ability to get students to recognize and "re-utter" the language of other students. (Elbow makes this point vis-à-vis Bakhtin and Vygotsky in "Reflections" 137.) But Stanley Fish complains about Bruffee, and by extension Elbow, in a way that pinpoints the problem of the creativity of hermeneutics (349–51). Quite simply, the "consensual move" does not necessarily enable us (or our students) to overcome the threats—and the material constraints—imposed by the "scarcity of food" or "the secret police" (Rorty, *Philosophy* 389), because it does not note the connection, direct or indirect, between language and the forces with which it is inevitably bound up. This antifoundational version of social constructionism only really allows us, and our students, to cope with the world by finding new ways of telling stories about their individual worlds. The philosopher Charles Guignon, in one of the most effective critiques of conventional antifoundationalism, has said in response to Charles Taylor that "we can always make our current views look good by cooking up some story about how those views supersede the older ones, but this fact shows us more about our skills at storytelling than about the validity of our beliefs" (89). The same charge might also be leveled at Rorty—and by implication, Bruffee and Elbow (see also Sprinker 49)—but this charge finesses Rorty because he does at some level recognize a role for a stronger kind of description than a narrative, hermeneutic one, as I will explain. Scientific description can in fact serve as a way to justify or guide belief, and it is the desire to include a "descriptive" moment in the hermeneutic enterprise of writing that distinguishes the "stronger" antifoundationalism from the just-described weaker one.

This stronger antifoundational position is espoused by Rorty in some of the work that follows *Philosophy and the Mirror of Nature* and precedes (and includes) *Contingency, Irony, Solidarity.* In this work (*The Consequences of Pragmatism,* "Epistemological Behaviorism," and others) Rorty recognizes a role for "normal" science or normal description even as we "act hermeneutical." Rorty is in part reacting to Charles Taylor's appraisal of Wittgenstein's and Heidegger's critiques of epistemology, and their valorization of hermeneutics. Following Wittgenstein and Heidegger, Taylor sees hermeneutics as providing a way to understand human interaction in a life-world, thereby avoiding the split between subject and object the West inherited from Cartesian epistemology (see *Philosophy and the Human Sciences* 38–40 and "Overcoming Epistemology" 473–83). The privileged insight we have into our own life-worlds does two things. First, it raises the human sciences over the natural sciences as a way to analyze human understanding and life; and second, it provides a way to guard against "distortion" and deceptions mediated by popular culture by contrasting the faddish and popular with lived life. Rorty accepts Taylor's repudiation of epistemology and his turn toward Wittgenstein and Heidegger, but follows Kuhn closely in suggesting that if human self-understanding is mediated, so must scientific description also be mediated. This leads also to the notion that it is difficult to guard against the deceptions of the popular unless we treat normal language as a background (normal language is understood here as "the popular") against which we create "ever more various and multicolored artifacts" (Rorty, *Contingency* 54). Philosophers like Charles Guignon and Joseph Rouse have tried to reconcile Taylor's distinction between the human and natural sciences and Rorty's more consistent hermeneutics by maintaining a role for the natural sciences while understanding and finding a way to use productively its mediated nature (as in standpoint epistemology; see Harding, "Rethinking Standpoint Epistemology," and Haraway, *Simians, Cyborgs, and Women*) and have tried to imagine a hermeneutic understanding as an operational one: in it, human activity is not seen as an active agent (subject) separate and capable of describing nature (object), but rather as a subject who has a being-in-time or who is part of a life-world. We cannot see subject apart from object, or object apart from subject. But in such a hermeneutic understanding, there is both an interpretive *and* a descriptive moment. It is particularly the recognition of this descriptive moment (and, more important, a material dimension to human activity) that distinguishes the materialist antifoundationalists from the "weaker" version of antifoundationalism. The work of people like Greg Myers, Patricia Bizzell, and Louise Wetherbee Phelps in composition studies points to this material dimension. But although I am sympathetic to it, this work—like Rorty's view of Heideggerian hermeneutics, less like Taylor's— often leaves unanswered the question of what systematic ways we have in order to *do something* with or about this material dimension.

Patricia Bizzell, in what is perhaps the strongest affirmation of an alternative to antifoundational theory for composition studies, suggests two models that incorporate the material dimension—and a more or less systematic descriptive analysis of it—into writing theory and pedagogy, in "Beyond Anti-Foundationalism to Rhetorical Authority." One of the alternatives she offers is the work of Linda Alcoff on "positionality" in feminist theory as a way to construe interpretation as one, but not the only, way to understand discourse. Positionality suggests that "woman," for example, is not defined "by inherent, biologically determined characteristics. . . . But neither is 'woman' constructed discursively of interpretations of gender that have no objective reality" (673). Rather, we should interpret discourses produced by women through positioning those discourses among certain historically contingent (and highly complex) circumstances that have a material effect on interpretation. Bizzell goes on to suggest that even positionality may underestimate the resistance students have to the "creative" dimension of the hermeneutic enterprise, although if we take what Bizzell has to say about Alcoff as consistently recognizing a student's complex position with regard to classroom practice and authority, it may be that such resistance can be pedagogically accounted for if not completely understood. Bizzell's theoretical statement on positionality makes sense until we come to the end of the essay, where she says, "I cannot conclude with any programmatic alternative to schemes for cultural literacy" (674), only that we can make highly ideological avowals for or against our view. Greg Myers, who is perhaps the strongest advocate for science in a rhetorical program, takes a similar backward step. In "Reality, Consensus, and Reform in the Rhetoric of Composition Teaching," Myers critiques what by 1986 had become the dominant platitude, if not method, in composition pedagogies, "process," and notes that reaching any kind of consensus, either inside conventional (that is, institutional or cultural) constraints or (in the positivist model) outside them is not particularly effective unless that consensus "express[es] deeper tensions that go beyond the rhetorical problems set" by one classroom assignment or another (163). He proposes a pedagogy different from Elbow's and Bruffee's (which he says is modeled after Kuhn and Rorty, in that change takes place only inside disciplines) that sees "change in terms of social and economic factors" (168). If a pedagogy works merely toward consensus, he says, it "may lead to a more readable and more academic sounding paper, but it will not tell us what" the students' lives are "really like": "When, for instance, the various students in a basic writing course at Queens College write comparisons of the places they live to the places their parents lived as children, what these places are 'really like' is determined by conventional frameworks of progress and nostalgia. . . . No careful attention to the description of stoops or wide lawns will reconcile these descriptions [loaded with ideological baggage] in one objective reality" (162). Myers urges, instead, a classroom strategy that is critical of the ideological baggage and at the same time grants individual descriptions an authority of their own to guide the broader hermeneutic work of interpretation. But Myers, like Bizzell, ends by saying, "I find I have no suggestions for assignments that are as innovative as those of the authors [Bruffee and Elbow] I am criticizing" (162).

We might just chalk up this lack of system to Fish's point: you cannot establish a composition pedagogy on an antifoundational foundation (351). But I think there is something else at issue here. Both in general and in composition studies particularly, antifoundational theory works actively against a "scientism" that believes that the world—and truth—exists independently "out there." Science (or at least the old-fashioned eighteenth-century empiricism of the Bacon-Newton-Lock triumvirate) is as context- and culture-bound as discourse, and so it cannot claim a legitimate role in human self-understanding, since hermeneutics is a much more discursively based strategy, one that recognizes that "language goes all the way down." And as much as Bizzell and Myers (or even Elbow and Bruffee) would like to suggest that there may be right and wrong answers, it is not up to scientific description to do this work. I want to be quite clear: I am not advocating a return to some scientific foundationalism based in the dualisms we have disposed of. I am also not suggesting that hermeneutics of the kind advocated by, say, Louise Phelps for composition studies will not work. In fact, the field is working all the better for it, and its forays into cultural studies and gender studies are in part the result of such groundbreaking work. I am saying, however, that hermeneutics—in both the weaker and the stronger versions presented here—runs the risk of disregarding the descriptive (i.e., scientific) role that is left for it, and as a result runs the risk of unhitching composition and rhetoric from any association with the "natural" sciences, relegating it to the "human" sciences. My point is that, like it or not, composition must engage science and scientific inquiry in stronger terms than has either version of antifoundationalism presented here.

I base this statement on the work of several postantifoundational philosophers of science who do not see things quite the same way as do those deriving their work from Rorty and Kuhn. Joseph Rouse, in an essay suggesting that there are no good reasons to divide the human from the natural sciences, has suggested, apropos of Kuhn and Taylor, that what we call "natural science proceeds quite well" in spite of "our self-understanding"—in other words, in spite of our hermeneutical interpretations of things (51). Rouse's conclusion is that we need to find a way to understand a role for science that is consistent with its methodology of observation, testing, and prediction and that at the same time functions alongside or within a hermeneutics of the life-world that implicates both human agents and natural processes that would proceed even if humans were not around to observe and test them. Richard Harvey Brown suggests that we see rhetoric as a mediation between "natural" and "human" sciences "by naming the conditions for possible kinds of knowledge, advocating certain procedures as correct and certain statements as true, and inviting and legitimating belief in a certain (version of the) world," a world nevertheless definitively "there" (326). But this valorization of rhetorical (or even hermeneutic) knowledge does not mean that we can dispense with normal science, or any science at all, simply because it does function alongside ideology or hermeneutics. It is often the scientific—or purely descriptive, or the "normal," or the brutal materiality of the extra-discursive world and systematic evaluations of its regularity and its effects—that gets shortchanged by antifoundational composition theorists.

I have already suggested that even the "stronger" versions of antifoundational composition pedagogy and theory, despite their claims to the contrary, stop short of a dialectical relationship of hermeneutics and science, one that recognizes a role for description and systematic scientific (and social scientific) investigation of phenomena, and social structures, and cultural artifacts. One version that does—and suggests a program for pedagogy that imbricates the material and the interpretive—is implied by Roy Bhaskar's transcendental realism. It takes up the notion of the dialectical relationship between the human and the social sciences implied by Rorty, by way of Heidegger, but remains firmly within a realist tradition, in the sense that it recognizes a world that operates on human agents *despite* human intervention. Bhaskar's realism is also consistent with an explicitly social theory of science like that explored by Sandra Harding, Evelyn Fox Keller, Donna Haraway and others, a theory that sees science as objective *from the vantage point of various distinct and identifiable social positions,* positions that at once guide scientific research and are subject to natural and scientific investigation themselves. It remains the task of this essay to suggest what a decidedly antifoundational composition theory and pedagogy looks like, one that acknowledges a role for science stronger than that advocated by either constructivists or materialists.

Transcendental realism begins with the hypothesis that extradiscursive phenomena operate according to certain regular laws, and that science may be one way to formulate these laws. Still, "events, for their part, whether the fall of an autumn leaf, the collapse of a bridge, the purchase of a newspaper, the composition of a poem or the decline of a civilization are not determined before they are caused" (Bhaskar 162). Though we may have the conceptual capacity and tools with which to understand these phenomena as phenomena (that is, as events that display some regularity or coherence), the event—the fall of a leaf—would have happened regardless of whether we *could* conceptualize it as event, and would do so outside of any explanatory capacity that a conceptual framework could offer. Of course, the conceptual tools we have at our disposal are the result of scientific work done at a particular historical juncture (that is to say, the conceptual tools are themselves cultural constructs and by definition at least in part subject to interpretation), but that does not mean they do not have some explanatory capacity. The more important point is that the conceptual framework does itself *partially* explain the workings of objects and phenomena that proceed without human observation or intervention; but it neither completely explains them nor fails to explain them. Moreover, we do not understand any phenomenon—again, in the example of the falling leaf—unless we understand *other* phenomena that work in conjunction with it (for instance, what we have come to know as gravity, the density of air, leaf structure, photosynthesis, and so on). All of this suggests, then, that a phenomenon—the falling leaf—can only be explained alongside other phenomena, and that they affect one another. If phenomena were determined before they were caused, Bhaskar suggests, then the only way we could change events would be to operate on their (subsocial) physical causes, and we do not have access to this level and so are rendered powerless. The problem with even strong antifoundational hermeneutics (like Rorty's) is that they are ambivalent about the relations between observation of events in constant conjunction and events outside observation. Without granting such a relation, this view leaves science without a real explanatory capacity—a capacity that is always acknowledged to be constructed, but which is also subject to scientific as well as hermeneutic explanation—and so we are left either with playing language games (purely normal science) that are not connected to physical entities that can affect our choices, or engaging in the fruitless activity of trying to find the line between hermeneutics and science, without finally being able to deploy either. For composition, this amounts to being left with a theory and pedagogy of writing that looks for but fails to find strong terms with which to link the activity of describing (both scientific and hermeneutic) with any change that might come of descriptions, or one that avoids making the link at all and trusts that changes in language will certainly lead to changes in everything else.

What is needed, and what transcendental realism provides (along with strong realist philosophies of science like Sandra Harding's), is a stronger theory of human agency that allows a connection between the situatedness of human activity and the material constraints (and the characteristics of that material and its role in the situatedness) that deflect and defer it, one that connects human activities like observation and work to the possibility of real social change. To understand a role for scientific description and a systematic analysis of change, Bhaskar sets down four principles that composition theorists and practitioners might follow. First, we should recognize that social forms are uniquely real, that they do play a role in causing "events," and that they do make a difference to the state of the material world. Because scientific activity is social work, that activity implicitly obeys the social conventions that have evolved normatively. This does not mean, however, that because of its obedience to social conventions it is unable to do the work it has set out to do. But the converse is also true: because science *is* able to tell us, with some success, how "the world" operates, its social conventions affect our view of that world. Harding makes this point: "In societies stratified by race, ethnicity, class, gender, sexuality, or some other such politics shaping the very structure of society, the *activities* of those at the top both organize and set limits on what persons who perform such activities can understand about themselves and the world around them" (442). Scientists should see their place in such structures objectively and as the "starting points" for scientific projects, from which to ask the questions that will lead them to observe, experiment, and test. Testing new strains of tuberculosis in the Five Points neighborhood of Manhattan leads researchers to ask rather different questions from those in the same kind of research done at the Centers for Disease Control in Atlanta. As scientists observe and experiment with the regularities of the world, authors similarly observe and redescribe their interpretations of it, and in each case, description guides interpretation, and those interpretations are later tested and observed, and so on. Both kinds of description—scientific and literary—are reformulated, retested, and redescribed, and both kinds of description must take into account the real (and objectively verifiable) social effect that the location of the test has on it. At the level of composition, we should have our students realize that notions of race, gender, and class are not just "made-up" ways of seeing the world, but that they have a physical aspect to them that must be measured and not simply "retold," and further that their physical aspect must in turn be described in relation to the other phenomena or events the students are writing about. Student writing needs to be seen not simply as a renegotiation of selves, but as a way to test the effect of the material dimension of those selves.

Second, we need to grant the existence and the *objectivity* of social struc-tures, which are not created by human beings, but which do preexist us. Inasmuch as we are born into families, or classes, and inasmuch as we are born male or female, we are already inside such structures. Any redescription of our selves must include the understanding—and systematic exploration—of this material circumscription *as preexistent.* The observation and description of the "behavior" of new strains of tuberculosis should come with a caveat: scientists are testing the disease under controlled conditions; they are not testing some entity called "tuberculosis," but rather are producing a constant conjunction with which to test the material reality of the disease in a particular time and place (such as the homeless shelters on Avenue A), realities that preexist the experimentation and will continue despite that testing. The corollary to this point is that the scientific testing of the disease (testing as social work) will have an effect on how the knowledge of it will be used to vaccinate the homeless on Avenue A. This is another way of saying that social life has a material dimension and leaves some physical trace. To go back to the example of Myers's students at Queens College, they were always already circumscribed by the material sur-roundings of their neighborhoods and the historical traces of their parents' neighborhoods; but they may (like our own students) be tempted to leave unexamined those physical traces and their effects. Perhaps the program with which Myers might have concluded his essay would include a constant back-and-forth movement between the (scientific) descriptions of the material aspects of the students' narratives and a hermeneutic assessment of how the students' own placement—as students at City College of New York, as African American or Hispanic, as men or women, as sons or daughters and fathers or mothers—has affected the testing itself, and more testing, and so on. That is, it makes sense to recognize that the descriptive dimension must be rigorous and must be understood as yielding valuable knowledge at the same time that we also recognize the conventions of that knowledge, and so test those conventions and their material traces.

Third, the notion prevalent in much antifoundational thought that social interaction consists of—in Rorty's formulation—"coping" with others is limited, since we cope not only with people but also with the social structures and the physical world in which they reside. We need to "find and disentangle the webs of relations in social life, and engage in explanatory critiques of the practices that sustain them" (Bhaskar 175): in writing classes, this means that our students should see themselves as authoring social practices that can be in turn examined scientifically as well as hermeneutically. Sad to say, but many male students in my own classes offer up the refrain "Feminist theory is so shrill," and any number of other students, male and female, are hard-pressed to say why this assessment may not be felicitous or accurate, particularly given my problematizations, in the same class, of normative or institutional codes of behavior. It is necessary to have a way to convince such students that this assessment and the language with which they offer it produce materially and socially real effects that have measurable impact. It may not be enough to assert—walking the path Clifford Geertz has scouted and which has been taken by many compositionists (see Smith)—that such an assessment of feminism or any other discourse is simply "a case among cases, a world among worlds," because such an assertion does not enable anyone to say what material effects it has or the results of those effects. I am not advocating, in the name of transcendental realism, that we put two incommensurable accounts of, say, the human acquisition of fire, side by side and suggest that a Javanese mythological account is inferior to a Western scientific account because the latter is more able to account for the phenomenon of fire. But I am also not suggesting that we simply set these two accounts side by side and note their juxtaposition because "every argument about theory-choice is ultimately and inevitably circular"

(Smith and Bernard-Donals 336). Rather, when we say that two theories conflict, we must suppose "that there is something—a domain of real objects or relations existing and acting independently of their (conflicting) descriptions—*over* which they clash," and so "incommensurable theories" of fire or anything else "must share a part world in common" (Bhaskar 19), and that our task at least in part must be to say something about that world which does, after all, have an effect on its observers enough to make us want to say something about it. In the same way, Rorty's "coping with nature" needs to be complicated, since we redescribe the social world within the natural world, and we need to recognize some of its absolutes: some natural resources are nonrenewable, for example; nuclear waste has a long half-life and has measurable effects. The social and physical worlds are intertwined, and we (and our students) need strongly to recognize this.

This leads us to a fourth guideline, which suggests that poetic or hermeneutic "redescription" does not render the sciences (social or physical) redundant: we may be able to "rewrite" our circumstances that change with a student's utterance of "Feminist theory is so shrill," for example, but there are other material circumstances that change as a result that we cannot be aware of hermeneutically; and though we cannot understand them in a hermeneutic analysis, we may observe and test those circumstances scientifically. The recontextualization of the stories Myers's students tell about life on the stoops in Queens may get his students only so far in recognizing the ideological "baggage" that their stories carry, particularly when those stories are recontextualized among the stories of other students who by and large are inextricably bound up in an institutional situation (i.e., as students at City College), a situation that may not be readily apparent. But if this situation *is* emphasized and subjected to the same kind of ideological (and descriptive) analysis the narratives themselves are subjected to—if hermeneutics gives way to science— then the results render new knowledge previously unavailable.

In short, in order to recognize that there are strategies students can use to do more than just redescribe themselves—as the weaker and stronger versions of antifoundational composition pedagogy suggest—teachers and researchers of writing need, in Bhaskar's words, to reclaim science on Rorty's own terms. We need to see how the conflicts and contradictions Myers talks about work between and among the utterances and discourses our students (and others) write. If we are going to change things, we have to understand that there are material constraints to account for—hunger, disease, poverty, racism, sexism, homophobia—and allow these considerations and analyses to guide hermeneutics as well as science. To deny this material dimension is tantamount to saying that any redescription looks as good as any other, and it leaves students saying, "I know how to write, but I'll be damned if I know how this changes anything."

Clearly, consensual pedagogies are in themselves not enough. We need a pedagogy that suggests not just how language is formative of a life-world, but how rigorous scientific inquiry allows us to see when hermeneutics masks and when it enriches understanding. We need not be scared away from controversial topics like war, poverty, AIDS, and other social problems, because these are the places where material constraints are most apparently working alongside the production of discourse. As I have tried to suggest from the beginning, I am not so much arguing against the antifoundational paradigm as I am trying to suggest how carrying it to its most logical ends can make for a stronger pedagogy—one that includes a role for scientific investigation and testing—than we so far have developed. I am suggesting for composition that we do not take the antifoundational revolution on faith, but that we understand the role for science and hermeneutics in the creation of a life-world, lest we do ourselves, our discipline, and our students a disservice.

Works Cited

Berlin, James. "Composition Studies and Cultural Studies: Collapsing the Boundaries." *Into the Field: Sites of Composition Studies.* Ed. Anne Ruggles Gere. New York: Modern Language Association, 1993: 99–116.

——. "Rhetoric and Ideology in the Writing Class." *College English* 50.5 (September 1988): 477–94.

Bhaskar, Roy. *Reclaiming Reality: A Critical Introduction to Contemporary Philosophy.* New York: Verso, 1989.

Bizzell, Patricia. "Beyond Anti-Foundationalism to Rhetorical Authority: Defining 'Cultural Literacy.'" *College English* 52.6 (October 1990): 661–75.

——. "Foundationalism and Anti-Foundationalism in Composition Studies." *Pre/Text* 7.1–2 (1986): 37–56.

——. "Thomas Kuhn, Scientism, and English Studies." *College English* 40.7 (March 1979): 764–71.

Brown, Richard Harvey. "Symbolic Realism and the Dualism of the Human Sciences: A Rhetorical Reformulation of the Debate between Positivism and Romanticism." *The Rhetorical Turn: Invention and Persuasion in the Conduct of Inquiry.* Ed. Herbert W. Simons. Chicago: University of Chicago Press, 1990: 320–40.

Bruffee, Kenneth. "Social Construction, Language, and the Authority of Knowledge: A Bibliographical Essay." *College English* 48.7 (March 1986): 773–90.

———. "Writing and Reading as Collaborative or Social Acts." *The Writer's Mind: Writing as a Mode of Thinking.* Ed. Janice N. Hays, Phyllis A. Roth, Jon R. Ramsey, and Robert D. Foulke. Urbana, Ill.: National Council of Teachers of English, 1983: 159–69.

Elbow, Peter. "Reflections on Academic Discourse: How It Relates to Freshmen and Colleagues." *College English* 53.2 (February 1991): 135–55.

Elbow, Peter, and Pat Belanoff. *A Community of Writers: A Workshop Course in Writing.* New York: Random House, 1989.

Fish, Stanley. *Doing What Comes Naturally.* Durham, N.C.: Duke University Press, 1989.

Guignon, Charles B. "Pragmatism or Hermeneutics? Epistemology after Foundationalism." *The Interpretive Turn.* Ed. D. R. Hiley. J. F. Bohman, and R. Shusterman. Ithaca: Cornell University Press, 1991: 81–101.

Hairston, Maxine. "The Winds of Change: Thomas Kuhn and the Revolution in the Teaching of Writing." *College Composition and Communication* 33.1 (February 1982): 76–88.

Haraway, Donna. *Simians, Cyborgs, and Women.* New York: Routledge, 1991.

Harding, Sandra. "Rethinking Standpoint Epistemology: What Is 'Strong Objectivity'?" *Centennial Review* 36.3 (fall 1992): 437–70.

Hiley, David R., James F. Bohman, and Richard Shusterman, eds. *The Interpretive Turn: Philosophy, Science, Culture.* Ithaca: Cornell University Press, 1991.

Myers, Greg. "Reality, Consensus, and Reform in the Rhetoric of Composition Teaching." *College English* 48.2 (February 1986): 154–73.

Phelps, Louise Wetherbee. *Composition as a Human Science.* New York: Oxford University Press, 1988.

Rorty, Richard. *The Consequences of Pragmatism.* Minneapolis: University of Minnesota Press, 1982.

———. *Contingency, Irony, Solidarity.* Cambridge: Cambridge University Press, 1989.

———. "Epistemological Behaviorism and the De-Transcendentalization of Analytic Philosophy." *Hermeneutics and Practice.* Ed. Robert Hollinger. Notre Dame, Ind.: Notre Dame University Press, 1985.

———. *Philosophy and the Mirror of Nature.* Princeton: Princeton University Press, 1979.

Rosenblatt, Louise M. "The Transactional Theory: Against Dualisms." *College English* 55.4 (April 1993): 377–86.

Rouse, Joseph. "Interpretation in Natural and Human Science." *The Interpretive Turn.* Ed. D. R. Hiley, J. F. Bohman, and R. Shusterman. Ithaca: Cornell University Press, 1991: 42–56.

Smith, Robert E. III. "Hymes, Rorty, and the Social-Rhetorical Construction of Meaning." *College English* 54.2 (February 1992): 127–39.

Smith, Robert E. III, and Michael Bernard-Donals. "Comment and Response on 'Hymes, Rorty, and the Social-Rhetorical Construction of Meaning.'" *College English* 55.3 (March 1993): 334–36.

Spellmeyer, Kurt. "Language, Politics, and Embodiment in the Life-World." *College English* 55.3 (March 1993): 265–83.

Sprinker, Michael. "Knowing, Believing, Doing; or, How Can We Study Literature, and Why Should We Anyway?" *ADE Bulletin* 98 (spring 1991): 46–55.

Taylor, Charles. "Overcoming Epistemology." *After Philosophy: End or Transformation?*
    Ed. K. Baynes, J. Bohman, and T. McCarthy. Cambridge, Mass.: MIT Press, 1987:
    470–84.

——. *Philosophy and the Human Sciences.* Cambridge: Cambridge University Press,
    1985.

Trimbur, John. "Consensus and Difference in Collaborative Learning." *College English*
    51.2 (February 1989): 602–16.

Contributors

James A. Berlin, late professor of English, Purdue University.

Michael Bernard-Donals, associate professor of English, University of Missouri, Columbia.

Patricia Bizzell, professor of English, College of the Holy Cross.

Michael Clifford, associate professor Philosophy, Mississippi State University.

Terry Eagleton, professor of English Literature, St. Catherine's College, Oxford University.

Melanie Eckford-Prossor, assistant professor of English, Mississippi State University.

Frank Farmer, associate professor of English, East Carolina University.

Stanley Fish, professor of English, Duke University.

Linda Frost, assistant professor of English, University of Alabama, Birmingham.

Ellen Gardiner, assistant professor of English, University of Mississippi.

Richard R. Glejzer, assistant professor of English, Albertson College of Idaho.

Michael Hill, assistant professor of English, Marymount Manhattan College.

David Metzger, assistant professor of English, Old Dominion University.

Patricia Roberts, assistant professor of English, University of Missouri, Columbia.

Richard Rorty, Kenan Professor of the Humanities, University of Virginia.

Charles Shepherdson, research fellow at the Pembroke Center, Brown University.

Robert E. Smith III, late of Auburn Associates, Florence, South Carolina.

Kurt Spellmeyer, professor of English and director of the Writing Programs, Rutgers University.

Michael Sprinker, professor of English and Comparative Studies, State University of New York at Stony Brook.

Index

Adequation, 143

Adler, Jerry, 161

Adorno, Theodor, 297

Aesthetics, 86, 87, 91, 92

Agency: 21–22, 324–37; essential, 326; instrumental, 327, 333; *passim,* 346, 447. *See also* Subject

Alcoff, Linda, 386–87, 443

Allegory, 323

Allen, Judson, 325, 326, 331, 333

Althusser, Louis: "Ideology and Ideological State Apparatus," 356–57; "Marx's Relation to Hegel," 130; *Reading Capital,* 349–50; on Generalities I, II, III, 349, 363; on ideology, 130–31, 143*n1;* mentioned, 129, 131, 143, 143*n1,* 341–65

Ambiguity, 94

Anachronism, 102

Anarchism, 360, 362

Anderson, Nels: *Urban Society,* 283

Anthropology, 230, 231, 232, 243, 252, 303, 309–10, 313, 375

Antifoundationalism: and composition studies, 438, 443, 446, 450; and cultural studies, 25–26; and literary criticism, 5, 320; and materialism, 442–43; and method, 3, 5, 8, 17; and positive assertions, 381; and science, 133, 437–38; and teaching, 1, 22–23, 433, 441; mentioned, 1–28, 118, 128–43 *passim,* 203–208 *passim,* 216–20, 239, 241, 319, 326, 331, 336, 337, 375–83 *passim,* 411–12, 413, 417, 419, 437–51 *passim*

Aquinas, Thomas: 238, 33l; on evil, 182

Archaeology, 302

Arendt, Hannah, 172

Argumentation: rules of, 173–78, 180

Aristophanes: *The Frogs,* 88

Aristotle: 3, 7, 8, 13, 17, 68, 79, 81, 89, 172–73, 327–28; *Rhetoric,* 34, 36, 38, 40; on causality, 182, 333; on probability and demonstration, 180

Arnold, Matthew, 91, 94, 95, 238

Aronowitz, Stanley: 21–22, 355, 357–60

Art: 293–94, 335–36; as imitation, 65; medieval, 323; and morality, 324; and rhetoric, 97; as self creation, 65; verbal, 230

Augustine, 35, 238, 327–36 *passim,* 408

Austin, J. L.: 173, 177; *How to Do Things with Words,* 49, 50, 51

Austin, Mary: *Earth Horizon,* 277–78, 284–88; 279, 280

Authority: 199; of academy, 275; construction of, 170–73, 175, 178, 183, 189; cultural, 275; and ideology, 378; and knowledge, 335

Baber, Asa, 158–59, 163

Bakhtin, Mikhail: 60; "Discourse in the Novel," 107; on carnival, 90; 126*n3,* 323

Balibar, Etienne, 129, 130, 142

Barthes, Roland, 1, 60, 260, 406

Bartholomae, David, 406, 434

Bauer, Dale M., 387

Bawden, C. R., 266

Being: 201; and language, 117–18;

Belanoff, Pat: *A Community of Writers,* 416, 440–41

Belief: as theory, 209–10

Berger, Peter: *The Social Construction of Reality,* 236

Berlin, James: 19, 25–26, 382, 384, 385, 412; *Rhetoric and Reality,* 297;

Bernard-Donals, Michael: 9–10, 19, 27–28

Bernstein, Richard, 205–7; 216

Bhaskar, Roy, 5, 21, 27, 341–65, 445–47, 450

Birmingham School, 390, 399, 405

Bizzell, Patricia, 19, 22–24, 27, 406, 411, 413, 421, 434–44 *passim*

Blitz, Michael: *Composition and Resistance,* 402–3

Bloom, Allan: 376–77, 380, 399; *The Closing of the American Mind,* 60

Blumenberg, Hans, 82, 83–84

Body: 311; and discourse, 312

Boethius: 327; *Consolation of Philosophy,* 264

Böhler, Dietrich, 173–74, 175–76, 191*n10*

Booth, Wayne: 172; *Rhetoric of Fiction,* 60–61; *Rhetoric of Irony,* 61

Bordo, Susan, 148–49, 158
Branagh, Kenneth, 431
Brecht, Bertolt, 426, 432–33
Brown, Richard Harvey, 445
Bruffee, Kenneth: 27, 236, 240, 398, 406, 439, 444; *Short Course,* 440–1
Buckley, William K., 377, 378
Burke, Kenneth, 7, 60, 227, 246, 265, 387
Bush, George, 134–36
Butler, Judith, 148, 165*n*9

Calhoun, Crain, 171
Calvinism, 182, 184
Canon, 23, 263, 272, 274, 283, 379–82, 387
Cantor, Norman, 318
Capitalism, 137, 143, 345–46, 355–60, 395, 396–98, 432–33
Carnap, Rudolph, 39
Cartwright, John, Major, 128
Causality: 19, 320–21, 333–34, 336; Aristotelian, 182–83, 327, 337; and contingency, 78–79; and language, 77; medieval, 327, 330; structural, 353–53
Chaplin, Charlie, 297, 299
Chaucer, Geoffrey: 322, 324–25; "Clerk's Tale," 337
Cheney, Lynn, 377–78
Chomsky, Noam, 37, 59, 173, 429
Chronotope, 126*n*3
Cicero, 42, 43, 87, 89 90, 408
Civil society, 133, 137, 141
Civility, 129, 133, 138, 141–43
Cixous, Hélène, 217
Class: 170, 178; and gender, 148; and rhetoric, 143; and struggle, 352, 354, 355
Clifford, Michael, 12, 13–14
Coleridge, Samuel Taylor: *Lyrical Ballads,* 91
Colish, Marcia, 331
Collier, Andrew: *Scientific Realism and Socialist Thought,* 355–56
Colonization: and education, 262, 274
Colquhoun, Patrick: *Treatise on the Police of Metropolis,* 137
Commensuration, 239
Common sense, 52, 274
Communication: conveying a message, 80; distortions in, 199–201, 203, 204; linguistic, 76

Community: 113, 129, 132, 133, 134–35, 212, 247, 250–51
Composition Studies: 4, 5, 255, 372, 389–408, 412; and antifoundationalism, 438, 444–46, 450; and cultural studies, 390, 393, 399, 401, 444; and rhetoric, 254, 408
Conrad of Hirsau: *Dialogue on the Authors,* 332
Conscience, 180
Consciousness: 21, 97, 211, 238, 323, 324; 326, 334; critical self-, 57–8, 204, 274; and cultural studies, 391, 393; false, 96, 131; and hermeneutics, 201; prelinguistic, 83; revolutionary, 199; and theory, 209
Consensus, 213, 220
Constraint, 129–42 *passim*
Constructivism: 439, 446; and language, 438; Social, 17, 27, 235, 236, 237, 243, 246, 250, 252, 441, 437
Context: 2, 209, 319; and meaning, 50–51; objective, 199
Contingency: 8, 129, 131, 132, 133, 250, 345, 347, 441; and causality, 78–79
Conversation: 415, 418–19
Corax of Syracuse, 86
Cotton, John, 179, 184–85
Critical theory. *See* Theory
Cultural literacy, 371–82 *passim,* 387
Cultural studies: 6, 23, 25, 102, 389–408; and composition studies, 390, 393, 401, 444; as lived activity studies, 392–93, 404; and rhetoric, 390, 393, 401; as text based studies, 392, 404
Cultural theory, 413
Culture: definition of, 256, 287; and difference, 245; and the individual, 254–88; and knowledge, 254–88
Cynicism, 25

Darwin, Charles, 78
Dasenbrock, Reed, 23
Dautermann, Jennie, 408
Davidson, Donald: 71–73, 75–78, 79–80, 82, 83; *A Nice Derangement of Epitaphs,* 75–76
Davis, Geena, 153, 155–56, 158, 166*n*13
de Man, Paul, 54, 93

Death drive, 311
Deconstruction: 71–73, 75–78, 79–80, 82, 83; and rhetoric, 53–55 93, 150, 375
Demand, 309–10
Demaris, Ovid, 156–57
Democracy: 25, 212–13, 217, 271, 282, 297–99, 310–11, 383, 396–408 *passim*; and philosophy, 214–15; and self, 213–14; and social theory, 211
Dennet, Daniel: Ryle-Dennet view of language, 77
Derrida, Jacques: 1, 2, 19, 51, 53, 72, 73, 83, 101–102; 118, 149, 216, 260, 278, 292, 298
Descartes, René, 235, 238, 330
Desire, 294, 299, 309, 310, 433
Dewey, John: 72, 211, 240, 383, 397
Dialectic: 4, 185–6, 188, 189, 302, 310; as logic, 89, 90, 91, 96; as logic and rhetoric, 7, 96; pre-Hegelian, 171, 173
Dialogue, 200, 217, 219
Didion, Joan: "Why I Write," 262
Dietrich, Linnea S., 148, 152
Dionysus, Pseudo-, 228, 333, 336
Discipline, 134, 135, 142
Discourse community: 440; national, 272–74, 276, 287
Discourse Theory: and rhetoric, 86
Discourse: academic, 23, 371–73, 403, 415, 439, 440; and the body, 312; classifying, 243; normal *vs* abnormal, 240, 241, 438–39, 441; and power, 390, 393; public, 170–191; as sexuality, 306; student, 433
Discursive practice, 116, 147
Domination, 199, 200, 202
Donahue, Patricia: *Reclaiming Pedagogy,* 401, 402, 403
Doxtader, Erik W., 190*n3*
Durkheim, Emile, 260, 261, 282
Dworkin, Andrea, 160
Dworkin, Ronald, 211

Eagleton, Terry: 5–12 *passim,* 21–25 *passim,* 55, 56, 130, 142, 143, 384–85, 393; *Literary Theory: An Introduction,* 6, 389–90; *Walter Benjamin: or Towards a Revolutionary Criticism,* 128
Eckford-Prossor, Melanie, 12, 13–14

Economics, 46
Edification, 129, 131, 141, 242, 343
Education: 261, 262, 274, 381
Eighteenth Century: 90, 101, 129, 170, 178, 179; novel, 135, 136
Elbow, Peter: 26–27, 411–22, 439, 444; *A Community of Writers,* 416, 440–41
Eliot, T. S.: 94–95, 285, 287
Eloquence: 35, 90, 92; and reason, 43
Emblem, 112–13
Empiricism, 348, 353, 354, 358
Empson, William: *Seven Types of Ambiguity,* 209
English Studies, 374, 384, 387, 389, 401, 436
Enlightenment, The: 65, 69, 83, 101, 129, 132, 135, 141, 148, 151, 206, 310; conception of self, 149, 212–13; and rationalism, 211–12, 214; and reason, 197, 199
Epistemology: 1, 2–3, 5, 6, 19, 109, 115, 197–220 *passim,* 229, 236, 238–39, 242, 319–37 *passim,* 343, 353, 362; cartesian, 442; foundationalist, 425; and Marxism, 341, 363; of natural sciences, 344; of presence, 321
Ethics: 112, 113, 324, 375, 394; communicative, 171–75 *passim,* 186, 191*n15;* of genealogy, 305; and transgression, 309
Ethnography, 17–19, 20, 231, 232, 243, 251, 393, 405, 407
Ethos, 172–73, 178
Etymology, 102–5; 109, 111, 112, 119
Eyes of Laura Mars, The, 427

Faigley, Lester, 411
Faludi, Susan: 148–149, 153, 158, 165*n4;* *Backlash,* 147
Fantasy, 324, 326, 425
Farmer, Frank, 16–17
Fatal Attraction, 427
Feiffer, Jules, 161
Feminism: 449; American *vs* French, 151; backlash to, 147–69; popular conceptions of, 147–169; postfeminism, 15, 147–169; and poststructuralism, 147–169
Feminist Theory, 60, 61, 148, 376, 381, 385–86, 443

Feyerabend, Paul, 20, 348, 350, 360–65
Fiction: 293–315 *passim*; and genealogy, 301; and image, 297; and language, 92; and truth, 293, 296, 301, 331–32
Fielding, Henry, 137, 139–40
Fish, Stanley: 1–23 *passim,* 125, 129, 131, 132, 136, 190*n4,* 203–20, 377–78, 411, 412, 437, 440, 444; "Consequences," 208–11, 213; *Doing What Comes Naturally,* 8
Fiske, John, 166*n14,* 407
Flax, Jane, 148
Folklore, 229, 231, 235
Fordyce, James: 140; *Sermons to Young Women,* 138
Formalism, 7, 319
Foster, Stephen, 178
Foucault, Michel: 2, 19–20, 46, 101, 106–18 *passim,* 132, 133, 149, 204, 278, 292–315, 406; *Archaeology of Knowledge,* 295, 316*n2; Birth of the Clinic,* 303; *Discipline and Punish,* 305, 308; *History of Sexuality,* 306, 308; *Madness and Civilization,* 297, 305, 306, 310; *Order of Things,* 103, 303, 305; "Preface to Transgression," 309–10; on geneology, 295
Foundationalism: 2, 16, 26, 43, 206, 217–220, 243, 322, 374–75, 377, 384, 386, 387, 411, 416, 419, 421, 437, 444; and natural sciences, 206; and philosophy, 207; and theory, 209
Frankfurt School, 196, 204
Fraser, Nance, 148
Freedom, 132, 134–35, 170, 345–47, 362, 364
French Revolution, 65, 69
Freud, Sigmund: 20, 83–84, 132, 294, 296, 310, 312, 395; *Five Case Histories,* 310; on the death drive, 311
Frost, Linda, 14, 19
Frye, Northrop, 95, 375

Gadamer, Hans-Georg: 17, 196–220, 249, 251; *Truth and Method,* 197, 205, 241; on *bildung,* 205, 206; on the fusion of horizons, 198; on method, 201; on *verstehen,* 198
Galileo, 74, 79, 81
Gallop, Jane, 162

Gardiner, Ellen, 25–27
Garland, Hamlin, 276
Geertz, Clifford: 61, 229, 235, 256, 260, 449; *The Interpretation of Culture,* 236; *Local Knowledge,* 236, 243, 286
Gender: 165*n11,* 170; and class, 148; and race, 148; and sexuality, 149
Genealogy: 293–315 *passim*; ethics of, 305; and fiction, 301; and memory, 295–96
Genre, 135–42 *passim*
Geoffrey of Vinsauf, 334–36
Gergen, Kenneth: "The Social Constructionist Movement in Modern Psychology," 236; *Toward Transformation in Social Knowledge,* 236
Glejzer, Richard R., 19–21
God: and truth, 67; and causality, 323–36 *passim*
Gordon, Robert, 57, 341, 357
Govermentality, 132, 133, 135, 136, 141
Grammar, 90
Great Awakening, The, 181, 191*n9*
Great Books, 376, 377, 379
Groundhog Day, 429
Guignon, Charles, 441, 442
Guilt, 313
Gumperz, John, 230, 252

Habermas, Jürgen: *The Structural Transformation of the Public Sphere,* 170–173; on domination, 202; on strategic action, 188–9; mentioned, 16, 19, 37, 58, 59, 132, 142, 144*n3,* 170–91, 196–220
Habermas-Gadamer Debate, 196–203, 205, 207, 210, 221*n2*
Hacking, Ian, 80
Hairston, Maxine, 408, 436
Hand That Rocks the Cradle, The, 153
Haraway, Donna, 148, 446
Harding, Sandra, 446, 447
Hate: and learning, 427, 433; and teaching, 425–27
Heath, Shirley Brice, 231, 405
Hegel, G. W. F. von: *The Philosophy of History,* 261; on science, 66: mentioned 69, 74, 79, 81, 130, 363
Heidegger, Martin, 14, 72, 73, 117–19, 239–40, 442, 443, 446
Heimel, Cynthia, 154–55, 162

Henricksen, Bruce, 11
Hermeneutic circle, 199, 202, 241
Hermeneutic retrieval, 119
Hermeneutics: 2–3, 8, 20, 21, 22, 175, 197–206 *passim*, 241–42, 249–50, 320; antifoundational, 437, 446; and consciousness, 201; and discourse, 438; rhetorical, 18; and science, 445–50, 451
Hesse, Mary, 78, 82
Heteroglossia, 107, 115
Higginson, John, 184
Hill, Michael, 14
Hirsch, E. D.: 256, 399; *Cultural Literacy,* 23, 60, 271–77 *passim;*
Historiography, 87
History: 19, 23, 53, 101, 128, 129, 143, 293, 295, 299–314 *passim,* 319, 327, 337, 391; and empirical claims, 171; and historicism, 354; and language, 103–15 *passim;* local, 283; and myth, 296; and self, 212; as signifier, 325; supra-, 108–9; and transgression, 304
Hooker, Thomas, 185, 188
Hovey, Kenneth Alan, 376–77, 379–80
Hugh of St. Victor: 333; *Epitome,* 330–31
Human sciences, 22, 202, 231, 302, 343, 352, 354, 442, 445, 456
Humanism, 130, 172, 318, 322, 324, 330, 401
Hurlbert, C. Mark: *Composition and Resistance,* 402–3
Hutchinson, Anne, 179, 184–85, 186, 188, 190*n7*
Huyssen, Andreas: on postmodernism, 149
Hymes, Dell: 17, 243, 246; "Ethnography of Speaking," 229–30, 232–33, 252*n1;* "Models of Interaction of Language and Social Life," 231, 233–34; "Toward Ethnographies of Communication," 251

Idealism: 73, 91–92, 343, 348, 351, 357; anti-, 343; German, 66; metaphysical, 206
Identity: 254, 283
Ideology: Althusser on, 130–31, 143*n1;* and authority, 378; bourgeois, 57–58, 432; effects of, 56; and identification, 322; and knowledge, 348; and Marxism, 357; and philosophy, 351; and power,

394; and rhetoric, 93; of sameness, 272–73; and science, 350–59 *passim,* 364; and struggle, 351, 359; and truth, 375; mentioned, 20, 23, 89, 93, 96, 199–204 *passim,* 287, 379, 445
Ignorance: 428; and learning, 433; position of, 431–32
Image: inverted, 301; and reality, 297–302 *passim;* and the word, 302–2
Imaginary, 131, 143–44*n1,* 293–303 *passim,* 321, 326, 399, 402
Imagination, 91, 335
Instrumentality, 326–37 *passim*
Interpretation: 1, 24, 201, 202, 205, 209; interpretive turn, 46
Intransitive dimension: of knowledge, 344, 348, 349, 358; of science, 354, 359
Invention (*inventio*), 89, and subjectivity, 322–37 *passim*
Iragaray, Luce, 151
Irony: 142; liberal, 129, 131
Isocrates: 433–44; *Antidosis,* 42, 44–45

Jakobson, Roman, 232
Jameson, Fredric: 109, 119–20, 126*n2,* 389; *The Political Unconscious,* 108; *The Prison House of Language,* 103–5
Jardine, Alice: *Gynesis: Configurations of Women in Modernity,* 150–51, 164, 165*n8*
Jargon, 107
Jerome, Jim, 156
Jesperson, Otto, 101
John of Salisbury: *Metalogicon,* 328
Johnson, Richard: "What Is Cultural Studies Anyway?," 391–93, 404–5
Johnson, Samuel, 141
Jouissance: 312, 314, 337; of the Other, 425; and punishment, 311
Judaism, 313
Justice, 211, 212–13, 214, 312, 314

Kant, Immanuel: 91, 116, 235, 238, 309, 313, 345–49 *passim*; "WhatI Is Enlightenment," 313–14; on categorical imperative, 181; on science, 66
Katriel, Tamar: *Talking Straight,* 231
Keller, Evelyn Fox, 446
Kelly, Douglas, 334

Khouri, Callie, 162, 164*n2*
Klawans, Stuart, 152, 166*n12*
Klein, Peter, 429
Knapp, Steven, 208
Knowledge: 20, 21, 96, 276, 295, 296, 306, 308, 445; authentic, 418; and authority, 335; and being, 325, 331, 336; changing, 271, 273; common, 263; definition of, 240–41; false, 320–21; foundational, 374–75; and freedom, 362; historical, 297, 314; intransitive dimension, 344, 348, 349, 358; and language, 3, 372; local, 277–79, 286; and love, 426; and meaning, 424–25; particular *vs* universal, 423; production of, 319–335 *passim,* 343, 349–50, 411, 418–19; and the real, 349–50; scientific, 5, 7, 374; semblance in, 431–34; subject of, 326; transitive dimension, 344, 348, 349, 350, 357, 358; true, 36; and truth, 130
Kristeva, Julia, 150, 164*n8*
Kuhn, Thomas: 5, 17, 18, 22, 36, 82, 238, 240, 243–44, 319, 358, 361, 436, 437, 442, 444, 445; *The Copernican Revolution,* 68; "The Historical Structure of Scientific Discovery," 244–45; *The Structures of Scientific Revolution,* 47–48, 237, 244–45; on theory-choice, 249–50
Kurosawa, Akira: *Ran,* 254–55, 263

Labor: and domination, 199; objectification of, 143
Lacan, Jacques: 2, 19–20, 292, 293, 299, 312, 313, 320–21, 329, 336; on jouissance, 314; on law, 311; on the real, 304, 314
Lackington, James, 36
Laing, R. D., 260–61, 271
Lakatos, Imre, 348, 361, 363
Lamaism, 265–66, 269, 270
Lang, Andrew, 37
Language: 3–14 *passim,* 21, 28, 36, 39, 302, 303, 401–2, 437, 441; and antifoundationalism, 1, 3, 24–25; and Being, 117, 323, 325; and causality, 77; centrifugal and centripetal forces in, 107; and cognition, 201; and contingency, 78; cultural determinants for, 230; democratic, 373; dialects, 255–56; exchange of, 414; and

fact, 82; and fiction, 92; games of, 67–68, 80, 419, 447; and history, 103–15 *passim;* idealization of, 260; and knowledge, 3, 5, 13, 372, 424, 436; made *vs* found, 69; as medium, 71–72, 75, 80, 83; and memory, 106; as meta-institution, 199, 200; and mind, 72; natural *vs* artificial, 49, 54; neutral, 49, 415, 421; philosophy of, 89, 101–26, 173; politics of 254–56, 260; and power, 390, 401; and the prelinguistic, 121–22; and reality, 6, 116–17; and rhetoric, 4, 5, 49, 92, 428; and self, 69, 72, 76, 81; and sexuality, 310; and social change, 101–26; and subjectivity, 334, 403; synchronic and diachronic, 103–5; and truth, 69; use of, 110, 119–20, 177, 439. *See also* Vocabulary
Lanham, Richard, 43–45, 275–76, 384
Laskas, Jeanne Marie, 157
Lavoisier, Antoine, 243, 245–49
Law: 7, 20; and civilization, 299–300; natural, 310, 311; and power, 314; and punishment, 313; and structure, 304; and symbolic, 312, 313; and transgression, 311–12
Lay, Mary, 408
Lears, Jackson, 383–84
Leeds-Hurwitz, Wendy, 230
Legal studies, 57
Leicester, Marshall, 325, 327
Leitch, Vincent, 391
Lenin, V. I., 362–63, 364
Lentricchia, Frank: 389; on de Man, 54
Leo, John, 158, 159–60, 163
Leupin, Alexandre, 335
Lévi-Strauss, Claude: 261; on bricolage, 256
Lewis, Matthew: *The Monk,* 140–41
Life-world, 18–19, 255, 267, 270, 271, 273, 442, 445, 451
Limit: 309, 311, 326, 328, 329; of formalization, 313, 314
Lindeman, Eduard C.: *Urban Sociology,* 283
Linguistics: 173, 175, 230–32; sociolinguistics, 230, 234; structural, 315
Literary criticism: 210, 319–20, 329, 375, 389, 397; feminist, 148; history of, 88–89; and rhetoric, 86, 87; and theory, 208
Literary theory: 6, 9, 392; and social theory, 13. *See also* Theory

Literature: 96; birth of, 91; fetishizing of, 92
Logic: 16; Puritans and, 180, 186; syllogistic, 184. *See also* Dialectic
Logos, 172–73
Longfellow, Henry Wadsworth, 278
Love: and knowledge, 429–30; and teaching, 425–27, 433
Luckman, Thomas: *The Social Construction of Reality,* 236
Lyotard, Jean François, 204

McCarthy, Thomas, 178
McCloskey, Donald: *The Rhetoric of Economics,* 46
Mach, Ernst, 362–63
Macherey, Pierre, 412, 420–21
Madness: and language, 310; and reason, 298, 304–5
Mailloux, Stephen, 9
Mann, Patricia S., 165*n11*
Marx, Karl, 96, 109, 118, 128–43 *passim,* 353–65 *passim*
Marxism: 86, 96, 97, 102, 107–10, 120, 128, 133, 142, 143, 196, 341–65, 376, 385, 398–99, 403; and philosophy of science, 341, 350, 352, 355, 357, 360, 365; and science, 129, 131
Mass culture, 149–50
Masses, 133, 134, 135, 142, 143
Materialism: 93, 128–32 *passim,* 329, 348–64 *passim,* 446; Cultural, 102; Historical, 92, 96; and material constraints, 447; and rhetoric, 96, 130, 141–43
Mathematics, 82, 309
Mather, Cotton, 187, 191*n11*
Mather, Samuel, 184
Meaning: 80, 105; construction of, 229, 236, 257–58, 400; and context, 50–51; and desire, 426; and fact, 75; and knowledge, 424–25; and language, 121–22
Medieval Studies, 20, 318–37
Medievalism, 318–21, 322, 326
Memory: 105; counter-, 306–8; and genealogy, 295–96; and language, 106; and philosophy, 295; of truth, 303
Men's movement, 160–61
Mendel, Gregor, 78
Menocal, María Rosa, 381

Merchant, Carolyn: 113, 115; *The Death of Nature,* 111–12
Metaphor: 39, 78, 320, 326, 335, 336; death of, 80, 83; and discourse, 240; *vs* literal, 79–80, 96; positivists on, 80–81; and reality, 81; and truth, 79
Metaphysics, 9, 207
Method: 206; and cultural studies, 391; and genealogy, 308; hermeneutic, 241, and rhetoric, 56; and theory, 314
Methodology: 229, 235, 238, 318–21; 333, 337, 341, 347, 362, 364; and antifoundationalism, 3, 5, 8, 17; Gadamer on, 201; of observation, 445; rhetoric as, 4–6, 8, 18, 25; and science, 27; and teaching, 417
Metonymy, 321–22, 326
Metzger, David, 24–25, 26
Michaels, Walter Ben, 208
Middle Ages: 20–21, 86, 89, 318–26 *passim*; as absence, 326–27; antifoundational, 326, 336
Mill, John Stuart, 91, 363
Miller, Joshua, 178–80, 187
Miller, Perry: *The New England Mind,* 180
Miller, Samuel, 135–36, 139–41
Milton, John, 33–36, 38
Mind: medieval, 319, 323, 326
Missionaries, 265–66, 274
Mob, 134, 136, 140
Modernism, 207
Modernity, 275–88 *passim,* 304, 310
Modleski, Tania: *Feminism without Women,* 149–50, 158, 161, 165*n5*
Moglen, Helene, 377, 378, 381
Moi, Toril: "Feminism and Postmodernism: Recent Feminist Criticism in the United States," 150–51
Momaday, N. Scott: 63, 271, 273; "The Man Made of Words," 256–58; *The Way to Rainy Mountain,* 256–59
Mooney, James, 267–70, 271, 273
Morality: 305, 323–24, 345, 384–85; and law, 311, 313; origin of, 292
Morgan, Thais, 11, 12
Morton, Donald: *Theory/Pedagogy/Politics,* 11
Multiculturalism, 263
Multitudes, 133, 139, 140, 141, 142
Murray, Bill, 429

Myers, Greg, 443–44, 448–49, 450
Myth: 232, 235; Oedipus, 299

Nancy, Jean-Luc: *The Inoperative Community,* 112–113, 114
Narrative: 108, 109, 298, 299, 300, 306–8, 315; false, 307; structure and, 296
Native Americans, 267–70, 271, 286
Natural sciences: 20, 344, 442, 445, 446; as foundationalism, 206; methods of, 197
Need, 307, 309–10
Negation, 297, 302, 428
Nelson, Cary, 11
New Criticism, 318, 375
New Historicism, 6, 274, 318, 319
Newton, Isaac, 68, 79
Ngugi wa Thiong'o, 261, 263
Nicholas of Lyre, 333–34
Nichols, Stephen, 318–19, 326
Nietzsche, Fredric: 54, 72, 79, 81–82, 83, 92, 93, 124, 216, 264, 292, 300, 301; on democracy, 214; on metaphysical comfort, 250
Norton, John, 181–82
Nostalgia, 113, 114
Nothing: as divinity, 83
Novak, Ralph, 156
Novel, 14, 128–42

Objectivity: 9, 204, 206, 247, 249; and literary studies, 209; pretense of, 412
Ong, Walter, 90
Ontology: 109, 121, 319–36 *passim*; of the natural sciences, 344; realist, 349, 352; and Rorty, 343–44, 346, 356, 358
Origin, 297–300, 302, 309
Ortiz, Simon: 263, 271; "Women Singing," 259–60
Orwell's Problem, 429
Other, the: 148, 312; and jouissance, 425; and teaching, 433–34
Overdetermination, 353
Overholser, Geneva: "What 'Post-Feminism' Really Means," 147
Owen, Craig, 151–52

Paradigms, 244
Park, Robert: on modernity, 280–84
Particularity, 117, 320, 423

Pathos, 172–73
Patriarchy, 150, 152, 160, 161
Patterson, Lee: 318, 326, 327; *Chaucer and the Subject of History,* 325; *Negotiating the Past,* 321
Pedagogy: 9, 401–2; antifoundational, 444–46, 450; of consensus, 440–41, 444–45; emancipatory, 271; oppositional, 284; and theory, 6, 10–12
Perelman, Chaim, 9
Performative utterance, 49–52
Perkins, William, 180
Perversion, 299, 312, 314
Phelps, Louise Wetherbee, 436, 443, 444
Phenomenology, 5, 302–3
Philology, 102, 106, 321, 327
Philosophy: 2, 19, 20,175, 207, 219–20, 235–43 *passim,* 295, 309, 327, 330–31, 343, 348, 350, 375; antifoundational, 8; definition of, 213, 216; and democracy, 214–15; edifying, 242; English *vs* Continental, 292; and foundationalism, 207; and ideology, 351; Marxist, 342, 350, 364–65; and paradigms, 244; and poetry, 70, 82; and reality, 293; and rhetoric, 89; and science, 66; and truth, 212
Philosophy of science: Marxist, 341, 350–60 *passim,* 365; post-antifoundational, 445; post-empiricist, 343; realist, 27; mentioned, 21, 66, 341–65
Physical sciences, 345, 347
Piaget, Jean: 176–77; and prelinguistic domain, 199, 201
Piscator, Erwin, 95
Plato: 7, 13, 17, 37, 90, 97, 214, 250, 408, 424; *Gorgias,* 3, 4, 9, 26, 34–35; *Lairs,* 88; *Meno,* 423; *Phaedrus,* 3, 9, 34, 87, 268; *Protagoras,* 41–42, 423; *Republic,* 33, 238; on art, 293; Plato's Problem, 429; on teaching, 425
Platonism: 80–81, 97; neo-, 327–28
Pluralism, 271, 272
Poetics: 322, 335; antifoundational, 331; medieval, 329
Poetry: 395; and philosophy, 70, 82; and rhetoric, 87, 90–92, 396; Romantic, 65
Policing, 136–37
Political science, 90
Politics: definition of, 254; of language,

254–56, 261, 263; and rhetoric, 55; of
   sameness, 272; utopian, 65, 66, 78
Pope, Alexander: *The Dunciad,* 137
Porter, James E., 408
Positionality, 386–87, 421, 443
Positivism: 197, 198, 348, 352, 354, 358;
   and metaphor, 80–81; new, 60
Postcolonialism, 261
Postmodernism, 6, 15, 102, 116, 147–69,
   204, 207, 254, 255, 261, 274, 320, 321,
   434
Poststructuralism: 6, 7, 10, 24, 25, 320,
   348, 392, 398–407 *passim*; and cultural
   studies, 391; and rhetoric, 53; and sub-
   jectivity, 283
Poundstone, Paula, 161
Power: 304, 308, 311, 393–401 *passim*; and
   discourse, 390, 393; and language, 390,
   401; and sex, 307; as structure, 304, 313;
   student, 417, 419, 421; theory of, 314
Practice, 209–11, 213, 214
Pragmatism: 5, 95, 96, 115, 203–5, 211–
   16, 219, 220, 397; neo-, 229; Transcen-
   dental, 174, 175, 188; and truth, 219;
   Universal, 59, 177, 205
Predestination, 181–82, 183
Prejudice, 197, 198, 201, 210
Printing, 90, 144*n*5
Probyn, Elspeth, 148, 164*n*2
Propaganda, 97, 385
Psychiatry, 306, 310, 313
Psychoanalysis: 7, 173, 175, 201, 300, 310,
   311, 314, 319, 320, 329, 355; and crit-
   ical theory, 200; and memory, 295; origin
   of, 296; and science, 2
Psychology, 178, 310, 375
Public sphere: 16, 171, 184, 187; definition
   of, 172; rational-critical, 170, 172, 178,
   179, 186, 189, 190
Puritans, American, 15–16, 171, 178–91
Puttenham, George, 8

Quandahl, Ellen: *Reclaiming Pedagogy,* 401,
   402, 403
Quinn, Sally, 159–60
Quintilian, 87

Race, 148, 178
Radical doubt, 131, 133, 142

Ramism, 89
Ramus, Peter, 4, 90, 184
Rape, 158–59
Rapping, Elayne, 152
Rationalism: 92, 96, 203, 211–12, 214,
   355; scientific, 348, 350, 351
Rationality, 172, 175, 177–89 *passim,* 269,
   270
Rawls, John: *A Theory of Justice,* 211–13
Reader Response Criticism, 61
Reader: amateur *vs* professional, 414–16;
   teacher as, 414–16, 420–21; and writer,
   411–422
Real: 2, 8, 25, 28, 55, 96, 97, 119–20, 131,
   328; and knowledge, 349–50; Lacan's,
   304, 313–15; and language, 440; as
   limit, 313; and science, 350; and symbolic, 312
Realism: 297, 298, 348, 354–58 *passim,*
   364; critical, 342–43, 344, 456; transcendental, 27, 445–48
Reality: 5, 115–18, 301, 302, 328; and appearance distinction, 81; and art, 293; and
   fantasy, 296; and image, 294, 297; and
   language, 76, 116, 117; and metaphor, 81;
   and self, 73, 75; and truth, 67–70
Reason: 18–19, 90, 116, 180, 197, 199,
   271; and eloquence, 43; and law, 313;
   and madness, 298, 304–5; obedience to,
   187; return to, 263–67
Reflection, 199, 200
Relativism, 47, 354
Religion, 94, 358, 361, 375
Renaissance, 89, 90, 322, 326
Representation, 117
Repression: 298; and language, 294; and
   power, 304–5, 314; and sex, 306–7
Repressive Hypothesis, 132–33
Reproduction: 138, 139, 140; of genre,
   135; novel as agent of, 141
Rhetoric and Composition Studies. *See*
   Rhetoric. *See* Composition studies
Rhetoric: 3–28 *passim,* 38, 40, 86–97 *pas-
   sim,* 125, 129, 131–33, 135, 189, 375,
   384, 387, 389–408 *passim,* 436–37, 445;
   and anti-rhetoric, 95; art of, 34, 97; and
   change, 21; and class, 143; Classical, 89,
   95; and cultural studies, 390–393; and
   deconstruction, 53, 55; and dialectic, 7,

Rhetoric (*continued*)
  96; and discourse theory, 86; of embodiment, 19; expressionist, 393, 395–96,
  397, 400; expressivist, 26; and foundationalism, 43; and geometry, 36; history
  of, 172, 189; and ideology, 93; and liberal
  culture, 394–95; and liberation, 57; materialist, 130, 141–43; medieval, 334–
  35; and method, 4, 8, 25; and morality,
  35; and philosophy, 40, 42, 45, 89; and
  poetry, 87, 90–92, 396; and politics, 55;
  Puritan, 189–90; of reading, 26–27,
  411–12, 419; and realist critique, 40;
  and sensibility, 92; social constructivist,
  393, 397–98, 400; social epistemic, 398–
  400, 401; and subjectivity, 394; of subsumption, 200, 203, 207, 217, 219, 220;
  and theory, 56; and truth, 34, 41
Richards, I. A., 94, 408
Richardson, Samuel, 138, 140
Ricoeur, Paul, 201
Riley, Denise, 148
Riot, 134–36, 140
Robbe-Grillet, Alain, 301, 303
Roberts, Patricia, 15–16
Robertson, D. W., 323–33 *passim*
Romance, 137–39
Romanticism, 65, 69, 73, 78, 80–81, 90–
  92, 110–11, 322, 326, 395
Rorty, Richard: 8–24 *passim*, 27, 61, 115–
  118, 121, 129–42 *passim*, 203–20, 229,
  237, 244, 246, 251, 252, 343, 362, 375,
  426–50 *passim*; *Consequences of Pragma-
  tism,* 237, 250, 343, 442; *Contingency,
  Irony, Solidarity,* 8, 343, 442; *Philosophy
  and the Mirror of Nature,* 2, 8, 26, 205,
  229, 235–43, 249, 343–47, 438, 442;
  "Pragmatism, Relativism, Irrationalism,"
  115; "The Priority of Democracy to Philosophy," 208, 211–16; "The World
  Well Lost," 217–18; on edification, 205–
  7, 241–42; on normal science, 238
Rosmarin, Adena, 209, 210–11
Rouse, Joseph, 442, 445
Ryle, Gilbert: Ryle-Dennet view of language, 77

Saccamano, Neil, 180
Sade, Marquis de, 313

Said, Edward, 109, 110, 389
Salem Witch Trials, 184
Sarandon, Susan, 153, 155–58, 162,
  166*n13,* 167*n15*
Satire, 292–301 *passim*
Saussure, Ferdinand, 101–7 *passim,* 111,
  132, 260, 261
Scheffler, Israel, 48
Schickel, Richard, 154, 166*n14*
Schlesinger, Arthur: on national identity,
  273
Scholasticism, 327, 331–33
Scholes, Robert, 59, 389
Science: 5, 19, 22, 89, 96, 322–23, 328–
  29, 331, 348–59 *passim,* 438–451 *passim*; antifoundational critique of, 133;
  creation of, 103; as a cumulative process,
  47–48; description in, 442, 444, 448;
  empirical, 66; and hermeneutics, 445,
  450, 451; history of, 78, 341; intransitive dimension, 354, 59; and Marxism,
  129, 131; and paradigms, 244; and philosophy, 66; proletarian, 359; and psychoanalysis, 2; and realism, 446; and
  rhetoric, 443; and speech acts, 235; transitive dimension, 358, 364. *See also* Philosophy of science
Scott, George C., 425
Scott, Ridley, 160, 163
Searl, John, 52–53, 126*n1,* 173, 177
Self: 38, 322, 323–24, 329, 333, 401; and
  art, 65; authentic, 395–96; constitutive
  selfhood, 214; creation of, 69; decentering of, 399; and democracy, 213–14; and
  difference, 273; divided, 38; Enlightenment conception of, 149, 212; and history, 212; intrinsic nature of, 69, 70, 82;
  and language, 69, 72, 76, 81; and modernity, 285, 287; and reality, 69, 73, 75;
  and vocabulary, 69
Semblance: of truth and falsity, 24, 431–34
Semiotics, 87, 93, 103, 132
Sex, 306–8
Sexuality: 19–20, 314; as discourse, 306;
  and gender, 149; identity, 148, 151; and
  language, 310; normal, 113–115; as sexuation, 430; and transgression, 308–9
Shakespeare, William, 263, 430–31
Shaughnessy, Mina, 372, 406

Shepherdson, Charles, 19–21
Shotter, John, 415, 418
Shuar, The, 227–52 passim, 17–18
Silence of the Lambs, The, 161
Silvestris, Bernard, 332
Sin, 182–83
Siskin, Clifford: on novelism, 130
Skepticism, 9, 383–84, 387, 434
Sledd, Andrew, 378, 381
Sledd, James, 378, 381
Smith, Adam, 136
Smith, Jeff, 382–83
Smith, Robert, 17–18, 19, 20, 21
Smith, William Kennedy, 158–59
Social change: 4, 13, 18, 21, 25, 101–26, 437, 447–48,
Social life, 119–20, 125
Social net, 121–124
Social sciences: 196, 202, 347, 353, 392; and intransitive objects, 359; knowledge in, 197
Social structures, 448–50
Social theory, 13, 356. See also Theory
Socialism, 95, 96, 97, 141, 343, 355, 356–57
Society: 353–54; bourgeois, 143
Socrates, 4, 8, 26, 87, 89, 186, 268, 264, 423
Sophism, 34, 41, 42, 87–88
Southern, R. W., 330
Space: and time, 67
Spatial field, 120–24, 126, 126n3
Speech Act Theory, 95, 126n1, 175, 177
Speech acts, 52, 58, 59, 232–35
Speech: community, 233, 234, 247, 249; components of, 233; event, 17, 233–35, 246, 247, 249; field, 233; ideal situation of, 203; network, 233, 247; situation, 233, 234, 247; styles, 233, 235, 247;
Spellmeyer, Kurt, 17–19, 20, 21
Sprat, Thomas: 88–89; History of the Royal Society of London, 37
Sprinker, Michael, 9, 21–22, 27
St. Paul, 79
Stallybrass, Edward, 269–70
State, The, 133, 254
Steinem, Gloria, 153
Sterne, Laurence: Tristram Shandy, 140
Stimpson, Catherine, 152

Structuralism: 7, 24, 314, 326, 392, 398–99, 406; and cultural studies, 391; topological, 320–21, 329, 337
Structure, 20–21, 298–313 passim, 319, 329, 331–36 passim, 353–54
Subject: 13–14, 18, 20–21, 25, 91, 108, 303, 319–37, 391, 395, 399–403 passim; cartesian, 245; instrumental, 326, 331–33; intersubjectivity, 137, 144; and language, 403; liberal, 283 297–99; masculine, 337; materialist critique of, 128–42 passim; moral, 297; and object, 143, 442–43; postmodern, 152; and power, 394; religious, 330; and rhetoric, 394; social construction of, 398, 403; split, 334
Subsumption, 16, 197, 200, 203, 207, 208, 211, 217, 219, 220
Superego, 311, 312
Swan, William, 265–74 passim
Swift, Jonathan, 292–301
Symbolic: 297–302 passim, 323, 325, 326, 328, 401; and art, 294; and law, 312, 313; and the real, 312; and symptom, 296
Symptom: 20, 299, 311; symbolic dimension, 296

Tambiah, Stanley, 272–73
Taylor, Charles, 216, 217–18, 441, 442–43, 445
Teaching: 22–28, 423; and antifoundationalism, 1, 22–24; and love and hate, 425–27; politics of, 255–56, 270, 273
Temporality, 67, 110, 115, 121–22
Thelma and Louise, 15, 147–69
Thematizing, 210
Theory: 6, 10–12, 197, 246, 249–50, 308, 309, 314, 323; and antifoundationalism, 5, 209; and belief, 209–210; and the composition class, 401; critical, 110, 200, 202–3, 304; definition of, 207–11; and foundationalism, 209; medieval, 327, 334, 335; and pedagogy, 6, 10–11; and teaching 9–12
Therborn, Goran: The Ideology of Power and the Power of Ideology, 394
Thomism, 81
Thuggery, 17, 196, 208, 215
Totalitarianism, 297–99, 310–311

Tradition, 199–200, 211, 213, 220, 285, 318
Transference, 427
Transgression: 308–310; and law, 311–12;
Transitive dimension: of knowledge, 344, 348–51 *passim,* 358; of science, 358, 364
Transparency, 119
Transtextual occupants, 121–24, 126
Trimbur, John, 390, 399, 400, 406
Truth claims, 173, 174, 177
Truth: 2–3, 8, 9, 36, 47, 70, 83, 118, 124, 132, 294; and belief, 428–30; with capital T, 195–96, 203, 207, 215, 217; and causality, 330; claims, 264; and contingency, 42; correspondence theory of, 81; and the Enlightenment, 206; and fiction, 293, 296, 297, 301; and God, 67; and knowledge, 130; and language, 69; making *vs* finding, 65–67, 374, 375; and metaphor, 79; nature of, 70; and philosophy, 212; and pragmatism, 219; transcendent, 375; universal, 308; usable, 375–76; *vs* world, 67

Unconscious, 20, 201
Underlaboring, 342, 354
Unger, Robert, 57

Vickers, Brian, 172
Victorians, The, 114, 306–8
Violence, 124, 195, 219, 254–55, 268, 297, 310, 312
Virgil: *Aeneid,* 332
Visibility, 302, 303

Vocabulary: 67–83 *passim,* 116, 131, 215, 216–17, 219, 372; incommensurable, 242; new, 245

Warfield, Ted, 429
Warnke, Georgia, 199, 206
Watt, Ian, 136
Weber, Max, 218
White, Hayden, 108
Wigglesworth, Michael, 182
Wilkins, Bishop, 39
Williams, Raymond: *Keywords: A Vocabulary of Culture and Society,* 102, 109–10, 111, 115, 119
Williams, Roger, 179, 184–5, 186
Winterawd, W. Ross, 407
Wittgenstein, Ludwig: *Philosophical Investigations,* 239; on language, 75, 197; mentioned, 73, 443
Women: attitudes towards, 178
Wordsworth, William, 91
World, 2–5, 8, 9, 13, 16, 17, 26
Writing instruction, 371–72, 381, 389, 411–22, 424–26, 433–34, 436–51
Writing: 129, 135–141 *passim,* 440, 448; academic *vs* popular, 149; and the human sciences, 436

Yale School, 93
Yeats, William Butler, 74, 79, 81

Zavarzadeh, Mas'ud: *Theory/ Pedagogy/Politics,* 11
Zizek, Slavoj, 25, 297, 310, 426